THE REVOLUTION IN SCIENCE
1500–1750

The revolution in science
1500–1750

A. RUPERT HALL

LONGMAN
London and New York

Longman Group Limited
Longman House
Burnt Mill, Harlow, Essex, CM20 2JE England

Published in the United States of America
by Longman Inc., New York

The scientific revolution
© A. Rupert Hall 1954, 1962
The revolution in science 1500–1750
© Longman Group Ltd 1983

The original version of this book was published as *The Scientific Revolution*
in 1954; a Second Edition appeared
in 1962.
The present volume was first published
in 1983.
Second impression 1984
Third impression 1985

British Library Cataloguing in Publication Data
Hall, A. Rupert
The revolution in science 1500–1750
1. Science–History
1. Title
509   Q125

ISBN 0–582–49133–9

Library of Congress Cataloging in Publication Data
Hall, A. Rupert (Alfred Rupert), 1920–
The revolution in science, 1500–1750.

Revision of: The scientific revolution, 1500–1800. 2nd ed., 1962.
Bibliography
Includes index.
1. Science–History.   2. Science–Methodology.
3. Science–Philosophy.   I. Hall, A. Rupert
(Alfred Rupert), 1920–. The scientific revolution, 1500–1800.   2nd ed.
II. Title.
Q125.H28   1983   509′.03   82–8978
ISBN 0–582–49133–9 (pbk.)   AACR2

Produced by Longman Group (FE) Ltd
Printed in Hong Kong

Contents

Preface

It is pleasant to re-think and re-write a work of one's younger days. *The Scientific Revolution* (1954) took shape from my first years of teaching in Cambridge, where my mentors had been Herbert Butterfield, Alexandre Koyré, Joseph Needham and Charles Singer. It is astonishing, looking back, how much solid scholarly work has been accomplished internationally since those days, and how greatly research and teaching in the history of science have been transformed in nearly thirty years.

This re-written book attempts to reflect the increased maturity of studies of sixteenth- and seventeenth-century science, studies both comprehensive and profound. The archival depth and technical richness of recent publications are beyond comparison with what was normal before about 1960, and certainly cannot be adequately reflected even in a revised volume of this scope and character. A survey may, however, convey something of the new spirit of this branch of history.

I now conclude my story near the middle of the eighteenth century. When Newton died the great creative phase of the scientific revolution was already finished, though its acceptance and assimilation were still incomplete. Therefore I now omit the successor phases of the eighteenth century in which the sciences of chemistry and electricity received their first coherent forms. On the other hand I have broadened the book's vision of history in other ways. In Chapters 9 and 13 I have reprinted a good deal of material from *The Scientific Revolution* because I could not, within the same scope, improve it. Otherwise this is a new book. Extensive 'Reading Guides' are now unnecessary, and so I have simply provided an entrance to the recent literature in the notes to each chapter.

I am grateful to Longman for suggesting that I might return to *The Scientific Revolution* and to Miss Fiona Cooper and Mrs Julie Hounslow for typing the result. I salute all the colleagues and friends from whom I have learned and borrowed, especially those whose kindliness has survived a measure of scholarly disagreement. Among all these I name again Joseph Needham, sole survivor of the heroic age of the 1920s and 1930s, whose massive learning time will not soon erode.

A.R.H.

Bibliographical note

A selection of 'Further Reading' was provided in the original version of this book, *The Scientific Revolution, 1500–1800* (1954), and in the Second Edition of 1962. Most if not all of those older works are still useful reading. Two recent publications contain very large numbers of references to sources and secondary literature; these are: Magda Whitrow (ed.), *Isis Cumulative Bibliography* (5 vols) and C. C. Gillispie (editor-in-chief), *Dictionary of Scientific Biography* (16 vols). Extensive current bibliographies appear in the journal *Isis*.

Introduction

The 'revolution in science' of this book concerns the natural sciences, that is, knowledge of the external world which we now presume to exist independently of man – though in the recent past the close relationship between nature and man was universally held to be one of the best reasons for studying nature – including in this the human body, which can be investigated objectively and which has long been compared with the bodies of animals. I shall not here consider either the sciences of mind and personality, or those of society, such as anthropology and economics. Considering science as knowledge means following the activities and writings of learned men: philosophers and mathematicians in the earlier centuries, astronomers, naturalists and chemists as they began to be called in the later ones. I shall not, in general, be analysing folkbeliefs (even though a good many of these were also current among some learned men, belief in astrology or witchcraft, for example) nor seeking to establish what knowledge of nature may have been, at least implicitly, expressed in the craftsman's command over living things and natural materials. Such topics have been investigated and are worthy of investigation, but lie apart from the literate and academic level which this book seeks to pursue. Nor is it merely snobbish to pursue the academic and neglect the popular. It is no modern aberration for the ordinary citizen's image of the world he inhabits to be a popularization of that held by academic pundits; most of Shakespeare's science can be traced back to perfectly good classical and medieval antecedents. It is no accident that the popular knowledge of his day about sex and reproduction was derived from a work entitled *Aristotle's Masterpiece*, or that seventeenth-century popular astrology still bore marks of its origins among the Babylonian mathematicians. Some pieces of scientific knowledge have grown upwards from the soil – Jenner's discovery of vaccination is perhaps the most famous of them – but an incomparably larger number of folk-beliefs have sedimented down from above. Moreover, it is in the learned works of a society that the historian finds its view of nature – even its errors and superstitions – most clearly and cogently presented. Indeed, just as today we could not discover from Samoans what it was like to grow up in Samoa fifty years ago but only learn this from the anthropological studies of Margaret Mead, so we can usually only discover what ordinary people

1

believed in the past because their more learned contemporaries – clerks, judges, scholars – recorded something of them, perhaps unwittingly.

Similarly, in writing of the scientific revolution I shall say little of the fully or partly magical view of nature nor dwell on 'pseudo-sciences' like astrology and alchemy which the scientific revolution tended to displace or devalue (they have adherents still). This is not because magical ideas, or hermetic ideas, or the principles of astrology and alchemy were not studied and expounded by men of impeccable learning. Quite the contrary: some of the great figures of the scientific revolution, including Kepler and Newton, took such things seriously.[1] Some historians, indeed, hold that the interest such 'moderns', as we might otherwise think them, took in alchemy or astrology, not to say the Christian conceptions of the divine origin and governance of the universe, profoundly affected their technical scientific work. To put it at the lowest level, the way in which the progress of thought is accompanied by a kind of atavism, of which the progressive thinker himself may be unconscious, is certainly a part of history. Almost all revolutionary thinkers – Newton, Robespierre, Florence Nightingale, Einstein – show some deep attachment or other to an older order of thought which seems almost inexplicable to a later age. Having rejected so many toys of intellectual infancy, why did they cling to *that*?

Here I unashamedly follow a positivist or even whiggish line, for it is impossible to write in the same sentence of the victors' and the losers' view of a battle. I do not believe that Copernicus is an important figure in history because he once names Hermes, that Kepler's astrological tract is his most important work, that Newton's name is immortal because he read alchemical authors, or that Miss Nightingale's rejection of 'germs' was an error fatal to her teaching. I have tried to analyse, to set in context, to understand the creative work of men and women; if one is interested in creativity one must, to a large extent, follow the victorious and not the defeated. Atavism must be accepted, but not supposed to be more interesting and significant than creativity leading to the abandonment of traditional ideas.

The historian may well leave to his philosophical colleagues the precise discussion of what the achievement of victory by one scientific system or theory over another actually entails: he will observe that it turns sometimes on the presentation of new factual information, sometimes on the consideration of equivalences and their plausibility (is it more easy to believe that the Earth moves, than that the Sun does?), sometimes on a preference for a new conception (as with 'atom' in the seventeenth century, not always 'new' in the simplest historical sense), or sometimes again on the acceptance of novel mathematical arguments. Some historians would argue that shifts of preference – changes, over a period of time, in those propositions which people are prepared to qualify by such terms as 'self-evident', or 'plausible', or 'rational' – are much conditioned by experience or thoughts that have nothing directly to do with science and its problems. What was obviously true to a medieval Christian might have seemed highly debatable to a Greek philosopher, for example, or one might argue that men's experience of machines might alter their notions about physics or even biology, or perhaps most broadly of all, some historians take it as a truism that just as the human study of society, its customs and its institutions is to some extent at least influenced by the students' knowledge of science, so inversely people's ideas about society may affect their ideas about nature. In the simplest example, the concept of God as creator of the universe has been generalized from human experience of what it is like to make things – so it was said (by analogy) that God had a purpose, that he followed a design as a boat-builder might do and so forth, and most elegantly observed geometrical principles. Whatever truth there may be in the view that the scientific beliefs of a society are conditioned by the context of that society itself – which it is not the business of this book to argue one way or the other – it is certainly the case that in broad terms any large group of people we study has its own 'idea of nature'[2] within which particular beliefs about matter and creation, the stars, living things and so on are roughly consistent. Thus many of the Greeks, especially the two giants Aristotle and Galen, saw the whole universe as organic, a whole which had grown and developed much as a living thing does, which had an internal, overriding drive to self-preservation like a living thing, so that none of its events could be arbitrary, stochastic, or self-destructive. To medieval Christians the universe was simply the theatre for the drama of man's fall and redemption: hence, for example, the belief enduring into early modern times that all living species were created for man's use in one way or another. The last two and a half centuries have witnessed the prevalence of an idea of nature quite different from either of these, for nature is seen as the product, in local areas like our planet perhaps the fortuitous product, of casual chains springing from the first constitution of existence. At one level, therefore, the scientific revolution is the phenomenon of the displacement – partial, as yet, rather than complete – of one idea of nature by an alternative; one 'world-view' by another. Teleology – the belief that the nature of a thing is to be explained by its excellence in being what it is – is weakened; the sense of phenomena arising from the logic of the fabric of the universe and the 'laws of nature' is strengthened.

But there is more to the scientific revolution than this: it is not simply analogous to the replacement of Baroque aesthetics by Romantic aesthetics: the observer cannot simply say 'each is perfectly good in its own terms'. The science of 1750 was still rudimentary, but it could both describe and rationally account for a far greater range of events in nature than had been possible in 1500. A great deal more was known about the universe – to take one simple fact, that some stars at least show observable cycles of change, and alteration of position, and so are not eternally constant as had always been supposed in the past – and the whole fell into a more satisfying pattern of thought. One can, of course, only make these comparisons because the nature of what was studied was the same, and because what counted as an explanation was still (up to a point) the same: where no dialogue between two philosophers, or as we might now say two scientists, is possible it is not possible to affirm that one has advanced intellectually beyond the other. We can never, obviously, in an absolute sense maintain that in the succession of scientific theories through time – let us suppose, to be concrete, regarding the influence of male and female parents on the morphology and behaviour of their offspring each 'model' has successively come closer to reality, if only because we do not know what the 'reality' is, or be confident that we shall ever know it. But we can be sure that whether our knowledge now (or indeed in 1750) is more 'real' or not, it is certainly far richer in its factual content than that of 1500, that the theories are much more finely structured, that they are incomparably more closely integrated with other well-known fields of knowledge (chemistry, physics, etc.), and finally that they permit more accurate predictions to be made about future events from given antecedents. This we may well call progress, and believe confidently that in the systems of scientific knowledge progress can be measured in terms quite independent of value-judgements. It is not simply a value-judgement to maintain that the Newtonian theory of the universe is superior to the Aristotelian, a more advanced type of theory; for the Newtonian theory is bigger, more exact, more precisely testable, and above all more mathematical, than its predecessor.

Though no less part of a world-view than any scientific system of the past, modern science differs markedly from any of them. It demands rigorous standards in observation and experiment. It excludes spiritual agencies from its province and accepts a pure materialism, but these characteristics of science were finally established only in the late nineteenth century. It distinguishes between confirmed theories, plausible hypotheses, and tentative speculations – three degrees of confidence and perhaps, inversely, three different degrees of intellectual excitement. It is highly mathematical in structure and argument. In modern science a good theory is general, but it also has to be precise, for most working scientists would probably agree that the best test of a theory is the verification of conclusions (predictions) drawn from it. Further, theories provoke research and the fruits of research enforce development of theories; there are 'inactive' areas of science where everything is fixed in textbook rigidity, but in the active areas where research is most lively change has tended to become more and more rapid. These characteristics were acquired by the study of nature during the period of transition conveniently known since the end of the seventeenth century as the scientific revolution, and retained through detailed development of both factual knowledge and its theoretical ordering.

It is pertinent to try to define, in general terms, the force and character of this revolution. Man's view of the external world was firmly established and confidently held at the close of the Middle Ages; expressed in many learned and some popular books, a proportion of which (of both sorts) had already been printed before the end of the fifteenth century, this view was widely supposed to be authenticated by its derivation from the Graeco–Roman world, in which the highest intellects of humanity had flourished and men had come closer to the truth of things than ever before or since. Nor was this all, for the classical age had witnessed also the greatest recorded feats of human skill and ingenuity. However, medieval people recognized as their ancient predecessors had done that tool-making and the useful arts had grown from invisible beginnings in the dawn of humanity, whereas philosophical and mathematical discussion of nature seemed to have begun only among the Greeks of the fifth century, rising

4

to rapid maturity in the writings of Aristotle (384–322 BC) and Euclid (c 300 BC). By one of the most extraordinary coincidences of history, by the sixth century BC, 'we are entering the greatest period of intellectual flowering of ancient China. The "hundred schools" of philosophers were at their height between −500 and −250' (Joseph Needham).[3] But of Chinese intellectual history the medieval West, despite Marco Polo, knew nothing. Similarly, knowledge of pre-Greek philosophy, medicine and science was limited to rumours of Phoenician and Egyptian sages, of whom the most celebrated was one Moschus, sometimes identified with Moses. These mysterious sages were not esteemed as physicians or astronomers – for the solid beginnings of these sciences in Egypt and Babylonia were only to be rediscovered in the nineteenth century – but as magi, for their esoteric skill in reading the stars and controlling natural agencies.

In short, there were four components in the late-medieval world-view, all supposedly (and in fact) traceable back to the ancient world: the *technical*, mastery of forces and materials, of wind, water, metals, wood and stone, in all of which very rapid and effective progress had recently been accomplished; the *philosophical*, of which medicine may be regarded as a part, addressing itself to the most general problems about the nature of the world we live in, and firmly basing itself upon the textbooks by Greek, Latin and Islamic authors read in schools and universities; the *mathematical* (including astronomy), junior in prestige to philosophy (yet serving it as, through astrology, it did medicine also) and limited in its most advanced departments to a small handful of experts; and finally the *hermetic* or *magical arts*, feared by almost all, known (at least by repute) to many, professed openly by a few. There were links, of course, between these different forms of knowledge: both astronomers and philosophers spoke of the heavens, and the former advised navigators and explorers how to find and chart their way about the surface of the globe; mathematics was closely allied to magic (to the grossly superstitious, all mathematical figures and symbols seemed cabbalistical) just as philosophy, through its discussion of qualitative change, was allied to alchemy. Architects and artists, though artisans in the social hierarchy of the late Middle Ages and Renaissance, might like Alberti and Leonardo da Vinci through their studies become learned men; so did printers. This made for fertility and richness in ideas, but also for confusion: what appeared as a clinching argument about the nature of things might equally well turn on a quotation from an ancient authority, a supposed piece of common experience, the testimony of travellers or of reputed experimenters whose stories could not easily be verified, or rarely on a geometrical demonstration. With argument shifting its emphasis from one sort of evidence to another it was difficult ever to reach solid conclusions – not least, because written authority when appealed to was far from unanimous, and because contemporary experience of the actual world did not exactly square with the reports of the ancients.

Above and beyond all forms of authority was religious truth, again expressed in a variety of sources, in the Old and New Testaments, in the writings of the Fathers of the Church, in the pronouncements of popes and councils, and certainly far from crystal clear. Salvation at the end of human life was the only important goal a rational man should propose for himself; destruction before the judging of men was to be the fate of the material universe. All authority agreed that the world had existed long in terms of human lives – several thousand years – but that it probably had little future, since God would soon accomplish his purpose with regard to humanity. The sense of an existence of things in time, save this little human time of one hundred or so generations, was utterly lacking as indeed it had been in antiquity too; if anything, it seemed that the world had been created perfect, and had since gradually deteriorated partly through the attrition of the years, partly because of man's wilfulness and greed. It would have been absurd to think of the universe without man, for whom it was created, and impious therefore to think of it without God. Even the attempt to distinguish a natural event from a divine intervention involved theological considerations: and there could be nothing of *science* until such a distinction had been drawn. The Arab says: 'Imshallah: it is the will of God': where was the Christian properly to say: 'It is the way of the World'? In a sense, this was the question on which all turned: this book might be said to be about the victory of rationality over religiosity. But in truth the situation in the fifteenth century was not nearly so desperate as such an antithesis might suggest, though it had been desperate indeed in the early Middle Ages, soon after the fall of the Roman Empire. The few vestiges of ancient learning current then, and its tremendous and swift revival in the twelfth and thirteenth centuries, had restored to Europe a pre-Christian rationality and intellectual expertise – together with a great deal of sheer factual information about nature – which was grafted on to Christian theology to form an uncomfortable amalgam. If it were possible to discuss the sacraments in terms of Aristotelian qualitative philosophy, even Thomas Aquinas could not make Aristotle declare that the universe was other than eternal. There had been strong reactions against Graeco–Arab learning: Aristotle's doctrines were condemned many times in the thirteenth century while Averroes, a Spanish Muslim who had taken Aristotelian positions to extremes, was never to become really respectable in the Christian West. The facts that the vast majority of learned men were clerics, that the awkward Aristotelian texts could be bowdlerized or buried under an invocation of spiritual authority, and that a harmonious and seemingly immensely profitable synthesis could be achieved had rendered these tensions latent rather than urgent: but the truth remained that the Greek and Christian epistemologies were, and are, irreconcilable; when tensions began to reappear with the revival of Platonism in the mid-fifteenth century, the result was in part creative, in part obstructive.

Finally, we might ask what did late-medieval Europe want the kind of knowledge we call scientific *for*? Certainly not in general because of its practical utility. Of all the established branches of learning only medicine recognized the distinction between *episteme* and *techné*, that between theoretical knowledge and practical skill which is so familiar to us: and university emphasis was naturally upon the former. Outside academic studies the practitioners of esoteric arts also invoked the notion that knowledge gives power; the magus who understood the nature of the mysterious hidden forces could also command them. Mathematics too was understood to possess some useful applications – the relation of arithmetic to mercantile accounts and of geometry to architecture is quite clear, for example, in late-medieval writings – but the full strength of this idea only began to emerge in the fifteenth century, as a feature of the renaissance mentality, especially after the 're-discovery' in 1414 of Vitruvius' book on architecture (the oldest extant manuscript had been transcribed at Bede's monastery of Jarrow in the ninth century). Vitruvius had catalogued the useful branches of mathematics in a way that proved very popular to renaissance scholars such as John Dee (in his Preface to Billingsley's *English Euclid*, 1570). Astronomy, as already noted, was godfather to astrology, and so was of professional importance to physicians, among others. But mathematics proper was a science having no application whereas the higher learning of philosophy, ranging far through the writings of Aristotle and all his commentators, led on to theology.

Men pursued philosophy – and we know it was eagerly pursued in medieval universities – because where there are books there will always be readers, because (in some of its branches) it promised intellectual techniques of universal application which might help to clarify the mysteries of Christianity, because (in others) it offered insight into the eternal problems of being and purpose, of continuity and change, and into the order or harmony which must surely underlie the seeming chaos and chance of the world of experience, and because (in other branches still) it offered guidance in understanding the vicissitudes of social and political life. Philosophy was secular wisdom, the wisdom of this temporary world (which was why the views of pagan authors could be treated with respect) just as theology was the wisdom of the eternal world. The two studies inevitably met; the Bible related certain things that had to be believed about this temporary world – as for instance, that our Earth is fixed at its centre, although as Oresme already remarked about 1370, reason alone might lead us to conclude that it moves likes a planet, did not Authority save us from this error – and, of course, religion had also much to say about morality and human conduct. To put it very crudely one might say that philosophy became the most important university study in the Middle Ages because of St Paul and the Fathers, who had made Christianity an intellectual religion, not simply a matter of faith and hope in Jesus' message; it was after all rather a question of philosophy than anything pertaining to the story of Jesus and his message that had fatefully divided the Eastern and Western Churches. However, if the most obvious justification for studying pagan philosophers was to be found in the nature of religion, paradoxical as this may seem (and, from time to time, fiery and simplistic reformers arose to denounce it), it seems more reasonable to suppose that it was the intrinsic, puzzle-solving fascination of natural knowledge that drew some men, if relatively few, to this aspect of philosophy. Some (perhaps we may include the Emperor Frederick II among them) were attracted by the huge variety and strange curiosity of nature, and the aesthetic beauty of living things; others by the mechanics of definition and logic hoped to arrive at the utmost precision of ideas, and rigour in deducing conclusions about problems of motion and change; others, building here on the work of a great Iraqi exemplar, ibn al-Haitham whom they called Alhazen (c 965–1040), plunged into the mysteries of light, closely connected with God's manifestations to man. Most were concerned to some extent at least with the deepest question of all: how can men form any coherent, rational image of the external world when it is so huge, in part inaccessible, and in constant flux?

This was, it is true, a bookish and literary investigation, made by academics for didactic purposes. Calculation had its place within it – indeed, the fourteenth-century English philosopher, Richard Swineshead, was known to posterity as 'Calculator' because 'mathematical functions and considerations pervade [his] major work' (Murdoch)[4] – yet such philosophy was always distinguished from mathematics. The starting-point of most lines of investigation was in some Greek or Arabic author, though the Latin philosopher might indeed leave that far behind; facts, arguments, and principles of explanation were all alike borrowed and all learning was essentially a commentary and elucidation of what the most talented learned men had written before. Refined analyses and delicate drawing of distinctions was followed through large treatises without taking a fresh look at the real world, in fact much of medieval 'natural philosophy' (including that of 'Calculator') is concerned with thought-experiments. It may be a libel that Thomas Aquinas debated how many angels could stand on the point of a pin, but the question, what would happen to a stone falling in the gap between the two halves of the Earth, if it could be divided and the two parts separated by a foot, was certainly asked. There is evidence of a very little first-hand observation of animals and plants amid the otherwise almost complete lack of interest in living things; and in the optical tradition experiments were certainly made. Another high point of empiricism was Petrus Peregrinus' *Letter on the Magnet* of 1269. Direct observation was certainly accepted by medieval logicians as a test of the truth of a proposition, and they recognized that by induction from repeated observations a generalization could be formulated; but the application of such a methodology to more than one or two exceptional cases had to await the scientific revolution.[5] The probing of phenomena was an intellectual exercise to be pursued on paper, not an experimental one to be pursued by searching for fresh information. There were three great technical innovations made during the Middle Ages each of which we might term 'scientific' – the use of gunpowder, of the mariner's compass, and of spectacles. The two former were introduced into Europe from, ultimately, China; the last derived from the Latin philosophers' interest in light and vision, which brought them awareness of the use of primitive lenses as magnifiers by Alhazen. Yet the invention of spectacles seems to have been made by some sensible, shrewd man, certainly not by one of the great authorities on optics, Roger Bacon for example.[6]

What changed in the character of learning, in the fifteenth and sixteenth centuries particularly? Some of the shifts in perspective are very subtle: it would certainly be erroneous to supposed that natural philosophers of around 1600 were less devoutly Christian than those of three centuries before, but in that period Western Christianity and its relations with philosophy had undergone

INTRODUCTION

profound changes. Again, it would be excessively simple to portray the scientific revolution as a revolt against Aristotle for, on the contrary, Aristotelian ideas and example could still stimulate creative innovation, as with William Harvey. Some points are fairly obvious and wide-ranging, however. Perhaps most important of all was a shift in the cultural base. The medieval intellectual heritage had largely been formed by the twelfth-century translators working at Toledo and other centres of multilingual skill: late, and better translations (like those made into Latin directly from Greek by Willem van Moerbeke, for the benefit of Thomas Aquinas) tended to have little circulation, and what was not translated early, like the works of Archimedes and the preponderance of Galen, did not enter that heritage at all. Much of the best technical science of the Greeks was missed out in this way, although Arabic commentary thereupon was much better represented. Of his Doctor of Physic in the *Canterbury Tales* Chaucer wrote

> Well knew he the olde Esculapius,
> And Deyscorides, and eek Rufus,
> Olde Ypocras, Haly and Galyen,
> Serapion, Razis and Avicen,
> Averrois, Damascien and Constantyn,
> Bernard and Gatesden and Gilbertyn.

Fifteen authorities, the names all more or less corrupted: five Greek (one mythical of course), seven Arab, one French and two English. The Arab contingent was the most numerous, and by far the most voluminous. The Renaissance brought to light a vast amount of forgotten classical literature – much of it transcribed in the centuries just following the barbarian invasions – in Greek Archimedes, Galen, Ptolemy, Plato, in Latin Celsus and Lucretius, for example. The Greek language, almost forgotten in Western Europe, was revived giving scholars a sense of immediate and vivid contact with the most philosophical of ancient societies.

Now the Arabs were – with a good deal of injustice – pushed aside as mere bunglers. The physician and radical theologian Michael Servetus writes (1537) of the brilliance of Galen, who, 'once shamefully misunderstood, is reborn and re-establishes himself to shine with his former lustre' and who 'has delivered the citadel which had been held by the forces of the Arabs, and cleansed those things besmirched by the sordid corruptions of the barbarians'.[7] Renaissance philosophers differed not at all from medieval ones in thinking that modern man should ground himself firmly on the teachings of antiquity, but he was meant to do this directly, ignoring all that had been written in between, and in a less narrow fashion. The hero of the Renaissance became Plato, rather than Aristotle, especially in Tuscany; analogously, but later, others took up the atomism of Epicurus and Lucretius in preference to Aristotle's qualitative theory. Dioscorides was another great hero: sixteenth-century botany was founded on study of his works. The pre-Socratic philosophers were read and quoted, so were the Pythagoreans. Copernicus found in Plutarch – another renaissance discovery – and quoted in Greek the information that Philolaus the

Pythagorean had supposed the Earth to move, as did Heraclides and Ecphantus; he also refers to Aristarchos of Samos, to Anaxagoras, Empedocles and Leucippus, displaying knowledge of a great tradition which the Middle Ages had virtually never considered. New horizons brought new varieties of thought and new problems to unravel.

The most powerful philosophical influence at work in the fifteenth century, that of Plato, pushed people towards mathematics; it was shameful to be ignorant of geometry. The rediscovery of ancient pure and applied mathematics urged in the same direction. In the thousand years or more since Greek mathematics had come to an end, a Martian seeking a mathematical genius would have had to look in India (especially), China or Islam – not in Europe. Now all this was to change: mathematics proper, and its close relation astronomy, were rapidly to flourish there as never before. Algebra on the one side, trigonometry on the other, took tremendous strides while mathematics was applauded everywhere as the key to navigation and exploration, military science, geography (rapidly shrugging off its legacy of travellers' yarns) and even aesthetics. Niccolo Tartaglia (1500–57) illustrates in his writings all the new trends: he was joint first in offering the solution of cubic equations, he studied the flight of projectiles, and he produced the first edition of Archimedes. Of greatest general interest, however, is the idea that mathematics offers a unique key for understanding the nature of things; yet this was not a *single* idea since it had two chief and distinct branches: firstly, the conviction that nature is inherently mathematical, because God eternally geometrizes, or in the words of Leonardo da Vinci

Proportion is not only found in numbers and measurements but also in sounds, weights, times, positions, and in whatsoever power there may.

This means that not only may we expect nature to be rationally ordered in some way because if it were not so to seek for understanding of it would be futile and because (as Descartes emphasized) if it were not so God would be, impossibly, deceiving men, but we may also expect this rationality to be mathematically realized. And secondly there is the purely logical conviction that mathematical reasoning is the most certain that we can command; to quote Leonardo again

There is no certainty where one can neither apply any of the mathematical sciences nor any of those which are based upon the mathematical sciences.[8]

Galileo, among many others, also emphasized both these characteristics of mathematics: he believed that the Book of Nature is written in the language of geometry and he also held that the mathematical proof of a proposition is, in logic, the best we can have. Neither of these positions was entertained in antiquity; not that the force of, for example, a geometrical demonstration was regarded as any more doubtful in antiquity than in modern times, but rather the ancients had supposed that the mathematical kind of reasoning was inappropriate outside strictly mathematical contexts (one may compare the modern canard about lies, damned lies and statistics). There was good reason for this seemingly perverse view: the physical conclusion of a mathematically formulated argument is only as sound as the physical premises on which it is based; it is illegitimate to argue that because the mathematical argument is sound the physical conclusion must be true. Greek philosophers held that the physical axioms posited by mathematicians – such as, that planets move uniformly in perfectly circular orbits – were so uncertain, or rather to be more exact, offered so great a variety in their interpretation, that nothing based on them could be confidently believed. They understood (correctly) that different mathematical models can be constructed in correspondence with the same physical principles, and that these different models may, indeed to be comparable must, generate many identical conclusions or predictions. (In principle, an infinity of such equivalent mathematical models may be discoverable.) Accordingly, being unable to decide whether (say) eccentrics or epicycles really exist in the sky, the ancients rejected mathematics as a guide to truth. except perhaps heuristically. A literate analysis, it seemed, was more likely than a numerical one to yield an answer one could put one's trust in: that is to say, verbal pictures seemed more definable, and therefore more realistic than mathematical models. The ancient mathematician, furthermore, could only handle rather simple and narrow aspects of a subject: circles in astronomy, straight-line rays in optics and perspective, ratios in music; and reality seemed always more rich and subtle than these artificial abstractions. In music, for instance, the performer's notes seem to blend harmoniously together, although mathematicians (here, once again, Ptolemy) teach that it is impossible to divide the octave into eight equal notes. The Greek was, in short, well aware both that the theoretical elements employed in a mathematical model may not exist at all and that the model gives only a *possible*, not a *definitive* account of the phenomenon: in the words of the Aristotelian commentator Simplicius, astronomers

have been unable to establish in what sense, exactly, the consequences entailed by [their geometrical] arrangements are merely fictive and not real at all. So they are satisfied to assert that it is possible, by means of circular and uniform movements, always in the same direction, to save the apparent movements of the wandering stars.[9]

In other words, mathematical science could not explain things by revealing the structure of reality and its inner logic, it could only give the possibility of predicting future results from stated antecedents.

The debates about mathematical models and access to reality have continued ever since. During the Renaissance, however, many mathematicians like Copernicus and Kepler and some philosophers like Galileo endorsed a view that was perhaps more naive than that of the Greeks but was also much more creative, as we have seen in Leonardo. It is a crippling restriction to hold that no theory about reality can be in mathematical form; the Renaissance rejected this restriction, holding that it was a worthwhile enterprise to search for mathematical theories which also – by metaphysical criteria – could be supposed 'real'. The outstanding instance of this is Copernicus, who explained that he had abandoned all existing mathematical theories of planetary motion not because they were unable to 'save the phenomena' but because they could not (being both incomplete and inconsistent) be taken as offering a real description of the heavens; the mathematical theory based on the hypothesis of the Earth's motion, however, is no less valid mathematically in 'saving the phenomena', is consistent, and has other advantages such as definitively setting all the planets in a spatial order; it may therefore be taken as 'real' in Copernicus' eyes. Kepler was even more explicit in arguing that the well-chosen mathematical model of reality, far from being arbitrary, is uniquely able to account for certain features of the universe, such as the number six for the planets (including Earth).

This characteristic of renaissance science – merging insensibly into the 'mathematical physics' (the expression is still, of course, anachronistic) of the seventeenth century – has been described in a variety of ways: to describe it as 'revived Platonism' emphasizes the more static concept of mathematical order or architecture in nature, and finds its most obvious success in crystallography; to describe it as 'revived Pythagoreanism' emphasizes the more dynamic concept of mathematically articulated theory with a more esoteric overtone (for the Pythagoreans, as Copernicus recalled, kept their discoveries secret), greater concern with how phenomena are produced, than with the composition of the world; or, more simply, one can speak with Alexandre Koyré of the 'mathematization' of nature. The most eloquent and full defence of this process was given by Galileo, whose mathematization of the science of the motion of real bodies furnished a model for physical science generally during the following century.

If this shift in the form of explanation from the verbal to the mathematical is the major epistemological change of the Renaissance, it is not of course the only one, nor the only intellectual change affecting science. The introspective, self-regarding tendency of medieval thinking was weakened: if man was still seen as the microcosm, this made the macrocosm, the universe, more rather than less interesting. If nature was still God's theatre for the human drama, this wisdom, goodness and providence were best discovered in the deepest scientific understanding and veneration of this marvellous creation. In the words of Francis Bacon:

all knowledge and especially that of natural philosphy tendeth highly to the magnifying the glory of God in his power, providence and benefits; appearing and engraven in his works, which without this knowledge are beheld but as through a veil. [10]

And the Renaissance, Bacon especially, tended increasingly to stress an aspect of this idea previously neglected: God had intended everything in nature for man's use or instruction, these 'messages' were only to be as it were deciphered by those who understood nature, and so science may and should improve the usefulness of nature to man, thus fulfilling God's providential intention. Were there not countless secrets in mechanics or the treatment of metals, for example, which once discovered by men might greatly ease and enrich their lives? The most obvious field for such improvement, without any compensating demerit that could be foreseen, was medicine; the New World especially must be furnished with countless plants of medicinal value, some few already discovered by the native Indians, which God had surely intended to be of value to the Europeans whom He had permitted to discover and occupy those hitherto hidden lands.

Geographical exploration and territorial expansion had been dramatic, forceful manifestations of a Europe shifting in many ways from a passive to an active mood. Fear of the ferocious Turk was to last as an outmoded legacy to the nineteenth century, but Christian Europe was now in the late fifteenth entering a phase of more than four centuries' duration in which it did not need to dread being squeezed by outside Great Powers. Carlo Cipolla has well explained how Europe's technical ascendancy in warfare brought her command of world-wide commerce, and the power by which a handful of men could subdue the Aztec Empire.[11] The aggressive European was both sceptical and superstitious, tolerant and narrow, barbarian and learned. Part of him rejected the non-European world as savage, or absurd, or ineffective, but part of him was eager to admire and borrow: porcelain first, for example, then tea-drinking. Especially the European was impressed by the artistic craftsmanship of alien peoples: the feathered work of the Aztecs (but their gold he simply melted into bullion), Persian rugs, Indian silks and cottons, but he found nothing to challenge the solid practical industry of his own continent, or its business acumen, or its science. Within a century of the passage of the Cape of Good Hope and the discovery of America, the European had begun to see himself as the great practical inventor to whom the combination of common sense, manual handiness and natural knowledge had brought power and wealth. Philosophically this vision is best presented by Francis Bacon, writing for example in the First Aphorism of his *Novum Organum*;

Man, being the servant and interpreter of Nature, can do and understand so much and so much only as he has observed in fact or thought of the course of nature; beyond this he neither knows anything nor can do anything.

But visually and symbolically it is best seen in the *Nova Reperta* ('New Discoveries') of Jan Stradanus (*c.* 1590), a series of engravings displaying Europe's mastery of cannon-founding, printing, wind and water-power, the compass and magnetism, paper-making, spectacle-making, gunpowder, silk-weaving and many other crafts, none known to the ancients though many had long preceded the Renaissance.[12] If we set aside the Greeks' interest in the mathematical analysis of machines, the fifteenth and sixteenth centuries were the first in which there had been any self-conscious literary interest in crafts and technology (architecture, machines, military and naval affairs, hydraulics, metallurgy and mining, indeed virtually the whole range not excluding agriculture), producing a host of books perfused by the belief that innovation and improvement in techniques is both possible and necessary. Authors from Agricola to Zonca drove home the lesson that man's way with nature is hardly less wonderful than nature itself.

By no means all these technical experts, and one might well call them propagandists also, had any faith in abstract or academic learning: some, like Bernard Palissy the potter and Paracelsus, the chemical physician, actively mocked book-knowledge and its futility. Indeed, the rising swell of technical progress and capital investment that brought Europe to the eve of the industrial revolution through the sixteenth and seventeenth centuries was maintained by practical men, engineers and industrialists, rather than by the scholars who (sometimes) wrote the books; by anonymous precursors of Thomas Newcomen and Abraham Darby. Hence the real facts of technical progress, and also the contemporary apprehension of them as an ideal to be aimed at – both of which can be exaggerated, for they are as yet invisible in imaginative literature, for example – both stand in a rather enigmatic relation to science. During the seventeenth century, following Bacon, the usefulness of science to the practical concerns of human life was to become a propaganda commonplace, yet the benefits were always future rather than actual. Before 1660, at any rate, the direct benefits to be recited as flowing from the scientific revival were few and dubious; for of the medical gains, to take a favourite example, such innovations as spectacles, couching for cataract or cutting for the stone seem to spring as much from manual daring and dexterity as from theory, and others seem in hindsight perhaps more powerful in their operation on the natural excretions of the body than truly curative of sickness. And where the thrust of scientific change seems most forceful, those who brought it about seem (so far as we can tell now) to have had little eye to any kind of application to craft or industry. The desire to solve old intellectual problems is more often to be noted than the desire to solve new technical ones. To the renaissance mind, it was not necessary to gain *new* knowledge, in order to acquire greater control over nature; indeed, in magic, still seen as the most obvious key to such power by learned and simple alike, the practitioner aimed only at emulating the power attained by the ancient magi. In an analogous way many mathematicians and natural philosophers, not least Newton, regarded themselves as recovering a wisdom that had been for long mislaid, rather than as discovering anything fundamentally new. Even in so apparently straightforward a case as that of Francis Bacon it is therefore anachronistic (as Paolo Rossi has pointed out)[13] to detect a naive line of thought such as: investigation brings new knowledge, new knowledge engenders new technology. The concept that the technical apparatus of society could itself progress in sophistication to infinity had yet to be framed. It is perhaps more promising to consider the fertility latent in the 'mixed' fields of learning that the Renaissance began to promote, not only in various forms of applied mathematics but in earth- and sea-sciences, mechanics, 'chemistry' and 'physiology', this last now about to cease to be merely the speculative counterpart to anatomy.

In these new 'mixed' disciplines the theoretical structure was weak, the empirical input strong if incoherent. Those who were most critical of ancient book-learning were also those who praised most highly the lore of farmers, miners, potters (all people who knew about the products of the soil), or bath-keepers, herbalists and alchemists (people who knew about the curative properties of spa and other waters, of plants, and of minerals), of glass-blowers, carpenters and shipwrights, and metal-workers (people who knew the properties of materials). They did not mind that this lore was disorganized and often unreliable, at least it went along paths that learned men had not pursued before. Modern historians like Edgar Zilsel[14] and Cyril Stanley Smith[15] have argued that such new subjects of enquiry as geomagnetism and metallurgy (to use anachronistic labels) sprang almost entirely from such roots as these; Francis Bacon had said much the same thing, and two generations after him Robert Boyle would discuss what the natural philosopher might learn from the trades-man. It seems certain that this more eclectic and less supercilious attitude to what might count as knowledge of the natural world had a considerable effect on natural history and stimulated interest in its curiosities (caves, strange min-erals, monsters and prodigies) and, as in the history of pneumatics discussed later, sometimes opened novel branches of systematic investigation. Not that this was happening for the first time, since Aristotle in his zoology had taken much information from fishermen, graziers, bee-keepers and so on, and Cte-sibios (the ancient founder of pneumatics) was the son of a barber in Alexandria. It may be doubted, however, whether this refreshing breath of empiricism was directly and uniquely responsible for introducing systematic experimentation into science; the 'hard' use of self-conscious, controlled observation and exper-iment seems rather to happen first in the traditional sciences (astronomy, optics, anatomy–physiology), though chemistry may present a rather different case. If one thinks of the early classical experiments in mechanics (on falling bodies, pendulums, collision), for instance, they do not seem very closely related to machines – though again one should note that the pendulum does first appear in machines designed by Leonardo, as an inertial device for storing energy.

At least in the broader perspective of history it is probably useless to try to be too definite on this question of the influence of technical progress – which is itself beyond doubt – on the modification of 'scientific' ideals and methods. Craft certainly broadened the horizons of philosophy; to suppose that modern science is an amalgamation of craft and philosophy is to propose too simple a formula, and to neglect those very large, indeed, preponderant aspects of the scientific revolution that had nothing to do with craft experience at all. But it is useful to consider a dichotomy in that revolution to which Thomas Kuhn has drawn attention:[16] between the quantitative or mathematical sciences and the qualitative or experimental sciences. If one examines the whole area of nat-ural knowledge in Newton's day – and even a century later, in the time of Laplace, the same situation prevailed still to a large extent – it is clear that no close definitions in terms of methodology, epistemology, ideals or any sort of generalization can be evenly applied over the whole area: the most precise branches of science, like astronomy and mechanics, were very different in kind from chemistry or geology. Without being naughtily Whiggish it is inevitable to feel that Newton's science has progressed more towards our own conception of science than has the science of Boyle, or *a fortiori* John Woodward. And this is no matter of personal genius or inventiveness in methodology: no one could have written a *Mathematical Principles of Geology* in 1700. Thus there arises the paradox: those sciences which were most rigorous in their appeal to facts, and most precise in their theoretical articulation, were also those that had possessed these characteristics outstandingly in antiquity and the Middle Ages; even mechanics, the most profoundly revolutionary of all forms of natural knowledge, had long and respectable antecedents. On the other hand, those lines of enquiry that the Renaissance had created or re-created (chemistry, earth sciences, most of biology) were still primitive at the end of the seventeenth century, from the point of view of structure, despite relatively very great advances. Critical facts were still uncertain, two or more rival theories disputed the allegiance of students, and inconsistencies abounded. The 'Newtonian synthesis' of chemistry was to be effected only about 1800, that of geology about 1830, and that of biology about 1860. (Of course, none of these syntheses was mathematical in form or argument.) In other words, those sciences which were most novel in character in the Renaissance, most vaunted by contemporary propagandists, most notable for their strong 'mixed' elements coming from the crafts, most Baconian as it is often said, in a sense made their critical transition to modernism last, following in the track of (and after Newton, consciously emulating) the mathematical or academic sciences.

How is one to understand this paradox, that the traditional was in a way the more revolutionary? It may seem trivial that an established science, like astronomy, should get on faster than geology: it possessed techniques, salaried experts in universities, and state patronage (because of navigation). All one can say is that this is not what most intellectual reformers of the Renaissance expected. (Descartes is an exception: but he was a gifted mathematician to whom empiricism and natural history counted for little.) It was certainly not what Francis Bacon expected: he looked for no intellectual revolutions in the areas of astronomy and mechanics; if Bacon did not perceive what was happening around him (in the writings of Galileo and Kepler, or the closer presence of William Gilbert and Thomas Harriot) it was not through blindness, but from the pre-conviction that the true growth-points lay outside the general area of mathematics, precisely *because* that area had been so long cultivated and brought to a sterile plateau. To put it otherwise, Bacon precisely did *not* foresee that the high road to the understanding of nature would be mapped by some future 'Newton' figure, whereas the generality of historians looking backwards have seen (with hindsight) precisely this. From the eighteenth century onwards, Newtonianism (in the widest sense) has been seen as the ideal of science; therefore the paramount success story of the scientific revolution is the achievement of the Newtonian world-view, with which in subsequent centuries the empirical sciences were also rendered consistent.

Today this historiography commands less universal respect than it did thirty years ago. There are those who think that natural science could, or should, have followed some alternative world-view. They take some comfort from the fact that the Newtonian view proved too simple. They may speak of indeterminacy. This debate is irrelevant here, for I have written this book in the belief that Newtonianism did provide the historical high road to the development of the sciences we actually have. And it is clear that though what has come to be called Baconianism – what I have here called the empirical cultivation of the 'mixed' sciences – made important contributions to modern science, it was not itself on this high road. If Galileo, Descartes, Newton (and others) had never heard the name of Bacon, it would have affected history little, before 1700. Which statement is by no means meant to deny the crucial importance of the ultimate, nineteenth-century reconciliation of Baconianism and New-tonianism.

All this turns not only on the nature of the materials that the various sciences have to cope with, but on the nature of the human mind that has to cope with these materials. What is at stake is not just the issue: are stars easier to under-stand than rocks, or vice versa? All science when it ceases to be merely descrip-tive is basically a study of motion and change, whether it is called biological evolution or the expansion of the universe. It happens that motion is something that the Western mind (at any rate) has found comprehensible, partly through the possibility of associating it with number, and so success with all its man-ifestations is the very nature of scientific evolution. Now macroscopic motion – the readily discernible movements of large things – is relatively easy to study, at least until speeds approach that of light, and the things are as large as gal-axies: this has formed the chief tradition of physical science, from Aristotle through Newton to Einstein. But microscopic motion – the normally unde-tectable movements in the structure of things that form the basis of the science of all living and inert substance – is almost impossibly difficult to develop at all; but especially mathematically. Aristotle found it so impossible that he rejected it (that is, atomism) completely; Newton saw its importance with crys-tal clarity, but could make no headway with it; the real beginnings were with Daltonian chemistry, and the kinetic theory of gases. Great depth of under-standing, and the possibility of unification of theory from atomic physics to molecular biology, are still within living memory. When historians speak of the Newtonian tradition and its success, they are of course speaking of macro-scopic kinetics, for at the microscopic level Newton enjoyed a temporary and illusory success only. By contrast, Baconian science – so far as it is more than an encyclopaedic description, and Bacon's own vision seems to have indeed risen beyond that – was concerned only with microscopic kinetics, this is the only kind of kinetic science in which Bacon had any interest. Macroscopic kinetics, as remarked above, he wholly ignored. 'Baconianism' in other words is a label that might be applied to that most recalcitrant of the two scientific paths in the study of motion, whose pursuit was to prove so perplexing, and whose fruits (in terms of mathematical theory) were to prove so difficult of attainment. Even yet, the worlds of Bacon and Newton, or Bohr and Einstein, are still not united, though they are closely reconciled.

There is perhaps yet another reason for the less strikingly rapid success of the Baconian branch of the scientific revolution, which yet might have been thought to bring strength to it. This was its positive social involvement. Far-rington's label for Bacon as a 'prophet of industrial science' is absurd, because Bacon could have no inkling of industrial society and science-based industry, but he certainly believed the betterment of the human condition to be a worthy and attainable objective, and measured knowledge by a practical as well as an aesthetic yardstick. The errors of philosophy for many centuries before his own time were not merely deplored by him because they had left men in a state of intellectual blindness (they had failed to produce *light*) but actively detested because they had left pain and misery unalleviated (they had been without *fruit*). There is a passion in Bacon's denunciation of intellectual barrenness which is quite lacking, say, from Descartes's account of the real ignorance of those who were supposed to be learned. The philosophical revolution that Bacon wishes to bring about is not one of ideas and methods only, but one that seeks to alter the whole course of human history, which had somehow begun to take a wrong turn even in antiquity so that the full potentiality of man had never been realized, and had in the Middle Ages receded further and further away. Bacon is as it were saying to the philosophers: 'Repent: change your ways before it is too late', just as Puritan divines would make the same appeal to the people, thinking of the coming apocalypse, and indeed just as Savonarola had urged repentance on the Florentines in the 1490s, crying

The Sword has descended; the scourge has fallen; the prophecies are being fulfilled ... It is not I but God who foretold it. Now it is coming. It has come![17]

Many English Puritans of the seventeenth century believed that the Millennium foretold in the New Testament had indeed already begun with the Protestant Reformation, and that they were living in the age of the 'Kingdom which shall never be destroyed', the last age of men on Earth, in which after the war between Christ and Antichrist had been won, men should enjoy the dominion of Earth and sea and stars, accepting the surrender of Mother Nature. The parallel with Bacon's philosophical revolution was natural and appealing; in the words of Charles Webster[18]:

the search for a new philosophy based on experience appeared to seventeenth-century [English] protestants to be thoroughly consistent with the religious reformation. The invention of printing and of gunpowder, and particularly the voyages of discovery, seemed to herald a revival of learning which was seen as thoroughly consistent with the envisaged utopian paradise and indeed capable of providing the means whereby the utopian conditions would be realised.

Some consequences of this identification of the philosophic with the religious millennium will appear later; the point here is, that while it gave a temporary and local boost to certain intellectual developments in England, it reduced the appeal of Baconianism to those of other religious persuasions, and different philosophical outlook. In Europe the metaphysical discussions of Descartes or Leibniz seemed far more pertinent as the substrate to a scientific worldview than any variety of millenarianism or utopianism, so that despite the immense discrepancies between Descartes and Leibniz (themselves very dissimilar thinkers) on the one hand, and Newton on the other, yet they had more in common with each other (all were concerned with macroscopic kinetics) than with Bacon. Moreover, the whole Puritan and millenarian outlook was to enjoy only a brief dominance, and its failing carried much of the force of Baconianism with it.

In simple analysis, one sees that Bacon's philosophy and its ideals became intertwined with a social activism that was not indeed, contrary to his own spirit, though he himself was Puritan neither in theology nor in his vision of history. Such an involvement may give power to a particular current in science for a time, but as society changes it becomes a fetter. Mathematical or 'Newtonian' science, free from social commitment, capable of a kind of chameleonism which enabled it to flourish in London, Paris, Berlin or St Petersburg, was universal. Despite its brilliant beginning, Baconianism and descriptive science left (in most people's minds) only the thin legacy of empiricism, *fiat experimentum*, and the story of Francis Bacon catching his death of cold through stuffing a hen with snow. Encyclopaedic natural history had to make a new continental start with the work of Buffon and Alexander von Humboldt; microscopic kinetics, equally on the continent, was to spring from such diverse roots as mathematical statistics, Lavoisier's chemistry, and the hybridization experiments on plants of Koelreuter, all in the eighteenth century, and preparing the way for a 'second scientific revolution' in the nineteenth century through which, at last, the age-old vision of a harmony between the microscopic and the macroscopic worlds at last came within reach of attainment.

NOTES

1. See B. J. T. Dobbs, *The Foundations of Newton's Alchemy*, Cambridge U. P. 1975.
2. R. J. Collingwood, *The Idea of Nature*, Clarendon Press: Oxford, 1945.
3. Joseph Needham, *Science and Civilization in China*, Cambridge U. P., I. 1954, 95.
4. *Dictionary of Scientific Biography*, XIII, 208, col. 2.
5. A. C. Crombie, *Robert Grosseteste and the Origins of Experimental Science*, Clarendon Press: Oxford, 1953.
6. Edward Rosen, 'The invention of eyeglasses', *Jour. Hist. Medicine and Allied Sciences*, XI, 1956, 13–46, 183–218.
7. 'The Syrups' in C. D. O'Malley, *Michael Servetus*, American Philosophical Society: Philadelphia, 1953, 60–1.
8. Edward MacCurdy, *The Notebooks of Leonardo da Vinci*, Cape: London, 1948, I, 634, 636.
9. P. Duhem, *To Save the Phenomena* (trans. E. Doland and C. Maschler), University of Chicago Press: Chicago, 1969, 23.
10. F. Bacon, *Philosophical Works* (ed. J. M. Robertson), Routledge: London 1905, 209.
11. Carlo Cippolla, *Guns and Sails*, Collins: London 1965.
12. A useful reprint of these engravings was issued by the Burndy Library, Norwalk, Connecticut, *c.* 1950.
13. Paolo Rossi, *From Magic to Science*, Routledge: London, 1968.
14. Articles in the *Journal of the History of Ideas*, 1940, reprinted in P. P. Wiener and A. Noland (eds) *Roots of Scientific Thought*, Basic Books: New York, 1957, 219–80.
15. C. S. Smith, *The Pirotechnia of Vannoccio Biringuccio*, Basic Books: New York, 1958, Introduction.
16. T. S. Kuhn, *The Essential Tension*, University of Chicago Press: Chicago, 1977, 31–65.
17. C. Hibbert, *The Rise and Fall of the House of Medici*, Lane: London, 1974, 185.
18. C. Webster, *The Great Instauration*, Duckworth: London, 1975, 1.

CHAPTER ONE

The problem of cause

Neither mutation nor fixity is inevitable in human affairs, including philosophy and science. Ideas, like societies, have sometimes changed rapidly, sometimes remained as it seems in the same state for many successive centuries. It is therefore a paradox of historiography that either mutation or fixity may equally seem to demand explanation, as though the other – which may be either – did not. Thus we might seek to explain why English political institutions, though plainly imperfect in many respects, remained unchanged from 1689 to 1832, while conversely seeking to explain the occurrence of a great political convulsion in France in 1789. This is partly because the historian may ask of any event: 'Why now, rather than earlier or later?' or 'Why here, rather than there?' so that the problem of the occurrence of one event may be simply the inverse of the problem of the non-occurrence of that event.

Unless the inevitability of historical events be accepted[1] – and if it is, no need of explanation remains – the scientific revolution of early modern times need not have occurred. Verbose and general as it was, the system of philosophy, science and medicine which had been formed by selection (sometimes capricious) from the intellectual life of the ancient world and which had satisfied the successor societies both Islamic and Christian for so long might have endured longer still. Perhaps subtly modified, as it had been in previous centuries, yet still preserving its essential homogeneity and sources of deep (if erroneous) appeals to the human consciousness it might have endured for millennia. That system still attracts the deep interest of specialist scholars, even though its validity be denied; no sensitive mind would dismiss it as so much outdated rubbish, while portions of it are still entertained as valid by the less sophisticated members of Western societies. Though we now know the premodern scientific world-view to be false, it was not and is not intellectually contemptible, and indeed can be seen as satisfying and adequate for many purposes. One cannot say that it was 'bound' to be exploded.

Therefore there must be special reasons for its breakdown, which indeed was powerfully resisted for reasons not wholly absurd or conventional. In political revolutions one sometimes feels that the coup succeeds because the forces of conservatism have lost conviction and so have lost courage: the defenders of established science in the sixteenth and seventeenth centuries lacked neither, nor were they stupid, and of course they possessed the power of the establishment. We ought therefore to ask not one question, but two: why did new scientific ideas and methods come to be introduced, and why did they prevail (or more exactly, why did *some* prevail, *at least for a time*)? And always we have to remember that the scientific revolution was an episodic process — we have no reason to believe that Copernicus' views on medicine were other than conventional. Philosophers like Bacon and Descartes levelled very broad methodological attacks on the past, but actual investigators of phenomena tended to be piecemeal in their approach (this is true for insistance of Descartes's own study of light).

The causes of the scientific revolution offered by historians fall into two well-defined classes: some relate to the degree of mismatch between established learning and the society of the Renaissance, and accordingly make a change in society precede a change in science. Other causes relate to the intellectual consistency of science either within itself, or with other intellectual activities such as religion and philosophy: we are here speaking very generally of a 'world-view' which contains many elements besides the scientific; if these alter, the scientific parts of the picture must shift also. Obviously these two classes of cause are, irrespective of the plausibility of particular discussions of them, complementary rather than antagonistic: we might, if we wished, seek the origin of new scientific ideas in shifts of intellectual perspective, while looking to changes in society for their acceptability. Equally obviously intellectual change relates to individuals — some one, or a small group, must propose a new idea or method in the first place — while discussions of social shifts relate in principle to large groups of people, such as most English Puritans, or speculators in foreign exploration, or practising physicians. One writes *in principle* because, in intellectual history, where 'society' is invoked there is in ordinary practice no employment of statistically significant samples, except where the techniques of prosopology are employed; argument usually turns on the discussion of a few supposedly typical individuals. A third obvious point is that the intellectual analysis is vulnerable on grounds of particularity (if we study as closely as possible the workings of the mind of a single individual, be it Galileo or Newton, this cannot tell us anything of the thoughts in other minds), while the social analysis is vulnerable not only technically (because of paucity of evidence) but because of the logical impossibility of making, say the perception of a problem the same thing as its acceptable solution. For of course the tackling of new problems is only one aspect of the evolution of ideas; the provision of new solutions to old problems is at least as important, perhaps more so, and few problems have unique solutions.

To begin with social analysis, which at least promises generality and not merely a host of individual case-histories, it is clear that historians have long discussed a multitude of changes denoting the transition from the 'medieval' to the 'modern' world, changes which may be symbolized geographically by the discovery of America in 1492, politically by the French descent into Italy of 1494, and in religion by the posting of Luther's theses in 1517. If there was indeed a turning-point in the character of Western civilization – never marked by long-term stability – then it is not unreasonable to suppose a connection between more flexible ways of thought and more flexible forms of society. Historians have written of the stimulus provided by world-wide exploration and the discovery of the strange fauna and flora inhabiting new continents: the one, through the dependence of navigation upon cartography and astronomy, ensured the importance of applied mathematical skills which were cultivated by a host of 'mathematical practitioners' in seaports and other large centres, from whom again grew some of the first professional schools training naval officers[2]; the other, through curiosity, through the prestige attaching to collections of exotic animals, and through the medicinal importance universally assigned to herbs, re-invigorated natural history and initiated anthropological interests.[3] In both instances what was chiefly involved was a broadening and reification of interests: a concern developing almost of necessity in real things like the times of rising of the stars or unfamiliar animals, yet without there being any tension between this new concern with a new reality and the old structure of astronomy and philosophy. If a wider experience of nature and sharper mathematical necessities aroused any scepticism with respect to the old categories of thought it was at most indirectly, through the conversion of academic professionalism into practical professionalism.

Rather the same conclusion seems to apply to another much-canvassed agent of intellectual ferment, technology. The purely indirect role of the printing press (1454), for example, is surely beyond dispute: the press did not incite people to write new books or put new ideas into them any more than the organized scriptoria which had existed for centuries. What the press did was to enlarge readership vastly: it was the multitude of copies of books, not their mode of production *per se*, which slowly led to an enlargement of the nature of the book, as by the writing of manuals for the autodidact, and of specialist books for people who previously, if literate at all, certainly had not bought books. Interlocking with that is the rise of practical mathematical professionalism, on land as well as at sea (surveyors, drainage engineers, architects, shipbuilders, gunners) thriving in an economically adventurous and bellicose Europe. The mathematization, rudimentary as it was, of these old arts (changing, in the Renaissance, in form rather than in essence) was itself expressive of a new attitude creating a positive feedback effect between the *idea* of what such a practitioner ought to be, and the *manner* in which he actually did his work, where the printed book plays a seminal reinforcing role. Again the main interest here for the historian of the scientific revolution is in the creation of a new population that was both 'learned' and practical, though not formally academic, a population capable of channelling knowledge of natural phenomena to effective intellectual levels, for example. Among the letters of Torricelli one finds a complaint that the ballistic tables he had published were not confirmed by practical trials (to which the mathematician replied that he wrote for philosophers, not gunners)[4] and a more celebrated instance is Galileo's learning that suction-pumps could not raise water more than some 9 m (30 ft). In the general field of engineering one observes mathematicians from Simon Stevin in the sixteenth century to Leonhard Euler two centuries later making a wide range of practical suggestions, to which this world of literate practitioners was able to respond by adopting some and rejecting others: up to a point, at least, the introduction of a workable steam-engine may be regarded as an example of this process, which was both commercially and philosophically lucrative.

No historian would wish to overlook the significance of numbers: no intellectual activity can thrive if those who pursue it are extremely few, isolated, and without support from others. Certainly the political, social and economic changes of the Renaissance provided a bigger literate (and to a much less extent, numerate) population than had ever existed before, whose concerns drew it towards an investigation of natural phenomena. One might also expect that this interest would tend to be more 'real' and less schematic or discursive than during the high Middle Ages. When one makes this point, however, it is again necessary to emphasize that novelty or originality was not at a premium: the most successful printed books in the fifteenth century (leaving aside almanacs, health tracts and other medical books) were medieval encyclopaedias like *De Proprietatibus Rerum, c.* 1230 (On the Properties of Things) by Bartholomew the Englishman, or Caxton's *Myrrour of the World* (1481), or the largely imaginary travels of 'John of Mandeville'. In astronomy easily the best seller of all time (relatively speaking) was Sacrobosco's *Sphere* (*c.* 1230). The historian can hardly overemphasize the conservatism of the substratum of culture, especially in the north (which accounts for Shakespeare's world-view).

In a weak sense, then, a Marxist proposition that the development of commerce and industry in the Renaissance, and perhaps particularly its global extent, stimulated a certain kind of intellectual activity in Europe may be taken as valid, though hardly adequate to account for any specific events (such as the Copernican revolution in astronomy) that one might care to name, whereas the strong form of the same proposition, that commerce and industry dictated problems for natural philosophers to solve seems (to me, at any rate) palpably false, for the most interesting scientific problems of the time tended to be still traditional ones — human anatomy, planetary motion, the fall of heavy bodies and so forth. One need not be long misled by the vulgar sophism that would see Leonardo da Vinci's studies of artillery or Galileo's lessons in fortification as evidence that 'science' had been overtaken by novel military necessities.

Science was linked with technology and religion by Robert K. Merton almost half a century ago in his classic case-history of the sociology of science[5]: the idea that the reformed religion (its Calvinist sects especially) favoured the cultivation of natural science in a way that the Roman Catholic Church did not, and indeed any church with bishops did not, is of course much older than half a century, and still attracts able exponents such as Christopher Hill, Reijer Hooykaas and Charles Webster.[6] Historians from Catholic, Mediterranean Europe seem not to have espoused it. At a first inspection the correlation asserted has much to commend it: the northern, Protestant half of Europe seems to have been rendered more fortunate in eminent scientific discovery than the south, and in countries like Italy and Spain scientific achievement seems to have followed, rather than preceded, the relaxation of the clerical ascendancy in educational and intellectual matters. No one could deny the distinction of research in Catholic France, but it is notorious that in that country intellectuals, especially the *lumières* of the eighteenth century, were for the most part anticlerical. Moreover, the case argued by Merton and others did not merely depend on accumulating instances (where weighting becomes alike important and impossible) but also on a detailed argument turning on the value of the work-ethic in the Protestant outlock, the belief in salvation by works, and the necessity to praise God understandingly: thus a coherent explanation was offered of *why* the Calvinist or Puritan in particular should be more likely to study nature than his more light-hearted or obscurantist Catholic contemporary. Thus Merton wrote[7]:

Puritanism transfused ascetic vigour into activities which, in their own right, could not as yet achieve self-sufficiency. It so redefined the relations between the divine and the mundane as to move science to the *front rank of social values*. As it happened, this was at the immediate expense of literary, *and ultimately, of religious pursuits*... Puritanism differed from Catholicism, which had gradually come to tolerate science, in demanding, not merely condoning, its pursuit.

However surprising these strong expressions (to which I have added emphasis) may seem to those with other views of the principal teachings of John Calvin and John Knox, they have not (to my knowledge) been repudiated by the recent upholders of the 'Protestant ethic' in relation to science, who indeed cite mainly seventeenth-century authors and sometimes, even, men who actually became bishops. But in any case, extrapolation backwards of the 'Protestant ethic' thesis to the fifteenth century is impossible, nor has anyone supported it by reference to Luther's celebrated Wittenberg theses of 1517. Calvin's dominance of Geneva began in 1541 but his *Institutes* were completed only in 1559. By this time, in the eyes of most intellectual historians, the history of thought in Europe had long been set on a new course. The great works of Copernicus and Vesalius had been printed (1543) and the former was dead. Tartaglia, Paracelsus, Fernel and many other pioneers of the new scientific movement were dead also by 1559. It would be strange indeed to claim that the reawakening of the European spirit had been effected by Calvin, who ordered the burning at the stake of Servetus in Geneva (1544). Moreover, it was to Italy and nowhere else that sixteenth-century intellectuals – even, much later, the arch-Puritan Milton – wished to travel. Italy formed Copernicus, and enabled Vesalius (another notherner) to do his work. The new botany, the new algebra, the new anatomy, came from Italy, whose universities attracted the most distinguished students from all countries irrespective of sect. The telescope and microscope were Italian, as eyeglasses had been before; pneumatics was Italian; the most highly paid engineers were Italian.

   Protestantism is totally irrelevant to the initiation of the scientific revolution. The influence it had on the character of seventeenth-century science is another matter. But no historian (I believe) has failed to see an essential continuity from Vesalius to Harvey, from Copernicus to Kepler, from Galileo to

Newton, bridging firmly over any stretch of time in which the new Protestant spirit might be supposed to infiltrate. Those historians who wish to write any kind of genetic account of the scientific revolution, or to trace its evolution from small beginnings through successive accretions and modifications, are surely right in looking back to the universally Catholic fifteenth century, in the youth of Leonardo and Copernicus, for the first portents of what was to come.

To say this is not to deny that other historical issues remain. As soon as we ask why the Mediterranean failed to retain, after the sixteenth century, the ascendancy in science and technology so marked during the Renaissance, why the names of northerners like Descartes, Huygens and Newton dominate the scene, clerical reaction against the new philosophy suggests itself as the obvious explanation. The tradition of Galileo, condemned by his Church, died in Florence[8]; those of the next generation like Borelli and Malpighi who continued to bring intellectual distinction to Italy were by no means universally praised there, or free from obstructions. Sectarian distinctions may well therefore have much to do with the continuation of the scientific revolution – though even the Protestant north had its reactionaries, like Sir William Temple and Dr Jonathan Swift, and its clerical criticism of the materialism of the new science – even though a simple association between Protestantism and science, Catholicism and non-science, is clearly untenable.

Investigations of the affiliations of those energetic either on behalf of intellectual innovation or in opposition to it have proved difficult and inconclusive, and there has hardly been agreement on how to conduct them in an illuminating manner. Almost every kind of person down to the level of clerks, tradesmen and apothecaries might be found upon the fringes of the scientific movement. The main centres of activity were, naturally, the universities and the great cities (some of which, like London, Venice and Lyons were not graced by universities), but there was a scattering of the *curious* or the *virtuosi* (as they were usually called in the seventeenth century) in provincial towns and even in the depths of the countryside. In some towns like Caen in Normandy or Spalding in Lincolnshire local societies flourished. Such groups and isolated individuals (old John Beale in Somerset, Martin Lister in York) who could rarely attend the meetings of national academies like the Royal Society kept in touch by means of the national postal systems which were already fairly efficient, though an *international* postal system was as yet a thing of the future; the periodicals coming into existence at the same time were also distributed by mail. Certainly the largest single class in the scientific movement was that of the medical men, preponderantly physicians, in all countries; some of them occupied academic posts, and there were other academics – professors of mathematics, for example – who eagerly advanced their subjects. Everywhere too the Churches gave learned men to science, not least (in Roman Catholic states) from the great teaching orders, the Jesuits and in France also the Oratorians. Some of these, like the astronomers Giambattista Riccioli in Italy and Giovanni Domenico Cassini in France, either from necessity or genuine conviction remained anti-Copernicans, while nevertheless carrying out professional work of first-class importance. (A very few astronomers, including Cassini and John Flamsteed at Greenwich, were the only men in the seventeenth century actually employed to carry out research.) Most of the scientific clergy, and all those private gentlemen who took part actively or passively in the development of mathematics and science, were of course strictly 'amateurs', but the idea of attaching professional scientific status to anyone before the nineteenth century is highly inappropriate, since it suggests a similarity with the present that really did not exist. There were not, in the seventeenth century, any sanctions on the 'professionals' who failed to justify their promise for research and publication, as there are today.

In any case, even if prosopological investigations of the sixteenth and seventeenth centuries could be made reliable or convincing, it would still not be evident whether noisy controversy or solid professional work counts for more in the progress of science, or whether it makes sense to compare the achievement of Francis Bacon, a programmatic writer in Protestant England, with the descriptive microscopy of Marcello Malpighi in Catholic Italy, two generations later. Equally incomparable, in the case of one individual such as Galileo, are the effects of scientific discoveries and polemical writings. It is too naive, historically, to ask where men stood in relation to some great question, whether of religious or scientific doctrine, as though there were simple tests of an individual being 'reactionary' or 'progressive', 'conservative' or 'innovatory'. In fact no such tests exist, people were then as always mixed in their thoughts and attitudes and a great deal of the most important work in mathematics and science was purely technical, lacking those overtones and complexities which some modern scholars are so anxious to detect everywhere, rather like psychiatrists searching for the fateful experiences of infancy.

On the intellectual plane, where historians have sought to find the origins of modern science in a new 'thinking-cap' (as Herbert Butterfield put it), an altered notion of how one might tackle one's problems as philosopher, astronomer or mathematician, the study of nature has long been accepted as derivative – in a rather unspecific way – from the widening horizons of the fifteenth-century Renaissance, and particularly 'humanism'.[9] Humanism is an ill-defined, and perhaps no longer very suitable concept: ill-defined, because it seems to imply a freedom from religious fervour and intolerance that was by no means to be characteristic of European society, and because preoccupation with humanity (whether it be literary, or psychological or social) is by no means necessarily linked with any sort of concern for nature, and no longer very suitable because it invokes a large, vague explanation for events that were quite precise, such as the search for 'lost' Greek scientific writings, and by no means unprecedented. There were, of course, two great textual transfusions into Latinate Europe: one in the twelfth and thirteenth centuries (this brought medieval science into being), the second, considerably more sophisticated in its scholarship, in the fifteenth and sixteenth centuries. We can reasonably argue that a great deal of science was learnt from this second classical revival, which gave Europe almost all Galen, the 'pure' Ptolemy, Archimedes and other Greek mathematicians, the pre-Socratics (p. 9) and above all Plato. Can we, therefore, regard modern science as the outgrowth of this larger, more varied, more exciting library – which, however, still included the great medieval philosophers as well?

To consider a straightforward case seems to make a direct positive answer possible. The new anatomy of the sixteenth century – from which slender root all our present panoply of medical science springs – was certainly 'caused' by the recovery of the anatomical texts of Galen. Its best known (and to bibliophiles most costly) monument, the *De Humani Corporis Fabrica* (On the Fabric of the Human Body) by Andreas Vesalius (1543) is solidly related, line by line, to Galen; but Vesalius does not *echo* Galen. He saw himself not merely as an editor or expositor – though he filled both these roles – but as a critic, and if need be an innovator. He had explored vastly more of the human body with his own eyes than ever Galen had. He did not hesitate to dispute Galen's contention that the great blood vessels of the body originate from the liver, for he saw them coming from the heart. Note that his test is one of observation, not reasoning, and that he seems to find the perfection of knowledge in the future, rather than the past. This was an important characteristic of the renaissance intellectual – Leonardo shared it – but it was not ubiquitous.[10] Moreover, Vesalius' work and that of other contemporary anatomists benefited from two other developments unrelated to scholarly humanism. In the first place, he enjoyed the freedom to dissect human cadavers and to become an academic professor of anatomy (at Padua) because the medieval world had institutionalized the teaching of medicine in universities and had countenanced dissection (of course, following Galenic precepts) as a necessary feature of medical education. Not the Renaissance, but the Middle Ages, gave Vesalius (as before, Berengario da Carpi, or later Fabricius) his opportunity, his vantage point in society for intellectual exploration. In the second place, the study of the human body and the permanent recording of its appearance as revealed by dissection had been developed by graphic artists. Nothing like the 'photographic' realism aimed at by the artists, of whom Leonardo was the most studious and the most pursuant of the relation between structure and function, and after them by the anatomists, had ever been seen before; there is no reason to imagine that the Greeks had ever possessed anything similar; medieval illustrations are either grotesqueries or at best artificial diagrams more useful as mnemonics than as visual images. It is easy to see how the new representational techniques – reproducible in print – transformed teaching and study, and indeed the vision of the anatomist himself.

Hence the story of the simple textual input of Galen's writings proves to have its complexities, even in this short analysis. At least one must recognize the significant difference in social setting – for antiquity, it is clear, viewed any form of dissection with utter repugnance, unless performed by gladiators at the public games – and the stimulus of technical richness. Similar complexities greet the historian in considering the contemporaneous but dissimilar innovation of Copernicus. His position is closest to that of Vesalius in that he too valued his own technical expertise, this time as a mathematician (the significance of new observations in his work is minimal). And like Vesalius too he has a model, Ptolemy's *Almagest* – three times translated into Latin, yet still inaccessible to fifteenth-century scholars – which Copernicus follows chapter by chapter. But the crucial difference between the two men is that Copernicus had found himself a new principle, a new point of departure for his mathematics in the treatment of the Earth as a planet. Vesalius' triumph was methodological, that of Copernicus intellectual, for he proved the validity of a new principle (though he did not of course prove that the Earth really moves). Moreover, whereas sixteenth-century anatomy owed nothing to the cognate civilization of Islam, it is at least possible that Copernicus in some way made use of mathematical devices developed in Persia nearly two hundred years earlier; at all events, certain technical, non-Ptolemaic features of his astronomy had been anticipated there.

Such evidence suggests that there was some unreality in the endeavour to seek a new, purer inspiration in Greek writings, just as there was artificiality in Machiavelli's contention that modern warfare should return to the weapons and tactics of the Roman legions. What had happened between 1100 and 1400 could not be thrust out, any more than Christianity itself. Humanism was one aspiration of a changing society, bringing it elegance, precision and a strong touch of materialism. It provided innovators like Copernicus or Harvey with excellent antecedents or authorities for departing from ordinary, common-sense knowledge – but humanism may not necessarily explain why such men wished to seek out new antecedents, why they were discontented with the conventional.

According to one well-known thesis, those conventions in learning (the fixity of the Earth, the primacy of the liver) which T. S. Kuhn originally called 'paradigms' ultimately fail and are replaced when counter-instances or counter-arguments multiply to the point where the tension becomes intolerable. This model has only partial applicability to the Renaissance, however, partly because although Aristotelian philosophy might be said to constitute a paradigm, internal dissension between scholars and universities was always strong, polemic being after all the heart of academic life; partly because the idea of 'paradigm' seems inappropriate for most technical aspects of late-medieval science, and partly because in them the processes of paradigm-establishment and paradigm-refutation seem to be concurrent. If Copernicus challenged the paradigm of terrestrial fixity and centrality, it was only by accepting every mathematical paradigm of Ptolemy's astronomy. Or to put this more generally, the intellectual world of the fifteenth century was so confused, inchoate, preoccupied with groping for some truth and certainty, that there could hardly be a conflict between 'truths' and 'refutations', and we cannot say that refutations sprang from new factual discoveries, or hitherto perceived inconsistencies, or factual or logical deficiencies of other sorts (though everyone knew that these existed – it is almost *never* the case, in any period, that the existing state of knowledge is held to be perfect). For example, the Aristotelian qualitative analysis of matter and change was no more defective in the sixteenth century than before, or more open to experimental refutation, yet the opinions of philosophers tended steadily to favour a more materialist analysis, modelled on that of the pre-Socratics and Greek atomists.

Here we should note and accept the point made long age by Collingwood that although the words in which a problem is expressed many remain the same, among different groups of men at distant intervals of time the questions asked are really very different.[11] To discover what the real question is we have not merely to read the words expressing it, but to interrogate the mind of the speaker. Thus, in relation to the theory of matter, we may well suppose Aristotle not to be asking the unanswerable question: 'what is stone made of?' but rather 'what is in stone that affects our senses with a feeling of coolness, hardness, roughness and so on?' to which his qualitative theory gives an adequate reply. Thus he can give an account of the world of substance to man the sentient being. But to the Renaissance – partly because they believed the world to have been made out of something by a Creator, it made sense to ask: 'what is the matter that precedes substance? And how does matter produce the qualities of substance, such as stone?' In term of this quite different question, the answers of atomism or the mechanical philosophy, rejected by Aristotle in relation to his question, make sense and the qualities, no longer reified, become names given to sensations in the sentient being. Materialism had the charm of freshness, it provided a new intellectual game to be played (the explanation of the real properties of things, like sweetness, in terms of the hypothetical movements of imagined particles), it had the merit of greater picturability as a model than Aristotle's qualitative theory, but it cannot be reckoned as logically superior to that theory unless we overlook the fact it is answering different questions from those posed in Aristotle's mind.

Unfortunately, Collingwood's historiographical strategy leading to the process of thought-reconstruction as the core of the historian's task, still leaves us with the problem: Why do the questions men ask change?

Questions may alter, though phraseology remains constant, for many reasons: because the persons asking them are different (astronomers, say, rather than philosophers: Copernicus provides a superbly illuminating example here); because material conditions alter (so Jellicoe's tactical problems of naval warfare were very different from those of Nelson a century earlier, though the objects of naval warfare and even the process of ship-by-ship annihilation remained unchanged), or because thoughts themselves alter by, for example, the refutation of what had previously seemed a strong proposition (so, in the game of chess, a popular attacking gambit or defence may fall into desuetude when a player thinks out a new and stronger response to it). It would be mistaken, however, to suppose that question-shifts occur *only* when the questioner has a different interest at heart (as when he is, say, a practitioner of of some skill rather than a philosopher), or conversely *only* because there has been some metaphysical change rendering a different answer more acceptable (which means, of course, that the real question asked is no longer the same), or still more that question-shifts only alter because some new facts have been discovered by chance, or experiment, or other means. The historical reality seems to be, and it is rather unsatisfactory, that question-shifts occur gradually, insidiously, and without anyone deliberating consciously on the wisdom or otherwise of altering the questions. A fine example is the 'Newtonian' theory of gravity during the eighteenth century, which began by asking 'can gravity, a force, be an attribute of matter?' (answer, no) and ended by asking 'can gravity, a universal property of matter, not be its attribute?' (answer, again, no). Yet there was no formal refutation of the earlier, and authentically Newtonian, position.

Perhaps the most obvious 'cause' for the scientific revolution that can be suggested is that it represents the selective flowering of certain medieval traditions. No one doubts that the scientific revolution was a departure from, indeed a reaction against, the mainstream of medieval learning as cultivated in the universities; but some great scholars have believed that there were currents in the mainstream carrying ideas forward in the direction that modern science was to take. Pierre Duhem (1861–1916), for example, believed that the science of mechanics – the science refounded by Galileo, and which he connected with cosmology – received such major improvements in the fourteenth century that it remained only for Galileo to rediscover, generalize and reformulate what medieval and renaissance 'precursors' had known before him; Galileo brought out the full power of the tool they had forged.[12] In particular, Duhem drew attention to statements in the Middle Ages closely analogous to the later concept of inertia, and to the successful mathematical analysis of accelerated motion. In fact, Duhem proved that some philosophers in medieval universities were teaching ideas about motion and mechanics that were totally non-Aristotelian, were consciously based on criticism of Aristotle's own pronouncements, and were far closer in spirit to the language of the seventeenth century. Similarly, Crombie has drawn attention to the importance of empiricism in medieval discussions of logic, and to the successful use of experiments in medieval optics, most strikingly in the early-fourteenth-century study of the rainbow colours by Theoderic of Freyburg.[13] Again, this certainly went far beyond the shadowy and jejune Greek ideas about light and colours, so as to leave Descartes in 1637 only one step to take. Like Duhem, Crombie has argued that the medieval philosophers had provided a 'model' of a new and more modern kind of science, which only needed to be developed and extended to push knowledge along new and unconventional paths.

The researches of such historians as these – there have been many others – have certainly, during the last century, rendered the former image of medieval intellectual life quite out of date. Scholasticism was not all cobwebs, as Francis Bacon thought, nor was it merely an endless rumination of what Aristotle and a few other authorities had written: it was critical, innovative, mathematical even experimental. We can indeed find in it all sorts of anticipations of later philosophy and mathematics – just as there were, in ninth-century India, mathematicians solving isolated problems that in the West had to await the time of Newton. But when we have taken the highest possible view of medieval learning, it still remains difficult to find an embryonic scientific revolution within it – except in the sense that the one necessarily preceded the other. For one thing there seems to have been an historical collapse, a breach of continuity between the late fourteenth century and the mid-sixteenth century. Much of the medieval achievement was forgotten or devalued – it is surely very unlikely that Descartes knew anything of Theoderic, or Galileo of Jean Buridan and Nicole Oresme.[14] In part this may have been due to the humanistic 'classical reaction'. Some of the exciting new themes of the fourteenth century survived the Renaissance, but not all, and their treatment seems to have remained static. At the least, the problem of the revival of a dying tradition would have to be faced. Even more seriously, on more through historical examination the parallels noted by Duhem between medieval and modern thinking have proved less than perfectly exact, that is, certain important differences between the medieval and the modern use of similar phrases remain. Notably, it has been necessary to emphasize the conjecturalism of most medieval mechanics, which was a subtle intellectual game, not an attempt to provide an account of the real natural world. It was based on assumptions which no one supposed to be really true, and though its more mathematical aspects give a deep impression of the power and acuity of human intelligence they still, set in their contemporary context, belong to some world of philosophical abstraction rather than to the world of mathematical physics. Similarly the discovery of new truths with the aid of water-globes or magnets, and the more general art of invention associated with Roger Bacon, seem not to have produced a lasting methodology nor to have created any enduring tradition.

We may well believe that the medieval culture was a necessary condition for the scientific revolution, without seeing how it can have been a sufficient condition. We can associate the decline of this culture with the economic and demographic decline following the Black Death (1345–46), which thus cut short the high-medieval intellectual promise. But it is difficult to be satisfied with unbroken or even periodic continuity as a sufficient explanation of the sixteenth-century outburst of original scientific activity. The historian is forced to look for some new impulses to account for the enormous change of philosophic character between the fourteenth and the sixteenth centuries, and for the progress made by the Renaissance in areas like pure mathematics, astronomy, or graphic anatomy where the medieval antecedence had been uninventive. It is surely significant that the fields of medieval triumph, mechanics and optics, did not initiate the scientific revolution but became active research fronts only in the late sixteenth century.

An equally powerful but totally different current of ideas in recent years has found a total change of mental perspective attributable to the ascendancy of Plato over Aristotle. The Middle Ages had accepted Aristotle's putting down of his teacher Plato (and all his other predecessors) at its face value and indeed had sought out nothing of Plato's writings beyond the *Timaeus*, which had made little impression. In the fifteenth century, most markedly with the Florentine neo-Platonists, all this changed – again, for no obvious reason except that Plato was new and intellectually exciting.

The significance of this Platonic revival of the sixteenth century for the development of modern science has long been recognized: 'magic, astrology and alchemy – all the outgrowth of Neoplatonism – gave the first effectual stimulus to the observation of nature, and consequently to natural science', writes one author.[15] Yet the various threads in the skein of ideas are confusedly mingled, and seem to lead from uncertain origins to very different ends. The most truly Platonic thread, stemming from the *Timaeus*, was that God the architect of nature is, like the human architect, a geometer. This can lead to the patterns of crystallography or the patterns of the periodic law in chemistry, or it can lead to certain elements in Freemasonry, where the neophyte is (or was) addressed in terms beginning thus[16]:

Adam, our first parent, created after the image of God, the great Architect of the Universe, must have had the Liberal Sciences, particularly Geometry, written on his Heart . . .

Other threads led through the neo-Platonist school of philosophers, writing many centuries after Plato's death in the third and fourth centuries AD, to numerology, magic and other esoteric arts wholly foreign to the mind of Plato himself, while others again produced a transcedental mysticism which was a little later absorbed by Christianity. Quite how the authentic philosophy of Plato or even of his late followers (of whom Plotinus and Proclus are the most distinguished) became the father of natural magic – magical operations without the aid of demons – seems to be somewhat obscure. As far as the Renaissance is concerned, however, it is certain that the neo-Platonic philosophy rediscovered by Marsilio Ficino in Florence was seen as derived from a much more venerable sage, Hermes Trismegistus (the thrice-greatest), who had himself been the world's first and chief authority on the philosophy of nature and the magical command over nature. His writings in the *Corpus Hermeticum*, supposedly at least coeval with Moses, were brought to Florence in 1460 for the benefit of Cosimo dei Medici; really they were composed by Greeks of the neo-Platonic period, as Isaac Casaubon first proved in the early seventeenth century. Hence Plato, together with the neo-Platonists, could be interpreted as magicians by Renaissance scholars, even though their works contain no overt magical elements. Upon this tradition Ficino's contemporary, the dubiously regarded Pico della Mirandola, grafted further magical ideas which he took from the Hebrew Cabala, ideas about talismans and the marvellous significance of letter-number transcriptions, which the adept could employ to control the flow of events. 'The profound significance of Pico della Mirandola in the history of humanity can hardly be overestimated,' Dame Frances Yates has declared: 'He it was who first boldly formulated a new position for European man, man as Magus using both Magic and Cabala to act upon the world, to control his destiny by science.'[17]

The argument of Miss Yates's now classical study of *Giordano Bruno and the Hermetic Tradition* (1964) was essentially, as in this last quotation, not merely that neo-Platonism induced Renaissance men to examine nature – they could, and did, learn this from many other sources, including Pliny and the Latin writers on agriculture – but that it induced men to examine nature with the intent of mastering it. The utilitarianism of Francis Bacon has been 'placed' historically in the same way by Paolo Rossi, through relating it to the natural

32

magic of the sixteenth century.[18] Dame Frances has a vision of modern science as being 'theoretical technology', as though men should study physics in order to devise steam-engines, or chemistry in order to compound explosives. She writes, with truth, that the Greek philosophers had neither possessed nor sought the power to operate on nature: to understand and ratiocinate had been the limit of their ambition. When they had gone so far in this way as Aristotle's comprehensive and consistent philosophy their intellectual ambition weakened and they went no further. Renaissance neo-Platonism gave a new ambition, a new objective for knowledge: power.

In this formulation the hypothesis of the 'magical origins of modern science' – a theme long ago taken up by the American historian Lynn Thorndike,[19] who similarly believed that natural magic led to scientific empiricism – comes very close to the 'craft origins of modern science', where technical progress is seen as the goal resulting from the study of nature. But Miss Yates, noting that some historians of science have voiced a certain despair concerning the causes of the scientific revolution, speaks also (and I believe rightly) of an 'emotional driving force' impelling Copernicus, and of 'emotional excitement'[20]:

It is a movement of the will [she writes] which really originates an intellectual movement. A new centre of interest arises, surrounded by emotional excitement; the mind turns where the will has directed it and new attitudes, new discoveries follow. Behind the emergence of modern science there was a new direction of the will towards the world, its marvels, and mysterious workings, a new longing and determination to understand those workings and to operate with them.

And she writes later[21]

The return to the occult this time stimulates the genuine science.

Miss Yates is surely correct in emphasizing the passion for a new kind of knowledge – the will to find something better than the 'barren rationalism' of scholastic philosophy – and in believing that the search to gratify this passion occasioned intellectual excitement in men like Copernicus or Vesalius. What seems doubtful is the strong association suggested as essential between this passion, and the sense of the barrenness of rationalism provoking it, and neo-Platonism, the occult and magic. Particularly (to take up the strong and more particular form of the proposition, advanced by both Miss Yates and Rossi) the link natural magic – applied science – pure science seems highly suspect. The concept of 'applied science' in the Renaissance is itself anachronistic, but the more important point is that if one looks in detail at the work of mathematicians, philosophers, physicians and so forth what they actually do seems to depart equally far from the magical and the utilitarian. It would be impossibly naive to believe that all mathematics existed for navigation and survey, that all astronomy was done for the sake of astrology, all botany to benefit the druggists and all anatomy for the sake of the surgeons, and so forth. The excitement, indeed, mentioned by Miss Yates seems often to relate not to any possibility of grasping *power*, but rather to understanding *order* in nature (astronomical order, botanical order, algebraic order). Copernicus made *order* (by which he meant nothing like a magical hierarchy) the criterion of truth in the universe; within the Copernican universe, for example, the great orbits of each planet are concentric, the periodic times increase steadily as the planet is more distant from the Sun, and it is possible to state the relative size of each orbit. None of this was possible before, so that (as Copernicus himself claimed) his seems to be a more symmetrical system than any preceding it.

So also with Kepler, *order* was the object of his search – when he writes of the snowflake as when he write of the cosmos. The ordering of the universe proposed by Kepler is capable of being tested against measured distances, and stands up well to the test. The magical order and occult harmonies proposed by John Dee – in his *Monas Hieroglyphica* for example – or by Robert Fludd, though they appealed strongly to the imaginations of some men, offer no ratios or proportions that can be scientifically tested.[22] They are mere assertions. Moreover, real mathematicians furnished solid technical improvements; from Copernicus' system improved ephemerides can be derived. On the other hand the magical mathematicians – at least, the English ones, Dee and Fludd – have no place in the history of mathematics written by mathematicians. This is not to deny that Dee taught Englishmen the principles of cosmography and navigation, and that he was a man of international reputation and influence; he simply discovered nothing new. (A century later another highly influential figure and bishop, John Wilkins, wrote a popular *Mathematical Magick*, yet as a mathematician he is utterly insignificant.) It is obvious that singing Orphic melodies or making cabalistical calculations are very different skills from discovering how to solve cubic equations, and possibly no one even in the Renaissance imagined otherwise; for a real mathematician to figure also in the history of the esoteric arts, as Girolamo Cardano does, is very exceptional. In general geometers and algebraists tried to detach themselves from any kind of taint of magic and mystery, which they regarded as harmful and deceptive.

Consider next an even broader issue. Much of the debate about the scientific revolution during the last twenty years has turned on the importance of new 'programmes' for knowledge – should knowledge be practical and realistic and down to earth (as the 'craftsmen' are said to have wished), or should it be centred upon magic and hermetic mysteries, or should it all be founded upon actual observation and experiment, or take mathematical demonstration as its test of rigour? We can properly regard Hermeticism and neo-Platonism, or Paracelsism, as programmes for knowledge, as well as the more clearly articulated and philosophically sophisticated programmes of Bacon and Descartes. Now, despite the tendency of authors to see one programme as *the* unique one which really made the difference, it is quite certain that each favoured one broad area of knowledge, and was irrelevent to others, just as one appealed to certain readers and meant little to others. Baconianism obviously had a great effect on natural history but none on observational astronomy – not to say mathematical astronomy. To make a trivial point, for history to emphasize one of these programmes at the expense of all the others must be misleading. There were many different, even opposed, currents all contributing ultimately to the same scientific revolution: at the very time when physical philosophers were endeavouring to jettison Aristotle, the first students of embryology in Europe (Coiter, Fabricius, Harvey) were adopting him as their very adequate guide. Similarly, astronomy was in one and the same period becoming more richly qualitative (Galileo) and more precisely quantitative (Brahe, Kepler). Such seeming paradoxes abound, so that no simple formula supposedly providing a mystic key to events will really turn. In each particular situation different factors were at work.

It is no less important to realize that a great deal of scientific growth occurred independently of any programme, unless we say that renaissance humanism constituted one. (If we do, then it must be clear that unlike the others it had no particular relevance to nature, or to the study of nature; indeed, humanists – Erasmus, for example – were contemptuous of contemporary philosophy.) Such figures as Copernicus and Vesalius cannot be readily linked with any epistemological or methodological movements, or with currents of social change, but clearly stand out as triumphant products of the classical textual Renaissance. Natural history was another branch of activity arousing great enthusiasm, enormously enriching man's knowledge of living things by means of careful field-study and exploration, stimulated by renewed attention to the ancient authors. It brought into existence a new learned institution of the sixteenth century, the botanic garden, parallel to the (private) observatory beginning to appear in astronomy. It is important also not to allow the controversial character of the ideas of an intellectual innovator like Copernicus to obscure the importance of the growing bulk of work of non-controversial character; there was no opposition to the revival of mathematical astronomy or scientific medicine as such, and exponents of science like Tycho Brahe or Jean Fernel – hardly to be dismissed as routine parrots – were not involved in intellectual crises at all. Botany, pure mathematics, geography, mechanics (before 1632), embryology and optics are all examples of types of scientific activity that flourished and made real progress in the fifteenth and sixteenth centuries without the creation of strong internal tensions, without the appearance of conflict between facts and theories, in short without obvious polemics about broad issues. Knowledge and its theoretical structure developed smoothly, particularly in that most conservative of environments (supposedly), the University, and there is hardly any need to look for such an explanation of catastrophic change within them as the attraction of new programmes might provide. A good deal of medievalism died in the sixteenth century – it was just quietly dropped from university courses – and if we ask what took its place, the answer must be: in part revived classicism (Aristotle as well as Archimedes and Lucretius), in part innovations, some of which (to a degree as yet uncertain) were influenced by the new programmes such as Hermeticism and Baconianism.

If, as Charles Schmitt has argued (justly, I think) universities were pushing on with important, non-controversial scientific work (as well as harbouring some radical innovators) then it is natural to suppose that much of the appeal of the non-traditional programmes was to non-academics[23]: Ficino, Pico, Paracelsus, Dee, Bacon, founders of new programmes for knowledge, were all extra-mural. Accordingly, one's views of the causation of the scientific revolution are intimately related to one's appreciation of its *dramatis personae*: is modern science (it might be said) born of an intellectual escape from *academe*? In a sense it obviously was: almost all the learned men of the Middle Ages had been clerics and academics – an exception was Geoffrey Chaucer, poet, writer on astronomy, and administrator. Despite the continuing importance into the eighteenth century of one group whom we may consider academic, the physicians, this was no longer the case even by the late fifteenth century. A literate population was being formed that was neither clerical nor academic. On the other hand the influence of the University was still persuasive, if more subtle, and the printing-press increased it. Leonardo da Vinci, for example, imperfectly educated, absorbed scholarly ideas and terminology from books. The autodidact would often seek out and read the material used by students, which the press made more freely available, especially as Latin became less and less essential even for advanced knowledge; there was, after all, in this period only one model of culture.

If we reject the hypothesis that growth and change in knowledge only occur by catastrophic processes, through the violent relief of mounting tension in earthquake-like fashion, then the need to introduce some single overwhelming factor to explain the scientific revolution becomes less than compelling. The evidence for a gradual breakdown of scholasticism – but not yet, of course, for departure from the Greek tradition – is not inconsiderable: in the rise of the professional university, like Bologna; in the mockery of Erasmus; in the preference for style over argument; in Peter Ramus's oft-quoted thesis of 1536 that 'Everything said by Aristotle was fictitious'; in the eager acceptance of unfamiliar classical authors and matching neglect of the 'Arabs'; in the revival of curiosity about the exotic world, about plants and animals and about unusual human skills; in all the aspects of a 'scientific renaissance' that lasted from about 1450 to about 1550 the historian can find the foundations of the succeeding scientific revolution. Tensions were indeed to appear after this latter date, but they seem to be rather epiphenomena of the scientific revolution itself, than in any way its causes.

There was no unique reason for the development of science in early modern Europe, since one is free to argue that every feature of European civilization was a contributing factor. It is tempting to suggest that this civilization was more intellectual than others, like the Chinese or Arab, yet this can hardly be true except in the sense that it was perhaps relatively more educated. No comparable civilization had produced anything like the medieval university, in form or size, and it is hard to see how our science could have been brought into being without the university of medieval and later times. It created a learned caste that was never composed only of priests or bureaucrats; it taught that truth was derived from argument and evidence, not mere authority alone; it throve on criticism and debate. (It also had its weaknesses, its pettifogging exercises, its thousand times recited platitudes, its endless verbiage.) The medieval university left men a great deal of freedom and there was variety between one and other centre of learning; there was no one imposed set of courses and procedures, no unified dogmatism (*local* dogmatism abounded). It was to be a great intellectual disadvantage for Islam that its philosophy was even more enmeshed with its religion than was the case in Christian Europe. The West, reading philosophy, science and mathematics in works by pagan authors knew that these authors could be wrong, many must be wrong in certain respects. They had the freedom to believe that everything was open to debate (except religion) for all propositions about the natural world could only be contingently true. This freedom, however, would have been worth little enough had not Europe's scholars also learned a feeling for reality. Galen's 'human subject' had been a fiction, pieced together from scraps of observation of men and animal dissection; Ptolemy's astronomy a mechanism to permit calculation. Even Aristotle's philosophy seemed to be more about definitions, concepts and abstractions than about solids, fluids and airs. The general characteristic of the reaction against scholasticism first, then later against conventional Greek science as then understood, was it seems to me a desire for testable propositions about the real world: a sense that natural philosophy was no intellectual game, in which those who gave the most fluent answers won the most prizes, but a result of the study of what is all around us. The best known instance of this is of course Copernicus' endeavour for a 'real' (physically valid) mathematical astronomy, but it is just as evident in the Italian botanists' endeavour to establish the 'real' flora of north and central Italy. Painstaking, accurate description is obviously the most elementary way of aiming at reality, and analysis or theory is bound to invoke entities (like atoms or forces) that are no longer in the immediate sense 'real'. Is motion more real than sweetness, and if so why? It was worth asking the question, because it could be answered, and indeed a great deal of the conceptual progress in science has simply consisted of asking 'Is X more real than Y?' In some cases the asking of the question has been more importance than the answer produced.

NOTES

1. It is classically refuted in Isaiah Berlin, *Historical Inevitability*, Oxford U. P., 1954.
2. For Britain, see the many writings of Eva G. R. Taylor, from *Tudor Geography* (Methuen: London 1930) onwards; for France, the work of F. B. Artz. Also F. R. Johnson, *Astronomical Thought in Renaissance England* John Hopkins University Press: (Baltimore, 1937).
3. W. T. Stearn, *Botanical Gardens and Botanical Literature in the 18th Century*, Hunt Foundation: Pennsylvania, 1961.
4. A.R. Hall, *Ballistics in the Seventeenth Century*, Cambridge U.P., 1952, 97–8.
5. Robert K. Merton, *Science, Technology and Society in Seventeenth Century England*, *Osiris* 1938, reprinted Harper: New York, 1970.
6. Christopher Hill, *Intellectual Origins of the English Revolution*, Clarendon Press: Oxford, 1965; Charles Webster, *The Great Instauration*, Duckworth: London, 1975.
7. Merton, op. cit., 86–7.
8. M. Torrini, *Dopo Galileo*, Olschki: Firenze, 1979.

9. Antonia McLean, *Humanism and the Rise of Science in Tudor England*, Heinemann: London, 1972.
10. Another progressivist was the French physician Jean Fernel (1497–1558) – see C. S. Sherrington, *The Endeavour of Jean Fernel*, Cambridge U.P., 1946, 16–17, 'Our age today is doing things of which antiquity did not dream.'
11. R. G. Collingwood, *Autobiography*, Oxford U. P. 1939, Ch 10.
12. Pierre Duhem, *Etudes sur Léonard de Vinci*, Hermann: Paris, 1906–13.
13. A. C. Crombie, *Robert Grosseteste and the Origins of Experimental Science*, Clarendon Press: Oxford, 1953.
14. Marshall Clagett, *The Science of Mechanics in the Middle Ages*, University of Wisconsin Press: Madison, 1959.
15. *Encyclopaedia Britannica*, 14th edn, 1929, 16, 220; the writer (perhaps Adolf Harneck?) emphasizes Platonism and neo-Platonism as encouraging empiricism in opposition to the 'rationalistic dogmatism' of the schools.
16. Frances A. Yates, *The Rosicrucian Enlightenment*, Routledge: London, 1972, 213.
17. *Idem, Giordano Bruno and the Hermetic Tradition*, Routledge: London, 1964, 110.
18. Paolo Rossi, *Francis Bacon: From Magic to Science*, Rouledge: London, 1968 (Italian edn, 1957).
19. Lynn Thorndike, *History of Magic and Experimental Science*, Columbia University Press: New York, 1923–58.
20. Frances A. Yates, op. cit. (note 17), 448.
21. Ibid., 450.
22. On Dee, see Miss Yates op. cit. (Note 16) – she regards Dee as the *de facto fons et origo* of Rosicrucianism; also see her *Theatre of the World*, Routledge: London, 1969. On Robert Fludd, *Mersenne on la Naissance du Mécanisme*, Vrin: Paris, 1943, 103–9, 367–70.
23. C. B. Schmitt, 'Science in the Italian universities in the sixteenth and early seventeenth centuries', in M. P. Crosland (ed.), *The Emergence of Science in Western Europe*, Macmillan: London, 1975.

CHAPTER TWO

The scientific revival of the sixteenth century

In the early seventeenth century Francis Bacon eloquently denounced the 'fine meditations. speculations and fabrications of mankind' that had hitherto passed for natural philosophy as 'unsound . . . useless for making discoveries of practical value', and the logic on which it was based as 'useless for the discovery of the sciences'.[1] Yet it is clear that the same logic, deriving from Aristotle's *Posterior Analytics* and the same natural philosophy had satisfied many philosophers of genius; clearly the difference between the men who taught the Aristotelian world-system and the men who later rejected it was not simply one of intellectual calibre. Only when the criteria of what contributed an adequate scientific explanation changed, and when fresh demands were made for the practical application of nature's hidden powers, could an effective scepticism concerning the validity of the earlier philosophy and its intellectual underpinning take shape. When that occurred, the cohesive strength of medieval science, and the extent of its consistency whereby one part reinforced another, became important in strengthening its resistance to criticism.

Medieval science was not wide-ranging in its factual compass, nor particularly accurate in stating the facts it did embrace. Even the most empirically-minded authorities could be curiously inexact; the greatest theoretician of medieval optics (after the Arab ibn al-Haitham), Theoderic of Freyburg, states the radius of the primary rainbow incorrectly, while his precursor in magnetism by some fifty years, Pierre de Maricourt (1269) gives as a fact the revolution of a circular lodestone in sympathy with the heavens.[2] In the one branch of science where exactitude of measurement had always been recognized as a desideratum, astronomy, the Latin West had made virtually no beginning at this practical level – certainly nothing comparable to what was done in the East. Thus, in the realm of facts, medieval philosophy and medicine might readily have been faulted, if accuracy as to facts had played a major role in its ultimate downfall. Theories, however, were much more firmly articulated and tightly enmeshed. The passage from the idea of elements (earth, water . . .) to qualities (hot, moist . . .) in physics, and so to humours (blood, phlegm) and then in medicine to temperaments (sanguine, phlegmatic . . .) is an obvious if elementary example: in fact, though Galen was by no means Aristotle's docile slave on professional points (Galen denied that the heart is the seat of sensation, for example) he followed Aristotle on most matters of general philosophy and *weltbild*. Similarly, Aristotle had made physics and cosmology a coherent unity to which mathematical astronomy, as we have seen, had been in no epistemological position to make a challenge of its own. The medieval world-view, bizarre and counterfactual as it may seem to us in most respects, had a sort of monolithic solidarity: it was not easy to make changes in it piecemeal. It had to be credible as a whole; even, say, to challenge the conventional doctrine on blood-letting might have tremendous cosmological repercussions. In other words, that doughty conservative argument: 'this is the thin edge of the wedge . . .' had tremendous force, and the *ad hoc* insertion of a new explanation in the place of an old one (as with Copernicus' theory of gravity) was extremely hazardous and ineffective. On the other hand, technical improvements of a seemingly non-philosophical kind could be accepted much more readily.

The sixteenth century shows these facets of the scientific revolution in two contrasted forms. In the year 1543 were published two books which have become classics in the history of science, the *De Humani Corporis Fabrica* of Andreas Vesalius (1514–64) and the *De Revolutionibus Orbium Coelestium* of Nicholas Copernicus (1473–1543). Neither of these books was modern in content, nor readily comprehensible even in English translation to a modern reader, for Vesalius was no more successful in escaping the limitations of Galenic physiology than was Copernicus in departing from the artificial system of perfect circles, but both inspired trains of activity which were to lead to the promulgation of quite other conceptions within a couple of generations. The two books and their authors, however alike in their broad impact upon the scientific movement, are totally dissimilar. *On the Fabric of the Human Body* is for the most part significant as a work of descriptive reporting, the beautiful dissections of a great anatomist immortalized by the new skills of draughtsmen and block-makers; the illustrations in *De Fabrica* are by no means naturalistic in the general sense – who has ever seen a skeleton moralizing over a tomb against a background of Paduan landscape? – but as renditions of structures and their dispositions in space they represent the first great step towards 'photographic realism' in science, which incidentally the herbalists were taking at just the same time in their books. *On the Revolutions of the Celestial Orbs* on the other hand is a work of philosophy and above all technical mathematics; Copernicus was not an observer, nor even a critical user of others' observations, nor did he aim at unprecedented predictive accuracy. Vesalius was a young man, showing astonishing precocity, fantastic speed of work in getting so much material into print in the six years since his arrival in Padua (1537) – most of the book was prepared after 1540. Copernicus was a dying man, already of considerable fame though he had little yet in print, who had nursed his great idea for nearly forty years. Vesalius was an ambitious and popular teacher who started the University of Padua on its rise to eminence as a centre for the teaching of medicine, while Copernicus was a minor ecclesiastical administrator who attracted only one real disciple, Georg Joachim Rheticus (1514–76). Vesalius

40

was the founder of a *method of discovery* – essentially, for almost two hundred years, all discussion of the working of living organisms was to be founded upon anatomy – while Copernicus exploited a great new principle, the principle that in the system of the heavens there is a perfect reciprocity between sun-centred systems and earth-centred systems. The fact that he himself favoured a sun-centred system of his own devising in which the Earth joined the number of planets, was in no way determined by observational evidence; his preference rested rather upon indemonstrable (though plausible) considerations of simplicity, order and harmony. As already mentioned, his own clearly stated acceptance of a heliocentric cosmology was for long disguised by Osiander's Preface, so that for most of a generation Copernicus appeared simply as the inventor of an elegant but inherently implausible mathematical model. Vesalius in the realm of opinion or theory was much more reserved. He had been a deep student of Galen, an editor of one of Galen's works, and he continued to respect him as the greatest early authority on human anatomy. True, he knew (and emphasized his knowledge repeatedly) that Galen had dissected only apes and other animals, he could differ from him and call him 'imbecile' (as in preferring to find the origin of the great central vein of the body, the *vena cava*, in the heart rather than the liver, where Galen saw it)[3]; he could insist again and again that Galen had been deceived, but he nevertheless left the understanding of the bodily functions little beyond the point to which Galen had taken it. It was Vesalius who drew attention to the absence of pores in the intraventricular septum of the heart, by which blood might pass from the venous to the arterial system, but it was left to his successor, Realdo Colombo (1510–59), to propose a new route for the blood's passage via the lungs. Neither theorist nor philosopher, Vesalius by his great book vastly improved the range and precision of knowledge concerning the structure of the human body, which he had probably explored more thoroughly and more frequently than anyone in history, and this was to be an essential foundation for the rational physiology that was to follow from Harvey's discovery of the circulation of the blood (1628) onwards; then, and only then, serious conflict between ancient and modern medical ideas arose. Yet it may be held that the beginnings of the scientific revolution are to be found as truly in *De Fabrica*, and the series of illustrated anatomics of which it was the first and outstanding member, as in Copernicus' *De Revolutionibus*. As examples of innovation the two books are complementary to one another.

From whatever philosophical, sociological or historical point of view one regards the history of modern science, the broad distinction between the *conceptual* line of advance of which Copernicus is the leading pioneer, strengthened by extreme theoretical competence, and the *factual* line exemplified by Vesalius, in turn reinforced by supreme technical competence, remains valid; any branch of science must touch ultimate sterility if there is an enduring mismatch between these two types of innovation. The former may be shaped in its course by considerations strictly, at the time, external to science (such as Copernicus' architectonic idea of the universe), the other be enriched by serendipity and chance, not to say instrumental and other techniques (as with the introduction

41

of the telescope to astronomy): no matter, intellectual fertility depends on a marriage between these two modes of enquiry. After the theorist Copernicus came Tycho Brahe; after the descriptive anatomist Vesalius, William Harvey.

During the Middle Ages the professional physician received a learned training in certain universities; the surgeon's was a much humbler craft acquired, like any other, by apprenticeship. (The people at large, of course, received their medical care from practitioners of folk medicine, from the 'wise woman' at birth onwards.) Medicine, like all university subjects was learned from books, by thorough acquaintance with the opinions and experience of the best writers. Of 'medical science' there was none, except (from the fourteenth century onwards, and perhaps only in Italy), the opportunity to see a criminal's body cut open by a surgeon over a period of four days. At this stage indeed the teaching of anatomy to students of medicine would have been a waste of time, for all the very sensible exhortations of Galen, since organic dysfunction was not introduced as a cause of ill-health but rather systemic dysfunction (made manifest by external signs, to be seen in the skin, blood, urine and stools). And of course the physician did not operate directly on the body: that was the business of surgeon and apothecary. The 'liver' (as the maker of one humour, the blood) was very important to the physician as a concept, but as a large, soft, red, bloody organ in a man's corpse he really need have no familiarity with it at all. While patterns of education have to lean heavily on the book and aim to make the pupils masters of existing systems of knowledge (for the so-called 'heuristic method' is, after all, a fake in that it lays out the questions and leads the student to the 'right' answers), the distinction between one and another is whether or not the pupil finds that the input to the systems of knowledge (constituting the vital, as distinct from the dogmatic aspect of them) derives in part from reality, that is experience, or wholly from criticism and scholarship devoted to texts. As in medieval natural philosophy which only so rarely – as in optics – took a fresh look at reality, so in medicine too the main effort was scholarly: to master the 'ancient' theories of health and disease and apply them to the relief of the suffering patient. To seek fresh enlightenment by searching into reality outside these systems would have seemed presumptuous, irrelevant and hopeless.

The principal authority in medical science and the actual practice of medicine until the seventeenth century was well advanced was that of Galen (AD 129–99). Other writers were of course studied by the would-be physician; Galen was more revered than read, in fact, and his authority was exercised through delegates, of whom the majority were Islamic (the Renaissance was to change this, to raise the status of Hippocrates and Aristotle, and to introduce the Roman physician Aulus Cornelius Celsus (c. AD 25)). Avicenna (980–1037), the greatest scientist of the Arab world and its foremost physician, unless we should award that title to Rhazes, produced in his *Canon* of about one million words probably the most successful medical compendium of all time, greatly favoured by physicians in both Islam and Christendom. It was translated into Latin by Gerard of Cremona in the twelfth century and its use as a textbook was only given up at the universities of Montpellier and Louvain in the middle of the seventeenth century. The same translator provided most of the versions of Galen's own writings that were to be current for hundreds of years, but his chief anatomical texts remained in Greek and Arabic: only a small digest of his anatomy was used in the West before the sixteenth century. Masses of other medical material was translated by Gerard and others from Arabic, especially from the writings of the great clinician Rhazes (854–925/935) including his book dedicated to the Caliph al-Mansur and his monographs on the particular diseases measles and smallpox. Before the sixteenth century these massive Islamic commentaries upon and additions to the Greek originals had a decisive influence upon the European understanding of Greek medicine; all figured among the earliest books to be printed, some many times over.

It is not easy to overestimate the strength and longevity of the Galenic tradition. When ladies of Miss Austen's day suffered from a putrid fever, when surgeons a couple of generations later spoke of 'laudable pus', Galenic ideas were still active. The London College of Physicians in 1559–60 could order the 'trial' of an Oxford doctor, John Geynes, who had publicly asserted that Galen had erred on a number of points, and force him into submission. Yet John Caius, its President, and second founder of the Cambridge College commonly known by his name, was a great humanist, and the first Englishman to write a monograph on a specific disease (the sweating sickness, sometimes identified with influenza). He was also author of the first book on English dogs. It is pleasant to record that the rashly-spoken Dr Geynes after his reconciliation with his colleagues became an officer of the College and was the first of its Fellows to die on active service abroad, at the siege of Le Havre (1563).[4] It is far more likely that the supposed mistakes committed by Galen according to Geynes related to the philosophical kind of medicine than to its scientific basis in anatomy: when even physicians were educated as logicians – and a university MA was entitled to practice – rather than as observers, it was infinitely easier for them to detect errors in philosophy than in anatomy or physiology. Admiration for Galen was so extravagant that early anatomists were more apt to attribute their failure to confirm his descriptions to their own lack of skill, than to his. One is reminded of the Aristotelian philosophers of a later day who attributed Galileo's discoveries with the telescope to defects in his eyes or his instruments. It was only tardily and hesitantly that Vesalius admitted to himself the simple truth that the formation of blood vessels below the brain then called the *rete mirabile*, properly found in the animal's head by Galen, does not occur in man:

Great things, sometimes surpassing reason, are attributed to Galen (who was easily the chief of the teachers of dissection) by the physicians and anatomists who have followed him, and (strongly) is that blessed and wonderful reticular plexus (*rete mirabile*) affirmed which he introduces somewhere in his books, which also the physicians prate of very commonly for even if they should never see it (as it is almost non-existant in the human body) they describe it on the authority of Galen. Indeed, to say nothing of others I can hardly wonder enough at my own stupidity and excessive respect for the writings of Galen and other anatomists, because I myself so laboured in my respect for Galen that I never undertook to show the human head at public dissections without that of a lamb or ox, in order to supply in the sheep's head the want of what I could absolutely not discover in man, and so impose on the audience rather than say that I could not find that plexus so well known to everyone by name. For nothing at all of such a reticular plexus that Galen reports is formed by the carotid arteries (in man).[5]

Only gradually could anatomists learn to see even these grosser structures of the body other than with Galen's eyes – he who had been one of the greatest medical scientists who have ever lived, demonstrating in Rome and roughly contemporaneously with Ptolemy at Alexandria, a city of learning which Galen admired but seemingly never visited, the residual vigour and quality of Hellenistic science at this moment of maturity when it was able to draw on six hundred years of thought and experience since Aristotle. Galen's technical deficiency, the fact that marvel as he was he had never himself dissected a complete human body as the renaissance anatomists did, was scarcely appreciated before the time of Vesalius. As Galen himself indicated, human dissection as an aid to science seems to have been practised only for a short period at Alexandria, hundreds of years before his own time. Nomenclature and classification also were defective in Greek anatomy, and of course since written texts only were transmitted there have remained to this day some doubts here and there about what exactly is being described. The Islamic transmission of Greek medical science had done nothing to improve the anatomical legacies, for the Arabs did not dissect and the few illustrations surviving in their medical manuscripts are of diagramatic crudity. In Europe the systematic study of anatomy seems to have begun in the twelfth century, at the time of the rise of the famous medical school of Salerno, though the actual practice of human dissection was a north Italian development. The reception of Aristotle's writings in the thirteenth century, temporarily halting the growth of a purely Galenic medical tradition, was counter-balanced by a stronger interest in dissection, flourishing within the wide privileges of the new *studia generales* (schools for 'general studies', or universities). The opening of the human body was given countenance partly by the needs of surgery and partly by legal recognition (stemming from the Law School of Bologna) of the value of forensic evidence derived from post-mortem dissection. There has been at all times and in all places a universal revulsion against the carving up of human bodies to serve mere curiosity (a practice closely regulated in all modern societies), so it is not so extraordinary that it was limited in the Middle Ages as that it happened systematically at all, for the first time in human history. At any rate public human dissection was a regular practice at Bologna by the early fourteenth century, the legal process of enquiry into the cause of death having been converted into a means of instructing students. In teaching anatomy at Montpellier in 1304 Henry de Mondeville used illustrative diagrams probably derived from those used earlier in the University of Bologna.

Medieval anatomical study reached its zenith in Mondino dei Luzzi (*c.* 1275–1326), teacher at that university and author of a textbook that was current for nearly two hundred years (being printed in Latin, Italian and French). Mondino stabilized the method whereby the professor read out the text (his own) with any appropriate additions, an *ostensor* pointed to the structure being described, and the *demonstrator*, a surgeon, performed the actual sectioning to show the structures, as also the regular six-day exposition that became habitual, starting with generalities and a discussion of authorities, beginning the actual dissection with the soft parts of the abdomen, then moving on to the organs of reproduction, the thorax and its contents, the head, the skeleton and the peripheral parts. His teaching was Galenic in origin, of course, and more directly Arabic: he perpetuated many gross errors including those like the five-lobed liver that derived from animals; he made errors of which Galen was not guilty. His object was pedagogic, not to add to knowledge. But he was the first anatomist in Western Europe.

It is easy to understand how Mondino's method degenerated into an academic ritual – though apparently in the fifteenth century a popular one. The book was far more important than the body, and the student was a mere spectator who was extremely lucky if he could see anything at all of the finer structures. The purpose of the demonstration was by no means to inculcate the virtues of empiricism as a method of science. In fact Galen himself while insisting often and picturesquely on the merit of anatomical learning in the physician, was far from being a simple empiricist. To interpret what he saw he necessarily had to introduce certain non-empirical principles of interpretation, such as the association between form and function (thus, we may believe the liver to be the blood-making organ of the body because it is itself the organ most like congealed blood: the arteries, exercising an active motion (pulse) are thick and strong, while the veins are thin and soft), and especially the great principle that nature does nothing in vain: therefore every feature of the body has a purpose which can be grasped, and the arrangement is indeed an optimum one for the life of men. Thus we may gather from study and experiment (by tying up the vessels) that the kidneys, not the bladder, are the primary organs of urinary secretion; and that though the mamalian heart has two chambers with four valves (while amphibia manage quite well with a simpler organ) this can be explained by the presence of lungs. For many centuries the demonstration of the perfect fitness of structures to function was to remain the objective of 'theoretical anatomy' – one can hardly yet speak of physiology in the modern sense – and experiment as well as observation was to be involved; only with the development of analysis of the organism in mechanistic terms and of *comparative* anatomy did alternatives to teleology begin to appear. Even more stongly than Aristotle, moreover, Galen was given to personifying nature, giving this word the sense of a wise, prescient, benevolent and omnipotent creative agency, indeed, Galen's nature fills the role of the Christian God, so that this manner of speech was readily comprehensible to the Christian naturalists and medical men of later centuries, who continued to feel comfortable with Galen's biological philosophy even when pouring scorn on his specific version of fact and explanation.

Here again one may note the general contrast between the biological and the physical aspects of the scientific revolution. While the latter seem to depend very much and from the beginning on shifts of metaphysical perspective – for this is the basis of Copernicanism, not to say the work of Kepler and Galileo –

the former seem rarely to rise far above the phenomenological level and in their highest theoretical flights, as with William Harvey, to extend only to embrace limited systems. Of a metaphysical shift in the principles of biology there is no sign, with the exception of Cartesian mechanism. But by no means all naturalists or physicians after Descartes were mechanists, and of those who were, many employed mechanism in relation to living organisms only in an instrumental fashion, ignoring or denying its metaphysical implications as indeed Descartes himself had done with regard to man: for if (with Descartes) we take the human body to be mechanical, but man not a machine, there is no non-solipsistic reason for not extending the same reasoning to animals, which clearly possess the senses of pleasure and pain and perhaps some faculty of reason, as man does. So that Descartes's biological mechanism became, after all (except for a few eighteenth-century philosophers) rather a universal transformation of systemic explanation, than a metaphysical shift.

But this is to run far ahead. To return to the Renaissance of anatomy in the late fifteenth century, it is associated with the printed text and the utility of the woodcut illustration, as well as the renewed vigour of medicine as a professional academic study (law was its only rival). The first half of the sixteenth century reveals a considerable group of able practical anatomists at work, mostly Italian: Berengario da Carpi, Johannes Dryander, Niccolo Massa, Charles Estienne, Giovanbattista Canano, besides Vesalius, one of the youngest of them. All of these save Massa (1536) used the new technique of printed figures. In the spirit of humanist publication of classical medical texts (the most famous new discovery was that of Celsus' first-century AD *De Medicina Octo Libri* in 1426, first printed at Florence in 1478) Johannes Guinter, then teaching at Paris where Vesalius was his pupil, published in 1531 the first Latin translation of Galen's chief textbook on dissection, his *Anatomical Procedures* (or, to be more exact, the portion of this book that had survived in Greek): Vesalius himself was to edit this important work later, and two lesser studies of dissection by Galen, in the Giunta edition of the works of the great ancient physician (1541). In England Thomas Linacre, founder of the College of Physicians (1518), was a very active translator of Galen's Greek into Latin, among his texts being Galen's major work on the principles of 'physiology', *On the Natural Faculties* (1523).[6] Linacre's translations were often reprinted on the continent, and Erasmus paid him a high compliment, saying that Linacre had made Galen 'so eloquent and informative (in Latin) that even in his own tongue he may seem to be less so'. Particular attention was devoted to exact nomenclature, the medieval Arab–Latin tradition having become thoroughly confused (two names being in use for the same structure, or one name for two structures), so that a great deal of the Greek-based terminology of gross anatomy was introduced at this time. However, one must of course distinguish those who were primarily scholars in this field (such as Linacre, Guinter and Massa) from those who were making actual discoveries in dissection, like Berengario, Canano (the first to discover valves in the vascular system) and especially Vesalius. Scholarship alone could not bring about the amendment of factual errors in Galen's observation. In some ways (as we have seen with Dr Caius) more exact

Greek scholarship might emphasize rather than weaken the tendency to idolize ancient masters, towards dogmatism.

Another important source of inspiration, as well as the means of communication, came from the naturalistic movement in art which also produced Albrecht Durer's rhinoceros and Hans Weiditz's illustrations for Otto Brunfel's *Living Images of Plants* (*Herbarum Vivae Eicones*, 1530). Italian painters and sculptors had studied the superficial anatomy of the human body in search of graphic realism even before the end of the fifteenth century – surviving sketches by, for example, Michelangelo and Raphael suggest that they occasionally practised covert dissection. Leonardo da Vinci (1452–1519) went much further along the same path leaving behind him a large quantity of anatomical drawings, ranging from rough sketches apparently drawn from the dissected member to elaborate drawings commonly incorporating traditional though erroneous beliefs about the content of the body. A proper judgement of these sheets requires an expert eye for, contrary to the naive supposition that such artists as Leonardo only depict with the pencil what they have seen with the eye, Leonardo's anatomical drawings look completely 'natural' and realistic even when they show forms that are impossible, as in his celebrated picture of the uterus. Indeed, whether accurate or not (and on occasion Leonardo was extremely acute in his observation) these figures constitute the first careful effort in all history to 'photograph' dissected structures, as also to study comparatively the forms – especially the skeleton – of different species. Beginning in the early 1490s, they precede Vesalius' comparable printed figures by half a century, and are enormously superior in quality to any other pre-Vesalian depictions. Presumably Leonardo started with an artistic impulse, but if so (as in all his other investigations) he was overtaken by philosophical curiosity, as is evident both from his acquisition of an academic familiarity with anatomy – the Galenic anatomy of books, especially the Italian edition of Mondino (1493) – and from his own notes and comments on the sheets, sometimes quite elaborate, which show him investigating with great care the mode of action of the four valves of the heart; Leonardo was the first to declare (contrary to Galen) that 'the heart is a principal muscle with respect to force'. He wanted to know how the body works, trying to apply hydraulic principles to the motion of food in the gut and of urine in its vessels. He even performed experiments on animals, including frogs and pigs. But not all his drawings are taken from life: some represent his imagination of what he found in texts (Plato's *Timaeus* among them), some his analytical comparisons between different species, some again are mechanical models of the body's functioning as he sees it.[7]

It is of course obvious that the artistic preoccupation alone could not have given rise to scientific anatomy, but that Leonardo moved (so far as the limited reading and the small amount of human dissection material available to him would allow) towards a reformation of anatomical knowledge. His own indisciplined methods of study and incapacity for organization and classification prevented his even beginning a systematic exposition of the human body: in any event, the secrecy in which his worksheets were shrouded prevented his having any significant effect upon his immediate successors, in this respect as in most others. What Leonardo does prove, given the possibility of human dissection, is the fertility and indeed the necessity of studying the book and the body at the same time. Leonardo spoke of *Anatome Naturale* – life-like anatomy – which one can see also attempted, to the point of parody, in Vesalius' *Fabrica*. Naturalism was the style of the day, for the student of nature as for the artist; both employed the same techniques of draughtsmanship and image reproduction, both followed the same aesthetic conventions. As Leonardo wrote, the anatomist needed 'the good draughtsmanship that pertains to representation' which must be 'accompanied by a knowledge of perspective'. Just as in the new ideal of teaching the structures were to be properly and systematically displayed to the student audience by the professor himself, so in making a book illustrations must go with text and illustrations could only be taken from the dissected body (who drew the figures in Vesalius' *Fabrica* is unknown, or how the collaboration between anatomist and artist, if such there was, actually worked). Thus the logic of naturalism, of the medical school, of the printing-press combined to bring a new kind of recorded, observational science into existence, and proceeding thus the anatomist found that the human body did not always correspond to Galen's descriptions; so in time he learned to depart with greater confidence from the Galenic text and to rely upon observation alone as his authority. A few conservative medical men were well aware of the dangers of illustrated texts: too great a reliance upon dissection and its visual record might lead to disregard of Galen's superior knowledge and wisdom. Indeed, with both Leonardo and Vesalius the illustrations are sometimes more accurate and less traditional than the words. It can hardly be too much emphasized that the enterprise of recovering the understanding of the full range of Greek medical exposition was itself one of great freshness and excitement – since what had been known of it before the Renaissance was so narrow, dry and pedantic, and if some of the great professionals of the period such as Vesalius in anatomy and Fernel in 'physiology' began to manifest a critical spirit, this was no more than a side-effect subsidiary to their main enterprise of assimilating the full richness of the Greek tradition. To study human anatomy, to prepare elaborate anatomical illustrations, was not in itself to be critical of Galen: the criticism only came with mounting experience. Thus investigation beyond Galen, even contrary to Galen, was the product of the attempt to realize his descriptions and comprehend his theories.

Vesalius' *Fabrica* is a large and handsome book: close, devoted cooperation between anatomist and printer (Johannes Oporinus of Basel) made it one of the dozen masterworks of scientific bibliography. No other anatomist of the time produced nearly so beautiful a book (Berengario's *Anatomy*, for example, is downright wretched); this assisted its success, yet the copper-plate anatomical drawings of Vesalius' contemporary Bartolomeo Eustachi (*c.*1505–74) were equally plagiarized in other books up to the late eighteenth century. The history of these engravings is curious: prepared in 1552, Eustachi himself printed eight small illustrations in 1564, then the remaining thirty-nine were lost for one hundred and fifty years until rediscovered, bought by a Pope (Clement XI) and printed in 1714. They are of the highest quality, particularly the illustration of the sympathetic nervous system is 'generally considered to be one of the best ever produced'. There was in a sense, then, no uniqueness about Vesalius and the magnificence of the *Fabrica* (a work whose hostility to Galen Eustachi resented); had the historical fate of Vesalius' and Eustachi's figures been reversed, history would surely not have been very different, despite the total failure of Eustachi to write a text to accompany his figures: perhaps, even, anatomy would have advanced still more rapidly. Eustachi was a highly experienced man of around forty-five years when he began his major task of illustration; Vesalius – if we date the beginning from his establishment at Padua in 1537 – only twenty-three. He could hardly claim to write with mature knowledge since, though he had studied medicine both at Louvain and at Paris, his experience of dissection must have been quite limited. There he had been grounded in humanistic Galenism, rather than in any independent spirit of criticism. Vesalius' first notable publications were a revision of Guinter's *Anatomical Institutions according to Galen* and his own *Six Tables*, both in 1538. The former needs no comment; the *Six Tables* – six sheets of anatomical drawings with explicatory notes – are Galenic expositions of human anatomy containing much that is imaginary, or of literary rather than dissecting-table origin. The illustrations contain many mistakes and Vesalian experts are agreed that they bear no comparison with those of the *Fabrica*. (Rather unfairly, the experts tend to assign responsibility for the rather feeble character of the *Six Tables* to the artist who drew them, the Fleming Jan Stephen van Calcar, whom nevertheless Vesalius praised highly, and they argue that the same hand could not have drawn the *Fabrica* figures.) We know that as Vesalius settled at Padua, and particularly to his great task from 1539 onwards, he had access to abundant raw material – enough to abandon the old stereotype of beginning with the soft inner parts (still followed by Eustachi). It seems reasonable to suppose that he owed the reputation of the *Fabrica* and his own growing confidence in disagreeing with Galen to this massive amount of evidence; yet Charles Singer opined years ago that 'A few of his comments reveal an active dissector less experienced than his contemporaries Berengario da Carpi, [Niccolo] Massa and Charles Estienne'.[8] Since Vesalius gave up research and teaching for the Imperial medical practice soon after completing the *Fabrica*, his main years of activity were indeed few.

Whereas the beginnings of experimental science were painful and fumbling, in the biological sciences of anatomy and botany there was an ample field for the development of observational skills within a relatively traditional and acquiescent academic context. Men like Vesalius and Eustachi rose to be top-ranking physicians. Aided by naturalism, stimulated by the printing-press, observation and record grew smoothly out of textual study. There was no powerful methodological drive beyond this, rather it was the case that the endeavour to emulate Galen's practice led to the abandonment of Galen's precepts. The anatomists who freed themselves, however partially, from their natural inclination to imitate classical masters blindly were, as it might be, accidently framing new techniques of observation and new criteria for judging both statements of fact (like the time-honoured but erroneous thesis: 'In man, the right kidney is constantly higher than the left', because in the Aristotelian system of values *right* is invariably superior to left, *sinister*) and theoretical propositions about, for instance, the functions of veins and arteries. In no real sense was this the moment of the birth of some novel, self-conscious method of observation and experiment in science, but it was a moment when an accepted narrative of fact and theory – rich at one level, sophisticated at the other – was first modified effectively and permanently by recourse to the actual evidence. A body of originally examined, carefully verified facts was, for the first time, in the middle of the sixteenth century measured against a traditional, literary account – and the latter was found wanting. The whole process was too slow and sporadic for there to be severe internal tension within the medical profession, at least before the time of Harvey, not least because there were other ancient authorities (Plato, Aristotle, Hippocrates . . .) even older and greater than Galen himself who could, at times, be appealed to as witness against his teaching. Yet slowly – and in botany the process was yet more gradual – the new discoveries combined to teach the leasson that the whole body of descriptive human anatomy, and much at least of the explanatory theory immemorially associated with it, must be reformed by the methods of meticulous observation and independent thought. While the facts of experience to which appeal had been made by anti-Aristotelian theorists of motion, such as the more effective throwing of a lump of lead than a similar piece of cork, had been commonplace and trivial, the new anatomy turned to the systematic exploitation not only of the refined technique of dissection itself (seen in the study of the ear ossicles, for example) but those of classification and descriptive nomenclature.

The most complete and striking use of these techniques, of great immediate impact, was certainly that of Vesalius in the *Fabrica*. All authors agree that his exposition of human anatomy was outstanding in early modern times, basing their judgement on his text – paraphrase of Galen's *Uses of the Parts* though most of it may be – as well as upon his even more eloquent illustrations. He was not unique, but he was the most successful exponent of a new procedure that was to win adherents all over Europe, some of whom Vesalius did not scruple to treat unfairly. Among Vesalius' immediate predecessors Berengario da Carpi, whose crudely illustrated *Commentary* on the already-printed brief anatomy of Mondino was published as early as 1521 was notable for hesitancy in following Galen. Another, Charles Estienne (1505–64) was at work on anatomical plates as early as 1530 though his 'Three books on the dissection of the parts of the human body' were published only two years after the *Fabrica*. A member of the Parisian printing family, he studied under Sylvius and received an MD from Montpellier; besides practising medicine he was a very active editor and translator. A number of original anatomical observations are credited to him. and he was as certain as Vesalius that the historian of the human body should report only what was manifest and evident to his eye; nevertheless (like Vesalius) he followed Galen pretty closely in his remarks on the functions which the structures were to serve. Estienne's repulsive figures (which fail alike to be 'photographic' or schematic) do not merit comparison with those of Vesalius or Eustachi (p. 48); however, his book had the advantage of translation into French – as, indeed, Vesalius' *Epitome* of anatomy (1543) was soon translated into English.

The effect of simultaneity is enhanced by Giovanbattista Canano (1515–79), who was indeed associated with Vesalius as well as with Gabriele Falloppio (1523–62), his pupil. Canano's very rare 'Illustrated dissection of the muscles of the human body' (1541 or 1543) in fact dealt only with the muscles of the arm, on twenty-seven copper-plates engraved by Girolamo da Carpi, a painter of Ferrara where Canano was born and studied. This was the most detailed study of the 'Vesalian' generation. There were of course many others of less note also at work, especially in Italy where the tradition was to be carried forward to the end of the century.

It is evident, therefore, that the study of anatomy by dissection was a natural growth-point, whose expansion and success were promoted not by one man, still less the force of a particular genius, but by the vigorous state of the Italian universities (especially their medical schools) and the freedom for investigation they offered; Fallopio even survived a false accusation of vivisection. Medicine was then (as always) of great importance and particularly so because of popular talk of new diseases and new remedies. The fresh revival of Galenism provided the intellectual framework and practical discipline by which anatomy could be prosecuted for the benefit of medicine and (as Estienne and others wrote) for the glory of God in His creation.

Vesalius was certainly not unique, if *primus inter pares*. Little is known of his personality. He was certainly less learned in Greek and other ancient tongues than other medical men of his age. He had a good conceit of his own powers, and lavished critical abuse on others in the fashion of the time. Nevertheless, the *Fabrica* is a monument of sixteenth-century science, revealing as truly as Copernicus' *De Revolutionibus Orbium Coelestium* the astonishing progress towards maturity and independence of investigation effected within the previous half century. In its own day the *Fabrica* gained immediate authority. It was the implementation, in a manner whose total effect is superior to that attained by any contemporary work of similar character, of a unitary conception of what a complete anatomical work ought to be, and nothing indicates that this conception as to both text and illustration was anything but wholly Vesalius' own. It aimed at a systematic, illustrated survey of the body part by part and layer by layer. The skeleton and the articulation of the joints, the muscles, the system of arteries, veins and nerves, the abdominal organs, the heart and lungs, the brain, were described and depicted with a detailed accuracy never attained before. The woodcuts are indeed on occasion better than the text they illustrate, though in one place it is admitted that a drawing had been modified to fit Galen's words. Falloppio was to draw attention to the fact that in treating the kidney Vesalius had silently substituted that of the dog for the human kidney (the latter, containing more fat, is less suitable for illustration). There were many other errors to be corrected by Falloppio and other successors of Vesalius. Some whole topics (the eye; the female reproductive system) were particularly defective in his treatment, due partly to want of material (Vesalius seems to

51

have dissected only three females), partly to inaccurate observation, partly to the persistence of false traditions. In a classical instance – to which we return later – Vesalius admitted that the so-called pores or pits in the wall (septum) dividing the two principal chambers of the heart were blind; therefore blood could not pass through them from the right (venous) side of the heart to the left (arterial) side. He left the passage of blood into the arteries, as he said, a mystery; yet it was easily solved by his successors, following a strong hint from Galen himself.

If Vesalius and his contemporaries effected a revolution in knowledge of the human body – the extent to which this was an individual or a collective achievement is of little long-term significance – then it was a conservative revolution, not daring to step beyond the testimony of the eyes to wider realms of theory: the revolutionaries were proud to assert their new discoveries, and shrill occasionally in the denunciation of past errors, but content to set their new descriptive accuracy firmly within a safe context of familiarity. As Charles Singer wrote of Vesalius:

If it be said that he often corrected Galen it may be rejoined that much more often he follows Galen's errors . . . The *Fabrica* is, in effect, Galen with highly significant Renaissance additions. The most obvious and important is the superb application of the graphic method.[9]

But the 'graphic method' – no invention of Vesalius' – of course does not affect the question of the accuracy of the descriptive (and functional) account given in the text. Singer was surely right to affirm that a great deal even in this mid-sixteenth century flowering of anatomy – certainly in the texts of Vesalius and Estienne which were the only ones aiming at a complete textual statement – was still to a large extent Galen pictorially realized: on the other hand, in detail, in tracing this structure on that, a much higher order of accuracy was coming in.

If Vesalius was pre-eminent among early anatomists he must not be made so at the expense of his contemporaries, who were also men of ability and precision, which can only be done by overlooking their discoveries and his mistakes. The tradition of anatomical study was not introduced to northern Italy by Vesalius during his few years there, for dissection was already practised, as we have seen, in several universities. As for the claim sometimes made that Vesalius was the first teacher of anatomy to carry out dissections before students with his own hands – the idealized scene at Padua is familiar from the frontispiece to the *Fabrica* – the view has been put forward that even as early as 1528, and in the humanistic medical school of Paris, 'the participation of students and doctors in the actual process of dissection was recognised'. Since anatomy had become a thriving branch of study, the old didactic and literary method of exposition necessarily fell into disuse, though Estienne tells us that he employed a surgeon to assist him in the laborious task. Vesalius must, however, be allowed his proper share of credit for introducing a number of innovations in the practice and teaching of anatomy which further extended its possibilities of discovery. And the *Fabrica*, more richly than any other anatomy of the time, attempted to integrate the visual examination of structure with the intellectual grasp of function even more closely than Galen himself had been able to do. Vesalius, like Galen and indeed Estienne, understood that anatomy is the necessary and inescapable foundation of medical philosophy; true, he himself was unable to progress far towards the perfection of physiology – Sherrington argued that Jean Fernel showed more insight in this way, perhaps with some injustice to both Galen and the *Fabrica*[10] – but he drew attention to the weak points in Galen's account that deserved attention in the future. Possibly one could believe that he took the content of anatomical description safely past a critical point: certainly there was no going back, only a steady increase in professionalism. It was an adequate basis, or work of reference, from which as a starting-point fresh voyages of discovery could be made. In a descriptive science such as anatomy, progress depends on *social* conditions – that human dissection can be carried out, that a context for it exists, and that the enterprise attracts workers forming (as in sixteenth-century Italy) a kind of research community – it also depends on a *methodological* condition, that the comparison between things-as-they-are-seen and the statements (in books or lectures) about things-to-be-seen can actually be made. There can be no descriptive science of invisible things. There were (and are) many difficulties in interpreting or verifying Galen's statements about the things-to-be-seen in the human body: partly because previous basic anatomical experience is needed, partly because the language is obscure (and the text sometimes corrupt), partly because Galen dissected animals, not humans, and not least (after all) because the Renaissance text of *On Anatomical Procedures*, being incomplete, did not cover the whole body. Therefore it was necessary to start again, to re-write the statement of things-to-be-seen, using Galen (because there was no other guide) and the actual body. Vesalius made this new start, he gave – but he was not alone in this – a new assertion of what-was-to-be-seen. Galen's anatomy (though not his physiology and medicine) could now be forgotten. Vesalius made the study of *On Anatomical Procedures* a purely antiquarian exercise, not by being more accurate, but by being (with text and figures) a very great deal more intelligible. Anatomy could now begin from a proper base in his statement of reality, not with explorations in classical philology to discover what Galen was writing about.

In that respect Copernicus' masterpiece is exactly comparable with that of Vesalius: 'Ptolemy' continued to be taught in a debased way in elementary courses on astronomy, and Sacrobosco's *Sphere* (*c.* 1230) remained the most popular astronomy text to the end of the sixteenth century and beyond, but as far as the development of the science is concerned Ptolemy's *Almagest* virtually ceased to have any effect or influence after 1543. (This did not, of course, also entail the acceptance of Copernicus' opinion of the reality of the Earth's motion.) Serious astronomy had begun afresh in Europe with *De Revolutionibus Orbium Coelestium* and even those who could not follow its physical principles accepted the fact.

Yet astronomy remained with Copernicus in that world of the artificial from which anatomy was trying desperately and with success to escape: Copernicus was interested neither in the practical reform of astronomy nor in making new discoveries in the heavens. He was a student of books rather than of nature herself: the few scattered observations he made himself are of no significance. He was a mathematician and made no other explicit claim for himself, though implicitly he claimed the right to philosophize, that is, to assert for himself what is more or less likely to be 'real'. Very often in the history of science profound theoretical changes have some kind of factual fulcrum on which they turn, however insignificant in itself: the valves in the veins for Harvey, the relation between electrostatic and electromagnetic units for Maxwell, the Michelson–Morley experiment (some would claim) for Einstein. With Copernicus there is no such fulcrum, unless we would claim for that role the factual discovery that the Julian calendar was at fault (that is, that the exact length of the tropical year must be somewhat different from $365\frac{1}{4}$ days). However, though Copernicus could make a fair point by saying that astronomers could hardly claim great competence while such a quantity was still undetermined, it is not one upon which the kinematics of planetary motion in turn depend. We have here what seems almost a perfect instance of a change of thought addressed to the resolution of no new problem, yet presenting a new solution.

It was medieval in Copernicus to base his work eclectically on a body of observations that were taken for granted as to accuracy and homogeneity, many selected from Ptolemy himself; medieval too that he should aim at improving the harmony of knowledge; in medieval philosophy the reconciliation of pagan science and Christian religion, the patient comparison of authorities, the explanation of contradictions and discrepancies had been an unending task. Copernicus' external aim was just such a fusion, in his case of the mathematical and philosophical traditions, and so (rather naively, perhaps) to construct a single image of reality. (His internal object will be considered later.) Faced with the incongruity between a philosophical account of the universe which was and seemed likely to remain wholly non-quantitative, and a mathematical model yielding predictions that was both unimaginable, inconsistent with the former, and incoherent, Copernicus preferred the mathematical model as an intellectual starting-point while recognizing plainly its incoherence:

in the course of the mathematicians' exposition of what they call their system we find that they have either omitted some indispensable detail or introduced something foreign and wholly irrelevant. This would of a surety not have been so had they followed fixed principles: for if their hypotheses were not misleading all inferences based thereupon might be confidently verified.[11]

This short passage makes two important points. In the first place Copernicus implicitly rejects the ancient opinion rehearsed by Osiander in his suppositious Preface to the Reader that incoherence in mathematical models was of no importance, because the models were not supposed to reflect reality. The whole of Copernicus' dedication of his book to Pope Paul III makes sense only if we start from this rejection, which in turn may have something to do with the thirteenth-century theological condemnation of the contention that the universe must necessarily correspond to the dictates of philosophical reason – that is, Aristotelianism.[12] Granted that Aristotle's picture of the universe was the most rational man could devise, yet God might have made it otherwise, for example according to the models of the mathematicians (if only these could avoid internal inconsistency and other weaknesses). Therefore an improved, harmonious mathematical model *could* – according to this theology – as well represent God's design as a seemingly more rational philosophical account and therefore make an equally potent claim to be realistic. No Greek could have followed such an instrumentalist line of thought.

Secondly, Copernicus is saying that the *principles*, not the analytical tools nor the data of the mathematical astronomers are at fault. Ptolemy's technique, based on his resolution of planetary orbits into multiple circular components, was fine: what was mistaken was his *philosophical* assumption that the Earth is the fixed pivot about which the universe turns. This must be a philosophical assumption, for mathematically as Copernicus writes

A seeming change of place may arise from the motion of either the object or the observer, or again of unequal movement of the two (for between equal and parallel motion no movement is perceptible . . .). If then some motion of the Earth be postulated, the same will be reflected in external bodies, which will seem to move in the opposite sense.

The mathematician then is free to choose his pivot, and the philosopher must leave him free to choose, since he has no authority to say that God could not have made a universe with a fixed central Sun. And once the mathematician adjusts to this freedom, and feels at home looking at the universe in this new way, he discovers that the consequent relative motions entail a logic and order all of their own:

if the motions of the rest of the planets be brought into relation with the circulation of the Earth and be reckoned proportionate to the orbit of each planet, not only do their (known) phenomena presently ensue but the orders and magnitudes of all the heavenly bodies and of the heavens themselves become so bound together that nothing in any part thereof could be moved from its place without producing a confusion among all the other parts and of the Universe as a whole.[13]

It surely cannot be an accident that Copernicus, who had lived in Italy at the same time as Leonardo da Vinci, here employs an anatomical metaphor contrasting the perfection of the properly assembled morphology with that of geocentric astronomy, wherein the bodily limbs and members seemed to be selected and put together at random, so as to constitute a monster rather than a man, as Copernicus had written on the immediately preceding page. It was, of course, natural for him to think of the microcosm (man) and the macrocosm (the universe) as cognate and parallel to each other.

How did Copernicus come to be an astronomical revolutionary, a role which he clearly found troublesome since he took so little trouble to make his ideas known, ripening them for thirty-odd years and preferring (as he says) to discuss mathematical matters only with mathematicians? His life in fact enjoyed a long preparation which could so easily have lacked any intellectual fulfilment. He was almost born into the Church, since from infancy he and his brother Andreas were brought up by their mother's brother, Lucas Watzelrode, their father (a merchant of Torún in Poland) having died early. Watzelrode, in time to become bishop of Varmia, secured for his promising nephew a canonry in the cathedral at Frambork where he was to spend forty years in the administration of church lands and other business. But meanwhile the astronomer, who was to remain discreetly active through those years, was formed at Cracow, his father's birthplace. In this, the richest city in the kingdom and (at that time) its capital, a university had been founded in 1364, possessing one of the finest libraries north of the Alps. There Copernicus acquired (as he acknowledged later) the knowledge and ideas that immortalized his name: between 1491 and 1496, when he left for Bologna. After a stay in Italy of about four years, during which he continued to pursue astronomy as well as law (his official study) Copernicus returned briefly to Poland, to seek and receive leave of absence to study medicine in Italy 'in order to advise our most reverend bishop and also the members of the chapter', choosing this time Padua though he was to take his doctorate in canon law at Ferrara.

He settled finally at Frambork in the summer of 1504, aged about thirty-three. Some years – evidently active ones – pass before there is a record of his buying materials for building a small stone tower, which he employed for observation. He remained in touch with the mathematicians at Cracow, and one of them already possessed by 1514 a 'Little Commentary upon the hypotheses of celestial motion' postulated by an anonymous, who surely was in fact Copernicus, for this 'Little Commentary' (*Commentariolus*) survives as Copernicus' first brief exposition of his extraordinary notions. We have no reason to believe that his six-page sketch enjoyed any wide circulation. At least ten years later, in 1524. Copernicus wrote for a friend a *Letter against Werner*,[14:1] criticizing the opinion stated in print by Johann Werner of Nuremburg that the eighth sphere in the heavens (that bearing the fixed stars) revolves with a uniform motion or precession. Here Werner was in principle right, and Copernicus in asserting a variability or reversibility of the eighth sphere's motion in error. Neither of these little papers was printed before modern times. Otherwise, our information about Copernicus' repute as a mathematician is very limited. Rheticus relates – it must have a proud memory with his master – that during Copernicus' first stay in Italy in the course of a visit to Rome he gave a lecture 'before a large audience of students and a throng of great men and experts in this branch of knowledge'.[15] There is also a record that one Widmanstad explained the Copernican theory to Pope Clement VII and several cardinals in the year 1533.[16] (But how did Widmanstad get his information – should the pope be Paul III and the year 1543?) Georg Joachim Rheticus certainly knew enough of some achievement in astronomical theory by Copernicus to make his way in 1539 from Wittenberg to Frambork in order to discover its nature. With his 'first account' (*Narratio Prima*) of what Copernicus had been doing, printed in 1541, the well-kept Pythagorean secret was out, at least in Germany; when this was soon followed by *De Revolutionibus* itself, all the world began to talk of Copernicus. He was already dead. A man who keeps his great work by him till he is seventy can hardly have wished to be energetic in its defence.

What were Copernicus' sources? Rheticus wrote of him as a master not inferior to Regiomontanus, adding

I rather compare him with Ptolemy, not because I consider Regiomontanus inferior to Ptolemy, but because my teacher shares with Ptolemy the good fortune of completing. with the aid of the divine beneficence, the reconstruction of astronomy which he had begun.[17]

whereas Regiomontanus died relatively young. Ptolemy was for Copernicus, as indeed for all astronomers for many ages, the ultimate fount of knowledge and source of inspiration, but as the *Almagest* or *Great Syntaxis* was not printed before 1515 Copernicus had no knowledge of it when he composed his *Commentariolus*.[18] In the *Letter to Werner* (1524), however, he refers to the *Almagest* extensively, and so thereafter. What did he read before 1515? The important book by Regiomontanus (to whom Rheticus alluded) appeared only in 1496, the year of Copernicus' departure from Cracow, though he was certainly to use it. But the book with which he began (if we set aside Sacrobosco's *Sphere*, the medieval *Planetary Theory* of Gerard of Cremona and other old favourites that were certainly read and discussed at Cracow) was the *New Theories of the Planets* (*Theoricae Novae Planetarum*) written by Georg Peurbach (1423–61) in 1454. This book was first printed about 1474; a commentary upon it by Wojciech of Brudzewo (1482) became a standard text at Cracow and must have been familiar to Copernicus, even though Wojciech was not his teacher. These *New Theories* were intended to replace the medieval summaries, and did, enjoying a long and useful life as a primer explaining the technical language of astronomy and the systems of circles whose combined revolutions represented the motion of each planet. Peurbach clearly showed, for example, how in the outer planets the motion of the planet in its epicycle exactly 'mimicks' the motion of the Sun about the Earth (according to Ptolemy), the radii being always parallel to each other. The circles were by him 'modelled' into a system of solid spheres (containing hollows for the epicycles) after the fashion of some Islamic astronomers, and Copernicus may have noted the difficulties that resulted. The Cracow astronomers – it was one of the best centres for this science in Europe – seem to have gone beyond Peurbach in questioning conventional assumptions, pointing out, as of course had far better known medieval philosophers like Nicole Oresme, that there were sound arguments for interpreting the apparent daily revolution of the heavens as a rotation of the Earth upon its axis, and that the Sun does not necessarily move because it seems to do so. Copernicus may well have been induced to think over such questions.[19]

He could not have learned mathematical astronomy from Peurbach, however, and here we must suppose his first resource and the basis of the *Commentariolus* to have been the *Epitome* of the *Almagest* printed in 1496, more than thirty years after it had been completed. This was the joint work of Peurbach and Regiomontanus, or Johannes Müller of Konigsberg (1436–76), who had joined

Fig. 2.1 How the motion of an outer planet on its epicycle mimics that of the Sun. After Peurbach, *New Theory of the Planets*. O is the central Earth. Each angular movement of the planet from P_1 to P_2, P_3 to P_4 and so on matches a similar movement of the Sun to successive positions 2,3,4 etc.

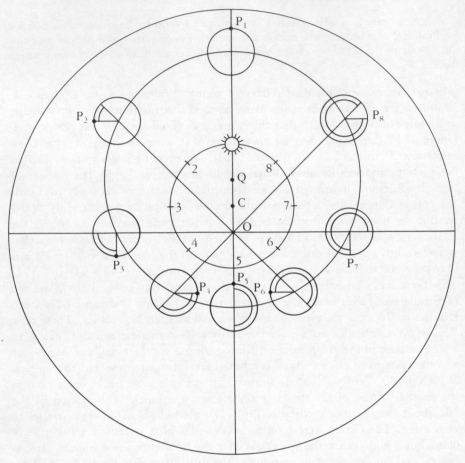

forces in Vienna and worked on the Greek manuscript that Cardinal Bessarion had brought from Constantinople (actually, *before* the fall of that great city to the Turks). Regiomontanus was not only a good Greek scholar, which Peurbach was not though according to the younger man he knew the Latin *Almagest* almost by heart, but active in actual observation and the publication of accurate texts, such as his *Ephemerides* giving the positions of the heavenly bodies for every day from 1475 to 1506, which Columbus took on his fourth voyage. He was also a fully competent mathematician (though his important trigonometrical work was to be printed only as late as 1533). The *Epitome* – qualified by one modern authority as 'the finest textbook of Ptolemaic astronomy ever written'[20] – could have given Copernicus all he needed to devise his heliocentric astronomy, and he would also of course have had access to the necessary volumes of astronomical tables.

Fig. 2.2

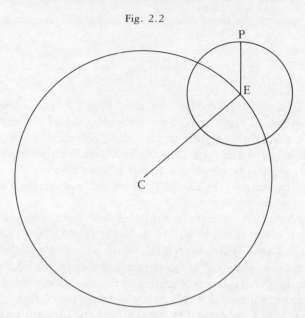

Much technical detail is needless here, but an outline of the principles of pre-Copernican planetary astronomy is essential for understanding Copernicus' revolution. The first essential is that while the system for the two inner planets (Mercury and Venus) mirrors that for the three outer ones (Mars, Jupiter, Saturn), there is a reversal of magnitudes. Thus, considering the former first, if C be the centre of the principal orb, a section through which in the plane of the ecliptic is represented by the deferent circle carrying E, the centre of the secondary orb or epicycle represented by the smaller circle; in turn, the epicycle transports the planet P. The most basic facts required to model the movements of Mercury and Venus are the *relative* sizes of the two circles, and the periods of revolution (in days, say) of each planet round E, and of E itself about C. These are readily tabulated (having been painfully established by observation and computation):

	Mercury	Venus
Ratio EP/CE	3.75 : 10	7.19 : 10
Period of P	88 days	225 days
Period of E	365¼ days	365¼ days

Here it is a practical though not a logical necessity of the scheme that wherever the centres E be placed in space – and they could be supposed either nearer than the Sun or beyond it in any order at will – they must, for Mercury and Venus, be placed on the line between the Earth and the Sun. Ptolemy's order was Earth (O), E_M, E_V, Sun: thus Mercury reaches a maximum elongation from the Sun every 44 days, and Venus every 112½ days roughly and then the planet moves back towards the Sun: on one side of the Sun it is of course seen as an evening star (setting after the Sun) and on the other side as a morning star (rising before the Sun). The Sun's own period is obviously 365¼ days.

59

Turning now to the outer planets, we can tabulate the same basic relations

	Mars	Jupiter	Saturn
Ratio EP/CE	6.58 : 10	1.92 : 10	1.08 : 10
Period of P	365¼ days	365¼ days	365¼ days
Period of E	687 days	4,332 days	10,750 days

From this it seems that though the ratio EP/CE *increased* from Mercury to Venus, it *decreased* again from Venus outwards, the two outermost epicycles being quite small by comparison with their deferents. Moreover, the outer epicycles all have the same period as the Sun, just like the deferent of the inner planets and, as already noted, the radius EP has always to be parallel to the line joining the Sun and the Earth. Thus the Sun mysteriously appears in both systems, but in different ways.

A further complication has to be remarked. Ptolemy like his predecessors found that to match observations he had to make the centre of the epicycle E in each case appear (as seen from the central Earth) to move at regularly changing speeds in its orbit; the most accurate match was obtained by a rather complex manoeuvre: the Earth (O) was placed upon the axial diameter of the orbit (AB) a little to one side of the centre (C), while another point (Q) at an equal distance on the opposite of C was taken as the centre of the uniform rotation of E; that is, the angle EQB varies uniformly as E moves round the circle. Consequently the peripheral speed of E is really greater near A than it is near B, while the greater nearness of O to A than to B contributes to making E near A (perigee) seem to move faster than it does near B (apogee), as seen from O. The eccentricity OQ 'halved' in this way (dividing it between OC and CQ) is never very great for any of the planets, so the change of distance of the epicyclic centre E did not enter into the theory, which was wholly concerned with angular positions and movements.

Fig. 2.3

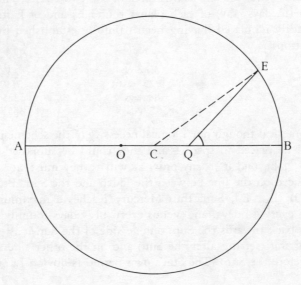

Copernicus found this mathematical treatment unsatisfactory for a number of reasons, although initially in the *Commentariolus* he insisted on one only; it seemed (he wrote)

quite doubtful, for these theories were inadequate unless they also envisioned certain equant circles, on account if which it appeared that the planet never moves with uniform velocity either in its deferent sphere or with respect to its proper centre. Therefore a theory of that kind seemed neither perfect enough nor sufficiently in accord with reason.[21]

Copernicus' difficulty is obvious. If E is carried on a real, solid sphere whose centre is C, then uniform motion of that sphere entails that E must move uniformly round C itself, not an equant-point such as Q. If the rotation round Q were to be uniform, then the sphere as a whole would have to be slowed down during one-half of each revolution, and speeded up during the other half, a process never conceived of in astronomy. Geometrically, the uniform rotation of E about Q is readily conceivable but in terms of mechanical spheres it is impossible. And Copernicus, it is clear, had his eye very much on such mechanical constructions as those of Peurbach: as he said in *De Revolutionibus* a circular motion must be uniform for it has a never failing cause of motion, which is the system itself.[22] In this mature work too he alleges other defects of a similar kind in the orthodox treatment of planetary motion; there is no explanation in it of why a disproportionately large volume is occupied by Venus' huge epicycle, nor is the position of the Sun between Mercury and Venus, and the other three planets, sufficiently argued. 'What cause can be brought forward by those who place Venus nearer than the Sun, and Mercury next, or some other order?' Why should not the lower planets, like the upper ones, be completely detached from the Sun:

Either then the Earth cannot be the centre to which the order of the planets and their orbits is related, or certainly their relative order is not observed, nor does it appear why a higher position should be assigned to Saturn than to Jupiter, or any other planet.[23]

In other words the customary order of the five planets with the Sun in the middle was a mere convention; nothing definitely tied the six systems of circles into a logically coherent order. Hence Copernicus is able to argue that it would be at least a step towards greater coherence to make Mercury and Venus circulate about the Sun (as indeed had been proposed long before); nothing is lost by this simplification save the idea of each planet having a separate deferent orb surrounding the Earth.

When this is done, it immediately follows that a ratio is set between the 'epicyclic' orbs of Mercury and Venus having the sun as their centre, and the Sun's own orb, because we can measure the maximum elongation of these two planets from the Sun. Suppose now that in search of still greater simplicity – and Copernicus considers this possibility too – we were to invert the circles for the outer planets, making the Sun's orb the deferent orb for each of these three (as already for Mercury and Venus), so that the 'epicycle' of each planet will now have the Sun at its centre, and these 'epicycles' respectively the periods

Fig. 2.4   The geoheliocentric system, the Earth fixed.

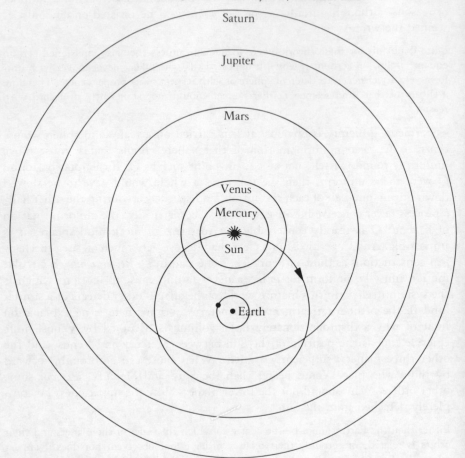

of 687 days (Mars), 4,332 days (Jupiter) and 10,750 days (Saturn) already found. As seen from the Earth the movement of each planet will be the same as before. Now, however, the dimension of each of these three outer planetary 'epicycles' has become proportionate to the size of the Sun's orb, as before with Mercury and Venus. We can work out – as doubtless Copernicus did – a sequence of planetary distances from the Sun (putting the Earth's distance from the Sun as 10):

Mercury	3.75	Mars	15.2
Venus	7.19	Jupiter	52.1
(Sun	10.00)	Saturn	92.6

The distances between the various celestial bodies (including the Moon, naturally) are now definitively fixed, a fact which may seem compelling to us, as it did to Kepler.

This is not yet the heliocentric system of Copernicus, rather it is often called the geoheliocentric system; many years later it was to become forever linked with the name of the Danish astronomer Tycho Brahe (1546–1601). Nor, though Copernicus was well aware of the fixing of dimensions – true in both the geoheliocentric and the heliocentric system at which he would arrive – did he insist very much upon it, perhaps because it is indifferently true of both. The geoheliocentric system has indeed all the advantages of order that Copernicus claimed for his own system, but it had (in his eyes) one overwhelming disadvantage: it cannot possibly be modelled with solid spheres, because the spheres would have to cut across each other.

What could have led Copernicus to explore different systems from those of Ptolemy, avoiding the illogical equant circles? If we rely only on his own account of the matter, he sought inspiration in the writings of other ancient authors besides Aristotle and Ptolemy 'to find out whether any of them had ever supposed that the motions of the spheres were other than those demanded by the mathematical schools'. And indeed in Plutarch – to whom Copernicus might have turned because of his well-known essay on *The Face in the Moon* – he found allusions to the fifth-century Pythagoreans like Philolaus and Heraclides who had supposed the Earth to move. 'Taking advantage of this I too began to think of the mobility of the Earth; and though the opinion seemed absurd . . . I considered that I might readily be allowed to try whether, by assuming some motion of the Earth, sounder explanations [than those of the Greek mathematicians] for the revolution of the celestial spheres might also be discovered'.[24] What Copernicus did *not* tell his readers, perhaps because he knew that the story carried unhappy associations, was that (as Plutarch also related on the authority of Archimedes) Aristarchos of Samos had devised a mathematical system, thus going far beyond the Pythagoreans, in which the Earth was treated as a planet. This problem, he may well have believed, had been solved in antiquity though prejudice had set Aristarchos' solution aside: we know this because of a passage that was deleted from the manuscript in the course of late editorial changes made by Copernicus himself.

It may well have been so. There is no need to doubt a story so circumstantially told by Copernicus. But Plutarch could not have set Copernicus *mathematically* on the road towards a heliocentric system. Here, as Noel Swerdlow has suggested, a hint he can hardly have overlooked in the Regiomontanus' *Epitome* (1496) may have proved crucial.[25] In Book XII of this work Regiomontanus showed how the motions of both the lower and the upper planets could be represented, not by means of the deferents and epicycles of Ptolemy, but by an eccentric circle whose centre is placed on the solar radius and revolves with it around the Earth at the centre of the universe. That is to say, the two figures below are equivalent kinematically as the dotted lines indicate: in other words, it is the same thing to have a big circle moving round a little one, as to have a little circle moving round a big one, *except* (and this is the important point) that now the 'little' circles for all five planets – actually, for Mercury and Venus they will be bigger than the eccentric or orbital circuits – have the same period as the Sun. Moreover, it is obvious though Regiomontanus did

Fig. 2.5   Regiomontanus' equivalence.

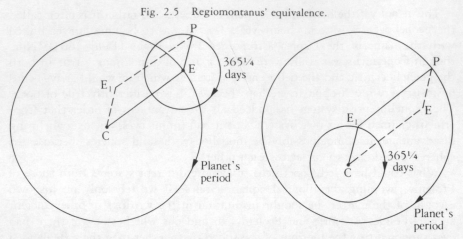

not say so explicitly, that the 'big' circles for all five planets may have the same centre, and this may be the Sun. If that choice is made, then we end up with the geoheliocentric system already described.

Swerdlow has presented evidence to show that Copernicus took this course, but inevitably Copernicus could not stop at the geoheliocentric model because that can only work for circles, not spheres. For some of the orbits around the Sun intersect the Sun's orbit around the Earth. Since Copernicus accepted the reality of the celestial spheres, being the only apparatus known to him by which the planets could be transported through space, he had to go beyond geoheliocentricity to the true heliocentric system,[26] for by making the Sun rather than the Earth the centre of motion, and putting the Earth into the Sun's orb, all the intersections disappear and a spherical model can be constructed.

However, one more grave difficulty remained before Copernicus could be satisfied, that of the equant-point. How should the motions of uniformly revolving spheres be arranged so as to give the same effect as Ptolemy's spheres which had to move non-uniformly, as we have seen? The answer was simple:

Fig. 2.6   Copernicus' alternative systems: (left) *Commentariolus*: (right) *De Revolutionibus*.

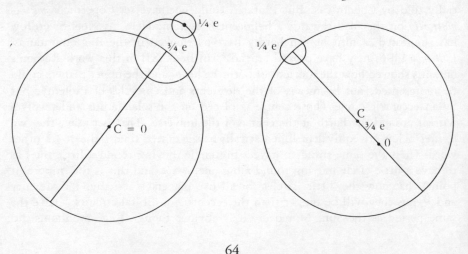

add more spheres to the system. In the *Commentariolus* he added to the con-centric orbital sphere of each planet a primary epicycle, then to that a secondary epicycle moving twice as fast. In the case of Jupiter the radius of the concentric is 52,166 units, that of the primary epicycle 4,040 units, and that of the secondary epicycle 1,347 units, the radius of the Earth's orbit being 10,000 units. In every case, in fact, the secondary epicycle was only one-third the size of the primary. In his mature book, however, Copernicus preferred for the three outer planets an equivalent system, making the deferent circle eccentric to the Sun with only one epicycle of the same size as the former secondary epicycle; the eccentricity was equal to the radius of the former primary epicycle. He said he did this because he now thought that the eccentricity of the orbits was variable. It can easily be shown that either of these devices is equivalent to Ptolemy's bisection of the eccentricity.

For about twenty-five years now it has been known that the *Commentariolus* geometry for the motions of Mars, Jupiter and Saturn was not first proposed by Copernicus, but by Ali ibn Ibrahim ibn al-Shatir (*c.* 1305–75) of Damascus, who devised it for just the same reason, to make a realistic spherical assembly possible. Some of the parameters used by Ibn al-Shatir are also identical with those used by Copernicus, possibly because both are worked out from the same Ptolemaic origin: some are different because Copernicus made an independent computation. It is also curious that Copernicus repeated in every detail of his lunar theory what Ibn al-Shatir had done before; elsewhere he employs two rolling circles to produce a straight-line motion in the manner of another Islamic astronomer, Nasir al-Din al-Tusi. Why this close correspondence should exist between reformers of Ptolemy in the East and the West is hard to understand: of course it did not extend to the heliocentric principle. Cop-ernicus surely read no Arabic nor Persian; yet in the diagram of the two rolling circles Copernicus for *De Revolutionibus* employed exactly the same lettering, point by point, as in the corresponding figure where it appears in manuscripts of al-Tusi's *Tadhkira*, a treatise on astronomy then accessible (it seems) in Italy.[27] Moreover, Copernicus never explained why the two epicycles in the *Commentariolus* and the single one of *De Revolutionibus* have to be of the proportions given to make the Ptolemaic equivalence work out.[28]

The last figure also makes another amusing point clear. Copernicus rightly claimed that in his system all the spheres moved uniformly, and so he had abolished the equant-circle; but it is not true (as we have just seen) that he abolished the equant-*point*. In fact there is, and there must be for the equiv-alence and correspondence with observations, uniform motion around an 'empty focus', Q Fig. 2.7. All the rest is elaboration. But Copernicus' claim that his system of spheres is mechanically constructable and so 'real' remains valid.

Hence we can see that Copernicus was far less of an isolated, totally inde-pendent genius than was once supposed. He was thoroughly trained by experts in Ptolemaic astronomy, in both Cracow and Italy, who seem to have been sufficiently free from dogmatism to make him aware of the true nature of the technical problems in treating the motions of the heavenly bodies, and to understand that other solutions to them than those of Ptolemy himself might

Fig. 2.7   The middle circle is the Ptolemaic eccentric deferent, with the Earth (or the Sun for
Copernicus – it is all one) at O. The planet is at P, revolving uniformly round the
equant-point Q. The lowest circle in the figure, drawn round O, represents the
deferent of the *Commentariolus*; the point M, the centre of the primary epicycle,
revolves uniformly around O, N, the centre of the secondary epicycle, moves uniformly and at the same speed but in the opposite sense to M, so that MN is always
parallel to the apse-line OQ. The planet P is carried by the secondary epicycle around
N at twice the angular velocity of M and in the same sense. The circle drawn through
the centres of the small epicycles is the deferent of *De Revolutionibus*. It will be seen
that all these three constructions are nearly equivalent – in fact, Copernicus' 'orbit'
for P is not exactly circular. It can be shown that MO and PQ are necessarily almost parallel, hence P always moves uniformly around Q, as Ptolemy
required.

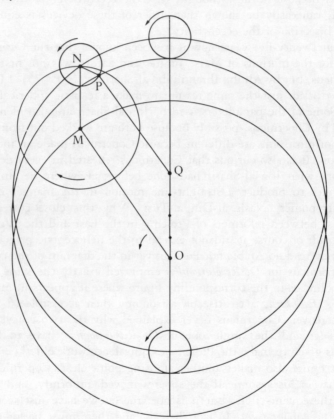

be examined. Moreover, he may have derived example and inspiration from the
studies of Persian astronomers in the previous century; though there is no
irrefutable evidence that this was so, it now seems more likely than not. All
this relates to the mathematical analysis that Copernicus effected, the aspect
of his work that a number of historians have already qualified as 'conservative'
in the sense that Copernicus continued to juggle with arbitrary circles which
he adjusted as he pleased to fit ancient observations, and without troubling
himself with the actual or resultant path followed by the heavenly bodies

through space. As Galileo was to point out later, for example, if Venus had been a self-luminous star (as Copernicus presumably supposed) then the great variations in her distance from the Earth postulated by Copernicus would have been not at all confirmed by the relative constancy of her brilliance as seen from the Earth. Nor did Copernicus account for the anomaly of the centre of the Earth's orbit being the centre of the whole system; while in other matters – such as his attribution of a variation in the rate of the precession of the equinoxes, and his ascription of a third motion to the Earth necessitated only by the fixing of its axis in his imaginary sphere – Copernicus was both old-fashioned and mistaken.

On the other hand, in proposing his great idea of the Sun as fixed and the Earth as a planet, which really has nothing to do with the technical astronomy one way or the other because a heliocentric and a geocentric universe can always be made equivalent by the same kind of devices, Copernicus was original and independent. His implied claim to have had no precursors since antiquity is quite just, and we may well doubt whether any of them, even Aristarchos, had ever worked out the heliocentric principle in the technically complete manner of Copernicus himself. Whether he began from the technical feasibility of a heliocentric universe, and then convinced himself of its physical elegance, or whether starting from the Pythagorean principle he discovered its technical feasibility (as he himself seems to indicate) we cannot tell for certain. In either case it does not look as though Platonic philosophy or obsession with the Sun had much to do with the course of his thought.

Copernicus well knew that though technical astronomy could perfectly assimilate the idea of the Earth as a planet, and to his mind derive advantages from it, the same could be said neither of philosophy nor of religion. To take the latter first, Copernicus appealed in his Preface for the protection of Pope Paul III against slanderers, sycophants and idle babblers, including those who might 'claim a right to pronounce a judgement on my work, by reason of a certain passage in Scripture basely twisted to their purpose'. He also hints at his knowledge that some early Christians, like Lactantius, held very absurd ideas about the universe. And that is all he has to say on the problem of the choice between revealed and rational truth which has proved of so much interest through many centuries. In fact besides the reference in *Proverbs* to the Earth being established fast, that it shall not be moved, numerous other passages (not least the account of Joshua's miracle at Jericho) make perfectly explicit the universal assumption of the scriptural authors and the early Fathers that the Earth is at the centre of the universe, as of course the pagan philosophers and mathematicians also believed. As a biblical statement about the observable world this was as well known and as definite as the creation of the world by God in six days, the appearance of the rainbow (unknown in the antediluvian world) as a sign of the ending of Noah's flood, on the miraculous star at Bethlehem; however tactful Copernicus' reluctance to argue the issue, it was to remain real and thorny.

The philosophical argument had been thoroughly canvassed in the fourteenth century, unknown surely to Copernicus. Nicole Oresme (1320–82) in the

French lectures he devoted to Aristotle's *On the Heavens* towards the end of his life argued that it is all one whether the skies move and the Earth stands still, or vice versa[29]; further, he said, neither experiment nor reasoning could prove which is actually the true case. Galileo was to say the same thing two hundred and fifty years later. Oresme quotes three contrary arguments, all of which were to be directed against the Copernican system. First, we actually see the Sun and stars curve around us in motion; second, if the Earth turned from West to East (rather than the sky from East to West) a great wind would be felt blowing steadily from the East; third, a stone flung vertically upwards would not descend to the same spot, because of the motion of the Earth meantime. Oresme has answers to all these arguments. He begins by emphasizing (as Copernicus was to do) the subjective relativity of motion: a man in a boat gazing at a second boat cannot easily tell which is moving, he seems to be at rest in his own little world. As for the wind, the truth is that the Earth, water and air of the sublunary world would all move together as a whole, and so there would be no wind other than those to which we are accustomed (only much later would the regular trade-winds be linked with the Earth's rotation). The difficulty about the rising and falling stone Oresme answered similarly: the stone moving through the air is carried along with the air and with 'all the mass of the lower part of the world which is moved in the daily movement'. This seems to mean that the stone moves along with the Earth beneath, and all else, though freely moving in the space of air.

Oresme also faced the contention that the motion of the Earth would be out of place in the texture of natural philosophy, arguing that although Aristotle had attributed no movement to the elemental Earth as a whole he had nevertheless declared that a single simple motion was appropriate to each element, so that the elemental Earth – and presumably the water too – might well turn in its place, as the heavens do in theirs, and the element fire below the heavens. Oresme agreed that if the Earth turns it must be endowed with a 'moving virtue' but this (he asserted) it must in any event possess already since pieces of earth removed from Earth return to it. To the objection that the movement of the Earth would falsify astrology he replied that all the conjunctions, oppositions and zodiacal events significant in astrology would be seen to happen as they do now, the tables of movements and the theories of celestial influence would remain 'true' without change, the only difference being that the reality of motion is withdrawn from the heavens and given to the Earth. Contrary to Oresme and most early followers of Copernicus it has often been alleged that he removed what scientific basis astrology may be supposed to possess. It was not so, for indeed astrology argues from the apparent configurations of the sky. not the mechanics by which they are produced or their physical nature. The constellations themselves are purely man-made, and the 'Houses' of the zodiac so important in astrology no longer correspond even to these. But the most learned astronomers, like Kepler himself, have not thought of this as affecting astrology adversely.

Even though Joshua's miracle did not discountenance Oresme, he finally affirmed that however philosophers may argue, we can be assured that the Earth does not move, because Scripture states as much. Moreover, Oresme's discussion seems to be limited to the Earth's axial rotation, since he did not contemplate a progressive revolution of the globe around the Sun; the arguments are the same in either case. To conceive of this annual or planetary movement was Copernicus' chief claim to originality and this movement was the more repugnant to those who believed that God had given the Earth a special position at the centre of the universe (with, curiously, Hell inside it). Thus Copernicus had even greater need for strong arguments on his side than had Oresme, who was after all only putting a philosophical position that ultimately he would safely abandon, yet Copernicus if anything made out a weaker philosophical case than Oresme.

He tells us first that the Earth is a sphere, and that rotation is natural to a sphere for by that very act its shape is expressed. While this may be true of planetary spheres (or not) it is certainly not true of all spheres. Next Copernicus argues that 'a simple celestial body cannot move irregularly in a simple orb': this is one of his statements against Ptolemy's equants, both justifying and justified by the conventional resolution into uniform spherical motions. Then he reminds us, wisely, that when we see motions apparently in the heavens, we must be careful not to attribute to them what is really happening on Earth: since the vault of heaven contains all things, should not movement be attributed to that which is contained? And, 'should we not be more surprised if the vast universe revolved in twenty-four hours, than that the little Earth should do so?' Here Copernicus seems to have forgotten that if there really are celestial spheres, and they do really move, the matter of 'slower' or 'faster' in human terms can have little meaning. Because the variations of the planets' motions indicate that these do not have the Earth as their geometric centre, 'it is justifiable to hold that the Earth has another motion in addition to the diurnal'. This is strictly a *non-sequitur*; however, Copernicus does go on to show correctly how, if the heavens are immeasurable compared with the Earth, an annual motion of the Earth would not be revealed by an opposite apparent circling of the fixed stars through the year: 'thus the Earth appears as a mere point compared to the heavens, as a finite thing to the infinite'. (This argument Copernicus may have read in Plutarch, reporting Archimedes' use of Aristarchos' 'immeasurable' universe in the *Sand-Reckoner*.) As for Ptolemy's fears that motion of the Earth would cause destructive instability to everything on it, Copernicus retorts that the Earth's motion is natural, 'a thing far different from an artificial action', and natural processes work smoothly. One could as well argue, he suggests, that the starry sphere would be disrupted by its stupendous revolution in twenty-four hours.[30]

Like Oresme, Copernicus treats the atmosphere as part of the Earth, rotating along with it. But heavy bodies falling, and light bodies rising upwards, through the atmosphere must have a double motion, not the single motion Aristotle deemed suitable: because, as Copernicus saw, the falling stone must go round with the Earth, as it descends towards the centre in a straight line. Here he offers an interesting generalization: simple bodies in their natural place and state only move in circles, for that motion is self-contained and 'similar to being at rest'. Only when a body is out of its natural place does rectilinear motion occur (or rather, he should have said, appear to occur) as with the falling stone; and these forced rectilinear motions are never uniform, whereas the natural circular motion of all things is uniform. Circular motion, he has just said, is like rest, and rest or immobility he prefers to motion, because 'immobility is nobler and more divine than change and inconstancy, which latter is thus more appropriate to Earth than to the (entire) universe'. There seems some imperfection in the argument here, for the planet Earth behaves as a planet no less perfectly than other planets: the change and inconstancy only relate to the displaced parts, partaking of (apparent) rectilinear motion. They have nothing to do with the question whether the Earth is a planet or not.[31]

Soon, however, Copernicus comes to a most important philosophical innovation, made to deal with the difficulty that because all the heavy stuff in the universe (according to Aristotle) – that is the earth and water – is no longer collected at its centre, one cannot say that heavy things fall to this centre as their natural place. Instead, Copernicus proposes that weight or gravity – which we perceive as the cause of falling – is simply a principle of coherence, 'a natural inclination bestowed on the parts of bodies by the Creator so as to combine the parts in the form of a sphere and thus contribute to their unity and integrity'. Further, as all bodies in the solar system are spheres, it is plausible that they too should have a similar property of coherence, or gravity.[32] We may doubt whether Copernicus had worked out the full implications of this far-reaching suggestion, which include the possibility of thinking of all the planets and the Moon (and indeed the Sun too) as physically similar, and of coherence/gravity as a universal property of matter. It would not be very long before someone would point out that something of the same sort causes small drops of fluid to run together into spheres.

But finally the core of Copernicus' argument for his system is given in Chapter 10 of his Book 1: 'On the order of the Heavenly Bodies', for it is in the fixing of the series of the planets and their distances that the heliocentric arrangement excels. Yet this perhaps is as much an aesthetic preference as a philosophical argument. Here also Copernicus tells us of the glory of the Sun enthroned at the centre:

He is rightly called the Lamp, the Mind, the Ruler of the Universe; Hermes Trismegistus calls him the Visible God, Sophocles' Electra calls him the All-seeing. So the Sun sits as upon a royal throne ruling his children the planets which circle round him.

In the one poetic passage of De Revolutionibus Copernicus seems carried away momentarily by the chiming of his ideas with the (very different) ones of ancient myth and wisdom: one might wonder what Sophocles' Electra had to do with the calculation of the length of the tropical year. At all events, he turns sharply to renewed emphasis on the geometrical symmetry of his system, and the 'clear bond of harmony in the motion and magnitude of the orbits such as can be discovered in no other way'. Nor does he fail to urge the principle of economy – Ockham's razor – 'We thus rather follow nature, who producing nothing vain or superfluous, often chooses to endow one cause with many effects.' And even here with virtually his final words on the rightness or wrongness of the method he had chosen, he honestly confesses that after all he must address the technically expert.

Though these views (of mine) are difficult, counter to expectation, and certainly uncommon, yet in the sequel we shall, God willing, make them abundantly clear at least to mathematicians.

What were Copernicus' thoughts as he received copies of the book he had polished through so many years, it is said as he lay dying? Did he think of its possible reception by mathematicians and scholars, and wonder whether they would use or neglect it? He certainly cannot have imagined that in the perspective of history it would seem, more than any other single book, to have introduced a new epoch in history.

NOTES

1. *Novum Organon*, Book I, x, xi.
2. A. C. Crombie, *Robert Grosseteste and the Origins of Experimental Science*, Clarendon Press: Oxford, 1953, 210, 252.
3. *De Fabrica*, Book III, Ch. 6.
4. Sir George Clark, *History of the Royal College of Physicians of London*, Clarendon Press: Oxford, 1964, 1, 109–10.
5. *De Fabrica*, Book VIII, Ch. 12; cf. C. Singer and C. Rabin. *A Prelude to Modern Science*, Cambridge U.P., 1946, xliii–iv.
6. F. Maddison, M. Pelling and C. Webster (eds) *Essays on the Life and Work of Thomas Linacre*, Oxford U.P., 1977.
7. Kenneth D. Keele, 'Leonardo's Anatomia Naturale', *Yale Journal of Biology and Medicine*, 1978 (reprint). C. D. O'Malley (ed.) *Leonardo's Legacy*, University of California Press: Berkeley and Los Angeles, 1969.
8. C Singer in *Studies and Essays in the History of Science and Learning offered to George Sarton*, Schuman: New York, 1947, 47.
9. Ibid., 81.
10. Sir Charles Sherrington, *The Endeavour of Jean Fernel*, Cambridge U.P., 1946.
11. J. F. Dobson and S. Brodetsky, *Nicolaus Copernicus, De Revolutionibus*, Preface and Book 1, Royal Astronomical Society: London, 1947, 4.
12. Edward Grant, 'Late medieval thought, Copernicus, and the scientific revolution', *Journal of the History of Ideas*, XXIII, 1962, 197–220.
13. Dobson and Brodetsky, op. cit., 10, 5.
14. Edward Rosen, *Three Copernican Treatises*, 2nd edn., Dover: New York, 1959, 93–106.
15. Ibid., 111.
16. Lynn Thorndike, *History of Magic and Experimental Science*, V, Columbia U.P.: New York, 1941, 410.
17. Rosen, *Three Copernican Treatises*, 109.
18. To elaborate: a medieval Latin version from Arabic was first printed at Venice in 1515. This Copernicus presumably used. Next, a Latin translation from a Greek manuscript made (1451) by George of Trebizond was printed also at Venice in

1528: scholars seem inclined to think poorly of this. Then the same Greek manuscript was printed at Basel in 1538 – this was too late to have been of service to Copernicus.

19. Paul W. Knoll in R. S. Westman (ed.), *The Copernican Achievement*, University of California Press: California 1975, 147–8.

20. Noel Swerdlow, 'The *Commentariolus* of Copernicus' in *Symposium on Copernicus, Proc. Amer. Phil. Soc*, 117, 1973, 426.

21. Ibid., 434.

22. Dobson and Brodetsky (op. cit., Note 11), 15.

23. Ibid., 17.

24. Ibid., 5.

25. Swerdlow (loc. cit., Note 20), 471–7.

26. Strictly the Copernican system is not heliocentric in that for Copernicus not the Sun, but the centre of the Earth's orbit (close to the Sun and moving round it) is the centre of the whole System. Neither, strictly are the Keplerian and Newtonian systems heliocentric. The pedantically exact term 'heliostatic' (apart from its unfortunate resemblance to the quite different *heliostat*) does not so well recall Copernicus' own glowing instance that the Sun was at the centre of the universe.

27. Willy Hartner, 'Copernicus, the man and his work' (in op. cit., Note 20), 421.

28. Swerdlow (loc. cit., Note 20), 469.

29. The *Livre du Ciel et du Monde* was edited by A. D. Menut and A. J. Denomy in *Medieval Studies*, IV, 1943; revised edition, University of Wisconsin Press; Madison, 1968.

30. Dobson and Brodetsky (op. cit., Note 11) 9–13.

31. Ibid., 14–15.

32. Ibid., 15–16.

CHAPTER THREE

A century of confusion

When the masterpieces of Copernicus and Vesalius were published the process of scientific and artistic Renaissance had continued for over a century, and their productions should be regarded as among its mature fruits, rather than as belonging to its beginnings. Printing too was almost a hundred years old, and had poured a wealth of learning upon the world; people were even becoming accustomed to the idea of the Americas, and learning of their strange plants and animals. Greek had ceased to be a great rarity, and the name of Plato was becoming almost as familiar as that of Aristotle. Courtly patronage was no longer to be enjoyed only in Italy, for the example of love for learning had been imitated in France and England, and was making headway in Germany, where a prince took up astronomy. But there was as yet no definable programme of work, no identifiable frontier of knowledge rolling forward. There was excitement, a ferment of activity, but also great confusion. A very few brash spirits were already daring to boast that the modern world was beginning to outstrip antiquity in knowledge, but most scholars around 1550 and for long afterwards thought it quite as important to study and understand old authors, as to try for new advances. Even in the late seventeenth century Newton, Leibniz and many of lesser fame prided themselves as much on their scholarship as on their scientific capacities. A programme of demolition and reconstruction in the realm of ideas seemed by no means generally appropriate; this kind of policy, and the great Copernican debate, only began to dominate the scene in the early seventeenth century.

By contrast, if we leap a century ahead to the years near 1640, a far more positive situation presents itself and the labours of the next couple of generations – the period of the scientific revolution *par excellence* – seem to follow in almost logical sucession. By 1640 the great methodological and programmatic statements of Bacon, Galileo and Descartes had been promulgated and were approaching realization. A battle between intellectual radicalism and conservation was already taking place on more than one front, and the defining characteristics of the 'new philosophy' as it began to be called – questioning of mere authority, acceptance of Copernicanism and mechanism, faith in empirico-rational arguments, and especially mathematics – were already clearly displayed. Organizational centres of the new scientific movement, as yet largely independent of the universities, became identifiable in some of the major European cities; though penetration into the academic world was making headway also, the strength of activity of the academically trained who had renounced university confines (Bacon, Descartes and Galileo all fall into this category, all were vigorous critics of academic philosophy) was even more conspicuous. New textbooks, compendia, astronomical tables, anatomical atlases dominated the scene. One could find everywhere confidence in past achievement as well as optimistic expectation for further intellectual conquests in the future, and their utility in everyday life. Some imagined that the human quest for understanding of the ultimate mathematical and natural truths might be completed in two or three generations if enthusiastically undertaken. The century of confusion ended with the death of Galileo and the birth of Newton and the century of fulfilment was beginning. Science was to be firmly linked with modern history.

The variety of sixteenth-century efforts made confusion inevitable. The respective 'modernists' who supported Vesalius, Copernicus or Paracelsus – to cite a third figure yet to be considered – had almost nothing in common except criticism of orthodoxy. Then there was tension between the objectives of emulating or surpassing ancient excellence. In 1594 Sir Hugh Platte wrote:[1]

Why then should we think so basely of ourselves and our times? Are the paths of the ancient philosophers so worn out or overgrown with weeds that no tract or touch thereof remaineth in our days whereby to trace or follow them? Or be their labyrinths so intricate that no Ariadne's thread will wind him out that is once entered?

Such backward-looking glances, though to be protracted right up to the dispute between the ancients and moderns (or 'Battle of the Books') of the late seventeenth century, were already yielding something to those who wrote of joyful news from a new-found world, or of the discoveries made in recent times unknown to the ancients, like Stradanus and Francis Bacon. More narrowly one might in the development of mathematics contrast the careers of Federico Commandino (1509–75) and Raphael Bombelli (1526–72). Commandino's lifelong labour as translator and editor of the Greek geometers (not forgetting also Hero's *Pneumatica*, so significant in physics), among them Apollonios, Archimedes, Aristarchos, Pappos and Ptolemy, made an enormous contribution to the sophistication of mathematics in Europe setting out for all the highest level of mathematical thinking that the Greeks had attained, and initiating the search for 'lost' works of merit which sometimes ended in their 'restoration' by the moderns, as with Commandino's completion of Archimedes *On Floating Bodies* as it was then imperfectly available. Bombelli – a man of a much lower social level – worked as a drainage expert on the reclamation of marshes (the parallel with Simon Stevin is obvious) and is remembered above all as a great algebraist, who could conceive of such utterly non-classical quantities as $\pm \sqrt{-10}$, and could operate with them. Certainly he studied (in manuscript) the great Diophantos, and was influenced by him, but his role was as the last great figure in the Italian school of analysis, which introduced algebra to modern Europe.

Similarly in the history of mechanics. Through Commandino's editions especially the writings of Archimedes made a great impact after about 1540, having been almost unknown (or at least uninfluential, for they were translated) during the Middle Ages. Statics and hydrostatics, most typically problems of the determination of the centre of gravity of bodies, suddenly blossomed: such studies attracted the youthful Galileo for example. Interest in the Aristotelian tradition of statics, dominant during the past few centuries, suddenly waned, although the practice of teaching the principle of mechanisms by means of the theory of the 'five simple machines' – all reducible to the principle of the lever – continued, again, for example, in the hands of Galileo who composed an important treatise in Italian on this topic, which also goes back to Aristotle's *Mechanics*.[2] On the other hand medieval achievement in the study of moving bodies certainly remained alive, though its precise importance in the late sixteenth century is still uncertain. At the time when Galileo was a student at Pisa the names of some of the great medieval philosophers who had studied the problems of motion, not least 'Calculator', were still known, and their language and ideas still employed, but their works were probably little read (even though they had, in part, been put into print). Indeed, Newton in the *Principia* makes use of this technical language when he speaks of the intension and remission of qualities, meaning their quantitative increase and decrease (of heat, for example). Curiously, the highly mathematical form that such discussions had taken in the fourteenth century was now quite abandoned, as though in preparation for their replacement by a quite different mathematical treatment of movement.

One post-classical concept that was of great importance in sixteenth-century mechanics is that of *impetus*. Aristotle in his *Physics* had categorized sublunary movements under two heads: if they occurred as part of the order of things they were *natural*, if contrary to that order (as when a weight is lifted upwards) *violent*. Both kinds of movement he thought to be resisted by the medium (normally air or water) through which the moving body has to pass, as when a leaf flutters down from a tree. Continuation of movement therefore required a cause or a force to produce it – only living things, Aristotle said, move spontaneously and of their own will. Nature's tendency towards order is the cause of natural motion in terrestrial things, while muscular effort or some unusual violence in nature itself (for example, a gale of wind) produce violent motion. All this is quite logical, Aristotle steadily following the maxim that there is no effect without its cause. Unfortunately experience suggests a complication: it is often just as hard to *stop* a violent motion, as to cause it to happen. Everyone knew that a boat does not stop dead as soon as the sails are lowered or the oars shipped, nor does the potter's wheel come to rest the instant he ceases to spin it round (the potter could not work single-handed if it did). Aristotle had no good explanation of why this continued motion occurred after the cessation of the applied cause, though it was clearly non-natural, and must cease after a time. He was commonly supposed to have taught that the medium (air in the case of the potter's wheel, the arrow, the cannon-ball and so on) carried the heavy thing along, and for this was roundly criticized by philosophers from Byzantine times onwards, probably unjustly. In any case, there was an awkward lacuna. Following earlier precedents, scholastic philosophers chose to introduce a new name for a postulated new cause, impressed virtue or impetus. They observed that some changes are inelastic: press a seal upon a piece of smooth, soft clay and its pattern remains on the clay in reverse. Place an iron bar in the smith's fire; it will retain a bright red heat for some time after it is withdrawn. Similarly, they argued, when some cause makes a body move, the quality of motion does not at once vanish from the body as soon as the cause ceases to act. In the words of Leonardo da Vinci

Impetus is the impression of movement transmitted by the mover to the movable thing.

Every impression tends to permanence or desires permanence. This is proved by the impression made by the sun on the eye of the spectator and by the impression of the sound made by the clapper as it strikes the bell.[3]

So a heavy projectile exerts a smashing effect even after travelling many yards from the machine that flung it into motion.

The new word did not alter the Aristotelian categories of motion (Leonardo also notes: 'Violent movement the more it is exerted the more it grows weaker: natural movement does the opposite').[4] It was generally supposed that the violent and the returning natural motions of a projectile were along straight lines, and that the fall was perfectly or nearly vertical as it is shown to be in Leonardo's sketches. Most philosophers (again, Leonardo follows them) – not all – imagined that impetus like red-heat or bright pigmentation or the vibration of a bell or physical beauty was a qualitative attribute that naturally and inevitably tended to zero unless it were somehow recharged by the original cause: this was one way of explaining why, for example, an arrow shot up in the air does not recede indefinitely from the Earth, but after a time falls back; of course its motion is also resisted by the air. It will be gathered that as a 'cause' that comes from nowhere, that is detectable only by the one effect attributed to it, and that vanishes away into nothing, impetus was an unsatisfactory notion.

Nevertheless, it did permit analyses of the phenomena of motion to be made that Aristotle could not make. Some writers (and their treatment leaves traces in Galileo) used impetus to account for the slowing down of projectiles in ascending, and the acceleration of falling bodies, in terms of an opposition between the constant downward pull of gravity and the waning force of impetus. While impetus prevailed the projectile shot up, with its excess over gravity ever diminishing; at equality of the two tendencies the projectile was momentarily at rest, vertically suspended, until the increasing prevalence of gravity over impetus brought it crashing down to Earth. Perhaps more interesting, however, was the attempt lasting over several generations to plot the line traced by a projectile shot off at an angle to the horizon. Leonardo, sketching mortar-bombs describing a high trajectory, shows an extensive curve linking the initial 'point-blank' straight line with an equally rectilinear vertical fall. Some supposed that such a line could be enclosed within a triangle, and the proportionality of ranges be computed from the proportionality of triangles. Many – including Leonardo – called the curvilinear part of the motion 'mixed'. Obviously the idea of a mixture of the Aristotelian categories of natural and violent is as confused as the idea of mixing celestial and terrestrial, and proved to be of neither physical nor geometrical value, yet it lingered on to the period of Newton's *Principia*.[5] A start towards a clearer conception was made by Niccolo Tartaglia (1506–57), who argued in the first book devoted wholly to the study of ballistics, *La Nova Scientia* (The New Science, Venice 1537), that gravity is operative along the whole trajectory, from the moment the cannonball leaves the mouth of the gun, for example, and therefore the ball's path is continuously curved downwards from the straight line along which it is shot. Most gunners of course believed in the illusory 'point-blank' shot. In his later book *A Variety of Discoveries and Inventions* (1546) Tartaglia put his conviction much more strongly: not only could a cannon not possibly shoot fifty paces in a straight line, it could not shoot even one. However, he had no success in analysing the curve traced by the projectile, nor did any one else in the sixteenth century. Mathematicians parroted phrases about simple motions following rectilinear paths, and mixed motions curved ones, which left them no wiser than at first, while gunners found wisdom in such philosophy as

> Every motion in the world endeth in repose.
> Every simple body is either rare and light
> or else thick and heavy and according to
> these differences it is naturally carried
> towards some part.
> Nothing worketh naturally in that
> which it is wholly like or wholly dislike,
> but in that which is contrary to it and
> more feeble.[6]

As now seems obvious to us, the definition of projectile motion required the prior definition of free fall under gravity since, as the impetus theorists had dimly perceived, a projectile is a negatively falling body when it ascends, and a positively falling body when it descends. Now the nature of uniformly accelerated motion had been intensively studied in the fourteenth century, and it was understood that equal increments of speed must be understood to be received by the moving body in equal increments of time or equal increments of distance from the origin. Leonardo for instance had this from the philosopher Albert of Saxony (1316–90), who may have been the first philosopher to use the relatively new gunpowder-artillery in an example. He was an intelligent follower of the Parisian and Oxford commentators upon Aristotle's *Physics*. If uniformly accelerated motion was defined in this way by equal changes of speed, then, certain mathematically minded philosophers perceived, in the second half of an accelerated motion of this kind three times as much distance would be traversed, as in the first half. This indeed follows readily from the 'Merton Rule' – so named by historians because of its association with the Aristotelian commentators of Merton College, Oxford – which posits that the motion of a uniformly accelerated body is equal to that of a second body travelling uni-

Fig. 3.1   Oresme's demonstration of the 'Merton Rule'. Ordinates on the base AB represent instantaneous movements, all uniform if the ordinates terminate at DE (speed constant), increasing from zero to the maximum BC if they terminate at AC (speed uniformly increasing). The totals of these ordinates – the rectangle ADEB and the right triangle ABC – are clearly equal if E bisects BC and so G also bisects AB. That is, if the uniform movement is equal to the accelerated motion at its mid-point (in time, we must add) the distances traversed by the two motions are equal. Now it is also obvious that the small right triangle AFG is in area one-fourth of the large triangle ABC; therefore, in the first half of the accelerated motion, up to the mid-point G (in time) one-fourth of the whole motion is effected, three-fourths in the second half.

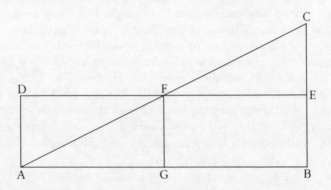

formly, when the second body has a constant speed equal to that of the first at the mid-point of its movement (mid-point in time, we should add, to be more specific than medieval writers always were). Oresme, who deployed a geometrical demonstration of this rule and also of its 1 : 3 distance consequence, also understood that if the division into equal parts of time were extended indefinitely, the successive distances traversed by the accelerating body would be as the continuing series of odd numbers: 1,3,5,7, . . .[7]

However, all this mathematization of accelerated motion was entirely abstract. It had nothing to do with falling stones or projectiles. The first person to propose that a naturally falling body might be supposed to be uniformly accelerating, so that the elaborate discussion briefly summarized above would apply to it, was the Spanish theologian Domingo de Soto (1494/5–1560) in a commentary on Aristotle's *Physics* (1551); he was a conservative in his philosophical opinions and apparently regarded the step he had taken as being of no great moment. Nor did anyone else, though Soto's commentary was several times reprinted and was known to Galileo: no one before Duhem referred to him as a possible forerunner of Galileo. It seems to be expressive of the muddled thinking of the sixteenth century that no one earlier than Galileo thought it interesting to define precisely the way in which a heavy body falls, even though Soto in a well-known book had essentially provided the answer, or went on from that to see that the step of defining the simple theoretical trajectory of a projectile followed fairly simply once the falling-distance could be plotted. (The other idea required is of course that of the vectorial analysis of motion.) Yet many writers were interested in projectile motion, and quite a few besides

Galileo in falling motion (G. B. Benedetti and Simon Stevin, for example): Galileo's well-known trials at the Leaning Tower of Pisa, to try whether bodies of different sizes fall at the same speed in air, are said to have aroused enormous interest. However there is no suggestion that Galileo was acquainted with Soto's definition of free fall at this time.

All the elements of what was to strike the next generation as a major success, a turning-point of innovation, were already present, but no one saw how to put them together. This was partly because of excessive realism: writers considering such problems as these were (in Aristotle's tradition) obsessed with the influence of air upon motion – which is indeed very great, as even the motorcar manufacturers have at last discovered. Pursuing this complexity, a simple, too simple truth eluded them. Secondly (and again following Aristotle) they were over-concerned about the particular characteristics of the heavy body – again, it seemed obvious to them that its *quality* must affect its behaviour in motion. And, thirdly, their eyes were rather on causal explanation of motion, than on describing the manner of motion: this one finds, for example, in Galileo's first notes on this topic (the so-called *Juvenilia*) written in the later 1580s or around 1590, close to the time of the trials at the Tower of Pisa.[8] Though these earliest known thoughts on motion contain arbitrary numbers (these, too, are found in Aristotle) they are preponderantly qualitative, not quantitative in their form. In his mature work, after more than twenty years of investigation and perplexity, Galileo was to abandon a historicist approach altogether and make a completely fresh start on the problems of motion, to all intents and purposes burying the medieval and renaissance discussions as if they had never been.

In mechanics, where Galileo was to inaugurate a new and different system of thought, nevertheless there was evident continuity: his definition of naturally accelerated motion is the same as Soto's, and the first two propositions of his geometrical treatment of it are closely related to Oresme's version of the 'Merton Rule' (p. 78). The situation is otherwise if we turn from the theory of motion, an established academic discipline, to a loosely integrated area of knowledge and speculation stretching from ideas of matter through 'chemistry' to medicine. Only within the last few years has a 'science of materials' begun to be so called. It is curious that though men have long been surrounded by a vast variety of materials essential to daily life, metals, minerals, earths, timber and so on, the systematic study of their properties is a recent occurrence: when in the late eighteenth century chemistry, emerging as an organized and discrete science, took charge of the composition and internal structure of substances it developed little interest in their gross properties (such as strength) which were resigned to the attentions of engineers and manufacturers. Before the emergence of chemistry there was no coherent body of knowledge relating to materials and substance at all – once more, because Aristotelian philosophy treated matter as formless, characterless 'stuff', attributing all differentiation and properties to the qualities impressed upon it.

Looking for the sources of eighteenth-century scientific chemistry, nineteenth-century metallurgy, and twentieth-century 'science of materials', the historian can go back only as far as a variety of craft skills (in metal-refining, ceramics and other branches of pyrotechnics) which began in pre-history, and to alchemical and iatrochemical writings which first constituted a recognizable literature in Europe during the second half of the fifteenth century. Academic, philosophical texts avail nothing in this context; technological texts, when these appear in the sixteenth century, contribute to our understanding of methods without illuminating the realm of thoughts. They have a real importance of their own, and the best of them like Vanoccio Biringuccio's *Pirotechnia* (1540) and Agricola's *De re metallica* (1556) achieved some deserved success of reprinting and translation, but their authors did not become leaders of schools or movements, and do not seem even to have given weight to the empirical philosophers like Francis Bacon. And this is to be regretted to the extent that such sober writers as these, rather than the tribe of alchemists, represented the true summation of 6,000 years of development in the pyrotechnic arts.[9] Their skills evidently did not captivate the imagination: perhaps, before researches into the properties of materials of the 'chemical' kind could attain any sort of éclat, they had to be associated with flamboyant claims for the prolongation of life and the manufacture of gold. At least, it seems to have been so in both China and the West – unless these two seemingly separate traditions are really closely related.

Traditional alchemists of the Middle Ages and Renaissance (if one may so describe them) kept quiet about their successes, in accordance with the most obvious suggestions of prudence. They sought neither enemies nor disciples. The man who was to set up a new cult of pyrotechnic art in Europe, Theophrastus Bombastus von Hohenheim who called himself Paracelsus 1493/94–1541) was a provocative, extravagant, inflammatory figure (literally: he once at Basel made a public bonfire of the printed works of Avicenna). He was contemptuous of authority, a forceful champion of his own merits, a trouble-maker of the most energetic kind in words and writings (largely in Swiss-German for he despised Latin). He had probably studied at Italian universities, he was an acute observer of diseases, and enjoyed some notable professional success especially in the treatment of wounds and chronic sores. But it was the legacy of his writings, many of which became known only after his death, which made this strange man one of the most influential thinkers of renaissance Europe.

Paracelsus was by no means a lucid author or one whose message was easily grasped. Nor are there any discernibly 'modern' elements in it, such as we may find in both Copernicus and Vesalius: there is nowhere a straight line from Paracelsus to modern science, and despite his 'chemical' skills he was (in Walter Pagel's words) 'neither a scientist nor a chemist in the modern sense'.[10] Perhaps the most obvious point to make is that he totally rejected the standard humoural theory of disease, which amounts to the belief that the symptoms of disease – difficulty in breathing or retaining food, pain, swellings, fever and so on – were all produced by one or more defects in the patient's internal constitution, defects which might be occasioned ultimately by heredity, or a wrong way of life, or casually by chills, over-exertion or over-indulgence, and so on. In humoural pathology diseases had no simple, identifiable causes and

certainly no casual agent in one-to-one correspondence with a complex of symptoms. Paracelsus on the contrary believed that specific causes of disease exist.
Goitre, he had found, had some cause in the water drunk by those afflicted.
Other ingested substances, especially minerals – Paracelsus' background was
in the mining regions of south Germany – could be disease agents: so also
might poisons in the atmosphere, coming from the stars. Particularly is this
so in the case of disturbance of behaviour and psyche: if a man is inclined to
miserliness, says Paracelsus, it is because he has chosen Saturn as his wife, for
each star is a woman; and if a man suffers from melancholy it is futile to seek
to purge his black bile: rather one must free him from astral influences.[11] Sometimes Paracelsus speaks of the 'seeds' of disease to which man is subject, created
by God at the beginning. In a very rough sense it might be said that the
Paracelsian pathogens are either poisons or astrological influences; neither is
'modern' and the latter chimes (in Paracelsus' own peculiar way) with a long
familiar belief about ill-health. But perhaps even more important than his
innovations in pathology and his general pronouncements on the relation
between man (the microcosm) and the universe was Paracelsus' new therapy,
his production of new and often dramatic weapons against disease. The traditional pharmacy traceable back to Dioscorides was herbal; indeed there was
no clear line of distinction during the Middle Ages between botany and pharmacy since Aristotle's and Theophrastus' more philosophical interest in plants
had been forgotten. Commonly, in polypharmacy, ingredients from many
plants were combined and a long process of boiling and heating was thought
necessary to extract their virtues. Animal substances were used too, notably the
vipers entering (with countless other things) into Venetian Treacle (*Theriacum*)
while minerals were largely limited to external applications. This armoury,
gentle for the most part not to say ineffectual, had been enriched towards the
end of the Middle Ages first by the discovery of the way to distil alcohol, highly
regarded as a great restorative in itself and still more as a solvent of active
substances ('tincture of iodine' is perhaps still with us). Moreover, by Paracelsus' time mercury had been introduced for the treatment of syphilis. (Judged
by contemporaries, probably rightly, to be a new disease, syphilis was supposed
to require a new medicament for its cure. Some found it in the wood guaiacum
brought from the New World, whence many believed the new disease to have
come. Mercury, with its dramatic effects on the patient, was found more effective, partly because of the normal tendency for the first distressing symptoms
to disappear.) Typically, Paracelsus disapproved of the massive administration
of mercury with its toxic consequences: he believed in the useful medical power
of the metals (including arsenic and antimony as well as mercury) but taught
that the dosage should be limited and the violence of the action mitigated by
change of chemical form. Metals and minerals are poisons, says Paracelsus, but
on the homoeopathic principle of like healing like, in proper usage they also
cure:

A hole rotting the skin and eating into the body, what else is it but a mineral? Colcothar – the *caput mortuum* of vitriol – mends the hole. Why? Because colcothar is the
salt that makes the hole.

Fig. 3.2 One form of the microcosm–macrocosm analogy, devised by Paracelsus. After Pagel, *Paracelsus*, 1958, p. 119.

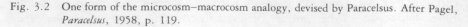

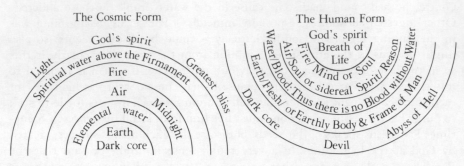

The Cosmic Form

The Human Form

In Paracelsus' philosophy this follows from the analogy between microcosm (internal) and macrocosm (external): the pathogenic colcothar or other substance internal to the body must be overcome by introducing the same healing substance from without. This may involve chemical treatment, as with arsenic (also a poison, as Paracelsus knows) which must be 'killed' before it is used as a drug: for example, white arsenic may be heated with saltpetre 'until it forms a deposit like lard at the bottom of the crucible'. This, poured off, takes on a golden hue and may be dissolved in alcohol or mixed with tartar. It is good against syphilitic and other sores.[12]

Without entering into further details and examples, it is certain that two historical consequences of great importance followed from Paracelsus' idiosyncratic therapy. First, his Renaissance followers formed in time an alternative school of medicine and pharmacy rivalling that of the Galenists: a revolutionary school, since the Galenists long held all academic and official positions and did their utmost to have the Paracelsians' practice declared illegal: at various times the course of dispute followed similar lines in different countries. In its particular way there was in medicine a battle between ancients and moderns that was quite as general and as noisy as that between Copernicans and Aristotelians: but in the end it led to a compromise, rather than a fundamental ideological change such as occurred in astronomy. Ultimately many Paracelsan remedies passed into official pharmacopoeias, while some traditional polypharmaceuticals, like treacle, were expelled or rationalized to inanity. As early as 1613 the Augsburg Pharmacopoeia allowed the use of chemical remedies when 'prepared according to the directions of and prescribed by fully experienced physicians who know how to combine rationality and experiment'. But drugs have always been taken from plant material, and much of Paracelsus' philosophical substructure vanished. On the other hand the idea of 'chemistry' (pyrotechnics) as a handmaiden to medicine expanded and flourished. Students of chemical reactivity now had a definite goal for their empirical operations (besides the alchemical delusion): they could hope to discover remedies that would be new, effective, palatable and safe. In their search they had certain guiding principles to assist them, weak and deceptive it is true, such as the belief in an 'arcane' principle in every substance which has to be *extracted*: do not mix things mindlessly, Paracelsus had taught, rather extract the pure *arcanum*. In this way 'chemistry' became a practical science of great importance, indeed, it was the therapeutic ambition of the Paracelsans that began the very gradual separation of 'chemistry' from alchemy.

One might argue that this group, the followers of Paracelsus, were historically speaking more important than the master himself, who has been described as 'Fasting in the morning, drunk in the evening, presenting every idea exactly in the order in which it came into his mind',[13] if only because the disciples gradually evolved a coherent, less extravagant system. Paracelsus' writings were collected by Johannes Huser, a physician of Baden, and printed at Basel between 1588 and 1590. But already some currency had been given to them in Germany by Leonhart Thurneisser (1531–1595/6), a quack doctor and faking alchemist, by Alexander von Suchten, Gerard Dorn and other minor figures. Although the centre of devotion to Paracelsus (and to alchemy) was to remain in Germany, some of his most influential early exponents were French, especially Quercetanus (Joseph du Chesne, ? 1544– 1609) and Theodore Turquet de Mayerne (1573–1655) who was to find refuge in England in 1606, for in Paris the defenders of traditional medicine proved vocal and powerful. Du Chesne was a competent chemist, using intelligible language; the introduction into medicine of calomel (mercurous chloride, a powerful purgative, the 'blue pill') has been ascribed to him. De Mayerne had much to do with the modernization of English medicine (notably through the London Pharmacopoeia, 1618) and the introduction of chemistry to England (he was the founder, much later, of the Company of Distillers of London). And after them came the string of early writers of 'chemical' textbooks – Oswald Croll, Jean Beguin and Andreas Libavius.

From this literature emerged the theory of the Paracelsan, 'spagyrical' or chemical principles, salt, sulphur and mercury, the *tria prima* in opposition to the four elements of the philosophers: in fact, the difference of *names* is not important, for salt continued to be the principle of earthiness, sulphur that of fire, and mercury that of fluidity, while chemists continued, like Aristotelians, to talk of 'airs' also. Nor was 'air' the only class (or 'state' of matter, to speak anachronistically) recognized by the 'chemists', yet not qualifying as a principle: metals – supposedly compounded of sulphur and mercury – acids, and in due time alkalis, were all regarded as important types of substance: from the very beginning, it seems, this recognition of types of active substances was as significant as the recognition of (ever unattainable) principles. The ancients seem never to have taken special notice of the fact that some materials are clearly more vigorously active than others (for example, wine and opium in relation to the animal body),[14] they knew nothing of acids and strong alkalis – not making soap from lye – and knew little of the active minerals, mostly metallic compounds, occurring naturally. Like soap, gunpowder and distilled alcohol were unknown to the classical world; what little acquaintance it had with the strange, beautiful and sometimes dramatic changes produced by combining two or three different substances (and perhaps heating them) was confined to technology – the manufacture of glass, for example – and fell quite outside the philosophical experience. If Paracelsus had any precursor, it was the fourteenth-century Franciscan John of Rupescissa. The most promising intellectual innovation of Parcelsus, therefore, was this notion of the activity – we woud say reactivity – of matter.

Paracelsus did not, seemingly, claim to be an alchemist in the ordinary sense: the alchemy he taught and practised, he said, was the preparation of 'secret remedies, by which one cures diseases that are regarded as desperate' and he believed that this was the business to which the ancient alchemists had devoted themselves. Of course he believed also in the possibility of transmuting metals, as evinced by the change of iron into copper (iron objects placed in water rich in dissolved vitriol became plated with the copper: this is the origin of 'Herrengrundt ware' from Bohemia) or by the yellowing of copper by calamine (the manufacture of brass by alloying zinc with copper). But he did not see the pursuit of factitious silver or gold as a proper object for one who sought to heal the sick, who should nevertheless be just as familiar with furnaces, coals, alembics and distillation as the traditional alchemist. Since the word *chemistry* (chimie, chemie and so on) to signify a practical art concerned with the preparation of useful substances, especially medicaments, was not in widespread circulation before the middle of the seventeenth century there was a long period in which the word *alchemy* had an ambiguous meaning, covering much more than the search for artificial gold and the philosopher's stone. Like Paracelsus, Andreas Libavius (d. 1616), not by any means his totally committed follower, defined alchemy as the art of extracting perfect magisteries and pure essences from compound bodies, an art useful in medicine, metallurgy and everyday life. The title of one of his works reads, translated:

The practice of alchemy, that is the method of the artificial preparation of the chief chemical medicaments explained in two treatises: of which the first was written by an anonymous author from his own experience concerning the distillation of waters and oils, of salts and essences; the second treats of the philosopher's stone, in which the method of preparing it is taught without metaphor and parable . . . Frankfort a.M. 1603.

Libavius is usually described as 'the author of the first chemical textbook' (his *Alchymia*, 1606), though all his writings combine 'chemistry' in our sense – a rational, experimental science – with alchemy in our sense; he was in fact very credulous.[15] That Paracelsus was still alive in his grave was only one of his tales. Few writers on 'chemistry' down to and including Robert Boyle (1627–91) regarded transmutation of metals as *in principle* impossible, though wiser heads tended to be sceptical about the many richly circumstantial tales about the production of alchemical gold that passed freely through the literature; indeed, there was yet no theoretical reason or theory of matter forbidding such transmutation; only common sense and experience were against it.

A consequence of Paracelsus' teaching was therefore to graft 'medical chemistry' (iatrochemistry) and alchemy firmly together, as nothing more than twin variants of the same art; some successors of Paracelsus even saw him simply as a deviant from the older and surer tradition of the alchemists, going back to

Geber among the Arabs, Mary the Jewess, and Hermes Trismegistus himself. (Authorities differ upon the degree of practical skill displayed by Paracelsus in his writings: Pagel thinks him very experienced, but Partington views his knowledge as drawn from books.) From the early seventeenth century a more strictly pharmaceutical line began to separate out, distinguished by such authors as Jean Beguin (*Tyrocinium Chymicum*, 1610), and from this in turn as its main (but by no means sole) root developed philosophical chemistry, that is, the objective study of reactivity and chemical change. However, in the early seventeenth century the transformation of 'chemistry' into a theory of matter was still far distant, and its natural alliance was with an esoteric rather than a mechanical philosophy. Just as the reality of mechanical marvels, automata especially, gave plausibility to tales of artificial birds or perpetual-motion machines, so the extraordinary genuine phenomena of chemical change gave colour to wonders even greater than that of transmutation. Persistent and striking is the story of the chemical phoenix; as Paracelsus tells it[16]:

Any man can bring the egg to maturity under his own arm and procreate the chicken as well as the hen. And here something more is to be noticed. If the living bird be burned to dust and ashes in a sealed curcurbit (vessel) with the third degree of fire, and then, still shut up, be putrefied with the highest degree of putrefaction in a *venter equinus* (horse-belly = blood heat), then that phlegm can again be brought to maturity and so, renovated and restored, can become a living bird, provided the phlegm be once more enclosed in its jar or receptacle. This is to revive the dead by regeneration and clarification, which is indeed a great and profound miracle of nature . . . This is the very greatest and highest miracle of God, which God has disclosed to mortal man . . .

This is similar to the later tale reported by Quercetanus of the growth of plants from ashes in hermetically sealed vessels under a gentle heat, accomplished by an unnamed Pole; others affirmed that the salts obtained from plant-ashes revealed in their crystals the shape of the plants from which the ashes had come.[17] Perhaps one may see the origin of all such stories in the fact that plants naturally spring up freely from burnt-over ground, certainly they may be taken as symbols of the mysterious processes of death and regeneration. (But that still leaves the problem of the mind that cannot distinguish between symbol and fact, myth and reality.)

The writings of Paracelsus and his followers were indeed perfused by magic – and not merely a high-level, esoteric, metaphysical kind of magic such as is associated with neo-Platonism, but a robust, operative magic. From the middle of the seventeenth century, through the combined influence of Descartes and Boyle, the beneficent action of chemical medicaments was interpreted in mechanistic terms – albeit fanciful enough in their own way. But in the earlier Paracelsan period they were regarded as having an essentially magical action, and the Paracelsans did not limit such virtue to mineral substances and their derivatives. They were quite prepared to find great merit in the older kind of magical material, like the bone from a dead man's skull, if only it was chemically prepared. In the same vein Paracelsus insists on the strict link between *form* and *use* known as the 'doctrine of signatures' (which is not unlike the anatomists' *a priori* faith in the deduction of function from morphology), of good medieval background[18]:

Behold the *Satyrion* root, is it not formed like the male privy parts? Accordingly, magic discovered it and revealed that it can restore a man's virility and passion. And then we have the thistle: do not its leaves prick like needles? Thanks to this sign, the art of magic discovered that there is no better herb against internal prickling . . . And the *Syderica* bears the image and form of a snake on each of its leaves, and thus, according to magic, it gives protection against any kind of poisoning.

So inevitably the stars too act magically upon men: 'A healthy man must submit to heaven and every day he must await what it sends him.' It is certainly not the case with Paracelsus that chemistry offers a new entrance to the rational study of nature (that is, one supposing a regular relationship between cause and effect), nor that chemical remedies offer a sure escape from that perilous world where disease is the effect of elf-dart, magical spell, or astral malevolence; on the contrary, Paracelsus simply uses the new world of chemical process and phenomena to enlarge the realm of magic. In the words of Lynn Thorndike[19]:

for Paracelsus there is no such thing as natural law and consequently no such thing as natural science. Even the force of the stars may be side-tracked, thwarted or qualified by the interference of a demon. Even the most hopeless disease may yield to a timely incantation or magic rite. Everywhere there is mystery, animism, invisible forces.

Walter Pagel, the foremost modern student of Parcelsus, agrees that he rejects rational thinking, is indeed 'inspired by a deep distrust of the power of human reasoning', and believes that the great truths of nature are rather learned 'in dream and trance fortified by a strong will and imagination'. This is because nature is best apprehended not by the brain which examines nature as something external, but by the 'astral body' of a man which is itself (as the microcosm) directly a part of nature and so apprehends these truths directly, intuitively: such an imaginative writer as D. H. Lawrence would presumably have agreed. For knowledge in the true Paracelsan sense is not a 'story' concocted in the brain about 'things' — that was the mistake of Aristotle — but is on the contrary (as Paracelsus writes) within things, seemingly as their essence or virtue. And he who has this knowledge of all things (the powers of the stars as well as the medical virtues of plants) is the Magus:

if a man go to no other school than that which is made of bricks and mortar and seek no schoolmaster other than him who teaches from behind the stove, he will come to nothing except superficially.

But the magi of the past never taught or sought the 'bookish learning of mortal man', and we should follow their example. Paracelsus resembles the religious mystics, and many alchemists, in regarding the truth that follows from enlightenment as transcendental, unattainable through the ordinary literary processes of study.[20]

One should not infer from this that Paracelsus developed no natural philosophy of his own, or that because he proclaimed himself untaught he refrained from trying to teach others. On the contrary, Paracelsus was the author of an 'alternative' natural philosophy, presenting a magical world-view that is not only different from that of Aristotle, Galen, and the Christian philosophers of the Middle Ages, but from the revived neo-Platonism which also contributed strongly to the Hermeticism of the Renaissance. The parallelism of microcosm and macrocosm appears in both, but neo-Platonism knew nothing of the three chemical principles, nor of the medical importance of the celestial influences upon which Paracelsus insists in his doctrine of correspondences. Paracelsus' conception of time also appears to be all his own, and is highly relativistic. Further, Pagel has pointed out that Paracelsus' emphasis on the organic – not characteristic of neo-Platonism – and the specific individuality of each organic being, is in contradiction with the microcosm–macrocosm theory, whose logic leads rather to the idea of a diffusion or sharing of life universally. Each being, according to Parcelsus, contains a Vulcan or Archeus who is the workman fabricating that being from primordial matter; plants are the living products of the Earth, formed by the 'Vulcan of the Earth', while in animals and man the Archeus is the chief inhabitant of the stomach where it presides over the functions of digestion and nutrition. (It is thus cognate to the Nutritive Faculty of Galen.) It 'directs everything into its essential nature', a function imitated by the physician (a sort of human Archeus) in his preparation of medicines. The seat of life, however, is in the heart – here, for once, Paracelsus agreed with Aristotle. Finally, besides this carnal body man also possesses an 'astral body' – perhaps meaning what others have called the spirit or soul in man – whereby man has a direct communication with the outside world and can predict events in it. It functions for instance in dreams, which

indicate certain works of nature that are in progress at the time. For example, a dream in which water or fish occur points to the maturation of minerals, salts, metals, sand, etc. which are all products of this element.[21]

If this attempt to characterize briefly the complex thought of a confused thinker seems barely intelligible, it is because the writer finds it impossible to attach meaning to many of the (translated) utterances of Paracelsus, or to perceive the force of their inspiration. What is the virtue of all the weird terms he coined for his discourse – the Oportet, the Archeus, the Iliaster, Truphat and Leffas? (The only one of such names that has survived is *gas*, devised by Van Helmont.) Why did he draw such a strong bond between innovation and absurd credulity, scepticism and superstition? Yet, at the simplest level of history, he had through his followers an immense influence upon pharmacology and so upon the course of the science later to be called chemistry. More subtly his influence and traces of his language turn up in all sorts of places, as in Bacon's writings. Though Bacon accused Paracelsus of making 'man into a Pantomime', and called him a fanatical breeder of phantasms, he also thought that he had encouraged men to experiment.[22] Clearly, unconventional thinking and reaction against authority, not to say the appeal to 'nature' and empiricism, could assume many forms and lead in many directions. Rational, scientific thinking was only one among several rejoinders to Aristotle, of which the two particularly associated with the names of Hermes Trismegistus and the other *prisci theologi*, that is neo-Platonism and Paracelsism, were perfused by magical conceptions, not only the idea of the magical universe but the idea of magic as a control of nature.

Of course to draw such distinctions is in a measure anachronistic: the lines between 'science' and 'magic' were as yet no more firmly drawn than those between astrology and astronomy. 'Natural magic' employing the extraordinary phenomena of magnetism, optics, pneumatics and so forth (as the unsophisticated judged them) was never magic in the true philosopher's sense at all. Many philosophers and mathematicians, as well as the followers of Paracelsus, were 'magicians' also, among them (as already noted) Girolamo Cardano, a man of powerful intellect and universal interests, but highly unstable; by no means an example of the progressive, right-thinking and future-building individual, he has an immortal place in the history of modern mathematics and, in the sixteenth century, he was widely read and influential. His *De Subtilitate* (Nuremburg, 1550) went through six editions in its first ten years. This is an encyclopaedia of natural philosophy embracing the natural and mental sciences, in which the nineteenth chapter is devoted to demons, of whose existence Cardano has no doubt, a confidence shared by Henry More (1614–87) the Cambridge Platonist, the 'sceptical' Joseph Glanvill, and of course many others. Indeed, many of the most learned of this age were unremitting enemies of the crime of witchcraft – such as, in the American colonies, Cotton Mather (1668–1728); indeed, the more learned a man the more stories of the activities of demons he could recite, as Cardano does from Philip Melanchthon and Erasmus as well as classical sources. Cardano was highly credulous too about astrology and all other ways of divining the future. But even his contemporaries regarded him as extravagant.

A figure somewhat similar in type, to whom great importance has been attached and who is certainly better known than Cardano in the English-speaking world, is the enigmatic John Dee (1527–1608). At the Court of Elizabeth I Dee secured patronage as a magus and astrologer – his fame in supposedly 'black arts' was to bring about the sack of his house at Mortlake just outside London by an irate mob; as an adviser on matters of geography and navigation to Elizabeth's sailors and explorers Dee played a practical historical role. Hence he is called a mathematician, though he made no contribution to the progress of mathematics, and he can at best be qualified as an influential teacher in a still-backward island. From a fairly early age what might now be called 'psychical research' became his main preoccupation, under the protection of his private medium or 'skryer' Edward Kelley (Dee did not claim to have personal familiarity with spirits), and he became a Faustian figure passing long years in European travel during which, it has been suggested, he founded the mysterious sect of the Rosicrucians. Dee – somewhat like Sir William Crookes at the end of his life – wandered right out of the sphere of matter and science into that ghostly invisible realm of demons and spirits (no judgement more perilous than that between the true and the false in this realm), separated from the material world by so thin yet to most impenetrable a veil, which was so fascinating and so plausible to the Renaissance mind. Dee, one must feel, for

88

all his mystic claims to power and wisdom, his *Monas Hieroglyphicas* and (in more rational moments) schemes for making Elizabethan Britannia rule the waves, for all his interest to scholars in many ages,[23] was more than a little insane and wrote reams of (unpublished) rubbish – whereas Cardano and Paracelsus, who published far, far more, at least expressed some good sense and were perhaps only on the edge of psychiatric disorder. But this again is an anachronistic classification; the Renaissance knew only of demons, the possessed, magi and mystics.

It must not be supposed that the innovators whether rational or, particularly, irrational had it all their own way despite the success of Cardano, Dee and Paracelsus; on the contrary, criticism was strong and persistent. Such of it as came from dull conventional upholders of established wisdom like the Paris doctors raised no important issues of principle; it was simply a defence of professional omniscience. On the other hand, the criticism of Paracelsus by Erastus (Thomas Liebler, 1523–83), a notable theologian, founded on a plain man's view of facts and words, makes a strong case for cautious rationalism against excessive imagination.[24] While accepting on theological grounds the existence of demons and witches, Erastus regarded magic as based either on demonology or on a mistaken conception of astrology: here he condemned Paracelsus and the neo-Platonists together. For the heavens are not controllable by men in their action upon the Earth beneath; rather they act according to a regular, constant pattern. He castigates Paracelsus' exaggerated idea of 'chemistry' – which is not a special art of controlling nature but simply a part of nature – and his introduction of the three chemical principles: here as elswhere Erastus points to the internal incoherence and illogicallity of Paracelsus' utterances; really, he says, the only logical idea of an element is that given by Aristotle – the least part of all things. All his talk of wonderful remedies from minerals simply boiled down to the suspect use of mercury. Erastus, it seems, is on the side of robust common sense and shrewd evaluation of experience against rant, bombast and folly. Are not, therefore, the friends of innovation and originality almost more dangerous and absurd than its enemies? Erastus was surely no friend to the scientific revolution or a new logic, and yet in many ways he seems to understand the 'scientific', sceptical spirit of later times better than Paracelsus did. The dilemma is very similar to that of mid-twentieth-century politics: the anti-Fascist too often finds the Communist his readiest ally. The critic of the magicians and the Hermeticists was all too likely to speak with the same voice as black clerical reactionaries, such as the theologians who condemned the elder Van Helmont for his attachment to the doctrines of Paracelsus and for 'perverting nature by ascribing to it all magic and diabolic art, and for having spread more than Cimmerian darkness all over the world by his chemical philosophy'.[25] Could rational, experimental science emerge without allying itself with this powerful force also demanding intellectual freedom and the right to choose new methods and systems?

The answer is still very much in debate. Many recent historians argue that it must be at least partly negative, that neo-Platonism, Hermeticism, Paracelsism – magic, in short – was essential to the development of science and the rejection of the past's philosophy. Apart from the many vocal defenders of the esoteric and Paracelsan, some of the leading 'new philosophers' of England and Germany seem to have leaned in the same direction, such as Kenelm Digby, Robert Boyle, Leibniz, even Isaac Newton. The French, Catholic, mathematical, Cartesian, avoided it for the most part though there were French 'adepts' and 'spagyrists' still long after Descartes's death. On the other hand, there were staunch rejections of the Hermetic tradition. One of the most celebrated came from Kepler, himself a Platonist and admirer of Proclus, a defender of astrology (after his own reformed model) and the son of a woman once accused of witchcraft. His opponent was Robert Fludd (1574–1637), a successful London physician who was also a Hermeticist and occultist; the complexity of intellectual relations is shown by the fact that Fludd supported for mystical reasons the circulation of the blood first described by his friend William Harvey (1627) on anatomical and experimental grounds. (Fludd's criticism of Galenic medicine, years before, had delayed his acceptance into the London College of Physicians; Harvey was not a critic of traditional medicine. To a forward-looking, liberal mind of c. 1620 Fludd might well have seemed a far more progressive, exciting and active figure than Harvey.) Kepler in 1619 thought it necessary to put him right both as to music and to celestial harmony. As to music, he says that Fludd has written as a musician, himself as a philosopher and mathematician; more important, Fludd thinks harmony is explained by numbers, Kepler by something that numbers measure (wavelengths, we would add, but this was not yet known). Moreover, when looking for the secret harmony of the universe (which for Fludd, curiously, is still Ptolemaic) the Englishman's numbers for the realms of Earth, Water, Air and Fire are merely imaginary while the German's numbers relating to planetary motion have been derived from measurement. The difference, briefly, is between numerology and mathematical physics.

This was one vital issue. While to the innumerate no doubt all mathematical reasoning was esoteric, it was essential for science as it has developed to distinguish between the occult and the rational endeavours to mathematize nature. (When Newton sought an analogy between the divisions of the colours in the spectrum and musical harmonies he was, regretfully, again confusing the two.) The numerologist reads significance into numbers everywhere, of his own devising: let us say, one, because it is unique; two, because everything comes in pairs or sides; three, because it is (as Aristotle said) the number of dimensions; four, because (says Fludd) everything can be divided into four quarters; five, because it is the ancient number of the planets; six, because it is the first perfect number, and so on. Then significance can be read into an infinity of ratios made of the integers. Here is an absurd (but true) example of numerology: in the Authorized Version of the Bible, turning to Psalm 46, we find that the 46th word is *shake*, and the 46th word backwards from the end (omitting Selah) is *spear*. Shakespeare was born in 1564: obviously he had a hand in the Authorized translation completed by 1611, five years before his death. The reversed order of the last two digits of the birthdate (46 for 64) is indicated by the reversed order of counting for the second word-element, *spear*. Perhaps more typical, however, is the kind of 'mystical' argument found in Grosseteste's *De Luce* ('on Light', *c.*1230) – for this kind of absurdity was common in the Middle Ages – where form is represented by unity, matter by the number two, their composition by three, and the resultant compound by four; since the sum of these numbers is ten (a triangular number) 'every whole and perfect thing is ten'.[26]

Kepler's attack on Fludd was supported by Marin Mersenne (1588–1648), a Minim friar who was to be closely associated with Descartes and the development of the mechanical philosophy in France. Mersenne's criticisms of 1623 were again supported against Fludd's rejoinders by the atomist philosopher Pierre Gassendi.[27] Mersenne chiefly condemned Fludd's cabbalistical arguments (which involved transposing letters into numbers and so 'proving' identities between words or names) and the animism of such neo-Platonist (and indeed Paracelsan) philosophy which put souls into everything. The microcosm–macrocosm analogy was to him a mere delusive figment and the idea of the 'harmony of the world' which Mersenne found also in a different form in Kepler was equally fabulous. Later, when Mersenne had become a Copernican like Kepler, he was to admit that Kepler's determination of astronomical constants was accurate, though he would never allow the spheres any audible music – but then nor did Kepler.

Mersenne was by no means uniquely opposed to Fludd, for he equally condemned a number of Italian philosophers – among them Giordano Bruno, Francesco Giorgio, Tommaso Campanella, and Francesco Patrizzi – whom he regarded as naturalists and animists, probably also deists or libertines, all tarred with the hermetic and cabbalistic stain. At this time before his meeting with Descartes (1623 or 1624) Mersenne was still strongly imbued with the spirit of Catholic reaction, and still regarded Lucretian atomists as atheists. His philosophy was soon to undergo a complete revolution, but it was never to admit magic. Thus about the year 1620 the line of division between rational-mathematical and mechanistic science on the one hand and an animistic or magical view of nature on the other was at last drawn, though hardly established; such a man as Kenelm Digby who defended the 'weapon-salve'[28] was to be, for all the similarity of his natural philosophy to those of Descartes or Hobbes, on the wrong side of it, and so we must probably reckon the elder Van Helmont also. Obviously this does not mean that after the close of this century of confusion everyone was consistent, one way or the other; they were not, any more than Bacon, or Kepler or Mersenne had been (in our eyes) consistent before. What did happen was that about 1640 mathematical, mechanical and experimental science became quite strong enough to need no magical or other esoteric prop, and also began to speak more confidently of its *own* utility. By the end of the seventeenth century – long after the whole legend of Hermes Trismegistus and the ancient fathers of wisdom had been exploded by Isaac Casaubon (1614) – astrology, alchemy, and magic were rapidly descending to the level of inferior subcultures. They were no longer respectable.

NOTES

1. Sir Hugh Platte, *The Jewell House of Art and Nature*, London, 1594, B1-B2.
2. I. E. Drabkin and Stillman Drake, *Galileo Galilei on Motion and on Mechanics*, University of Wisconsin Press: Madison, 1960.
   The 'five simple machines' were the lever, pulleys, windlass, inclined plane (wedge) and screw: the question at issue, the gaining of mechanical advantage. Aristotle – or the author of *Mechanics* whoever he was (*c.* 300 BC) – already understood that the gain in force exerted is balanced by greater distance moved in all cases. The study of the inclined plane was to prove particularly illuminating to Galileo.
3. Institut de France, MS. G 73r, quoted in Edward MacCurdy, *The Notebooks of Leonardo da Vinci*, Cape: London, I, 1938, 567.
4. *Codice Trivulziano*, 30a, quoted in MacCurdy, op. cit., 536.
5. A. R. Hall, *Ballistics in the Seventeenth Century*, Cambridge U.P., 1952, 81–3.
6. Robert Norton, *The Gunner, shewing the whole practise of Artillerie*, London, 1628, 3–4.
7. The non-specialist needs nothing more here than Marshall Clagett, *The Science of Mechanics in the Middle Ages* (University of Wisconsin Press, Madison, 1959) and appropriate articles in *D.S.B.*
8. See Drabkin and Drake (above, note 2). According to the accepted date, Galileo was in fact twenty-six years old when *On Motion* was composed. The Leaning Tower trials, long discredited, have recently been validated by Stillman Drake: there is no record of them outside Viviani's biography of his master. Certainly at this time Galileo already believed – like Benedetti before him – that two differently sized bodies of the same material would fall at very nearly equal speeds without being interested to define the change of speed in falling.
9. On this topic, see the books by Cyril Stanley Smith beginning with his edition of Biringuccio's *Pirotechnia* (trans. Martha T. Gnudi), 1942, reprinted Basic Books: New York, 1959.
10. Walter Pagel, *Paracelsus: An Introduction to Philosophical Medicine in the Era of the Renaissance*, Karger: Basel and New York, 1958, 344.
11. Ibid., 150, 138.
12. Ibid., 147, 145.
13. F. Hoefer, *Histoire de la Chimie*, 2nd edn, Paris, 1866, II, 5.
14. The name *laudanum* was given to the alcoholic extract (tincture) of opium by Quercetanus.
15. J. R. Partington, *History of Chemistry*, II. Macmillan: London, 1961, 248, 250.
16. A. E. Waite, *Hermetical and Alchemical Writings of Paracelsus*, London, 1894, I, 121.
17. Partington (loc. cit., Note 15), 169.
18. Paracelsus, *Selected Writings*, ed. J. Jacobi, Routledge: London, 1951, 196–7.
19. L. Thorndike, *History of Magic and Experimental Science*, V, Columbia University Press: New York, 1941, 628.
20. W. Pagel (op. cit., Note 10), 50–51, 63.
21. Ibid., 72–81, 104–6, 121.
22. Paolo Rossi, *Francis Bacon. From Magic to Science* [1957], Routledge: London, 1968, 31, 57.

23. In the *Dictionary of Scientific Biography* Dee is dismissed in half a page. For Dee and the Rosicrucians see Frances A. Yates, *The Rosicrucian Enlightenment*, Routledge: London, 1972.

24. W. Pagel (op. cit., note 10), 311–33.

25. *Idem*, in *D.S.B.* VI, 254 col 2, quoting.

26. L. Thorndike, *History of Magic and Experimental Science*, II, Columbia University Press: New York (1923), 1947, 444. I was told the peculiarity of Psalm 46 by Charles Singer.

27 Robert Lenoble, *Mersenne ou la Naissance du Mécanisme*, Paris, 1943, 103–5, 367–70.

28. It was described in 1608 by Rudolf Goclenius; the ointment was applied to the weapon, not the wound that it had caused, and was supposed to heal the wound by magical action over long distances. According to some, the victim's dried blood on the weapon was essential to the efficacy of the salve. Digby described his 'powder of sympathy' (the same thing, in his case simply a dried solution of vitriol, copper sulphate) in a lecture at Montpellier in 1657, which proved very popular in print.

CHAPTER FOUR

The new science of motion

Until the end of the sixteenth century, outside medicine, the mood of scientific criticism and innovation was modest, even humble. Though Vesalius called Galen hard names for descriptive errors, he had adhered to his physiological scheme even when that appeared to conflict with observation; like the botanists, such zoologists as Pierre Belon (1517–64), Conrad Gesner (1516–65) and Guillaume Rondelet (1507–66) were chiefly notable for achieving greater accuracy and range in the descriptive part of natural history, showing little tendency to find fault with their ancient master, Aristotle; similarly also with those who attempted to follow the immature development of creatures, the chicken in the egg or the embryonic animal in the womb. Hieronymus Fabricius of Aquapendente (c. 1533–1619) was to publish the finest renaissance studies in embryology, superb volumes, magnificently illustrated, attaining a level of detail going far beyond the ancient model; but all the essential thought is Aristotle's.[1] In mathematics also there was no conflict between the spontaneous development of algebra on the one hand and the Greek-inspired exploration of geometry and mechanics on the other. Philosophy was more disputatious, since the neo-Platonist school came under severe criticism from conservatives such as the early-sixteenth-century physician of Lyons, Symphorien Champier (d. 1537), a journalistic writer on many topics who printed a *Dialogue in Destruction of the Magic Arts* (? 1498). Then there were controversies between the so-called 'Averroists' (that is, philosophers who accepted the fact that Aristotle taught pagan doctrines) and the Christian Aristotelians who were shocked to be told that Aristotle did not believe in the immortality of the individual soul. Representative of the former group was Pietro Pomponazzi (1462–1525) who taught at both Padua and Bologna, and who while accepting the reality of occult powers (among them, curiously, the capability of some people to move their ears at will) argued sceptically against the power of magicians to summon demons to do their bidding: much more, he suggested, was effected by natural magic. And later in the century there were rows between the followers of outright critics of Aristotle, such as Ramus (p. 36), and the Peripatetics.

It was in medicine, rather than in science and natural philosophy, that controversy raged in the sixteenth century, in language rather appropriate to Billingsgate than *academe*. Vesalius was not mealy-mouthed in his views of rivals. Paracelsus swore that his shoebuckles knew more medicine than Galen and Avicenna, and that his beard had more experience than the university doctors. Such rant was typical of his age and was echoed by his followers. Other battles were fought between Arabists and Humanists, between (in surgery) cauterizers and anti-cauterizers (this gentler school of wound treatment was founded by Ambroise Paré, 1510–90). The new drugs from the Americas were attacked and defended. Violence in language seemed an easy way to make a reputation.

In astronomy, which seems to us to offer a more interesting and important instance of the conflict between ancients and moderns, there was little noise until the close of the sixteenth century, in part because it was far from clear, so long as the 'Wittenberg interpretation' went unquestioned, that there was any need to defend the traditional position warmly. If Luther called Copernicus a fool this was just the plain reaction of an ignorant man; scholars did not think him one. The English pedagogue Robert Recorde (1510–58) advised his 'scholar' not to leap to conclusions about the apparent absurdity of the motion of the Earth.[2] No one yet saw that *De Revolutionibus* was a bomb destined to destroy the ancient House of Learning, and few even perceived how ramshackle that structure really was. The work of demolition was in fact begun by the neo-Platonist, metaphysical philosopher Giordano Bruno (1548–1600), who found in Copernicus' doctrine of the fixed Sun a convenient fulcrum for his crowbar, without having either interest or competence in the technical astronomy wherein Copernicus had excelled. The Nolan was no scientist, and his impact, his historial importance, his ultimate influence upon the development of non-scientific attitudes to science, were all the more startling for that reason. We must not suppose that the intellectual world of the sixteenth century was at once shaken to its roots by the criticism of its pillars by such men as Copernicus, Vesalius and Paracelsus. Debate and dissension, the call for change and improvement, had been going on in that world for centuries. There was never a time of monolithic fixity, in any realm of learning. Men did not yet feel that a moment of crisis or revolution had come where every argument, discovery or demonstration was to be weighed as counting either for or against the tradition. Only the Paracelsans adopted such a 'root and branch' position. Most scholars saw a process of gradual change in the content of books and lectures continuing, as the wheat was sifted from the chaff in the harvest of innovation. Only when the narrowly formulated proposals of Copernicus (emasculated by the Wittenberg experts) were vastly opened out by the bubbling philosophical imagination of Bruno, disclosing a vision of endless worlds, endless souls, endless Redeemers, and when Galileo (some twenty years after Bruno) went on to paint a whole new observed vision of the cosmos in which Copernicus' Earth moved, did innovation assume a massive, threatening character. The crisis came in 1615–16 and again in 1633 when it became clear to the responsible authorities of the Roman Church that the synthesis of theology and philosophy which had served Christianity since the time of Augustine was now seriously called in doubt. Of course Catholics were not the only Christians to be disturbed by the thought of a whirling, gyrating Earth – John Donne's famous lines are evidence to the contrary[3] – but the papacy was the only religious organization that attempted to supress Copernicanism. Its policy flourished only in Italy; Johannes Kepler, a Protestant Copernican, was tolerated in Catholic Austria and while Frenchmen displayed some natural nervousness at the condemnation of Galileo, none suffered for his beliefs.

Galileo's persecution made his name immortal; his astonishing astronomical discoveries of 1609–10 had first made it known; yet in sheer intellectual quality and importance his investigations into motion outweigh all the rest. Although *The Dialogue on the Two Chief Systems of the World* was widely read in Latin and Italian (and translated into other languages) and had a vast public influence – this was the only book of Galileo's that Newton is known to have read, for example – that book had no message of comparable importance for the future of science: its polemical structure, a model for all time, conveyed most to its own age. Yet we must not forget that the two branches of Galileo's transforming activity, astronomy and mechanics, were firmly united; indeed, the *Dialogue* of 1632 already lay down the elements of Galileo's mechanics. For only a clear understanding of the true principles of motion, which Galileo had attained for the first time, could dispose of the apparently fatal objections against the motion of the Earth, while (on the other hand) only a 'Copernican' view of the universe could be consonant with the new knowledge of Moon and planets that Galileo had acquired. Though superficially the two lines of investigation pursued by Galileo seem far apart, in fact there is a unity running through all his creative activity: besides its characteristic instrumentalism (through its employment of telescopes, thermoscopes, pendulums, inclined planes, floating bodies and so on) there is a deeper philosophic unity in Galileo's realism – the properties of natural bodies are determinate, demonstrable and explicable – and especially in his aiming at a single, consistent philosophy of nature. The great principle on which he built – much more profound than his dictum that the language of science is geometry because the book of nature is written in squares, triangles and so on – was the principle of the physical homogeneity of the universe. There are local differences, obviously: chalk differs from cheese, the surface of the Sun from the surface of Jupiter, but in Galileo's eyes the same matter exists everywhere, the same definitions of motion are valid everywhere, no one place is more privileged or singular than another. With hindsight this unification seems an inescapable corollary of Copernicanism, for if the Earth is a planet the other planets may be Earths, and so the Sun a star like other stars (as several late-sixteenth-century astronomers seem to have accepted without difficulty). But no one in fact had yet seen and obeyed the unity of nature as Galileo did, unless reference be made to Giordano Bruno. Bruno certainly perceived that Copernicans opened a door to the plurality of worlds (through which Galileo firmly refused to look) without, however, examining the principle of unity within one world, which was what mattered to Galileo. Note that it is in the *use* of this principle that these two philosophers differ: Galileo uses it to justify the Copernican universe, Bruno to project soul through infinite universes. But though Galileo's use of the principle is scientific, the principle itself is just as metaphysical as Aristotle's carefully argued dualism of Heaven and Earth. There could be no question of *proving* it. As well try to argue that the Sun is merely a large coal-fire, which the least thought indicates it cannot be; celestial heat and terrestial heat could only be equated in the twentieth century.

In the last few years, through the researches of Stillman Drake, another distinction between Galileo's two fields of innovation has appeared. When he made his discoveries with the infant telescope Galileo, within a few months, set them before the world: here, he said, is what I have just seen. True, in the mature *Dialogue on the Two Chief Systems of the World* the argument for Copernicus is presented in complex fashion, and the 'new' solar system plays a relatively small part in it. In mechanics, in the *Discourses on Two New Sciences* (1938) no such experiential base appears at all. Yet, we now know, it existed: Galileo had systematically experimented over a number of years to elucidate the properties of moving bodies. Yet of this background he made no mention and no use, though of the telescope discoveries, to which he had been led accidentally, he claimed proud ownership. He washed it all out in favour of a purely axiomatic presentation, perhaps in order to follow the 'Archimedian' model. In this he was, in a sense, justified for it is given to very few men to lay down the axioms of a new science.

Unlike his predecessors Galileo consciously assumed the attitude of a publicist and a partisan. Writing more often in his native Tuscan than in Latin (for he was one of those who led the way in abandoning for science the official academic language), he shaped his arguments to a wide audience. His dialogues were lively, his irony biting, and he did not scruple to make debating points in his own cause. Zealously he magnified the weaknesses of conventional science in order to pour ridicule upon them. Almost alone among the ancients the mathematician Archimedes was singled out for Galileo's commendation; Aristotle he treated for the most part as a logic-chopping ignoramus, as though the subtlety and complexity of Aristotle's mind had composed fantastic webs of artificiality while blind to the simple truths of nature. Galileo was emphatically a modernist. He had a sure touch in sensing the falsity of common beliefs, and apparently this scepticism went back to his early years. The critical attitude evident in his 'juvenilia' was to generate his original ideas later. Born in 1564, securing himself a training in mathematics in opposition to the wishes of his father (who pressed the safe profession of medicine upon him), by 1589 Galileo was already teaching at the University of Pisa. Two of the most famous stories about his unconventional activities belong to these Pisan years: here he observed the equality in time between the large and small swings of the cathedral lamps, and carried out from the Leaning Tower the famous experiment of dropping large and small weights, that hit the ground at the same time. Modern opinion seems more favourable to the truth of these stories than that of fifty years ago, and we now feel confident also that it was at Pisa that Galileo began to take an interest in the measurement of motion, and perhaps to experiment, though the critical phase of his experiments on motion was to be between 1604 and 1609. Unlike most academics of this time, Galileo remained a layman, though he did not marry. After only a few years, in 1592, Galileo procured a change of employment at treble salary to Padua; according to his later pupils and biographer, Vincenzo Viviani, this was because of his colleagues' animosity and a court intrigue against him. The University of Padua, though it represented exile to Galileo from his beloved Tuscany (whither he returned for almost every summer vacation) was within the anticlerical Venetian state; doubtless Galileo hoped to prosper better in a freer atmosphere and certainly he made many close friends there among men of liberal opinions, among them Paolo Sarpi (1552–1623), head of his Order, yet excommunicated because he supported Venice against the papacy. At Padua Galileo laid the foundations of all his future work on mechanics, had some success as a teacher, but yet – until almost the end – won no fame for himself. However, his construction of an improved telescope, following reports of a spyglass brought from the Netherlands to Venice, and the astronomical discoveries he made with it, brought the success he had long sought. Venice rewarded him richly, but he opted to return to Florence in 1610 under the special patronage of the Grand Duke. From that moment until 1633 he was deeply engaged in the defence of his discoveries and of the Copernican hypothesis which was to end in his trial and condemnation at Rome for publishing *The Dialogue on the Two Chief Systems of the World*. Only then, after a quarter of a century, did Galileo return to 'writing up' his early investigations into motion, the result incorporating a Latin text which may well have been drafted at Padua not long before Galileo first heard of the telescope. The result was *The Discourses on Two New Sciences* (1638).

Galileo's biographer, Viviani, relates that already at Pisa Galileo was conscious of the need for a true knowledge of the nature of motion for the investigation of natural phenomena, and so 'gave himself over to its study', following the example of Aristotle in his *Physics*. But Galileo, it is clear, did not take his start from Aristotle's text, which he set out to refute in a number of particulars, but rather from the current sixteenth-century versions of fourteenth-century natural philosophy. At least three of the professors at Pisa during the time when Galileo was a student there – Girolamo Borri (1512–92), Francesco de' Vieri (*fl.* 1550–90) and Francesco Buonamici (d. 1603) – published books bearing on the philosophy of motion (Buonamici's is of vast size) and presumably lectured in a similar vein. Galileo was also aware of the work of Tartaglia (p. 77), of Francisco Toledo (1532–96) and of Giambattista Benedetti (1530–90), the two last-named being authors of *Commentaries* upon the *Physics*. We may well doubt, indeed, whether he had any *first hand* knowledge of medieval natural philosophy; the ideas he had received had been modified, simplified and added to by the succession of expositors.[4] Between 1586 and 1591 Galileo composed a series of drafts of a work *On Motion* (never completed, nor printed before the nineteenth century) in which he addressed himself, as a philosopher, to a discussion of the causes of the (supposed) attributes of motion: for instance, why is natural (falling) motion faster at the end than at the start, while for a violent (upwards) motion the reverse holds? Or: does a stone come momentarily to rest between ascent and descent? Galileo's approach is not, of course, mathematical but there is a tendency for the mathematical content to increase through the drafts. He 'proves' that in the same medium all objects of the same substance fall at the same speed (the Leaning Tower theorem), as Benedetti had done before; he argues that for different materials speed of fall is related to the ratio between the density of the material and the density of the medium (so, the lightness of cork makes it fall more slowly in air than stone, and float on water, in which stone sinks more slowly than lead). He attributes the violent upward movement of heavy bodies to an 'artificial lightness' (he still thinks of fire as 'naturally light'): the artificial lightness is caused by a force or impetus. A very interesting passage attempts – incorrectly – to relate the speed with which a body slides down a frictionless inclined plane to its speed of fall through the same vertical height: they are as the lengths of the lines inversely.[5]

In Padua, Galileo took students into his house as boarders and gave private instruction to young noblemen and others (it was for long supposed that the great warrior King Gustavus Adolphus of Sweden was one of these, but it was not so). He lectured on the celestial sphere, fortification and practical mechanics. Italian engineers and artisans had excelled in both these latter subjects since the fifteenth century; Galileo himself took out some patents for machines and otherwise displayed his ingenuity. About 1596 he wrote a treatise, *On Mechanics*, which again touches on the problem of the inclined plane: this time Galileo tells us that the force acting downwards of a body on the plane is to its weight as the height of the plane to its length – a similar rule to that given for speeds. Even more interesting is the first suggestion of Galileo's restricted principle of inertia: on a frictionless, horizontal plane a body would preserve its motion indefinitely, and when at rest the least force would suffice to move it.[6]

When there is next firm evidence of Galileo's thoughts on motion, some six years later (1602), he had made considerable advances. During this interval – or indeed somewhat later – he may have been stimulated by the interest of his patron, the Marchese Guidobaldo del Monte (1545–1607), in the shape of the trajectory of a projectile. Guidobaldo, a pupil and friend of Commandino (p. 74) at Urbino, was the foremost authority on motion and mechanics in Europe at this time, always looked favourably on Galileo, and was instrumental in his move to Padua. Guidobaldo, however, was on many points the more conservative; for example, he taught in accordance with everyday experience that more force is required to start a motion than to continue it uniformly. In 1602 Galileo wrote to Guidobaldo (evidently as part of a more extended correspondence) of his discovery of the isochronism of the pendulum (the period of each swing is independent of its amplitude); he was unable to demonstrate this mathematically, he admitted, showing Guidobaldo how it could be seen experimentally but he could prove something analogous, that the descents along all chords to the base of a vertical circle are isochronous.[7] At this time Galileo, like all his contemporaries, was unaware of the importance of acceleration in thinking about motion for, like everyone since Aristotle, he tended to associate force ('the push') with the continuation of a steady motion.

The next landmark is a letter, to Paolo Sarpi in October 1604. Here we find great news: the law of fall; distances fallen increase as the squares of the times taken, it might be 16, 64, 144 . . . feet in 1, 2 and 3 seconds. This of course is the rule also known to Oresme (but not applied by him to real bodies) and to Domingo da Soto. How did Galileo discover it? It seems that in 1603 Galileo concluded that the important thing to know about movement on inclined planes was not the average speed of descent – related to the length and the total time taken for planes with the same vertical height – but rather *the way in which the speed increased*, that is, the distances passed over in successive equal time intervals. Stillman Drake has found evidence that he set out to ascertain this by experiment, using his sense of musical time (his father had been a professional musician) to establish the intervals and a very gradual slope so that position at successive beats could be marked. In a manuscript dated by Drake to 1604 the following numbers appear: (1) 33, (2) 130, (3) 298, (4) 526 . . . eight in all, which he interprets as experimental measures, and obviously they follow closely the series 1,4,9,16 . . . of the squares. Yet, curiously enough, Galileo may already in the previous year have noted his 'double speed rule', that is, the rule that a body having accelerated from rest at A down the slope AB would, in the same time when moving uniformly along the horizontal plane DC, cover a distance BC = 2AB. The argument is much like that justifying the equivalent 'Merton Rule': Galileo says that 'all the (increasing) speeds at single points' will be to uniform speeds of the maximum value (that is, at B) as a right triangle to a quadrilateral of the same sides, that is, as one to two.[8] From this 'rule', as we have seen before, the odd-number series and so

Fig. 4.1   Galileo's 'double-speed' rule.

the square-law for falling bodies can at once be generalized. Apparently Galileo did not do this, nor does he explain further the source of his 'double speed' argument. We can be fairly sure, though, that Galileo did not simply borrow and apply the medieval 'Merton Rule', which he rediscovered, and redeployed in his *Discourses on The Two New Sciences*. The 'Merton Rule' had been forgotten by north Italian philosophers, by whom even 'the ideas of the Merton tradition were very largely ignored, or, at best, made the subject of cursory and ill-informed antipathy'. It may well be that if Galileo owed anything to the Oxford philosophers ultimately, it was not a calculus but the idea of velocity as an intensity of motion, continuously variable.[9]

Whatever the exact details, it is certain that Galileo was now striking out on a highly independent line and, what is more, re-creating that bond between mathematics and motion which had been so long severed; further, he was already (it seems) becoming aware that this bond could be explored in a geometrical way, through the development of a logical series of propositions, and not in merely verbal disquisitions.

However, as Galileo went on to explain in his 1604 letter to Paolo Sarpi, he was far from satisfied to propound the law of falling bodies ($s \propto t^2$) as an empirical generalization, though he had from this time no doubt of its truth; he felt, and we may believe rightly, that to be convincing and intellectually satisfying he should be able to prove that this generalization followed from some sound theory of motion. How could he claim to measure an (accelerating) motion if he did not know how to define an accelerating motion? He was still hardly better off than with his 'double speed rule' which gave him the equivalent to an accelerated motion, but left him in ignorance of its properties. Whatever he knew of the Merton tradition, he did not feel that it provided him with an immediately usable argument to justify his law of fall, as Soto had done, and so he did not elaborate the reasoning justifying the 'double speed rule'. Instead, he took an analogous but different (and mistaken) line: that he could define a uniformly accelerated motion as one wherein the speed at any point B is proportionate to the distance AB from the origin, A. It seems just as extraordinary as Galileo's ignorance of the convergence of his own ideas with those of medieval philosophers that he now failed to perceive the inconsistency between this 'distance-law' of acceleration and the principle to which he had groped that change of motion is continuous. For according to the distance-law if a body possesses a degree of motion, however small, it must have already moved a distance, however small; or inversely, however slowly a body moves it can not come completely to rest without a discontinuity, a jerk, because it would approach its stopping-place infinitely slowly. The case is the same as that of Zeno's Paradox of the hare and the tortoise. For the present, be that as it may, Galileo provided Sarpi with the assurance that the law of fall could be mathematically deduced from this distance-law. A manuscript containing this purported, and very strange demonstration, has long been known; it entails that the *average* velocity of fall also increases with the square of the distance fallen, that is, as the fourth power of the time taken.

Then followed five critical years. By the end of this time Galileo had totally rejected the distance-law of acceleration and had instead adopted a time-law: the velocity of the body at any instant is proportional to the *time* lapsed since the acceleration began. The date is fixed in letters, notably one of February 1609 to Antonio de' Medici in Florence in which Galileo writes of his new theory that projectiles describe parabolas, and another (June 1609) to Luca · Valerio (*c.* 1552–1618), a mathematician, now lost but reconstructable from Valerio's reply (July). Both inform us that Galileo was writing a treatise on motion, starting with accelerated motion on inclined planes. Datable manuscripts dealing with all of these topics clearly relate to the Paduan period before Galileo's telescope studies began; from these we learn of his intense interest in and experiments on projectile motion – not using crossbows or guns, but balls sliding down an inclined plane. Possibly he was stimulated by the views of Guidobaldo del Monte, also derived from experiment, that the 'up' and 'down' sections of the trajectory were strictly symmetrical and that the curve so formed was like a parabola or catenary.[10] But there is no evidence that these (unpublished) opinions were imparted to Galileo, whose experiments were certainly different. At any rate, to simplify a complex story, Galileo concluded from careful measurements that the curve is a parabola, the horizontal component of motion being uniform and the vertical accelerated in accord with the law of falling bodies.[11]

Such experiments interpreted in the light of the law of fall provided Galileo with both real and imagined numbers to apply to time, speed and distance in accelerated motion; to these numbers he could apply tests of consistency with his other ideas, such as the (false) distance-law. In such ways – scholars disagree as to the precise details – Galileo came to realize that the distance-law required the ratio of increase in speed of a falling body to be greater than it is, and that the average velocity is not related to the fourth power of the time, but to the time directly. As he clarified his thinking and methods of calculation, he at last realized fully that time is the essential base, that is, 'the supreme affinity of time and motion'. Despite the pre-cognition of this fact by medieval philosophers, Galileo was indubitably the first to use this truth as the foundation of an organized theory of the movements of real bodies: this is how he formulated it in the *Discourses* of 1638[12]:

We shall call that motion equably or uniformly accelerated which, abandoning rest, adds on to itself equal moments of swiftness in equal times.

He was also to adopt as a postulate (for he knew no way to prove it) an equivalence already noted as involved in his study of inclined planes: the speed acquired by a body in descending through any given height (without friction) is the same, no matter what the angle of descent. He argued this from what is essentially the conservation of kinetic energy. Upon these foundations, and now deriving the law of fall by reasoning essentially involving his 'double speed' or the old 'Merton Rule', Galileo was able to set out the science of motion in an ordered series of geometrical propositions.

One can hardly dispute the view that 'only by means of a repeated process of comparison of theory and experiment and the analysis of theory was Galileo able to bring this work to a successful conclusion'.[13] That serendipity played its part, as in so many successes, is no doubt true also. Galileo succeeded by means of *two* carefully planned series of experiments – this we did not know even ten years ago, before Stillman Drake examined neglected, hopeless-looking papers in Florence – by making a series of computations (some of an almost trial-and-error kind), and by thinking of the compatibility of one generalization with another. Precisely how Galileo reasoned, in what words he would have expressed his ideas or processes, we do not know because the critical pages lack explanatory prose, and because though all may reasonably be dated to Padua 1605–9, it is impossible to be certain of their order. At first, Galileo was probably proceeding in the manner of the ancient astronomers by seeking only to 'save the phenomena' or construct an algorithm, such as his 'double speed rule' actually is. So, in his *Treatise on the Sphere*, Galileo distinguishes from the philosopher who considers the qualities of things the mathematical scientist who deals with observed phenomena, structural hypotheses and geometrical demonstrations; as a first step it was enough, and indeed a great thing, to treat motion in this fashion only.[14] To the extent that Galileo's subject was always the description of motions (kinematics) rather than the action of forces in producing motion (dynamics) he never quite renounced this limitation: in the *Discourses* (1638) he was to insist that questions about the cause of natural acceleration should be set aside in favour of questions about its 'attributes'. But of course this avoidance of the cause of force does not imply Galileo's avoidance of the effect of force in motion altogether, nor avoid the necessity for Galileo to formulate what he meant by 'speed' (uniform or non-uniform), 'equal' (in terms of speed or motion), 'instantaneous' and 'average' speed, momentum and so on. These are neither observed phenomena, nor structural hypotheses (like the light ray or astronomical spheres of the ancients) but concepts, and to the extent that he was redefining concepts Galileo was certainly acting as a natural philosopher, not a mathematician. The geometry could only come later, or be useful in the process of evolving the concepts. Galileo himself did not despise the title of 'Philosopher' despite his quarrels with the many Aristotelians who bore that title; indeed, he claimed it for himself as the Grand Duke's servant, saying that he had devoted far more years to philosophy than to mathematics.

Accordingly, in his mature *Discourses* Galileo does not offer an algorithm for dealing with hypothetical inclined planes, but an analysis of the accelerated motion 'that nature employs' as evinced by 'that which physical experiments show to the senses', and 'by consideration of the custom and procedure of nature herself in all her other works'.[15] Certainly, no more than Newton does Galileo say what 'gravity' (in the sense of the cause of weightiness) is, or explain why the heavy body descends towards the centre of the Earth (it is because it does this that we call it 'heavy', and 'gravity' too as Galileo says is only a name). Though he uses many dynamical terms (gravity, force, momentum, collision) Galileo never despite Newton's contrary belief generalized a proportionality between force and acceleration ($f = ka$), indeed, he limits himself conceptually to a constant force and a constant acceleration, that which is 'natural' even though (in fact) he makes both variable by means of the inclined plane. That Galileo was constantly grappling with problems of theory and explanation is evident from his letters to Guidobaldo (where he explains that he cannot quite account for the pendulum theoretically) and Paolo Sarpi (where he explains that he cannot quite deduce the law of fall theoretically). Moreover, it is evident that at times he did not know how to make immediate sense of the data he himself compiled in his experiments; he had to elicit the pattern that made sense, for example the parabola. Finally, it is undeniable that just as Archimedes constructed a theory of statics, so Galileo constructs a theory of motion. Just as the former necessarily idealized the concepts of perfect equilibrium or perfect fluid, so Galileo had to geometrize (make perfect) the physical reality of inclined planes and pendulums. And the realism – despite this – of Archimedes' statics and Galileo's kinematics is justified by experiments. It is surely significant that Galileo, like Archimedes and for that matter the Greek writers on optics and astronomy, prefers an axiomatic to an inductive exposition: he does not tell us how he found things out by experiment, but only explains how he used experiment to confirm the truth of what he already knew. When we read Galileo's *Discourses on Two New Sciences* we cannot learn how he discovered the propositions in the book, but we can surely learn something of his ideas about the methodological nature of science, science meaning here not the process of discovery but a communicable body of knowledge. Indeed, the supposed ideal of science as the product of simple induction implicitly rejected by Galileo had not yet been promulgated.[16]

If we compare Galileo and Aristotle with respect to motion, the mere attainment of an algorithm or even a law appropriate to measure accelerated motion marks no great point of difference. There is no reason to imagine that Aristotle would have been surprised at the notion of measuring changing as well as uniform speeds, or that he would have thought natural acceleration irregular in its manifestations. Similarly, the truth of the affinity between time and motion, crucial though it is, does not immediately entail profound philosophical innovations: time has always seemed a vaster, more mysterious, more morally loaded concomitant of our lives than space. We have many familiar proverbs about time, a few about distance, none about space generally. The deep concerns touched on by Galileo's theory of motion relate rather to matter, force and inertia. On all of these topics his views were far from limpid, and though he left many fecund hints there was much for his successors to clarify and to add.

Galileo devised no coherent theory of matter in the later sense of the term, that is, a theory of means of which the gross physical and chemical properties of things could be derived from a universal substructure: the atomic theory is one example. However, in *The Assayer* (1623) Galileo did, in effect, declare that such a theory is necessary for, he asserts, the phenomena of substance are no guide to its reality.[17] The distinction he introduces between primary and secondary qualities has Greek roots; Galileo connects it with a subjective psychology and, obliquely, thus refutes the Aristotelian qualities. Such qualities as sweetness, sound, smell have no absolute existence in the sweet or scented object but exist only in the nervous system of the subject: without the senses as our guides, reason or imagination unaided would probably never arrive at qualities like these. Thus the sensation of 'tickling' is not at all in the feather, but in the sentient skin stroked by it. The 'real' attributes of matter, according to Galileo, are shape and motion:

I think that if ears, tongues and noses were removed, shapes and numbers and motions would remain, but not odours or tastes or sounds.

Or for that matter heat and cold as the body experiences them. This argument, whether deriving directly from Galileo or other later writers like Descartes, was to be a common place of the later scientific revolution, a conceptual foundation of the mechanical philosophy. It vitiated the realism of Aristotle – the assumption that the attributes we find in nature like the redness of roses or the humming of bees are really there in nature, rather than names we give to sensations in us. The realities, says the doctrine of Galileo or Boyle or Locke, are the shape of a sucrose molecule, the vibrations of an insect's wing or of an air molecule. We can as little apprehend the pigment of a flower by naming it yellow as the nature of a star by calling it twinkling. The world of direct sense-experience is, almost universally, a texture of deceptions for physical reality is totally different and cannot possibly be described in the language of sensations. Here Galileo and modern science, rejecting Aristotle, adopted the philosophical position of the Greek atomists.

What is the point of this claim, apart from making the observer humble and sceptical about his sensations? Perhaps to us the chief advantage of the rejection of qualities is that shape, size, number and motion can all be measured, where subjective sensations cannot; but the early tradition emphasized rather the intellectual simplicity of materialism: all substances and all sensations could in principle be reconstructed from a small group of postulates, typically of the form: matter is composed of particles varying in size, shape and motion; and further each property is capable of modification. Thus the requirements of a theory of matter serving for the reconstruction of sensations of the direct kind (like sweetness in honey) and also of the phenomena of nature (for example, eclipses) are, first, the specification of the structure (a series of rules about the properties of atoms, particles or whatever) and, second, the description of procedures for the process of reconstruction from the specification.

Galileo undertook neither of these tasks. He did not commit himself to an invisible particulate substructure for substance, nor declare whether the particles are atoms or not. In *The Two New Sciences* (1638), though he speaks plainly enough of atoms and indivisibles, he seems to confuse the issue by a discussion of the paradoxes of infinity. And having asserted dogmatically that only the three properties of the substructure that he had enumerated were real, he provided no rules for inferring from the microscopic to the macroscopic world. As with Bacon, Galileo's views are best expressed in relation to the theory of heat, of which motion is the cause:

Those materials which produce heat in us and make us feel warmth, which are known by the general name of 'fire', would then be a multitude of minute particles having certain shapes and moving with certain velocities.

The minute particles and their velocities are brought into existence by the antecedent process, such as combustion or friction accompanied by attrition; further, the most minute fire-particles, Galileo suggests, become light-particles (obviously some link of this sort is essential). In order to explain the action of heat in rendering substances fluid, which become solid again when cool, Galileo suggests that[18]

Penetrating through tiny pores of the metal, between which (on account of their narrowness) the smallest particles of air and other fluids could not pass, these fire-particles might, by filling the very small vacuities between the least particles of the metal free them from the force by which those vacuities draw one particle against another, so that they cannot separate. Being thus able to move freely, their whole mass would become a liquid.

We observe here two notions introduced without comment that will be of much service to later mechanical philosophers: that of particles having relative sizes, and of moving particles breaking up cohesive larger particles. Galileo's idea of the 'active vacuum' was not, however, to survive as an explanation of cohesion.[19]

How, in general, the motion of matter is created cannot be understood from Galileo's writings. He simply postulates that the fire-particles, previously inert in an ignited piece of charcoal, become suddenly active and mobile. (Nor, on a larger scale, does Galileo explain the source of planetary movement.) So, if we re-name the cause of a particle's motion *force* in general, Galileo has no occasion to consider the relation of matter and force either macroscopically or microscopically, or to address himself to the question of what variety of such forces there may be. He does not, apparently, even touch the question whether matter is active (with internal forces, as the alchemists and Paracelsans supposed) or purely passive, so that 'force' must have a source or existence independent of matter. Possibly he would have regarded such questions as metaphysical, while the existence of indivisible particles seemed to be justified by reason. All he tells us is that no change of motion can occur without a cause (or force) effecting it,[20] and so rest or uniform motion only can be consistent with the absence of cause. The heavy body as such is indifferent: it can neither move itself quicker nor faster nor be in any other state without cause. It has the quality that Newton later called inertia.

But there is a problem, as Galileo was aware, and he could not resolve it. If the heavy body is indifferent to motion, then all heavy bodies should behave identically. In natural accelerations they do, because (as Newton discovered) the operative gravitational force is proportional to the mass in each case. But in violent motions the magnitude of the moved body is very relevant, even though (as Galileo correctly argued) the least little force will give some acceleration to an object no matter how great. Yet

He who shuts the bronze doors of San Giovanni will try in vain to close them with one single simple push; but with a continual impulse he impresses on that very heavy movable body such a force that when it comes to strike and knock against the jamb, it makes the whole church tremble.[21]

The heavy body is *not* indifferent to motion now – however well oiled the hinges and so on – even though it is not being urged further from the centre of the Earth. A light cupboard door swings with the least touch. Lacking the concept of mass, in this case where the concept of weight is useless Galileo could not deal with the matter clearly.

Inertia is the first mechanical property of matter. The word has many meanings. Originally for Aristotle as later for Kepler it signified 'sluggishness', the reluctance of heavy matter to be moved. With Newton inertia develops two aspects for it becomes resistance to a change of motion; the heavy body resists acceleration or retardation equally and so as 'innate force' propels a once-moved body in free, uniform motion (in the absence of resistance). Galileo seems to employ no such abstract noun as inertia. Rather, he makes everything depend on the behaviour of the natural heavy body which accelerates towards the centre of the Earth and decelerates away from it, in the absence of impediments. (In principle, the natural light body would act inversely.) Therefore, he can say that where the effect is natural acceleration, since every effort requires a cause, the cause is descent (or, inversely, ascent). How then can *uniform* natural motion arise? What is its cause? Galileo replies that it happens when the heavy body neither ascends nor descends, that is, when it is upon a horizontal plane or what might be the same thing, the perfectly smooth spherical surface of the Earth itself, *provided the body is moving already*, for then it is in a state of indifference:

If the plane were not inclined, but horizontal, then this solid sphere placed upon it would do whatever we wish: that is to say, if we set it down at rest, it will remain at rest, and given an impetus in any direction it will move in that direction, maintaining always the same speed that it received from our hand and having no propensity to increase or diminish this speed, there being neither rise nor fall along the plane.[22]

Again, Galileo omits to note that whereas a thumb might impel a marble, a strong shove indeed would be needed to propel a cannon-ball at the same speed: matter *does not* behave indifferently 'as we wish'; but, more to the point, is not this uniform motion, continuing indefinitely, itself an effect and if so what is the cause? Here is the old problem of impetus mechanics again, and Galileo speaks indeed of the body 'having an impetus' (elsewhere he uses the word 'momentum' analogously). Yet Galileo is correct in his discussion, if not wholly unambiguous in his language (no more was Newton): there is no cause of uniform motion under these ideal conditions.

Since rest and uniform motion are equivalent, we can say that bodies sharing the same uniform motion are mutually at rest. This too Galileo will argue at length, as we shall see.

In Aristotelian physics, rationalizing experience of the world of affairs, rest was normal and motion a state requiring special explanation; in Galileo's physics where space has been idealized to an empty, geometrical world as hard and crystalline as Aristotle's spheres only changes in the state require explanation. Thus the concept of impetus or 'impressed force' as the cause of continued motion became redundant, indeed erroneous. Its abandonment was already foreshadowed in the early treatise *On Motion*, where Galileo discussed the neutrality in motion of a sphere placed upon a horizontal plane, where the motion is neither natural nor forced and 'it can be made to move by the smallest of all possible forces'.[23] Here, however, he did not yet foresee the uniformity of its continued motion. So early, too, he had satisfied himself that even in the total absence of resistance motion could not be infinitely swift. In Galileo's revised thinking a moving body could contain no more 'impressed force' than an unmoved one; movement should rather be supposed to generate what he was the first to call *momentum*. While the *Dialogue on the Two Chief Systems of the World* and even the *The Two New Sciences* preserve much medieval language, nevertheless Galileo from 1608 completely abandoned medieval conceptions of motion, at the expense (as Koyré saw long ago)[24] of the claim maintained by the Peripatetics of describing the real world of experience. For the real world knows friction, air-resistance and other complications of the ideal theory of motion, hence that ideal theory can never be perfectly verified by experiments made under conditions that are less than ideal. Of this Galileo had a clear understanding, and he explained how the ideal structure and relationship of things can be both discerned and verified beneath the pattern of small discrepancies arising from the greater complexity of our experiments; when challenged in the *Dialogue* by the opinion that

these mathematical subtleties do very well in the abstract, but they do not work out when applied to sensible and practical matters

he made the reply that, if one first remembered that real spheres and planes lacked the perfection of the geometrical forms, then

what happens in the concrete up to this point happens in the same way in the abstract. It would be novel indeed if computations and ratios made in abstract numbers should not thereafter correspond to concrete gold and silver coins and merchandise. . . . the mathematical scientist, when he wants to recognise in the concrete the effects which he has proved in the abstract, must deduct the material hindrances, and if he is able to do so I assure you that things are in no less agreement than arithmetical computations.[25]

So far has Galileo come beyond the search for an algorithm merely permitting calculations of natural accelerated motion, so far beyond the ancient desire to 'save the phenomena', that he is now entering upon a coherent theory of mathematical physics as capable of constructing ever more refined accounts of reality, approaching ever more closely to experience. Mathematics could provide not merely arbitrary models capable of grinding out predictions and 'idealized' versions of a geometrical universe, but in principle an analysed account of the world as it experimentally is found to be.

Once the vague, causal concept of impetus had been supplanted by the complementary concepts of inertia and momentum, however incomplete and imperfect as yet, the potentialities of the geometric method in kinematics could be greatly extended. With the addition of a definition of natural acceleration and the law of fall the basic structure was complete, hence Newton (rather too generously, for once!) allowed to Galileo the discovery of the first two laws of motion. What Galileo left wanting, in fact, were the exact definition of inertial motion and the generalized concept of force. Both defects were due, in part, to Galileo's inability to render his view of motion completely homogeneous and consistent.

In the *Dialogue of the Two Chief Systems of the World* Galileo twice refers to a classification of motion originating with Copernicus:

if all integral bodies in the world are by nature movable, it is impossible that their motions should be straight, or anything else but circular; and the reason is very plain and obvious. For whatever moves straight changes place and, continuing to move, goes ever further from its starting point and from every place through which it successively passes. If that were the motion that properly suited it, then at the beginning it it was not in its proper place. So then the parts of the world were not disposed in perfect order. But we are assuming them to be perfectly in order, and in that case it is impossible that it should be in their nature to change place, and consequently to move in a straight line.

And so it seems that rectilinear motion

is assigned by nature to its bodies (and their parts) whenever these are to be found outside their proper places, arranged badly, and are therefore in need of being restored to their natural state by the shortest path.[26]

Obviously this is a revision and amplification of the Aristotelian dichotomy between celestial and terrestrial motions, not excluding the circular revolution of the Earth nor (as Copernicus had hinted) the vertical fall of Martian stones on Mars. Galileo's words do not seem to be unconsidered, and they are consistent with the complete absence from his writings of any suggestion that either rectilinear or accelerated motion could ever be conceived of as belonging to the heavenly bodies. Indeed, Galileo seems to have held that their circular motion required no explanation. On the other hand, where he speaks of continued rectilinear motion it is always as a terrestrial event, in an 'Archimedian' situation (where the Earth's surface is taken to be a flat plane, and all lines drawn to its centre perpendicular). In this situation inertial motion must be rectilinear. By extension, Galileo seems to hold that a ball rolling round the perfectly round sphere of the Earth, neither approaching towards nor receding from the centre, would maintain uniform speed for ever: where the infinite plane bends round into a circle there is no difference between them. Galileo makes no difficulty in arguing that the least force suffices to hold a loose object to the Earth, precisely because at its origin the angle of contact between the sphere and the plane is infinitely small. Yet he knew that the stone escapes from the string along a straight line, and connected this correctly with the inverse relation between this endeavour and the size of the circle of revolution.[27]

The universal restriction of inertial motion to a straight line was effected by Descartes (1644), who realized that a perfectly undisturbed movement must be straight, and that therefore a curve of any sort implies an influence (force) acting upon the motion. Once more it is clear that a dynamical approach clarifies Galileo's kinematics. It is curious that having so successfully perceived the folly of qualitative distinctions between 'natural' and 'violent' motions, Galileo should have preserved something of the Aristotelian privilege of the former wherein (as we have seen) the problem of the relation between applied force, weight (or strictly mass) and acceleration does not arise. Galileo's difficulty here was one of geometry, as well as ideas. He maintained the strict Greek principle that ratios can only be established between similar quantities; as there can be no ratio between chalkiness and cheesiness, so for him velocity could not be a ratio between time and distance. In his geometrical representations, the time-axis (vertical) is AB, and ordinates to it represent instantaneous speeds; distance fallen is represented by a separate line HI. The constant acceleration is implicitly measured by the angle $\angle$BAC (Galileo does not say so) while the force is not represented at all. Galileo never represented distance by area ($v \times t$) or, still less, as the sum of instantaneous speeds. He makes no bow in the direction of mathematical indivisibles, and wholly disregards algebra. So the relation, simple to us, between the effects of a static weight (mg) and a falling weight (mgh) completely eluded him. But besides this procedural difficulty Galileo –

Fig. 4.2   Acceleration and distance.

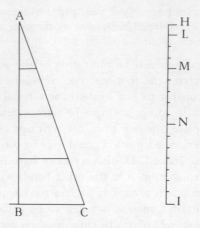

after writing *On Motion* in which acceleration is linked to medium-resistance – developed a philosophical reluctance to admit force into the natural scheme of things. The supreme, most violent example of force was that of gunpowder and the immense velocities it produced; these 'supernatural' effects he more than once specifically excluded. He did not see force as a part of the natural order, which was above all his concern and to have brought force into his geometrical scheme of time, velocity and distance would have been like adding a fourth dimension.

The bold title of the *Discourses on Two New Sciences* is amply justified. Galileo did show for the first time how the strength of beams and structure made from them might be geometrically related to their shapes and sizes; he did also provide a quantitative science of the gravitational movements of heavy bodies, including projectiles. He had solved the problem of the trajectory and invented the time-keeping pendulum. But it had not been his aim ever (or not since 'On Motion') to provide a complete philosophy of movement, or even (in that book) to integrate his new science completely into natural philosophy. He does not conceal many remaining difficulties towards whose solution he had at least offered hints – rotational force, the real path of descent of falling bodies, the isochronism of the pendulum and the force of percussion, for example. And although he had attached so much deep significance to microscopic motions, he had not in the least revealed how the mathematical science of motion could be made to penetrate to the roots of physics. What did turn out to be interesting, in the wider context which Galileo almost wholly neglected otherwise, was the bearing of the theory of motion on the Copernican dispute, to be considered in the next chapter.

Before passing on to that, something should be added concerning the Galilean method in physical science. One might ask both what Galileo sought to discover, and how he thought this desideratum should be sought. In trying to answer either of these questions it must be recalled that Galileo himself, and the objects of his intellectual explorations, changed greatly during the years.

The strongest influence in his early philosophical notes or *Juvenilia* was that of the Jesuit Fathers in the Collegio Romano, of whom only one, Christopher Clavius, was a mathematician[28]; in later life he was to act strongly against this Aristotelian tradition in which he had been brought up and even to decry the whole school of 'philosophers', even though he claimed this title for himself and could never wholly renounce his education. Crombie emphasizes the legacy studied by Galileo with his customary thoroughness in youth when he writes of 'the longevity and depth of the Aristotelian knowledge from which Galileo approached the search for the true cosmology which became the overriding intellectual preoccupation of his (mature) life', while Drake emphasizes Galileo's reaction against philosophical and anti-Copernican conservatism when he declares that Galileo's 'opposition to philosophers in scientific questions was already active several years before the telescope'.[29] Then again, Galileo began in the tradition of late-scholastic argument (in *On Motion*), went on to Archimedian, propositional reasoning, then explored the resources of experiment, and only late in life made the Copernican issue his own. It would be foolish to look for complete consistency and total absence of change in Galileo's attitude to natural knowledge through his life. Unlike most men, he seems to have become more radical and more sceptical as he grew older.

Unlike Descartes among his near-contemporaries, Galileo did not write a complete treatise explaining the metaphysical and logical basis of natural philosophy, nor, unlike Gassendi, did he adopt a non-Aristotelian view of nature ready-made from antiquity. Galileo's opinions have to be gathered piecemeal from many writings, perhaps most obviously from *The Assayer* (1623) and the *Dialogue on the Two Chief Systems of the World* (1632) – works, however, which, like others, Galileo wrote for polemical not epistemological purposes. Galileo was no systematist, he offered no single conceptual key to the mysteries of nature, such as the mechanical philosophy was to be later. If as we have said, he is to be numbered among the early mechanists, the fact is almost incidental to a consideration of his achievement. It is reasonably clear what is meant by 'Newtonian science' or 'Cartesian science', but there may be doubt about what 'Galilean science' would mean, or how it could be extended to a universal view of nature; yet one certainly feels that Galileo was much more than the founder of kinematics and telescopic astronomy. Sometimes it has been argued that the very lack of a systematic Galilean science is a measure of Galileo's modernity, but my own view is that, as with Aristotle, Galen, or Descartes, systematizers like Newton, Darwin and Einstein have continued to perform an essential function in the evolution of science.

Most important is Galileo's insistence on studying what is, and what is knowable, the realism discussed before (p. 103). In this sense Galileo possessed very little of the Platonic belief that experience gives only a shadowy idea of the true relations that govern the universe. Here is the reason for Galileo's antipathy to Kepler's writings, for Kepler was convinced that deep understanding required an apprehension of the Archetypes of nature. In his later, vehemently anti-scholastic writings especially Galileo seems sometimes to argue that the only valid test of a proposition must be an experimental one, and so the philosophers' forms and qualities, and Archetypes, and the influence of the Moon upon the sea, all those things that cannot be directly observed must be dismissed as nonsensical.

In *The Assayer* Galileo ridiculed such appeals to the unobservable and his rhetoric is the more striking in that the drift of his argument – to show that meteors could not be heated to incandescence by friction in the Earth's atmosphere – happens to be incorrect:

If Sarsi wants me to believe that the Babylonians cooked their eggs by whirling them in slings [he wrote] I shall do so, but I must say that the cause of this effect was very different from what he suggests [i.e. friction]. To discover the true cause I reason as follows: 'If we do not achieve an effect which others formerly achieved, it must be that in our operations we lack something that produced their success. . . . Now we do not lack eggs, nor slings, nor sturdy fellows to whirl them, yet our eggs do not cook, but merely cool down faster if they happen to be hot. And since nothing is lacking to us except being Babylonians, then being Babylonians is the cause of the hardening of the eggs, and not friction in the air.'[30]

Natural philosophy, Galileo holds, is not a matter of verbal argument, like an orator's speech or a defence counsel's plea in mitigation; it is not a matter of repeating what others have declared, or rehearsing what the ancients could do, or dreaming of wonders now lost. Men are as they were, nature is as it was, and its secrets are as accessible and demonstrable to us, now, as at any time. The natural marvels in books are often based on errors of fact, while the true marvels of nature (such as those he recites from time to time, like the floating of a needle on water) can be seen with the eye.

Yet Galileo is no naive realist. He does not assert that everything must be visible or touchable. He argues from the least parts and vacuities of matter, for example, which are no more directly demonstrable than forms. He is prepared to idealize nature, as though the surface of the Earth were a flat plane. Above all, he rejects the naive-realist objections against the motion of the Earth; here crude experience as he insists again and again is deceptive and we must learn to interpret our experience of the Earth's motionless solidity to discover what is truly the case (here Galileo is at his most Platonic). In fact Galileo is obviously aware – at least in astronomy – that all our judgements in knowledge are theory-laden: otherwise we would believe the Sun, the Earth and the Moon to be all the same size, and so it obviously is also in the pure science of mechanics since we lack experience of perfect bodies, or of absolutely vacuous spaces. Experience, then, is not to be naively accepted as authoritative but to be critically examined so that apparent inconsistencies (like the floating of the steel needle) can be resolved by better understanding, for example, in terms of a more complex theory than that 'only bodies less dense than water float upon it'. In Crombie's phrase: 'Galileo's rational experimental science was defined by its integrated search at one and the same time both for reproducible practical results and for corresponding principles of theoretical explanation'[31]. Explanation, however, was by reference to a procedure of justification rather than to a system of ideas in the manner of Aristotle or Descartes.

It is certain therefore that the scope and character of Galileo's physical science must be more restricted than those of Aristotle, or Descartes, or Newton, having no system furnishing universal terms of explanation, no laws of nature, no theoretical models capable of fresh application. His explanations of phenomena – of buoyancy, of the cohesion of matter, of fire, of the reflection of light, of the optics of telescopes, of harmony in sounds – seem disconnected and casual, while on some of the traditional deep issues of natural philosophy (light, gravity, planetary motion) Galileo is silent or enigmatic. Synthesis on the grand scale did not appeal to him. On the other hand, his work is united as *mathematical* philosophy. Repeatedly Galileo emphasizes the superiority of mathematical (quantitative) over rhetorical (qualitative) arguments. Why try to prove by words what can be demonstrated geometrically? In 1605 Galileo published anonymously a whole burlesque dialogue in Paduan dialect to prove this point against the philosophers who attacked the 'expressed view [of Galileo himself] that it is bad judgement to abandon the senses and go searching for reason [or cause]'. The traditional view was that mathematics had nothing to do with truth; Galileo believed the opposite, and that therefore the application of mathematics to phenomena (as revealed to the senses) would yield truth.[32] He did not, like Plato and Kepler, see the esoteric morphology of nature mirrored in geometric forms or still less believe that mathematics provided a symbolic key to nature; his conviction rather was that because nature is necessarily geometric in pattern, understanding of it most easily and correctly results from geometrical reasoning. This is most obviously true – in the eyes of mathematicians like Euclid, Galileo, Kepler and Newton – of space: the three-dimensional space in which we live and breath must necessarily (when ideally freed of the imperfections of rulers and theodolites) correspond to Euclidean space; so again with any physical phenomena describing a curve: if like a point on a wheel, a planet, or Galileo's projectile, it describes a definable curve then reasoning valid for the geometrical curve is valid for the physical path; and Kepler (not Galileo) would have extended the same idea to crystal form: the angles and planes of crystals must correspond to solid geometry.

Not all of this was new. No philosopher had argued that geometrical optics produced false results: he would have argued (correctly) that there are questions about vision, light and colour, that geometrical optics cannot answer, and (incorrectly) regarded these as reserved for philosophy. What was fundamentally original and revolutionary in the conception of Galileo (and one may add, of Kepler and Descartes also) was the assurance that, in principle, the potentialities of mathematical reasoning went far beyond the narrow limits allowed by traditional philosophy; so that (in the final extension involving a change of definition) there was no proposition belonging to natural knowledge that should not be argued *more geometrico* – in the mathematical way – though for such philosophers as Descartes and Spinoza (but not Newton) this did not necessarily mean arguing in terms of magnitudes. And obviously if one by definition should exclude non-mathematical reasoning from natural knowledge, then one excludes verbal philosophy. I do not suggest for a moment that either Galileo or Descartes took so extreme a view, but it was towards this direction that Galileo first set the trend. Where possible the natural philosopher should deal with numbers and measures: to the extent that the realm of quantitative and mathematical reasoning could be increased, so would natural philosophy become the more certain.

This was the message that Galileo carried to his successors and which they understood, seeing him (as he would have wished to be seen), as a new Archimedes: Borelli, Castelli, Huygens, Wallis and Newton, mathematicians all, were the natural expositors of Galilean science. Descartes, the great systematizer, and perhaps too much his rival to judge his merits quite impartially, thought Galileo's treatment of motion too unphilosophical, too opportunistic because it lacked a deep consideration of the nature and function of motion in the universe; yet he himself left the problems of kinematics quite unresolved (having at an early stage, as Koyré has shown, fallen into the same traps that snared Galileo).[33] Indeed, having founded his system of the world on the partition of movement between its component particles, he was quite unable to offer any mathematical account of motion, microscopic or macroscopic, at all. The followers of Galileo's model, however, not only improved the axiomatization of mechanics, but showed how, macroscopically, the same treatment could be extended to the problems where Galileo himself met defeat (for example, pendulum motion and the collisions of bodies); further, particularly in Newton's *Principia*, it is proved that Galilean kinematics is valid for all bodies, including the least particles of matter. Here, at last, Galileo and Descartes meet, the former providing the mathematical theory, which the mechanical philosophy had, up to the time of Huygens and Newton, completely lacked.

NOTES

1. See Howard B. Adelmann, *The Embryological Treatises of . . . Fabricius* (Cornell University Press: Ithaca, 1942); that on the animal foetus was published in 1604, that on the chick posthumously in 1621.
2. *In The Castle of Knowledge* (1556). Recorde says Copernicus has 'renewed the opinion of Aristarchus Samius' and was perhaps the first so to do: 'the understanding of that controversy dependeth of profounder knowledge than in this Introduction may be uttered conveniently'.
3. John Donne, *An Anatomy of the World*, 1611, contains oft-quoted lines beginning:
   'And New Philosophy calls all in doubt,
   The Element of Fire is quite put out;
   The Sun is lost, and th' Earth, and no man's wit
   Can well direct him where to look for it . . .'
4. Christopher Lewis, *The Merton Tradition and Kinematics in late 16th and early 17th century Italy*, Padua, Antinore, 1980, especially Ch. VI
5. In truth, vertical fall and the equivalent frictionless descent of an inclined plane end with the same instantaneous velocity, and the average velocity (distance/time) is the same in each case also. Hence the times taken are as the distances, which Galileo proved later.

6. This principle was explicitly enunciated by Galileo only in his *Dialogue* of 1632.
7. Stillman Drake, *Galileo at Work, His Scientific Biography*, University of Chicago Press: Chicago, 1978, 69–71. Drake argues (55–6) that the finished form of *On Mechanics* was written in 1600–02. Clearly, Galileo entered a new period of intense interest in this topic about this time.
8. Drake, ibid., 82, 86–90; *idem; Galileo's Notes on Motion* (Monografia No. 3 dell' Istituto e Museo di Storia della Scienza, Firenze), Firenze 1979, 19, 23. *Two New Sciences*, 196. Drake's researches over many years have greatly modified and enriched our knowledge of Galileo's mechanics. Particularly: he has provided unassailable evidence of the experiments Galileo made.
9. Lewis, (op. cit., Note 4), 280, 282.
10. R. H. Naylor in *Physis*, 16, 1974 and *Isis*, 71, 1980.
11. The precise meaning and ordering of the manuscript notes cannot be established beyond doubt. The interpretations of scholars also differ considerably in detail; see Drake (op. cit., Note 8), Naylor (op. cit., Note 10 and elsewhere) and W. Wisan in *Archive for the History of Exact Sciences*, 13, 1974. No one doubts that, as Drake first discovered, the experiments were made and shaped Galileo's thoughts.
12. Galileo Galilei, *Two New Sciences . . .* trans. with Introduction and Notes by Stillman Drake, Wisconsin University Press: Madison 1974, 162.
13. R. H. Naylor, *Isis*, 71, 1980, 570. Until recently many historians, including myself, took a far more 'idealistic' view of Galileo's process of discovery. He appeared to be a theoretical rather than an inductive scientist. We were wrong: Galileo discovered fundamental principles from what Bacon or Newton would have called 'induction from experiments'. The most important of these were never described in his printed writings.
14. Drake, *Galileo at Work* (Note 7 above), 52.
15. Galileo (op. cit., Note 12), 153.
16. By 'ideal' here I mean the simple series of steps that runs: (1) statement of the object of the investigation; (2) the means of effecting it; (3) the apparatus used; (4) the results obtained; (5) analysis in relation to the object.
17. Stillman Drake, *Discoveries and Opinions of Galileo*, Doubleday: New York, 1957, 274–8. Marie Boas (Hall) in *Osiris*, X, 1952, 435–7.
18. Galileo Galilei, *Two New Sciences* (Note 12 above), 27, slightly altered.
19. The hardness of fundamental particles seemed to be guaranteed by their durability, moreover, softness would imply internal structure. Variations in size are hypothetically convenient, but not essential. Variations in shape were abandoned as unnecessary and arbitrary. The concept of molecules – clusters of fundamental particles of various numbers and spacings, arranged in a variety of patterns – not mentioned by Galileo, gave great flexibility. Of course there was no better basis than 'reason' for accepting these speculations rather than Aristotelian theory, nor any possible method of verification available.
20. 'Motion in the horizontal plane is equable, as there is no cause of acceleration or retardation'. *Two New Sciences*, 196, and many other places.
21. Ibid., 305–6.
22. Ibid., 297.
23. 'On Motion', Ch. 14. I. E. Drabkin and S. Drake, *Galileo on Motion and Mechanics*, Wisconsin University Press: Madison 1960, 65–6.
24. Alexandre Koyré, *Etudes Galiléenes*, Hermann: Paris, 1939, 71.
25. Galileo, *Dialogue concerning the Two Chief World Systems*, trans. Stillman Drake, University of California Press: Berkeley 1953, 203–8.

26. Ibid., 19, 32.
27. Ibid., 216–7.
28. A. C. Crombie in J. Hintikka, D. Gruender and E. Agazzi (eds) *Pisa Conference Proceeding*, I, Reidel, 1980, 279.
29. Stillman Drake, *Galileo against the Philosopher*, Zeitlin & Ver Brugge: Los Angeles, 1976, xii.
30. *Idem, Discoveries and Opinions of Galileo*, Doubleday: New York 1957, 272.
31. Crombie (loc. cit., note 28).
32. Drake (op. cit., Note 29).
33. Alexandre Koyré, *Etudes Galiléenes*, Hermann: Paris, 1939, 1966, Part II.

CHAPTER FIVE

The revolution in astronomy

The period of comparative silence in which little important comment, favourable or unfavourable, was made on the new celestial system proposed by Copernicus lasted for more than a generation after the publication of *De Revolutionibus*. Although the book was published from Nuremburg Rheticus, Copernicus' only disciple, came from Wittenberg and the early readers were guided by the fictionalist interpretation emanating from that centre of Lutheran orthodoxy: Copernicus was to be taken as propounding a mathematical, not a physical system. No ordinary reader needed to be troubled about the instability of a whirling Earth. For example, in 1584 Rembert Dodoens – celebrated as a botanist – published at Antwerp a little textbook *On the Sphere* naming Copernicus five times and praising his estimates of the sizes of the Moon, Earth and Sun without any hint that Copernicus did not, like Dodoens, believe the Earth to be fixed at the centre of the universe.[1] Some leading professional astronomers, like Johannes Praetorius (1537–1616) of Wittenberg and the great Tycho Brahe, rationalized their position by so re-inverting the Copernican geometry that the Earth again became the centre of the system.[2] With one or two exceptions such as the Englishman Thomas Digges (p. 119) – who was not a professional astronomer and exercised no influence – it was only in the last decade of the sixteenth century that true Copernicans began to appear, and with them the possibility of a conflict between realist astronomy on the one hand and philosophy and religion on the other.

From this time until the latter part of the seventeenth century there was a noisy and not always lofty dispute between the adherents of the new and the old opinions, in which astronomy served as the touchstone. Its warmth produced the genial (but vain) comment from John Wilkins in 1638:

'Tis an excellent Rule to be observed in all Disputes, That Men should give *soft Words* and *hard Arguments*; that they would not so much strive to *vex*, as to convince the *Enemy*.

The triumph of the innovators did not come rapidly: Copernicus' masterpiece was to grace the *Index of Prohibited Books* (perhaps the best bibliography of literary and philosophical originality ever compiled) until 1822. In Tuscany and Naples Copernicanism was vehemently condemned until the early eighteenth century, while in many places the Earth appeared in books, in models, upon clocks, in its traditional position, or this was expressed as one of two possible alternatives. Indeed, no known phenomenon nor principle required the Earth to be in motion before Newton, in 1687, showed how the Earth and the Sun must rotate round their common centre of mass which, because of the huge disparity between the two bodies, must lie near the centre of the Sun.[3] This was the first positive argument either way. One must judge that the Copernican innovation vastly promoted the development of the science of mechanics, but there was nothing in Galileo's study of it to justify his Copernicanism (though indeed he thought otherwise). In particular, nothing could be done for it with the mathematical arguments that Galileo valued so highly; yet the persistence of the Copernicans in arguing their unprovable case as being more plausible than the rival geocentric view was to be productive of enormously valuable changes.

The first conflict between the innovators in thought and authoritarian learning, which was full of future significance for the attitude to be adopted by the Roman Church towards the Copernican question, and also (in part) for the spirit of the scientific movement, at once defensive against allegations of irreligion and hostile to the older, literary form of scholarship, had strictly no connection with natural science, though partly inspired by the Copernican revolution: defending Copernicanism at Oxford in 1584 Giordano Bruno (1584–1600) argued that Copernicus himself, a mere mathematician, had failed to appreciate the true nature of his re-discovery of the ancient sun-centered system. Modern scholars see Bruno, who renounced his religious ordination, as above all a Hermetic magician; through restless travels which took him from Italy to France, London, Wittenberg, and, fatally, Venice he upheld with extraordinary openness and rashness a vision of a revised 'Egyptian' religion older than Christianity, allied to neo-Platonic philosophy whose origins he traced back to the same source. He made himself the most dangerous man in Europe, whom even the Emperor Rudolph II would not keep long by him, and was widely reputed to be a devil-worshipper. His reputation was enough to bring about his arrest in Venice, and after years of trial and imprisonment his execution by fire at Rome on 17 February 1600. Compared with his other offences against religion his linking of Copernicus with the total animation of nature and Sun-worship, or his peopling of an infinity of space with innumerable worlds, were probably rather minor crimes. (The judicial documents were destroyed by Napoleon.)

Speculations such as these in Bruno's *De l'Infinito, Universo e Mondi* (1584),[4] naturally fascinating to some thinkers, had occurred very early in the history of thought – for why should men be so petty-minded as to suppose their world and its life unique in the immensity of things? – and had been strongly attacked by Aristotle. It had always been regarded by Christians as theologically dangerous. Yet Nicole Oresme in his *Livre du Ciel et du Monde* (c. 1370) gave considerable attention to it. He envisaged the possibility of there being in time or space a plurality of worlds so that there might be one world enclosed in another or separate worlds scattered in space, for example beyond 'our' universe, all the work of one Creator. Aristotle's argument that the earth-material of another world would be drawn to a natural place at the centre of ours he confuted by rejoining that the natural place for such earth would be at the centre of its own world. He regarded the restriction of the divine creative power to the fabrication of a unique universe as a denial of omnipotence. Further, Oresme was so bold as to declare that it is natural for men to believe that there is space beyond the fixed stars bounding 'our' universe: in this space God could make other worlds exist. From this discussion he concluded that reason alone could not eliminate the possibility of a plurality of worlds, but in fact there never had been more than one, and probably never would be.[5] The whole of Oresme's purpose, as one might expect, seems to be to demonstrate the superiority of faith and revelation over fallible reason. In Bruno, or in the authors of such scientific fantasies of the seventeenth century as John Wilkins's *Discovery of a World in the Moon* (1638), the mood is different, and the contemplation of other worlds and other men no longer totally forbidden.

The allied belief in the infinity and eternity of the whole cosmos was also ancient. Expounded by Lucretius, who had them from Democritus, these doctrines were further developed by an important group of Muslim and Hebrew philosophers of the Middle Ages, though little favoured by Christians. Oresme seems to hint at the infinity of space. Nearer to Bruno's own time the impossibility of conceiving a boundary to space was asserted by Nicholas of Cusa in the fifteenth century: and it was from him that Bruno received his inspiration. In his own time the idea was specifically related to the Copernican hypothesis by the English mathematician Thomas Digges. Digges believed the fixed stars to be infinitely remote from the Earth, a notion he was free to adopt since it was no longer necessary to suppose them fastened to a revolving sphere. Yet Digges still placed the abode of God and the elect outside and beyond the stars in the uttermost realm of space. The Copernican hypothesis made no other demand than that the distance to the nearest fixed star should be very large indeed compared to the Earth's distance from the Sun; had this ratio been far smaller than it actually is, the sixteenth-century astronomer would still have failed to detect any evidence of the Earth's motion in his celestial observations. As for the infinity of space outside 'our' universe, it was perfectly reconcilable with Ptolemaic astronomy and not at all a Copernican innovation. However great the interest of Bruno's ideas in themselves, the idea of the plurality of worlds was not inspired by the scientific Renaissance, it was not a logical deduction from heliocentric astronomy, and it was totally irrelevant to the progress of science.

It is well to attempt to define the contemporary appreciation of a situation such as this. That the introduction of religious considerations into a question of quasi-scientific speculation is quite distinct from a similar intervention in the interpretation of observations or experiments was perfectly clear to philosophers of the Middle Ages and the early modern period alike. A very high proportion of scientists up to the mid-seventeenth century were men of unusually profound religious conviction, and none used science as a lever against religion. Thomas Hobbes won no countenance from the Royal Society. The furtherance of science and of religion were commonly regarded as inseparable objectives. The English scientists of the seventeenth century, especially, were far more complacent than medieval scholastics in their belief that reason and research properly conducted could never conflict with religious dogma. The attitude of the Middle Ages had been that where reason was incompetent to decide, faith should pronounce: and that in many instances faith must even prevail against reason. Why not? God's power and purposes could not be measured in human terms, and just as the mysterious workings of providence and of miracles defied logic and the ordinary course of nature, so that ordinary course must often be judged incomprehensible to man.

Although the denunciation of atheists was a standard routine, they were a tiny, almost non-existent group in the seventeenth century, when those who were so denounced were often, like Spinoza, not atheists at all. Natural philosophers were content to prefer the orthodox beliefs of their respective countries, and genuinely gave religious truth a higher status than natural truth: the Sermon on the Mount possessed incomparably greater authority than did the sermons of stones and brooks. Which is not to say that individual men be they theologians or bishops or even popes, being human, could not be held to have committed grave errors. In principle, there could be no general conflict between science and religion, both because the supreme importance of Christianity was universally recognized and because no one accepted a double standard of truth – God could not have written for men to read different messages in the brooks and stones from those in his Holy Book. If such discrepancy seemed to exist it must arise from the weakness of the human intellect. Though a theologian might specialize in the one and a natural philosopher in the other, there was no formal barrier between their studies, and indeed the development of love and awe for God was the most universally urged reason for the study of nature; professionally, many mathematicians and experimenters were clerics and some, like Isaac Barrow, were at least as much famed for their sermons as their theorems. Robert Boyle's devotional writings, today impossible for all but the most single-minded scholar, were gravely admired. For him, as for Newton and many others, the marrying of scientific and religious considerations – to discourse of God in relation to the appearance of the things of this material world – was certainly part of natural philosophy.

Moreover, the natural philosophers would never have dreamed of impugning the validity of universal moral and religious laws, as being even more rigorous than scientific laws. To the Protestant mind of the late seventeenth century the judgements upon Bruno and later upon Galileo might seem full of human error and expressive of the narrow, blinkered outlook of the unreformed Church, but the principle that Bruno and Galileo were subject to moral law in what they did was not doubted. The 'scientist' by his skills and knowledge was not exempt from the tribunals that might judge other men. No sympathizer with the views of Galileo believed any man to possess a complete liberty of thought and expression or doubted the right of 'just' societies to impose 'just' restrictions on the communication of pernicious or irreligious ideas, and the Puritans who burned witches would probably have burned Bruno as cheerfully, had he preached his magical philosophy among them. Galileo himself, though he never surrendered his inner conviction of rectitude, both in his scientific opinions and in his attempt to divert his Church from error, seems not to have contested the principle that the ecclesiastical authorities had a right to censure his arguments. He lived and died in the Catholic faith, and according to his biography by Viviani repented his own rashness. When Galileo recanted, under threat of dire penalties, he may as well have been submitting to the then universal belief that moral and religious truths are higher than scientific ones, as yielding to a natural weakness. Galileo could only regret the weak intellects of those to whom it fell to balance biblical quotations against scientific reason.

Although the defensive pronouncements of the Holy Office were not opposed to any positive scientific fact of the time, and in the case of Bruno were not directed against science at all, they had a deep effect upon the scientific movement, especially in Italy. They were widely interpreted as a final declaration of the Church of Rome against the Copernican hypothesis, and there is evidence that some philosophers (like Descartes) who were disposed to favour the heliostatic model openly, were artificially compelled to express their ideas in guarded and ambiguous terms. Some active astronomers like Giambattista Riccioli (1598–1671) and Giovanni Domenico Cassini (1625–1712) – the latter even in Paris – loyally defended Tycho's geocentric system when perhaps the logic of their own science would have taken them the other way. It seemed as though innovations in natural philosophy must lead to outbreaks of dangerous and heretical opinions, as reactionaries had long predicted; they thus became particularly suspect in Italy, where men of original mind had to learn to look abroad for encouragement and positive criticism. Even in England, critics of the newly-founded Royal Society did not fail to assert that its methods were subversive of the Church of England. An odium, which had not existed in the early sixteenth century, was for a time attached to any originality in astronomical thought. But the challenge provoked a powerful reaction in men like Galileo and Kepler. It created a situation in which the new doctrines had to be effectively vindicated; it was no longer possible for the two systems of the world to exist peacefully side by side.

The pre-Newtonian development of heliostatic astronomy may be analysed as involving four principal steps. Firstly, the dissolution of the prevailing prejudice against allowing any motion to the Earth, which involved a careful criticism of all existing cosmological ideas in order to create a new pattern in which such a motion would no longer seem implausible, and a broad discrediting of Aristotle's authority. A necessary auxiliary to this was the most important second step, in which physical theories were revised to show the invalidity of objections against the Copernican hypothesis arising out of terrestrial mechanical phenomena. Thirdly, the new astronomy was greatly enriched by qualitative observation, which suggested that the old teaching was very inadequate. Fourthly, exact quantitative observation provided new materials for recalculating the planetary orbits, thereby leading to the abandonment of the ancient preconception in favour of perfect circular motion, and to the enunciation of new mathematical laws. Kepler's discoveries might have been expressed in the terms of the geostatic system; but as Kepler was a staunch Copernican, his whole discussion of the solar system was constructed in such a way as to give further force to the heliostatic hypothesis. The accomplishment of these four steps extended over a period of roughly half a century (*c.* 1580–1630), while their assimilation and particularly the gradual recognition of Kepler's laws of planetary motion occupied another generation. During the middle period of the seventeenth century the nature of the problem was again slightly changed under the influence of Descartes's natural philosophy, which tended to enlarge the disparity between the natural-philosophical and the mathematical-astronomical approach which the discoveries of the first third of the century seemed rather to diminish.

The contributions of Galileo to the first three of these steps were of major importance: to the fourth, quantitative observation, he brought almost nothing. Galileo was not an astronomer as the word had previously been understood, he was never interested in the traditional procedures of positional astronomy, but as a philosopher he applied new astronomical techniques, mostly of his own invention, to the examination of cosmological problems. Before 1609 his studies were largely, as we have seen, devoted to mechanics. However, he had taught 'the sphere', or elementary astronomy in private lessons at Padua, and when a new star ('Kepler's supernova') burst forth in 1604 he devoted three public lectures, now lost, to the problems of its nature and position. Naturally he made the case for the mathematicians against the philosophers in arguing that new stars, as well as comets, were celestial not atmospheric phenomena. It is unlikely that on this occasion Galileo indicated his preference for the Copernican system, since such a preference was irrelevant to the problem of the new star, but it is probable that he had changed his mind some eight or nine years earlier. At any rate, when in 1597 he received a copy of Kepler's *Mysterium Cosmographicum*, published in the previous year, which a friend of Kepler's had brought into Italy, Galileo wrote to thank the author (whose personal gift to himself he mistakenly took it to be). In this letter Galileo professed himself a secret fellow-Copernican. We have no other evidence bearing on this, nor is it likely that Galileo ever plunged deeply into the details of heliocentric mathematical astronomy as set out by either Copernicus or Kepler – it was the general scheme that attracted him.

Next, Galileo learned while on a visit to Venice in July 1609 of a spyglass which a Frenchman had brought, as a Dutch novelty, which was seen by some of Galileo's friends. He hurried home without having examined it himself and by reflecting on the properties of lenses – convex ones make objects larger but blurred, concave ones make them appear smaller but clear – duplicated the Dutch invention of a small, poor telescope with a convex objective and a concave eye lens, giving an erect image. (Hans Lipperhey of Middelburg had applied for a patent for such a device in October 1608; curiously, the tradition of practical optics from which the magnifying spyglass sprang had been transferred to the Netherlands from Italy.)[6] By 21 August Galileo was back in Venice with an improved instrument, magnifying about eight times, which enormously impressed the gentlemen and merchants there: the government promised to double his salary. By the beginning of November he could magnify twenty times; in January 1610 he completed a × 30 telescope, his finest instrument.

Months of lens-grinding work and demonstration of the results preceded Galileo's first astronomical observation of the Moon on 1 December 1609. He was not the first to turn the telescope to the heavens; the English mathematician Thomas Harriot (1560–1621) had done so the previous summer, probably using an inferior instrument. Several of Harriot's moon-maps survive. He also went on, with better telescopes made by Christopher Tooke, to study Jupiter's satellites and sunspots. Unlike Galileo, Harriot did not publish so his work remained unknown. Galileo issued his first report on his astonishing observations in March, 1610, after only four months. The *Sidereus Nuncius* ('Starry Messenger') was Galileo's first real book; small as it is, no scientific work has ever contained news more unexpected by the average reader. He showed that the Moon was rugged like the Earth, with surface features such as mountains and valleys and perhaps seas; he estimated the height of the mountains from the shadow-lengths. His telescope resolved part of the Milky Way into a dense cluster of stars, and showed everywhere minute stars invisible to the naked eye. Galileo described in detail how Jupiter was surrounded by four hitherto unsuspected companions, the 'Medicean stars' as he called them in honour of the House of Tuscany; he first saw them in early January 1610 and it took him several days to understand that they were perpetually circling the planet. He remarked that they might comfort those Copernicans who were troubled by the singularity of the Earth in that it alone possessed a Moon. Now, and throughout most of his life, Galileo observed the motions of Jupiter's satellites very carefully, trying to reduce their appearances and disappearances to rules: he hoped, by using the rapidly revolving satellites as clocks, to be able to measure longitude at sea. In Saturn Galileo was to detect a peculiar variation of shape – interpreted, half a century later, as an enclosing plane ring – while in Venus Galileo discerned phases resembling those of the Moon. This demonstrated that Venus was in orbit around the Sun, and not between the Earth and the Sun. He was also one of the first to observe sunspots, which are of course sometimes visible to the naked eye: Kepler had failed to identify the phenomenon when looking for a transit of Mercury across the Sun in 1607. Johann Fabricius was perhaps the first observer of a sunspot, while Christoph Scheiner wrote the biggest book about them, but it was Galileo who realized first their astronomical significance, as indicating changes on the surface of the Sun and also its rotation upon an axis.

Almost all the new discoveries about the solar system that could be made with a low-power telescope were made by Galileo and a few other astronomers soon after 1610. The next discoveries – resolution of Saturn's rings and discovery of its satellite Titan, observation of the great red spot on Jupiter and so on – required better telescopes which became available from about 1645, all being of the 'Keplerian' or 'astronomical' type with two or more convex lenses. Naturally this new, qualitative branch of astronomy attracted immense interest in all parts of Europe, and a great deal of work was done, such as the painstaking mapping of the lunar topography by Johannes Hevelius (1611–87) – a rich brewer of Danzig who set up a fine observatory – and again by Riccioli (who provided the names like Copernicus (a crater), and Sea of Tranquillity, which the American astronauts were to make household words). Telescopic astronomy and the old business of establishing positions by measured angles remained quite distinct until the late 1660s, when micrometers were devised for use with the more powerful telescopes, and telescopic sights were fitted to instruments intended to measure angles. The result then was an increase in accuracy of between ten and one hundred times. Meanwhile, the telescope proved almost at a stroke how inadequate all philosophical (and popular) accounts of the universe had been. It demonstrated too how much such innovators of the previous century as Copernicus and Tycho Brahe had missed.

The former had left ideas about the physical nature of the heavens unaltered, save for hints that the Moon and planets might be bodies composed of ordinary matter possessing their own gravity. The planets were still carried by quintessential spheres – leaving the problem of the Earth's evidently non-existent sphere unsolved. Tycho Brahe, on the other hand, had publicly denounced the spheres for the reason that their solidity was inconsistent with the passage of comets through the heavens, and indeed with the interweaving of his own geoheliocentric system (Fig. 5.1). He had also taken a firm step towards homologizing the Earth and the heavens by maintaining that both new stars (as in 1572) and comets (as in 1576) were true celestial bodies, that is, changes and unexpected appearances could occur in the regions that philosophers had held to be eternally the same and totally constant in their motions. Now, to anyone who was prepared to think, the discoveries that followed upon the invention of the telescope would suggest a train of thought both anti-Aristotelian and non-Copernican. Evidently the heavens were far more complex than any astronomical system supposed. It would seem that the stars were not quite close, nor infinitely remote, but somehow distributed through space at a great distance beyond Saturn, and incredibly numerous. All the planets, and the Moon, were to be understood as dark bodies (perhaps not unlike the Earth if that could be seen from afar) shining by the reflected light of the Sun, which was not itself an unchanging and immaculate fire. Such thinking tended towards some general conclusion, that the universe was a physical structure, not composed of light and a matter totally different from the matter of the terrestrial region, but rather of two types of physical body. The first, the stars, were incandescent sources of light and plainly physical since they were not invariable. The second, of which more could be learnt, the planets, were physical bodies practically indistinguishable at this stage from the Earth itself, which could now be placed without hesitation in the class of solar satellites on physical grounds as well by reason of its motion. Physical astronomy was thus a creation of the telescope, for in the past the sole subject of astronomical science had been the analysis of the positions and motions of the heavenly bodies without consideration of their nature, which had been resigned to the speculative discussions of philosophers, while astrology had embraced the supposed influences of these bodies

Fig. 5.1   Tycho Brahe's System of the World, 1588; compare Chapter 2, p. 62.

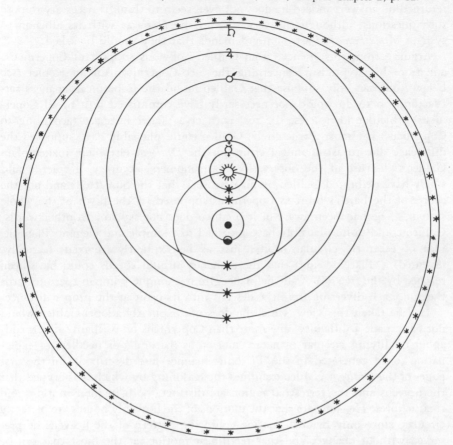

upon the terrestrial region. The concept either of physical astronomy or of celestial mechanics (which came later) was completely irreconcilable with the philosophical background of sixteenth-century practical astronomy, and it was necessary to reinterpret the Copernican heliostatic universe in this new light.

This reinterpretation was achieved in Galileo's *Dialogue on the Two Chief Systems of the world – Ptolemaic and Copernican* (1632) which was, therefore, far more than a defence of the heliocentric mathematical system as defined by Copernicus. For the first time Galileo gave that system philosophical being and physical substance. Above all he showed how the new motions of the Earth posited by Copernicus could be consistent with a treatment of motion in general that was different from Aristotle's. Yet in another respect the *Dialogue* failed to advance beyond *De Revolutionibus* with respect to motion – that is, to the defined movements of the heavenly bodies. Galileo had nothing to say about the complexities of planetary motion with which mathematicians had contended for two thousand years, and on which his contemporary Kepler was to spend his life. Whereas Copernicus and after him Kepler directly challenged Ptolemy's seemingly definitive masterpiece, Galileo's target was Aristotle, the philosopher. To the question: how and by what are the planets moved? Galileo returned no answer, indeed he does not even seem to think it necessary to pose such questions, although the very title to the *Dialogue* with its allusion to systems of *mathematical* astronomy demands that they should be asked.

Arguing from this silence, from Galileo's obvious support of Copernicus, and from his scepticism concerning the 'neo-Copernicanism' of Kepler (see below), one can only suppose that Galileo found the Copernican analysis satisfactory. So to do would not necessarily have committed him to all Copernicus' orbicular intricacies; the real path of a planet in space (according to Copernicus) is almost a true circle; Galileo could plausibly have supposed the difference due to astronomical error, for the *Dialogue* elsewhere makes plain Galileo's distrust of the observational astronomers' accuracy. Kepler would surely have delighted Galileo by his discovery that the Sun itself, and not the centre of the Earth's orbit as Copernicus supposed, is the pivot of the whole system, if he had been aware of it (Galileo does not say so). In other words, Galileo could quite plausibly have returned to a simple and elegant 'Platonic' idea of eccentric circular orbits, just as he explicitly 'revived' (actually, invented) a 'Platonic' idea that the planetary orbital speeds could have been reached by the free fall of all the planets from a unique point in space towards the Sun, each diverting from the descent into its orbit at the proper distance.

Had he taken this view (which he does not explicitly adopt) Galileo would not have made a difficulty, any more than Copernicus or William Gilbert did, about qualifying circular planetary motion as 'natural', or needless of explanation (once generated in the 'Platonic' manner just described). In the first pages of the *Dialogue* Galileo examines the reasoning by which it is argued that the heavens and the terrestrial region are distinct, both in their motions and their natures. He concedes that the motions of the heavenly bodies are perfectly circular, since only by such motion could the pattern of the heavens be preserved without change, and that rectilinear motion 'at the most that can be said for it, is assigned by nature to its bodies, and their parts, at such time as they shall be out of their proper places, constituted in a depraved position, and for that cause needing to be reduced by the shortest way to their natural state'. But he denies that terrestrial bodies do, in fact, move along straight lines, and so the antithesis is not a true one. As for the Aristotelian contention that the elements move directly towards and away from the centre of the universe along straight lines, Galileo replies:

If another should say that the *parts* of the Earth, go not in their motion towards the Centre of the World, but to unite with its *Whole*, and that for that reason they naturally incline towards the centre of the Terrestrial Globe [a notion distinctly reminiscent of William Gilbert], by which inclination they conspire to form and preserve it, what other *All*, or what other Centre would you find for the World, to which the whole Terrene Globe, being thence removed, would seek to return, that so the reason of the *Whole* might be like to that of its *parts*? It may be added, that neither *Aristotle* nor you can ever prove, that the Earth *de facto* is in the centre of the Universe; but if any Centre may be assigned to the Universe, we shall rather find the Sun placed in it.

A number of propositions in mechanics are carefully elucidated, and it is made apparent that the opposition of the Copernican to the traditional world-picture will depend upon his completely different analysis of the properties of moving things. Mechanics in fact is the foundation of cosmology:

> . . . none of the conditions whereby Aristotle distinguisheth the Coelestial Bodies from Elementary (i.e. terrestrial), hath other foundation than what he deduceth from the diversity of the natural motion of those and these; insomuch that it being denied, that the circular motion is peculiar to Coelestial Bodies, and affirmed, that it is agreeable to all Bodies naturally moveable, it is behooful upon necessary consequence to say, either that the attributes of generable or ingenerable, alterable or unalterable . . . equally and commonly agree with all worldly bodies, namely, as well to the Coelestial as to the Elementary; or that Aristotle hath badly and erroneously deduced those from the circular motion, which he hath assigned to Coelestial Bodies.[7]

That is, if the Earth moves, all Aristotle's physical theory of cosmology is baseless. Soon after this, Galileo makes the general discussion of the 'architectonics' of the world break down on the argument that hot and cold are not qualities proper to the heavenly bodies. That sort of dictum (he remarks) leads to 'a bottomless ocean, where there is no getting to shore; for this is a Navigation without Compass, Stars, Oars or Rudder'. Accordingly the debate shifts to the evidence for or against the changelessness of the heavens, in which the new observations made with the telescope are fully discussed, and a detailed comparison is made between the optical properties of the Earth and the Moon. From this their physical similarity is deduced. Incidentally Galileo points out the futility of the notion that changes in the celestial region would be impossible because they would be functionless in the context of human life, the purpose of the heavenly bodies being sufficiently served by their light-giving and regular motion. Nor does he pass over the curious judgement which made sterile immutability a mark of perfection: rather if the Earth had continued 'an immense Globe of Christal, wherein nothing had ever grown, altered or changed, I should have esteemed it a lump of no great benefit to the World, full of idlenesse, and in a word, superfluous'. By such asides as these, in a strictly scientific argument, the values of conventional thought were challenged in turn, its texture made to seem weak and strained.

The second *Dialogue* opens with caustic mockery of foolish deference to Aristotle's authority: 'What is this but to make an Oracle of a Log, and to run to that for answers, to fear that, to reverence and adore that?' Those who use such methods are not philosophers but historians or doctors of memory: our disputes, says Galileo, are about the sensible world, not one of paper. As for the motion of the Earth, it must be altogether imperceptible to its inhabitants, 'and as it were not at all, so long as we have regard only to terrestrial things,' but it must be made known by some common appearance of motion in the heavens; and such there is.[8] But in so far as motion is relative, the science of motion cannot decide whether Earth or heaven really moves. Consequently opinion turns on what is 'credible and reasonable'. It is more reasonable that the Earth should revolve than the whole Heaven; that the celestial orbs should not have contradictory movements; that the greatest sphere should not rotate in the shortest time; that the stars should not be compelled to move at different speeds with the variation of the poles. On all these points Galileo's view of what is 'reasonable' supposes a different perspective from that of anti-Copernican philosophers; but Simplicius is not allowed to argue the matter, and merely remarks that 'The business is, to make the Earth move without a thousand inconveniences.' The first group of 'inconveniences' to be dealt with includes the usual mechanical phenomena, the stone falling vertically, the cannon-ball ranging equally far east and west, which it was thought would not occur if the Earth moved beneath. They naturally lead Galileo into a long exposition of his new ideas on mechanics, in which a partial version of the law of inertia is enunciated. Much of this reasoning against the Aristotelian doctrine of motion had already been exactly anticipated by the impetus philosophers of the Middle Ages. There is a long discussion of the so-called deviation of falling bodies – a problem which attracted attention intermittently throughout the seventeenth century as affording a possible proof of the Earth's rotation. It had been alleged, for example by Tycho Brahe, that if a stone were to be allowed to fall freely from the top of the mast of a moving ship, it would not strike at the foot of the mast, but well aft. Galileo shows that this is inconsistent with the true principles of mechanics. In spite of Simplicius' cry 'How is this? You have not made an hundred, no not one proof thereof, and do you so confidently affirm it for true?' Galileo here says that he places his trust in *a priori* reasoning to give the correct answer.

I am assured that the effect will ensue as I tell you, for so it is necessary that it should, and I further add that you yourself know that it cannot fall out otherwise, however you feign or seem to feign that you know it not.[9]

Whether or not Galileo had himself made this crucial experiment – as it was certainly made satisfactorily by others – in the printed book he goes out of his way to make experiment redundant, even though he has previously taken pains to point out that experiment is always to be preferred to to ratiocination. This is just one example, an extreme one, of an epistemological ambiguity in Galileo, caused by his inability to reconcile completely the competing claims of mathematical rationality and visual experience.

Or, one might say, of illusion and reality. For Galileo has to prove that in the Copernican context all observed motion is illusory and must be understood in the light of reason. We cannot observe the 'true' path of a body, even if we could define what it could be. The apparently vertical descent of the stone on shipboard, parallel to the mast, is an illusion which a shore-based observer could (in principle) detect; but the path seen by this 'motionless' observer is an illusion also, apparent to a third observer fixed in space. So – making the same shift from the mast of a ship to a tower built upon the Earth – Galileo writes:

We only see the simple motion of descent [of a falling stone]; since that other circular one common to the Earth, the Tower and ourselves, remains imperceptible, and as if it never were, and there remaineth perceptible to us that of the stone, only not participated in by us, and for this, sense demonstrateth that is by a right line, ever parallel to the said Tower.[10]

For Galileo to have relied upon empiricism in this discussion of the trajectories of falling stones would have been inept, for it was precisely his object to bring out the rationality of motion, not to discover whether anything let fall by a careless sailor in the rigging would hit the deck or sink in the sea.

Surely the most elegant and perhaps the most interesting of all the ideas about motion due to Galileo is this of its relatively, or more strictly, of the independence of motions within a given frame as a whole. Galileo illustrated the idea appositely by the image of a man in the cabin of a ship sailing *perfectly smoothly*; anything he can do like bouncing a ball or tossing a coin happens just as it would in his room at home: experience cannot decide whether the 'frame' moves smoothly or is at rest. That motion can be subjectively an illusion had long been recognized – does the ship advance or the shore recede? – but Galileo was the first to prove that *objectively* the distinction between fact and fiction cannot be made.

In the absence of accelerations, we would say, though Galileo does not and the lack of precision in his language of smooth and natural motion is important. To decide whether a ship's cabin is moving smoothly in a circle (on the globe) or in a straight line may seem highly pedantic; certain fairground machines, however, prove that the point is not without interest. Galileo never faced this issue quite squarely, nor resolved it. He never lays it down that smooth and natural motions must in principle be long straight lines, or that motions in curves must involve accelerations and so, forces. In general, a reader would conclude from Galileo's books that the geometric shape of a motion is not very important or interesting – because such shapes are illusory, as we have seen. To an earth-bound observer earth-related projectiles move in parabolas, but again to an observer fixed in space they do not – perhaps, Galileo hints, they *really* move in circles.[11] It is a curious fact, emphasizing Galileo's inability fully to reconcile the small-scale Archimedean and rectilinear world of immediate experience with the large-scale, Copernican and circular cosmos of which the Earth was now a full member, that (as Marin Mersenne was to point out in some disgust in 1644) he completely ignores in the *Dialogue* the parabola as the product of simultaneous uniform and accelerated motions. To complete such a reconciliation in kinematic terms alone, without reference to the operative forces and their directions, is indeed impossible.

What is more important in the *Dialogue*, however, is that with one exception the mechanical objections that could be raised against the Earth's diurnal revolution are disposed of by appeal to the principles of inertia and of the relativity of motion which Galileo illustrates with a variety of ingenious examples. Other problems in mechanics auxiliary to the main argument are touched upon, such as the conception of static moment, the isochronism of the pendulum, and the law of falling bodies, here quoted by Galileo without proof. In replying to the objection that the rotation of the Earth would hurl down buildings, etc., Galileo makes the first investigation into centrifugal forces. Using the idea of virtual forces, enunciated in connection with static moment, he proves that with equal peripheral velocities the force is inversely proportional to the radius. He points out that the angular velocity of the Earth is very small, and its radius very large: therefore the force set up would not be sufficient to overcome a body's natural gravity. From Galileo's argument ('thus we may conclude that the Earth's revolution would be no more able to extrude stones, than any little wheel that goeth so slowly, as that it maketh one turn in twenty-four hours') it is clear that he did not realize that when *angular* velocities are equal, the centrifugal force is *directly* proportional to the radius. It was not indeed till much later that the rotatory stresses in equatorial regions were detected.

The extensive illustration of the perfect agreement between the Copernican theory of the planets and a natural philosophy that is wholly rational and in part mathematical was certainly Galileo's major contribution to the cosmological debate, after his telescope discoveries. Achievement of the agreement demanded the supreme importance of mathematics, both the mathematics of astronomy and the mathematics of motion, whereas in the ancient and medieval world mathematicians had perforce to dance to the philosophers' tune. Galilean mechanics was thus the necessary complement to Copernican astronomy, and though nothing could have been more surprising and grateful to seventeenth-century natural philosophers than this discovery that the same mechanical principles could be developed to embrace both terrestrial and celestial movements, alike on the smallest and the largest scale, the discovery was not fortuitous since it was for precisely this kind of harmony that Galileo (and Kepler) sought, in justification of Copernicus.[12]

There could be no question – as Galileo frequently emphasizes in the course of the *Dialogue* – of proving that the Copernican hypothesis was necessarily true; but with the readjustment of physical ideas effected by him it could be shown to be at least as plausible as the Ptolemaic. Aristotle's physical theory of the cosmos, terrestrial and celestial, had been an integral whole; for Galileo astronomy and physics were so far independent that he acknowledged the incompetence of purely physical observations to determine the system of the world, but he had no doubt that the same laws of motion were universally applicable, to celestial and terrestrial bodies alike. A true mechanical theory, besides wholly destroying all physical objections to the heliocentric system, actually created a preponderance of belief in its favour.

In the third *Dialogue* Galileo takes up the arguments for and against the annual motion of the Earth. Beginning with purely astronomical considerations, he makes plain his distrust of the quantitative measurements of his own time, from which, however, he confirms that the new star of 1572 was truly celestial. The irradiation of light, exaggerating the stars' and planets' apparent diameters, is next explained, and the observations are proved to verify the Copernican arrangement. Galileo then discusses, in an eloquent and lucid exposition, the problem posed by the absence of a detectable stellar parallax. He was not of the opinion that the stars are infinitely remote, but he does argue that the size of the universe is such that its dimensions are beyond human standards of magnitude. If its immensity can be grasped, then it cannot be beyond the power of God to make it so immense; if its immensity is beyond comprehension, it is none the less presumptuous to suppose that God could not create what the mind cannot comprehend. Simplicius objects that a vast region of empty space between the orbit of Saturn and the fixed stars would be superfluous and purposeless, so that Galileo can again condemn the introduction of theological reasoning into science. He appears to think that the remoteness of the fixed stars, though vast, is not to be exaggerated, and calculates that even if the radius of the stellar sphere bore the same proportion to the semi-diameter of the Earth's orbit, as that bears to the radius of the Earth, a star of the sixth magnitude would still be no larger than the Sun, which is, according to Galileo's reckoning, five and a half times as big as the Earth. The assiduity and skill of astronomers in making observations of stellar parallax is in any case doubtful, since these would demand 'exactness very difficult to obtain, as well by reason of the deficiency of Astronomical Instruments subject to many alterations, as also through the fault of those that manage them with less diligence than is requisite. . . Who can in a Quadrant, or Sextant, that at most shall have its side 3 or 4 *braccia* long, ascertain himself . . . in the direction of the sights, not to erre two or three minutes?'

Galileo's general explanation of the manner in which the heliocentric theory 'saves the phenomena' is modelled on that of Copernicus, save that he denies the reality of the third motion which Copernicus had ascribed to the Earth in order to account for the parallelism of its axis. Thus, for instance, the principle of relativity of motion solves the appearance of stations and retrogressions in the planets. But Galileo nowhere indicates that their orbits, which Copernicus had made eccentric, are other than purely circular about the Sun, nor does he attempt to justify particular orbits from the records of positional astronomy. He further differs from Copernicus in making the centres of the orbits coincident with the body of the Sun. It cannot be said, therefore, that Galileo improved the Copernican argument in terms of technical astronomy in the *Dialogues*, except through his use of the new qualitative evidence derived from the telescope, which had already been commented upon in his earlier writings. Indeed, the extremely simple astronomical model described is flatly incompatible with precise observation. Galileo, it is clear, was far more confident of the truth of the mechanical principle that bodies possess the property of inertial rotation in a perfect circle than of the accuracy of astronomical measurements. It was a characteristic of his scientific method of abstraction that it could more easily analyse, and describe in mathematico-mechanical language, a version or model of the real phenomenon which was less complex than the phenomena themselves; and Galileo was not always sufficiently conscious of the genuine significance of the greater complexity. In this instance Galileo was deceived, partly by his imperfect definition of inertia (only implicitly rectified in his discussion of centrifugal force) and partly by lingering cosmological ideas. It is noteworthy that, while he does not debate whether the spheres are real or not, the word itself he uses naturally and without comment. No more than Tycho Brahe long before did Galileo believe that the heavenly bodies are supported by solid crystalline orbs, yet it seems that Galileo, whose approach to the problem was kinematic rather than truly dynamic, did not sufficiently reflect upon the consequences of taking away the heavenly spheres, and leaving the stars and planets as free bodies in space. Unlike Newton, Galileo never compared the motion of a planet to that of a projectile; unlike Kepler, he did not know that the geometry of planetary orbits vitiated any kind of spherical model. Unlike both of them, he rejected the idea that the Sun affects the planetary motions.

Galileo's *Dialogue* brought to the end the period exceeding twenty years during which his chief, indeed passionate concern had been the open defence of his own scientific outlook, of his own discoveries made in the heavens, and of Copernicanism. His most usual target was academic philosophy, but he had not hesitated also to challenge the right of conservative critics to cite Scripture against himself as an overwhelming scientific authority. The notoriety established by the *Starry Messenger*, pushed to unprecedented heights, made Galileo's name the most famous in Europe among readers of books. For his own purposes he made three visits from Florence to Rome: the first, in 1611, was to demonstrate the things seen through his telescope to the Jesuits of the Collegio Romano of whom the senior was Christopher Clavius, reformer of the calendar (1582). It was a great success, for the Fathers agreed that Galileo had reported truly and Galileo was fêted by the new Academia dei Lincei (Lynxes) founded by Prince Federico Cesi, of which he was there and then made a member. In December 1615 Galileo returned in more sombre circumstances and in ill health to defend himself against charges (uttered publicly in Florence and imparted privately to the Inquisition in Rome) of spreading dangerously irreligious ideas; he had already been advised privately more than once to speak only as a mathematician and not to meddle with theology; in Rome, during February 1616, the authorities decided to condemn the stability of the Sun and the movement of the Earth as erroneous beliefs, and to place *De Revolutionibus* on the *Index of Prohibited Books*.[13] As instructed, Cardinal Bellarmine advised Galileo privately of this decree, obtaining his submission to it and his promise not to hold or defend these beliefs. Further, a commissary of the Inquisition there and then ordered him in the Pope's name not to hold, defend or teach such beliefs on paper or in speech; this last admonition was possibly given unofficially but nevertheless recorded. Early in 1624 Galileo was again in Rome, partly to meet Cesi and show off his newly devised microscope,[14] partly for the more important purpose of winning permission to write a new book on cosmology. As a result of six audiences with Pope Urban VII, on whom he made a good impression, Galileo left with his permission granted (so far as astronomical and mathematical reasoning went), without having revealed the 'unofficial' but express injunction laid on him by the Inquisition in 1616. The future book was, of course, the *Dialogue*, which Galileo finessed through the clerical licensing process: it was not quite what the Pope had in mind. The treatment was popular, not mathematical; it poked fun at the philosophers and appeared to ridicule an argument against Copernicus which the Pope had thought decisive; it seriously proposed the argument from tidal motion to show that the Earth really moves. True, Galileo formally claimed to prove nothing, but his sentiments were as obvious to any non-naive reader as his reluctance to accept the Bible literally. Galileo's attempt to publish a good-tempered book which would persuade rational men in the Church (and he believed there were such, friendly to himself) of the necessity to accept Copernicanism as a fact of nature blew back in his face. His fourth visit to Rome, in 1633, was involuntary. The record of 1616, and all the other accusations, were brought to light, the Pope was furious, and Galileo was made to repent and recant. The decisions of 1616 were more firmly established than ever. Galileo was condemned to isolation in his village house at Arcetri (an easy walk from the centre of Florence) and forbidden communication with other scholars – though this last penality was not strictly enforced. No notice was taken when the manuscript of the *Discourses on Two New Sciences* was smuggled abroad and printed in the heretical Netherlands (1638). Galileo certainly felt that, from the age of sixty-nine it was true, his life was in ruins, made more miserable by ill health and final blindness, but enhanced by the loyalty of pupils, friends and admirers.

The life of Johannes Kepler (1571–1630) ended hardly more cheerily, for after succeeding Tycho Brahe as Rudolph II's Imperial Mathematician, the latter part of his life (being a Protestant) was made wretched by the Thirty Years War; he died after many wanderings in an inn at Regensburg where, like Mozart's in Vienna, his grave is now unrecorded.

Like Galileo, Kepler sought relief from personal distress in ceaseless scholarly toil with little hope of reaching a wide readership through his six astronomical treatises, two on optics, and other works, all idiosyncratic, geometrical and difficult, to the degree that the acceptance of his ideas was impeded by their presentation. He did not expect to be understood by his contemporaries:

I have stolen the golden vessels of the Egyptians to make from them a Tabernacle for my God far from the confines of the land of Egypt

he wrote metaphorically of the book which, he went on, might be

either for my contemporaries or posterity to read, it does not matter which; let the book await its reader for a hundred years, if God himself has waited 6000 years for his work to be seen. [15]

Moreover, he was fully aware that after abandoning combinations of circular motions to represent the planetary orbits, he now made almost impossible demands on the mathematical competence of astronomers for they were not thoroughly grounded in the *Conics* of Apollonios of Perga, nowadays still described as one of the most difficult of ancient mathematical texts. Nor were his ideas such that, when discerned, they were likely to prove readily acceptable. For, although we think of Kepler as the mathematician who discovered the three basic descriptive laws of planetary motion – Newton was to say disparagingly that Kepler had *guessed* them! – as a result of tens of thousands of hours devoted to the reduction of observations and to computation, in fact he was a man of vivid and original scientific imagination who possessed strong physical intuitions about the way the universe works which powerfully directed his mathematical labours. Kepler certainly would not have earned his immortal fame had he been simply a capable mathematician, like so many others in his age, churning out tables.

To his chief objective, the revelation of the deep harmony and order in the sun-centred universe as roughly defined by Copernicus, and to the main principles of his response, Kepler was always faithful. At Tübingen University, where his principal reading was in theology, he studied mathematics with Michael Maestlin (1550–1631) from whom he acquired an elementary grounding in mathematical astronomy embracing a brief account of the Copernican system (when he left the university Kepler had not as yet made a thorough examination of *De Revolutionibus*). Kepler at once went beyond Maestlin in seizing upon that system as really true and offering a new key to wider interpretations, then deciding – perhaps with some prompting from his pastoral superiors – to renounce the life of religion in favour of mathematics. His first book, the *Cosmographic Mystery* (1596), written while teaching at Graz in Austria, followed straight from his student days; and Kepler maintained a long and fruitful correspondence with Maestlin. Copernicus' first appeal to him (as he relates himself) was in the physical, rather than the mathematical elegance of Copernicus' vision; therefore, he believed, convinced of the truth of the system, it should be possible to demonstrate it a *a priori* – that is, from some antecedent principles – as well as *a posteriori* from observations in the manner of Copernicus himself. (This, of course, means the mathematician whacking the philosopher's ball right off the court.) We may state Kepler's antecedent principles as being: (1) God created the universe; (2) Since creation must follow a plan, and God is pure intelligence, God in creating followed a rational plan; (3) Since God's plan is rational, it is also intelligible to man. In a general way, such principles are no doubt much older than Kepler, and certainly would have commended themselves widely at any time between the seventeenth and the nineteenth centuries. Words like design and plan became stereotyped. For Kepler, however, they signify as it were the Divine Architect's working drawings, necessarily geometrical, and he often prefers the word Archetype to convey this rigorous sense. As he put it near the end of his life:

The Creator does not depart from his Archetype, the Creator being the true source of Geometry and, as Plato wrote, always engaged in the practice of Geometry.[16]

Thus Kepler's fourth and most important antecedent principle from which the Copernican system is to be generated *a priori* is that the divine plan or Archetype is mathematically expressible. And so Kepler went to the origin of one of the deep roots of modern science. The immediate task, as he saw it, was to account for what Copernicus had taken as given: the number, dimensions, and motions of the planets. All of these are quantifiable: 'quantity', he writes, was created at first, with body, the heavens being created on the second day'. But there is more, reflecting Kepler's deep religious mysticism, when he explains further:

This I was made bold to attempt by the beautiful harmony that exists between the parts [of the Universe] that are at rest, that is, the Sun, the fixed stars, and the intermediate space, and God the Father, the Son, and the Holy Ghost.[17]

Taking the relative sizes of the orbits as defined by Copernicus, Kepler tried without success to find any proportionality between them, or to discover any pattern at all. Then it struck him that no series or pattern could define just *six* dimensions – why not fewer, or more? Then, on 19 July 1595, tracing for his students the pattern of the occurrence of the great conjunction around the zodiac, he saw how the same triangle repeated round a circle defines a second, interior circle; a square does the same, but the proportions are different. Could this be the clue? Plane figures of 3, 4, 5, 6 . . . sides could be considered . . . but why only six of them, which six? Suddenly he saw; if, instead of plane figures, he took solids, the unique group of *five* regular solids associated with *five* intervals defines *six* circles. The idea was enhanced by the association of the five regular solids with Plato, whose *Timaeus* had (in Kepler's view) come closer than any other work to the perception of the true mathematical Archetypes of creation, a book which was

beyond all possible doubt, a commentary on the book of Genesis, otherwise the first book of Moses, transforming it into Pythagorean philosophy, as will easily be apparent to an attentive reader who compares it with Moses' own words.[18]

With this idea, it was childs' play for him to calculate the ratios between the diameters of the inscribed and circumscibed spheres for each solid, and choose an arrangement suiting the successively larger planetary orbits, as it happens remarkably accurately[19]:

PLANETS	SOLID	RATIOS	
		Theor	*Obs.*
Mercury	Octahedron	86	88
Venus		122	122
Venus	Icosahedron	122	121
Earth		153	153
Earth	Dodecahedron	153	145
Mars		192	192
Mars	Tetrahedron	192	192
Jupiter		577	577
Jupiter	Cube	577	635
Saturn		1000	1000

Only in the case of the interval between Saturn and Jupiter did the solid fail to fit very well, but the good agreement for Mercury and Venus did depend, it must be added, on a special adjustment. Nor was this all: Kepler examined also the relationship between periods of revolution and distances, finding that for any adjacent pair of planets $D_1/D_2 = \sqrt{(P_1/P_2)}$, though in this case the agreement with observed numbers was less good and ultimately he would find a better law.

Believing that the agreement between his theory of the five archetypal solids – which he was to maintain throughout his life – and the measured distances might be improved by the use of observations more accurate than those of Copernicus, Kepler addressed himself to Tycho Brahe, the most exact and most active observer in Europe during more than a thousand years, and ultimately joined him as an assistant at Prague (or rather at the castle Benatky near that city). This was the turning-point in Kepler's career, which brought him the post of Imperial Mathematician on Tycho's death in 1601. The huge, largely undigested mass of Tycho's observations during thirty years thus passed into the hands of the man best fitted to exploit them.

In many ways the Danish astronomer's role in the early history of modern astronomy is analogous to that of Vesalius in anatomy. Perhaps he was even more fully than the anatomist the first modern exponent of the art of disinterested observation and description. For if Tycho imported into his astronomical theory dominant factors which were physical in nature, it cannot be said (as it may of Vesalius' physiological preconceptions) that the evidence to confute them lay before his eyes. The problem of attaining precision was no less real for him than for Vesalius, and the methods he devised to solve it were probably more original. And certainly Tycho was unique among early modern scientists in his insistence upon the crucial importance of accurate quantitative measurement; always a desideratum in astronomy, certainly, but never previously handled with the analytical and inventive powers of Tycho, who first consciously studied methods of estimating and correcting errors of observation in order to determine their limits of accuracy. The most accurate predecessors of Tycho were not Europeans, but the astronomers who worked in the observatory founded at Samarkand by Ulugh Beigh, about 1420. Their results were correct to about ten minutes of arc (i.e. roughly twice as good as Hipparchus'); Tycho's observations were about twice as good again, falling systematically within about four minutes of modern values.[20] This result was achieved by patient attention to detail. The instruments at Hven were fixed, of different types for the various kinds of angular measurement, and much larger than those commonly used in the past, so that their scales could be more finely divided. They were the work of the most skilful German craftsmen, whom Tycho encouraged by his patronage and direction. He devised a new form of sight, and a sort of diagonal scale for reading fractions of a degree. In measuring either the ecliptic longitude of a star, or its right ascension, it is most convenient to proceed by the way that requires an instrument measuring time accurately, and Tycho studied the improvement of clocks for this purpose: but he found that a new technique of his own by which observations were referred to the position of the Sun was more trustworthy. He was the first astronomer in Europe to use the modern celestial coordinates, reckoning star-positions with reference to the celestial equator, not (as formerly) to the ecliptic. Another innovation in his practice was the observation of planetary positions not at a few isolated points in the orbit (especially when in opposition to the Sun), but at frequent intervals so that the whole orbit could be plotted.

Tycho himself reckoned three phases of increasing refinement in his techniques of measurement; those that he made before his twenty-first year (1567) he regarded as childish and doubtful; those of the years 1567–74 as juvenile and fairly reliable; while those made during his twenty-odd years at Uraniborg 'with the greatest care and very accurate instruments at a more mature age, until I was fifty years old', he called 'the observations of my manhood, completely valid and absolutely certain'. The techniques and standards of precision in positional astronomy, thus re-established by Tycho in modern Europe, were evolved to fulfil a very simple ambition. When he was seventeen, in 1563, there had occurred a great conjunction of Saturn and Jupiter for which he had watched eagerly. When it came, it showed that the Alphonsine (Ptolemaic) astronomical tables were in error by a whole month, while the more recently computed Copernican tables were out by some days: 'For his calculation does not deviate very much from the true motion in the sky in the case of these two planets.' This demonstration of inadequacy persuaded the youthful astronomer to undertake the task of mapping afresh the positions of the brighter stars (for even star-maps were badly at fault) and with the fundamental chart of the sky thus established to observe the motions of Sun, Moon and planets in relentless detail so that the elements of their orbits could be calculated without mistake, and accurate tables compiled for the future. When young he travelled widely to perfect his knowledge of astronomy and of instruments, becoming rare enough among the Danish nobility for his intellectual interests to receive from King Frederick II of Denmark a grant of the island of Hven, in the Sound, whereon to settle himself to his task. There, from 1576, he built the castle Uraniborg ('City of the Heavens'), the first scientific research centre in Europe, for Tycho there set up besides his many instruments an alchemical laboratory and a printing-press: he took in students 'all the time, one class after another, and taught them astronomy and other sciences' while they laboured as assistants to this aristocratic master:

Thus by the grace of God it came about that there was hardly any day or night with clear weather that we did not get a great many and very accurate astronomical observations of the fixed stars as well as of all the planets, and also of the comets that appeared during that time, seven of which were carefully observed in the sky from that place. In this way observations were industriously made during 21 years.[21]

Today nothing coherent remains of Uraniborg. The end came after Frederick's death: Tycho quarrelled with his successor, Christian IV, and left Hven for the service of the eccentric Emperor Rudolph II, patron of alchemists and astrologers, at Prague.

It seems unlikely that Tycho launched out on his lifework with any strongly partisan intent, though he may well have wished to prove that even greater accuracy in prediction than that of Copernicus could be linked with a geostatic system. For we know that Tycho early followed a path similar to that of Copernicus himself, though in the reverse direction, so arriving at the geoheliocentric model in which all the planets (except Earth) gyrate about the Sun, which in turn circles the fixed Earth (p. 125). To vindicate this 'Tychonic' system (briefly described in 1588) as a valid alternative to the Copernican was the last ambition of his life which he charged Kepler to fulfil; and indeed for a century it occupied this position. However, Tycho was no slavish adherent to conventional ideas. He did not believe that apparent changes in the sky were due to meteors in the Earth's atmosphere; he proved that comets were celestial bodies, and that the spheres could have no real existence as physical bodies since comets pass through them; and his description of the planetary motions is relativistically identical with that of Copernicus. As an astronomer indeed, Tycho in no way belonged to the past: it was as a good Aristotelian natural-philosopher that he believed the Earth incapable of movement.

Tycho's observations, including his catalogue of one thousand star positions, have not proved of enduring value. The earliest observations that have an other than historical interest are those of the English astronomer, Flamsteed, early in the eighteenth century (error c. 10 seconds of arc), for within about sixty years of Tycho's death the optically-unaided measuring instrument, still ardently defended by Hevelius of Danzig, was beginning to pass out of use. Within a century Tycho's tables had been thoroughly revised by such astronomers as Halley, the Cassinis, Roemer and Flamsteed. In the interval, however, Kepler's discoveries based on Tycho's work had become recognized. To appreciate the relationship between Kepler and Tycho – the inventive mathematician and the patient observer – it must be realized that the balance of choice between Keplerian and Copernican astronomy is very narrow. Until measurements were available whose accuracy could be relied upon within a range of four minutes, or even less, there was no need to suppose that the planetary orbits were anything other than circles eccentric to the Sun. Kepler, in plotting the orbit of Mars, from which he discovered the ellipticity of planetary orbits in general, was able to calculate the elements of a circular orbit which differed by less than ten minutes from the observations. It was only because he knew that Tycho's work was accurate within about half this range that he was dissatisfied and impelled to go further. Kepler's famous 'First Law' was thus the first instance in the history of science of a discovery being made as the result of a search for a theory, not merely to cover a given set of observations, but to interpret a group of refined measurements whose probable accuracy was a significant factor. Discrimination between measurement in a somewhat casual sense, and scientific measurement, in which the quantitative result is itself criticized and its range of error determined, only developed slowly in other sciences during the course of the scientific revolution.

While Kepler's discoveries would have been impossible without the refinement of observation attained by Tycho Brahe, more than mathematical precision was involved in them. Before the telescope, the only materials available for the construction of a planetary theory were angular measurements – principally determinations of the positions of the planets in the zodiac when Sun, Earth and planet were in the same straight line. Consequently the most that a planetary theory could achieve was to predict the times at which a planet would return to the same relative situation, and its position at those times. The mathematical analysis of the solar system as a number of bodies moving in three-dimensional space had never been attempted, as such, by the older astronomers, who had been content to assign such problems to philosophers. They had never concerned themselves with the real path of a planet in space, so long as their model predicted with tolerable accuracy the few recurrent situations in which observations could easily be made. The whole tendency of the scientific revolution was to rebel against this view of the astronomer as a mathematician, a deviser of models to save the phenomena, and to see astronomy as a science comprehending the totality of knowledge concerning the heavens and the relations of the Earth to the celestial regions. Copernicus had abolished the equant because it was a mathematical fiction, an unphilosophical expedient. Galileo modified Copernicus' universe even further in the direction of physical explicability. Kepler had a true conception of the universe as a system of bodies whose arrangement and motions should reveal common principles of design – or in more modern language, be capable of yielding universal generalizations – which were to be demonstrated from the observations, not from physical or metaphysical axioms. For Kepler the astronomer's task was not to study the universe piecemeal – to construct models for each separate planet – but by studying and interpreting it as a whole to prove that the phenomena of each part were consistent with a single design. His aim was to provide a fitting philosophical pattern for the new discoveries of mathematical astronomy: 'so that I might ascribe the motion of the Sun to the Earth itself by physical, or rather metaphysical reasoning, as Copernicus did by mathematical', he remarked in the preface to the *Cosmographic Mystery*. Exact science might properly make inroads upon the established prerogative of philosophy; it was far from being his purpose to expel natural-philosophical considerations from quantitative science altogether.

However, as Tycho's paid assistant Kepler was not free simply to prove that Copernicus had been right: he was initially directed to perfect the theory for the motion of Mars calculated in accordance with Tycho's observations by Tycho's other assistant, Longomontanus. The result was to be published in 1609 (though the work was done four years earlier) as the *New Astronomy or Celestial Physics in Commentaries on Mars*, eight years after Tycho's death set Kepler at liberty to defend which system he chose. His first discovery was that the plane of the orbit of Mars passed through the Sun – not through the centre of the Earth's orbit as Copernicus had supposed – and that its angle of inclination to the ecliptic was invariable. He also experimented with giving up the little epicycles of Copernicus, reintroducing instead the equant-point (p. 65) but though this permitted adjustment of the angular velocity of Mars with respect to the Sun, Kepler found that no single position of the equant-point would satisfy all the observations. Turning to the Earth's (or Sun's) motion – for any error in stating this would be reflected in all the planets – Kepler made the important discovery that it resembled the planets in requiring an equant-point for an exact representation. Mars remained intractable: Kepler could represent the orbital motion 'in longitude' very accurately by a sliding equant, but the consequent errors 'in latitude' (that is, the planet's supposed distances from the ecliptic) were intolerable. On returning to the Ptolemaic bisected eccentricity he found maximum errors of about eight minutes of arc presented: of these he wrote:[22]

Divine providence granted us such a careful observer in Tycho Brahe that his observations convicted this Ptolemaic calculation of an error of 8'; . . . because these 8' could not be ignored, they alone have led to a total reformation of astronomy.

Progress seemed almost impossible by means of these arbitrary or as Kepler called them 'vicarious' hypotheses, and he was indeed far from his goal; but he was also guided by different, 'physical' principles of which the root was his belief that a 'moving spirit' in the Sun itself causes the revolutions of the planets in a sort of vortex of force. Supposing this force to be confined to the ecliptic plane, and acting as it were in circles, its strength at any distance from the Sun would be inversely proportional to that distance, from which Kepler thought to deduce the result (which he later knew to be false in general, though it is true for the regions near the apsides of the orbit) that the planet's speed also is inversely proportional to its distance from the Sun. Because the speeds of motion at different points in the orbit are known from observation, this relation provided another way of working out distances. In actual use, however, derivation of instantaneous speeds from the various radii is not convenient and so Kepler modified the rule to the proposition – since known as Kepler's Second Law of planetary motion – that the radius-vector drawn from the Sun to a planet sweeps over equal areas of the orbit in equal times. Though his first proof of the Law was questionable Kepler was later to assure himself that the various errors in it cancelled out, so that the Law was rigorously true.[23] He enunciated it definitively in his *Epitome of Copernican Astronomy* (1621).

At this stage in his complex and tedious calculations – involving the geometrical analysis of many theoretical possibilities, as well as the continual checking of the predicted motions against observations selected from Tycho Brahe's great store – Kepler was already convinced that the orbit of the Earth or a planet could not be a perfect circle eccentric to the Sun. As he said:

The reflective and intelligent reader will see, that this opinion among astronomers concerning the perfect eccentric circle of the orbit involves a great deal that is incredible in physical speculation . . . My first error was to take the planet's path as a perfect circle, and this mistake robbed me of the more time, as it was taught on the authority of all philosophers, and consistent in itself with Metaphysics.

In calculations of the Earth's angular velocity he could assume the orbit to be circular, because its ellipticity is small (*nam insensibile est . . . quantum ei ovalis forma detrahit*), but in the orbits of the other planets the difference would become very sensible. His next problem, obviously, was to define the nature of this non-circular orbit more closely. He therefore returned to the investigations on Mars, in a far more secure position now that he had worked out the movement of the observer's platform – the Earth – with greater accuracy than before. Experiment showed that the orbit of Mars could not, indeed, be circular, for this when compared with the observations made the motion of the planet too rapid at aphelion and perihelion, and too slow at the mean distances. After many trials Kepler wrote: 'Thus it is clear, the orbit of the planet is not a circle, but passes within the circle at the sides, and increases its amplitude again to that of the circle at perigee. The shape of a path of this kind is called an oval.' Again, the development of Kepler's thoughts was influenced by his idea of the physical mechanism which could produce such a departure from the perfectly circular form. He supposed that the oval path was traced by the resultant of two distinct motions; the first being that due to the action of the Sun's virtue, varying with the distance of the planet, and the second a uniform rotation of the planet in an imaginary epicycle produced by its own virtus motrix. The hypothetical orbit would be an oval (or rather an ovoid, since its apsides would be dissimilar) enclosed within the normal eccentric at all points save the apsides. It seems extraordinary that having earlier abandoned the whole conception of solid spheres and epicycles, and satisfied himself of the absurdity in his own physical terms of the vicarious hypothesis,[24] Kepler should now have returned in 1604 to the old idea of compounding the planet's real path from circular motions. He spent much labour in vain attempts to geometrize this strange hypothesis so that it could be compared with observation; he even used an ellipse – its eccentricity too great – as an approximation to the ovoid. Yet finally no exact fit could be made: Kepler had to confess that the oval orbit and the theory of its physical causation had 'gone up in smoke'.[25] Enlightenment, after much more tedious struggle, was at last to come as the result of happy accident, as he wrote himself; he perceived a numerical congruity

Fig. 5.2   The ellipse: R the radius vector, *e* the eccentricity (SB/BC), β the eccentric anomaly.

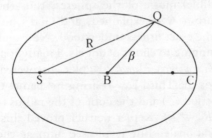

between the excess of the eccentric circle over the true orbit at the mean distances and the excess of the secant of the optical equation in the same region over the radius: or (in modern terms) he perceived that the length of the radius-vector of the planet could be written in the form $R(1 + e\cos\beta)$; *this is one form of the equation for a true ellipse.*[26] The ellipse thus arrived at, having the Sun at one focus, fitted the area-law and the observations exactly. For some time he was much disturbed by his inability to give a physical meaning to the elliptical orbit:

to show that the celestial machine is not so much a divine organism as a piece of clockwork, with all the variety of motions carried out by means of a very simple magnetic force in the body, just as in a clock all the motions derive from a simple weight.

He was 'almost driven to madness in considering and calculating this matter' until it struck him that a simple to-and-fro motion (libration) of the planet along a short straight line, while it also revolved round the Sun in a circle, would generate the ellipse.

With Kepler's first two Laws – the First defining the elliptical orbit – the old mathematical astronomy was finished, though full acceptance of the fact was to take two generations. Kepler's physics and Tycho's observations had been united in a novel and elegant definition of planetary orbital motion. But Kepler was still some way from his goal of disclosing the 'harmony of the world', a subject which (he had told a correspondent in 1601) 'I have long meditated upon and which I could only complete if Tycho were to rebuild Astronomy or if I could use his observations'.[27] After the realization of this last ambition Kepler was to repay his debt to Tycho with *The Rudolphine Tables* (1627) – which set, for almost a century, the standard of predictive accuracy – meanwhile, after preparing this work but long before its publication Kepler returned in the *Harmony of the World* (*Harmonices Mundi*, 1619) to his original interest. The thought of the Creator (ignored by Ptolemy) and of the Archetype of the world 'which lies in geometry and expressly in the work of Euclid, that thrice-greatest philosopher' had never left his mind.[28] He revised his regular-polyhedra Archetypal model in this book (and was to repeat it again in his *Epitome of Copernican Astronomy*, 1621) and also devised a rationale for the 'just' musical scale recently accepted among musicians that likewise depended on the geometry of polygons. Now a further unification presented itself to him: when he formed ratios between the extreme velocities of the planets (at perihelion and aphelion) he found the musical consonances to reappear, the true (though forever to man inaudible) music of the spheres; thus the magnitudes of the eccentricities of the orbits were explained, and God's means of adjusting the polyhedral model to the exact fitness understood. No wonder that Kepler could compare polyphonic singing to choirs of angels. Finally, only twelve days before he finished writing *Harmonices Mundi*, Kepler discovered by considering the powers of certain ratios the Third Law bearing his name: the ratio between the square of a planet's period (T) and the cube of the radius (R) is constant within the solar system ($T^2/R^3 = K$). Kepler neither proved this Third Law by exact data, nor gave it a rationale. But it pleased him as the final link between velocity and distance, and in the *Epitome* proportioned the 'masses' of each planet so that the solar spirit (or 'species') would give the right 'push' at the right distance (he supposed that if the 'push' were taken as constant, the speed conferred by it would be inversely proportional to the 'mass').

The simplicity and directness which these relations introduced into astronomy need no emphasis. The shapes and dimensions of the planetary orbits, and the velocities of the planets' motions, could now in principle be calculated with certitude, if not with ease, for there is no simple solution to the problem raised by Kepler's Second Law, that of dividing the area of an ellipse into determinate fractions by radius-vectors from a focus. Accordingly, astronomers during the next half century devised alternative methods of defining the planets' orbital speed relating it to the *empty* focus of the ellipse (about which, as Ptolemy had unknowingly discovered, the revolution is more nearly uniform than it is about the Sun). The diffusion of Kepler's discoveries is itself an intricate topic: published as they were far from the main centres of intellectual activity in Italy and France, composed sometimes in a diffuse and awkward manner (whose 'autobiography' is perhaps more interesting for us than for contemporaries), containing esoteric ideas that younger men were to find as unacceptable as Galileo did, Kepler's books were inaccessible to those unskilled in mathematics. As he admitted himself[29]:

It is extremely difficult nowadays to write mathematical books, especially astronomical ones. For unless use is made of an exact precision in the proportions, explanations, demonstrations and conclusions the book will not be mathematical; if such use is made, then the reading of it becomes very difficult especially in Latin which lacks articles and the grace of Greek . . . That is why nowadays there are few suitable readers; the majority generally despise and reject such works. How many mathematicians are there who will undertake the labour of reading through the *Conics* of Apollonios of Perga? Yet his material is of a kind which lends itself to explanation by figures and lines much better than Astronomy does. I myself, who pass for a mathematician, tire my brain in reading my own work . . .

The Rudolphine Tables were relatively soon accepted in competent circles as surpassing their predecessors and contemporary rivals; the diffusion of Kepler's Laws, on the other hand, depended very much on summarises of his astronomy in such works of general instruction as Pierre Hèrigone's *Course of Mathematics* (*Cursus Mathematicus*, 1644) or Thomas Streete's *Astronomia Carolina* (1661) – in English – from which Newton learned all he knew of Kepler. The great natural-philosophical systems of mid-century, those of Descartes and Gassendi, took nothing from Kepler and so understanding of his ideas was at the mercy of secondary interpreters who readily accepted the elliptical orbit but rejected the Second Law while (largely) ignoring the Third, to which only the slow evolution of dynamics could give significance.

With Kepler a tradition of mathematical astronomy which (in the Western tradition) had begun with the Babylonians came to an end. It was not only the case that the primacy of the circle had been destroyed but that, once Kepler had solved it, the problem of planetary motion which had fascinated scholars and illiterates alike for thousands of years ceased to be interesting, save to the experts. This was partly due to the shift to problems of physical astronomy, by means of the telescope, partly due to the decline of astrology. (London almanac-makers would, of course, prolong the Babylonian tradition which Kepler had abruptly ended in serious science.) Not that Kepler opposed astrology – and Galileo also cast horoscopes. Since Kepler believed firmly in the integrity of the universe and the centrality of the Sun, rejecting all notions of an infinite space containing a uniform distribution of stars, he also took it for granted that the heavens had some influence upon the Earth. The Sun and the Moon certainly affect our planet, why not stars and the other planets also? On the whole, while taking this rational view (incapable, indeed, of disproof since we have no notion of what terrestrial experience would be without stars and planets) Kepler distrusted the astrologers' conventional baggage. 'I am a

Lutheran astrologer', he told Maestlin, 'I throw away the nonsense and keep the hard kernel'. Even in this he ran counter to the spirit of the coming age.

But Kepler was more than a mathematician. Perhaps the importance of his work, apart from the three famous Laws, has not been sufficiently esteemed. The older historians passed politely over Kepler's theorizing on physical mechanisms, his love of analogy, and all that was ancillary to the main mathematical argument, as so much dross that was best left buried. Now it is not difficult to see that Kepler was as original and stimulating in his sidetracks as when following the plain mathematical road. Certainly his ideas on gravity, on the action of forces at a distance, are important factors in the prehistory of the theory of universal gravitation. The Cartesians ridiculed Kepler's mysterious forces seated in the Sun, and his appetites of matter, just as they later resisted the notion of gravitational attraction. Kepler does make odd equivalences between 'soul' or 'spirit' and force, nevertheless his cosmological theory and his astronomy were designed to follow firm principles of physical causation, and designed also to give a far more accurate model than those of either Galileo or Descartes. It was Kepler who, in the *Cosmographic Mystery*, followed the example of Tycho Brahe in denouncing the traditional belief in material spheres which had been left unchallenged by Copernicus:

Neither indeed is to be feared that the lunar orbs may be forced out of position, compressed by the close proportions of (other celestial) bodies, if they are not included and buried in that orb itself. For it is absurd and monstrous to set these bodies in the sky, endowed with certain properties of matter, which do not resist the passage of any other solid body. Certainly many will not fear to doubt that there are in general any of these Adamantine orbs in the sky, that the stars are transported through space and the aetherial air, free from these fetters of the orbs, by a certain divine virtue regulating their courses by the understanding of geometrical proportions.

He went on to ask, by what chains and harness is the moving Earth fastened to its orb? and to point out that nowhere on the surface of the globe do men find it embedded in a material medium, but always surrounded by air. Kepler, too, must be credited, at least as much as Descartes, with the perception that there must be some source of force, or tension, within the solar system. It could not be a complex of entirely independent bodies without mutual interaction. It could not be accidental that the planes of all the orbits passed through the Sun, nor could the variations of a planet's motion – the differences in its velocity at perihelion and aphelion, for example – be explained without the supposition that some force was acting upon it. For Galileo the natural motions of the universe were basically simple, eternal and force-free; in Kepler's far more realistic picture these motions were complex and resulted from an interplay of 'bodily forces' which by analogy (rather than identification) he called magnetic or gravitational. In this sense Galileo still belonged in a geometrical universe which Kepler had rejected for a physical universe in which purely geometrical notions without physical counterparts had no place. I call my hypotheses physical, he wrote, because 'I prove that the irregularity of the motion (of the planets) corresponds to the nature of the planetary sphere, that is, it is physical'.[30]

Thus Kepler set men (when they began to understand him) directly on the road to celestial mechanics, though their progress along it was to involve a deep revision and clarification of the concept of force, and new ideas about the nature and physical activity of universal matter. Kepler had proved, if idiosyncratically, that mathematics, measurement, and physical principles could be united in a certain synthesis, even if he had left the business incomplete. Natural philosophers could not indefinitely ignore the challenge to be (a) mathematically demonstrative and (b) observationally exact in the Keplerian manner. Kepler had gone far beyond the bounds of the astronomical problem of two generations – does the Earth move or not? – to assert principles of celestial motion, set in a pattern of theorizing about cosmic physics, which were thoroughly to displace traditional notions of what either philosophy or astronomy should be.

NOTES

1. I have not seen the first issue of this book, of 1548. Dodoens's acquaintance with *De Revolutionibus* was obviously very superficial.
2. Robert S. Westman in R. S. Westman (ed.) *The Copernican Achievement*, University of California Press, 1975, 285–345.
3. *Principia*, Book III, Proposition 12.
4. English translation in D. W. Singer, *Giordano Bruno, His Life and Thought*, Schuman: New York, 1950.
5. *Medieval Studies*, III, 233, 242, 244.
6. Albert Van Helden, *The Invention of the Telescope, Trans. Amer. Phil. Soc.*, **67**, 1977. Part 4. Rival (but posterior) claimants were Jacob Adriaenszoon Metius of Alkmaar and Sacharias Janssen also of Middelburg.
7. Here I retain the language of Galileo's seventeenth-century English translator, Thomas Salusbury, see Giorgio di Santillana, *Dialogue on the Great World Systems in the Salusbury translation*, Chicago University Press: Chicago 1953, 37, 40, 45.
8. Ibid., 125 ff.
9. Ibid., 159.
10. Ibid., 177.
11. Ibid., 178–80.
12. Werner Heisenberg, *Philosophic Problems of Nuclear Science*, Faber: London, 1952, 35.
13. The only phrases forbidden the eyes of Catholic readers were those few in Book 1 where Copernicus speaks of the Earth's motion as physically real.
14. This was a modified form of Galilean telescope, arranged to focus the image of an insect placed near the objective lens. The usual form of microscope – a modified Keplerian telescope – originated at about the same time in Holland.
15. Kepler, *Gesammelte Werke*, VI, 290, I have learned much from theses on Kepler by Drs A. E. L. Davis and J. V. Field.
16. *Harmonices Mundi*, 1619; ibid., VI, 299.
17. *Mysterium Cosmographicum*, 1596, ibid., I, 9.
18. *Harmonices Mundi, Gesammelte Werke*, VI, 221. In his explorations of solid geometry, Kepler discovered two further regular geometric solids.

19. I have recalculated the numbers given by Kepler himself to make a more coherent series of ratios.

20. Projection of modern determinations backwards indicates that the chief fixed stars, whose positions were taken repeatedly and averaged, were placed by Tycho to within about one minute of their true values. In fact, without optical aid it was hardly possible to be more exact.

21. H. Raeder, E. Strömgren and B. Strömgren, *Tycho Brahe's Description of his Instruments and Scientific Work*, Copenhagen, 1946, 106–118 (Tycho's scientific autobiography).

22. *Astronomia Nova* (1609), Ch. 19; *Gesammelte Werke*, III, 177.

23. Ibid., III, 263–70.

24. The 'vicarious hypothesis' (eccentric circle with arbitrarily placed equant) works well for the Earth because its orbit is almost circular ($e = 0.017$) but with Mars, whose eccentricity is about five times as great, the error will become more evident.

25. *Gesammelte Werke*, III, 345: 'causae physicae in fumos abeunt'. A. Koyré, *La Revolution Astronomique*, Hermann: Paris, 1961, 250–3.

26. *G. W. III*, 345b; Koyré, 254–6. R is the radius of the eccentric circle, e the eccentricity, β the angle of rotation of the radius vector. The difference was an excess of 429 parts over 100,000.

27. To Magini, 1 June 1601.

28. To Heydon, October 1605, *G. W.*, XV, 235.

29. *Astronomia Nova*, Preface; trans. by A. R. H. from Marie Boas Hall (ed.) *Nature and Nature's Laws*, Macmillan: London, 1970, 67, *G. W.* III, 18.

30. Gerald Holton, 'Johannes Kepler's universe: its physics and metaphysics' (1956), reprinted in *Thematic Origins of Scientific Thought: Kepler to Einstein*, Harvard University Press: Cambridge, Mass. 1973, 69–90. Arthur Koestler's *The Sleepwalkers*, Hutchinson: London 1959, contains a sympathetic picture of the complexity of Kepler's life and thought.

CHAPTER SIX

Innovation in biology

For the influential French historian of science Alexandre Koyré, who died in 1964, the centre of the stage on which the scientific revolution was enacted was occupied by the physical sciences, and the drama enacted turned upon their mathematization. To most historians of science today this would seem a very narrow point of view. They would argue for the importance of the mechanical philosophy (Ch. 7), standing quite apart from the mathematical trend, for great shifts in ideas and methods that were independent of physical science altogether and for changes in social attitudes to science as being all aspects of a revolutionary situation which the historian cannot ignore. In fact, Koyré was not arguing against such an inclusive view of the scientific revolution, but rather for the special importance of those currents which led to Newton, and so by ways that were relatively direct to Maxwell, Planck and Einstein. Einstein was certainly conscious of direct intellectual descent from Galileo in a manner evidently not shared by (let us say) Crick and Watson in relation to Harvey. A dialogue on questions of space and time between the seventeenth century and the late twentieth century is possible and indeed one might almost say normal; but such a dialogue about life and living processes seems virtually unthinkable. The conditions of the present debate about life were established only in the nineteenth century.

Such thoughts suggest others. Would the historian perhaps properly speak of a 'negative revolution' in seventeenth-century biology, for example, one which certainly destroyed the ancient basis of confidence without creating an effective 'research programme' permitting rapid cumulative development? One thinks of the comparative sterility of microscopy and of the even more striking interval between Harvey's discovery of the heart's true function and the beginnings of medical investigation of imperfections in cardiac action – by the simplest of means – two centuries later. We have ample testimony from the age of Newton that ideas and knowledge relating to the human body seemed then no less advanced beyond those prevailing in antiquity than their analogues in physical science, and if progress is to be measured by intensity of interest it is beyond question that there was more endeavour to innovate in medicine and natural history than elsewhere. It can hardly be doubted therefore that a 'revolutionary' situation existed but that for a variety of reasons – among which the intrinsic difficulty of the phenomena and a lack of the intellectual coherence enjoyed by mathematical sciences may certainly be numbered – it was much less successfully exploited. The depths of life were not plumbed to the same distance as those of space and time.

Should the historian conclude that the mathematical (Newtonian) sciences served as a model for others? Indeed, as we shall see in more detail later, by the early eighteenth century Newton was judged to offer ideals of knowledge and of method; not that these were seen exclusively in mathematical terms, however, for the Newtonian method proposed for chemistry or biology was thoroughly experimental and qualitative. Yet approximately one hundred years before, with Descartes, scientific mechanism as applied to living organisms seems to have developed hand-in-hand with the mechanization of the universe, and while biological mechanism (Descartes, Borelli, Willis) was necessarily based on physical analogues it could hardly be described as depending upon an antecedent development in physical science. Rather there was parallelism and interaction. Early attempts to model biological investigation upon physics often led to a dead end. So with the well-known investigation of Sanctorio (1561–1636) into the changes of body-weight by ingestion and excretion: his weighing-chair technique, ingenious and carefully pursued, led to the interesting discovery that the body loses much fluid steadily by insensible transpiration, yet it could hardly be argued that the experiment did anything to advance knowledge of metabolic processes or even offer evidence against conventional ideas of digestion and assimilation. In this context the elucidation of the lymphatic system by Gaspare Aselli (1622), Jean Pecquet (1651) and other anatomists, using the traditional method of opening dead and living animals, bore far more fruit. Similarly, in terms of theory, the physical explanations of muscular action which invoked such chemical reactions between the two substances, as 'explosion' or acid–alkali neutralization were totally *a priori* and though suggestive quite unhelpful in the long run. Where (as in these instances) the independent integrity of biological thinking was compromised at best only a kind of scaffolding could result. For all the interesting results obtained by experiment and the exploitation of physical–scientific analogies in the seventeenth century, anatomical study was to remain as it had been since the time of Galen the chief and safest basis for ideas of physiological function, right down to the early nineteenth century.

Historians have long employed a chronological scheme in which Lavoisier (*c.* 1787) is seen as the 'Newton' of chemistry and Darwin (1859) as the 'Newton' of biology.[1] Recently, Thomas Kuhn has pointed out that even within seventeenth-century physical science the completeness of the revolution in mathematical science stands beside an incomplete degree of progress in the experimental branches where, again, mathematization was 'postponed' to the nineteenth century. Agreeing with Koyré that:

If one thinks of the Scientific Revolution as a revolution of *ideas*, it is the changes in these traditional, quasi-mathematical fields which one must seek to understand, while nevertheless believing that 'other vitally important things also happened to the sciences during the sixteenth and seventeenth centuries (the Scientific Revolution was not merely a revolution in thought)' Kuhn finally concludes that a complete historical symmetry between even the mathematical and experimental departments of physics is impossible since 'the cleavage between mathematical and experimental science' seems 'rooted in the nature of the human mind.'[2] It is hardly surprising, therefore, that even greater historical asymmetries exist between the mathematical and the chemical, geological and biological sciences, where the 'Baconian' features of evolution are even more marked than in experimental physics.

In fact, while the greatest physical theoreticians like Huygens and Newton endeavoured, with success, to extend the domain of mathematical science into such experimental branches as optics, pneumatics and acoustics, thereby increasing homogeneity, in the biological sciences speculation ascended further than ever from the simple collections of natural history. Speculation ranged to the possibility of animals in the Moon or planets, to wild geological interpretations of the Book of Genesis, and (most extensively) to the reinterpretation of physiology and medicine in terms of fanciful mechanisms. Descriptive natural history broadened its character from microscopic pond-animals to the comparative anatomy of the largest mammals, embracing a huge and amorphous literature of geological curiosities, animal monstrosities, meteorological singularities and regional accounts. This often sensational literature has attached a pejorative tone to the epithet 'Baconian' inappropriate to the botanical collecting, microscopy and comparative anatomy which no less followed accumulative patterns in an organized and critical manner. In the good sense all these sciences, as well as (for example) mineralogy and pneumatics, could be described as 'Baconian', being descriptive, enumerative and a-theoretical.

The historical bases of the sciences of living nature – apart from Bacon's own didactic writings and examples, as in the *Sylva Sylvarum* (1627) which did much to influence the British especially – were double: human anatomy and the encyclopaedic natural history of the Renaissance. The revival of anatomy has already been discussed; it was logical, if by no means inevitable, that this should branch out into the more thorough study in particular of those animals that are like man, or of special interest to man, such as the horse (in the *Anatomia dei Cavallo*, 1598, of Carlo Ruini) or the dog (whose embryological development was described by Fabricius of Aquapendente). With Pierre Belon (1517–64) and Guillaume Rondelet (1507–66) the monographic treatment was extended to fishes, while the first specialized book on insects was the work of a group of Englishmen (*Theatrum Insectorum*, 1634, published by Thomas Mouffet).[3] A coherence dignifies such studies right through to the famous monograph on the chimpanzee of Edward Tyson (1699) deriving partly from the professional anatomists' techniques of dissection and analysis, partly from the parallel with the human model, the apex of the morphological scale. The advance of the encyclopaedic naturalists towards a 'modern' scientific method was more limited in character. The naturalist's ideas concerning the origin of organic life, the distribution of plants and animals, and the reason for their wide range of structure and form, were still for the most part non-scientific in origin, or at best derived from very ancient sources. On the other hand, he was progressing towards modern ways of classifying and describing organisms and of defining the subject-matter of natural history. He became less interested in nature-study as an exercise in morality; he made a partial distinction between the *Flora* and the *Pharmacopoeia*. This brought the disadvantage, however, that as botanists and zoologists became progressively more efficient in classification and description, they came near to losing interest in all other problems posed by the organic world. The naturalist was limited, in the main, to a particular kind of activity – ultimately inherited from the apothecaries' need to distinguish medicinal herbs – partly, of course, because it was one task worth doing which was within his competence, but partly also because he lacked the imagination which would have freed him from the influence of tradition, which was still highly literary. The works of such writers as Conrad Gesner (1516–65) and P. A. Mattioli (1500–77) are at least as much scholarly compilations as works of observation. A different kind of biology – for example, the very simple experiments by which Francesco Redi, a century later, confuted the universal belief in the spontaneous generation of insects – would certainly have been possible, but the intellectual context in which that might have flourished did not yet exist in their day. Aristotle's writings were still, in relation to life, very much more a source of stimulation than of doubt, and it did not seem necessary to seek to define new questions, or search for novel means of obtaining answers.

The vast range of biological and medical investigation which was to open out during the nineteenth century was, therefore, professionally represented in the Renaissance only by medicine and scholarly natural history (itself, of course, with strong medical connections). Therefore it is natural enough that physicians played a major creative part in the biology (to continue with this anachronistic but indispensable term) of the sixteenth and seventeenth centuries, nor that the course of events was shaped by medical interests. What is remarkable is the extent and diversity of intellectual endeavour within the profession of medicine. Many physicians, of course, sought to make their contribution and to distinguish themselves by publication relating to the actual practice of medicine or to the medical sciences (anatomy, pharmacology and so forth) but many devoted themselves to more marginally connected studies of plants and animals. Among the distinguished botanists most were medical men – to name only Fuchs, Cesalpino, Bauhin, Morison and Tournefort. All the work in comparative anatomy and a great deal of microscopy was carried out by physicians. Such notable names as those of Otto Brunfels (1489–1534), John Ray (1627–1705), Robert Hooke (1635–1703) and Antoni van Leeuwenhoek (1632–1723), those of major 'lay' contributors to knowledge of living things, are few and far between. The organization of the scientific movement and the structure of the universities perpetuated the mutual relationship between medicine and biology long after the separation between 'medical' and 'scientific' interests had been effected, simply because of the fossilization of formal instruction within any of the life sciences outside the medical curriculum. Teachers of botany (or, for that matter, of chemistry) were appointed only to fulfil the needs of the medical faculty.

To the young and ambitious physician of the late sixteenth and seventeenth centuries, eager to distinguish himself and to add to knowledge, many courses lay open. He might venture on original methods in practice, collect case-histories, perhaps contribute to the growing literature of abnormal observations and remarkable cures. Or he might, in the humanistic vein, seek to improve the general understanding of the magisterial texts. Or he might practise anatomy, in which case he would certainly dissect many animals. Or he might embark upon descriptive natural history. But the texture of the scientific work involved in all these courses was far from identical. The humanist-physician was easily assimilated to the type of the scholar, the naturalist-physician to the type of the lexicographer – admittedly with the development of specialized powers of observation. Neither of these courses, at this time, led naturally to the act of experimenting. The problem, however, which comes nearest to the physician's work, the understanding of the functioning of the human (and, by analogy, the animal) body in health and disease, is one that lends itself to observation and experiment. The physician must observe and classify diseases, he must also experiment in his therapy. Admittedly the physician found his normal ratiocinative background in Galen's ideas, admittedly he proceeded in accordance with the accepted theory of the nature of disease and of the measures requisite to effect a remedy; even the ascription of symptoms to the humoural condition, the amount and timing of blood-letting and the preparation of drugs were laid down by rules for his guidance more dogmatically than they are today. Yet, whatever the teaching, in any age a physician must be something of an empiric. He must learn to use his own judgement. He must adapt general principles to particular cases. And in the sixteenth century the art of medicine was far from static. Apart from the great variety of herbal medicaments among which the physician had to make his choice, there were the new inorganic remedies, such as mercury, and new drugs from the East and West Indies. There was a great controversy over the correct procedure in venesection. There were new problems – syphilis, gunshot wounds, scurvy ravaging crews on long ocean voyages, and plagues flourishing with the growth of cities. A physician's practice could be guided by principles – the use of contraries to restore the balance of the humours, or analogy (dead man's skull, powdered, in cases of epilepsy) – but he could be no mere follower of the book, if only because the book was an inconsistent and insufficiently specific guide. The most important part of medicine was learnt through experience, and profitable experience depends on experiment.

Perhaps this lesson was the most enduring contribution made by Paracelsus to true science. Naturally when Paracelsus writes, for example, 'From his own head a man cannot learn the theory of medicine, but only from that which his eyes see and his fingers touch . . . theory and practice should together form one, and should remain undivided . . . Practice should not be based on speculative theory,' it has to be remembered that 'practice' for Paracelsus meant something very different from the rationalist practice of the modern physician

151

(Ch. 3). Nor do empirical methods alone constitute a new philosophy of science. Ambroise Paré's use of ligatures and dressings instead of cauterization by fire is not to be put forward as an example of a conscious experimental science – though it was a genuine instance of empiricism. Paré knew no Latin: he was only the royal surgeon. But it is to a certain degree inevitable that the originally minded men who adhered to the more practical aspects of medicine, who were compelled to be empirical (Glauber, after all, must have tested his *sal mirabile*), should have moved more naturally in the direction of experiment than their colleagues whose interests ran otherwise. From dissection for research to experiment of a limited kind is not a great step. Anatomical observations on the veins and arteries suggested simple experiments on the behaviour of the blood in the living body – with which venesection made the surgeon necessarily familiar. Observations involving vivisection had been made long before by Galen and Aristotle, and were repeated in the sixteenth century: wounds occasionally gave opportunities for a glimpse beneath the surface. There was almost a tradition by which poisons and their antidotes were tested upon small animals (and sometimes condemned criminals). Moreover, the Hellenistic tradition in zoology and physiology offered perhaps the best model of experimental science that could be found in the whole corpus of transmitted learning. The Aristotle of the *Generation of Animals* and the *History of Animals* was an experimenter as well as an excellent observer. Galen's account (in *On the Natural Faculties*) of experiments made on a living dog to show the way in which urine flows in the ureters and the urethra could almost have served as a direct model for Harvey's analogous demonstrations of the way in which blood flows in the arteries and veins. In embryology especially – again leaving aside all questions of theory – the sixteenth-century heritage of careful observation is clear: Aristotle had opened eggs at different stages of hatching, as had Albert the Great in the thirteenth century, just as Fabricius and Harvey were to do. The men of the Renaissance had only to follow and extend well-marked paths.

Perhaps it is not stretching imagination to see practical medicine playing somewhat the same role in the development of biology as that of technology in the evolution of the physical sciences. The physician, engineer and manufacturer had that practical skill in their encounters with nature which was lacking to the reflective, generalizing philosopher of the study. They wove a strand of empiricism into the web of theory. They were equally (if honest and intelligent men) more interested in the attainment of tangible results than the discussion of means by which such results ought to be attainable. And just as experience with cannon or in industrial chemistry had no simultaneous, directly positive effect upon ideas of motion or the four-element theory of matter, so also empiricism in the medical sciences could not immediately and proportionately modify the broad theory of physiology or pathology. The impact of empiricism was in all cases gradual, subject to variations in emphasis and liable to be different from that which posterity might deduce merely by treating practical experience as the 'cause', and change in theory as the 'effect'.

In the history of the discovery of the circulation of the blood is an illuminating instance of the way in which the change of biological ideas was wrought by observation and experiment rendered fertile by a shifted perspective of thought. Harvey in arriving at his new concept had little in the way of anatomical information or medical experience available to him that had not equally been available to others for twenty years at least. According to a well-known story related by Robert Boyle it was Fabricius' monograph (1603) on the valves in the veins that first set him thinking of an inward, and therefore circular, motion of the blood; but the valves had been known to anatomists for many years – to Fabricius since 1574 – and had nevertheless been reconciled by them with traditional notions of outward flow in the veins. Harvey's great merit was to re-order known but misunderstood facts and observations into a new and comprehensive generalization. As he constantly reiterates in his book *On the Motion of the Heart and Blood in Animals* (1628) – for he was no eager destroyer of idols – many of the observations on which he relied were already known to Galen, who had in particular made a careful attempt to explain the function of the valves in the heart (he had been ignorant of those elsewhere). Other observations noted by Harvey appeared commonly with phlebotomy; and indeed anyone stroking the veins on the back of the hand (after the manner Harvey described) can discern both the presence of a valve and the inward direction of the vascular movement. Thus Harvey resembled Galileo in insisting upon a new view of what everyone thought he understood and also introducing a quantitative, mechanical aspect into this view, though this was by no means the essence of his method.

Harvey, however, made a far more precise appeal to experimental evidence than did Galileo, and his use of a 'critical instance' (though there seems to be nothing to suggest that Harvey was at all influenced by his great patient, Francis Bacon) is not paralleled in mechanics. The greatest physiologist of the sixteenth century, Jean Fernel, had not known how to apply the experimental method. Sir Charles Sherrington has expressly pointed the contrast between him and Harvey:

Fernel, it would seem, in order to do his work, must find it part of a logically conceived world. His data must be presented to him in a form which, according to his own a priori reasoning, hangs together. In that demand of his lies his inveterate distrust of empiricism. 'We cannot be said to know a thing of which we do not know the cause. 'And under 'cause' he included not only the 'how' but the 'why'. With Harvey it was not so. When asked 'why' the blood circulated, his reply had been that he could not say. Fernel welcomed 'facts', but especially as pegs for theory; Harvey, whether they were such facts or not, if they were perfectly attested.[4]

Of course, Harvey was to use observed and experimental 'facts' to demonstrate the circulation of the blood, whereas Fernel suggested that 'in passing from anatomy to physiology – that is to the actions of the body – we pass from what we can see and feel to what is known only by meditation', as though passing across a frontier. But Harvey himself twice tells us that his approach to his discovery *began* with meditation upon the large volume of blood passing into the heart. Sherrington exaggerated Harvey's positivism and made his thought-processes seem less subtle than they really were: some 'facts' surely known to Harvey (like the difference in colour between arterial and venous blood, often mentioned by Galen) were neither mentioned nor explained by him, while the peripheral completion of the circulation by passage from arteries to veins was as much an unseen act of faith for him as the transmission of blood through the septum of the heart was for Galen. As Pagel has emphasized, Harvey was no mere empiricist or mechanist but a biological philosopher. Pagel – in opposition to Sherrington – argues that 'the *final cause* – the reason for the sake of which something is done – is for Harvey the primary and principal of all causes in art as well as in nature and for this he invokes the authority of Aristotle'.[5] In Harvey's mind the blood circulated to conserve the heat of the animal body, the vital warmth generated and maintained by the heart. If Galen and Fernel found the origin of bodily process and motion in the soul, a non-material entity controlling the material structure, so too did Aristotle and Harvey, a matter nowhere more clear than in Harvey's work *On Generation*.

Traditional wisdom (to which our French friends are still attached) made the liver the principal functional organ of the whole body, for it was in the liver that the ingested food was made into blood. Blood was the material out of which all the structure – bones, flesh, nerves – was formed: therefore blood moved outwards from the central liver to all these parts. Attraction towards the part, assimilation by it, onward transmission beyond it, were the three prime faculties of Galenic physiology, effected in the veins (according even to Vesalius) by three different sets of fibres. In comparison with this primary nutritive function the role of respiration or that of the heart-beat was minor and obscure. By the sixteenth century physicians like Fernel commonly spoke of three 'coctions' or processes of qualitative change by heat; by the first, the food received by the stomach was turned into chyle, transported through the veins of the intestine to the liver. The second coction was the sanguification of this chyle within the liver itself. In the peripheral parts blood was in the third coction made flesh. The coctions were promoted by the animal heat (hence the term) and in the sixteenth century writers had begun to compare the second coction to fermentation, which thus provided the first 'chemical' analogy to any part of the digestive process (Galen had already likened respiration to burning). While the main course of the nutritive blood was radially outwards from the liver, revulsions of the blood inwards might occur (as when an elevated limb is drained and becomes numb or a person faints) and it was well known that matter could move inwards with or through the blood from the periphery of the body. 'Blood-poisoning' could rise up a sufferer's arm from a damaged finger, while the Ghost in Hamlet laments the

> . . . cursed hebenon
> That swift as quicksilver it courses through
> The natural gates and alleys of the body.[6]

Thus there was some traditional concept of a complex motion of blood in the body, even though the main idea of it was as a nutriment soaked up by the outlying parts.

The course of the blood from the liver was through the great central vein

Fig. 6.1 Diagram of the structure of the heart and lungs, illustrating the Galenic physiology.

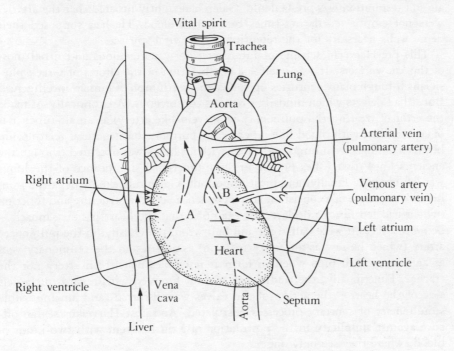

of the body, the *vena cava*, whose upper portion passes close by (but not directly through) the heart; the inferior portion was thought to nourish the legs and lower abdomen. Physicians supposed that by its active dilatation or diastole the heart attracted some small part of the blood into itself through the connecting vein to the *vena cava* (Fig. 6.1). By the same dilatation air was drawn down the vein-like artery into the other or left chamber (ventricle) of the heart. When the heart contracted again in systole the contained blood was squeezed (as Galen had perceived from the construction of the valves) from the right ventricle into the artery-like vein (pulmonary artery) which conveyed nourishment to the lungs, and also squeezed (as Galen thought) through small passages within the septum, or strong interventricular wall, of the heart into the air-filled left ventricle. Also by its systole the left ventricle expelled a fume or vapour of uncertain origin (constituting the expired breath, in fact) back to the lungs. Thirdly, in systole, some blood was forced from the left ventricle into the aorta and so generally into the arterial system of the body. In short, while it was the function of the right ventricle of the heart to supply nourishing blood to the lungs, and introduce some also into the arterial system, the distinct function of the left ventricle was to enable this arterial blood to be enriched by a *pneuma*, or 'vital spirit' as it was sometimes called, necessary to life and derived from the atmosphere. Thus, anatomically, the close connection between heart and lungs was perceived and, physiologically, interpreted as a relation between air and arterial blood. Further, the fact that asphyxiation causes swift death was accounted for, as well as (more vaguely) the modified or tainted character of the expired breath. This association of the arteries with air and respiration was pre-Galenic; Galen had rightly insisted that the arteries were not empty ventilating-tubes but full of blood. He had supposed their dense walls necessary for the retention of the 'vital spirit'.

This pre-Harveian scheme of interpretation was ingenious and fitted most of the known facts. It was itself – a combination of the efforts of Greek physicians through many centuries up to Galen – a triumph of human intelligence. But it had defects which hindsight renders conspicuous. Anatomically, it made the error of treating the pulmonary vein (vein-like artery) as an air-tube: it is of course filled with blood like other veins. Further, the structural relationship between animals with lungs and those without lungs was obscured (though the ancients knew that fishes breath air); the functional significance of the lungs was left obscure. Finally, and most important, Galen mistakenly departed from his own principle of a consistent correspondence between structure and function (which had led him to declare, for example, that the heart is not a muscle – being in this as it were half-right and half-wrong) in classifying the pulmonary artery (which he saw as an artery in form) as a vein and the pulmonary vein as an artery or air-pipe when in form it resembles neither an artery nor the trachea. Functionally, the traditional account fumbled with regard to the left side of the heart – the action of the valves was distorted, and an impossible simultaneity of contrary processes postulated. And post-Harveians see an offence against simplicity in the postulation of a dual system with two kinds of blood, where they see only one.

Post-Harveians also know that the pulse of the arteries is effected by the impulse of blood arising from the contraction of the left ventricle of the heart. The traditional account – wherein Galen had relied upon a single misleading experiment – supposed the arteries to expand and contract independently, though in sympathy with the heart. Fernel had argued that if the swelling of the arteries was produced by the outflow of blood from the heart the pulse would not be simultaneous along the length of the arteries, as it is found to be – a shrewd contention, but again hydraulically mistaken (so far as time-intervals that he could measure are concerned). Fernel added that the active contraction of the arteries helped to squeeze out vital spirit (through those thick walls!) into the surrounding flesh.

The theory first perfected by Galen – but not always taught in precisely his way – was universally adopted by subsequent medical authorities, and became familiar to the Latin West from the writings of Avicenna and Averroes long before the original Greek texts were available or thoroughly understood. Therapeutic directions drawn from the theory varied, but the basic facts were common to all. The two chief physiological statements of the theory: (1) that venous blood nourishes the parts; and (2) that arterial blood supplies the parts with vital spirits, were of course beyond the experimental enquiry of the sixteenth century. The anatomists were, however, able to check upon the agreement between the Galenic conception of the blood's motion and the observed structure of the venous and arterial systems, and of the heart itself. The operation of the valves in the heart offered no problem: their opening and closing was perfectly accounted for. But the density of the septum imposed an act of faith upon Galenic theorists. Berengario da Carpi credulously described the pores or pits in it through which blood passed from right to left ventricle, but Vesalius, probing the pits of the septum, was unable to find a passage, and in the first edition of *De Fabrica* he wrote: 'none of these pits penetrate (at least according to sense) from the right ventricle to the left; therefore indeed I was compelled to marvel at the activity of the Creator of things, in that the blood should sweat from the right ventricle to the left through passages escaping the sight'. In the second edition he expressed his failure to discover Galen's pores even more firmly, and remarked that he doubted somewhat the heart's action in this respect. At least one experiment on the heart is recorded by Vesalius, in which the heart-beat of a dog was restored after opening the thorax by artificially inflating the lungs. Some anatomists, however, still maintained that the passages were easy to find in very young hearts, though concealed in the adult body. Meanwhile, the structures in the veins, later known as valves, had already been observed by Estienne, and from about 1545 were studied by a number of anatomists, such as Amatus Lusitanus (1511–68) who dissected twelve bodies of men and animals at Ferrara in 1547 from which he derived a wholly false theory of their action.

One major modification to the Galenic account was well understood when Harvey was a student at Padua which, strangely enough, had been first recorded (but probably quite unknown to the Renaissance anatomists) by a thirteenth-century Syrian physician, Ibn al-Nafis al-Qurashi who like Vesalius had asserted the impenetrability of the cardiac septum:

It neither contains a visible passage, as some have thought, nor contains an invisible passage which would permit the passage of blood, as Galen thought.

He therefore proposed, in accordance with strong suggestions from the Galenic texts themselves and just as the Renaissance anatomists were to do, the exclusive transmission of *some* blood to the lungs by the pulmonary artery from the right side of the heart, through the lungs, and so back to the left ventricle by the pulmonary vein. The sole object of this revision was to obviate the unlikely passage of blood through the septum; air was still supposed to reach the heart and fumes leave it so that the triple function of the pulmonary vein was impossibly confused.

In Europe an account of this 'lesser circulation' of the blood was first printed by the Spaniard Michael Servetus (? 1511–53) in a work expounding his Unitarian views of the Deity, *Christianismi Restitutio* (1553); for this book he was burned to death by Calvin at Geneva.[7] Servetus' main interest was his purified Christianity and though he practised medicine for many years after study at the University of Paris, he never qualified academically. In Paris his skill in anatomy had (like that of Vesalius, his near-contemporary there) won particular praise. The lesser circulation is introduced into his last and fatal book in an account of the way in which the Holy Spirit enters the human body. Servetus tells us that the natural spirit originates in the liver and is carried by the venous blood, while the vital spirit has its seat in the heart and is diffused by the arteries. Thirdly, the soul-spirit, 'a ray of light, as it were', is found in the brain and nerves. 'In all these resides the energy of the one spirit and of the light of God.' Then Servetus details the origin of the vital spirit from the left ventricle of the heart, though it is rather actually formed in the lungs 'from a mixture of inspired air with elaborated, subtle blood which the right ventricle of the heart communicates to the left'. This communication is established not as commonly supposed through the septum between the ventricles, but through the pulmonary vessels and the lungs. The function of the lungs is to 'elaborate' the blood while the mixture with air takes place in the pulmonary vein. Servetus postulates channels connecting artery and vein in the lung itself and argues that the artery is far too large for the supply of the lung alone. His physiological conceptions are clearly not very different from those of Galen; he still imagines air as well as blood present in the pulmonary vein, and the generation of vital spirit is placed, as by Galen, in the left ventricle. A careful reader notes that Galen did not exclude the possibility that some blood might reach the left side of the heart by this route on which Servetus insists: such at least was Harvey's understanding when he wrote:

From Galen, that great man, that father of physicians, it appears that the blood passes through the lungs from the pulmonary artery into the minute branches of the pulmonary veins, urged to this both by the pulses of the heart and the motions of the lung and thorax.[8]

To a modern reader the most striking point in Servetus' brief account is his insistence upon the elaborative, qualitative change in the blood effected by its passage through the lungs, which indeed explains the necessity for that passage. Harvey provided no such explanation; the future treatise of his own *On Respiration*, referred to once in *On the Motion of the Heart*, has not survived. As though arguing directly against Servetus (whom surely he had never read) Harvey was to argue in his *Second Disquisition against Riolan* (1649) that the differences between arterial and venous blood are inconsiderable and that hypothetical analyses of the fluid in the vessels into 'blood' and 'spirits' of various sorts were simply imaginary; again and again he repeats that 'arterial blood differs in nothing essential from venous blood'; if it is more florid to the eye – that in the lungs most of all – 'we know how it is strained through the pulmonary tissue'.[9] And the reason for these assertions is plain: Harvey believed that the purpose of the circulation was to return the exhausted blood to the heart whence, revivified and warmed, it returned to the body. The lungs, for Harvey, are an adjunct to the heart, not vice versa.

In any case, for Servetus as for Galen only a part of the blood in the veins passes through the heart and lungs to the arteries. To this extent his conception of the pulmonary transit (as it should be called, rather than 'lesser circulation') only partially extends to the truth, and the same may be said of all other presentations of this idea before Harvey's. In spite of the almost complete destruction of *Christianismi Restitutio*, there is some record of its being read. It has been argued that the treatment of the lesser circulation by another Catalan physician, Juan Valverde, in 1556, is imitated directly from that of Servetus, since he stated, like Servetus, that the pulmonary vein contains both blood and air (later, in 1560, he wrote that it contained a copious quantity of blood). Valverde had studied under Realdo Colombo from about 1545 at Pisa and Rome; remarking that he had frequently observed the anatomical appearances with Colombo, he seems to claim no originality for himself. Colombo in turn had been a pupil of Vesalius, succeeding him for a short space in the teaching of anatomy at Padua, and it is possible that the genesis of the idea of the lesser circulation took place there, and so was made known to Valverde. Colombo certainly claimed the new idea as his own, and hitherto unknown, in a treatise published posthumously in 1559, which may well have been written before Valverde's printed in 1556. Colombo's reasoning on the circulation is superior to any that had preceded it. He made the plain statement that the blood passed from the right ventricle through the pulmonary artery to the lung; was there attenuated; and then together with air was brought through the pulmonary vein to the left ventricle. He relied particularly upon the observation that when the pulmonary vein is opened it is found to be full of bright arterial blood.

From this time the circuit through the lungs from the right side of the heart to the left was described by a number of anatomists, down to the time of William Harvey. It is important to recognize that though the physicians who invoked it are correctly spoken of as being his precursors, in the sense that the passage of blood through the lungs was to be an essential element in the whole circulation, the anatomical recognition of this fact did not confer a partial glimpse of the whole truth of the circulation. Anatomically, the pulmonary route simply bypassed the septum; it changed nothing else. From one point of view Servetus' talk of a qualitative change in the blood taking place in the heart and lungs was itself seriously misleading, since it impeded apprehension of the idea that there is but one volume of blood in the body, moving rapidly from veins to arteries, from arteries back to veins. None of Harvey's predecessors considered the problem from which (as he relates in Ch. VIII) Harvey began: 'what might be the quantity of blood which was transmitted, in how short a time its passage might be effected, and the like . . .' They were, on the other hand, still much bemused with the problem about spirits which he set firmly to one side: they still left the operations of the pulmonary vein, the left ventricle of the heart and the whole arterial system extremely obscure, all of which Harvey was to clear up once and for all at what one might call the 'hydraulic' or 'fluid flow' level. In fact, the earlier anatomists were attempting to solve a different problem from that of Harvey. They were concerned only to find the route by which blood and vital spirits entered the arteries in view of the impenetrability of the septum. Harvey's problem was twofold: firstly, to account for the function of the valves in the veins (which, as was realized before his time, obstructed the flow of blood outwards along the veins), and secondly, to dispose of the large quantity of blood which he knew must enter the heart. The novelty of his approach was that it ignored the question of vital spirits altogether, concentrating upon a wholly mechanical, and partly quantitative, difficulty latent in the accepted doctrine. This difficulty had occurred to no one before, because no one had doubted that the contents of the veins and arteries respectively were absorbed by the parts which attracted them outwards from the central reservoirs, the liver and the heart. The early theory of the lesser circulation was, therefore, useful to Harvey in that, at the proper stage in the development of his own ideas, the transfer of blood from the right side to the left side of the heart could be fitted in as a partially complete portion of the puzzle; but that theory in itself was a cul-de-sac so long as it was no more than a variation on Galen's.

Of the writers on the cardiovascular system between Servetus and Harvey he who most nearly attained the concept of the systemic circulation was Andrea Cesalpino (1519-1603), who departed from Pisa, where he had been professor of medicine and director of the botanic garden, in the same year as Galileo (1592). Unlike Galileo but like Harvey Cesalpino was a fervent admirer of Aristotle, and in his tradition made the heart the central organ of the body. His *Two Books of Medical Questions* (1593) indicate an understanding that the valves in the veins predicate an inward flow of the venous blood, without a consequential remodelling of Galenic theory. 'In other words', writes Walter Pagel, 'Cesalpinus stopped short of following up a line that should have led him to anticipate Harvey's discovery'.[10] True, he envisages a *circulation* of the blood, but this to him was a quasi-alchemical term indicating the elaboration of blood in the lungs, as in the reflux vessel called a 'pelican'.

William Harvey (1578-1657) began his medical studies at Padua in 1597, the year of his graduation from Cambridge. He remained there until 1602: 'he was very choleric', Aubrey relates, 'and in his young days wore a dagger (as the fashion then was) but this Doctor would be apt to draw out his dagger upon every slight occasion'. His teacher was Fabricius, and as 'the first that was curious in Anatomy in England' he could hardly have had a better: Harvey's discovery sprang obviously and directly from the Italian school, to whose members he often alludes. Whether Harvey's admiration for Aristotle's biological philosophy was acquired in England or in Italy it is impossible to be certain, but Pagel attributes it to his Paduan experience: 'far from this indicating intellectual backwardness on Harvey's part', Pagel continues, referring to the distinguished study of epistemology at Padua during the sixteenth century, Harvey's allegiance 'shows how open he was to the Aristotelian scientific modernism of a continental school' – a modernism that embraced the technical methods of comparative-anatomical dissection as well as scientific methodology.[11] While Harvey's admiration for the ancient master is most explicit in his later book *On Generation* (1651) it is obvious also in the final chapter of *On the Motion of the Heart*, where Aristotle is indeed named several times and Harvey revels in a rich variety of comparisons of cardiovascular arrangement among different kind of animals, following his own precept that they plainly do amiss who, while pretending to speak of animal morphology generally, confine their researches to the human cadaver. 'Thus nature', he concludes in what might have been Aristotle's own words, 'ever perfect and divine, doing nothing in vain, has neither given a heart where it was not required, nor produced it before its office had become necessary'. Of this reversion, as it were, from Galenic physiology to that of the earlier master Harvey, 'steeped in Aristotle' (writes

Pagel) 'deeply rooted in his personality', was fully conscious, and never more so than in the closing paragraphs of his great work, where he declares:

Nor are we the less to agree with Aristotle in regard to the sovereignty of the heart, nor are we to enquire whether it receives sense and motion from the brain? Whether blood from the liver? Whether it be the origin of the veins and the blood? and more of the same description. They who affirm these propositions against Aristotle overlook or do not rightly understand the principal arguments, to the effect that the heart is the first part which exists, and that it contains within itself, blood, life, sensation, motion, before either the brain or the liver were in being or had appeared distinctly or, at all events, before they could perform any function.

The heart, Harvey goes on, a kind of internal creature, is anterior to the body it serves; as the Sun for Copernicus, it is 'like the prince in a Kingdom', just as the Sun 'might well be designated the heart of the world.'[12]

As Archimedes for Galileo, so a non-Galilean Aristotle, a Renaissance Aristotle almost unsuspected by the Middle Ages, for William Harvey. Viewed against this background (to quote Walter Pagel yet again) Harvey was 'not a modern'. Old Aubrey said as much: instructed personally by the great physician 'what company to keep, what books to read, how to manage my studies, in short, he bid me go to the fountain-head and read Aristotle, Cicero, Avicenna and did call the Neoterics shit-breeches'. And though he refers to the cardiac valves as 'clacks in a bellows', Harvey was far from treating the blood simply as a fluid, the heart as a pump: rather he conceived of both as endowed with vitality, the blood regaining in the heart its 'fluidity, natural heat and [becoming] powerful, fervid, a kind of treasury of life, and impregnated with spirits, it might be said with balsam'. As cold precedes death while warmth belongs to life, he saw the heart as 'the cherisher of nature, the original of the native fire' whence new blood, imbued with spirits, was sent through the arteries to bring warmth to the whole body (Chs VIII and XV *On the Motion of the Heart and Blood in Animals*).

Nevertheless, Harvey *was* a modern, and never more so than in the experimental and mechanical aspects of his investigation of the heart, where to modern eyes (at any rate) his theory of the circulation seems most fully developed and most perfectly demonstrated. When describing the 'harmony or rhythm' of the near-simultaneous contraction of auricle and ventricle, where but one motion is apparent, he explains

Nor is this for any other reason than it is in a piece of machinery in which, though one wheel gives motion to another yet all the wheels seem to move simultaneously . . . So also in swallowing: by the elevation of the root of the tongue, and the compression of the mouth, the food or drink is pushed into the fauces . . . Yet are all these motions, though executed by different and distinct organs, performed harmoniously and in such order that they seem to constitute but a single motion and act . . .[13]

To say that Harvey compares such swift, concentrated and involuntary bodily movements to the linked, automatic operation of the parts of a machine *except* in the sense that both trains of events can be consecutive although to the eye simultaneous would be going too far, yet how pregnant is the comparison.

Again, Harvey does not say that the cardiovascular system is no more than a complex of pumps and pipes — on the contrary, he makes it clear how much more it is — but a large part of his argument depends on the validity of hydraulic analysis: in fact, it silently invokes the principle of hydraulic continuity that the rate of flow through all successive parts of the system must be constant. Harvey does argue *as if* the heart is a mechanical pump, the valves clacks, the veins and arteries pipes, the blood an ordinary fluid and so forth, though again we may well believe that this 'as if' belongs rather to the stage of demonstration than that of primary discovery. Even so, Boyle's story of the valves, Aristotelian as it is in showing us Harvey's confidence that 'so provident a cause as Nature had not pleased so many valves without design' also shows how primary was Harvey's concern with the nature and direction of the fluid flow, and Harvey himself records that the volume of flow presented itself as a primary problem. At a later stage, perhaps nothing in all seventeenth-century science strikes as more obviously modern, more paradigmatic of the scientific approach, than Harvey's in-principle computation of the rate of flow of blood through the heart 'assumed merely as a ground for reasoning' from which he concludes that in one half hour the quantity passing through the heart must at the very least exceed that contained in the whole body (Ch. IX). It is difficult to think of Aristotle, that staunch enemy of the mechanistic and quantitative in biology, making such an evaluation; Galen would have understood it, but set it aside on the ground that the attribution of such massive, swift flow in the blood was absurd. Here again a (modern) hydraulic analogy suggests itself: the ancients saw the rapid exsanguination of the body from a severed artery as the emptying of a tank, while Harvey saw the living, spurting blood as pumped out by the heart. The idea of the possibility of fluid *motion* (the first word of Harvey's title) must logically precede any other notion of circulation and its purpose, and to this extent at least we may say that Harvey started with a prejudice in favour of kinematics rather than statics.

Of the genesis and inception of Harvey's discovery, of the course of his human dissection and vivisection of animals, whether the investigation presumably begun in Padua was continued in London in the midst of a busy and successful professional life we do not know. The well-known allusion to the circulation written in his manuscript *Lectures* dated 1616 is now regarded as an addition of some later date (Harvey's book notes the presentation of his views in such public lectures). However strongly metaphysical was Harvey's own predisposition in favour of the solution he ultimately propounded, his statement of the case for it is strongly positivist. Consider the facts, he keeps telling his reader, reciting them in great detail. If the purely anatomical evidence contained little that was really new, nevertheless he made every point tell, as with the study of the action of the vascular valves, and of the correspondence of cardiac diastole with arterial systole. A mass of formerly discordant observation was made consistent on the single hypothesis of the circulation of the blood, as is most clearly seen in his remarks on the foetal circulation. The existence of an intercommunication between the pulmonary artery and veins in the mammalian foetus that disappears after birth was familiar to all anatomists, but no one before Harvey had correlated this short-circuiting of the lungs with either the supposed sweating of blood through the septum, or its passage through the lungs. It was left to Harvey to show that the foetal circulation avoids the lungs because they are collapsed and inactive. He is most original and striking when he uses the comparative method: 'Had anatomists only been as conversant with the dissection of the lower animals as they were with that of the human body, the matters that have hitherto kept them in a perplexity of doubt would, in my opinion, have met them freed from every kind of difficulty.'[14]

His admonition was accepted by a host of biologists in the later seventeenth century, including Marcello Malpighi who first observed the blood passing from the arteries to the veins through the capillary vessels in the lungs of a frog – the final link that clinched Harvey's motion in a circle. Harvey found that the action of the heart could be most easily studied through experiments on small animals or fishes, as for instance by observing the effect of tying ligatures about the great vessels, in suffusing or draining the chambers of the heart. He correlated the single-chambered heart correctly with the absence of lungs, and the double-chambered heart with the possession of lungs, pointing out that the right ventricle, which only sends the blood through the lungs, is slightly weaker than the left which sends it round the whole body. By experiment Harvey proved that the heart receives and expels during each cycle of expansion and contraction a significant quantity of blood, not a few drops only; by calculation he proved (as we have seen) that the whole volume of blood must circle round the body at least fifty times a day. In his second group of experiments, Harvey further demonstrated that the blood moves away from the heart through the arteries, and towards the heart through the veins. These experiments mainly relate to the human subject, and are such as would naturally suggest themselves to a physician practised in phlebotomy. Examining the superficial veins of the arm, he showed that the limb is swollen with blood when the veins are compressed, and emptied of blood when the arterial flow is obstructed. He found that the valves in these veins prevented the flow of blood away from the heart, and that by arterial manipulation it was impossible to force blood through them except in the contrary direction. Blood always filled an emptied vein from the direction of the extremity. Again, he showed that in the jugular vein the valves were so constructed as to permit a unidirectional flow towards the heart only, and that therefore their function was not (as some thought) to prevent the weight of blood falling down to the feet. The experience of wounds and venesection was cited by Harvey to the same general effect, and he further alleged the experience of physicians as proof that the blood was the mechanical agent by which poisons or the active principles of drugs are rapidly distributed about the whole body.

As Galileo remarked in another context, once a discovery such as that of the circulation of the blood has been made and accepted its demonstration seems obvious; the difficulty is to hit upon it in the first place. It is certainly more easy for a modern reader to follow the experimental and anatomical reasoning whereby Harvey enforces the principle of the circulation – all that was missing to him being the sight of blood-cells moving through the capillaries, first described by Malpighi in 1661 – than to understand the philosophical and medical context from which his discovery of it emerged, to perceive the subtle interplay of the factors within Harvey's early thought and experience which may have both favoured and impeded his making it, especially because we can only reconstruct that interplay from the *post-factum* account written by Harvey when all was clinched. One measure of the difference between the outlook of even the mature Harvey and ourselves is the comparatively little attention given by Harvey to the function of the double circulation, which seems to us to cry out for comment: How could he be content to leave this aspect of the matter where the Greeks left it? More than once Harvey laments that anatomists had been historically misled by the close association of heart and lungs, and he is right; yet fails to perceive the inadequacy of the Greek idea of 'refrigeration' of the blood (here Servetus seems more prescient). If such points in Harvey's investigation puzzle us, it is because we cannot understand with his pre-chemical mind, or distinguish correctly those expressions in Galen's *Use of the Parts* which Harvey would have found sensible from those he judged absurd. Another measure of the difficulty of understanding the medical science of Harvey's day is our problem in appreciating the objections against a doctrine that seems so obvious a summation of the anatomical history of the two preceding generations. His discovery, sought presumably through a number of years of patient research, then greeted with scorn and incredulity, was in debate for at least twenty years. Some critics, as he said, opposed him because they preferred to endanger truth rather than ancient belief. Others thought that they had discovered technical anatomical arguments against the circulation; or that only a portion of the blood circulated; or that venous and arterial blood could not be the same fluid. Even the basic anatomy of blood-supply to the chief organs of the body (especially the liver) was still doubtful, and its physiological interpretation barely begun; the capillary circulation, and the change in colour of blood, were to remain mysteries long after Harvey's death. His originality was that he preferred to face these new problems, rather than tolerate longer the inconsistencies of the old system, but in this he was followed by few contemporaries. As so often in science, one advance was made not by completely solving an old problem so that no question remained, but by transposing the problem into an answerable form, creating fresh problems by the very act of transposition. Harvey asked a question which, in his precise terms, had perplexed none of his predecessors, and the answer that he worked out was important, not only because it was correct, or because it challenged prevailing ideas, or even perhaps because it introduced a new kind of scientific enquiry. Harvey's influence in this last respect was significant (as much in his book on generation as in *On the Motion of the Heart*) but it was not wholly unheralded, and some of the new methods exploited by later seventeenth-century physiologists, such as 'biochemical' research and microscopy, were altogether unknown to him. Perhaps the most important of his achievements was to leave unsolved problems – not blind, impregnable problems, but questions that could be answered in the way he had himself declared. Just as seventeenth-century mechanics was based upon the unsolved (or imperfectly solved) problems left by Galileo, so the experimental problems of biology were inherited from Harvey.

While Harvey's biological philosophy was of the Renaissance, Aristotelian, creating the future from a richer evaluation of the past, once his physiological discovery was propounded it could be set into a very different intellectual context. Some signs there are in his writings of impatience with the teleological functionalism of Aristotle and Galen ('the means exist because the end is good') yet this was not a general reaction and in his book *On Generation*, for example, he insists that conception can occur without a material agent. One could view his Aristotelian position there as being positivistic – he could find no material agent – and certainly his onslaught on the protean doctrine of 'spirits' in the *Second Disquisition to Riolan* (1649) seems to bear something of that character: 'Persons of limited information', he writes austerely, 'when they are at a loss to assign a cause for anything, very commonly reply that it is done by the spirits; and so they introduce spirits upon all occasions'. As Harvey argues at some length, in a passage that again speaks straight to the modern reader, the doctrine of spirits even when it is more than 'common subterfuge of ignorance' embraces a multiplicity of things from the spirits of wine (alcohol) to the spirit of fortitude; what is 'spirit' he asks but an unseen, unknown cause of actions? If there is an active spirit in the blood, Harvey argues, with an intent that is as much anti-Greek as anti-alchemical, it is an essential component of the complete blood: he comes near to saying (but does not say) that 'blood plus spirit' is just a needless and useless duplication of 'blood' alone.[15] René Descartes (1596–1650) did not similarly hesitate, eschewing altogether such a dubious concept. He himself made some study of anatomy, especially of the eye, and wrote a treatise *On Man*; though not, in the *Discourse On Method* (1637), the first open supporter of Harvey's discovery, he was the first to take it out of a narrow professional context and demonstrate its perfect coherence with a totally new idea of nature: the mechanical philosophy. Indeed, Descartes obviously supposed – to the vast irritation of all medical historians since! – that he understood the true essence of Harvey's discovery much better than Harvey himself did.[16]

For two thousand years, in reply to the question: what makes the body internally active, able to respond, to move, to speak and so on? the answer had been 'the spirits', with endless elaboration of the basic three (natural, vital, and animal or as we would say psychic). Descartes abolished the lot: the principle of movement lay in motion, of which an enduring, unchanging quantity resided in the universe. Some of this constancy of motion which Descartes found in the universe is of course apparent in the perpetual circulation of large bodies like the planets, but for the most part it was to be found in the invisible motions of the smallest particles of matter (see further pp. 198–207). Of such particles, large and small, at rest or in motion, the animal and human body was also made and as such behaved as one complex in the great natural scheme. If the animal body, or the human body lacking its rational soul, were supposed purely material in its composition but properly ordered in its structure so as

165

to form, as it were, a machine, then it could perform all the functions of which animals or men are capable save that of thinking and consciousness of its own sensations. So the animal heat of the heart could arise, like the natural heat of fermentation, from the invisible motions of particles. Descartes indeed described the heart as an automatic pump worked by its own heat (anticipating by some hundreds of years the Humphrey pump of modern times!): on contraction, a little blood would be drawn into each ventricle, which being suddenly vaporized in the hot chamber would cause the whole heart to expand and close the inlet valves. This expansion of the blood would also open the outlet valves so that the blood would pass out into the lungs and arteries, where it would again condense to liquid and the cycle would be repeated. The heat of the heart, about which Harvey had written, thus accounted for its purely mechanical cycle of expansion and contraction. In his speculations about the heart (which show Descartes being by no means scrupulous to reproduce Harvey's careful analysis exactly, nor hesitant in imagination) Descartes went far beyond Harvey in assigning functions to the organ. It supplied heat to the stomach to concoct food; it completed the concoction by distilling the blood in the heart 'one or two hundred times in the day' (according to Descartes, the lungs were the condenser in which the blood was restored to the liquid state); it forced by compression of the blood 'certain of its parts' to pass through pores specially designed like sieves to admit them into the various parts of the body where they formed humours; and it was the hearth where burned a very pure and vivid flame which, ascending to the brain, penetrated through the nerves (imagined as hollow tubes) to activate the muscles. In *On Man* Descartes developed the theory that the flow of the spirits was controlled in the brain by the pineal gland, a sort of valve acting under the direction of conscious volition. According to Descartes's study of the physiology of behaviour, volition played a minor part even in man, who was alone capable of abstract thought and true sensation (that is, sensations capable of objective judgement), and none in the activity of any lesser creature. He devoted much attention to the study of motor mechanisms and reflex actions – as for instance tracing the involuntary mechanisms by which, when the hand is burnt, the muscles of the arm contract to withdraw it from the fire, the facial muscles contract in a grimace of pain, tears flow, and a cry is uttered. He regarded the greater part of bodily activity as due to mechanical processes of this kind, as automatic responses to external stimuli effected by the nervous system; but, though Cartesian physiology was to some extent supported by anatomical investigation of the relations of nerve, brain and muscle, it was in the main a purely conceptual structure. Descartes anticipated some of the conclusions of nineteenth-century physiology without its careful experimental foundation.

Harvey's work was an important step towards a mechanistic approach to biological problems, containing a tentative challenge to the supremacy of spirits founded on a particular experimental investigation. Descartes's more comprehensive and more speculative writings elevated mechanism to a universal truth, in physics and biology alike. Soul and material body could have nothing in common save a single mysterious point of contact; nothing could be attributed to the soul but thought. The old physiology postulated a variety of non-material souls or spirits each charged with the management of a set of bodily functions; for Descartes those functions were the result of mechanistic processes, as much as the different appearances and movements of an elaborate mechanical clock. This, he said in the *Discourse on Method*, would not appear strange to those aquainted with

the variety of movements performed by the different automata, or moving machines fabricated by human industry, and that with the help of but few pieces compared with the great variety of bones, muscles, nerves, arteries, veins, and other parts that one finds in the body of each animal. Such persons will look upon this body as a machine made by the hands of God, which is incomparably better arranged, and adequate to movements more admirable than is any machine of human invention.

The body was not maintained alive and active by one or more life-forces, or spirits, or souls, but solely by the interrelations of its mechanical parts, and death was due to a failure of these parts. Therefore, with no non-material factors involved, everything in physiology was potentially within the range of human knowledge, since no more was required than the investigation of mechanistic processes, complex and elaborate indeed. This conception of Descartes's was of course premature, far beyond the scope of the scientific equipment of his age, and it led to no immediate physiological discovery. Except perhaps in his work on the eye, the factual content of his biological theory was wholly mis-leading. But the influence of his general conception upon the anatomy and physiology of the later seventeenth century was profound.

Inevitably, direct attempts to apply Cartesian principles to physiology, though full of interest, produced naive results. *On the Motion of Animals* (1680–81) by Giovanni Alfonso Borelli (1608–79), a mathematician and astronomer of note, was the most elaborate essay coupling geometry and phys-iology in a way indicated by Galileo and Gassendi as well as Descartes. He attempted to compute the mechanical pull exerted by muscles, to analyse their action in leverage, and to explain the complex actions involved in running, walking, flying and swimming (Harvey too had gone into this in studies pub-lished only recently, following Aristotle long ago). He made some attempts to look at the heart and vascular system as a single hydraulic system, calculating speeds of flow on the vessels and so on, in a way which doctors only took up again in the nineteenth century. He thought that the inspired air played a purely mechanical part in the body: air-particles, compressed in the arterial blood, vibrated and so like a pendulum in a clock controlled the periodic functions of the body.

the automaton (clock) has a certain shadowy resemblance to animals, in so far as both are self-moving organic bodies which employ the laws of mechanics and are moved by natural powers.[17]

However, Cartesian mechanism and the 'iatrophysics' and 'iatromechanics' descended from it form only one theme in seventeenth-century biological think-ing, other currents of thought like the Aristotelian tradition of which Harvey was a member favoured vitalism and an ultimate scepticism about reducing living phenomena to physical and chemical explanations. Reactions against the too-easy hypotheses of Cartesian science and the intractability of living nature itself ultimately favoured the vitalistic philosophy of nature for a long period (roughly, 1730–1840) until, in turn, fresh knowledge, new ideas and the promising evolution of chemistry prompted once again a more hopeful return to reductionism, now far removed from the old Cartesian pattern. Yet for all its faults and absurdities Descartes's philosophical justification of experimental enquiry in biology was of permanent value; transformed by Newton's influence it was the original inspiration behind such major experimental investigations as those of Stephen Hales (*Vegetable Staticks*, 1727). Descartes created the notion of the biological 'model'. We cannot experiment on the living animal heart without disturbing or destroying it; we can experiment on the dead heart as a model for the living one, or even apply purely engineering concepts of pump and hydraulic flow to it (as Harvey himself had begun to do). Experiments on organisms of a quantitative kind from which the concepts of 'life' or 'vital force' were excluded were not valueless, nor were the analogies between inorganic and organic which the 'model' approach made possible. On Cartesian principles it was to be supposed that what was true of an organ or a tissue in the laboratory would also be true in the whole living body, and that particular results obtainable from certain experimental processes when observed in the living specimen must be produced by similar processes in its own organization. The basic axiom of experimental science is that, circumstances being unchanged, a like cause will produce a like result because the 'cause' releases a chain of events following an unchanging pattern. If this is not so, then the experimental method of enquiry is not one that can usefully be applied to the problem. It was Descartes's discovery (ratiocinative, not empirical) that this was true of physiological phenomena; it could be assumed, prima facie, that circumstances were unchanged (e.g. between the living body and the chemist's vessel), and that since functions were automative, like result followed like cause.

Thus the same message, that the living organism is not beyond analysis, came from two natural philosophers as disparate as William Harvey and René Descartes. Descartes's scientific writings, even more than Harvey's, suggested a host of enquiries into physiological processes. We can detect his influence in the development of comparative anatomy (especially in France and Holland) and still more in the development of neuromuscular studies by Borelli, Thomas Willis, Sylvius, Nils Steno and others. Even more effective was the experimental study of respiration, producing a theoretical elaboration of the old analogy with combustion. From the members of the Accademia del Cimento (1657–67) in Florence through Robert Boyle into the eighteenth century a series of investigators examined the effect on small animals of enclosing them in confined volumes of air, in 'elastic fluids' (gases) or in a partial vacuum. It was observed that in the vacuum both combustion and respiration were impossible and death came quickly, and also that some air-like 'fluids' were just as noxious. The English physician John Mayow (1641–79) insisted that only a *part* of the air was essential to life or combustion, being used up when an animal or flame was placed in a closed vessel over water; for the water-level rose up in the vessel, and the residual air was inert and useless. Amalgamating various earlier ideas, Mayow argued that a 'nitro-aerial' spirit in the atmosphere was essential to life and burning. (Among the evidence, a persistent story told that when the Dutch inventor Cornelius Drebbel navigated his submarine deep in the waters of the Thames before the astonished eyes of James I and his courtiers, he had revivified the confined air with nitre.) More mechanically, Robert Hooke showed (1667) that a dog could be kept alive by blowing air into its lungs with a bellows even with the ribs and diaphragm removed, from which experiment (which he refused ever to repeat) he concluded that the animal 'was ready to die, if either he was left unsupplied, or his lungs only kept full with the same air; and thence conceived, that the true use of respiration was to discharge the fumes of the blood'. Other members of the Royal Society satisfied themselves by experiment that 'the foetus in the womb has its blood ventilated by the help of the dam'; and that the foetal circulation depended directly on the maternal.

For a time, as Hooke's words suggest, there was doubt whether the presence of fresh air in the lungs was necessary to remove something from the blood (the 'sooty impurities' of Galen's physiology) or to add something to it. On this point the investigations of Richard Lower (1631–91), a physician and an experimental as well as a theoretical physiologist, threw new light. In his *Treatise on the Heart* (1669), the most distinguished successor to Harvey's masterpiece that the seventeenth century produced, Lower defended and extended the original pre-Cartesian form of the theory: the heart was not caused to beat by a fermentation of the blood, but by the inflow of spirits from the nerves, and if the nerves were severed the pulsation stopped. The blood, not the heart, was the source of heat, and of the activity and life of bodies – in this Lower, more clearly than either Descartes or Harvey, seems to see the heart as nothing but a mechanical pump. Nor has the heart anything to do with the change in colour of arterial blood, for this can be produced by forcing blood through the insufflated lungs of a dead dog, or even by shaking venous blood in air:

. . . that this red colour is entirely due to the penetration of particles of air into the blood is quite clear from the fact that, while the blood becomes red throughout its mass in the lungs (because the air diffuses in them through all the particles of blood, and hence becomes more thoroughly mixed with the blood)

venous blood in a vessel only becomes florid on the surface. Lower concluded that the active factor in this transformation of the blood was a certain 'nitrous spirit' (elsewhere called a 'nitrous food-stuff') which was taken up by the blood in the lungs, and discharged from it 'within the body and the parenchyma of the viscera' to pass out through the pores, leaving the impoverished dark venous blood to return to the heart. Respiration, therefore, was a process whose function was to add something to the blood (Lower remarked that since 'bad air' causes disease there must be a communication between the atmosphere and the blood-stream); but the fuller understanding of the nature of this addition had to await the chemical revolution of the eighteenth century.[18]

The new ideas of blood as a 'mechanical' fluid, a vehicle for carrying alimentary substances, constituents of the air, and warmth around the body, suggested the new therapeutic technique of blood transfusion, of which also Lower was a pioneer. The blood had still a semi-magical quality, and as it was thought that 'bad' blood could cause debility, frenzy or chronic disease, it seemed logical to suppose that if the blood of a human patient could be replaced by that of a healthy animal, an improvement must result. An Italian who claimed to be the inventor of the method of transfusion (though he admitted that he had never tried the experiment) even suggested that it would effect a rejuvenation which should be the prerogative of monarchs alone. Christopher Wren (1632–1723), when an Oxford student, made experiments on the injections of fluids into the veins of animals, by which, according to Sprat, they were 'immediately purg'd, vomited, intoxicated, kill'd, or reviv'd according to the quality of the Liquor injected'.[19] Suggestions for transfusions of blood between animals, and actual attempts to effect it, were made by various Fellows of the Royal Society in 1665, and Lower went into the matter thoroughly, successfully reviving a dog which had been exsanguinated almost to the point of death. Finally, in 1667, Lower performed before the Society the experiment of transfusing the blood of a sheep into a certain 'poor and debauched man . . . cracked a little in the head', which the patient luckily survived without any change in his condition. In this Lower had been anticipated by the French physician Jean Denys, whose practice soon after caused the death of a patient, which led to a prohibition of transfusion in France and the abandonment of the English experiments. Several accounts of this time describe the violent reactions produced by the introduction of animal protein into the human blood-stream, which rapidly proves fatal, and doubtless much of the apparent success of these early experiments may be attributed to the clotting of the blood in the tubes used, preventing the passage of more than a small amount. Experiments on transfusion were only resumed in the nineteenth century, when the use of animal blood was abandoned.[20]

While one important aspect of the expanding experimental biology of the seventeenth century was the mechanical and biochemical study of the blood, whose functions figured so largely in the therapeutical theories of the time, in another the essential mystery of 'life' was no less involved, and was more directly explored. This was the investigation of generation and the embryonic development of creatures, including man. Just as interest in the motion and functions of the blood may be traced to its prominent place in the Galenic theory of humours, so these embryological researches return in a continuous tradition to the work of Aristotle. Fabricius of Aquapendente, the first great student of reproduction and embryology in modern times (1604, 1621), had of course largely followed Aristotle as the only authority though he had introduced discoveries and new ideas of his own (for example, he appears to have believed that the blood is formed in the embryo *before* the heart) and on occasion, as in his own treatment of the foetal circulation in mammals, followed Galen. Harvey also, as we have seen, was very much a follower of Aristotle, but in one important matter Harvey contradicted Aristotle altogether (in this partly anticipated by Fabricius) for he was sceptical of 'spontaneous generation', and if he did not coin the phrase *omne vivum ex ovo*, it epitomizes his thought. The partial discredit of spontaneous generation (not complete, for the idea was to be revived in the eighteenth century, when it was refuted experimentally by Spallanzani, and again in the nineteenth century in opposition to Pasteur) was one of the most important changes in biological thought of the time; a first step towards modern conceptions of the living state. Formerly all living things had been divided into four broad classes: (1) those generated sponta-neously fron non-living matter, usually in putrefaction; (2) plants; (3) animals; (4) man. As we have seen, the three latter classes were distinguished according to their 'souls' corresponding to their observed capacities (respectively in higher additive order) for nutrition and reproduction, locomotion and sensation, and rational thought. The spontaneously appearing group, crossing the boundary between non-living and living, to which were assigned insects, worms, para-sites of all kinds and non-flowering plants, the ignorance of later centuries adding even bees, frogs, mice and 'barnacle-geese', was not further classified although the likeness of some to animals and of fungi and seaweeds to plants might have suggested such a division, and all were said by the learned (contrary to the most obvious experience of, say, edible and non-edible fungi) not to maintain their specific continuity. Clearly, the whole doctrine of spontaneous generation sprang from some old and primitive ordering of non-human life, from which even Aristotle (though he endorsed it, and endeavoured to give it philosophical coherence) could not remove the contradictions: for how can a group – so miscellaneous – of creatures be called *living* and yet otherwise denied all the attributes of living things? Why assign a natural history to the bee (as Aristotle does, and studies it scrupulously) and refuse it to the wasp? Even apart from the superstitions and fables later given refuge by the notion of spon-taneous generation, one must judge it one of the most counter-factual and irrational elements in the picture of nature inherited from antiquity.

Harvey, it is true, wrote in *On the Motion of the Heart* that the heart is not found 'as a distinct and separate part in all animals; some, such as the zooph-ytes, have no heart', and he continued, 'I may instance grubs and earthworms, and those that are engendered of putrefaction, and do not preserve their spe-cies'. If this was not merely a careless phrase Harvey changed his opinion, for in his later work *On the Generation of Animals* (1651), he declared:

. . . many animals, especially insects, arise and are propagated from elements and seeds so small as to be invisible (like atoms flying in the air), scattered and dispersed here and there by the winds; and yet these animals are supposed to have arisen sponta-neously, or from decomposition, because their ova are nowhere to be seen.[21]

Before such a statement could be given real force and meaning, the arts of natural observation, of comparative anatomy, and of simple controlled biolog-ical experimentation must be developed to, or beyond, the level which they had reached among the ancient Greeks. Aristotle's biological knowledge was in many respects far superior to anything that was available in the sixteenth century – indeed some of his observations were not to be verified before the nineteenth century. It is astonishing to find, for example, that Aristotle's sensible and penetrating observation of the process of reproduction among bees – which itself was not quite correct – was universally ignored up to modern times, while credence was given to fabulous tales of their generation in the flesh of a dead calf or lion which, besides appearing in the works of many Roman poets and writers on agriculture, were retailed in the sixteenth century and later by naturalists like Aldrovandi, Moufet and Johnson, and by the philosophers Cardan and Gassendi. Even the relatively simple life-cycle of the frog was a mystery, at least to academic naturalists.

Harvey had conjectured that in some cases the invisible 'seed' of creatures was disseminated by the wind. The man who set himself to confute the widespread fallacy of spontaneous generation systematically was Francesco Redi (1626–78), an Italian physician who worked at Florence under the patronage of the Duke of Tuscany and was an important member of the Accademia del Cimento. His observations and experiments were varied and numerous, but the most telling were the most simple. Thus he was able to prove, by the simplest means, that decaying flesh only generated 'worms' when flies were allowed to settle on it; that the larvae turned into pupae (which he called eggs) from which hatched flies of the same kind; and that the adult flies which infested the putrefying material possessed ovaries or ducts containing hundreds of eggs. Generalizing from such results, Redi pronounced that all kinds of plants and animals arise solely from the true seeds of other plants and animals of the same kind, and thus preserve their species. Putrescent matter served only as a nest for the eggs, and to nourish the larvae hatched from them. However, he had to admit that there were some examples of generation which he could not explain. Intestinal worms and other parasites puzzled him, and he failed to discover the cause of the growth of oak-galls on trees, which were traced later by Malpighi. This led Redi to speculate somewhat loosely on possible perversions in the 'life-force' of host organisms which might produce parasitic growths.

Despite their logical and factual incompleteness – for Redi certainly had proved neither that spontaneous generation never occurs in nature nor that it is impossible that it should occur – Redi's demonstrations were generally regarded as compelling. They fitted the more exact, more ontologically rigid spirit of the age, and were supported by the careful studies of other naturalists such as Malpighi and Swammerdam. That the products of death and decay might spontaneously yield life, however acceptable in other philosophies, was not a plausible notion for either a Christian or a Cartesian to accept: if God had populated the world with living things his creation could not have been indeterminate and confused, nor (if life were simply a highly organized form of motion) could this organization appear without cause or antecedent. The whole tendency of seventeenth-century thought about the living state was to distinguish it inviolably from the non-living; in fact, to confine life to the unchanging lines of specific descent. Every new discovery – the mammalian eggs of De Graaf or the spermatozoa of Leeuwenhoek – only served to emphasize the scrupulous and universal mechanisms by which these lines of descent were established and safeguarded. Since, to a Christian, the origin of life by special creation presented no problem and since, moreover, he also believed the newly created world identical with the experienced world of his own time – save, as it were, for the wear and tear of a few millennia – the immutability of living forms on the one hand and their non-proliferation on the other seemed necessarily to follow. Few supposed the *creative* power of God to have extended beyond the sixth day of the universe, and with that the power of matter to generate new life of its own had ceased for ever.

Furthermore, the second half of the seventeenth century was a period in which, partly through animal and vegetable anatomy, partly through the use of the microscope, and partly also through experiment, many of the mysteries concerning the less obvious processes of reproduction were being cleared up. The sexuality of plants, first asserted by Nehemiah Grew, was established experimentally by Camerarius before 1694. But if the general tendency was for the exclusion of pangenesis, the experimentalists were not inclined to hasten towards a purely mechanistic interpretation. The embryological speculations of Gassendi and Descartes found few followers. Harvey had written, 'he takes the right and pius view of the matter who derives all generation from the same eternal and omnipotent Deity, on whose nod the universe itself depends . . . whether it be God, Nature or the Soul of the universe', though this did not prevent his studying the phenomena with all attention. Similarly, John Ray in the *Wisdom of God* (1693) related his discussion of the fallacy of spontaneous generation to the fixed, created nature of species. Ray's world was a machine in the sense that he doubted – from the cessation of creation on the sixth day – the divine institution of new species (or the endowment of matter with life *de novo*) but for him life was transmissible only through the recurring generations springing from the original ancestors; since the power of living was confined to the whole group of creatures extant at any moment, it could not be born of any conjunction of purely mechanical circumstances.

Despite the limitations in philosophic outlook which denied to many experienced naturalists and to Harvey in particular any vision of the ultimate potentialities of the admittedly crude physico–chemical speculations of the time, the history of embryology offers a useful example of the critical application of observation and experiment to the consideration of scientific concepts of a complex order. This was possible for a variety of reasons, which point to some significant analogies between the situation in this science, and that in the physical sciences where so much progress was made. It was important in this branch of biology that there were ideas to be challenged or confirmed, problems that demanded enquiry, far more obviously than in the purely descriptive departments. What were the respective contributions of the male and female parents to their offspring? Were the parts 'formed' or did they merely 'grow'? What was the function of the amniotic fluid, or the foetal circulation? How was the embryo nourished, or enabled to breath? Aristotle's systematic account had attempted to deal with such questions; his exactness in biological observation and his acuteness in biological reasoning were examined no less thoroughly in the sixteenth and seventeenth centuries than were his doctrines relating to the physical sciences. As Galileo had wielded the method of Archimedes against Aristotle, so in effect Harvey and Redi applied the methods of Aristotle as observer against the conclusions of Aristotle as theorist. In embryology there was as effective a classical tradition to focus attention on the critical points as in cosmology or mechanics. Of course the strategic gains were far fewer – there was no Copernican revolution in embryology, no shift of ideas as major and permanent as that effected by Harvey in relation to the heart – but the tactical advances in method and analysis were no less real. The conceptual and the methodological steps forward in science do not necessarily occur in phase, and a long period of cumulative, undramatic development may sometimes be an essential prelude to a major shift in ideas, to the opening of some new door. Brilliant as were the flashes of biological insight illuminating this period, the problems of biology were too manifold and too complex to permit the formulation of any comprehensive and stable interpretive structure; many limiting-factors, technical and conceptual, were to be gradually removed only in the nineteenth century. Not least was that true of that wonderful, esssential, but deceptive tool of the biologist, the microscope, whose history and effects will be discussed in a later chapter.

NOTES

1. Perhaps the emphasis on Darwin is unfair to the cytologists, physiologists and neurologists working in his lifetime with enormously productive results; however, Darwin produced the most universal biological idea of all time.
2. T. S. Kuhn, *The Essential Tension*, University of Chicago Press: Chicago, 1977, 41, 64 (first published 1972).
3. Mouffet (or rather his daughter) is the only 'scientist' (if we except Dr Foster) immortalized in English nursery verse. His book was largely the production of Thomas Penny (1530–88) and Edward Wotton (1492–1555).
4. C. S. Sherrington, *The Endeavour of Jean Fernel*, Cambridge U.P., 1946, 143.
5. Walter Pagel, 'William Harvey Revisited. Part 1', *History of Science*, 8, 1969, 6.
6. 'Gates' is of course here an ultimately Danish word signifying road or way, not doors or valves.
7. Only three copies of the book survive. It was printed in January 1553; Servetus was executed on 27 October 1553. The appropriate passage is translated into English in C. D. O'Malley, *Michael Servetus*, American Philosophical Society: Philadelphia, 1953, 202–8.
8. William Harvey, *On the Motion of the Heart and Blood in Animals*, trans. Robert Willis, Ch. VII; Everyman Edition, 1907, 53.
9. Ibid., 140, 146.
10. Walter Pagel, *William Harvey's Biological Ideas*, Basel and New York, 1967, 175.
11. Ibid., 19.
12. Harvey, (loc. cit., Note 8), 57, 104, 105.
13. Ibid., 37.
14. Ibid., 42.
15. Ibid., 141–3.

16. The accusation that Descartes claimed the discovery of the circulation for himself is unjust: he attributed it to 'an English physician'. He claimed only for himself his mechanical account of the heart's diastole and systole.

17. G. A. Borelli, *De motu animalium*, Rome, 1680–81, II, 226.

18. Richard Lower, *Tractatus de Corde* (1669), English translation by K. J. Franklin in R. T. Gunther, *Early Science in Oxford*, IX (Oxford, 1932), especially pp. 164–71.

19. T. Sprat, *History of the Royal Society* (3rd. edn, London, 1723), 317.

20. See A. R. and M. B. Hall, *The Correspondence of Henry Oldenburg*, IV, Madison, Milwaukee and London 1967, and *eidem* in *Medical History*, 24, 1980, 461–5.

21. Robert Willis, *Works of W. Harvey*, London, 1857, 321.

CHAPTER SEVEN

New systems of scientific thought in the seventeenth century

No doubt time's telescope has the effect of making the intellectual history of the Middle Ages seem more monolithic than it really was. Apart from the theological schisms that produced bloody massacres like the Albigensian Crusade, apart from the ever-present tension between Christianity and Islam, there were less violent disputes between Realists and Nominalists, between the Dominican and Franciscan Orders, between the literally faithful Aristotelians and such innovators as the followers of Averroes or the Oxford mathematical school. But at least so far as the philosophy of nature is concerned the historian is inclined to feel that an essentially Aristotelian consensus dissolved in the latter part of the sixteenth century, to be replaced not by one but a multitude of schools: atomists, Cartesians, Hermeticists and Paracelsians, Helmontians, Platonists and Pythagorean mathematicians, eclectics and individualists of many types. Aristotelian logic and ethics were still taught in schools and colleges, indeed Aristotle's natural philosophy, like the medical texts of Galen, was still widely read as part of the normal course of study, fossilized already in the educational system; such texts no longer had any intellectual creative force, however, so that by the middle years of the seventeenth century the independent efforts of young men like Christiaan Huygens, Robert Boyle or Isaac Newton took off not from such well-trodden and dusty ground but from the books of the recent mathematical, mechanical and chemical philosophers. The first public teaching of modern natural philosophy, with experimental demonstrations, began at the University of Utrecht in 1672, that is, a generation after the first discussions of Descartes's philosophy there; more modestly, disputation topics drawn from modern rather than time-hallowed texts began to creep into the academic exercises of other universities also.

René Descartes was the modern who most nearly succeeded in claiming Aristotle's stolen mantle, for he was universally read and widely followed. He created a metaphysical foundation, an epistemology, and a complete system of nature embracing the explanation of all phenomena. He promised an unfailing method of discovery. His reputation was increased by the labours of skilled and patient expositors, notably Jacques Rohault (1620–73) and when the imperfections of his own accounts of natural phenomena began to be notorious fresh life was given to his system by the writings of extremely able 'neo-Cartesians', of whom the chief were Huygens, Malebranche and Leibniz. In fact, for all the powerful counter-influence of Newton, the light cast by Descartes was to extend right into the broader glow of the eighteenth-century Enlightenment, and the Diderot–Dalembert *Encyclopédie* which is its chief monument. Moreover, Descartes was a pure mathematician of genius who also did work of immortal worth in mathematical physics – if he had not been a philosopher at all he would still have had great rank in the history of science. In every respect but one, systematic experimental investigation, Descartes stood out at the time of his death, and thereafter in the eyes of all who at that moment were capable of understanding his books, as the great luminary, the man who had opened up a broad path for posterity.

One of the closest in type though not in strength of influence to Descartes was his fellow-countryman and near contemporary Pierre Gassendi (1592–1655), co-founder of what Boyle was to call the 'mechanical philosophy'. Both as pure philosopher and pure 'scientist' Gassendi's achievements were of a lower order than Descartes's, but before these two Frenchmen no one at all combined philosophy and science in an integral way. Galileo, for example, was a natural philosopher of the highest quality, but were it not for this he would have no place in the history of general philosophy. According to Stillman Drake Galileo was impatient of conventional rhetorical philosophy in much the same manner as many of his later successors. ('The questions asked by philosophers are either unanswerable or else are better answered by other means than verbal discussion'.)[1] Certainly Galileo avoided metaphysics as far as possible and distrusted all universal systems of thought. He was chiefly concerned – even in defence of the Copernican universe – with scientific matters and the discussion of specific problems. He did not construct a methodical philosophy of science, though the elements of such a philosophy may be extracted from his works. On the other hand he may properly be described as an epistemologist, for his conscious reflection on the obstructions to be overcome in arriving at a clear and confident understanding of nature is explicit in a number of passages and implicitly conditions the revolution in ideas that he effected. Like other major critics of Aristotle, Galileo was faced with two inescapable problems: on what foundations was the intellectual structure of science to be built, and what criteria of a satisfactory explanation were to replace those of Aristotle ? With Galileo these questions were not answered in prolonged metaphysical or logical analyses – though his ideas were no doubt influenced by just such analyses carried out by his predecessors – but the answers were given as they became necessary in the progress of his attack on the prevailing idea of nature. As a scientist Galileo's aim might be to detect Aristotle's errors in fact or reason, while as a philosopher he demonstrated more fundamentally how these errors had arisen from weakness in method that could be avoided by taking a different course. The negative exposure of an isolated mistake by means of experiment or measurement was not, in Galileo's view, the sole advance of which the new philosophy was capable.

Galileo's two greatest treatises are polemics. They do not relate how certain conclusions were reached, instead they seek to prove that these conclusions are certainly true. Their arguments are therefore synthetic, and the texture of reasoning and experience is so woven that experience appears less as a peg upon which a deduction depends, than as an ocular witness to its validity. It is universally the case that the methods by which a discovery is made and expounded differ, in varying degrees, and Galileo rarely used the direct technique of reporting and inference, so much favoured later by the English empiricists. We now know, from Stillman Drake's careful analysis of Galileo's disordered and unprinted notes,[2] that quantitative experiment played an essential role in the generation of Galileo's mathematical theory of motion, and that one should be inclined to trust his reporting of particular experiments (like those on floating bodies, for example) as reliable; in exposition, however, Galileo concealed a great deal of patient, factual work – this is true of astronomy also. Rather, in both the *Dialogue* and the *Discourses* the foundations of scientific knowledge are shown to reside in phenomena and axioms conjointly. By its attention to actual phenomena Galilean science was made real and experiential; by its use of the capacity of the mind to apprehend axiomatic truths its logic was made analogous to that of mathematics. The latter were indeed generalized from the former, but the process might involve historical as well as philosophical elements. Thus a fundamental axiom of the *Dialogue* is that heavenly bodies participate in uniform circular motion, while in the *Discourses* successive propositions in dynamics are deduced from the axiomatic definition of uniform acceleration. Such axioms, illustrated and confirmed by experiment, become the starting-point for arguments through which their implications are unfolded (in the manner of Euclidean geometry or Archimedean statics) and again in turn verified by experience, or applied to specific problems, such as the isochronism of the pendulum.

Galileo's remarks on the procedure to be adopted in arriving at these principal generalizations are therefore of special interest. The most important step is that of abstraction. The essential generalizations are not to be taken as the end-product of the logical examination of an idea, in the manner of Aristotle, but are obtained by abstracting everything but the universal element in a particular phenomenon, or class. So far Galileo agrees with Bacon, though he offered no comparable set of logical rules for effecting this operation. He went on, however, to insist emphatically that by abstraction it is learnt that the real properties of bodies are purely physical, that is, size, shape, motion, propinquity, etc., not colour, taste or smell, so that as he stated in the *Saggiatore*, the 'accidents, affections and qualities' attributed to them are not inherent in the bodies at all, but are names given to sensations stimulated in the observer by the physical constitution of that which he perceives. Galileo noted that this failure to abstract from sensations to the underlying physical reality had given rise to much confusion in the study of heat; physically considered (he says) there is no mystery in heat, which is merely a name applied to a sensation produced by the motion of a multitude of small corpuscles, having a certain shape and velocity, whose penetrations into the substance of the human body arouse such a sensation. In these opinions the influence of Epicurean atomism is evident; one might say that this whole approach to the question of primary and secondary qualities is determined by a mechanistic notion of the composition of matter. The explanation of a scientific problem is truly begun when it is reduced to its basic terms of matter and motion – the transformation which remained the ideal of classical physics. The name *heat* could not be a cause, since as Galileo pointed out there is nothing between the physical properties of bodies with the varying motions and sizes of their component particles and the subjective perceptions of the observer. He found other instances in conventional science of this tendency to believe that matters could be explained by juggling with abstract names, as when in the *Dialogue* gravity is defined as only the name of that which causes heavy bodies to fall; naming does not contribute to understanding. The world of Galileo's mechanics was in fact Euclid's geometrical space in which move bodies endowed with weight and momentum. The secret of formal science in Galileo's outlook – discovery being a private and informal process, so to speak – was to transfer a problem, properly defined, to this abstract world of science which, as ever greater elements of complexity were in turn added to it, could be made to approximate more and more closely to the experiential universe. Such also, but with even greater exactitude in the process of approximation, was Newton's method.[3]

The roots of such axiomatic, mathematical science were of course as Greek as Aristotelian physics. The clearest ancient precedent is to be found among the writers on optics who had identified rectilinear light-rays with geometrical straight lines and reflecting mirrors with mathematical surfaces; similarly, Archimedes had constructed statics and hydrostatics with the fewest possible physical axioms concerning equilibrium and the definition of a fluid. In such an axiomatic science the course of the argument was as impeccable as the geometry with which it was conducted, and it was the province of the user of the argument, so to speak, to determine how nearly real bodies in water, say, might match in their behaviour the axiomatic bodies in the axiomatic fluid of Archimedes. However, the ancients including Archimedes himself had signally failed to extend the same pattern of philosophy to motion, and no ancient mathematician would have declared that the axiomatic method was the sole method by which motion and change and all problems of physical science ought to be studied. Even Galileo does not go quite so far, rather he asserts that the mathematical method should be preferred to all others, as that which alone offers certainty. When a problem has been set out in mathematical form and a given conclusion reached, that conclusion must be true if the problem had been correctly formulated and the mathematical steps correctly taken. In such a case the logical rigour of the argument is guaranteed by its mathematical form, while its contingent truth or conformity with experience depends on the choice of the axioms, which may have to be determined as the result of experimental investigation, and is to be confirmed or refuted by further experiments. Galileo well knew how deceitful experiments and observations can be, unless interpreted in a suitable theoretical matrix. However, he argued that this method did not desert the reality of the physical world, since to Galileo the book of nature was 'written in mathematical language . . . the letters being

179

triangles, circles and other figures without which it is humanly impossible to comprehend a single word.'[4] The architecture of the real world was no less geometrical than that of abstract Euclidean space. Nor was there any distinction between 'real truth' and mathematical truth. If efforts to mathematize nature fail, it is merely because the task has been undertaken improperly. A physical plane is not a geometric plane, indeed, but its departures from geometrical planeness are in turn expressible in mathematics. It is a question simply of having skill to unfold the successive layers of mathematical complexity in nature. Reasoning thus, Galileo has been called a Platonist because he sought for the mathematical ideal in nature; but Galileo also perceived that while mathematical logic is infallible, it may rest on false assumptions, like those of the Ptolemaic system, which although it may satisfy a merely mathematical astronomer, could afford no satisfaction to a philosophical astronomer.

By the method of abstraction, moreover, the scientific concept of 'laws of nature' was simply and neatly accommodated. This concept, unknown both to the ancient world and to the Far Eastern peoples, seems to have arisen from a peculiar interaction between the religious, philosophic and legalistic ideas of the medieval European world. It is apparently related to the concept of natural law in the social and moral senses familiar to medieval jurists, and signifies a notable departure from the Greek attitude to nature. The use of the word 'law' in such contexts would have been unintelligible in antiquity, whereas the Hebraic and Christian belief in a deity who was at once Creator and Law-giver rendered it valid. The existence of laws of nature was a necessary consequence of design in nature, for how otherwise could the integrity of the design be perpetuated? Man alone had been given free-will, the power to transgress the laws he was required to observe; the planets had not been granted power to deviate from their orbits. Hence the regularity of the planetary motions, for example, ascribed by Aristotle to the surveillance of intelligences, could be accounted for as obedience to the divine decrees. The Creator had endowed matter, plants and animals with certain unchangeable properties and characteristics, of which the most universal constituted the laws of nature, discernible by human reasons. This conception is clearly capable of association with a mechanistic philosophy, and irreconcilable with animism; as Boyle put it:

God established those rules of motion, and that order amongst things corporeal, which we call the laws of nature. [Thus] the universe being once framed by God, and the laws of motion settled, and all upheld by his incessant concourse and providence, the mechanical philosophy teaches that the phenomena of the world are physically produced by the mechanical properties of the parts of matter.[5]

If this transcendental status be granted to the laws of nature – so that one may enquire what they are, but not why they hold – the question may still be asked, 'How may a given proposition be recognized as a law of nature?' In other words, how does a law of nature differ from any other generalization which happens to be true because no instance to the contrary has yet been discovered? Modern philosophers of science, having deprived the laws of nature of their transcendental status, present their own answers to this problem. Galileo, and after him Newton, obtained an answer to it by application of the method of abstraction. When Galileo created by abstraction the essential model of the phenomena of motion which he studied, he transformed the pragmatic validity of a generalization contingently true in the world of experience into the absolute validity enjoyed by an axiom or definition within the theoretical model. So Galileo offers (as he says) a single definition of equable or uniform motion:

Equal or uniform motion I understand to be that of which the parts run through by the movable in any equal times whatever are equal to one another

and to this he adds four consequences or as he calls them 'axioms'.[6] The definition is of motion which we can certainly conceive as occurring in nature, but Galileo does not say in what bodies it may be found; in fact, it appears from numerous places in Galileo's writings that he sees natural uniform motion as only taking place in very special, not to say impossible conditions. The properties of uniform motion are then elucidated, and it is of course clear that real moving bodies will possess such properties approximately in so far as they approximate to the state of uniform motion. Thus Galileo can also treat the ideal projectile as possessing a component of uniform motion. Galileo therefore has no *law* of uniform motion here; to write for him a law defining the circumstances under which uniform motion may occur would mean writing out a long statement of experiential conditions. Newton, however, was able to embrace all these in three words: *absence of force*; he then, so to speak, inverts the Galilean situation by stating as a law of nature that all bodies moving in the absence of force are moving uniformly in straight lines (adding this last essential proviso). Of course, it still remains for the user of Newton's First Law to determine what experiential conditions guarantee absence of force, which brings one back to the Galilean position, full circle. For neither Galileo nor Newton is it conceptually essential to define exactly when the conditions of the definition or the Law are realized (they are unrealizable: only a unique body existing in the empty universal space could be force-free, since any other body in the universe exerts a force on the first): it is sufficient to be able to build a systemic theoretical structure upon Definition or Law, and utilize this in (for example) investigating the behaviour of pendulums or projectiles.

Hence laws of nature could be considered as being rigorously exact within a theoretical structure founded upon appropriate definitions, as with Galileo or Newton, even though the laws can never be verified (or, for that matter, as Karl Popper would have it, falsified) with complete certainty in the experiential world. The perfect fluid of Archimedes, the perfect gas of Boyle and Charles, the force-free, dimensionless mass-points of Newton, cannot be found under experimental conditions, partly because the conditions cannot ever realize certain requirements (for example, a perfect vacuum), partly because all real substances are more complex than these ideal entities. Such limitations were quite early experienced in the case of experiments in mechanics, for Galileo's elaborate geometry of projectile motion is only crudely realized by actual projectiles flying through the air, which resists their passage. An even greater

181

surprise was the discovery of birefringence in optics, by Erasmus Bartholin in 1669; for some two thousand years men had confidently supposed that there was just one kind of refraction to which a ray of light was subjected in crossing the boundary between two different transparent media, such as air and glass, or water and air; moreover, it had been a recent triumph of mathematical science to define this refraction (we still refer to the definition, first published by Descartes in 1637, as 'Snel's' Law) and even to account for it in various physical hypotheses of light. Bartholin had demonstrated that in some transparent materials refraction could occur not in one way only, but in two. Thus light and matter both must be more complex than ordinary experience with the more common materials revealed, and than Snel's Law allowed: a useful reminder that mathematical theories may enclose but can never prescribe the range of experiential date.

How can the investigator in mathematical physics be sure that his theorems are applicable to the real world of experience? Galileo's answer, prepared by a long line of earlier logicians, was to make a practical trial. If from the theorems we can generate some predicted result of a verifiable kind, then if we see this result to appear in the test we can be confident that the theory is sound. So, in the *Discourses on Two New Sciences*, Galileo shows how the law of acceleration for freely falling bodies may be indirectly confirmed by experiment: the theory tells us that bodies descending a frictionless inclined plane accelerate according to the same law, though at a slower rate; we can therefore test the theory by setting up a plane that is as nearly without friction as possible, and letting a brass ball roll or slide down it. Then we should find that different distances traversed should be as the squares of the times. Galileo says that results consistent within the tenth part of a pulse-beat could be obtained by his method, and that in a hundred trials the theory was confirmed every time. (For reasons he could not have analysed, it was impossible to derive the acceleration of free fall from that on the plane, a fact that caused some confusion among Galileo's readers.) In Galileo's public writings such a formal and quantitative appeal to experimental verification is rare indeed, whereas (by contrast) Newton was to devote the entire third book of his *Principia* to just such a validation and exemplification of the mathematical principles of natural philosophy established in the first two books. Galileo more often describes tests in a vague and general way, as with the demonstration of the principle that bodies ascend to the height from which they fall, no matter what the shape of the path. He liked in exposition – if not necessarily in his private investigations – to exploit the faith of Plato's *Meno* that common sense and logical understanding exist in every mind and only need to be elicited. In some passages he refers readers to their experience of mirrors, of the smoothness of motion in a ship gliding through the water, of the flow of fluids. There are glancing hints at many experiments by way of demonstration or confirmation that might be made, but Galileo does not assert that he has really made them, perhaps believing that a book should be complete in itself and not require the reader to take a laboratory course. Whether 'thought-experiments' as well as the actual experiments he made played an important part in the evolution of

Galileo's ideas we cannot tell, but certainly they are essential elements in his exposition, for he does not really expect his reader to go on a sea-voyage to India, or shoot crossbows from carriages at the gallop, to climb the Leaning Tower of Pisa to drop weights, or mount the mast of a speeding galley for the same purpose. Galileo does not often, if ever, tell his readers: 'Here is a new fact that I discovered by experiment' – except when reporting his astronomical observations, for again he meant to convert the reader to his own point of view not by affirming truths of which the reader had remained hitherto ignorant (and therefore might well continue to doubt in the future) but by teaching the Simplicio of his dialogue to reason rightly. Being above all things (as he himself said) a natural philosopher (or theoretical scientist) he was no crude empiricist and accordingly he sought not only for more facts, but for deeper understanding. He was well aware that experimentation is a double-edged weapon, deceiving those who use it crudely, as when he writes of the 'sublime wit' of Copernicus, who

did constantly continue to affirm (being perswaded thereto by reason) that which sensible experiments seemed to contradict; for I cannot cease to wonder that he should constantly persist in saying, that Venus revolveth about the Sun, and is more than six times further from us at one time, than at another; and also seemeth to be always of equal bigness, although it ought to shew forty times bigger when nearest to us, than when farthest off.[7]

Sheer empiricism, therefore, could not uncover physical reality, which could only be glimpsed through the alliance of analytical reasoning (especially of the mathematical kind), scientific imagination, and cautious experiment always safeguarded by reason.

From the critique of empiricism it emerges that in Galilean science experiment is incompetent to confirm the whole intellectual structure, whose conceptual elements transcend experiment. For example, the concept of acceleration which science owes to Galileo cannot be proved in the laboratory, though its applicability in representing phenomena can be illustrated. For the definition of acceleration involves the further concepts of time and velocity, the latter a function of time and the concept distance. There is periodicity in nature, and there are intervals in nature, but nature offers no ready-made dimension-theory embracing the concepts of time and distance. These can have no other status than that of ideas or mental constructs which help to form the world-picture, having the advantage that unlike concepts of beauty and justice they can be understood in the same sense by all men. But their definition is of mind, not innate in the fabric of the universe. The concept time gives order to certain kinds of experience, the concept distance to others, and from these arise velocity and acceleration rationalizing others still, so that the first test for a definition of acceleration must be its assimilability in logic to existing dimension-theory; moreover, in a second test, by experiment, the usefulness of the new construct cannot be distinguished from the usefulness of the existing constructs, time and distance, so that effectively the whole system of constructs must be tested together, if at all. Though the Galilean scientist seeks to penetrate ever deeper into physical reality, the nodes of his exposition of nature can never be more than mental constructs, time, acceleration, the chemical element, or the electron, which give order and significance to the experimental data.

A view of the natural world that would exclude from reality every feature not directly verifiable by experiential test ('*This* is an apple, therefore apples exist') might be called realist–empiricist. The ancient view of nature transmitted to Europe was not wholly of this kind, since it included the heavenly quintessence and the planetary intelligences, the elements of matter and the faculties of the organs in the body, entities or concepts whose existence cannot be verified by inspection like the existence of apples or even camels. But that ancient view had characteristically been reluctant to depart from realist–empiricism with respect to the observable form and structure of things; it allowed the economical introduction of what could not be directly experienced (but seemed to be required for explanation) only when the introduction was of a psychic or non-material kind. Thus the dominant ancient legacy of science had accepted an organic view of nature (which in Galen for example becomes a personified nature) while rejecting the Pythagorean and Platonic non-realist traditions, and equally atomism with its divergence between appearance and reality. On the other hand, the fundamental metaphysical position of the scientific revolution (at least in the mathematical–physical sciences) excludes realist–empiricism. Such is the basis of Copernicanism: our Earth appears to be at rest at the centre of the universe whereas in reality is a planet; this is the message that Galileo confirms and justifies. Such is the basis of the mechanical philosophy, as we shall see shortly – such one might say was the prerequisite for the 'new' science of chemistry, studying the real process of chemical reaction so different from the appearance of burning, solution, fermentation and so forth. Galileo's concepts of acceleration and of locomotion generally are far from realist–empiricist and necessitate ultimately Newton's distinction between the appearance of time and movement and their ultimate, absolute reality. When the philosopher commits himself to deep investigation he must expect to find that the world he must construct for his level of enquiry will be quite other than the world of ordinary experience. That egg-laying mammals or spiral nebulae exist he can see by looking: but no seeing can determine the existence of electrons or black holes. 'Seeing' correctly and comprehensively is of course the fundamental necessity of science without which all the rest is speculation; but theories of the unseeable are the essence of the science which is to be created. The increasing sophistication of what is seen has entailed constantly more sophisticated theories of what is unseeable.

At every stage in a growing science tensions exist between the experiential seen and the theoretical unseen (if there is no such tension, then development depends upon accidental discovery, as with Bartholin and the birefringence of Icelandic spar). Thus, Galileo's study of the inclined plane left unsolved the problem why we cannot (in his simple, but within its limits correct, theory) determine from experiments on the near-frictionless inclined plane a value for free, natural acceleration. Thus too, later, Newton's calculation of the speed of sound from his theory of the unseen structure of the air fails to agree precisely with the physical measurements. Ultimate resolution of the tension may (as in these last two cases) simply reveal the need to add a new term to the former theory, or (as in the case of seventeenth-century optics) reveal the utter inadequacy of the original theory about the unseen structure of things.

In the form of science begun by Galileo and perfected by Newton, if we leave aside its practical or operational success in working with instruments and materials towards the discovery of new facts about the natural world, we are left with a body of theory in which the material entities were intellectual constructs (perfect gases and fluids, ideal particles, void spaces) and the concepts applied to the organization of these constructs (acceleration, forces in general, gravity in particular), equally idealized. We can experience none of these things directly: we know heavy bodies, but not the force of gravity save by inference. Sometimes (as with Galileo's concept of acceleration) the correspondence between experience and concept might be made quite close, in other cases (as with Newton's ideal gas) though a physical model for an experimental law results, artificiality obtrudes and such artificial models were to be quite displaced later. Moreover, not only were constructs and concepts both highly intellectualized, they were set in a theoretical structure which involved even by the end of the seventeenth century mathematical operations of considerable complexity: physics then ceased to exist in a literary form, which it still possessed in the time of Galileo and Descartes, or rather the literary form only continued to exist in the newest and least organised branches, such as the study of electricity. Considering the effect of these changes upon the nature of scientific explanation, four chief consequences suggest themselves. First 'common sense', that is realist–empirist, criticism of propositions became, at least in the physical sciences, completely invalid from the late seventeenth century onwards: Galileo, Descartes and Newton each successively demonstrated this so far as the Copernican theory in particular and the universal theory of motion were concerned. The only valid explanations of observed phenomena were those derived from the idealized constructs and concepts of theoretical science. Take the phenomena of tides for example, of which Galileo produced a mechanical explanation treating them as inertial oscillations (this was later adopted by Wallis and others), while Descartes attributed them to his 'aether' and Newton to gravity: it was agreed by all three philosophers that tidal patterns at particular places depended upon local geographical formations as much as on the mechanical theory although this was adequate (each claimed in turn) for the universal effects of periodicity, relationship to the moon's motion, and so forth. In other words, the tides presented an extreme example of the obvious fact that all scientific theories have to be rendered specific by the insertion of suitable parameters before they can yield particular explanations. Secondly, since a Galilean (and more emphatically a Newtonian) science consists of constructs, concepts and an appropriate mathematical articulation, and is in principle if not always in strict logic of axiomatic form, there is a close correspondence between description (now idealized) and explanation. The description (or theory) is attained by the process of analysis, while explanations are reached by the inverse process of synthesis. As Newton wrote in a famous passage of *Opticks*, here following the Greek mathematician Pappus:

As in mathematics, so in natural philosophy the investigation of difficult things by the method of analysis ought ever to precede the method of composition [synthesis]. This analysis consists in making experiments and observations, and in drawing general conclusions from them by induction . . . by this way of analysis we may proceed from compounds to ingredients, and from motions to the forces producing them; and in general from effects to their causes, and from particular causes to more general ones till the argument end in the most general. This is the method of analysis: and the synthesis consists in assuming the causes discovered and established as principles, and by them explaining the phenomena proceeding from them, and proving the explanations.[8]

Thirdly, and an essential feature of the system, a descriptive universal concept possesses an explanatory function. Clearly related to the general process of induction, this rule of reasoning as one might call it serves to frustrate the objection that causal chains can be indefinitely prolonged, to the point when nothing can be explained unless everything can be explained. Thus for Galileo the descriptive generalization that heavy bodies accelerate uniformly towards the centre of the Earth has great explanatory value, for example in relation to pendulums and projectiles, yet he explicitly refrained from attempting to unravel the cause of this acceleration:

At present it is the purpose of our Author merely to investigate and to demonstrate some of the properties of accelerated motion (whatever the cause of this acceleration may be) [9]

And Newton, advancing from kinematics to dynamics, defining gravity as a force operating according to a certain law and making gravity a universal force of many diverse manifestations still leaves the material cause of gravity undiscovered, if it has a material cause. Similarly Charles Darwin in a different world of thought will reveal the vast explanatory power of the concept of biological evolution, even with total ignorance of the physiological mechanisms which cause those variations in specific forms to occur, upon which the evolutionary process works. No matter: one gains so much by precisely ordered thinking at one level, irrespective of the philosopher's inability to define the entailed phenomena at some deeper level. For the inverse relationship between explanation and description is to be seen as demanding a certain hierarchical order: that is, the concepts and constructs that serve as explanations at one level can only count as descriptive at a deeper level: so, to understand some biological process chemistry is invoked, to understand chemical theory we investigate the atom, and atomic physics leads into the study of fundamental particles.

Fourthly, it is implicit in Newton's methodological doctrine, just quoted, as in the writings of other seventeenth-century philosophers following Galileo, that what is not reached as an antecedent in the process of analytical investigation, that is, some event or process not encountered in the successively deeper layers of the hierarchy of theory, cannot be invoked as a cause in the explanation of phenomena. Thus if we judge inertia to be a sufficient cause of the continued planetary motions, as Galileo seems willing to do, we have no need of intelligences to control their revolutions. But this was a stern principle to apply, especially for philosophers who firmly and sincerely accepted the creation of the universe as a divine artefact. When everyone in the seventeenth century agreed that God was the First Cause of the universe and all its phenomena, at what point was the philosopher to invoke God as the specific cause of this or that phenomenon? It was not doubted that God was the cause of Adam and Eve, but was he also (for example) the direct cause of gravity? Newton and Leibniz, Spinoza and his Christian critics, differed fundamentally and irreconcilably on such issues as these, for no method of physics or metaphysics could draw the precise boundary between these two phases of thought.

The early years of the eighteenth century, the epoch of the great dispute about the discovery of the calculus and of others between the British and continental schools of thought, constitute one period of philosophical polemic concerning the appropriateness (or otherwise) of certain scientific arguments[10]; there had been an analogous and not unrelated discussion some half-century earlier with Descartes and Gassendi as the controversial pivots, which in turn had succeeded the dispute over Copernicanism. At least at first sight it seems as though the philosophical critics of Copernicus, Galileo, Descartes and Newton were mere obstructionists blocking the proper progress of scientific theory in accordance with the necessities of new discoveries in phenomena. Reflection suggests that such a view is too naive: scientific speculation is no more exempt from criticism on grounds of logic, coherence and general plausibility than any other, and it is by no means necessarily the case that novel speculation about the way the world is made is either plausible, consistent or well informed. Philosophical criticism of scientific theories has indeed performed a useful function in enforcing their statement in a strong and clear manner, and has contributed to the elimination of weak theories.

This negative, critical role of philosophers, their defence perhaps to put it too broadly and bluntly of metaphysical positions against empiricism and functional mathematicism, is very well known and involves the equally well-known effect in any historical movement whereby the disciples of the wild radicals of an early generation became the conservatives entrenched in opposition to a new set of young Turks. But did philosophers also contribute positively to the course of scientific development in the sixteenth and seventeenth centuries? (Obviously there were philosophers who were also 'scientists', like Descartes, and 'scientists' who were also philosophers like Galileo and Newton; there were also philosophers who wrote as propagandists for Cartesian or Newtonian science; but one is looking for something more emphatic and fundamental.) It does not seem that the mathematical approach to natural phenomena, which all historians now recognize as being so fertile, was of much interest to philosophers; almost by definition, as it were, those who took this up would be classified as in some modest sense at least mathematicians themselves. There were Hermetic philosophers who were not mathematicians, such as Giordano Bruno, and others who were pseudo-mathematicians like Robert Fludd, but the Pythagoreans (if it makes any sense to form them into a class) were all mathematicians. It seems that the historian can most confidently look for a positive re-shaping of scientific thought and activity by philosophers in relation to the development of empiricism and of the mechanical philosophy.

To us, these seem closely related themes, because Francis Bacon and later British authors (including Isaac Newton) brought them firmly together, employing reductionism as a link. As Newton wrote in the second (1713) edition of the *Principia*:

Because the qualities of bodies are only known to us through experiments, we are to posit them as being general only so far as they concur generally with experiments, . . . We are acquainted with the extension of bodies only by the senses, which do not respond to it in all bodies, but because we perceive extension in all bodies of which we have sensation, we must affirm it of all. We find by experience that very many bodies are hard. However, the hardness of the whole originates in the hardness of the parts, and therefore we rightly infer the hardness of the atomic particles of all other bodies, not of those alone whose hardness we feel. That all bodies are impenetrable we infer not from thought but from sensation. We find those bodies which we handle to be impenetrable and so we come to the conclusion that impenetrability is a property of bodies in general. That all bodies are mobile, and that by means of certain forces (which we call the forces of inertia) they persist in either motion or motionlessness we infer from these properties in observable bodies. The extension, hardness, impenetrability, mobility and force of inertia of the whole body originate in the extension, hardness, impenetrability, mobility, and forces of inertia of the [component] particles, and accordingly we conclude that the fundamental particles of all bodies are extended, and hard, and impenetrable, and mobile and endowed with forces of inertia. And this is the foundation of all Philosophy.[11]

Although Newton, very correctly, notes that philosophers have no empirical proof of the existence of atoms (fundamental, indivisible particles) in Nature – and, he might have added, as modern theoretical physicists now realize, the experimental proof of the indivisibility of any particular days of particles is very hazardous – it is perfectly clear that he identifies the ultimate data of experiments with the ultimate postulates of the mechanical philosophy: hardness, extension and motion in particles. But experimental science and reductionism were not always so linked as they are in this passage by Newton, for empiricism was originally linked rather with a 'natural-history' approach to nature than with the rational approach, and was not by any means regarded as non-Aristotelian. The argument in favour of experimental methodology as a medieval precursor of modern science has already been touched upon (Ch. 1); this methodology, however, was directed to that search for causes which Galileo and his successors rejected, and in no way involved reductionism.

A more direct claim for philosophic planning of new scientific action was made by J. H. Randall, who dismissed the medieval traditions of Oxford and Paris as inadequately relevant to the revolution effected by Galileo, which he preferred to connect rather with the dissident Aristotelian tradition of Galileo's own university, Padua.

'What Paris had been in the thirteenth century, what Oxford and Paris together had been in the fourteenth, Padua became in the fifteenth: the centres

in which ideas from all Europe were combined into an organized and cumulative body of knowledge.' If this seems a somewhat optimistic distillation of
historic reality in which, over a long period of time, a large number of teachers
spoke with disparate voices, it is certainly true that Padua had a distinguished
tradition of Averroism, that it united active philosopical and medical traditions, and that in Galileo's time it was the most lively and frequented university
in Europe. Attention to problems of method in relation to medicine, following
in the steps of Galen, in Randall's view enabled the Paduan philosophers over
a period of some three centuries to build up 'a detailed theory of scientific
method which the Aristotelian scholars, themselves holders of medical degrees,
incorporated into their version of the nature of science' and formulated at last
as 'a completed statement in the logical controversies of [Jacopo] Zabarella
[1533–89], in which it reaches the form familiar in Galileo and the seventeenth-century scientists.'[12]

Though this is a neat and attractive thesis, it is historically unsatisfactory.
One can hardly accept the implication that Galileo was the sole intermediary
between the Paduan tradition and 'the seventeenth-century scientists', while
the alternative view that the Paduan tradition not only affected Galileo and
Harvey but Bacon, Descartes and others as well seems equally untenable. Randall's thesis deliberately excludes the earlier, mathematically-minded school of
philosophers of whom, at least superficially, Galileo's own writings bear more
obvious traces (Duhem's thesis); necessarily so, since Zaberella was a-mathematical, but Galileo was completely the opposite. Moreover, few students of
Galileo of the present or any earlier generation would find acceptable Randall's
assertion that 'in method and philosophy if not in physics he (Galileo) remained
a typically Paduan Aristotelian', if only because of the tacit incongruity contained within it between Galileo's 'philosophy' and his 'physics'. Historians
have always – rightly or not – perceived a close dependence of Galileo's scientific achievements upon his novel methodology: Randall's own argument
would seem to reduce the significance of method to zero if it led Zabarella to
one kind of physics, and Galileo to another kind. The logician discusses questions of epistemology and method for their own sake, whereas to the natural
philosopher they are significant only for the knowledge of nature they yield.[13]

The improbability inherent in the claim that any one philosopher – Zabarella
or Francis Bacon, or indeed Descartes – 'invented' a true and unique scientific
method, first fruitfully practised by his seventeenth-century successors, is that
it is impossible to prove either that the philosopher concerned exercised a creative influence upon all his successors, or that any one statement of method
was so complete as to embrace all facets of the new science. The twentieth-
century historian would expect any complete programme for the still future
seventeenth-century science to have included at least recognition of the following elements: conceptual originality, experimental exploration, mathematical
analysis. If we may agree that Galileo is an early example of a natural philosopher endowed with all these elements of success, we can discover no systematic
methodologist who propounded the necessity for each of them. Just as in the

arts the roles of artist and critic are normally diverse (Saint-Beuve and Balzac, Whistler and Ruskin) so in the investigation of nature the roles of interpreter and creator have rarely been well performed by one individual. Real creative power in science depends on much more than a working knowledge of the relevant branches of philosophy (logic, epistemology, methodology), just as creation in the artist depends on more than his knowledge of aesthetics, perspective, colour-science and so forth. Of course working scientists have always been inspired to see their own work in terms of a prevailing philosophy, from Aristotle's onwards, and so rationalize their activity according to an acceptable code of sound thinking and prudent theorizing, but one may doubt the relevance of such *post hoc* rationalizations to the process of discovery.

It is therefore doubtful whether it is worth while looking for any methodologist of the late Renaissance who offered a unique key to later successes in science. Francis Bacon (1561–1626) is the philosopher who has more often than any other been placed in such a position of eminence, as one who foresaw the future eminence of natural science, predicted the process by which it might be attained, and to some slight extent even showed by example what was to be done. Bacon, it has been claimed, was not only the founder of a whole new branch of philosophy, inductive philosophy, as against the traditional philosophy of deduction, but also perceived and taught a great truth about knowledge itself: that knowledge is power. In other words, whereas the object of medieval scholastic philosophy had been a passive reconciliation of man and nature, the Baconian philosophy taught that man should actively explore nature and, having discovered its secrets, exploit them for his own purposes.

The simple picture of Bacon as the methodological forerunner of industrial science has been treated with considerable scepticism in recent times,[14] not least because the description of the science which Bacon presumptively pioneered seems, if anything, more suited to the nineteenth century than to the seventeenth century. When Bacon is set more firmly in his historical context, not only the closeness of his relation to other logical philosophers of his own time but the distance between him and contemporary natural philosophers (Gilbert and Harvey as well as Kepler and Galileo) seems the more striking. The operative element in Bacon's philosophy appears at least as much in the tradition of natural magic as that of technology. Further, the simple picture of Bacon's historical influence subsisted on Bacon's own view of the historiography of science: that scholasticism had prevailed virtually unchanged and unchallenged down to his own day, that the whole task of reconstructing knowledge lay still ahead in the future, and that the only way towards a successful reconstruction was that described by himself. Our contemporary view is very different: we see development in European thought from the thirteenth century onwards, we see the extent of the development of the sciences before and during Bacon's lifetime, and we estimate the share of mathematics in that development highly. We no longer accept Bacon's historiography, and with that the traditional picture of what Bacon's writings signified must be unacceptable also; which is not to deprive these writings of a considerable real importance.

Bacon's first charge against conventional natural philosophy was that it was excessively rational and synthetic:

There are two ways, and can only be two, of seeking and finding truth. The one, from sense and reason, takes a flight to the most general axioms, and from these principles and their truth, settled once for all, invents and judges all intermediate axioms. The other method collects axioms from sense and particulars, ascending continuously and by degrees so that in the end it arrives at the most general axioms. This latter is the only true one, but never hitherto tried.[15]

(Note that Bacon, unlike say Pappos or Newton, contrasts analysis and synthesis as alternative methods, not regarding them as complementary.) It has been argued that, on the contrary, induction and the experimental method were known and practised in scholastic science: 'in fact the thorough-going conception of natural science as a matter of experiment as well as of mathematics, may well be considered the chief advance made by the Latin Christians over the Greeks and Arabs'.[16] There are notable examples of this in magnetism and optics; but it would clearly be impossible to say that the main emphasis of medieval natural philosophy was on experimental investigation. Fond as medieval students had been of compendia and encyclopaedias, Bacon was surely justified in maintaining that the storehouse of factual knowledge about the physical universe was pitifully empty; and that while facts were so thinly garnered, theories might well be presumed fallacious. Nevertheless, Bacon was himself a logician (hence the title, *Novum Organum*, New Instrument) and a rationalist. The only experiment personally made by him, it is said, was that which brought about his death: stuffing a chicken with snow, to see if that would preserve meat as well as salt. Hence Harvey's sneer: that he wrote of science like a Lord Chancellor. His own non-methodological writings such as *Sylva Sylvarum* and *The History of Winds* were literary compilations, far from the *Nullius in Verba* (on the word of no man) later chosen by the Royal Society as its motto.[17] But this low-level empiricism, this writing down of data about tides or storms or the migration of birds or the aurora borealis was the least of Bacon's philosophical concerns: his main problem was not the avoidance of factual error – on the contrary, he had hardly if any more awareness than his predecessors of the subtle difficulties involved in getting facts right, as by precise measurement and critical assessment of the experimenter himself – but the avoidance of intellectual error. How should men think correctly? How should they reason from the facts once amply collected? How can we distinguish a good explanation of phenomena from a poor one? Such were still his problems, as for methodologists before. The object of the exploration of nature was to *know*, but knowing meant not only the natural histories, the rudiments of knowledge, but being possessed of sound theories and deep understanding. So, in the most famous and complete of his procedural analyses, Bacon reaches the 'anti-commonsense' view that heat is a mode of motion. He was very far from being a philosophical technologist; if he wrote

the true and lawful goal of the sciences is none other than this: that human life is endowed with new discoveries and power.

he also declared, more emphatically, that as

the beholding of the light is itself a more excellent and a fairer thing than all the uses of it – so assuredly the very contemplation of things as they are, without superstition or imposture, error or confusion, is in itself more worthy than all the fruit of inventions . . . we must from experience of every kind first endeavour to discover true causes and axioms, and seek for experiments of Light, not for experiments of Fruit.[18]

Many passages in Bacon's writings indicate that he had a philosophic appreciation of the value of knowledge for its own sake, not merely for its utilitarian applications. The test by works, in Bacon's thought, assumed a particular importance not because works were the main end of science, but rather because they guaranteed the recititude of the method used. A discovery or explanation which was barren of works could hold no positive merit not because it was useless to man, but because it lacked contact with reality and possibility of demonstration. Since Bacon's science was to deal with real things, its fruits must be real and perceptible. Unfortunately, his philosophy left little example of the form of experimental science, or how the study of a subject by experiments might lead to the formation of a plausible theory. Bacon demonstrates the weakness of teaching by precept rather than example.

Certainly he did not regard the true, inductive method of science as merely a matter of compilation or of experimenting 'to see what happens'. This method must emulate both the ant and the spider, Bacon writes, or rather the bee, taking a middle course

it gathers its material from the flowers of the garden and of the field, but transforms and digests it by a power of its own. Not unlike this is the true business of philosophy: for it neither relies solely or chiefly on the powers of the mind, nor does it take the matter which it gathers from natural history and mechanical experiments and lay it up in the memory whole, as it finds it, but lays it up in the understanding altered and digested. Therefore from a closer and a purer league between these two faculties, the experimental and the rational, such as has never yet been brought about, much may be hoped.

Bacon was well aware that the logical articulation or intellectual cohension that makes an argument tight comes from thought and not from the mere recitation of facts or 'instances':

the induction which proceeds by simple enumeration is childish: its conclusions are precarious, and exposed to the danger of a contradictory instance . . . But the induction which is to be available for the discovery and demonstration of the arts and sciences must analyse nature by proper rejections and exclusions; and then, after a sufficient number of negatives, come to a conclusion on the affirmative instance, which has not yet been done or even attempted . . . [19]

Worse, says Bacon, 'no mortal has yet thought' of what must be provided for the method of induction so that it may work properly, when it will be able to generate not only axioms but concepts: 'it is in this (sophisticated) induction that our chief hope lies'.

What Bacon meant by this becomes clearer in Book II of the *Novum Organum* and especially in its Aphorisms 13 to 20. There he sought as the object of knowledge not a theory about something – theories he was inclined to distrust as too idiosyncratic and subjective, as with William Gilbert and his magnetic philosophy – but rather its 'Firm and true definition'. If the philosopher could once capture the true definition and nature of things then he had them within his power, just as a herbalist had a plant medicinally within its power when he knew its nature, not merely its morphology or outer form but its constitution or inner form also. One can savour something of a kinship with magic in this, though Bacon had no such conscious thought. After a wordy discussion of the particular case of heat he concludes that

Heat is a motion, expansive, restrained, and acting in its strife upon the smaller particles of bodies.

Even this is not quite complex enough: though the expansion tends all ways, it has an inclination upwards: and the strife of the particles is not sluggish but hurried and with violence.

Much as Bacon's kinetic acuity in these Aphorisms was to impress future generations, deeply interesting as his role as a pioneer of the seventeenth-century's mechanical philosophy may be, it remains true that his own natural history was commonplace and his theoretical natural philosophy of a kind unique to himself. No one has emulated his use of *Clandestine Instances* or *Instances of the Twilight* though, with a little modification, the expression *Crucial Experiment* (for instance) does come from Bacon. As a logician and a lawyer Bacon loved to let his pen run on, to classify, to draw distinctions, to label, remaining always as much as a man of the desk himself as were the schoolmen he criticized. His writings perpetuated into the late seventeenth century and beyond a distinction between natural history (the compilation of descriptive information) and natural philosophy (the interpretation of phenomena), the former being always prior and subservient to the latter, which has never accurately represented the whole character of scientific investigation. The science of the *a priori*, mathematical science, any systematic development of a theory in propositional form, had no appeal to him. Bacon did not deny that provisional hypotheses could be useful mental crutches or that the experimental testing or hypotheses could be a useful activity, but he gives little indication of seizing the crucial fact that the value of experimental work is wholly proportionate to the value of the idea giving rise to it – the most technically accomplished experimenter will contribute little to progress without good ideas about what experiment to do next. Bacon thought that having one's foot on the right path to knowledge was more important than a great intellect ('it is obvious that when a man runs the wrong way, the more active and swift he is the further he will go astray') and so declared that in his proposal for the discovery of the sciences little was left 'to the acuteness and strength of wits', rather all were nearly on a level.[20] Here the method appears almost as a kind of logical machine that only requires to be assiduously cranked – a notion which however contrary to historical experience has appeared again and again. If this seems an aberration, he must conversely be allowed merit as a prophet of organized, cooperative research – no one has a better claim than Bacon to be the father of the Institute and the Clinic and the professionalization of science. This element in his message was actively heeded by the scientific societies.

The historian may perhaps opine that what Bacon's near successors took from him was, after all, rather elementary: the idea of socially-related science, the justification of propositions by induction, the importance of experimental range and accuracy. A great deal more elaboration in Bacon's writings belongs rather to the history of philosophy than to that of science. It may also seem that this Baconian legacy was minor compared to the revolution in natural philosophy itself effected by such as Galileo, Kepler, Descartes and Newton, to cite only the physical sciences. Although the British especially revered and echoed Bacon, their models of scientific work were found elsewhere. Newton owned not one of Bacon's major writings, and though his predecessor in experimental science, Robert Boyle, was a fervent admirer of Bacon he rarely referred to him.[21] Those 'who followed, as nearly as they could, the precepts of their Master, Lord Bacon' tended to be, like Joshua Childrey, author of *Britannia Baconica* (1661), collectors of curiosities, marvels, and prodigies, finding their example and authority in *Sylva Sylvarum* and the rather absurd catalogue of natural histories drawn up by Bacon himself and ranging from the History of the Heavenly Bodies to (No. 130) the History of the Natures and Powers of Figures. Grass-roots enthusiasm is certainly never to be despised, and if the English now took pride in Wookey Hole (Somerset) and fell to collecting butterflies and fossils, this kind of interest like the antiquarianism with which it was linked in such figures as John Aubrey was itself an authentic facet of a changing civilization: many who began as mere collectors ended as expert entomologists. Natural history was, and still is in a highly professionalized form, a proper and serious part of scientific activity and just as the method of collection and classification was inappropriate to physics, so one may conversely regard it as essential to the sciences of life. Even in astronomy it had a place, for there was much natural history of comets, of the variability of stars, and of their motions which was still to be written. No Galileo could have defined in advance the strategic ideas of physical astronomy, still less of geology or physiology, as these sciences were to emerge in the nineteenth century on the basis of an immensely wider and deeper knowledge of the facts. Bacon's advice that a vast range of solid facts, certified by experiments, should be collected and recorded was sound and practical, and precisely this activity defines a great deal of the useful part of science during two hundred years after his death; though into this too as it progressed penetrated qualities of technical expertise and specialized language that Bacon himself would never have contemplated.

Thus if, as the French Encyclopaedists recognized, Bacon stood out as the first self-conscious author of a new programme for philosophy, it was Descartes after him who first established an anti-scholastic system of nature, a positive alternative. Though Descartes was some thirty-five years junior to Francis Bacon the disparity of their literary careers was such that he could barely have been influenced by the Englishman, and in fact their minds were utterly unlike. To a modern reader that interval of thirty-five years seems to separate the Middle Ages from post-Renaissance Europe. Descartes wrote in the vernacular, and as an individual appealing to other men like himself facing the problems of philosophy. He did not write 'Man thinks, therefore he exists' but *Cogito, ergo sum*. He proclaims not the submission of the individual to authority or system, but his right to believe what he must of philosophy, and no more. As Descartes relates in the *Discourse on Method* (1637), after completing a thorough education, in which, 'not contented with the sciences actually taught us, I had read all the books that had fallen into my hands, treating of such branches as are esteemed the most curious and rare', he found himself involved in many doubts and errors, persuading him that all his attempts at learning had taught him no more than the discovery of his own ignorance. In philosophy, despite all the efforts of the most distinguished intellects, everything was in dispute and therefore not beyond doubt, and as for the other sciences 'inasmuch as these borrow their principles from philosophy', he reasoned that nothing solid could be built upon such insecure foundations.

The realist philosopher might have argued at this point the necessity of extroversion because the natural world is surely real and existent: it is only necessary to discover it more completely and exactly. But as a programme (if not altogether as a procedure) Descartes avoided the line that would have taken him parallel to Bacon. Since we know the external world only by the mediation of our sense-perceptions, and these may betray our confidence (making the large seem small, the alike different and so on) we have no guarantee of such a direct access to reality as induction seems to postulate. The mind, being outside nature, is capable of doubting everything within nature.

In this perplexity, Descartes proposed to himself four 'rules of reasoning' which he applied in the first instance to that branch of knowledge which alone seemed to him logically sound, mathematics, treated in the most general way by combining the lines of geometry with the symbols of algebra.[22]

In this way I believed that I could borrow all that was best both in geometrical analysis and in algebra, and correct all the defects of the one by the help of the other. And, in point of fact, the accurate observance of these few precepts gave me such ease in unravelling all the questions embraced in these two sciences, that in the two or three months I devoted to their examination, not only did I reach solutions of questions I had formerly deemed exceedingly difficult, but even as regards questions of the solution of which I remained ignorant, I was enabled as it appeared to me, to determine the means whereby, and the extent to which, a solution was possible.

This account in the *Discourse on Method* is not biographically exact in that it omits the influence of the modernist Isaac Beekman (1618) and the studies undertaken by Descartes in advance of his former Jesuit education at La Flèche before the famous days of self-revelation in Bavaria. But it is certainly true that Descartes worked on pure mathematics and mathematical science for many years, postponing the extension of his method to philosophy proper. His success in pure mathematics – from the basic ideas of analytical geometry onwards – had persuaded Descartes that his mind was capable of entertaining clear and distinct ideas, and reasoning upon them. 'Since my method was not bound up with any special subject-matter', he wrote, 'I hoped to apply it to the problems of other sciences as usefully as I had to algebra'. However, as Descartes was well aware, whatever progress he had made towards logical clarity, the problem of ontology remained. Mathematics is about what may be, philosophy is about what is. How do we know what is, in order to form the clear and distinct ideas with which alone we can reason profitably? The *Discourse on Method* offers a metaphysical answer: the first certainty in existence is the enquirer himself:

I concluded from that, that I was a substance whose whole essence or nature is only in thinking, and which has no need of place or dependence on any material thing in order to exist; in such a way that this 'I', the soul, through which I am what I am, is utterly distinct from the body and is even easier to know than the body is, and that even if it were not it [the soul] would not cease to be all that it is.

Descartes then examined further the nature of his conviction of the truth of *I think, therefore I am*, whence he discovered that all things clearly and distinctly perceived as true, are true, 'only observing that there is some difficulty in rightly determining the objects which we distinctly perceive'. Further, he declared that since the mind is aware of its own imperfection, there must be a being, God, which is perfect and that since perfection cannot deceive, those ideas which are clearly and distinctly perceived as true are so because they proceed from a perfect and infinite Being. So much more certain are the fruits of reason, says Descartes, that we may be less assured of the existence of the physical universe itself, than of that of God, 'neither our imagination nor our senses can give us assurance of anything unless our understanding inter-vene . . . whether awake or asleep, we ought never to allow ourselves to be persuaded of the truth of anything unless on the evidence of our reason'.

After this denunciation of empiricism, this declaration that all knowledge of truth is implanted by God, this assertion that the task of the scientist is to frame propositions as clearly and distinctly true as those of geometry, what suggestions can be made for the deciphering of the enigma of nature? According to Descartes, it is necessary to follow exactly that procedure which Bacon had condemmed in Aristotle, that is, to establish the prime generalizations that are 'clearly and distinctly true'.

I have ever remained firm in my original resolution . . . to accept as true nothing that did not appear to me more clear and certain than the demonstrations of the geometers had formerly appeared; and yet I venture to state that not only have I found means to satisfy myself in a short time in all the principal difficulties which are usually treated of in philosophy, but I have also observed certain laws established in nature by God in such a manner, and of which he has impressed on our minds such notions, that after we have reflected sufficiently on these, we cannot doubt that they are accurately observed in all that exists or takes place in the world.

Newton was to declare later, echoing Bacon, that his laws of motion were learnt by induction: Descartes's laws of nature were deductive and he would have been surprised, perhaps, to be told that such universal laws could be other than rationally apprehended. Descartes was so confident of his method that, he asserted, the main features of his philosophy could not be otherwise, as with a theorem in mathematics:

In physics I should consider that I knew nothing if I were able to explain only how things might be, without demonstrating that they could not be otherwise. For, having reduced physics to mathematics, this is something possible.[23]

Now in fact it hardly needs to be stated that Descartes reduced only a little of physics to mathematics, at the cost of employing quite arbitrary assumptions; in the passage just quoted he goes on to admit as much, but his view of his own philosophy saw it as all mathematical and all founded on clear and distinct ideas. Hence, as a tightly logical system, it could not be false.

Thus the science of Descartes is a centrifugal system, working outwards from the certainty of the existence of mind and God to embrace the universal truths or laws of nature detected by reason, and then from the 'concatenation of these truths' revealing the mechanisms involved in particular phenomena. It is systematic, unlike the 'new philosophy' of Bacon or Galileo, because its aim is not to enunciate a correct statement here and there as it becomes accessible to intellect, but to provide an unchanging fabric whose relevance to particulars is the sole remaining subject of enquiry. In this respect, despite his contempt for scholasticism, Descartes sought for himself the commanding authority of a new Aristotle. Indeed, among Cartesian scientists, and still more among Cartesian philosophers of later generations, a new scholasticism flourished through the dissection, embroidering and expansion of Descartes's doctrines, until they, like Aristotelianism in the sixteenth and seventeenth centuries, were in turn regarded as a bulwark against dangerous innovations and as the philosophic justification of religious orthodoxy.

Although claiming for his science the formal, axiomatic truth of mathematics, only the two physical essays annexed with *Geometry* to the *Discourse on Method*, that is, *Dioptrics* and *Meteors*, possess this character, though not cast in the propositional form. For the rest of the expression of his philosophy Descartes chose narrative prose. The two optical essays – for the principal 'meteor' of the second is the rainbow – exerted enormous influence by developing a form of mathematical physics different from Galileo's because firmly tied to physical hypotheses, indeed, to the mechanical philosophy. For every student of dioptrics (that is, of refraction) in the early seventeenth century the touchstone was 'Snel's Law' ($\sin i / \sin r = k$); Thomas Harriot got it first (1601), without ever revealing the law; Kepler almost got it; then came Willebrod Snel (1621 plus) and finally Descartes who published it in his *Dioptrics* (1637). The first three worked inductively, that is, by making careful experiments; how Descartes discovered 'Snel's Law' is unknown, but he presented it as a rational discovery from his theory of nature of light and as such it was widely accepted as a justification for his method.[24] Later, successively, the Toulousan mathematician Pierre Fermat (1601–65) and Isaac Newton were to show that 'rational reconstructions' of 'Snel's Law', both quite different from each other and from Descartes's could be developed from alternative physical principles, and consequently neither the physical principles nor the rational reconstruction could be held to be proved by their agreement with experimental facts. However, it was (and is) always possible to maintain that, for one reason or another, improbabilities ruled out all but the writer's preferred set of ideas.

For Descartes to have created a grand system of nature on the model of his three mathematical essays of 1637 would have been quite impossible: he lacked technique, method, information and ideas to fulfil such a grandiose ambition. Notably, though he was to propose a completely kinematic philosophy of nature, he failed to devise a kinematics of his own and was to criticize that of Galileo as merely superficial, and displaying ignorance of the true reality of motion. Descartes was all too conscious that the mathematical approach to philosophy could range all the way from the absurd (Fludd – the opponent of Descartes's ally Marin Mersenne) to the fanciful (Kepler) and the unnatural (Galileo); he himself wanted to describe no unreal world – for such he took Galileo's world of abstraction to be – but the world of experience. However, he did not reject the axiomatic approach proper to mathematics: there must be first principles to be accepted as true because clear and distinct, so that no man could doubt them; but then the rest was to be demonstrated, not mathematically, but using verbal arguments 'in the geometrical way'. Thus, confusingly, *more geometrico* came to mean the opposite of its literal statement. Further, Descartes preferred to introduce the device of the model: he described, he says, not our own world but one having exactly the phenomena of ours; not the actual human body, but a mechanism having all the properties of a man's body. The point of using the model was (and is) that such a sceptical demand as: 'show me a blood-corpuscle' (which Descartes could not have done) becomes meaningless; the only correspondence to be expected is between what blood is and does in the model and what it is and does in a man. Descartes could present carefully detailed, indeed elegant mechanisms which he imagined as responsible for the phenomena without being defeated by the demand to produce a particle of magnetism. In other words, just as 'rational reconstruction' is consistent with the mathematical treatment of *Diotrics* and *Meteors*, so it is made possible in the context of non-mathematical theory by the device of the model. And considering the latter as an instrument of further research, it provides the possibility of finding out by comparison what the hitherto imperceptible causes or parts of things really are.

What did Descartes take to be the fundamental idea of philosophy? So far as the physical make-up of the universe is concerned we must begin, he thought, with the concepts of matter, which must both be divided into parts and capable of motion. The primary idea of matter is that it occupies space; hence, he argued, there can be no space unoccupied by matter, or vacuous. He further defined the subdivisions of matter, the least of which was analogous to the aether of later philosophers in filling all space otherwise empty of matter and playing an active role in phenomena; he also (incorrectly) laid down the way in which motion is shared between material particles when they collide one with another. The Cartesian model universe had evolved in time to its present observed state, planets being solidified minor stars, for example, as a closed system.[25] the original matter had changed in form but no matter or motion had ever been added. Being a closed system experiencing neither loss nor gain of motion (which is for Descartes the equivalent of the energy of later physics) the history of the universe is written in the redistribution of motion by means of the impact of particles; the distinct kinds of redistribution that occur occasion the huge diversity of phenomena that we classify qualitatively as living, falling, magnetic, chemical and so forth. (Since Descartes could operate with three kinds of matter, capable each of fulfilling many roles, and an infinite variety of motion, he could never lack hypotheses.) Thus the ultimate nature of every kind of observed change in the universe from the upheaval of a mountain to the birth of a mouse is the same, but each goes along its own path in the categories of action and reaction that Descartes devises and it is only in an ineffable ultimate balance of things, preserving constancy amid change, that all space remains always full and the sum total of motion constant. The assertion about totality in the Cartesian universe – which would be invalid, obviously, for merely local or restricted systems like the planet Earth, whose isolation or closure is merely naively apparent since it receives light and heat from the Sun, for example – entailed the consequence that this fundamental kinematics of Cartesian physics must remain forever unquantifiable. Not without strain and distortion could it ever be adapted to Galilean mathematics.

In building his models, experimentation was for Descartes no more than a weak substitute for rational reconstruction, when the mind starting from clear and distinct ideas could perceive multiple routes to the given explanation, and was forced to try to discover which Nature seemed to have chosen. Since the principles of philosophy were ideas, it was to fit these, and not experimental evidence, that its subsidiary theories were shaped. It was essentially deductive from these natural laws, and if knowledge did not supply the requisite materials, then they had to be invented with the aid of reasoned deduction, as the celestial vortices carrying the planets about the Sun, the three kinds of matter and the variously contrived pores of substances were invented in accordance with the exigencies of experience and reason. Of course, experience was respected in the sense that Descartes sought to explain in his model the sum of the phenomena of nature as he knew them, for it is obvious that he could not have deduced magnetism within his system had he not known of its manifestations. But Descartes made no attempt to confirm his mechanisms in detail by experiment. The foundations of knowledge, he thought, were best settled without it:

for, at the commencement, it is better to make use only of what is spontaneously represented to our senses, and of which we cannot remain ignorant, provided we bestow on it any reflection, however slight, than to concern ourselves about more uncommon or recondite phenomena; the reason for which is, that the more uncommon often mislead us so long as the causes of the more ordinary remain unknown . . .

Experiments indicating some conclusion detached from a deductive system Descartes distrusted. This must not be taken to mean that either Descartes or his successors were totally blind to the merits of experimentation, though it could only be an adjunct when the application of clear and distinct ideas failed, or in an obscure enquiry, or in order to demonstrate truths more convincingly. Within ten years of Descartes's death organized experimentation was set on foot in England, in Oxford and in London, in Paris and other intellectual centres in France, in Italy and in Germany, encouraged partly by the writings and example of Galileo and his pupils, partly by the precepts of Bacon, partly by the excitement of the newly-born science of pneumatics, and partly by the early patient work of Gilbert, Harvey and many others. The practice as distinct from the methodology of experimenting had many diverse and scattered origins. Cartesian philosophy was overtaken by its independent vigour and necessarily borrowed its assertion that the superiority of the new philosophy over the old was experimentally verifiable by the eyes. During the last decades of the seventeenth century Cartesians and neo-Cartesians actively adopted experimental demonstration as a means of vindicating their philosophy, and empirical confirmation of the truth of its broad tenets at least was being eagerly sought by such gifted practical scientists as the French academician Edmé Mariotte (d. 1684), as well as by the modernist teachers of philosophy who were forcing Cartesianism into reluctant universities.

The kinematic or as it is more usually termed mechanical philosophy of Descartes constitutes the core and character of scientific innovation for the second half of the seventeenth century, indeed until it was put down by the rising authority of Newton. In this half-century virtually everyone was, or had been, a quasi-Cartesian, not least such English inductivists as Robert Boyle and Isaac Newton. The immense fertility and range of Descartes's review of nature in his essays, in the *Principles of Philosophy*, in *On Man*, in his letters and other writings gave him a powerful voice on every topic; he was more universal than such 'specialists' as Kepler or Galileo, more compelling than rival authors of universal systems like Kenelm Digby (1603–65).[26] Moreover, in his version of the mechanical philosophy, more uncompromising, more rigorous, more emphatic than any other, Descartes seemed a more decisive and further-reaching thinker than Bacon or Galileo, or even Gassendi, or Thomas Hobbes or any other general theorist of nature contemporary with himself. Mechanism seemed to all such critical, innovating spirits the proper alternative to the Renaissance world of qualities, magic and mysticism: we have a kind of case-history in Marin Mersenne (1588–1648), friar and religious apologist, scientific organizer, friend and ally of Descartes, of a mind's passage from abhorrence of materialism to a joyful exploration of mechanism.[27] Descartes was its leading spirit.

It is obvious that the ultimate parent of the seventeenth-century mechanical philosophy was Greek atomism, now known in considerable detail from the writings of Epicuros and his Roman follower, Lucretius.[28] The fearsome stigma of atheism which those writings carried with them tinged Cartesian and other versions of the mechanical philosophy till the end of the century and resonate still in the philosophical debate between Newton and Leibniz (1710–16). The question: can a mechanistic universe also be a divine universe? Was never to be clearly answered within the terms of that age. Nevertheless, a great many devout philosophers thought it no derogation of the divine majesty to define

God as the Transcendent Artificer. The purer, more scholarly line of atomism runs through seventeenth-century thought in parallel with the freer imaginings of Descartes and others. Its major exponent was Pierre Gassendi (1592–1655), otherwise moderately celebrated in astronomy and physics. From about 1625 he was the first philosopher to attempt to develop a completely mechanistic physics founded in Epicuros and rejecting Aristotle; to a large extent he loosely paraphrased and expanded Lucretius, save that Gassendi was a Christian. As with the Greek atomists, the complexities of substance were to be explained without making any assumptions of a non-material kind, indeed postulating the existence of atoms in the void as the sole true reality; physical properties were traced to the imagined size and shape of component particles, which might be imagined round and smooth for fluidity, or hooked together for strength. In Bacon and Galileo, however, there had already been (as mentioned before) the beginnings of a truly kinetic theory of particles, especially in relation to heat. Isaac Beeckman, the Dutch philosopher who influenced the young Descartes, was another who noted that the three variables, size, shape and motion, should all be considered in a theory of particles.[29] Although one finds already in Galileo the famous distinction between primary and secondary qualities immortally associated with John Locke, and much other supporting evidence, for him as for Bacon the mechanical philosophy was of relatively minor importance in the whole reformation of knowledge; for the one less important than mathematics, for the other less essential than induction. While neither doubted that the Aristotelian qualities must be replaced by particulate mechanisms, neither was a strict atomist; Bacon indeed wrote that the proper method for the discovery of the 'form or true difference of a given nature, or the nature to which nature is owing, or source from which it emanates' would not lead to 'atoms, which takes for granted the vacuum, and immutability of matter (neither of which hypotheses is correct), but to the real particles such as we discover them to be'.[30] Many later natural philosophers shared Bacon's view that the atomistic version of the particulate or corpuscular theory of matter was unnecessarily dogmatic: it was, indeed, always to be both logically and experimentally true that the definition of 'atom' is entirely a function of the tests of divisibility to be applied. Many also found the concept of vacuum repugnant and incomprehensible. Only at the turn of the century was Newton to lead the way back to a much modified Epicurean atomism; he had in youth been influenced by the *Physiologia* (1654) of the most important English atomist of mid-century, the physician Walter Charleton (1620–1707), and found in terms of ultimate physics just as much trouble with the concept of 'aether' as with that of vacuous space.[31]

Meanwhile, for the greater part of the century, the stronger trend was towards the Cartesian, or kinetic version of the mechanical philosophy put forward with varying degrees of eclecticism, emphasizing the effects of motion in the particles rather than their hypothetical size or shape; the idea that phenomena could be effected by the motions of one or more extremely tenuous but material aethers (otherwise known as effluvia, spirits and so forth) was by no means uncongenial or inconsistent. From mid-century experiments in the 'vacuum' (that is, air pressure reduced to 2.54 cm (1 in) of mercury or less), indicating that light and magnetism at any rate traversed it unaffected, suggested the existence in space and within the pores of solid bodies of some universal medium far more subtle than the air. It is not too much to say that experimentalism grew to maturity around mid-century in association with such undogmatic Cartesianism, or eclectic version of the mechanical philosophy, detectable (for example) in the work of Borelli in Italy, of Huygens and Mariotte in Italy, and of the early Fellows of the Royal Society in England, above all Robert Boyle. Thus Descartes (principally) and Gassendi created a common, modern language for European science, which enjoyed by 1670 or thereabouts a community of progressive spirit and basic natural philosophy which had been quite absent at the beginning of the century. That there were very significant differences in detail between individuals in their epistemology, metaphysics and methods should not obscure the equally real ability of men of all nations to talk to each other fruitfully, to identify common problems and to have the same conceptions of what solutions would be like. Descartes was a far more truly international figure than either Galileo or Bacon, and the very fact that he wrote as a philosopher gave his scientific ideas greater currency; to many places where intellectual conventionality had lingered untroubled Cartesian ideas brought the first breath of a new outlook, a fresh vitality in natural philosophy. Thus, Oxford, because the reading of Descartes was encouraged there, was regarded about mid-century as being much in advance of Cambridge. Descartes's was the pre-eminent intellect behind the ebullience of ideas and discoveries which made Paris the scientific focus of Europe from about 1630 to the end of the century, and which provided the background for the English empirco–mathematical dominance later. Even such critics of Descartes as Robert Boyle and Isaac Newton, who discovered through their confidence in the experimental or Galilean method the speciousness of his physical theories, had found in those same theories their point of departure; indeed, the main activities in physical science for more than a generation after Descartes's death can be interpreted, without gross distortion, as a commentary upon Descartes's works. And if the *Principles of Philosophy* proved ephemeral compared with Newton's *Mathematical Principles of Natural Philosophy* – even the title suggests a reaction – its influence in leading later seventeenth-century science to entertain ideas of mechanism, of the corpuscular structure of matter, of the importance of 'natural laws', was creative of further progress.

Descartes's *Principles of Philosophy* (1644) was the major foundation of this common heritage shared by physical theorists, just as his *Geometry* was to be among mathematicians. Starting from the assumption that there are in nature neither magical powers nor such occult forces as gravity and magnetism were supposed by some to be, and supposing that the universe is continuously and completely filled with particulate matter in motion, Descartes developed an extraordinarily elaborate mechanical model to represent all its actions. His particles, of which there were three species, were not atoms, because he imagined them as divisible, though in nature not normally divided. The first element was a fine dust, of irregular particles so that it could fill completely the interstices between the larger particles. The second element (*matière subtile* or aether) consisted of rather coarser spherical particles, apt for motion, and the third element of still more coarse, irregular and sluggish particles. These three elements corresponded roughly to the Fire, Air and Earth of Aristotle, and as they were composed of the same matter, the elements could be transformed one into another. This was regarded by the Cartesians as no arbitrary hypothesis, but as a truth (according to Rohault) 'necessarily follow(ing) from the Motion and Division of the Parts of Matter which Experience obliges us to acknowledge in the Universe. So that the Three Elements which I have established, ought not to be looked upon as imaginary Things, but on the contrary, as they are very easy to conceive, and we see a necessity of their Existence, we cannot reasonably lay aside the Use of them, in explaining Effects purely Material.' The nature of a substance was mainly determined by its content of third element, its properties by the second. Since Descartes denied that the third-element particles had intrinsic weight or attraction, hardness (the cohesion of these particles) was attributed to their remaining at rest together, fluidity to their relative motion; but this motion was not intrinsic but imparted by the first and second elements. Thus in solution the grosser particles of the solvent by their agitation dislodged those of the dissolved material; if however the particles of the solvent were too light, or the pores of the solid material too small to admit them, the latter would not dissolve. When the pores between the third-element particles were large enough to admit a large quantity of the second element, the substance was an 'elastic fluid' (air), whose tendency to expand was caused by the very free and rapid motion of the second-element particles. Flame itself consisted of matter in its most subtle form and under most violent agitation, and was therefore the most effective dissolvent of other bodies, while the sensation of heat increased with the degree of motion in the particles of the heated body. Rohault notes that, when filed, copper grows less hot than iron because, copper being the softer metal, its particles do not require such violent agitation to separate them as do those of iron. The greater motion associated with heat was also the cause of thermal expansion. Light was thought to be 'a certain Motion of the Parts of luminous Bodies whereby they are capable of pushing every Way the subtil Matter (second element) which fills the Pores of transparent Bodies', and secondary illumination was attributed to the tendency of this matter to recede from the luminous body in a straight line. Transparent bodies had straight pores through which the *matière subtile* could pass, opaque bodies blocked or twisted pores. If this exertion of pressure by the luminous body were confined or resisted, it would grow hot. Refraction and reflection of this pressure (or rather pulse) which is light were explained by analogy with the bouncing of elastic balls. In dealing with magnetism Cartesians were careful to emphasize that 'though we may imagine that there are some Particular Sorts of Motion which may very well be explained by Attraction; yet this is only because we carelessly ascribe that to Attraction, which is really done by Impulse'; as when it is said a horse draws a cart, whereas it really pushes it by pressing on the collar. Magnetic effects were actually caused by streams of screw-like particles, entering each pole of the earth and passing from pole to pole over its surface, which passed through nut-like pores in lodestone, iron and steel, and thus were capable of exerting pressures on these magnetic materials.

By theorizing in this way on the different motions of the three species of matter the Cartesian physicists tried to account for all the phenomena of physics as known in the second half of the seventeenth century. They had some striking contemporary discoveries on their side: for instance, the discovery that the rising of water in pumps and analogous effects were not due to *horror vacui* or to attraction, but simply to the mechanical pressure of the atmosphere. They also explained gravitation mechanically as a result of pressure, and extended their corpuscular ideas to chemical reactions. The idea of particulate matter-in-motion was therefore the very foundation of Cartesian science, the basis of a homogeneous system of explanation. The fact that (in Rohault's words) 'the few Suppositions which I have made . . . are nothing compared with the great Number of Properties, which I am going to deduce from them, and which are exactly confirmed by Experience' was a strong reason for believing 'that That which at first looks like a Conjecture will be received for a very certain and manifest Truth'. As expounded by Descartes and his successors this 'mechanical philosophy' was illustrated by many qualitative experiments; but these could hardly be said to prove the Cartesian system, which always remained, in addition, entirely non-mathematical.[32]

The great neo-Cartesian Christiaan Huygens (1629–95), so long a principal ornament of Parisian intellectual life and mainstay of the French Royal Academy of Sciences, was to describe the *Principles of Philosophy* as 'un beau roman de physique'. Indeed, the Cartesian machines of nature and men were to receive little experimental validation. Clearness and distinctness in ideas, however rationally impeccable, proved irrelevant to the question of contingent truth. The deductive method, attacked by Francis Bacon in the schoolmen, was to be once more subjected to destructive criticism by the English Baconians of the Royal Society. Perhaps it may justly be said that Descartes's successes in science were due less to any merits in his method, than to his native genius for investigation. There is one point, however, both in the method and the texture of his thinking on scientific subjects that deserves to be singled out. Descartes well understood the importance, in any work of research, of scientific imagination, a faculty with which he himself was so well endowed that he hardly perceived its limitations when controlled by reason alone without cautious experimentation. Bacon had recognized that imagination or intuition might surmount an inconvenient obstruction; Galileo also admitted that in demonstrative sciences a conclusion might be known before it could be proved:

Nor need you question but that Pythagoras a long time before he found the demonstration for which he offered the Hecatomb, had been certain, that the square of the side subtending the right angle in a rectangle triangle, was equal to the square of the other two sides: and the certainty of the conclusion conducted not a little to the investigating of the demonstration . . .[33]

In Descartes there is a more overt appreciation of the function of directed imagination, playing on the problem in hand, in formulating hypotheses to be tested by experiment or other means:

. . . the power of nature is so ample and vast . . . that I have hardly observed a single particular effect which I cannot at once recognize as capable of being deduced in many different ways from the principles, and that my greatest difficulty usually is to discover in which of these ways the effect is dependent upon them; for out of this difficulty I cannot otherwise extricate myself than by again seeking certain experiments, which may be such that their result is not the same if it is in one of these ways that we must explain it, as it would be if it were to be explained in another.[34]

Here experiment is put forward, not as by Bacon to uncover the unknown, or as by Galileo to confirm the known, but as a means of eliminating all but one of the mechanisms suggested by imagination as the explanation of a particular phenomenon. And as Descartes correctly stated, the imagination is directed because it is referred to certain known principles (or constructs), and further because the mechanisms suggested must be susceptible in the first place of deductive check, since science does not admit of idle guessing. If Descartes had realized that even when only a single hypothetical mechanism seems deductively feasible it remains hypothesis until confirmed by experiment, and if he had applied this test more meticulously, his thought would have been less liable to have run into erroneous speculation. In any case the liberty to frame hypotheses (in spite of Newton's famous dictum), with the rigorous attention to the findings of experiment and observation which Descartes himself neglected in his encyclopaedic survey of nature, was to prove a creative factor in the accelerating progress of science.

Another point might be made. Though the physics of Descartes's *Principles* was a-mathematical it did, like his *Dioptrics*, disclose a possibility of mathematization. In a kinetic theory, whose basis was the continual redistribution of motion (or momentum) among particles by impact, it would in principle have been possible to compute gross changes in motion – that is, in phenomena – from the redistribution among the particles, once the simple laws of the distribution of momentum between pairs of colliding particles were known. To this topic Galileo, Descartes, Huygens, Christopher Wren, John Wallis, Borelli and Newton addressed themselves, as the fundamental mechanical phenomenon. The laws of change of momentum were found, but their application to near-infinite numbers of particulate collisions was never even attempted in the seventeenth century. The statistical approach to such problems was never perceived, and so Descartes's principle of the conservation of motion remained sterile, unlike the principle of the conservation of energy on the nineteenth century. But the ideal of mathematically integrating physics and mechanics was clearly understood, if unrealistic before Newton, who realized it by shifting the basis of action from the redistribution of motion to the action of force – in this way opening the path from the simplistic case of a single pair of particles to the physical consideration of gross bodies containing near-infinite numbers of particles. Newton was to render quantifiable the integration of action which remained for ever speculative in Cartesian physics.

The scientific method of the seventeenth century cannot be traced to a single origin. It was not worked out logically by any one philosopher, nor was it exemplified completely in any one investigation. It may even be doubted whether there was any procedure so conscious and definite that it can be described in isolation from the context of ideas to which it was related. The attitude to nature of the seventeenth-century scientists – especially their almost uniform tendency towards a mechanistic philosophy – was not strictly part of their scientific method; but can this be discussed except in connection with the idea of nature? In large part the character of the method was determined by the mental range of the men who applied it; hence Bacon's method bore fewer fruits in his own hands because his conception of the facts of nature was still Aristotelian. The influence of Descartes, too, was so great because he produced a mechanistic world-system of infinite scope (enriched with some genuine discoveries) which was welcomed by his age, not because he outlined a remarkably clear or satisfactory way of proceeding in scientific research. Even Galileo's observations on method were probably less important than direct imitation of the kind of mathematical analysis he initiated in mechanics. Over the broad area of scientific activity the influence of content on form was more significant than the reverse effect. Methods changed because different questions were asked, and a new view of what constitutes the most useful kind of scientific knowledge began to prevail. Perhaps this is most effectively revealed in the biological sciences, where the century witnessed a progressive change in the content of investigations unaccompanied by conscious discussions of the methods to be employed. Here there was no parallel to the criticism of the methods of Aristotle and the scholastics in physics, though of course the medieval neglect of the descriptive sciences was often commented on adversely. The far-reaching interaction between the content and the techniques of science was also uncontrolled by any very explicit conceptions of method. This interaction had a profound effect on the quality and extent of the information available; but Bacon alone explicitly recognized the importance of accurate fact-gathering in science. It seems most natural to believe that in any effective step the method, the philosophy and the discovery itself were carried along together in the subsequent impact, for though there is nothing that can reasonably be called a specific method of science to be found in the works of Harvey, or Kepler, or Gilbert, these men changed the character and form of future studies. Who, for instance, could ignore the challenge of the phrase with which Gilbert opens his Preface to *De Magnete*: 'Clearer proofs, in the discovery of secrets, and in the investigation of the hidden causes of things, being afforded by trustworthy experiments and by demonstrated arguments, than by the probable guesses and opinions of the ordinary professors of philosophy . . .' Yet the meaning and weight of experimental testimony was still open to discussion a century later. A scientific approach to problems must be the sum of its many aspects – experimentation, mathematical and conceptual analysis, quantitative accuracy, and so on – varying according to the nature of the problem; and this the seventeenth century drew from many varied sources. Its implied implementation in practice was more important than its explicit formulation. with the some-

what curious result that scientific method, shaping itself to the needs of practising scientists and vindicated rather by results than by preconceived logical
rigour, has remained something of an enigma to philosophers from Berkeley
onwards. In the long run the obstinate empiricism of a Gilbert or the unpre-
dictable intuition of a Faraday have successfully broken the rules of both
inductive and mathematical logic.

NOTES

1. Stillman Drake, *Galileo against the Philosophers*, Zeitlen and Ver Brugge: Los
   Angeles, 1976
2. *Idem, Galileo's Notes on Motion*, Istituto e Museo di Storia della Scienza, Florence,
   Monograph No. 3, 1979
3. I. Bernard Cohen, *The Newtonian Revolution*, Cambridge U.P., 1980
4. Galileo, *Il Saggiatore*, 1623; Stillman Drake, *Discoveries and Opinions of Galileo*,
   Doubleday: New York, 1957, 237–8 (The Assayer).
5. Robert Boyle, *Of the Excellency and Grounds of the Mechanical Hypothesis*, 1674; T.
   Birch, *Works*, 1772, IV, 67–8 (condensed).
6. Galileo, *Two New Sciences*, trans. Stillman Drake, Wisconsin University Press:
   Madison, 1974, 147–8.
7. Galileo, *Dialogue*, ed. G de Santillana, Chicago University Press: Chicago, 1953,
   347
8. Newton, *Opticks*, Dover reprint, 1952, 404–5.
9. Galileo (loc. cit. Note 6), 159.
10. A. Rupert Hall, *Philosophers at War*, Cambridge U.P., 1980.
11. I. Newton, *Principia*, London, 1713, 357–8.
12. John H. Randall Jr, 'Scientific method in the School of Padua' [1940], *Roots of
    scientific Thought*, (eds P. Wiener and A. Noland), Basic Books: New York, 1957,
    144–6.
13. Charles Schmitt, 'Experience and experiment: a comparison of Zabarella's view
    with Galileo's in *De motu*', *Studies in the Renaissance*, 16, 1969.
14. Benjamin Farrington: *Francis Bacon, Philosopher of Industrial Science*, Schuman:
    New York, 1949; R. F. Jones, *Ancients and Moderns*, Washington U.P.: St Louis,
    1936; Paolo Rossi, *Francis Bacon, From Magic to Science*, Routledge: London,
    1968.
15. F. Bacon, *Novum Organum*, Bk. 1, xix.
16. A. C. Crombie, *From Augustine to Galileo*, Heinemann: London, 1952, 217.
17. A more vernacular rendering would be 'Show me', the words attributed to the
    Missourian. Sir William Petty once jokingly proposed that Doubting Thomas
    should be the Society's patron saint.
18. *Novum Organum*, I. Aphorisms 81, 129, 70.
19. Ibid., I, 95, 105.
20. Ibid., I, 61.
21. Newton owned the *Essays* and the *Opuscula varia posthuma* (1658), which he had
    read and marked.
22. The four rules were: (1) to accept nothing as true that was not evidently so; (2)
    to analyse problems into the smallest elements; (3) to order his thoughts by start-

ing always with the simplest objects, moving gradually to the more complex; (4) to make full lists and reviews so as to be sure of omitting nothing.

23. To Mersenne, 11 March 1640.

24. It is well known that Descartes employs different language, and hence it seems variant models, in explaining the physical action of light in the *Dioptrics* and the later *Principles of Philosophy* (1644): in the latter the passage of light is instantaneous, in the former it occupies time. Commentators differ on the importance of this inconsistency.

25. Descartes taught that though God had indeed created the universe as it is, he created it as though it had evolved from a primitive state, that is, with a built-in past. This idea later reappeared geologically.

26. Digby's chief work has a long title: *Two Treatises, in one of which, the Nature of Bodies; in the other, the Nature of Man's Soule, is looked into: in way of discovery, of the Immortality of Reasonable Soules* (Paris, 1644). In 1644 neither Galileo's nor Descartes's works had been widely read, especially by Englishmen.

27. Robert Lenoble, *Mersenne, ou la naissance du mécanisme*, Paris, 1943.

28. There were before 1600 about thirty printings of *De natura rerum*, first published in 1473.

29. *Journal tenu par Isaac Beeckman de 1604 à 1634*, ed. C. de Waard, La Haye, 1939–45, I 216 (1618).

30. *Novum Organum*, Bk. II, Aphorisms 1 and 8.

31. Charleton paraphrased from Gassendi's *Animadversiones* of 1649, the first full statement of his atomist physics. Charleton also wrote on Stonehenge as a Danish structure.

32. The quotations in these two paragraphs are all from John Clarke (trans). *Rohault's System of Natural Philosophy Illustrated with Dr Samuel Clarke's Notes mostly out of Sir Isaac Newton's Philosophy*, London, 1723, I. 115–7, 156, 201 ff. II, 166; I, 203; II, 169. Jaques Rohault (1620–72) was the leading exponent of Cartesian physics at this time, whose *Traité de Physique* had first appeared in 1671. The careless fallacy of the argument against attraction – as though compressive and tensile stresses are identical – is quite typical.

33. Galileo, *Dialogue*. (Note 7), 60.

34. *Discourse on Method Part VI*.

CHAPTER EIGHT

The organization and purpose of science

Philosophy and science have always flourished in their own context, changing from age to age, and in particular institutional forms. In the oldest civilizations all learning, and especially astrology and medicine, flourished in the temples in association with religion: medical cults attracted many sufferers in Greece and Rome, and indeed down to our own day. The oldest secular institutions of learning existed in Greece: Plato's Academy, Aristotle's Lycaeum (continued by his pupil Strato), the great Library at Alexandria which endured through many centuries. Schools and universities founded in the Middle Ages are still teaching, however much altered their style. Lastly, the learned society and the academy, bodies that exist to promote science and learning and encourage their protagonists, were creations of early modern times. Their evolution was closely linked with that of science, not least because the idea of a *research institute* was very much in the first place a scientific rather than a literary or humanistic idea. Its prime function is not teaching and it charges no fees; its purpose is to augment knowledge rather than to diffuse it; the research institute is both a building with proper material facilities and a team, usually working towards some common scientific purpose under the leadership of its director. There are older non-European precedents for it, but the first research institute in modern Europe was undoubtedly Tycho Brahe's observatory at Uraniborg (p. 137). It is surely unsurprising that the first examples should appear in astronomy, the second being the Observatory of Paris under the direction of Jean-Dominique Cassini (1625–1712). Perhaps we would look next to the Paris Arsenal at the time of the French Revolution. Only in the nineteenth century was the reality of the research institute to emerge as a characteristic scientific form, though, as we shall soon see, the idea was often presented before.

From the sixteenth through to the eighteenth centuries the common form of learned and scientific grouping was looser, more discursive, and voluntarist. By 1700 only the French and Berlin Academies were composed of salaried members. The amount of institutionally determined and financed investigation was also small: academies and societies existed to stimulate research by inciting individuals to undertake investigations privately, to reward those who under-took research successfully, and to communicate research reports. They also served in a minor way as a vehicle for the state's concern with scientific or technical matters like marine navigation. By the end of the seventeenth century most men who were active in the scientific movement were members of such bodies, which were also beginning to undertake the publication of journals for the dissemination of reports and criticism. The academies and societies had by then won a considerable prestige: in science they enjoyed much more prestige than the universities – and attracted more obloquy. To some extent they profited from the failure of the universities to retain during the Renaissance that leadership in all philosophical, scientific, and medical matters they had established during the Middle Ages – which may in turn be connected with the odd geographical fact that the old universities were rarely to be found in great court cities (with such obvious exceptions as Paris and Vienna). In the community of medieval learning the scholar had enjoyed free intercourse with the members of other universities, from Cracow to Salamanca, and migration to hear the best masters was normal. The sixteenth century saw the novel phenomenon of scholars, poets and philosophers whose interests were no longer embraced within the pattern of academic studies, and who flourished in the service of a prince, or in the professions.[1] The nobleman and the merchant became more important as patrons of learning, while physicians, soldiers, apothecaries, lawyers and tradesmen began to contribute to its advancement. It was no longer essential to read Latin and Greek to have some learning, and as the number of vernacular readers especially grew rapidly during the sixteenth century, the market for mathematical and philosophical books in the spoken languages (as were those of Galileo and Descartes) flourished: consequently, in Northern Europe markedly (for here universities were both fewer and slower-moving with the times) intellectual leadership began to pass to a group which, if usually university educated, had passed from the academic to a wider world. Not surprisingly, the old studies were mocked by the young radicals:

> Oxford and Cambridge are our laughter
> Their learning is but pedantry;

wrote the author of the *Ballad of Gresham College*, adding typically enough 'Aristotle's an Ass to Epicuros'. (However the joke was to be turned on the new-fangled ways by Samuel Butler in *Hudibras* and Jonathan Swift in *Gulliver's Travels*.)

Moreover, towards the end of the Middle Ages a group of 'learned craftsmen' had begun to appear, many of whom were literate (some, in Latin), and others skilled in mathematics also. As leaders of this group the engineers (of whom Leonardo da Vinci is by far the most famous) select themselves; others were pharmacists, metal-workers (like Cellini), surveyors and navigators, assayers of precious metals and gunners. These men were not only practitioners of technical skills but writers of books, from which those of more philosophic outlook like Galileo or William Gilbert borrowed on occasion. Some who were practitioners at least for a period of their lives (like Thomas Digges and Thomas Harriot) were important figures in the evolution of science, many more were at least quasi-scientific. They helped to form a social and intellectual environment which the natural philosophers and mathematicians began to find congenial: sometimes a great nobleman might patronize men of all three types. It was widely recognized by the mid-seventeenth century that grammar-school and university did not provide the only valuable education, especially as schools and colleges were (on the continent) often controlled by conservative religious orders, while modernization of university teaching proved a painfully slow process. Scientific knowledge was no longer limited to the religious and medical professions, but was widely diffused through a diversifying and exuberant society. Many autobiographical accounts describe the exhilaration experienced by a young man in passing from the dull sterility of formal education to an acquaintance with the new philosophy and mathematics. As with Descartes's almost mystical experience in Bavaria or Galileo's conversion to the Copernican system or Pascal's independent 're-discovery' of Euclidean geometry, the shift to modern views and methods was highly individual since instruction and tradition all leant the other way; but those who acquired novel and independent intellectual tastes naturally clubbed together or were brought together by patronage. Inevitably informal groups tended to seek stability, encouragement and privileges. As scholars had gathered round the Medicis in fifteenth-century Florence, so the last Valois in France supported an 'Academy', or rather academies, whose discussions moved from poetry to mathematics and the Copernican system. Learning was also an aspect of life in a court or great household in the circles associated with Sir Walter Raleigh and Henry Percy (1564–1632), the 'wizard Earl' of Northumberland (most of his wizardry seems to have consisted in his patronage of such mathematicians as Harriot). At Rome the expert on optics and natural magic, Giambaptista Porta (d. 1615) assembled a group of colleagues and disciples called the Academy of the Secrets of Nature. All of these groups were too ephemeral and chaotic to be regarded as societies in the modern sense; they were also very restricted and private, like the most famous of this early group, the Accademia dei Lincei (calling themselves lynxes because of their own clear-sightedness). The lynxes rose to the relatively large membership of thirty-two, and formed ambitious plans for institutional activities. These were never realized, and the society can barely be said to have had a corporate existence at all; they were rather a number of individuals selected by the founder, Prince Federigo Cesi. Galileo was the outstanding member of the early Lincei.

There are again hints far back, for instance in More's *Utopia*, of the alternate scheme of communal living and activity, whereby a group of men, perhaps with complementary expertise, would work together towards a common objective. If we call this an 'experimental college' we see the lingering medieval idea of the learned community, now shifting from the school and scriptorium to the idea of the research institute. Bacon's *New Atlantis* contains the classic statement of an ideal that was to haunt the seventeenth century, and was to be satirized in Swift's Grand Academy of Lagado.[2] Salomon's house in the New Atlantis is devoted to 'the knowledge of causes, and the secret motions of things; and the enlarging of the bounds of Human Empire, to the effecting of all things possible', and if to a reader three hundred and fifty years later Bacon's free imagination of the most extravagant possible armoury for enquiring into nature seems to have rather missed the point, to his contemporaries the very idea of such organized and rich programmes of research was immensely inspiring. The mere provision that 'For every invention of value, we erect a statue to the inventor, and give him a liberal and honourable reward' appeared as a shining and almost unattainable ideal of generosity and prudence. Bacon certainly believed that the enormous realm of natural knowledge was far too vast for one man to tackle single-handed, while concentration on a single line of enquiry or exploitation of one idea of nature was all too likely to prove unbalanced and myopic. The way to combine individual expertise with breadth of vision was to employ many men in the same task. So, as Thomas Sprat put it later speaking of the Royal Society, to the efforts of individual pioneers, however splendid their genius, 'we prefer the joint Force of many Men'. And there was the strong practical advantage (of which the century was becoming increasingly conscious) that rare and costly apparatus like telescopes and burning-mirrors could profitably be shared between investigators. Bacon's influence was, naturally, strongest in England where the Royal Society's official apologist, Thomas Sprat, expressed in 1667 the opinion that in Bacon's writings were 'everywhere scattered the best Arguments, that can be produced for the Defence of experimental Philosophy, and the best Directions, that are needful to promote it'; what is usually recognized as the first formal scientific Academy, the Accademia del Cimento (Academy of Experiments) in Italy, founded in 1657, drew its inspiration from sources much nearer home, namely, Galileo and his associate Evangelista Torricelli (1608–47), who had remained at Florence after Galileo's death. The moving spirit behind it was Prince Leopold de'Medici, brother of the Grand Duke Ferdinand II, over whom he enjoyed considerable influence. Having such august backing the academicians were able to assemble the finest collection of scientific equipment ever seen in Europe, much of which still survives.[3] There were only nine of them, for this was emphatically a court academy, dependent upon and aiming to satisfy the whims of its patrons, which never succeeded in forming a coherent, long-term programme of scientific research although it included some of the most distinguished scientific talent in Italy at this time: Vincenzo Viviani (1622–1703), who of all living men had best known Galileo, G.-A. Borelli (1608–79), a man of many varied achievements, Francesco Redi (d. 1697) whose studies of insects have been mentioned already, and (briefly) Nicholas Steno (1638–86) from Denmark. The Academy began soon after Borelli's arrival from Sicily at the University of Pisa, and collapsed soon after his departure, but experiments had been shown at Court before 1657, and the noble brothers continued to maintain personal laboratories even after its demise ten years later.

The easiest way of summarizing a large and miscellaneous body of work, recorded in the *Saggi* of the Academy published in 1667,[4] is to say that it recapitulated and demonstrated experimentally the scientific work of Galileo, Torricelli and Viviani. There was a long series of pneumatic experiments, many others on heat and cold, and on sound; experiments on the motions of bodies, on magnetism and electricity and other varied topics. The Academy did not employ an air-pump; instead, tests were made in the 'vacuous' space formed by the descent of a column of mercury, as in a barometer. Extensive and strange work was done on thermometers and other devices, requiring exquisite glass-blowing. Everything was recorded anonymously under a most positivist label: if any speculations should be found in the *Saggi*, the reader is warned, these should 'be taken always for the thoughts and particular sense of some one of the Members, but not imputed to the whole Academy, whose sole Design is to make *Experiments* and relate them'. Hence, though the Academy confirmed some modernist opinions – such as that of atmospheric pressure – it did little to form the theoretical structure of modern science, which rather developed in association with analogous investigations carried out (for example, in pneumatics) by Blaise Pascal in France and Robert Boyle in England. Galileo's theorems on projectile motion were, as far as they could be, verified by trials; the time-keeping properties of the pendulum were studied and (after the independent application of the pendulum to clocks by Christiaan Huygens in 1657) Galileo's abortive, though workable design for such a clock was exhumed. The 'radiation' of cold from ice, the incompressibility of water, the passage of magnetic virtue (but not sound) through the experimental vacuum, and capillary attraction were all thoroughly investigated – not all were novel topics. The origins of the physical laboratory may be said to lie with the Accademia del Cimento.

Unfortunately, the poverty of communications prevented more than vague rumours of the activities at the Tuscan Court spreading beyond Italy before the publication of the *Saggi*, and by the time that account was being read experimental science was well established in France and England, where the climate for it was more propitious. The pious attempt to perpetuate the Galilean tradition in Florence was totally counter to the general current of clerical reaction in Italy, which was to cause even the most respected of investigators, like Malpighi, to tread very circumspectly.[5] Prince Leopold's enthusiasm for the Academy may have lessened when he was made a Cardinal; Borelli and two other members decided to leave Tuscany – one of these, Antonio Oliva, was soon (1668) to take his own life in the prison of the Inquisition at Rome; Steno gave up science after his conversion to the Roman faith. Such events show the tone, yet some scientific vigour survived in Italy, notably in an unbroken tradition at Naples (now represented by Tommaso Cornelio) and in the rising group at Bologna active in astronomy as well as in microscopy.[6] Bologna had its own scientific circles: a Philosophical Academy existed in the 1660s, to be revived near the end of the century and formalized in 1714.

Local enthusiasm for the new philosophy, which in England was typically expressed by country doctors, parsons and landed gentry, somewhat tenuously linked by acquaintance and correspondence, in Italy and France where the traditions of urban cultural activity were stronger encouraged the formation of such short-lived but discernible societies as this at Bologna, and others at Naples, Caen, Rouen, Castres and Montpellier. In Italy the existence of many universities promoted such assemblies: in the south-west of France Protestantism was an additional bond. But the most obvious feature of the scientific movements in both England and France is the dominance of the capital city, even though a great deal of the talent was found in the provinces, because both national societies were closely linked to the court. The Royal Academy of Sciences in Paris was composed of the King's pensioners, while the Royal Society in London was always hoping for a royal bounty it never received. Perhaps one of its most solid privileges was that of carrying on its foreign correspondence by the diplomatic bag, for the exchange of news, books and journals not only within countries but between countries is a barometer of intellectual health that was rising rapidly in the late seventeenth century. Because the ordinary public postal services left much to be desired, especially with respect to the transport of packages, communication often depended upon the passage of travellers and diplomatic channels. Tycho Brahe, Galileo and Kepler are the first scientists whose correspondence survives in any considerable volume, then from about 1640 such material becomes extremely copious. This is very much so with the French group of mid-century (Descartes, Gassendi, Fermat, Roberval, Pascal) and especially with that very energetic correspondent, Marin Mersenne. From his religious house in the Place Royale, Paris, which was also to some extent it seems a place of regular if informal discussion, Mersenne energetically spread news and criticism between his friends. At a time when travel provided few opportunities for direct personal contact, when newspapers and learned journals were not in circulation (though, by 1660, the latter were about to come), this private summarizing of new books, reporting of new experiments, or retailing of Brown's lecture critical of Robinson's published work, or mere accounts of who was doing what where, played an exceedingly important role in minimizing the isolation of individuals and in creating a real scientific movement with its own momentum and standards. Those who were painfully touched by reported criticism (or still more, reported suggestions of prior discovery elsewhere) were likely to call those who made correspondence a business 'intelligencers' or 'philosophical merchants' or worse, but these men were the founders of an international scientific community and pioneers of the scientific journal.

After Mersenne, the most important of them were another Parisian, Henri Justel (1620–93), officially one of the King's secretaries but in practice a kind of Figaro in French scientific circles who knew everyone and everything, was for long the end of the link connecting London and Paris; Henry Oldenburg (? 1618–77), who from 1662 to the end of his life was the active Secretary of the Royal Society, and who in 1665 began to publish the *Philosophical Transactions, giving some Accompt of the present Undertakings, Studies, and Labours of the Ingenious in many considerable Parts of the World;* and John Collins (1625–83), a minor English government official and enthusiast for mathematics, who made it his special concern to keep mathematicians alert and busy. Of these three men Oldenburg, a German by birth who had settled permanently in England in 1653, was by far the most important, by his office, his tireless industry, and his robust common sense. He had, by and large, a good eye for what has proved to be enduringly interesting, he understood and tried to implement inter-

214

nationally the Baconian programme, and he perceived the necessity of working up a sketch for a good piece of work into a 'research programme' to which many could contribute. Oldenburg not only made the Royal Society's ambitions and achievement known abroad; he constantly made his Society aware of progress on the continent.

The island which produced Bacon, Napier, Gilbert, Harvey, Harriot and Briggs was hardly unproductive of originality and talent during the first two decades of the seventeenth century; but some of this talent was at least half-hidden and the possessors of it were isolated individuals, either ignorant of or indifferent to each other's endeavours. An observant traveller would have thought the English genius tended rather to poetry and music than to science, and though many bright young men came down from the universities, institutionally these were exceedingly dull and backward. The main focus for scientific interest was Gresham College, opened in 1597 under the will of a great London merchant in his own town house. The object was to lay sound learning before the citizens in vernacular lectures, London wholly lacking any such vehicle of education for the young or mature. The subjects were traditional: the mathematical sciences of geometry, astronomy and music; rhetoric, or the science of expression; and the three professional studies: divinity, law and medicine. Sir Thomas Gresham had formed no modernist utilitarian or progressivist view of the knowledge to be purveyed by his lectures. In nearly four centuries of existence – for Gresham Lectures are still delivered – the College has been more notable for survival than intellectual distinction: from the beginning the professors scamped their duties. Some distinguished men held the office: in geometry Henry Briggs (1556–1630), popularizer and one might almost say second inventor of logarithms, Isaac Barrow (1630–77), first Lucasian Professor of Mathematics at Cambridge and Newton's patron, and Robert Hooke (1635–1703); in astronomy particularly Christopher Wren (1632–1723); the influence of such men as these, even if only during a brief period, was sometimes decisive for others. Moreover, 'Gresham' brought men of mathematical and scientific tastes together, becoming the natural focus for the club. The Royal Society and Gresham College were to be inseparably associated until near the end of Newton's lifetime.

As noted before, London sea-captains and navigators had sought to perfect their skills in geography, cartography and navigation from the start of Elizabeth's reign, with John Dee as their best known mentor. Humphrey Gilbert had sought for an establishment to teach practical mathematical sciences to 'her Majesty's wards, and others the youth of nobility and gentlemen' in 1572, Dee sought something similar, and so with equal unsuccess did Richard Hakluyt, compiler of the *Voyages*. However, the Armada threat in 1588 inspired the founding of a Mathematical Lectureship in London, held until about 1595 by Thomas Hood (c. 1560–98). The same practical line remained strong at Gresham College, notably in the person of Edmund Gunter (1581–1626). Outside the College of Physicians, with which William Harvey was naturally associated, this was probably the strongest scientific group in London during the early seventeenth century. Evidence shows that young men came to the lectures and made personal contact with the professors; that there were regular meetings or discussions at Gresham College almost from the beginning is, however, much more dubious.[7]

The best near-contemporary narrative connecting Gresham College and the Royal Society, that of John Wallis the Oxford mathematician (1616–1703), takes his knowledge of such meetings no further back than 1645, to the end of the First Civil War in England:

We did, by agreement, divers of us, meet weekly in London on a certain day and hour, under a certain penalty, and a weekly contribution for the charge of the experiments, . . . of which number were Dr John Wilkins . . . Dr Jonathan Goddard, Dr George Ent, Dr Glisson, Dr Merrett (Drs in Physick), Mr Samuel Foster . . . Mr Theodore Haak . . . (who I think first suggested these meetings) and many others.

Wallis further recollects that the group met either at the lodgings of Dr Goddard, because he kept an 'operator' to help with experiments, or at Mr Foster's lectures: both men were Gresham professors: the former of medicine, the latter of astronomy; or they assembled in the Bull Inn, Cheapside.

Besides this circle, to which we shall return, there were others who would also take part in the national scientific movement. In a northern group of astronomers the outstanding figure was Jeremiah Horrocks (1618–41), who spent most of his life near Liverpool. He was an early and effective observer with the telescope, uniquely recording the 1639 transit of Venus. Even more important was his extension of Kepler's elliptical theory of planetary motion and correction of Kepler's tables: he was the first astronomer to treat the Moon's orbit as elliptical. William Gascoigne (c. 1612–44), a Yorkshireman linked with Horrocks by their common friend William Crabtree, was also known to Christopher Towneley of Lancashire, who preserved the papers of this whole group. Gascoigne was the first to use the telescope in refined instruments for angular measure; the micrometer he devised was to be passed on to the Royal Society by Christopher's nephew, Richard Towneley (1629–1707), more than twenty years after Gascoigne's premature death. During the Restoration this younger Towneley was also to work with the natural philosopher Henry Power (1623–68) of Halifax, the first English microscopist, and with John Flamsteed (1646–1719) who was to publish Horrocks's lunar theory and become the first Astronomer Royal. His home was in Derby.

This little network of personal relationships (extending over some fifty years) has been described – with some omissions – to illustrate the kind of personal connections in pursuit of science and mathematics that existed in several parts of Britain, and of course equally in other countries. In this northern connection of astronomers – tending to Royalism in politics and Catholicism in religion counter to the prevalent trend – there was no one dominant figure. It was otherwise with a second London group, different from that described by Wallis, which assembled round Samuel Hartlib (d. 1662), also a German Protestant refugee, as was his friend Theodore Haak mentioned in Wallis's narrative, and in a sense Henry Oldenburg also. Perhaps Hartlib could best be described as a social philosopher, for he was not the least active in the formal sciences like astronomy and botany. He was one of those worthy and energetic souls, active in every generation, who believe that a secular millennium will be inaugurated if only a series of straightforward and obviously desirable reforms can be effected. In 1641 – at which time he was perhaps in his early forties – he described the enlightened state of the future in *A Description of the Famous King-dome of Macaria*: this was one of sixty-odd publications by Hartlib towards the public good (not all from his own pen). His ideas on the way to reform society were varied and changing; at the time of *Macaria* he hoped for much from the programme of the Czech reformer John Amos Comenius, advocate of universal education and peace, whom he caused to visit England (mistakenly, Comenius thought the invitation came from the Parliament). Later in life he was more occupied with agriculture and technical inventions of a very miscellaneous character. Hartlib and his associates were men of the winning political side – Parliamentarians and Cromwellians – Hartlib himself receiving for many years a pension in aid of his beneficent purposes. Like many other groups, such as the Levellers, each in its own way, some having a more definite religious enthusiasm than others, they regarded the downfall of the monarchy and the established Church as signs that a new and better age was beginning: for some, the 'Rule of the Saints', for others, the education of women, or universal suffrage, or mastery of the elusive perpetual motion to ease men's toil for ever. The time when Wallis's friends were meeting soberly at Gresham College to discuss the new philosophy was also a time of wild and generous visions, which Bacon's writings played some part in shaping. These reforming Baconians were not logicians, like Bacon himself, nor were they scientific experimenters; perhaps what they chiefly drew from him (rightly or not) was the view 'that values no knowledge but as it hath a tendency to use' to borrow Robert Boyle's words of 1646.[8]

For all his lack of firm direction, Hartlib carried an atmosphere of inspiration, warmth and optimism impressing the politicians and the intellectuals working with them (like John Milton and John Pell, a mathematician and Original Fellow of the Royal Society), as well as much younger men like Boyle and William Petty of whom a great deal more would be heard. Under the Commonwealth Hartlib hoped to organize his disciples into a state-funded 'Office of Address' – an international agency for correspondence and invention – and, this failing, his circle extended to take in another little group, of whom the leading figures were Boyle and Benjamin Worsley (*c.* 1620–73); their chief concerns were for useful applications of chemistry and natural history.[9]

London clearly provided a rich soil for the growth of the scientific plant. On the whole, it seems that the men with whom Wallis met around Gresham College survived the Restoration of 1660 successfully and figured in the Royal Society; they were also 'academic', that is, physicians, anatomists, mathematicians, astronomers, botanists. With the notable exceptions already mentioned, Hartlib's friends, more sincerely committed to puritan ideals and social innovation, fared less well after 1660 and did not become Fellows: they had gone for practical, non-academic things. Such a one was Johann Sibertus Küffeler, son-in-law of the Dutch inventor Cornelius Drebbel who was for many years a technical consultant to the English navy. Küffeler too was brought over by the Council of State to display his destructive torpedo, which greatly impressed Cromwell in the last year of his life. More pacifically, Küffeler managed the production of the 'Bow-scarlet' dye invented by Drebbel – so long the colour of British army uniforms – and invented the thermostat for furnaces. He was greatly pushed by Hartlib, who thought the terrible effects of his invention such 'that the nation that should be first master of it' would be able 'to give the law to other nations'. Küffeler was never to be found in the Royal Society circle.

In the late 1640s and 1650s a new centre of enquiry developed at Oxford, initiated (as John Wallis in his narrative went on to say) by the installation there of John Wilkins (1614–72) as Warden of Wadham College, in 1648. Of the original Gresham group, Goddard and Wallis followed Wilkins to Oxford before long; Robert Boyle took up residence there in 1654; and the young talent of the University was strengthened by hosts of able men, Seth Ward, Thomas Willis, William Petty, Robert Hooke, Richard Lower and many more. Wilkins, a divine by profession, had like Hartlib the personal quality to give him ascendancy, though his published work was trivial enough: *The Discovery of a World in the Moone* (1638) and *A Discourse tending to prove that 'tis probable our Earth is one of the Planets* (1640) were skilful vulgarizations of Galileo. Robert Hooke, one of Wilkins's protégés, thanked God that 'Dr Wilkins was an Englishman, for wherever he had lived, there had been the chief seat of generous knowledge and true philosophy'. This seat was to be found at Oxford, as Wallis recalled, at the lodgings first of Petty, then of Wilkins himself, and finally (after the latter's removal) at those of Boyle. Some writers, including Thomas Sprat the first historian of the Royal Society and another protégé of Wilkins, have seen in these Oxford meetings 'the foundation of all this that followed'. For with the Restoration, being for a brief moment on the wrong side, Wilkins was out of a job and back in London. Most historians believe that, as Wallis stated, the London meetings had continued through the 1650s, and that the two parties now joined to form the Royal Society, in amity with such returned Royalists as Sir Robert Moray and Lord Brounker. On 28 November 1660, twelve men met together in the rooms of Lawrence Rooke, professor of geometry, at Gresham College after a lecture given by Christopher Wren, professor of astronomy, and there made a formal resolution to inaugurate 'a more regular way of debating things, and according to the manner in other countries, where there were voluntary associations of men in academies, for the advancement of various parts of learning' by meeting weekly and inviting others to join them.[10] This was the birth of the Royal Society, though it was chartered by Charles II only in 1662.

The Journal-Book, just quoted, makes it clear that the twelve founders were conscious of foreign precedents. Almost certainly they knew of the Accademia del Cimento in Florence, from recent travellers abroad such as Henry Oldenburg and Robert Southwell, and from books of earlier Italian groups like the Lincei. But perhaps they were thinking chiefly of Paris. Both Wilkins and Theodore Haak (to whom Wallis attributed the original suggestion for the

Gresham meetings) had corresponded with Mersenne; Wilkins had continuing contacts with Holland also. Most relevant, Oldenburg (who had become a client of the Boyles, especially Robert) while travelling in France had acquired a detailed picture of French intellectual life, and had attended meetings in Paris.

The middle-class intellectuals, who in England combined to form their own clubs in which they met as equals, were in France, as in Italy, more dependent on the good offices of a patron. Thus, at the beginning of the seventeenth century, one of the group most notable in Paris for literature and learning met regularly at the residence of the historian de Thou. His patronage, which included the use of his valuable library, was continued by his relatives the brothers Dupuy to about 1662. Less exalted gatherings met at the Bureau d'Adresse managed by the journalist Renaudot. At these, as at the Cabinet of the Dupuys, literary and political news was more eagerly awaited than discussion of scientific topics. Mersenne's circle, however, confined its attention almost entirely to mathematical and scientific affairs: it was he, for example, who made the discoveries of Galileo and his pupils known in France, who gave currency to the Cartesian system, and publicized Pascal's problem on the cycloid. After Richelieu's foundation of the Académie Française there was some feeling among those who cultivated the sciences that encouragement ought to be given to a similar non-literary institution. Among their number was Habert de Montmor, a man of great wealth who had offered his patronage to both Descartes (who declined it) and Gassendi. Not long after the death of Mersenne in 1648 weekly meetings were taking place in his house, presided over by Gassendi. Their discussions were not limited to science, and it was required only that those who took part should be 'curious about natural things, medicine, mathematics, the liberal arts, and mechanics'. The Montmor Academy, which gave itself a formal constitution in 1657, soon became a fashionable resort, as shown at a meeting in 1658 when the exciting news of Christiaan Huygens's elucidation of the nature of Saturn's ring was read out: the room was full of doctors of the Sorbonne, noble Abbés, secretaries of state, lawyers, officials, and others of high rank and social distinction, besides mathematicians, scientific amateurs, and literary men.[11] Science, even the most abstruse mathematics, had become respectable, and apparently interesting, even in the upper levels of Parisian society. The new philosophies of Descartes and Gassendi were victoriously allied against Aristotelianism. But the course of the academy was not altogether smooth; the amateurs were more ready to discuss the latest marvels in science than to work for its advancement, and there were sharp clashes of personality.

Mazarin, who had shown far less concern for the intellectual eminence of France than his master Richelieu, died in 1661 and the supreme power was then committed to the young King, Louis XIV. There was thus the possibility of acquiring for science the greatest of all patrons. Since the Royal Society had begun to take shape in 1660 the Montmor Academy had followed its fortunes with some envy, and had even to some extent modelled its own proceedings upon the Royal Society's example. The links between the two bodies were close, for Oldenburg corresponded with several members of the Montmor Academy.

Huygens and Sorbière (the Secretary of the Academy) were members of both societies, and a number of the Parisians visited London.

The works of Boyle and other Englishmen were carefully studied in Paris, where the usefulness of the empirical attitude was gradually more highly esteemed. Sorbière pointed out in 1663 the advantage of experimentation over verbal wrangles, but opined that 'only Kings and wealthy rulers or a few wise and rich republics can undertake to erect a physical academy where there would be constant experimentation'. The French seem to have been even more impressed than were the Fellows of the Royal Society, which had grown from its own independent and varied origins, with the need for large subventions if an experimental society were to succeed. About the end of 1664, when the Montmor Academy had collapsed through inanition, personal rivalries and lack of money, Melchisédec Thévenot (1620–92), traveller and polymath, inventor of the spirit-level, with the astronomers Adrien Auzout and Pierre Petit formed a plan for a Company of Arts and Sciences which was, virtually, a research institute equipped with laboratories, observatories, translators, corresponding secretaries and so forth. For a time Thévenot himself tried to provide a base for such activities at his own house, until the expense proved too great. Of the various, inharmonious subgroups forming the intellectual milieu of Paris, among which were Cartesians, Gassendists, mathematicians, philosophers, astronomers and experimentalists the two last pursued a successful initiative with Louis XIV's great minister, Jean-Baptiste Colbert, who was not unconscious of the precedent set in letters by his great forerunner, Richelieu. He had already begun to patronize distinguished foreign men of science. He was not displeased by the advances made to him on behalf of experimental science by Sorbière, Auzout and Thévenot, each individually. The very elaborate scheme for a 'Company' was much cut down, but in the end salaries were provided for fifteen academicians, divided into two classes: the mathematicians (including astronomers and physicists) and the natural philosophers (including chemists, physicians, anatomists); they met in two rooms assigned to their use in the Royal Library on Wednesdays and Saturdays. The first assembly took place on 22 December 1666.[12]

Louis XIV had most serious reasons of state for founding the Academy of Sciences, while Charles II's favour to the Royal Society had a trivial basis. The French Academy was intended to add lustre to the French crown; the official engraving depicting Louis's state visit to his academicians perfectly makes the point: all excellence, all distinction, all achievement draws its inspiration from the monarch, and reflects stronger light upon him. The King was to be the centre and patron of all cultural activities within the state. The Academy was an intellectual Versailles, another setting for the crown. In addition, Colbert, authoritarian, mercantilist, pioneer of the managed economy, was surely convinced by the rhetoric of utility with which the experimental scientists tempted his generosity. In the techniques of war and seafaring, of shipbuilding, of architecture and engineering, it could be expected that these inventive experts would place their skills at the service of the state, and so give it in manufacture and trade, as well as in war and the arts of magnificence, an ascendancy over all other nations. In later years Colbert did indeed direct the academicians to such enquiries, to which they submitted with good grace if little obvious advantage to any one. There was also some early idea that the institution would unite the separate merits of theoreticians and practitioners, to the common good of the useful arts. It is difficult to imagine the cynical Charles taken in by these self-interested claims. He put his money on the shipwrights of Deptford rather than the double-bottomed boat of Sir William Petty. (The French, on the other hand, were by the end of the century to bring their shipyards under outside, expert control.) Moreover, Charles clearly ensured that the Royal Society never cost him a penny, nor imposed any tedious obligations upon his own royal person. It amused him to gratify painlessly the vanity of those few about his court who found philosophy an amusing hobby: he probably took a real if whimsical interest in some works of ingenuity such as Hooke's watch and Newton's reflecting telescope. No doubt it amused him also to be regarded as a patron by those to whom, in fact, he gave nothing. Mostly, as Pepys and others have recorded, he spoke of the Royal Society as a comedy, thus deeply offending the Italian visitor Lorenzo Magalotti, former secretary of the Accademia del Cimento, when he came to London in 1667:

I have become greatly disillusioned about my reception by the King [he wrote later], for whereas I was given to understand that the effective patronage that he affords the famous Royal Society is the effect, if not of goodwill, at least of esteem towards those studies, I have learned that he is accustomed to call his academicians by no other name than *mes fous* (my jesters). [13]

Yet if he laughed at them, Charles did talk to his jesters at Whitehall, which Louis XIV did not do at Versailles.

In both countries the new foundations signified new beginning. Neither the Academy nor the Royal Society was a simple royal ratification of what had gone before. In England the Restoration ended millenianism and many beneficent projects collapsed. Some men like the poet Milton and the naturalist John Ray (1627–1705), then a tutor at Trinity College, Cambridge, took to retirement for reasons of prudence or conscience; others, like the educationist and chemist John Webster or the mathematician John Pell found their career opportunities blocked, while for others like Samuel Pepys and Henry Oldenburg life opened fresh promises. Some men of the right interests and talents were certainly excluded from the Royal Society on grounds of personal unsuitability. [14] The outstanding example is Thomas Hobbes (1588–1679), one of the greatest of English philosophers, who had written a materialist philosophy somewhat in the same manner as Descartes and Digby, and who fancied his abilities as a mathematician. The persistent taint of atheism damned him in the eyes of conservatives, while his reactionary attacks on Boyle and others offended the moderns. The election of the Cambridge Platonist philosopher Ralph Cudworth was carried, but he did not become a Fellow; perhaps, as a provincial, he did not wish to make the effort. Some other provincials were probably excluded for the same reason, though regular correspondents of the Society. However, it is hard to understand why the Londoners Vincent Wing and Thomas Streete, the best writers on astronomy in England, were never elected Fellows; the latter was very closely associated with those who were.

The Fellowship of the Royal Society was very numerous compared with that of the French Academy of Science – more men had been elected to the former by 1690 than to the latter by 1800. It is therefore possible to ask questions about Englishmen interested (in some sense) in science which could not be asked of the French.[15] Nearly half (41%) of the early Fellows were noblemen, landed gentry, or courtiers; one may presume that many of these were drawn into the Society for social or careeristic reasons. A large proportion showed no further interest in its meetings and declined to pay their subscription. About the same number (40%) were professional men of one kind or another, most being either MDs (14%) or scholars (10%); many – but by no means all – of the solid workers of the Society came from these strata of the community. The rest were either merchants (6%) or foreigners (rather numerous at 10% the Royal Society was not, at first, a national society), or are undefinable.

Clearly, the Royal Society was not a professional group in the seventeenth century as it is today, or as the French Academy of Sciences already was. Not one in fifty of the Fellows could be said to have earned his living from science, at any time in his life; but there were others, like Robert Boyle, Martin Lister or John Ray who gave very large fractions of their life to science without office or remuneration. Neglecting half the seventeenth-century Fellowship as useless and inactive (many were in time expelled), there remains a large group (over 200) – much larger than the known scientific population of any other country – plus at least another fifty non-Fellows who demonstrated some positive scientific interest. What induced men to take trouble that was so unprofitable? For only a very naive person can have supposed that application to astronomy or natural history would lead to any sort of career. A few, like Newton, became deeply engrossed in such studies at the University; for others, like Samuel Pepys who was much more deeply committed to nautical history, it was one occupation of an active and receptive mind. Others again found science a natural offshoot from their profession as physician or apothecary, though to say this leaves many problems unsolved. Others seem to have been drawn in by the countryman's observation of planets and animals, seventeenth-century Gilbert Whites. All such as these seem to have been little inspired by the usefulness of the knowledge they hoped to acquire, or of the activities that were to be inspired. Others did certainly have an eye to results: such was Hartlib's legacy, for example. There was some of this in Boyle (who wrote an early treatise on the *Usefulness of Experimental Natural Philosophy*) and even more in Hartlib's former associate, the verbose country parson John Beale. As in Beale and John Wallis, the pious ambition to improve nature's works for men could merge into intellectual chauvinism – the spirit that animated Louis XIV and Colbert showing itself in private men. Having said this, if we ask what works, or which individuals, were most highly regarded by the Royal Society contemporaneously, we find a judgement closely corresponding to that of their remote prosperity. The Society published Newton's *Principia*, Ray and Willughby's book on fishes, and Malpighi's embryological studies. With some hesitation about the second, these are among the productions of the time most highly valued by historians. Newton, Ray, Malpighi, Boyle, Huygens, Cassini, Leeuwenhoek, James Gregory – all such great names have preserved the reputation they already enjoyed in their own day. Of course there were those whose worth was then almost unperceived, like the Czech philosopher Marcus Marci (1595–1667) – forerunning the fate of his better-known countryman Gregor Mendel – but the historian can hardly argue from such changes in reputation that the concept of what a scientific achievement should be has changed fundamentally since the late seventeenth century. Equally one would not argue that because Newton or Malpighi was highly praised, every one was aiming at the same achievement; this was not so. Very often men undertook tasks or wrote reports, that seemed to their contemporaries as well as to us hopeless, or futile, or misguided. It would be difficult to find anything of great value which was excluded from publication in the *Philosophical Transactions*, easy to find many included pieces of low quality. Again, the general sense of that age about such things seems to agree very much with ours. Though there was a lot of waste motion or tentative groping in this direction or that, when a major positive step forward was made it was (roughly speaking) as apparent then as it is now.

The selection of the first scientific academicians in Paris was made by Colbert, at first guided by the mathematician Pierre de Carcavi (d. 1684) and the man of letters Jean Chapelain (1595–1674). Much about the inner history of the institution before 1699, when a complete reconstruction took place, is now obscure. No rules or constitution exist before 1699. Christiaan Huygens was brought from the Netherlands to be its most distinguished scientific light. The systematic Cartesians were carefully excluded, and even some of the Frenchmen whose earnestness was responsible for its existence, such as Auzout and Thévenot, had little or no importance within the actual Academy. This was partly because Colbert brought from Bologna another foreigner, Giovanni Domenico Cassini, who was to become Director of the Observatory opened in 1669. Rising French talent was recognized by the Crown, notably in the astronomers Jean Picard (1620–82) and Jean Richer (1630–96), and the experimenter Edmé Mariotte (*c*. 1620–84). However, when a general account of the scientific movement in France outside Paris is written, it will be clear that it had little to do with the Academy, which was neither representative nor inclusive.

The Academicians were not only pensioners but functionaries of the state, whereas the Fellows of the Royal Society were free in discussion to follow the whims of the afternoon. Nevertheless, their proceedings were orderly, to the admiration of such foreigners as Sorbière who noted (1663):

There is no body here eager to speake, that makes a long Harangue, or intent upon saying all he knows: He is never interrupted that speaks, and Differences of Opinion cause no manner of Resentment, nor as much as a disobliging Way of Speech: there is nothing seemed to me to be more civil, respectful and better managed than this Meeting.

Such had not always been the case in Paris. The weakness of the Society (setting aside lack of money, apparatus and laboratories) was instability in attendance at meetings, and consequent inability to follow any theme or plan. So often an experiment to be performed or a book to be reviewed seems to be forgotten subsequently; only rarely was any continuous line of discussion maintained through two or more consecutive meetings. An attempted committee structure, intended to render groups of individuals responsible for such topics as agriculture, mechanics, trade, botany and so forth soon disintegrated.

A Curator of Experiments, Robert Hooke (1635–1703) was appointed in 1662 to produce experiments of his own or others' devising or as ordered by the assembly: Hooke was fertile, ingenious and assiduous; the variety of material he produced was fantastic, but it can hardly be said that as a 'director of research' he showed consistency or persistence. He was brilliant in ideas, low in concentration of effort. The Society drifted on, rarely without an interesting meeting, but reaching no conclusions, initiating no line of investigation. Attempts were from time to time made to make the proceedings more methodical, as by requiring Fellows in turn to bring in a 'discourse', without regulation ever having a permanent effect. The Royal Society became, as it has remained, a place of report rather than a research institute. The discursive note was clearly sounded in Wallis's narrative of the early Gresham College meetings:

Our business was (precluding matters of theology and state affairs) to discourse and consider of Philosophical Enquiries, and such as related there unto; as Physick, Anatomy, Geometry, Astronomy, Navigation, Staticks, Magnetics, Chymicks, Mechanicks, and Natural Experiments; with the state of these studies, as then cultivated at home and abroad. We then discoursed on the circulation of the blood, the valves in the Veins, the Venae Lactae, the Lymphatick Vessels, the Copernican Hypothesis, the Nature of Comets and New Stars, the Satellites of Jupiter, the oval Shape (as it then appeared) of Saturn, the spots in the Sun, and its turning on its own Axis, the Inequalities and Selenography of the Moon, the several Phases of Venus and Mercury, the Improvement of Telescopes, and Grinding of Glasses for that Purpose, the Weight of Air, the Possibility or Impossibility of Vacuities and Nature's Abhorrence thereof, the Torricellian Experiment in Quicksilver, the Descent of heavy Bodies, and the degrees of Acceleration therein; and divers other things of like nature. Some of which were then but New Discoveries . . ..[16]

There was no programme there, nothing to hinder the spontaneity of lively minds eager to canvass the newest ideas and discoveries; so it remained; one could draw up just such a list of topics, only far longer, to represent the Royal Society's interest during the thirty years after the Charter.

It was somewhat the same in Paris. The academicians there took a New Year's resolution annually to devote themselves to certain projects, but in fact their meetings were quite discursive. They had some general objectives such as solving the problem of determining longitude at sea, effecting the cartography of France, practical hydraulics and mechanics but in fact devoted themselves at will to other topics catching their interest, such as the air-pump or the reflecting telescope or the theory of light. Some specific problems were, however, put to the Academy, including the optimum design of gun-carriages. In two ways, however, the Academy differed very much from the Royal Society.

First, the construction of the Observatoire de Paris (1669) provided a perma-nent base for the astronomers and the possibility of a continuous programme of work; Cassini was highly systematic and embarked (with his assistants) on long projects such as codification of the motions of the Moon and of Jupiter's satellites, while Picard undertook the measurement of a degree of the meridian near Paris. Extensive trials of Huygens's marine chronometers were made at sea, partly under the supervision of the astronomers, while Jean Richer's voy-ages to French Canada (1670) and Cayenne (1672) enabled the longitude of the eastern American seaboard to be discovered accurately for the first time. At Cayenne, Richer observed the position of Mars at perigee simultaneously with colleagues in Paris; from their measurements the Sun's distance was worked out, nearly correctly, for the first time. Further, he found it necessary to shorten the pendulum of his astronomical clock, in comparison with Paris: this fact was to prove an important confirmation of Newton's theory of gravitation. Sec-ondly, the Parisians developed a responsibility for certifying the merit of new inventions and technical processes, starting with schemes for finding a ship's longitude at sea or removing the salt from sea-water, and going on especially to the consideration of proposed new machines. In the new regulations for the Academy of 1699 this was imposed as a duty: the collection of models deposited by inventors formed the origin of the Museum of the Conservatoire des Arts et Métiers in Paris. In a somewhat similar vein the Academy also controlled the publications of its members much more closely than did the Royal Society, though this body did deliberately signify its approval of certain books, includ-ing Newton's *Principia*.

In some such ways, perhaps most of all in its mounting of scientific expe-ditions and astronomical team-work, the Academy was actually closer to the Baconian ideal than was the Royal Society. As Henry Oldenburg in his letters from London was constantly urging natural philosophers in all countries to combine their labours to fill a great storehouse of natural knowledge, from which a true philosophy of nature could be extracted, so Huygens wrote in 1666 that the principal and most useful occupation of the new Academy must be 'to work in natural history somewhat in the manner suggested by Verulam [Bacon]'. They were just as conscious as he had been of the importance of cooperative effort and ample means of investigation, and preferred anonymous publication of their official enterprises like the *Mesure de la Terre* (by Picard, 1671) or the *Mémoires pour servir a l'Histoire Naturelle des Animaux* (also 1671). They were just as certain as Bacon that fact-collection must precede theory, so that Fontenelle could write of the 1699 reform with the authentic Baconian ring: 'Systematic Physics must refrain from building its edifice until Ex-perimental Physics is able to furnish it with the necessary materials.' The academicians found that they could agree on the 'undigested observation of some phenomenon' when agreement on cause and theory was unattainable. The Royal Society, most self-consciously Baconian in its 'histories' (narratives) of trades, some of which were printed in Sprat's *History* and in the *Philosophical Transactions*, never reached the same level of team-work in investigation, its collaborative effects being brought about rather by Oldenburg's industry in managing the Society's correspondence, for example in the form of answers to natural-history enquiries obtained from various parts of the world.[17] The Society could never become anything remotely like a research institute, though it did endeavour to speak as a collective authority on the validity of experiments, as when Newton's reflecting telescope and early accounts of his optical investigations were reported in 1671–72, and indeed commonly, in accordance with the Baconian precept 'Let the experiment be tried'. With only Hooke (as Curator of Experiments) and Oldenburg (as Secretary) serving it as partly-salaried officers, with neither place nor means for active investigation, a continued research programme was almost impossible, unless performed by the enthusiasm of an individual.

So, for example, all the astronomical telescopes and observatory clocks in Britain were private possessions. When Charles II resolved to emulate his cousin in France by founding a national observatory, he literally provided a building only (designed by Wren). When John Flamsteed began his career as Astronomer Royal in 1675 he had to bring in his own equipment, together with what he had in gifts from friends, notably Jonas Moore (whose clocks still survive). He himself was forced to take a country living for support, and could never afford proper assistance. His main work in determining the positions of the stars was not available for more than thirty years, but he supplied observations on the Moon used by Newton in his gravitational theory. The credit for Flamsteed's great achievement in reducing the errors of astronomical measurement to a new low order, despite all the obstacles he had to overcome, clearly attaches to himself alone. The Royal Society had other Observers of note, such as Robert Hooke and Edmond Halley (Flamsteed's successor at Greenwich), but these had to do what they could with their own resources, as did observers outside the Society, like Thomas Streete. The Royal Society had no share in the running of the Greenwich Observatory, or use of the instruments there, though Fellows from time to time visited Flamsteed privately. As a result, though good private work continued to be done in England in astronomy, by Flamsteed before he went to Greenwich, or by Robert Hooke in observing the Great Red Spot on Jupiter and determining its period of rotation at the same time as Cassini in Paris, it could not be doubted that the Paris Observatory was the European centre of excellence in its field. The same might be said of comparative anatomical research, for similar reasons, despite the very fine efforts of such individuals in the Society as Nehemiah Grew (1641–1712) and Edward Tyson (1650–1708), first anatomist of a higher ape.

Everywhere in Europe the formation of scientific societies illustrates a dual tendency, on the one hand towards the crystallization of a specifically scientific organization out of informal groups having broader and more superficial intellectual interests, and on the other towards the preponderance of the experimentalists within the organization. In Italy, France and England there was a transition from the discussion of natural-philosophic systems or hypotheses to the verification and accumulation of fact; as the course of the scientific revolution laid more emphasis on deeds than on words, on the laboratory rather than the study, and as the preparation of commentaries and criticisms of ancient texts gave place to the writing of memoirs describing the results of systematic investigation, so the characteristics of scientific organization changed accordingly. In the first half of the seventeenth century the function of a scientific assembly had been to promote discussion and dissemination of the new idea of science, and to provide a forum in which, not merely before an audience of enthusiasts, but before the broadest cross-section of educated and literate society, the original thought of a Galileo or a Descartes could challenge conventional opinions of science. Patrons like the Medici brothers, or a newsgatherer like Mersenne, amassed the accumulative weight of innovation against the science of colleges and textbooks. They presented the total case fot the 'new philosophy', in an intellectual environment whose dogmatic traditions were already disintegrating, to a new learned class freed from the sterner discipline of the old professional scholar, ready to admire acuity of wit, subtlety of reasoning and fertility of imagination more than allegiance to orthodox 'sound' views. If the 'new philosophy' was obstructed in the university, there was appeal through the scientific assembly to the more tolerant, eager and wealthy intellectual circles of court and capital. But the alliance between modern science in its early stages and the whole turbulent current of cultural development in the seventeenth century was inevitably incomplete and of short duration. Important, creative scientific work rapidly outdistanced the dilettante and virtuoso: rarely, for example, does the name of John Evelyn occur in the proceedings of the Royal Society printed by Birch in his *History*. A man of general culture could not see the point of detailed scientific labours, for whereas he might enjoy a debate on Descartes's concept of the animal as machine, he tended to find the naturalist grubbing in ditches for insects' eggs merely comic. The exploitation of the shift of intellectual perspectives, so fascinating in general outline, inevitably sank to a tedium and pedantry in the eyes of those who sought entertainment and striking novelty. As a result, the Montmor Academy broke up, and the Royal Society failed in wide appeal after its first fifteen years.

During roughly the last twenty-five years of the seventeenth century, a period that one might loosely qualify as that of the 'Cartesian consensus' – during which the most interesting development of a broad character was that of experimental and mathematical neo-Cartesianism as represented by Huygens, Leibniz and Malebranche – there was no deep issue of principle dividing intellectuals, such as the Copernican question had been before, or the Newtonian philosophy was to present in the future. Consequently, in the second half of the seventeenth century the role of the scientific society changed considerably. Having become a thoroughly professional body, it served as a focus for the discussion of works rather than ideas. Its aim was to develop the sciences, rather than to promote a 'new philosophy'. Opposition from Aristotelian university teachers, or the medical profession, was hardly serious any longer. The scientific movement required countenance less than means – buildings, apparatus, money for the maintenance of research, and methods for exchanging its results. It was found, for instance, that as scientific books became more truly technical, more fully devoted to describing research (rather than useful textbooks or practical manuals), the publishing trade refused to handle them unless large sums were laid down. Or again, while there was an expanding commercial market for ordinary watches and clocks, navigational instruments, and even telescopes and microscopes, financial encouragement alone would induce craftsmen to hazard their profits in efforts to improve instruments for the advancement of science. In short, the task before a scientific society was less to secure the scientific revolution, than to maintain its momentum and to reap its harvest. It was now surely clear that, however much the scientific society might aid and encourage the scientist, the real innovations – in ideas or methods – had to come from individuals. The great ascendancy of Boyle, or Helmont, or Malpighi makes the point; Newton would underline it strongly. The Royal Society rapidly became individualistic. The 1699 reform of the French Academy of Sciences formally recognized the limitation of works undertaken in common, and ordered that each academician was to choose a particular object of study so that his reports upon it might enlighten the whole body.[18] The notion of the research institute was hardly to return again until the French Revolution.

Meanwhile, Germany was somewhat late on the scene. Not to mention Kepler, who had no worthy successor in central Europe, or the numerous and influential chemists such as Johan Rudolph Glauber (1604–70), Germany in the persons of the intellectual mayor of Magdeburg, Otto von Guericke (1602–86), of Caspar Schott (1608–66) and even the ceaselessly outpouring Athanasius Kircher (1602–80) made her contributions to the development of experimental science. The territorial divisions in Germany, its backward social and economic conditions, the Thirty Years War, reduced the effectiveness of its many excellent schools and universities. The first society to be formed there was the Academy of the Investigators of Nature (*Academia Naturae Curiosorum*), whose descendant is still in existence; technically this was born in 1652, but really developed from 1661 by the efforts of a strange individual, Philipp Jacob Sachs von Lewenheimb (1627–72) of Breslau (Wroclaw) where he was city physician. It was a society of physicians, whose only real function was to publish their contributions in an annual volume, the *Miscellanea curiosa;* these were largely descriptive of curious experiences in medical practice or natural curiosities, but there were accounts of books and a few other papers of wider view. If this enterprise 'hardly deserves to be classed as a learned society' – though the *Miscellanea* enjoyed some contemporary (Baconian) repute, and the Academy was adopted by the Emperor in 1677 – then the other seventeenth-century German group, the *Collegium Curiosum sive Experimentale* of Altdorf, modelled upon the Accademia del Cimento, was no more than the private club that had existed in Italy long before.[19] It did, however, work through a series of the physical experiments typical of the age, and print a description of them.

The creation of a national academy in Germany, modelled upon the French example, was the work of one man, the philosopher and mathematician Gottfried Wilhelm Leibniz (1646–1716). For many years he had been in the service of the small state of Hanover, but found near the end of the century a patron for his long-considered scheme in the Elector (later King) of Brandenburg-Prussia, Frederick I. The Berlin Academy was created in 1700. The city was far removed from the main centres of learning in Germany, its university not being founded until more than a century later, and certainly no group of scientific amateurs, virtuosi or curiosi, existed there from which it could have derived spontaneous existence; the vigour of the Berlin Academy was to owe much to imported talent (some members being like Leibniz himself Germans from other states). Leibniz had long wished to further the interests of his nation and raise its technological standards by encouraging the vernacular language – hitherto, and for long thereafter, Latin or French were the learned and polite languages in Germany – and the reform of education towards practical subjects. To attain these ends a national academy which should concern itself with practical applications as well as with the pure sciences was the first necessity, in Leibniz's opinion. Where earlier exponents of the usefulness of scientific discovery had rather aimed to shift the whole balance between man and nature for the universal good, and so improve the condition of all mankind, Leibniz in his arguments for the new academy looked to an objective that Bacon had regarded as less noble, the exaltation of one nation as compared with others.

In Leibniz's view Germany had once enjoyed pre-eminence in useful arts, especially in mining and chemistry, but also in horology, hydraulic engineering, goldsmith's work, turnery, forging, etc. Astronomy was restored by the Germans, and the 'Nieder-Deutschen' (Netherlanders) had invented the telescope and mastered navigation. The only remedy for the subsequent deterioration was the generous encouragement of science, which Leibniz coupled with the enforcement of a strictly mercantilist economic policy, by which the state should become self-sufficient. As he put it in a letter to Prince Eugene, discussing the proposed scientific academy in Vienna:

In order to perfect the [practical] arts, manufactures, agriculture, the two kinds of architecture [civil and military], the topographical description of countries, and mining, as also to provide work for the poor, to encourage inventors and entrepreneurs, and finally for everything to do with the economy or mechanics of the civil and military state, observatories, laboratories, herb-gardens, animal-menageries, cabinets of natural and factitious rarities, and a physico–medical history for each year based on the reports and observations that the salaried doctors would be under an obligation to furnish, are requisite.[20]

Though one may perceive a measure of naivety in his choice of means and functions, Leibniz, historian, mathematician, philosopher, diplomat and confidential adviser of princes, in his dual devotion to science and Germany saw the scientific academy as a necessary instrument of the modern state, through which science could be made to play its part in social and economic policy. He had little patience with those who 'consider the sciences not as something very important for human welfare, but as an amusement or a game' and criticized the French Academy of Sciences for this reason.[21] Science as a factor in creating national prestige, its role in war and in the commercial rivalry of states, were appreciated in England and France as well as in Germany; but no one who could claim high rank as a philosopher and scientist announced the importance of scientific organization to jealous statesmen more clearly than Leibniz.

Thus, one alleviation of the obstructions to scientific progress was sought through the conversion of Bacon's appeal to the interests of humanity into an appeal to the interests of the state, addressed to a monarch or great minister. Quite a different approach, in societies very different from that of Prussia, was to seek to arouse the enthusiasm and support of the public through a direct appeal, using the relatively new technique of weekly or monthly publication. Perhaps it is natural that the most successful use of this technique was made in England, the most open society, in association with the open Royal Society. True, the French were first in the field with the *Journal des Sçavans* (January 1665), but this was never specifically a scientific journal for it covered all fields of knowledge. Its main and useful purpose was to summarize new books. With fair regularity the proceedings of the Academy of Sciences were reported and some papers submitted by the academicians were printed, as were extracts from Henry Oldenburg's *Philosophical Transactions*, issued in London. Under its founder, Denis de Sallo, the *Journal des Sçavans* appeared for just three months without benefit of royal licence:

Erudite without pedantry or jargon, occasionally witty, even lightly malicious when the occasion justified it, allusive and deriving from the learning and science of the day, the reviews which fill the pages of these [13] weekly brochures are still worth reading as one attempts to capture the temper and climate of the age.[22]

De Sallo's freedom from bigotry injured clerical sensibilities; from March 1665 to the beginning of 1666 the *Journal* was suppressed; it re-emerged, much more dull, under the Abbé Jean Gallois.

As the original *Journal* died, the *Philosophical Transactions* were born, an enterprise no doubt stimulated by the French example, for Oldenburg had for some time been considering the issue of a scientific newsletter to contributors, based on his large correspondence, the books he received from abroad, and the proceedings of the Royal Society. He adopted instead the French model of a monthly periodical, intended to keep the 'virtuosi' and 'curiosi' informed of what was happening in London and other chief centres, but limited to mathematical and scientific topics. The journal was to be for the public good, but it was also a way in which Oldenburg as proprietor and editor could make extra and much needed profit from his labours on behalf of the Royal Society: the *Philosophical Transactions* was not to become an official organ of the Society for nearly a hundred years, nor was it intended to print only the Society's proceedings. From the first issue (March 1665) Oldenburg did this, but he also culled much from the letters he received from correspondents at home and abroad, translating if necessary. Oldenburg allowed his correspondents to speak for themselves though, like many editors since, he could not resist introducing improvements of style and grammar. He also borrowed from the *Journal des Sçavans*. Most of the accounts of books he prepared himself, with no little diligence and skill, reproducing sometimes the judgement of regular correspondents like John Wallis which he had sought by letter. Obviously Oldenburg's task would, in principle, have been impossible or at least far more difficult had he not been able to rely on regular and printable advice from such prompt and businesslike coadjutors as Wallis, John Beale, Robert Boyle, and especially John Collins. Possessing perhaps a bare understanding of mathematics, Oldenburg certainly had no real proficiency in that subject and here Collins was his mentor, both with respect to books and the content of letters. Collins provided most of the matter for the London end of Oldenburg's mathematical correspondence. Hooke was close to Oldenburg for many years of their association as Officers of the Society without offering the same support: clearly, Hooke was not eager to supply material for the *Transactions* – reasonably preferring to publish himself in his own time – nor was he generally cooperative about returning answers to questions or comments on books. And it must be said that his judgements of the work of others tended to be abrasive.

Rapidly, because its publication was regular (that of the *Journal des Sçavans* was not), because its level of interest was consistently high, and because its content was varied so as to appeal to many tastes, the *Philosophical Transactions* acquired status and was much sought after abroad. The earlier volumes were translated into Latin and reissued from Amsterdam; the Paris Academy of Sciences had some translated into French for their private use. Oldenburg created the scientific journal and the scientific paper as means of communication. He had his pages to fill, his readers to satisfy, and he chose whatever came to hand as most suitable for the purpose, sometimes to the surprise of a letter-writer who had not expected to see himself in print. This proved an ideal way of recording and communicating pieces of information or ideas whose expression did not demand a larger compass; Newton's letter about the development of his investigations into light and colour, occupying thirteen pages of *Transactions* No. 80, published on 19 February 1672, is a celebrated example. It immediately aroused interest elsewhere, and possibly (the point is arguable, of course) brought forward public knowledge of Newton's work by many years.[23] Newton had himself studied the *Transactions* and almost certainly prepared his letter in anticipation of its publication in them, though his own correspondence with Oldenburg had begun only at the beginning of the year. At his request, Oldenburg made some changes in the printed version of the letter – this was by no means unusual and indicates another feature of journalistic practice.[24]

Hopeful contributors abroad as well as colleagues nearer home began to write to Oldenburg specifically with the object of seeing their letters published in the *Transactions*. The most voluminous and distinguished of the former was the Dutch microscopist Antoni van Leeuwenhoek (1632–1723), who knew only his native Dutch tongue; fortunately Oldenburg, competent in Dutch among other languages, was able to translate his letters for publication in either English or Latin. The successful example set in London and Paris was soon imitated elsewhere: in Rome by the *Giornale dei Letterati* (borrowing heavily from its two predecessors, and in intermittent direct contact with Oldenburg); in Leipzig much later by the *Acta Eruditorum* (1682) of which Leibniz was a co-founder. The *Acta* resembled the *Journal des Sçavans* in its wide range and book-reviewing function, while also like the *Transactions* publishing original articles, of which those on mathematics were of first-class importance as coming from Leibniz's own mathematical school. One might note also Pierre Bayle's *Nouvelles de la*

Republique des Lettres (1684) as one of the most influential journals ever issued, and the *Mémoires de Trevoux* (1706) as an example of a conservative journal, for it was produced by the Jesuits and for long led the opposition to Newtonianism in France.

Though the journal was vital to the continued health of the scientific movement from the seventeenth century onwards, the book remained the vehicle by which the major impact of new work was conveyed, from Newton's *Principia* (1687) and *Opticks* (1704) through Lavoisier's *Traité Elementaire de Chimie* (1789) to Charles Darwin's *Origin of Species* (1859) and even beyond. The situation prevailing in the past was different from that of the present in many ways, not least because the understanding readers of journals were so few in number and the more massive effect of the book was required to effect a change on received ideas. There was, one might say, a distinction between the tactical gains (articles) and the strategic advances (books) of science no longer evident – and indeed not universally true even by the end of the eighteenth century. There is also the point that the book reflecting the latest movement of ideas also served as a textbook – as selections of the *Principia* did for over a century. Not that there was a total absence of scientific texts directed solely at the needs of beginners: rather that these tended to be relatively few and highly conservative. The paramountcy of the scientific journal in modern times has had a consequential effect on the character and quality of expository texts.

The free transfer of matter from one printed periodical to another by the time that three or four were in being during the latter part of the seventeenth century is strong evidence of the community of the scientific spirit, especially in that quarter-century (roughly) when, as already mentioned, a broadly neo-Cartesian philosophy of nature was dominant. If the historian applies his microscope to study the day-to-day contacts and thoughts about each other of the natural philosophers of Italy, Britain, France and Germany he will find, before the 1690s, little evidence of national style or prejudice, less in mathematics. An Englishman might naturally have done what Malpighi did – indeed, Nehemiah Grew's botanical microscopy ran parallel with Malpighi's; Huygens felt himself even more at home in London than among the academicians in Paris. The astronomers, like the mathematicians, worked on a completely international footing one with another. This was really an extraordinary change since the beginning of the century, and the rise of Newtonianism would in turn introduce new features. The community of intellect in Europe in the late seventeenth century was perhaps greater than at any time since the fourteenth century. The publication of the works of a Scottish mathematician (James Gregory) at Padua, those of Italian and Dutch microscopists in London, or that of a Dutch mathematician and physicist in Paris; the careers of Cassini and Leibniz (for a time) in Paris, of Oldenburg and Nicolas Mercator in London, the maintenance of scientific correspondence between countries even in the time of war, all go to show that the Baconian talk of cooperation between individualists and societies across national frontiers was not mere rhetoric, and that despite differences of organization and objective the scientific academies were all moving towards a common goal.

Perhaps a few words should be added about the institutional relations of science and medicine, at least as far as England and France are concerned, both because organizations at the various levels of the medical profession were far older than in any other science, and because the physicians were the largest professional group displaying scientific activity in the seventeenth century. However, the individual eagerness of a Harvey or a Malpighi to make new discoveries in anatomy and physiology, or of Martin Lister (? 1638–1712) to study fossils, stands out against the general conservatism of the medical institutions, which existed above all to protect the interests of their members.

In England, the Barbers' Company was founded in 1462; it joined with the Surgeons under a new Charter in 1540. Meanwhile, Henry VIII had already granted a Charter to the College of Physicians founded by Thomas Linacre in 1518. The 'Art and Mystery of Apothecaries' was chartered in 1617. In these matters as in others England was behind the times, for on the continent barber–surgeons and apothecaries had been organized on a guild basis since the thirteenth century in some places. The object of the company or college was to restrict entry to the profession to those properly qualified by apprenticeship or otherwise in a given region, to prevent practice by interlopers from elsewhere without proper admission, and to penalize unqualified practitioners. As regards physicians specifically, the normal situation on the continent was that in university towns the practice of medicine was regulated for the town and region by the Medical Faculty of the University; in non-university towns like Nîmes (1397) and Bordeaux (1411) colleges were founded, often only admitting to membership the graduates of specified universities.

It is sufficiently clear [writes Sir George Clark] that London was exceptional (it might be rash to say unique) among the greater European cities in having no medical organization (before 1518), and that in some of the places known to English men of affairs there was a kind of organization suited to cities which were like London in having no university.[25]

All these bodies were, like the trade and merchant guilds, essentially monopolistic. They conferred privileges upon their members and had powers to protect them. Even in the early sixteenth century the atmosphere created by the Faculty of Medicine of the University of Paris was so stifling that François Rabelais preferred to journey south to Montpellier, a great medical university. A century later the Paris Faculty was the greatest opponent of Paracelsan medicine in the whole of Europe, at a time when the pure Galenism of the London College of Physicians, instilled by Linacre and cherished by Caius, was already weakening, witness the London Pharmacopoeia (1618), and the admission of such dissidents as Theodore Turquet de Mayerne and Robert Fludd. The former had been forced by the Faculty to leave Paris in 1611 as a renegade, tarred with the brush of Paracelsism, after the assassination of Henry IV; he became James I's physician. Fludd (1574–1637) was never anything but philosophically extravagant, a Rosicrucian; he entered the College only with difficulty yet was four times elected its Censor. The battle between the chemical physicians or followers of Paracelsus and the Galenists was occuring all over Europe; Harvey was hardly less of an eminent target for abuse, though for a much shorter period before the acceptance of the circulation of the blood became universal. In Germany Caspar Hoffman, in Italy Giovanni della Torre, in France Primrose, Riolan and Guy Patin (1601–72) were enthusiastic opponents of Harvey, who troubled to respond formally only to Riolan. Patin's epithets for Harvey's theory were 'paradoxical, useless, false, impossible, absurd, harmful'. Dominating the Paris Faculty, he proclaimed its irredeemable opposition to every innovation in science, medicine and philosophy, though of course other Frenchmen like Jean Pecquet (1622–74) of Dieppe, discoverer of the thoracic duct, were working in a different direction.

The Colleges of Physicians, having no interest in research and progressive change in medical practice, were firmly looking backwards. In Paris the Faculty of Medicine, after the death of Louis XIII (1643), succeeded in closing down the meetings or *Conférences* organized by Theophraste Renaudot at his *Bureau d'Adresse*, where all kinds of topics had been discussed in a popular way, because Renaudot had favoured new remedies and dispensaries to provide free medicines for the poor.[26] The Faculty seemed a possible enemy to scientific societies in Paris during the 1660s, though in the end royal patronage and its concentration on non-medical sciences made the Academy of Sciences respectable. Everyone knows the scorn that Molière poured on the medicine of the Faculty in *Le Malade imaginaire* (1673) and other plays; less familiar is the story that Nicolas Boileau in the following year wrote (with Racine) a burlesque decree declaring the doctrine of the circulation of the blood to be heretical and had it laid before the First President of the *Parlement de Paris* for his signature in place of a decree promoted by the University of Paris to prohibit the teaching of the philosophy of Descartes, thus by ridicule blocking the genuine decree. Boileau, however, was by temperament a conservative, and like many scholars (as well as physicians) a staunch defender of the 'ancients' against the innovating 'moderns'.[27]

In London the history of the College of Physicians is likewise for the most part a record of its staunch defence of its Fellows' privileges against the incursions of quacks, apothecaries, surgeons, foreigners, midwives and King Charles I. Not until Harvey made a benefaction at the close of his life (1651) did the College possess a library or a museum of herbs and specimens; the former was much enriched a few years after by the learned Marquess of Dorchester. A chemical 'operator' or 'laborant' had been employed to make medicines since 1648 (the Apothecaries had taken this step twenty years before), but this did not mean that 'chymical physicians' were now everywhere accepted. Although Harvey hoped that the College would become a centre for medical science, and ordered his Orators to exhort its Fellows to search out and study the secrets of nature by means of experiment, he was himself (so Aubrey tells us) one of those who distrusted chemical remedies.[28]

In other ways, however the London College of Physicians served in the republican period as a nursery of research in medical science. Its annual lectureships were devoted to reports of new discoveries, and according to Walter Charleton its members were assiduous in the dissection of animals and in confirming Harvey's 'incomparable invention'. Charleton saw the College (of which he was of course himself an active member) as a realization of Bacon's dream of Salomon's House; yet he and others were soon to transfer their main allegiance to the Royal Society.[29]

On 15 July 1662 the College of Physicians ceased to be the only chartered learned body in the capital, when the Royal Society was brought into legal existence. The particular association of the origins of the Society with Dr Jonathan Goddard, a respected FCP since 1640, the membership in it of other physicians such as William Petty, Thomas Willis, Walter Charleton and Sir George Ent (Harvey's nearest heir), and the Society's interest in anatomy and physiology – indeed, questions of therapy also – seem to suggest a close relation between the two corporations. The Royal Society even enjoyed, like the Physicians and the Surgeons, the right to obtain the bodies of executed criminals for dissection. But in fact there were no official relations between the two; the Royal Society is never mentioned in the records of the College. They are firmly connected – apart from distinguished dual memberships – by the story that an elder statesman of the College, Baldwin Hamey the younger, hired a vitriolic pamphleteer, Henry Stubbe (himself, ironically, an unqualified practitioner of medicine at Bath, which was outside the College's sphere of authority) to attack the Royal Society, which he did (in part) by asserting that it proposed to undermine the established privileges of the College of Physicians and of the Universities. Stubbe seems to have had some success in stirring up feeling at Oxford against the Society, but no echo of his malice in the London College has been found.

It might be tempting to affirm that the one belonged to the past, the other to the future, but the proposition hardly bears examination. New corporations of physicians were to be founded even in the eighteenth and nineteenth centuries, and they still today perform important professional functions not wholly dissimilar from those they have always exercised. In fact, organizations to encourage research in medicine and those to enforce professional standards are both necessary. If the conservatism of Guy Patin or Hamey seems egregious, it can be paralleled easily enough among men of affairs like Sir William Temple, writers like Swift, philosophers like Sir Robert Filmer, not to mention crowds of theologians. Perhaps rather than deploring or emphasizing conservatism, the historian should note the flexibility of a society in which so great varieties of strongly-held opinion could exist, if not peaceably, at least without mutual destruction.

Finally, it is perhaps worth noting that the eclectic and large Royal Society never found room for two of the most famous of English physicians – Thomas Browne and Thomas Sydenham. Nor did the College of Physicians ever include England's most famous seventeenth-century Doctor of Medicine, John Locke.

NOTES

1. Of course there were earlier exceptions: Petrus Peregrinus (Pierre de Maricourt, 1269) was a soldier, Geoffrey Chaucer (writer in English on technical astronomy c. 1390) a courtier, official and poet.

2. However Swift's instances of the folly of learning are said to be modelled on Rabelais, though given a contemporary twist.

3. In the Museo di Storia della Scienza, Florence.

4. Englished by Richard Waller as *Essayes of Natural Experiments made in the Academie del Cimento* (1684), but the word *Saggi* would now be rendered as 'Tests' or 'Trials' in this context. See W. E. Knowles Middleton, *The Experimenters: A Study of the Accademia del Cimento*, Johns Hopkins University Press: London and Baltimore, 1971.

5. Maurizio Torrini, *Dopo Galileo*, Olschki: Florence, 1979

6. The astronomers were J. D. Cassini (1625–1712 to be director of the Paris Observatory), Eustachio Manfredi (1674–1739) and Geminiano Montanari (1633–87). All were men of international repute.

7. F. R. Johnson, *Astronomical Thought in Renaissance England*, Johns Hopkins University Press: Baltimore 1937; his view of Gresham College is too rosy.

8. Hartib, his associates, his times, Baconianism and the endeavour towards reform about mid-century are all very fully treated in Charles Webster, *The Great Instauration*, Duckworth: London, 1975.

9. Scholarly debate defining the meaning of Boyle's words 'Invisible College' in letters of 1646 and 1647 has become unprofitable, and I have therefore avoided this label in the text. It is certain that Boyle did not apply it to the group described by Wallis, with which he was then unacquainted. Boyle's range of associates in 1646–47 is known. Sooner or later Hartlib was much interested in the efforts of all of them, including Boyle. A high minded utopianism of the 'Invisible College' type was widespread, as well among those acquainted with Hartlib in 1646, as among those who were not. See the articles collected in *Notes and Records of the Royal Society*, **23**, No. 2, 1968.

10. The twelve included four returned *emigrés*, and at least five men who had done very well during the Republic. Four had been at Oxford. Two (Wilkins and Goddard) figure in Wallis's 1645 list. Two (Boyle and Petty) had been closely linked with Hartlib.

11. Harcourt Brown, *Scientific Organizations in Seventeenth Century France* (1620–80), Williams and Wilkins: Baltimore, 1934, 84.

12. Roger Hahn, *The Anatomy of a Scientific Institution: The Paris Academy of Sciences, 1666–1803*, University of California Press: Berkeley, 1971.

13. W. E. Knowles Middleton in *Notes and Records of the Royal Society*, **32**, 1977, 14. I have slightly reworded Dr Middleton's translation.

14. See Webster (Note 8) and Michael Hunter in *Notes and Records of the Royal Society*, **31**, 1976, 9–114, the latest study of the early Fellowship. With exceptions, notably Petty, Hartlib's associates had little to do with the new Society, though Haak was both active and respected.

15. There is scattered material for this in A. R. and M. B. Hall, *The Correspondence of Henry Oldenburg*, University of Wisconsin Press: Madison and London, 1965 (continuing).

16. Sir Henry Lyons, *The Royal Society*, Cambridge U.P., 1944, 8–9.

17. See Hahn (Note 12), Ch. 1 and Marie Boas Hall in Harry Woolf (eds) *The Analytic Spirit*, Cornell University Press: Ithaca and London 1981, 177–94.

18. Hahn, op cit., 30.

19. Martha Ornstein, *The Role of Scientific Societies in the 17th Century*, University of Chicago Press: Chicago 1913 [1938], 175.

20. Foucher de Careil, *Oeuvres de Leibnitz*, Paris 1859–75, VII, 317.
21. To Tschirnhaus, January 1694 (C. I. Gerhardt, *Math. Schriften*, in *Ges. Werke* hrsg. von G. H. Pertz, IV, 519).
22. Harcourt Brown, *Science and the Human Comedy*, University of Toronto Press: Toronto, 1976, 83.
23. No. 80 contained, besides Newton's letter, eight pages giving accounts of three books and the annual index – another innovation. To compress the whole into twenty-four pages the printer was forced to print the last review page in very small (though legible) type.
24. See A. R. and M. B. Hall, *The Correspondence of Henry Oldenburg* (University of Wisconsin Press: Madison and London, 1965 onwards, XI vols published). See also Marie Boas Hall in *British Journal for History of Science*, **2**, 1965, 177–90.
25. Sir George Clark, *History of the Royal College of Physicians*, Oxford U.P., 1964, I, 65.
26. Harcourt Brown, *Scientific Organizations in Seventeenth-Century France*, Johns Hopkins University Press: Baltimore, 1934, 24, 30.
27. *Idem, Science and the Human Comedy*, Toronto University Press: Toronto and Buffalo 1976, 102–3.
28. Clark, op. cit., 309–12.
29. W. Charleton, *The Immortality of the Soul*, London, 1657, 34–5; Robert G. Frank Jr., *Harvey and the Oxford Physiologists*, California University Press: Berkeley, Los Angeles and London, 1980, 24–5.

CHAPTER NINE

Some technical influences

The renaissance of science in the sixteenth century, and the strategic ideas of the first phase of the scientific revolution, owed little to improvements in the actual technique of investigation. Before the beginning of the seventeenth century there is little evidence, except perhaps in anatomy and astronomy, of any endeavour to control narrowly the accuracy of scientific statements by the use of new procedures, still less to extend their range with the aid of techniques unknown to the existing tradition of science. Even the refinement of observation, begun in anatomy by Vesalius and his contemporaries and in astronomy by Tycho Brahe, hardly involved more than the natural extension and scrupulous application of familiar methods. Since the apparatus and instruments available were crude and limited the means were not at hand for gaining knowledge of new classes of phenomena, or eliciting facts more recondite than those already studied. Though greater reliance was placed on observation and experiment, the change in the content of science could not be dramatic and other sources of information were, at least till the latter part of the sixteenth century, largely traditional. Aristotle, Pliny, Dioscorides, Theopharastus and Galen were still very highly respected. Gradually, however, the tendency to supplement this book-learning, checked by personal examination where possible, by the experience of various groups of practical men gained ground. The wealth of fact was augmented by admitting the observations of craftsmen, navigators, travellers, physicians, surgeons and apothecaries as worthy of serious consideration, and thus the status of purely empirical truths, hardly inferior to that of the systematic truths of physics or medicine, was in time enhanced.

In this respect, as in others, the work of Galileo gives a useful indication of a turning point, displaying in various ways the operation of new technical, as well as conceptual, factors in the development of science. Galileo's conceptual achievements were of the greater importance, and imply a new metaphysics rather than the total absence of metaphysics, but he also admired the technological achievements of his time and appreciated the scientific problems suggested by them. By revealing the value of mathematics as a logical instrument in scientific reasoning, he transformed, if he did not actually create, an important method of enquiry. His exploration of the potentialities of the telescope and other instruments shows his concern for the enlargement of the scope of observation and experiment through newly invented techniques. It is typical of the evolution of the apparatus of science during the seventeenth century that Galileo's results were more notable for their qualitative originality than for quantitative accuracy, since the necessity for precision in measurement was less apparent than the strange novelties which the new techniques unfolded. Though the perspective in which science regards nature changed markedly in the sixteenth century, it was only in the seventeenth century that a significant qualitative change occurred in the image itself, to which the technical resources used by Galileo contributed profoundly.

It has already been pointed out that the ideal of social progress was also a commonplace among seventeenth-century scientists, and that with varying degrees of assurance the attainment of this ideal was linked with the application of scientific knowledge to technology. Conversely, it is clear that scientific research is itself dependent upon the level of technical skill, especially when the endowment or organization of science compels the experimenter to rely upon the skills acquired by the craftsman in the normal course of his trade, as was the case before the nineteenth century. Perhaps, in the early stages of a science, it is even more important that the investigator should be amply provided with both problems and the materials for solving them by the technological experience to which he has access. This is partly a question of attitudes – the ability to receive the stimulus from a merely practical quarter – partly of the richness of the techniques. Galileo makes Sagredo remark, on the first page of the *Discourses*:

I myself, being curious by nature, frequently visit [the Arsenal at Venice] for the mere pleasure of observing the work of those who, on account of their superiority over other artisans, we call 'first rank men'. Conference with them has often helped me in the investigation of certain effects including not only those which are striking, but also those which are recondite and almost incredible. At times also I have been put to confusion and driven to despair of ever explaining something for which I could not account, but which my senses told me to be true.

It can hardly be doubted that the dialogue of the First Day in this work was influenced by such practical observation, and it was from a workman that Galileo learnt of the breakdown of the *horror vacui* theory when the attempt was made to lift water through more than 9 m (30 ft) by means of a suction pump. Bacon also wrote of the knowledge concealed in skilled craftsmanship. In the next generation Boyle thought that only an unworthy student of nature would scorn to learn from artisans, from whom knowledge could best be obtained; for

many phenomena in trades are, also, some of the more noble and useful parts of natural history; for they show us nature in motion, and that too when turn'd out of her course by human power; which is the most instructive state wherein we can behold her. And, as the observations hereof tend, directly, to practice, so may they also afford much light to several theories.[1]

Such opinions did not spring from theoretical reasoning alone. They express the new philosophy's concern for *realia*, but they also recognize a genuine historical fact, that many of the ordinary operations of household and workshop were quite beyond the reach of scientific explanation. To remedy this, Galileo began the theory of structures and Boyle the study of fermentation in foodstuffs. Many of the problems suggested by the 'naturalist's insight into trades' could not, of course, be very profitably handled in the seventeenth century and some of the most intractable – like fermentation – were in any case very old. On the other hand, the enquiry into geomagnetism begun in the late sixteenth century is an example of a branch of science originating in the recent observations of practical men and followed up with profit to both theory and practice. Time-measurement also was both a scientific and a commercial problem, especially in relation to navigation. More obviously, skill in glass- and metal-working, especially grinding, turning and screw-cutting, could be readily applied to scientific purposes. Improvements in such arts were sought by scientists and craftsmen together, as when Robert Hooke collaborated with the famous clock-maker, Thomas Tompion.

In three related sciences, chemistry, mineralogy and metallurgy the pre-eminence of art over science was very marked at the opening of the sixteenth century. In natural philosophy there was a rudimentary knowledge of the classification of gems, earths and ores together with a wholly useless theory of the generation and transformation of substances. The pseudo-science, alchemy, had its own theory of the nature of metals and their ores, and contained some sound information on chemical processes and the preparation of simple inorganic compounds. But during the previous three centuries its originally useful content had become garbled and obscured through the growth of esoteric mysticism and the propagation of absurdities in its name. By contrast, great progress in chemical industry, at a time when this represented almost the only rational body of chemical knowledge, was scarcely reflected at all in scientific writings before the mid-sixteenth century. There were changes, permitting the use of new materials, economy of manufacture, or the improvement of the product, in a long list of trades, all of which depended on chemical operations, such as the extraction of metals and the refining of precious metals, glass- and pottery-making, the manufacture of soda and soap, the refining of salt and saltpetre and the manufacture of gunpowder, the preparation of mineral acids, and distillation. Other chemical arts, like dyeing and tanning, were probably less improved; some later innovations, like sugar refining, immediately aroused scientific interest. The knowledge of the craftsmen concerned was, of course, wholly empirical; they were uninterested in theory, and given to superstition and prejudice. Part of their skill may have derived from the Greek scientific tradition through Islamic sources – the art of distillation was clearly derived in this way, but it was perfected by artisans, not by philosophers or alchemists. Much of their skill was the tardy fruit of long experience. Taken altogether, craft knowledge in chemistry and related sciences implied a far greater acquaintance with materials and command over operations than were available to the philosopher or the adept.

By the end of the sixteenth century something like a rational chemistry was coming into existence, though sixty years later Boyle could still write:

There are many learned men, who being acquainted with chymistry but by report, have from the illiterateness, the arrogance and the impostures of too many of those, that pretend skill in it, taken occasion to entertain so ill an opinion as well of the art as of those that profess it, that they are apt to repine when they see any person, capable of succeeding in the study of solid philosophy, addict himself to an art they judge so much below a philosopher . . . when they see a man, acquainted with other learning, countenance by his example sooty empirics and a study which they scarce think fit for any but such as are unfit for the rational and useful parts of physiology [science].[2]

In the course of that century a number of books had appeared which, although primarily concerned with technological processes, had a significant influence on the chemical group of sciences. Avoiding theory, they threw off the air of mystery. They described in a matter-of-fact way how mineral substances were found in nature, extracted, and prepared, and how further commercial products were obtained from them by the operations of art. The processes described required mineralogical and chemical knowledge, manipulative skill, and often a complex economic organization. Some of the German mines already absorbed heavy capital expenditure, and some processes, like the manufacture of nitric acid needed for the separation of gold from silver, were conducted on a considerable scale.

The first of these treatises was a small German work known as the *Bergbüchlein*, printed at Augsburg in 1505.[3] Before this, in the fifteenth century, there had been in circulation manuscripts written in German dealing with pyrotechnics, the preparation of saltpetre and the manufacture of gunpowder, but these were never printed and seem to have been unimportant in science.[4] Possibly there were similar 'handbooks', earlier than the invention of printing, dealing with mining and metallurgy. The *Bergbüchlein* describes briefly the location and working of veins of ore, and is followed in the *Probierbüchlein* (first printed about 1510) by an account of the extraction, refining and testing of gold and silver. Their usefulness is proved by the many editions published. The same subjects were treated by Biringuccio in 1540, by Agricola in 1556, and by other German authors later in the century. The best informed of these was Lazarus Ercker, superintendent of the mines in the Holy Roman Empire, whose *Treatise on Ores and Assaying* (Prague, 1574), was translated into English as late as 1683.[5] Ercker's thoroughly practical book is chiefly concerned with the precious metals, but has chapters on working with copper and lead, on quicksilver, and on saltpetre. The *Pirotechnia* of Vanoccio Biringuccio and the *De re Metallica* of Agricola both cover a wider range of topics.[6] Biringuccio, for instance – the only Italian author of an important work of this type – describes the blast furnace, bronze- and iron-founding, and glass manufacture, but the technical information is somewhat unspecific. Agricola's book, massively detailed in its account of geological formations, mining machinery and chemical processes is justly regarded as the masterpiece of early technological writing. Agricola [*germanice* Georg Bauer] was a scholar, corresponding with Erasmus and Melanchthon, writing good Latin, enriching his observations with appropriate quotations from classical authors. He wrote also *On the Nature of Fossils* and on other scientific subjects. His knowledge of mining and industrial chemistry was gained through long residence, as a physician, in the mining towns of Joachimsthal in Bohemia and Chemnitz in Saxony. About the first third of *De re Metallica* is given to a discussion of mining methods. Then Agricola passes on to describe the assaying of ores to determine their quality, and the operations of preparing and smelting them. Iron, copper, tin, lead, bismuth, antimony and quicksilver are considered as well as the precious metals. The testing of the base metals for gold and silver content is the next topic, followed by an account of the separation of precious and base metals, and of gold from silver. Here the various processes of cupellation, cementation with saltpetre, liquation with the use of lead, amalgamation with mercury, refining with stibnite, and extraction with what Agricola calls *aqua valens* are described at length. This last was, apparently, a mixture of mineral acids prepared by distillation of different mixtures of vitriols, salt, saltpetre, alum and urine. The last section of the work treats of the preparation of 'solidified juices' – salt, potash and soda, alum, saltpetre, vitriols, sulphur, bitumen and glass. Here Agricola was on less firm ground and was guilty of some confusion and error.

This series of technical books reflects a tradition in applied science that had grown slowly in the later centuries of the Middle Ages, that was still gradually increasing in skill, and was capable of producing new techniques for handling the unprecedented richness of the South American mines. The authors, like the contemporary anatomists and herbalists, took full advantage of the art of wood-cut illustration. They did their work so well that it lasted into the early eighteenth century, when a new era of technology was beginning; it was over Agricola's great folio that Newton pored when he was investigating the chemistry of metals. Chemical industry did not merely furnish the chemists of the late sixteenth and seventeenth centuries with the materials in their laboratories; it supplied them with a factual account of the occurrence of minerals in the natural state and the methods of their preparation. More than this, the technical treatises provided, in contrast with the fanciful symbolic language of the alchemists, a precise account of basic chemical operations and reactions. Besides the works already mentioned, the philosophical chemist and virtuoso could turn to the *Distillation-book* of Hieronymus Brunschwig (1512) and its successors for instruction in this most necessary, and most difficult, of chemical arts. The alchemists, even when honest, wrote on the principle that if the reader had not been admitted to the secrets he would fail to understand, and if he had he would scarcely need further guidance. These writers, however, set forth the best of their knowledge as plainly as possible; and it was likely to be sound, for as Boyle remarked, 'tradesmen are commonly more diligent, in their particular way, than any other experimenter would be whose livelihood does not depend on it'. Only in its practical applications, stripped to its bare essentials of preparing this from that, was chemistry on a really solid foundation, independent of the misleading implications of false, and often fantastic, theories. But the chemical operations of industry were not merely qualitatively reliable and instructive. The application of *quantitative* methods to a chemical reaction was the essence of assaying, for example in calculating the quantity of gold in any alloy by carefully drying and weighing a precipitate.

The assayer deserves as much credit as the observational astronomer for providing numerical data and establishing the tradition of accurate measurement without which modern science could not have arisen. Though more of a craftsman than a scientist and more concerned with utility than with intellectual beauty, the assayer nevertheless collected a large part of the data on which chemical science was founded.[7]

When, in the eighteenth century, the balance was recognized as an invaluable tool in research the chemist was only extending a technique whose specialized usefulness in assaying was long familiar. Even the law of the conservation of mass was no more than a theoretical statement of a truth on which the operations of this craft were founded.

Boyle once spoke of German as the 'Hermetical language', because so many alchemists had used it. It is perhaps a more useful observation that rational chemistry began with accounts of the elaborate chemical industry in Germany, and was continued by German experimenters, some of them inspired by Paracelsus, himself a German-Swiss. Here there seems to be a clear case for believing that the development of a technical art to the necessary point in complexity and achievement provided much of the basis of fact and method from which experimental sciences could arise. Of course, the roots of modern chemistry, mineralogy and metallurgy are also to be found in alchemy, in pharmacy, and in philosophy. To the formation of chemical theories in the seventeenth and eighteenth centuries the description of practical operations contributed very little. Ideas were derived from different sources; and there was even a muddled, wrong-headed tradition of laboratory work in alchemy parallel to operations on the industrial scale. Yet in many ways the outlook of Black or Lavoisier resembles that of a practical assayer more than it does the esoteric perspective of Raymund Lull, Paracelsus or 'Basil Valentine'. The influence of the artisan, conceived as closer to the realities of nature than the abstracted philosopher, was an important element in many of the nascent sciences, but nowhere more than in chemistry, which most of all required an alliance of same thought and reasoned activity.

So far this chapter had discussed only some instances of what might be called the unconscious technical roots of science, that is, the information about the practical mastery of nature that was to be found in printed books before the beginning of the seventeenth century, and which might have been supplemented by actual visits to shipyards, workshops and foundries, and talks with those who worked in such places. For whom the various books just described, and their successors in the seventeenth century of which Joseph Moxon's *Mechanick Exercises* (1678) is an obvious English example, were written, is far from clear; but they are surely more likely to have been aimed at aspirants in craft or profession rather than at amateurs, philosophers or mathematicians. If Newton at Cambridge in the 1680s really pored over the large folio of Agricola, *De re Metallica*, in search of insight into the philosophy of metals, this was surely a use of his book that author cannot have foreseen. In the seventeenth century, however, books about techniques began to appear which were directed specifically towards the gentleman amateur, the curious, the rural philosopher, and perhaps especially the improver; one of them, by Walter Blith, is actually entitled *The English Improver, or a new Survey of Husbandry* (1649) and was re-issued as *The English Improver Improved* (1652). Bettering an estate required all sorts of technical arts: accountancy, surveying, land-draining, field geology, practical mechanics, agricultural chemistry and botany, animal breeding and (for the owner's house at least) architecture. During the Commonwealth period much effort was devoted by Hartlib and his associates precisely to encouraging the improver by such publications as Sir Richard Weston's *Discourse of Husbandrie used in Brabant and Flanders; shewing the wonderful improvement of land there* (1650), or *An Essay for the Advancement of Husbandry-Learning. Or Propositions for the Erecting a College of Husbandry* (1651) and Ralph Austen's *Treatise of Fruit-Trees* (1653). Hartlib himself put together from information supplied by Weston (who was the chief pioneer in England of the cultivation of leguminous plants such as sainfoin for animal-feed), the mysterious Cressy Dymock and others *Samuel Hartlib his Legacy* (1652).

This interest in agriculture was continued by the Royal Society, which distributed *Enquiries* about English farming practice to which a number of detailed replies were received. The chief object was to compile 'a Good History [Account] of Agriculture' and to recommend the best practices of particular regions for general use everywhere;[8] the country people, however, seem sometimes to have regarded such 'curiosity' with suspicion, fearing perhaps some fresh imposition of tax on their prosperity. No public result emerged from this activity, though private encouragement may well have been given to the improvement of farming, as by the cultivation of the turnip as a fodder-plant which was beginning at this time, until John Houghton FRS published two series of *Collections for the Improvement of Husbandry & Trade* (1681–83; 1692–1703). The long run of the second series in nineteen volumes indicates that it found readers. At first, at any rate, Houghton drew heavily on the traditions going back to the Hartlib circle.

In the same circle originated the parallel 'histories of trades', some printed in Sprat's *History of the Royal Society* (1667), and some in the *Philosophical Transactions*. William Petty's programme for this enterprise in *The Advice of W.P. to Mr S. Hartlib for the Advancement of Some Particular Parts of Learning* (1648) had been called the principal textbook for the history of trades.[9] Other famous names equally involved in it are those of Boyle and John Evelyn (1620–1706), the diarist, whose long fight for the re-afforestation of England should not be forgotten in this same context. In later years Evelyn became particularly interested in the craft of gardening, translating a successful French work on this topic by Jean de la Quintinie, who was also in direct correspondence with the Royal Society. Evelyn's artistic taste induced him to write *Sculptura* (1662), an account of the art of engraving on copper. He also prepared narratives of bread-making and the 'marbling' of paper. Boyle wrote enthusiastically about the history of trade and the utility of craft knowledge in his *Usefulness of Experimental Natural Philosophy* (1663) – a book written many years before its publication. When Sprat was compiling his book in the mid-1660s interest was still strong:

The Histories they have gather'd are either of Nature, Arts, or Works, These they have begun to collect by the Plainest Method, and from the plainest Information. They have fetch'd their Intelligence from the constant and unerring use of experienced Men of the most unaffected, and most unartificial kinds of life. They have already perform'd much in this way, and more they can promise the world to accomplish in a very short space of Time.[10]

But by the time his *History* was published in 1667 the main drive had already slackened. The narrative of craft methods was being supplanted by other interests, such as the air-pump: 'its contribution to science was no longer needed when laboratories increased in number and efficiency, and when the method of hypothesis supplanted the mere collection of experimental data'.[11] Or perhaps one should rather say, when precise scientific investigation supplanted the discursive collection of second-hand information.

All this was very much an English development, having few or no continental analogues, though the indefatigable Oldenburg did secure a few accounts of crafts from his correspondents abroad, just as the publication of 'machine-books' was very much a mainland tradition without parallel in England.[12] As already noted, in Paris the Academy of Sciences, perhaps not altogether of its own volition, took far more interest in the development of machinery than did the Royal Society. On the other hand, at various times matters of shipbuilding and navigation were of concern to many countries. Galileo perfected his observations of Jupiter's satellites to a very high degree of accuracy, having in view partly the utility of their appearances and disappearances, if they could be correctly predicted for future times, as a celestial clock to be used in determining longitude at sea.[13] He designed an observer's chair for use on shipboard and entered into discussions impartially with the Spanish and Netherlands governments. Later, the search for the longitude was energetically pursued by Christiaan Huygens, employing the mechanical clock: his principles were perfectly correct save that he chose to ignore the problem of temperature-compensation which was in fact drawn to his attention by Sir Robert Moray, but his clockmakers did not attain a sufficiently high level of workmanship.[14] Another who tackled the same problem was Robert Hooke, that versatile philosopher and experimenter, who unlike Huygens never actually produced a chronometer for sea-trials[15]; Leibniz too published a design for this purpose. Navigation and the problem of longitude were among the most powerful incentives to the foundation of national observatories in France and England; Cassini continued the intensive study of Jupiter and its satellites begun by Galileo, while both he and Flamsteed at Greenwich tried to plot and solve the lunar motions, the moon being an even more obvious potential timekeeper. Precise measurement of the occultations of the planet's satellites led to Ole Rømer's discovery (1676) of the finite velocity of light, detectable as the line of sight to Jupiter crosses, or does not cross, the diameter of the Earth's orbit.[16]

Both the construction of ships and the sailing of them seemed matters capable of analysis by application of the principles of mechanics. For example, the seaman may have to try to answer the question, when the wind is adverse: should he always sail as close to the wind as possible and so, by tacking, make the distance covered as short as possible, or should he choose to increase the mileage and speed by sailing further off the wind? This was first tackled as a problem in mechanics by the French Jesuit Ignace Pardies (1636–73) – who had a gentlemanly dispute with Newton about optics[17] – then by Huygens, and after him by many excellent mathematicians of the eighteenth century including Johann Bernoulli, Pierre Bouguer and Leonhard Euler. Construction, so far as it concerned the physicists, turned upon the shape of ships (the ease with which they move through the water) and their stability: loaded as they were with cannon, warships in particular were in peril of capsizing, as happened with the just-commissioned *Vasa* of the Swedish navy in 1628. In all countries the methods of the shipyards were traditional and unreliable, at least to the extent that for no obvious reason a new-built ship would on occasion prove very different from expectations and sometimes so dangerous that modifications had to be made to her. Some study of resistance was made by Huygens, Newton published in the *Principia* the first geometrical proposition about the ideal shape for the bows of a ship, while Johann Bernoulli was the first to investigate stability. Before the end of the century also suggestions had been made that experiments on models could well lead to improvements in design.[18] This was, in a sense, the policy followed by Sir William Petty, who in succession built a model and then four small sailing-vessels to vindicate his belief in the twin-hull or catamaran type of construction. Of the three constructed in 1662–64 the last, *The Experiment*, was lost in a great storm in the Bay of Biscay; the fourth boat never did well.

Another field of activity for the mathematicians was ballistics. After Galileo had first discovered experimentally, then demonstrated geometrically, that the trajectory of a projectile is a parabola – provided that air-resistance, the curvature of the Earth, Coriolis forces and so forth be neglected – a series of writers, Torricelli among the earliest, worked out the implications of this simple theory: how range is affected by the upward or downward slope of the terrain, for example. A number of writers, among whom perhaps the best known was François Blondel, in *L'Art de Jetter les Bombes* (1683), presented the parabolic theory in an elaboration of tables so that it could be used in the field by a reasonably literate gunner (whether it *was* much used there is another matter). In private, the parabolic theory was independently discovered by Thomas Harriot, who also, realizing that the perfect form of the parabola must be distorted by the air-resistance against the projectile, thought that this lack of symmetry might be represented by tilting the axis of the parabola, thus rendering the descent of the projectile (correctly) more steep than the ascent – as, indeed, Leonardo da Vinci had realized long before. Curiously, the first mathematician to open the subject of air-resistance publicly, James Gregory (1672) adopted exactly the same device for representing it as Harriot. Analytical studies of the effect of air-resistance on motion were made (privately) by Huygens and in the *Principia* by Newton; neither gave the curve for a realistic case in general form.

This was done by Johann Bernoulli in 1719. None of this sophisticated mathematical analysis was of the faintest interest to practical artillery-men, since it was simple a training-ground for skills in the calculus; the simple parabolic theory would give at least a rough guide to the behaviour of slow-moving mortar bombs.[19] Seventeenth- and eighteenth-century projectiles were delivered from the gun or mortar with so much uncertainty as to precise direction and velocity, and were so unsteady in their progress through the air, that precision in ballistic calculations was completely useless, nor could they (in general) have been assimilated into the actual conditions of warfare.

The object of the last few paragraphs has been to show how 'trades' suggested problems to natural philosophers and mathematicians, or (to put it the other way) how in pursuing lines of enquiry these men came across propositions in which they recognized the possibility of practical application. This happened, in a classical instance, when Christiaan Huygens realized that if the 'elastic fluid' in a vessel could be greatly rarefied by heat, on cooling the external atmospheric pressure would do work, for example by forcing down a piston. Thus the principle of the atmospheric heat-engine was known from at least 1675. Alternatively, the recognition might come to a third person, like the unknown seventeenth-century inventor of the air-rifle, from the air-pump: perhaps a toy to some, but issued to Austrian soldiers fighting against Napoleon and regarded by the French as a deadly accurate and unnatural weapon. Of course, one might also argue that interest in animal reproduction and the physiology of plants is at least as much 'practical' as 'philosophical'; certainly interest in the medical sciences (anatomy, physiology, pharmacology, pathology and so on) could very well be classed as 'practical' in the sense that the preservation of health is very much of direct interest to all men. Physic and surgery could in this sense be grouped with the 'trades'.[20]

To say that a fairly wide range of questions possessing at least an apparent relevance to the wide world of ships and cabbages and sealing-wax were investigated by philosophers and mathematicians is not to argue that this is *all* they did, or wrote about. A very great deal of writing in the mathematical, experimental and medical sciences was highly didactic: it conveyed instructions about facts and techniques, not about problem-solving. So far as men wrote or talked about problem-solving activities, they seem to be far more concerned with advancing knowledge than with reaping benefits. An enormous amount of effort was devoted to pushing forward existing lines of thought or developing new ones, or simply making more contributions to the stock of recorded knowledge. In Newton's *Principia* there are almost two hundred numbered propositions, not counting lemmas and corollaries; of these, one glances at a possible relevance to gunnery, another states its possible usefulness to shipbuilding. That does not seem a high proportion. Many years ago, as one element in a classical study, Robert K. Merton drew up, for four sample years of the seventeenth century, a tabulation in terms of 'pure science' and 'science related to socio-economic needs' of the topics raised or treated at the meetings of the Royal Society: his conclusion was that only about 41% fell into the category of 'pure science' while 59% were (potentially) useful in some way or other.[21]

No one is more aware than Merton that his ratio could not possibly be extended to an evaluation of scientific achievement, or that if one piled up 'pure' books on one pan of a balance, and 'applied' books on the other, the former would greatly preponderate. The talk at Royal Society meetings is only one barometer of the pressure of science upon society, not necessarily completely faithful or judicial, since it depends on the classifier's subjective appraisal. Nor, qualitatively, should too much credence been given to such a rhetorical statement as Hooke's

they [the Fellows of the Royal Society] do not wholly reject Experiments of meer light and theory; but they principally aim at such, whose Applications will improve and facilitate the present way of Manual Arts.[22]

The exaggeration is almost absurd. Certainly no such selection is evident in the book Hooke was introducing or in the later body of his own work. The much-discussed utilitarianism of the Royal Society must be diminished by appreciation of the vast distinction between what men say, or even suppose themselves to be doing, and what they naturally achieve.

Moreover, in the words of a great historian examining this issue:

The disinterested desire to know, the impulse of the mind to exercise itself methodically and without any practical purpose, is an independent and unique motive

to the study of mathematics and natural philosophy, as of other topics. Such a desire to know was already institutionalized in the universities of Europe, at the foundation of whose existence lay the disinterested love of truth. If some of the results of the scientific movement percolated down into practice and were applied:

On the other hand, the greater part of the scientific labour then done brought no practical return until long afterwards; the growth of science, limited by the laws of its own coherence and that of the universe, touched the needs of human life only here and there.[23]

The invention of numerous scientific instruments during the seventeenth century, and their fertile use in many capacities, has long been associated with the revolution in scientific thought and method. The idea of science as a product of the laboratory (in the modern sense of the word) is indeed one of the creations of the scientific revolution. In no previous period had the study of natural philosophy or medicine been particularly linked with the use of specialized techniques or tools of enquiry, and though the surgeon or the astronomer had been equipped with a limited range of instruments, little attention was paid to their fitness for use or to the possibility of extending and perfecting their uses. More variants of the astrolabe, the most characteristic of all medieval scientific instruments, were designed during the last half-century of its use in Europe (c. 1575–1625) than in all its preceding history. The Greeks had known the magnifying power of a spherical vessel filled with water, but the lens was an invention of the eleventh century, the spectacle glass of the thirteenth century, and the optical instrument of the seventeenth century. Navigational instruments also were extremely crude before the later sixteenth century. It was not that ingenuity and craftsmanship were wholly lacking (for many examples of fine metal-work, for artistic and military purposes, prove the contrary); rather the will to refine and extend instrumental techniques was absent. On the other hand, it has justly been pointed out that the early strategic stages of the scientific revolution were accomplished without the aid of the new instruments. They were unknown to Copernicus, to Vesalius, to Harvey, Bacon and Gilbert. It is clear that, great as was the influence of the instrumental ingenuity of the seventeenth century upon the course of modern science, such ingenuity was not at all responsible for the original deflection of science into this new course.

Thus it would seem that the first factor limiting the introduction into scientific practice of higher standards of observation and measurement, or of more complex manipulations, lay in the nature of science itself. Only when the concept of scientific research had changed, as it had by the end of the first quarter of the seventeenth century, was it possible to pay attention to the attainment of these higher standards. A number of the new instruments of the seventeenth century were not the product of scientific invention, but were adopted for scientific purposes because the new attitude enabled their usefulness to be perceived. The balance was borrowed from chemical craftsmanship. The telescope was brought into use by artisans, initially for military service. The microscope was an amusing toy before it became a serious instrument of research. The air-pump in the laboratory was an improved form of the common well-pump or syringe. And inevitably the techniques used in the construction of the new scientific instruments were those already in existence; they were not summoned out of nothing by the unprecedented scientific demand. Some instruments were only practicable because methods of lathe-turning and screw-cutting had been gradually perfected during two or three centuries, partly owing to the more ready availability of steel tools, others, because it was possible to produce larger, stronger and smoother sheets or strips of metal. The techniques of glass grinding and blowing which provided lenses and tubes might have been turned to scientific use long before they were. The established skill of the astrolabe-maker could be devoted to the fabrication of other instruments requiring divided circles and engraved lines, that of the watch-maker to various computers and models involving exact wheel-work, and so on. Common craftsmanship held a considerable reservoir of ingenuity, when scientific imagination arrived to draw upon it.

On the other hand, once interest in the kind of result that could be obtained from the employment of specialized instruments had been created, particularly as this employment began to extend under a more disciplined direction towards a greater qualitative depth of information and a greater quantitative accuracy of measurement, the limitations of normal craftsmanship were soon reached. Then it was necessary to begin a more conscious examination of the instruments themselves. Descartes was virtually the founder of the scientific study of the apparatus of science, in his investigation of the causes of the distortions present in the images of crude telescopes. (At the same time, purely empirical measures were also being adopted to remedy their defects.) Descartes concluded that

249

lenses should be ground to a non-spherical curvature, which would introduce greater complexity into their manufacture. Some scientists (including the astronomer Hevelius, and the microscopist Leeuwenhoek) became masters in the art of grinding the lenses they required for their work; others, like Newton, experimented with an alternative form of optical instrument. Towards the end of the century a scientist wishing to have a really good telescope or microscope could no longer simply make use of craftsmanship; he had to direct the work in accordance with a pre-determined specification. Astronomy had already at the end of the sixteenth century reached the point where further advances in precision involved great effort. Devices like the vernier scale and the tangent screw were major steps, and the attachment of telescopes to instruments for measuring angles reduced sighting errors. But the advantages gained by increased complexity in mechanical construction were all dependent on progressive refinement in workmanship, and the forethought and supervision of the scientist. The astronomer, in fact, had to consider his observatory as an exercise in design; he had to build walls, duly orientated, that would not settle; to design quadrants that were rigid, yet light, and true; to ascertain the probable errors of divided scales; to collimate his telescopes and rate his clocks. He had become aware that the limitations to his work were imposed by factors that were, in the main, technical and mechanical. As such, they deserved, and received, increasingly meticulous attention.

From the historical point of view, instruments may be divided into two classes: those which render qualitative information only, and those which permit of the making of measurements. Naturally, these uses of an instrument are not necessarily exclusive, in fact a little consideration makes it obvious that in their evolution most early scientific instruments tended to move into the second class. Thus, devices like the micrometer could be added to telecopes and microscopes so that very small or very distant objects could be measured; or alternatively these optical systems could be added to other measuring instruments to improve their performance. But the *first* use was purely qualitative. Similarly, in the eighteenth century, the electrometer designed in the first place for the detection of charges, was later applied to their comparison and measurement. The balance was first used in chemistry to establish a simple loss or gain in weight; its employment to determine accurately the masses involved in a chemical reaction came much later. It is therefore a natural and plausible proposition that the quantitative potentialities of a new instrument or piece of apparatus are generally appreciated less readily than the qualitative, and this was particularly the case in the seventeenth and eighteenth centuries. The invention of instruments, therefore, did not have that immediate effect of inducing greater rigour, and greater interest in refined measurement, which might be anticipated *a priori*. The barometer, for example, was invented by Torricelli in 1643. It was used originally to demonstrate the existence of atmospheric pressure, and secondly as a means of exhausting a small chamber formed at the top of the tube in which experiments could be made. Only about 1660 was the correlation between barometric pressure and climatic conditions discovered, and only after this were attempts made to improve the readability of the instrument and collect a 'history of the weather'. Later still, Boyle employed the barometer as a gauge to measure the quality of the vacuum formed by his air-pumps, and the amount of 'air' evolved from fermentations. The thermometer has an even longer, and more surprising, history as a merely qualitative instrument. The thermoscope, an instrument in which the expansion of air in a bulb moved a column of water in a narrow tube upwards when heat was applied, was invented by Galileo about 1600. Liquid thermometers were introduced about the middle of the century, and were extensively used by the Accademia del Cimento, but none of these was calibrated. The first suggestions for systematic calibration with the use of two fixed points were made about 1665; Fahrenheit's scale was devised about fifty years later, and the modern centigrade scale only in 1743. Thus the first century of thermometry yielded no quantitative measurements which can now be interpreted with any degree of confidence.[24]

While seventeenth-century astronomers, continuing a long tradition, effected a refinement of angular measure which bore fruit in Flamsteed's *Historia Coelestis Britannica* (1725), in physics and biology qualitative results were far more significant. Even the allied science of terrestrial angular measure (in surveying and geodesy) remained rather crude until vernier scales and telescopic sights were introduced at the close of the century. Consequently it can scarcely be maintained that *technical* limitations to accuracy of measurement were significant in any other branch of science than astronomy before the early part of the eighteenth century. Certainly it has been argued that chemistry would have progressed faster, and the science of heat have been more systematic, if greater attention had been paid to the quantitative aspects of experiment; but the reasons for the neglect of these aspects are to be sought rather in the nature of scientific activity in the seventeenth century, than in instrumental deficiencies. The importance of accurate measurements was not adequately understood, and therefore they were rarely made; so that it was the texture of science that hindered the effective exploitation of devices already in being, rather than vice versa.

On the other hand, with regard to the two qualitative instruments which most strikingly opened up great new fields of activity, the telescope and microscope, it is plain that technical limitations rapidly became serious, and that the nature of these limitations was well understood. Both instruments began in very crude form.[25] Systems of convex lenses replaced the concave–convex combination (the so-called Galilean arrangement) only gradually from about 1640, when rules for working out the appropriate focal lengths and apertures were better understood. The first true compound microscopes date from about this period, and the new (Keplerian) telescope brought more detail of the solar system into visibility. Additional satellites were discovered; the mysterious appearance of Saturn was accounted for; transits and occultations could be observed with higher accuracy. But the great desideratum of seventeenth-century astronomy – an observational proof of the earth's rotation – was not accomplished. To increase magnification without a corresponding vitiating increase of the aberrations the astronomer was compelled to use enormous focal lengths and small apertures. The light-gathering power of such instruments was poor, and a practical limit to length (about 30 m (100 ft)) was soon reached. Non-spherical curvatures for lenses were theoretically desirable, but technically impracticable. Newton's optical theory explained the nature of chromatic aberration without suggesting an appropriate remedy, for he found that the separate colours into which white light can be resolved could not be brought to a single focus by a simple lens. The reflecting telescope, free from chromatic aberration, was suggested by James Gregory and first constructed by Newton, but it was hardly of serious value to astronomers before the later years of the eighteenth century.

Similar problems were encountered in the microscope. Simple glasses, with a magnification of about ten diameters, were used early in the seventeenth century; by Harvey, who observed the pulsation of the heart in insects, and by Francesco Stelluti who published in 1625 a microscopic study of bees. The small tubular 'flea-glass', with the lens mounted at one end, and the object set against a glass plate at the other, became popular among the virtuosi. Towards the middle of the century the compound microscope attracted renewed interest, being now constructed with a bi-convex objective and eye-lens, with a plano-convex field lens placed between to concentrate the rays. In the improved design of Hooke (described in *Micrographia*, 1665) the body, containing extensible draw-tubes, was mounted so that it could be tilted to a convenient angle; a long nose-piece engaged in a large nut, so that the body could be brought to focus on the object by screwing it in or out. The lead-screw and slide method of adjustment was invented later by Hevelius. To illuminate opaque objects Hooke used an oil-lamp and bull's-eye lenses; before the reflecting-mirror was fitted (about 1720), transparent objects were examined by placing a lamp or candle on the floor beneath the instrument, which was often pierced through the base. The compound microscope was complicated and extensive, but it was easy to handle, and in mechanical design became steadily more efficient. Optically it was less satisfactory. Magnifications exceeding 100 diameters could be obtained, but the uncorrected lenses, made of poor glass, gave low resolution. As a result, the point was soon reached where, though the object could be made to appear larger, no finer detail in it could be seen. From 1665 until about 1830, when satisfactory corrected lenses became available, the compound microscope made comparatively slight advance in optical properties. The limitation imposed, on biological research in particular, is obvious.

Nevertheless, the compound microscope was eminently a scientific instrument, and Hooke's *Micrographia* the first treatise on microscopy. Since his objects were fairly coarse (insects, seeds, stones, fabrics, a razor's edge, leaves, wings, feathers, etc.), and since he did not seek to penetrate into anatomical structure by dissection (though he examined the compound insect eye, and discovered the cellular composition of cork) he was able to produce a series of admirable illustrations despite the limitations of his microscope. Most of the discoveries of the time in minute anatomy, associated with the names of Malpighi, Swammerdam and Grew, such as the capillary circulation of the blood, could also be demonstrated with the compound instrument. For the very finest observations, however, another technique was required, in which the Dutch microscopist Antoni van Leeuwenhoek excelled. The compound microscope had stimulated the grinding of very small bi-convex lenses of short focal length for use as objectives. It was found that better results could be obtained by mounting such highpower lenses, or even tiny fused glass spheres, as simple microscopes than by using them as elements in an optical system that multiplied the aberrations. For considerable magnification the lenses had to be less than 2.5 mm (0.1 in.) in diameter; they were proportionately difficult to grind and manipulate, and they imposed severe eye-strain. But Leeuwenhoek reported, in his letters to the Royal Society, observations obtained by this means which were only repeated with the achromatic microscopes of the nineteenth century. His skill as an optician is further shown by the fact that one of his few surviving lenses has been proved, by recent tests, far superior to any other known simple lens; others of his own make are good but not outstanding. This skill enabled him to study more thoroughly than any other observer spermatozoa and the red corpuscles in the blood and to become the first to discern protozoa and bacteria. Despite some contemporary incredulity, aroused by the great number and disparity of Leeuwenhoek's original discoveries, and the difficulty of confirming them, his work was astonishingly accurate. At the end of the century Leeuwenhoek was alone in his investigation of microscopic creatures, although others were engaged on the study of the microscopic parts of larger creatures; his results, therefore, remained largely isolated curiosities. In the eighteenth century the description of various animals, visible to the naked eye but capable of being studied only with the aid of the microscope, was taken up both in England (Baker, Ellis) and in France (Réaumur, Bonnet, Lyonet). Trembley, whose monograph on the hydra has become a classic, worked in Holland and was closely associated with both the English and the French groups of naturalists. All these worked with the simple microscope but at a much lower magnification than that frequently employed by Leeuwenhoek. This instrument thus became established in familiar use among zoologists and botanists for much the same purposes as it serves at the present time, when the higher powered compound microscope, given a beautiful mechanical construction by the English instrument-makers, was still of little scientific value. The continuation of the sciences of histology and cytology, begun by Malpighi and Leeuwenhoek, depended upon the perfecting of lenses which proceeded swiftly in the early nineteenth century.

It would be possible to develop other, comparable, instances of the way in which, after an initial seventeenth-century invention, a long interval followed before, in a stage of higher proficiency in instrumental techniques, observations or measurements of a different order became practicable. The greatly enlarged Newtonian reflecting telescope, with Herschel's improvements, for the first time enabled the astronomer to escape the confines of the solar system. If the 'chemical revolution' of the eighteenth century was to be effected without profound modifications of apparatus, on the other hand the chronology of electrical science was fixed by the discovery of instruments for the creation and measurement of charges and currents. Also during the eighteenth century a considerable literature grew up dealing with the manufacture and use of scientific instruments of all kinds, and teaching the technique of making experiments and observations, while the actual manufacturers strove intelligently to improve their wares. John Dollond, the practical man who solved the problem of making achromatic telescope objectives which had baffled mathematicians, was an instrument-maker. The marine chronometer, in the perfecting of which so much was due to another practical man, John Harrison, imposed a close collaboration between watch-makers and astronomers. Science, therefore, entered into a promising situation with the early nineteenth century, being able to call upon the services of a skilful and progressive specialized craft, and realizing far more pertinently than hitherto its own dependence upon its material equipment. In nearly every respect its progress was to be involved in that of some instrument, or in that of a variety of laboratory techniques.

NOTES

1. R. Boyle, *Considerations touching the Usefulness of Experimental Natural Philosophy*, *Works*, 1772, III, 443 (as abridged by P. Shaw, I, 129–30.)
2. R. Boyle, *Works*, 1772, I, 354.
3. A. Sisco and C. S. Smith (trans. and ed.) *Bergwerk-und Pröbierbuchlein*, American Institute of Mining and Mechanical Engineers: New York, 1949.
4. W. Hassenstein, *Das Feuerwerkbuch von 1420*. Verlag der Deutschen Technik: München, 1941.
5. A. Sisco and C. S. Smith, *Lazarus Ercker's Treatise on Ores and and Assaying*, Chicago University Press: Chicago, 1951.
6. M. Gnudi and C. S. Smith, *The Pirotechnia of Vannoccio Biringuccio* [1942], Dover: New York, 1959; H. C. and L. H. Hoover, *Georgius Agricola, De re metallica* [1912], Dover: New York, 1950.
7. Sisco and Smith (op. cit., Note 5), xv.
8. They were printed in *Phil. Trans.* No. 5, July, 1665, 82–94. For answers, see A. R. and M. B. Hall, *Correspondence of Henry Oldenburg*, VII, 294–9 (1670), VIII, 344–8 (1671).
9. Walter E. Houghton Jnr. in *Journal of the History of Ideas*, 2, 1941, 33–60.
10. T. Sprat, *History of the Royal Society*, London, 1667, 257.
11. Houghton, loc. cit., 60. It is odd to imply that Boyle, Grew, Ray and Newton used the 'method of hypothesis'.
12. See A. G. Keller, *Theatre of Machines*, Chapman and Hall: London 1964, and M. T. Gnudi (*trans.*) *The Various and Ingenious Machines of . . . Ramelli* [1588], Johns Hopkins University Press: Baltimore, 1976.
13. Stillman Drake, *Galileo at Work*, University of Chicago Press: Chicago and London, 1978, 193–4.
14. M. Mahoney in H. J. M. Bos *et al.* (eds) *Studies on Christiaan Huygens*, Swets and Zeitlinger: Lisse, 1980, 234–70.
15. A. R. Hall in *Studia Copernica*, 16, 1978, 261–81.
16. René Taton (ed.) *Roemer et la Vitesse de la Lumière*, Vrin: Paris, 1978.
17. A. Ziggelaar, *Le physicien I. G. Pardies*, Odense University Press: Odense, 1971, 137–8.

18. See A. R. Hall, 'Architectura navalis' in *Transactions of the Newcomen Society*, 51, 1979–80.
19. A. R. Hall, *Ballistics in the Seventeenth Century*, Cambridge U.P., 1952. I owe my knowledge of Harriot's work to D. T. Whiteside.
20. G. N. Clark, *Science and Social Welfare in the Age of Newton*, Clarendon Press: Oxford U.P., 1937, 1949.
21. Robert K. Merton, *Science, Technology and Society in Seventeenth-Century England, Osiris*, IV, 1938; New York, 1970. Table 13, p. 204.
22. Robert Hooke, *Micrographia*, London, 1665, Preface.
23. G. N. Clark, (loc. cit., Note 20), 186–9.
24. Although the tubes of early thermometers were marked with divisions, these were arbitrary and non-comparable. An inch division on a barometer, by contrast, is meaningful – provided one knows the standard inch employed!
25. The evolution in 1608 of the Dutch (or Galilean) telescope or spyglass from attempts to improve defective vision by combinations of lenses has been traced by A. Van Helden in *Trans. Amer. Phil. Soc.*, 67, 1977.

CHAPTER TEN

The progress of experimentation

Philosophers have often emphasized the distinction between discovery and demonstration in science: reflection and cursory investigation of a problem may make the explanation appear, without suggesting a convincing demonstration that it is correct, which may have to be obtained in some different way. On the other hand it may be the case that the discovery and the demonstration are identical. With a rather elementary discovery of fact, such as that made by the young Isaac Newton (in which he had been anticipated by Marcus Marci) that blue rays of light are more refracted – in a prism, for example – than red rays are, this is commonly the case: for the demonstration of the effect is simply the repetition of the original experiment, which may be varied infinitely to show that it holds in all cases. Or, to show that oxygen supports combustion better than ordinary air, one repeats some variant of Priestley's experiment by which this fact was discovered. The real difficulty lies in the demonstration of an explanation, or theory. So, to go back to colour and refraction, Newton's conviction that refrangibility is an inherent property of the ray, and that the rays are thus as it were characteristically labelled by a definite proportionality as well as by their individual colours, is much harder to demonstrate than the original property it seeks to explain. For it is not rationally necessary that the rays should be thus labelled, nor each existent as a separate, elementary and unchangeable component of ordinary white light, as Newton argued. This he recognized from the first: one can imagine theories of the physical nature of light in which this property does not hold, just as well as other alternative theories in which the property does hold true. Accordingly, the truth of the property inferred by Newton from his original experiment with the prism (p. 268) must be contingent, and made evident from different experiments concerning colour and refraction. In his first optical paper, in which he asserted the heterogeneity of white light, Newton offered no such evidence from further experiments and accordingly certain critics doubted the necessity for the inference he had asserted.

This is one example of the difficulties that can arise in the experimental confirmation of theories: the more precise the confirmation sought, the more difficulties arise. When a theory is argued on the basis of inherent likelihood and common knowledge, as with Greek atomism, for example, the question of experimental confirmation does not present itself. The Cartesian mechanical philosophy was of a similar kind – it could be illustrated by suitable experiments, but not confirmed, since its foundations were metaphysical assertions (a vacuum is impossible in nature) and invisible entities (the three types of matter). The theories to which experiments relate must always be of a more restricted range. There must be a fit between what the theory predicates and what the experiments determine, if either experimentation or theorization is to be of maximum usefulness. Without such a fit, experiments can only be randomly chosen empirical trials and theories can only be untestable assertions.

Such a fit was hardly obtained at all in the first half of the seventeenth century, hence the scientific work of that time cannot be typically qualified as experimental, though of course there were experiments. Consider William Gilbert's celebrated book *On the Magnet* (1600), for example: certainly it contains very many experiments on lodestones and iron, many instruments specially devised for Gilbert's purposes, many factual confutations of erroneous beliefs such as the possibility of obtaining perpetual motion from some kind of magnetic machine. But Gilbert was a natural philosopher as well as the father of English experimental science: and as he extends his treatment to the terrestrial globe and the universal principle of magnetism he leaves experiment far behind. Early in the book he tells us that the spherical lodestone (shaped with the poles on a diameter) having 'the orbicular form which nature granted from the beginning to the common mother Earth [possesses] many virtues, by which many obstruse and neglected truths in philosophy buried in piteous darkness may become more readily known to men'. In short, the supreme merit of this terrella (or little Earth, as he calls it), much employed in Gilbert's investigations, is that it served him as a laboratory model for the Great Magnet, the Earth. Though he investigated the variation of the magnetic declination from true north, and also dip, he carried out little experimentation on geomagnetism otherwise (effectively, this study began in the nineteenth century) and his reliance on his terrella as a model was in some respect misleading. Thus Gilbert's magnetic philosophy was founded, not on massive experiments, but upon an analogy, confidence in which takes him to heights of quasi-Copernican animism, as he explores the idea of a magnetically organic universe:

A lodestone is a wonderful thing in very many experiments, and like a living creature. And one of its remarkable virtues is that [causing rotation] which the ancients considered to be a living soul in the sky . . . For they suspected that such various motions could not arise without a divine and animate nature . . . We, however, find this life in globes only and in their homogenic parts . . . We consider that the whole universe is animated, and that all the globes, all the stars, and also the noble Earth have been governed since the beginning by their own appointed souls and have the motives of self-conservation.[1]

Clearly, what began as a factual study of the attractive and repulsive properties of matter has ended as a very different metaphysic; experimentation, seemingly

257

a guarantee of realism and defence against wild-ranging speculation, has proved (at least with Gilbert) to be nothing of the kind. And for this, it seems, Bacon blamed him, not appreciating as we may the force of Gilbert's imagination.

With others of the same early period, experimentation was so little trusted that it was deliberately concealed. Of the three discoverers of Snel's Law (p. 197) we know – and at that only very recently – of the empirical process of only one, Harriot. The lost trials or experiments attributed to others by contemporaries are legion. The supreme case is that of Galileo: we now know (Ch. 4) that he made extensive series of experiments on falling bodies and projectiles, which he chose not to cite as evidence, but to suppress or at least only glance at in the most brief and general allusions. Nor did Galileo ever specifically claim for himself the Leaning Tower of Pisa trials immortally linked with his name; it is his biographer Viviani who does so. What Galileo had discovered by experiments he preferred to justify rationally in his books.

Perhaps he was right not to jeopardize his credit, at a time when a man could be accused of lying if his reports lay outside the common belief. For this is precisely what had happened when Galileo published the *Sidereus Nuncius* in 1610; because he had seen through the telescope what had never been observed in the heavens before, the satellites of Jupiter, a myriad new stars in the Milky Way, theoretical astronomers like Antonio Magini of Bologna who had never looked through a telescope accused Galileo of being deceived by the instrument. The new phenomena were accepted as real only after Galileo in 1611 showed them to the Roman astronomers, Jesuits, through his own telescope. One should not altogether lack sympathy for the critics' scepticism, while deploring their manner of expressing it, for the literature of the day was full of such marvels which he who pleased might believe. Not to speak of mathematics, where evaluating π was still a common sport (the great scholar Julius Caesar Scaliger 'proved' it to be equal to $\sqrt{10}$), or at the other extreme the strange tales of witchcraft and possession, there was a long tradition of optical marvels. What is to be made of the claim by the respectable English mathematician and engineer Thomas Digges that by means of lens and mirrors, as it seems,

you may not only set out the proportion of an whole region, yea, represent before your eye the living image of every town, village, etc . . . but also . . . by application of glasses in due proportion cause any particular house or room thereof (to) dilate and show itself in as ample form as the whole town first appeared . . . or read any letter there lying open . . .

Had the inventor, his father Leonard Digges, devised before 1571 a telescope with zoom lenses?[2] Should this account of an experimental device – one of several – have been accepted as credible or put in the same class as other tales of optical marvels? Then there were the numerous and plausible-sounding stories of the alchemists. Most writers on alchemy claimed at some point not necessarily to have made gold themselves, or even to have seen it made, but at least to have examined specimens of factitious gold, of whose alchemical origins they could have no doubt. Among them, though rather physician than alchemist, was Johann Baptist Van Helmont (1577/80–1648), a man much admired and read in his day and still the subject of considerable interest; he tells us that he has several times seen and handled the Philosopher's Stone:

it was of colour, such as is in Saffron in its powder, yet weighing, and shining like unto powdered Glass; there was once given unto me one-fourth part of one Grain . . . being rolled up in Paper, I projected [it] upon eight Ounces of Quick-silver made hot in a Crucible; and straightway all the Quick-silver, with a certain degree of Noise, stood still from flowing, and being congealed, settled like unto a yellow Lump: but after pouring it out, the Bellows blowing, there were found eight ounces and a little less than eleven grains of the purest Gold.

Was Van Helmont himself deceived, or attempting to deceive his readers? For whatever he himself believed – and he told this tale more than once – the experiment never happened as he described it. But then Van Helmont was credulous: witness his story of the church-tower near Leiden in Holland, wholly destroyed by thunder (!) so that nothing of it remained; when two weeks later a grave was dug

behold under an unmoved and green Turf, first the Brass Weather-Cock with the Iron Crosse, appeareth, and then a Pinnacle of the Tower, and at length the whole Tower is digged out.[3]

It was by no means the case in the early seventeenth century that the literature of nature consisted merely of dry, rational Aristotelianism; on the contrary it was rich in stories of what men had seen and done, told with the most assured authority and not infrequently with the added, clinching admonition: Try this for yourself and you will see that it is true.

The mere relation of an experiment is not enough. It needs credible eye-witnesses, circumstantial support, context, quantitative measurement. Above all, organized experimental science, if it is not to be as confused as Van Helmont's animal whose parents were a dormouse and a rabbit, needs a group of men (such as the Accademia del Cimento and the Royal Society were) devoted to the verification of experiments. However, the different characteristics of these two bodies emphasize an important point. Sporadic checks to see whether this writer or that has told a true tale will hardly conduce to organized science; what is most profitable is the situation where the relation between experiment and theory can be explored. In this one may find an explanation of the fact that chemical science and chemical technology made only a gradually-maturing and ambiguous contribution to the development of experimentation. On the one hand, one has quite rational and reproducible literary accounts of chemical and metallurgical trades – say the manufacture of brass or gunpowder – as in Biringuccio's *Pirotechnia* (1540), and also accounts of quite exactly quantitative chemical analyses and tests, such as are to be found in Lazarus Ercker's *Treatise on Ores and Assaying* (1574).[4] The artisans practising these trades controlled many of the techniques and materials necessary for an exact experimental science, not least the use of the balance. On the other hand, the vastly greater bulk of chemical writing, shading into pharmacy and alchemy, was elusive and confused. It was written for adepts and mystics rather than laboratory scientists.

And above all there was no general theory of the constitution of matter, or of chemical change. One could of course test the assayers' instructions about the parting of silver and gold with nitric acid; one could, perhaps with more difficulty, test certain narratives in Paracelsus or Oswald Croll or Van Helmont. But how to test whether Butler's Stone really cures all diseases? And what would be tested, in many such specific instances, beyond the credibility of the author? So much is this case, that though the historian can point to a moment in time beyond which the influences of Paracelsus or Helmont have ceased to be significant, he cannot say when or by when they were effectively refuted.

The earliest and perhaps finest example of organized experimental science in the seventeenth century is offered by pneumatics. Not that all was new, for the Greeks had been familiar with a number of pneumatic devices, including the syringe and force-pump (but not the suction-pump) and had discussed the difficult question of void spaces in nature. Their ideas, principally expressed by Hero of Alexandria, became familiar in the sixteenth century. A new turn was given by the discovery that nature's mechanical resistance to the formation of a vacuum – the resistance felt in withdrawing a well-fitting piston from a closed cylinder – was limited: even the best made of suction-pumps could not draw well-water upwards through more than some 9 m (30 ft). Galileo, the first to record this observation in print (in his *Discourses*, 1638) rather curiously compared the column of water in pipe and barrel to a thread which, if long enough, breaks under its own weight.[5] A mathematician at Rome, Gasparo Berti (d. 1643), of whom little is known, repeated the situation in a long lead pipe set up vertically; after it had been filled from the top, and the top sealed tight, when the stopper at the bottom was removed the water-level in the tube fell to the height stated by Galileo. It is not really clear whether Berti and his friends thought of the space left vacant by the descending water as void, or whether they realized that the column of water was pressed upwards from the bottom, not suspended from the top. The arrangement made at the bottom which was to become classical, plunging the tube into a bucket of water, suggests that the latter point may have been understood. When Evangelista Torricelli at Florence heard of Berti's trial he at once repeated it with mercury, arguing that as mercury is about fourteen times as dense as water, the column should be somewhat more than 0.5 m (2 ft) high: and so it was proved. What counted was the weight/surface-area ratio at the base of the column, that is, the pressure: from which Torricelli guessed that the column was upheld by the counter-balancing weight of the atmosphere, a guess supported by his observation that the barometric height (as we may call it) was not invariant but altered from day to day. Not nature's resistance, but simply the weight of the atmosphere held back the plunger in a syringe.

In 1644 this Torricellian experiment made in the previous year became known to Mersenne in Paris, who gave it widespread European currency, overshadowing independent trials made elswhere. Many were anxious to repeat it; it was almost as exciting as Galileo's wonderful observations with the telescope had been. One who did so was Blaise Pascal (1623–62), a mathematical prodigy who at the age of sixteen wrote a treatise on conics, and at nineteen constructed the first arithmetical calculating machine. He also, at Rouen, set up the corresponding water-tube experiment. He proved that it was the vertical height, not the length of the tube that mattered, by inclining it, and devised many other variations. When he learned, after a year or so, that the weight of the atmosphere was supposed by some to support the column of fluid – air being considered philosophically a material substance, indeed, one of the four elements, the attribution of weight to air was no innovation – he deduced that if one supposed the layer of air surrounding the Earth to be quite thin, on high mountains the height of the barometer column would be less because a part of the atmosphere's weight would be below the apparatus. He further saw that the atmosphere is, as it were, a compressed ocean of air in which men move and breath like fishes in the ocean of water; strictly, the barometer is not held up by the *weight* of air, for it will retain its height when placed in a perfectly closed container at atmospheric pressure, but rather the pressure of the air, which must be elastic or spring-like. This fact could be neatly illustrated by the rather tricky contrivance of fitting the base of one barometer into the 'void' space at the top of another: the height of the mercury in the first then varied inversely with the height of the mercury in the second. But far more dramatic than the Rouen experiments was Pascal's commission to his brother-in-law, Perier, who lived near the 1,460 m (4,800 ft) Puy-de-Dome in Auvergne; on 19 September 1648 he and a company of observers measured the height of the barometer in the town of Clermont-Ferrand as 67 cm ($26\frac{1}{4}$ in.) (French); having ascended the mountain its height on the summit was several times measured as 59 cm ($23\frac{1}{8}$ in.), while about halfway down it had the intermediate value of just 64 cm (25 in.). Repeated trials allowed Perier to compute that while at ground level the change in pressure was about 0.13 cm (0.05 in.) of mercury for each 15 m (50 ft) difference in altitude, at around 900 m (3000 ft) above the town the same alteration in the mercury occurred for about each 30 m (100 ft) difference in altitude. This demonstration – for such it was taken to be – that nature's resistance to a vacuum was no magical or organic effect, but simply the mechanical consequence of atmospheric pressure, seemed in its day as epoch-making as the astronomers' confirmation of Einstein's theory of relativity.

Meanwhile, a quite different type of pneumatic experiment was being developed by Otto von Guericke, who came to his interest in air and the vacuum from cosmology. Von Guericke, a university-educated man who practised as an engineer and also as a diplomat, was a convinced Copernican: he asked himself what fills space in a Copernican universe, and how are the heavenly bodies moved in it? From 1646, when he first gained an idea of Cartesian physics with its assertion of the plenitude of space, and also of Torricelli's barometric experiment, he determined to test Descartes's assertion more effectively. In the following year he tried in vain to pump all the water out of a tight barrel: air was heard to leak in. His first copper vessel imploded. Finally with a sphere he succeeded; by now he had found that air itself could be exhausted, using a simple syringe-type pump with two valves. His experiments showed the elasticity of air within the vessel, and the enormous force of the atmosphere upon a large surface when the air behind it was reduced to a lower pressure by the pump. In the famous 'Magdeburg' experiment teams of horses failed to separate two large metal hemispheres thus held together after the air had been highly rarefied inside.

Von Guericke was a self-conscious experimenter who quotes St Basil, Galileo and Athanasius Kircher (but not Bacon) in defence of experimentation, but he was content to defer publication of his own account of demonstrations made before a number of grandees until 1672, when he embedded them in the middle of a large work on cosmology and speculative physics, in which (for example) he argues that empty space necessarily preceded God's creation, as being its receptacle.[6] First printed news of his work came in Caspar Schott's *Mechanica hydraulica pneumatica* (1657) and *Technica curiosa* (1664). The former book, widely circulated, fell into the eager hands of Robert Boyle, then living at Oxford and a member of Wilkins's circle there. It inspired him with the determination to explore the properties of the vacuum more thoroughly himself.

Robert Boyle (1627–91), youngest son of a noble and intellectual family, had been introduced to the intellectual circles of Commonwealth London by his sister, Lady Ranelagh; soon he was intimately associated with Samuel Hartlib (p. 216) who became for a time his mentor and remained a friend, but the heart of Boyle's interest was always natural philosophy, and the usefulness of natural philosophy, rather than organization, education and other plots for the common weal. He plunged deep into chemistry with Benjamin Worsley, Gerard Boate, Robert Child and the Helmontian 'philosopher by fire', George Starkey, some of whom talked of forming a chemical club. In the early 1650s Boyle was acquiring technical skills with furnaces and apparatus, reading hard, and already himself beginning to write copiously, though not to publish. He settled in Oxford in 1654, having first met Wilkins in the previous summer, and became by virtue of his intellect as well as his rank a leading member of the group there, and with them his range of interest widened further. He was always able to employ scientific assistants and secretaries: the man who devised the successful air-pump for Boyle was Robert Hooke, who had come up to Oxford as a poor student in 1653, and was recommended to Boyle by the anatomist Thomas Willis. What made Boyle's pump a laboratory instrument was that one man could work it (by means of a rack-and-pinion), it had proper valves, and the space evacuated was a glass globe. This vessel was even fitted with a device so that simple movements could be made within it after exhaustion. Pumps essentially like Boyle's continued to be made well into the nineteenth century; when new and original it was the cyclotron of its age.

Boyle and Hooke thoroughly investigated all the usual phenomena of pneumatics as known hitherto, to illustrate the 'spring and weight of the air'; they are described in Boyle's book with that title, published in 1660.[7] For example the effect of reducing or increasing the external pressure on the mercury cistern of the barometer could be made evident simply by plying the pump (in this case, the glass vessel was perforated to allow the barometer tube to be passed through and sealed into it). This part of the investigation produced its best known result: Boyle's Law. Curiously, while Boyle recognized that a mathematical relation must exist between a closed volume of gas and the incumbent pressure, he did not state it until (as he acknowledged) it had been worked out independently by Hooke and Richard Towneley. Boyle's Law was first enunciated in his 'Defence of the Doctrine touching the Spring and Weight of the Air', where it was magisterially demonstrated, in the second published series of air-pump experiments. There was to be a third series many years later.

Qualitatively, the more interesting part of Boyle's laboratory work was that in which he experimented on the properties of things *in vacuo*. Magnetism and light were unaffected; sound ceased. Birds and animals died as fast as the pump could be worked. Flame expired (but gunpowder could still be fired). Warm water boiled fiercely. It became obvious that air was far from being the inert substance it had sometimes seemed to be in philosophy – even a hint of its having a chemical significance began to appear. Further, in his last experiments with the air-pump, Boyle showed that substances can evolve an ordinarily imperceptible air *in vacuo*, which had as it were been concealed or fixed in their substance – a pregnant suggestion for the future.

The 'Boyleian vacuum' became one of the great commonplaces of science of his own age and the next, to be immortalized in Joseph Wright of Derby's painting of 'The Philosopher'. Everyone wanted at least to have witnessed the experiments, though few could actually own so costly a piece of apparatus. Boyle gave his own first pump to the Royal Society. But a great many people could and did own barometers, and chart their irregular ups and downs, soon associated with changes in the weather. From this sprang two of the strangest of all seventeenth-century pneumatic observations: the first was noted by Christiaan Huygens and aroused great interest in the 1660s. The 'anomalous suspension of mercury' is a surface tension effect: under exceptional conditions the mercury will stand in a long tube, at a height of 1.5 m (5 ft) or so, instead of forming a barometer in the usual way. Did this prove the existence of a Cartesian aether, since the pressure of the atmosphere alone could not explain the effect? Of greater interest was the observation of triboluminescence, or electrical glow in the barometer. It was first perceived by the astronomer Picard about 1676; when his barometer was shifted from one room to another, the inevitable oscillation of the mercury in the tube caused a slight glow in the empty space above the column.[8] The effect was difficult both to verify and explain – the mathematician Johann Bernoulli tried to relate this also to the Cartesian aether – but early in the next century it suggested another experiment to the London scientific lecturer Francis Hauksbee. He mounted a dry, evacuated glass globe as a triboelectric generator, using his hand as the rubber (in the manner devised by von Guericke, who had employed a solid, cast ball of sulphur for the purpose) – when a charge was built up, a glow was seen in the hollow sphere. Thus, to the great interest of Newton, light and electricity were strongly linked, the electric friction having previously been known only to cause attraction and repulsion.[9] Hauksbee's experiment was to open a vast realm of thought and experiment during later centuries.

It is rather rare for one investigator to have produced such a rich and complete series of results as those obtained in the course of the various series of air-pump experiments made by Boyle and his associates, among whom, after Hooke, was the forefather of the steam-engine, Denys Papin (1647–1712). One might add that the original atmospheric steam-engine of Newcomen (1712) was itself a peculiar air-pump, utilizing the vast lifting-force of atmospheric pressure that von Guericke had first displayed. Contrary to Charles II's jests, the philosophers' weighing of the air did in the end, by mediation of the sound mechanical sense of Thomas Newcomen, produce results of industrial importance.

Pneumatics was a wholly new science; experimental optics had a respectable tradition going back to the Greeks. One aspect of it, concerned with the making of lenses for instruments, will be discussed in a later chapter; another, to be considered now, the study of the refraction of light, had been effectively begun by Alhazen in the tenth century, taken further by Theoderic of Freyburg and his predecessors during the thirteenth and fourteenth centuries, and revived by Baptista Porta and others in the sixteenth century. Theoderic had shown how a glass carafe full of water could serve as a model for the rainbow; though his work may have been forgotten, the practical experimental tradition certainly continued, strengthened indeed by the practical utility of the spectacle-lens from Theoderic's time onwards.

However, optics was also in an even more important sense a mathematical science: the putative equation of a single (hypothetical) light-ray with a straight line made it so. From Ptolemy's time onwards arbitrary tables – supposedly but not in fact founded on actual measurements – correlated the angle of emergence from the interface with the angle of incidence upon it. Astronomers well knew that rays from the stars are refracted through the atmosphere also, but not exactly in what proportions. As we have seen, the general law of refraction – Snel's Law – must have been derived from measurements; Descartes, possessing it, and before him Kepler, who had it not, opened up the mathematical theory of refractions taken further by Barrow and Newton. Meanwhile, the physical problem of the origin of the colours in the rainbow and other spectra, or for that matter the problem of the nature of colour in general, had progressed not at all. In qualitative terms it had been supposed since the Greeks that colour was a function of intensity: all dim colours seem less bright, and the blue end of the spectrum shades into darkness. Despite the immediate and urgent objections to this view, it was still the best that the early seventeenth century could offer: it implied, obviously, that any coloured light was somehow weakened or modified as compared with white light. Descartes made the latter hypothesis specific. Defining light as a pressure (or motion) of the particles of his aether, he further hypothesized that in white light the particles do not have spin, whereas the colours are our various responses to varying degrees of spin in the particles. The spin was acquired by the oblique passage (refraction) of the rays through an interface – an event only consistent with the linear motion or translation of the aether particles.

In his *Micrographia* (1665), a book on his microscope and observations made with it, mostly or wholly at Oxford, Robert Hooke devoted a few pages to light and colours. Rejecting Descartes' hypothesis of the streaming of particles,

Hooke argued that a light-ray consisted rather of a succession of pulses propagated through the aether from the source. Each pulse or vibration in the flame
or other source of white light would form an expanding concentric sphere about
it 'just after the same manner (though indefinitely swifter) as the waves or rings
on the surface of water do swell into bigger and bigger circle about a point of
it, where, by the sinking of a stone, the motion was begun'. When expansion
of the spheres was obstructed in such a way that only a beam of light could
proceed, the successive pulses or vibrations would be at right angles to the
beam. On considering the passage of the beam through an interface between
two transparent media, and hypothesizing (like Descartes) that the optical difference between them lay in one allowing the light-pulses to travel more
quickly than the other, he reasoned that if the beam fell obliquely upon the
interface, one end of each pulse on passing through it would be accelerated or
retarded as compared with the other end, passing later through the interface.

Fig. 10.1 Hooke's Theory of Refraction. *aaabbb*, incident ray; *cccddd*, refracted ray. *ab, ab* perpendicular pulses, *cd, cd* oblique pulses.

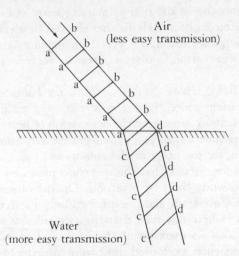

Consequently the pulse would become oblique to the beam, and in this physical
difference between the refracted and the unrefracted beam resided, he thought,
the colours of the former and the whiteness of the latter. Hooke reasoned that
in a whole beam of light there would be some confusion of the oblique pulses,
and that one 'edge' of each pulse would be weakened or blunted through having
to initiate the vibration in a medium at rest, thus:

Blue is an impression on the Retina of an oblique and confus'd pulse of light whose
weakest part precedes, and whose strongest follows. Red is an impression on the Retina
of an oblique and confus'd pulse of light, whose strongest part precedes, and whose
weakest follows.

For example in Fig. 10.2, towards *a* the leading edge of each oblique pulse,
being adjacent to the undisturbed medium, is weakened, whereas towards *d* the

Fig. 10.2   Hooke's Theory of Colours.

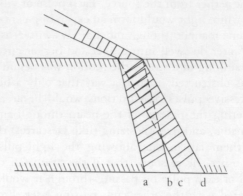

a   b c   d

lagging edge of the pulse is weakened for the same reason. Hence the colour blue will be seen about *a* and red about *d*. Hooke thought that the intermediate colours of the spectrum 'arise from the composition and dilutings of these two' produced by the confusion of the two primary types of oblique pulse towards the middle of the refracted beam. He further showed by a very ingenious analysis that when a ray passes through a very thin medium a similar succession of strong–weak or weak–strong pulses is created, according to its thickness, producing colours.

In this theory of light, Hooke devised a simple mechanism by which colours might be derived from white light considered as a train of uniform and homogeneous pulses. It accounted for the association of heat, light and motion in a crudely sketched kinetic theory; for the fact that refraction is always accompanied by coloration; for the order of the colours as produced by refraction or by interference; and for the fact that the spectrum produced by one prism can be re-converted into white light by a second. On the other hand, it was not very clearly conceived in detail, and it explained only a selection of the known facts. Hooke seems to have observed that the two sides of a refracted ray are not parallel, but makes no mention of the fact (cf. Fig. 10.2) Probably no experiments on homogeneous coloured light were made by him, since he seems not to have known that further refractions have no effect upon such light; this would certainly have been difficult to reconcile with his theory. The most serious objection against its broad form was that it failed to account for the rectilinear propagation of light. If a ray was a train of pulses, why did not these spread out into the surrounding medium, as sound-waves do? This was, indeed, for long a profound objection against any pulse or undulatory theory, having been thoroughly discussed by Newton in the *Opticks* (1704).

Neither Descartes' theory nor Hooke's was enriched by experimental evidence, though both appealed to several supposed analogies (like Hooke's between light-waves and water-waves) and Hooke later claimed to have made hundreds of experiments on refraction and colour. He described none. To support his views that mixtures of red and blue would create all colours, he cited an experiment upon two wedge-shaped glass boxes, positioning these so that light passed through varying thicknesses of each, the boxes being filled with blue-dyed and red-dyed water. It is hard to see how he could have produced a bright yellow or any sort of green; in fact, Hooke's theory is only a modification of the old hypothesis that colour was a function of intensity. Hooke's important experimental discovery, which justified his assigning periodicity to the fundamental motion of light, was that of 'Newton's rings', as they are unjustly known. He observed them in the laminations of mica and in plates of glass pressed hard together, and appreciated their relation to the spectral series.[10] In the year of the publication of *Micrographia* a posthumous book by an Italian experimenter, Francesco Maria Grimaldi (1613–63), also appeared in which he described a third way in which colours could be produced: when a ray of light was deflected by passing over a sharp edge. (This was later called *diffraction*, while Newton's rings were to be known much later as *interference* colours). Grimaldi had previously made, on behalf of his astronomer colleague G. B. Riccioli (1592–1671) – both were Jesuits – a series of experiments on the fall of bodies from the leaning Asinelli tower at Bologna which confirmed Galileo's times-squared law, and had originated the present system of naming 'seas' and 'mountains' on the Moon. Grimaldi understood that the diffraction bands of his experiments were quite different from the spectral bands, and that they refuted the strict rectilinearity of the light ray. Much of his book, *A Physicomathematical thesis on light, colours {and} the rainbow* debates an Aristotelian philosophical question about whether light is a substance or an accident; it is a turgid and difficult book. Grimaldi, like the English experimenters, thought that 'Colours are not any thing permanent in visible things, not of themselves lucid when they are not illuminated; but that they are the light itself, under some peculiar Modification made sensible by the sight'. This modification Grimaldi supposed to be 'a most finely furrowed Undulation . . . a kind of tremulous diffusion, with a certain very subtle floating', by which (it seems certain) he did not mean anything like the pulse- or wave-theory of Hooke and Huygens.[11]

The diffraction of light was to remain a mystery for a century and a half – Newton had no very good idea of the phenomena and probably never read Grimaldi's book. He certainly did read Robert Boyle's *Experiments and Considerations touching Colours* (1664); his notes on this book are immediately followed by his own first experiments, which preceded his examination of *Micrographia*. Boyle was chiefly interested in the colours of opaque bodies, and in particular the relationship between colour and chemistry (he was the first to see the significance of colour-indicators like the now familiar litmus). However, he did also write probably the clearest account that Newton read of the 'Triangular Prismatical Glass being the Instrument upon whose Effects we may the most Commodiously speculate the Nature of Emphatical Colours (and perhaps that of others too;)' and he anticipated Newton in the idea that the superficial colours of bodies are somehow caused by their mechanical surface texture.

Spread over a series of years from 1664, perhaps ten years, and finally writing up his experiments and theory only in the early 1690s (*Opticks* was then further to await publication until after Hooke's death in 1703) Newton effected the greatest experimental investigation in all seventeenth-century physical science – indeed, one of the greatest of all time. Its place in his evolution as a philosopher will be discussed more fully later. What is important now is that Newton created completely novel standards of scientific method both with regard to the accuracy and detail of an investigation, and of the closeness of relationships between experiments and theory. Ultimately his research into light and colours – heightened, gilded and retouched not a little, it must be said – was to be set out in rich detail in *Opticks* and so become a subsequent model of experimental science; his first announcement was laconic and to many unconvincing. This was partly because at this stage he hardly knew how to express his idea of what he took to be unavoidable theoretical inferences from his investigation without tying himself to deeper pronouncements about the philosophy of light which he was anxious to escape. A certain perhaps inevitable ineptitude then led him directly into the controversies he sought to avoid.

Newton had also read Descartes, and understood the mathematical treatment of light thoroughly. Like so many others, he tells us, he was much interested in the improvement of lenses, for which Descartes had proposed aspherical curvatures. Newton followed the same path. But when he obtained a prism he found reason to do otherwise and leave off his 'glassworks'. At first he looked through the prism, as through a lens, and to see the effect of refraction upon colours painted a thick straight line, part red, part blue; when looked at through the prism, the line no longer seemed to be straight. It seemed that 'the rays which make blew are refracted more than the rays which make red'. On darkening his room (in the First Court of Trinity College, Cambridge) admitting direct sunlight through a small round hole, and shining the beam thus formed through his prism, the spectrum of 'vivid and intense colours produced thereby' was a 'pleasing divertisement' until he stopped to ask, why was the spectrum not round, like the beam, but elongated in the direction normal to the axis of the prism? Was the beam after refraction curved or otherwise distorted? The answer proved to be rather that the blue ray had been more refracted than the red ray, so that that the light was now dispersed in one direction (indeed, if there were no dispersion the distinct coloured patches of the spectrum could not be separated at all). Newton found that while rays delimiting the breadth of the prism diverged at $31'$ of arc, corresponding to the Sun's diameter, those delimiting its length diverged at $2°\ 49'$. Using two pierced diaphragms in his 'crucial experiment', and a pair of prisms, he satisfied himself directly that an isolated red ray was less refracted in the second prism than a blue ray, and that each separate colour was labelled by its characteristic degree of refraction. Colour, Newton had discovered, was not only a qualitative but a mathematical property of light.

From this it followed, for Newton, that each colour, of which he detected seven in the spectrum, was a physical identity, marked quantitatively by its characteristic physical x. For physicists since Thomas Young x has signified wavelength (or its equivalent, frequency); in one of his papers Newton contemplates just this idea of identifying colour. But if, continuing the Cartesians model, light be rather supposed a stream of particles, then the physical

x could be spin, in the manner of Descartes, or mass, or velocity. Newton steadily rejected the wave-theory of light because (he argued, missing the point of diffraction) light always moves in straight lines, while waves curve round obstacles; otherwise he had no idea what the physical x might be, and could never settle the question. This was the issue he desired to avoid in his first letter about his optical discoveries. Instead, Newton went on to his next inference: if each ray has a physical identity this cannot have been created by refraction, but must have existed before refraction. That is, 'Light itself is a heterogeneous mixture of differently refrangible Rays', the prism simply acting as an optical filter (as we would say) to separate out these seven constituent members of white light, which could be recombined by passing through a second prism inverse to the first or in the focus of a lens. If one of the constituent rays was blocked then white light could not be re-formed.

Newton now saw that it was impossible to bring white light to an exact point focus with a lens, for the focal length for each constituent colour was slightly different: hence the annoying coloured fringes in the images of telescopes and microscopes. Though aspherical lenses could indeed correct for spherical aberration, they still would not take away the fringes:

This made me take Reflections into consideration, and finding them regular . . . I understand that by their mediation Optick instruments might be brought to any degree of perfection imaginable, provided a reflecting substance could be found, which would polish as finely as Glass, and reflect as much light, as glass transmits, and the art of communicating to it a Parabolick figure be also attained.

In 1668, it seems, Newton constructed a tiny reflector,[12] having an aperture of 2.5 cm (1 in.) – at this size accurate parabolization was not important – choosing a hard white bronze for the mirrors which he made himself. It magnified about thirty times – the same as Galileo's best telescope – and made the satellites of Jupiter visible (these are indeed not far below the limit of visibility to a good unaided eye). It was this astonishing little instrument that made Newton suddenly famous in the winter of 1671–72, and brought about the writing of his first optical letter, dated 6 February 1672, to explain the experimental and theoretical background to his invention.[13]

An enormous controversy exploded, for Newton's doctrine of the homogeneity of the seven coloured spectral rays and the consequent heterogeneity of the white light formed by their addition appeared very shocking to contemporaries. The simple nature of white light had always been accepted as axiomatic. The proof that all the colours of the spectrum are equally primary and necessary in white light cut directly across notions which supposed them the product of mixtures of red and blue, or blue and yellow. While some theorists of empiricism welcomed Newton's Baconian use of experiment, many who had prided themselves on their knowledge of optics were hostile. The reactions of the critics, Hooke and Huygens among them, are interesting. When Newton's first paper appeared in the *Philosophical Transactions*, they judged initially that he was merely speculating, and tried to answer with irrelevant arguments. Then they denied that the experiments gave the results described by Newton, or maintained that if the experiments were correct the conclusions drawn from them were false. Finally, it was alleged that if Newton's ideas were justifiable, they were not original. Neglecting the minor critics, it may be doubted whether either Hooke or Huygens – two of the leaders of the scientific movement – ever succeeded entirely in adjusting their thinking in accordance with the evidence of Newton's experiments. The former never understood that his own pulse-theory could not account for them. The latter, in his *Traité de la Lumiere* (1690), tactfully omitted the subject of colour completely. Their failure is not more surprising than that of other scientists in more recent periods who have equally resisted an innovation which has inevitably overwhelmed their criticism. Newton's propositions were revolutionary, not only in their content, but because they were founded straightforwardly on new experimental evidence. It is, in one sense, an indication of the superficiality of the change in spirit effected by the scientific revolution that such obvious conclusions drawn from such easily repeatable experiments should have been treated as matters for argument.

When this has been said, we must recognize certain complexities. First, Newton's own thought – the path by which he reached the conclusions about the nature of light published in 1672 – was not so simply inductive as he wished to make out: that is, he was helped along by theoretical crutches whose help, in public, he disliked acknowledging. He always believed that the emission, or particulate, theory of light must be true. Some features of his complete optical system make no sense unless this is so. On the other hand, he never publicly or privately established a definitive link between colour and the hypothesis of light-particles, so that nothing in his treatment of colours can be said to have covertly depended on that hypothesis. Secondly, when Newton wrote his first optical letters he already knew about the colours of thin plates – interference colours, Newton's rings. Therefore, in accordance with Newton's 'doctrine' of the heterogeneity of white light, the thin plate too must act as a filter, the filtering action depending on the thinness of the plate, or more accurately on multiples of thinnesses. Newton did not mention this phenomenon at all in his 1672 letter, but did so in a much longer optical paper submitted to the Royal Society at the end of 1675. Here he gave a detailed account of interference rings, and proposed the arbitrary hypothesis that 'light' being not the aether filling space, nor even a vibration of this aether, nevertheless (whatever its nature) is to be supposed capable of creating vibrations in the aether.[14] These vibrations then, in a wholly unexplained way, when they match the dimensions of a plate cause that plate to transmit one colour only. Thus, in a peculiar manner, the wave-theory was reintroduced *ad hoc* at a secondary level, and though Newton says he has no commitment to this theory he repeated it in *Opticks*, slightly disguised as the 'fits of easy reflection and easy transmission'. Newton's basic doctrine of heterogeneity was not sufficient for all phenomena of colours without reinforcement by an auxiliary mechanical hypothesis.

In Newton's own words his belief that 'whiteness is a dissimiliar mixture of all colours' was regarded as 'the most Paradoxical of all my assertions, and

[has] met with the most universal and obstinate prejudice'. Yet to himself it was 'infallibly true and certain'.[15] Had Newton proved that the nature of light is not modified by any colour-creating process, such as refraction? Some historians have asserted that he did not:

[experiment] does not prove that the properties of the refracted light exist primarily and unaltered in white light. It might well be that those properties are manufactured out of white light by the prism but, once generated, they are not alterable by further refractions.[16]

The second sentence is unjust to Newton's technique, for he showed (though not indeed in the first printed letter) that a similar prism, placed inversely to the first, recombines the dispersed coloured rays so that they reconstitute white sunlight – two prisms, separated, act like a single square-section piece of glass. This is just like the chemical analysis of water by electricity into hydrogen and oxygen, and the synthesis by electric spark of the gases into water. Would not the claim that the two gases had been 'manufactured' out of homogeneous water be regarded as casuistical? Newton's mistake was not in the logical interpretation of his experiments, but in his careless assurance that a narration of two or three of them would satisfy critical readers. In fact, partly because of Huygen's criticism of the Newtonian theory, partly because Mariotte incompetently repeated the experiments in Paris in 1679, finding that the coloured rays from the prism showed further dispersion and colour-separation, Newton's theory was not accepted on the continent until after 1707. In subsequent years his experiments were verified several times, both at the Royal Society and in France; a French translation of *Opticks* appeared at Paris in 1722.[17] By this time, of course, the English had long subscribed to the view that the incomparable Newton had

invented and established the Theory of Light and Colours; and by Demonstrations founded on Experiments and Observations, at once begun and finished that great Discovery, and advanced that Part of Opticks . . . of which there was little, if any thing, before known, to a Perfect and Compleat Science.[18]

The most important of Newton's discoveries, because they were unconventional and because his own natural philosophy had shaped itself from early years against the prevalent neo-Cartesian system, aroused in many of his contemporaries the feeling that the accepted ideas about natural processes were being wantonly disturbed in order to account for phenomena that could well be embraced within that system without the need for intellectual upheavals. Leibniz in the new century was to accuse Newton of putting the clock back and renouncing the advantages that Cartesian mechanism had grasped. Already before the end of the seventeenth century the former antithesis between 'ancients' and 'moderns' was becoming lifeless, and the divisions between the various groups of moderns were becoming far more critical. The appeal to experiment and observation had played a useful part in resolving the former antithesis, but the appeal to a new conception of what science should be, to a new image of nature, to a new mathematics and structure of reasoning, in short to a new appraisal of familiar facts, had achieved far more sweeping results. In many ways, genuine observation and experiment had been the pivots of seventeenth-century biology far more than they had been of its mechanics and physics. With the empiricist reaction against Cartesian Science, which had seemed for a moment almost to sum up the whole revolt against tradition, and especially with the discoveries of Newton, came the test of the ability of the heirs of Copernicus and Galileo to resolve their own internal contradictions. If these were not in turn to lead to endless debate, such as had embroiled the heirs of Aristotle, it could only be by a more rigorous attention to the criteria of experiment. The fundamental significance of Newton's scientific method was that it achieved this exactly; it did not show merely that a theory roughly agreed with a selected group of facts, but that a group – however limited and restricted – of theoretical propositions could be associated with a range of experimental facts, carefully checked and often repeated. Confidence could be granted to such a group of propositions because it was unique, and the minimum necessary; because it claimed only to comprehend a limited range of phenomena that had been exactly studied, and not to extrapolate from a few particulars to universal truths. Against such a method the kind of criticism directed towards Newton's theory of colour was unavailing in the long run, as was that directed against Lavoisier or Joule. If, with regard to Newton, expressions of incredulity were less well founded, it was perhaps because his precise use of the experimental method was not yet understood.

Before considering Newton's place in the history of experimental science more deeply, it is well to return to the achievements of the man rightly held to be Newton's major predecessor in this respect, Robert Boyle. For Boyle's pneumatic researches, already mentioned, were but episodes in a life devoted to chemical experimentation.

The idea that there is a peculiarly chemical 'science of materials', or rather of the transformations of substances, was almost totally absent before the late sixteenth century, and even then gained ground but slowly. Early speculations about the nature or composition of matter, and about the processes involved when one kind of stuff is turned into anther kind of stuff, were a part of physics, as little empirical as the rest of physical theory. They were scarcely at all connected with the practical knowledge of certain groups of craftsman. In a similar manner it was far from obvious that a distinct science was required to explain how the bread that man eats is transmuted into flesh and bone. A pre-scientific physiologist might speak of 'concoction' in the stomach, but the term, though frequently used by chemists, had no specific meaning. It was an empty word that described nothing and explained nothing. When, however, certain experimenters adopted the belief that all metals are variously compounded of sulphur and mercury – using the names sulphur and mercury in a particular sense distinct from that of ordinary language – it does become possible to speak of a chemical attitude to substance. Robert Boyle frequently applied the word 'chymist' in this way, as describing those who thought and worked in accordance with the three-principle theory. Otherwise the chemist was only distinguished from other men by the nature of his methods: 'What is accomplished by fire', wrote Paracelsus, 'is alchemy – whether in the furnace or in the kitchen stove.' The chemist was indeed primarily a pyrotechnician, who knew (or tried to discover) how to obtain certain results by long and gentle, or short and fierce, heating. To the end of the seventeenth century chemical analysis was practically confined to destructive distillation by fire, in which the substance to be analysed was forced to yield its waters, oils, sublimates, salts and *caput mortuum*. In this sense the metal-refiner, the soap-boiler and the distiller were chemists; the practices of more learned men in the early modern period were hardly less haphazadly empirical than theirs, and owed little more to the guiding influence of a distinctive theory. And, as chemical ideas were but slowly differentiated from those generally current in natural philosophy, so chemical techniques were very gradually differentiated from those of the kitchen and workshop. Even in the time of Lavoisier they still bore strong marks of their craft origin. That symbol of chemical science, the balance, was itself borrowed from the assayers of precious metals.

The immediate practical background to mid-seventeenth-century chemistry was provided by the iatrochemists, or medical chemists, who prepared drugs. These were men of learning and wrote Latin. Their view was narrow, being limited by the doctrine of the three principles, and they were often subject to the delusions of alchemy, but their books were meant to be understood. They created no secret language. Instead they began to describe, as plainly as their knowledge and terminology allowed, how the operations of chemistry are performed, from what materials and by what methods a large number of compounds are prepared, and for what purposes they might be employed. They began to compare the method used in one case with that used in another, to detect analogies between different compounds, and to try to explain what happened when a chemical reaction occurred by means of concepts which they invented or adapted. Here was the beginning both of a 'natural history' of chemistry, and of a chemical theory.

However, the iatrochemists presented no natural philosophy, only the loose system of the three principles (salt, sulphur, mercury) to set against the four elements of the alchemists. Natural philosophy was, it is true, richly and amply presented by Van Helmont, but in a way that has remained largely unintelligible from that day to this. Boyle, who greatly admired him as the first real chemical philosopher, confessed his frequent inability to follow his meaning and the impossibility of believing many of his tales of experiments and cures. Van Helmont taught that there are but two elements, air and water. Fire is not a body, and therefore not an element. All solid bodies, of which the type is earth, are generated from water by the action of seeds or ferments: 'The first beginnings of bodies, and of corporeal causes, are two and no more. They are surely the element Water, from which bodies are fashioned, and the ferment by which they are fashioned.' These divinely created ferments were the specific organizers of water, the *prima materia*, into minerals as well as living things; they were immaterial, though the seeds to which they gave rise were not. A famous experiment illustrated this last belief: a willow-tree in a tub gained 75 kg (164 lb) weight by its growth during five years, though nothing but water was added to it. Like Boyle later, van Helmont attacked the three principles of orthodox chemists on the ground that some bodies could not be resolved into them. He accepted the existence of vacua in solid matter: for this explained how metals could be more dense than water. Air, however, could not be turned into water, even by great compression, and was therefore a distinct element. Two other important features of Van Helmont's system were Blas and Gas, the former a principle of movement or vitality, the latter word having by no means its modern connotation but denoting a state of water finer than steam or vapour, but more dense than air, in which Water was redistributed about the universe. He also called 'gas' the exhalations given off by fermenting grapes or by the solution of silver in nitric acid, and recognized that these various 'gases' were not all identical.

Both the experimental justification and the theoretical usefulness of the term 'gas' were to be made known only in the late eighteenth century, after a long period when the word 'air' (qualified, if necessary, by such adjectives as 'fixed', 'inflammable' or 'eminently respirable') was used in the same sense as the general name for a state in which matter is dispersed, fluid and elastic. That aeriform or gaseous substances play an essential role in the phenomena of chemistry only gradually became apparent from the experiments of Stephen Hales, published in 1727 (Ch. 13). That subsequent historical development owed nothing to J. B. Van Helmont.

Thus, about the middle of the seventeenth century the position in chemical theory (to use what is still an anachronism) was that the Aristotelian doctrine, now moribund and opposed to the broad trend of the scientific revolution, was still respectable; practising chemists, as a class, stood by their three principles and the general tenets of iatrochemistry; van Helmont's double-element theory aroused much interest, but won few adherents. Meanwhile a fourth approach to the problems of chemical combination, based on the mechanical, particulate view of matter was taking shape, and was soon to be developed elaborately by Robert Boyle. Factual knowledge of chemical reactions and processes had also ramified considerably since the time of Beguin and Libavius. Van Helmont himself was a skilled practical chemist, who reported a good number of new preparations. He taught that matter was indestructable, illustrating this belief by the recovery of the original weight of a metal from the compounds in which it was apparently disguised. It is said that he made much use of the balance: his famous tree-experiment shows how deceptive quantitative methods may be when applied within an inadequate conceptual scheme. A younger iatrochemist (who also pursued the philosopher's stone) was Johann Rudolph Glauber (1604–70). He described for the first time the preparation of spirit of salt (HCl), sodium sulphate, and perhaps chlorine. Glauber had a sound insight into certain types of chemical reaction, such as double decomposition; for example, he explained the formation of 'butter of antimony' with sublimation of cinnabar from stibnite heated with corrosive sublimate by saying that the spirit in the latter, leaving the mercury, preferred to attach itself to the antimony in the stibnite; the mercury then united with the sulphur in the stibnite to form cinnabar. From this example it is also clear that Glauber employed the concept of chemical affinity – he understood that one unit in a reaction might attract another more than a third.

In 1675 there was printed for the first time a new textbook on chemistry by a practical man, Nicholas Lemery (1645–1715), which remained popular for upwards of half a century. The title of the *Cours de Chymie contenant la maniere de faire les operations qui sont en usage dans la Medicine* sufficiently indicates it purpose. It was a straightforward recipe-book, dealing first with the metals, then with salts, sulphur and other minerals, and finally with preparations obtained from vegetables and animals. Lemery was not given to theorization, but he taught that there were, in addition to the three active principles mercury (spirit), sulphur (oil) and salt, two passive principles, water and earth. He also accepted the theory due to Otto Tachenius that salt=acid+alkali, and occasionally followed the particulate ideas of Descartes, at least to the naive extent of supposing the component particles of acids to be sharply pointed, those of alkalis to contain hollows, and so forth. Theoretically, Lemery is eclectic to the point of incoherence. By the end of the seventeenth century the best accounts of experimental chemistry – and there were by now many, an English example being George Wilson's *Compleat Course of Chemistry* (? London, 1699) – were still those written with medical applications in mind and though the old, esoteric iatrochemistry deriving from Paracelsus had perished, future progress was to owe much to physicians and apothecaries, among them Boerhaave, Cullen, Scheele and Black. It is of significance also that the teaching of chemistry in universities, beginning *c.* 1700, everywhere placed it as an auxiliary to medicine. Even at the close of the eighteenth century most of Black's pupils at Edinburgh were medical students. From the time of Boyle to that of Priestley and Cavendish the role of the 'amateurs' in chemistry was relatively insignificant, and the reason is not far to seek. This was a period of rapid practical development in the subject, but of minor theoretical expansion.

The rational application of chemistry to medicine was what first captured the imagination of Robert Boyle, nor was this ambition ever wholly to desert him. But this modestly utilitarian object was through the years to be overtaken by a much wider ambition to embrace chemistry (a body of empirical knowledge and skills) within experimental natural philosophy, indeed, to establish it as the core of such a true philosophy. Boyle was both one of the outstanding theorists of the mechanical or corpuscular philosophy, though he preferred to treat this in a characteristically general or eclectic form than to embrace the atomist, Cartesian or other system, and a consummate experimenter in both physics and chemistry. His works are among the first to consist largely of descriptions of experimental research: he contributed powerfully to the development of precise technique, the principles of chemical analysis, and the study of chemical composition. Boyle's writings may seem haphazard, even (deceptively) casual in their selection and arrangement, prolix almost beyond bearing and in the last resort seemingly indefinite – for though Boyle's own view of things was decisive enough, he hated to be publicly dogmatic – yet in experimenting he knew his objects precisely, and how far he had attained them. He fully controlled the extensive work done in his own research laboratory, noting and recollecting the precise details of each experiment. He was probably the first chemist to appreciate the importance of using pure substances and of viewing operations critically. For example, of one 'famous chemist' and his method of preparing the crystalline salts of vegetables involving solution in nitric acid, Boyle wrote:

for divers years before I met with his process, I have, with fixed salts of more than one kind of vegetable, by joining them with aqua fortis, and after a while exhaling the superfluous moisture, made good inflammable saltpetre; by which you may easily guess, how judiciously the solution in aquafortis is prescribed [by the 'famous chemist'] only as a depuration and how fit such authors are to be credited when they ascribe to these crystalline salts the several virtues . . . of the respective vegetables, from which the alkalies were obtained. [19]

Boyle clearly saw how the final product of a chemical procedure might be an artefact, deriving nothing from the valued primary ingredient. He was well aware too of the importance of repeating experiments, and the difficulties of reproducing effects that may be thus met with, especially when different individuals perform the same experiment. He did not take the results of a single trial to justify sweeping conclusions, in the manner of his predecessors.

The task Boyle set himself was to examine philosophically the natural phenomena made known by chemical art; to determine the underlying nature of the material transformations of which a cumulative description had been built up since the time of Libavius, and of the processes by which they were brought about. He undertook to prove to philosophers that chemistry could be more than a collection of recipes, and to the 'chymists' that in revealing nature's secrets they would have a more noble aim than the concoction of medicines, for he was aware that natural philosophy as a whole is greater even than the cure of disease. Boyle wrote no textbook of chemistry, like Lemery's, rather he usually assumed such a level of knowledge in his readers; nor was he greatly interested in the piling up of more and more empirical knowledge for its own sake. Almost always he wrote with a definite problem in mind, some aspect of his ambition to restore natural philosophy as a unified whole, in which chemical knowledge should pay its due part. He sought to build a bridge between chemistry and physics, the two sciences concerned with the properties of matter, which ought to start from common ground and be explicable one in terms of the other. In this respect Boyle had much in common with Van Helmont; but whereas Van Helmont had criticized natural philosophers for their ignorance of ideas to which he himself had been brought by his own quasi-Paracelsan development, Boyle proceeded quite differently. Endowed with an up-to-date philosophical outlook, Boyle possessed the idea that the phenomena of chemical change were to be accounted for in terms of underlying physical structure, by the theory of matter-in-motion. He was unique among physicists in wishing to master all the details of chemical technique and nomenclature, unique among chemists in substituting for their vague qualitative notions the precise, and potentially quantitative, mechanical concepts of the p'lysicists. So he distinguished between 'a chymical explication of a phenomenon, and one that is truly philosophical or mechanical', the former being in terms of substances, the latter in terms of the displacements of particles.[20]

In the first of his major works to be printed, which is also the most widely read, this is certainly not very clear. The purpose of the *Sceptical Chymist* (1661), as its title suggests, is negative, not positive. It was to clear the ground of the three theoretical attitudes to chemistry which were then in vogue. Boyle disposed rapidly of the four Aristotelian elements, for they were no longer plausible entities (at least to the progressive experimental scientist). His main attack was on the three principles of the orthodox chemists, his real target. In this connection there was nothing novel in his own definition of a chemical element, nor in his insistence on the importance of discovering what the ultimate constituents of compound bodies are. He argued that none of the chemists' principles could be extracted from metals like gold or mercury; that their criterion of analysis by fire was in any case faulty, since it could not divide glass into its own constituents, sand and alkali. He pointed out (like Van Helmont) that the natures of bodies are not changed by entering into combinations, since the same bodies could sometimes be recovered separately in their original state. He emphasized acutely the illogicalities and contradictions in which the ideas commonly entertained by chemists were involved. The criticism was warrantable, but in the *Sceptical Chymist* Boyle equally proved that he could create nothing to take the place of that which he would destroy. No more than any other contemporary did he believe that ordinary substances – gold, mercury, sulphur – were elements, though they resisted analysis. He used Van Helmont's tree-experiment (which he repeated) to show that vegetable matter could be formed from water alone, without the participation of earth and fire, or salt and sulphur, but he did not believe that all things were made of water. In the end Boyle failed not only to draw up his own list of chemical elements, but even to decide definitely whether such simple substances do exist at all. There was, indeed, sufficient reason in his corpuscular physics why he should have been doubtful, why he should have thought that anything might have transmuted into anything else, by nature if not by art. Some of the evidence is set forth in the *Sceptical Chymist*. Boyle believed, with most of his generation, that metals and minerals like saltpetre 'grew' in the earth. These substances were not themselves elements; neither were they formed from pre-existing elements, for such elements could not be traced in the earth where the growth occurred. 'From thence' wrote Boyle 'we may deduce that earth, by a metalline plastick principle latent in it ("seed"), may be in process of time changed into a metal' – a common enough opinion. From a survey of phenomena of this kind he came to the conclusion that transmutations in the chemical sense were possible by means of this 'plastic power' in the earth, as also by the 'seminal virtue' in seeds (for the salts, etc., in wood were certainly not present as such in the water with which the tree was nourished). However puzzling this might be from the chemist's point of view, it was not at all inexplicable to the physicist in Boyle, for his physical theory of matter taught him that all substances are made up of the same fundamental particles. Since, therefore, substances differ from one another only in the 'various textures resulting from the bigness, shape, motion and contrivance of their small parts, it will not be irrational to conceive that one and the same parcel of the universal matter may, by various alterations and contextures, be brought to deserve the name, sometimes of a sulphureous, and sometimes of a terrene or aqueous body'.[21]

The theory of matter which Boyle favoured led him to believe (as he acknowledged in the early pages of the *Sceptical Chymist*) that in its basic and primitive form matter existed as 'little particles, of several sizes and shapes, variously moved'. These were further organized into 'minute masses or clusters,' being the 'primary concretions' of matter, some of which were in practice indivisible. Hence the clusters that compose gold, being inviolable by the ordinary chemist's art, could always be recovered from any compound of the metal. But a mass of such corpuscles was not an element, for as Boyle stated, the particles of two sets of corpuscles might so regroup themselves that 'from the coalition there may emerge a new body, as really one, as either of the corpuscles was before they were mingled'. Thus vinegar acting upon lead formed 'sugar' of lead (lead acetate) but by no means could the acid spirit of vinegar be recovered from the new compound; Boyle thought its corpuscles were destroyed. The indivisible corpuscles of glass were formed by a 'coalition' of those of sand and ashes; so that resistance to chemical analysis by fire or acids was not a test of elementariness: for such indestructible corpuscles could as well be found in the bodies due to art, as in those due to nature. The same experience that taught Boyle that glass was not to be numbered among the elements, prevented him from knowing whether gold was one or not: he thought it was probably not.[22]

Plainly, Boyle's experimental natural philosophy prevented his attaining what has been generally regarded as one of the essential concepts of nineteenth-century chemistry – the pragmatic concept of the chemical element, formally defined by Lavoisier (1789). No body made of particles in the manner conceived by Boyle could possibly be regarded as simple, homogeneous, or elementary. And unfortunately chemical kinetics was to remain as much beyond his grasp as that of Newton, surely better qualified to succeed in that line of thought since Boyle had no natural aptitude towards the mathematization of nature.

That Boyle's chemical theory was predominantly shaped by his corpuscularian physics is apparent from many works beside the *Sceptical Chymist*. He was no dogmatist, nor a follower of systems, he believed that hypothesis should be framed to fit the facts, but it was quite clear to him that complete scepticism and abhorrence of all theory were antithetical to true philosophy. Indeed, his ambition to bring chemistry into natural philosophy would have been meaningless had he not had a theory of natural philosophy, essentially a theory of matter, to hand for the purpose:

I hoped I might at least do no unseasonable piece of service to the corpuscular philosophers, by illustrating some of their notions with sensible experiments, and manifesting, that the things by me treated of may be at least plausibly explicated without having recourese to inexplicable forms, real qualities, the four peripatetick elements, or so much as the three chymical principles.[23]

278

Thus for Boyle solution always represented the interspersions of the corpuscles of the solvent among those of the dissolved body, fire consisted of material particles, and 'air' of all kinds mainly of elastic corpuscles of a particular type, among which the mingling of other corpuscles gave each 'air' its own character. He constantly attributed the properties of acids, oils, salts, etc., to the nature of their component corpuscles. In fact the theory was brought into play whenever Boyle commented on a chemical experiment. Instances are particularly numerous in the *Origin of Forms and Qualities* (1666), where (as examples chosen at random) he spoke of 'the body of silver, by the convenient interposition of some saline particles [being] reduced into crystals' of Luna cornea (silver chloride); or, of another experiment, 'considered that the nitrous corpuscles [of nitric acid], lodging themselves in the little spaces deserted by the saline corpuscles of the sea-salt, that passed over into the receiver, had afforded this alkali', or again declared that

the more noble corpuscles which qualify gold to look yellow [and to resist nitric acid] . . . may either have their texture destroyed by a very piercing menstruum, or, by a greater congruity with its corpuscles, than [with] those of the remaining part of the gold, may stick closer to the former and . . . be extricated.[24]

Corpuscularian ideas were especially developed by English scientists in relation to the allied reactions of combustion and calcination. Both were anciently regarded as separations: the ash or calx (oxide) remaining was an earthy residue left after the more volatile parts of the combustible or metal had been driven off by fire. It was well known, however, that the calx (oxide) exceeded the original metal in weight: whence Jean Rey was led to believe (in 1630) that though the calx was lighter than the metal in nature, it became heavier by the attachment to it of air which had become thickened in the furnace. Boyle later thought that the increased weight came from fire-particles penetrating the walls of the crucible and impregnating the calx. This explanation was widely accepted until it was decisively confuted by Lavoisier. With regard to combustion it was well known to Boyle and others that bodies would not burn without air, unless (like gunpowder) they contained some nitrous material. A familiar experiment (originally described by Van Helmont) showed that when a candle was burnt in a closed vessel over water, the air within diminished and the water rose up inside. From these and other observations Robert Hooke sketched a theory in *Micrographia* according to which combustible bodies were dissolved by a certain substance present in the atmosphere, this solution (like others) evolving great heat, and thus flames, which Hooke took to be 'nothing else but a mixture of Air, and volatile sulphureous parts of dissoluble or combustible bodies, which are acting upon each other'. This aerial substance he identified with 'that which is fixt in Saltpeter'.

As has been discovered in recent years, Hooke's theory of the aerial nitre was far from original: probably he (and others) derived it from Sir Kenelm Digby but its literary origins (as known so far) are in a book of 1604 by a Polish alchemist, Michael Sendivogius.[25] Its empirical origins are in the fertilizing action of nitre and animal manure, the known connection between manure and nitre, and the power of nitre to support combustion (and some said, human life). An English physician, John Mayow (1645–79) was to elaborate the idea of 'nitro-aerial particles', supposed to be present in air and nitre and indeed very widely distributed in nature, into a large speculative philosophy; these particles, and their violent reactions with 'sulphureous' particles in organic and combustible bodies, acccounted for not only fire and flame and respiration, but lightning and the fiery body of the Sun, as well as animal heat (Ch. 6).[26] Although Boyle, with the guess of an active 'Quintessence' in the air and his own experimental studies of combustion, had been one who translated the aerial nitre from metaphysical alchemy (where it was known as a 'dew' or 'balsam') into the mechanical philosophy, he was not at all impressed by the idea of nitre as a universal causative agent in nature, indeed he very reasonably (in view of the difficulty of volatilizing nitre) doubted if it existed in the atmosphere in great quantity:

I know that divers learned men, some physicians, some chemists and some also philosophers, speak much of a volatile nitre that abounds in the air, as if that were the only salt where with it is impregnated. But though I agree with them in thinking that the air is in many places impregnated with corpuscles of a nitrous nature, yet I confess I have not been hitherto convinced of all that is wont to be delivered about the plenty and quality of the nitre in the air; for I have not found that those that build so much upon this volatile nitre, have made out by any competent experiments that there is such a volatile nitre abounding in the air.[27]

Boyle's objection could not apply, of course, to the assertion that an unknown ingredient x is common to both air and nitre; this is the assertion some suppose Mayow to have made. However, until samples of x derived from air and from nitre had been produced and shown to be identical, Boyle would have regarded such an assertion as a hypothesis not to be taken seriously by an experimental philosopher.

Though Boyle never declared *Hypotheses non fingo*, and indeed (like Newton also) proposed many hypotheses, he was well aware of the difference between speculations (however favourite) on the *ultimate structure* of matter – necessarily beyond the reach of direct experiment – and positive statements about the *substantial composition* of things, which were worthless if unverified. Air, he thought, should be considered as a single substance until its components had been experimentally identified in the ordinary chemical way. This caution pervades his vast scientific output. He believed in a physical layer of explanation deeper and more real than the chemists' qualitative talk in terms of reacting substances of his own day, but he could not himself offer exact examples of how this form of reductionism would work, as Mayow and others sought to do. For this philosophers like Spinoza and physicists like Huygens blamed him; in the latter's words,

It seems strange enough that he built nothing on the basis of the many experiments with which his books are filled.[28]

To them the mechanical philosophy in its neo-Cartesian dress seemed self-evidently true: what need was there to demonstrate it in a merely general way from the phenomena of chemistry? Such assessments missed the point of Boyle's endeavour as a natural philosopher, not to explore reason, or to fabricate systems, but to investigate nature herself experimentally. Systematic ideas were a guide to research, perhaps, but not its product.

Recalling the dull recipes or eccentric mystery-making of almost all chemical writing in this period, recollecting the repetitive analyses of plant-material into earth, oil and water made by the chemists of the Paris Academy of Sciences, Boyle's stature as an experimental and philosophical chemist swells to greatness. No one else in his field in his century was equally lucid, intelligent and rational. No one else, it has been said,

did so much to effect the shift from thinking in terms of chemical elements and principles to thinking in terms of simple substances and real entities which preserved their individuality as corpuscles throughout many chemical vicissitudes . . . The amalgamation of chemistry and physics, and the development of rational mechanical theory in chemistry, amply indicate that seventeenth-century chemistry deserves a place in the seventeenth-century scientific revolution.[29]

That is to say, Boyle like his friend Isaac Newton was an intellectual leader in that revolution.

As a method of experimental investigation, Boyle's lifelong examination of chemical mechanism may seem defective in two chief ways, though the former certainly and the latter possibly was made inevitable by the nature of his experiments; Boyle's results were stated in a non-mathematical, non-quantitative form, and the relation between result and theory was loose, lacking in sharp definition. If Henry Power in his *Experimental Philosophy* (1664) aimed only at some deductions, and probable hypotheses, in avouchment and illustration of the atomical hypothesis, had Boyle set his sights much higher? Or, to use Hooke's expression, was more in question than 'the explication of these phenomena by various hypotheses'? Setting aside Boyle's self-confessed gentlemanly carelessness (losing samples from his pocket, leaving papers where the maid could use them for fire-lighting) he was more definite about certain results – the constitution of nitre, the isolation of phosphorus – than appears from such discursive pieces as the *Sceptical Chemist*. His defence of the spring and weight of the air was precisely argued. And some numerical experimental investigations – for example, that elaborately conducted by Mariotte of the laws of impact – were neither exciting nor illuminating: merely routine.

Nevertheless, Henry Guerlac's words are surely apposite:

For Newton . . . experiment is essentially a device for problem solving, for determining with precision the properties of things, and rising from these carefully observed 'effects' to the 'causes'. More clearly than Bacon was able to do, Newton showed by his method that experimentation could lead with at least 'moral certainty' to axioms, principles, or laws,[30]

That is, if we apply them to Newton's fully successful investigations leading (and the distinctions are his own) to the enunciation of certain 'doctrines', propositions quite distinct from causal or explanatory hypotheses. Examples of such doctrines are the heterogeneity of white light and the existence of universal gravitation. These, as he said, were

evinced to me, *not by inferring tis thus because not otherwise* that is not by deducing it onely from a confutation of contrary suppositions, but *by deriving it from Experiments concluding positively & directly.*[31]

In conformity with this remarkably anti-Popperian declaration Newton took infinite pains to achieve exact numerical concordance between the results of theoretical computation and careful measurements; sometimes he went beyond discretion in 'adjusting' his figures to obtain an exact match. Obviously for such a concordance to be realized, and the perfection of experimental science attained, it is no less essential that the theory should be capable of yielding quantifiable predictions, than that the experiments and measurements should be scrupulously made. In the fields of optics and mechanics the genius of Newton could raise theory to such a height of excellence, but in chemistry he was no more successful than Boyle in doing so.

Newton added an important hypothetical dimension to chemical kinetics, that of preferential attraction or affinity, but neither he nor his successors (Keill and Freind) could quantify *this* attraction fruitfully. To read Query 31 of *Opticks* is to read an essary in theoretical chemistry going beyond Boyle, but not possessing a different character from Boyle's essays. It is indeed one of the few extensive passages in Newton's works that might well have come from the pen of Robert Boyle.

NOTES

1. William Gilbert, (trans. S.P. Thompson) *On the Magnet*, repr. Dover: New York, 1958, 12–13, 208.
2. F. R. Johnson, *Astronomical Thought in Renaissance England*, Johns Hopkins University Press: Baltimore, 1937, 175–78 quoting T. Digges, *Pantometria*, 1571, Ch. 21. It is more likely that Digges employed some kind of *Camera Obscura*.
3. J. B. Van Helmont (trans. John Chandler) *Oriatrike*, or *Physic Refined*, London, 1662, 752–3, 91
4. Both of these works have been well edited in English translation by Cyril Stanley Smith.
5. I, at least, have never understood how Galileo could attribute tensile strength to a fluid – some confusion with viscosity, as in honey?
6. The pictures in *Experimenta nova (ut vacantur) Magdeburgica de Vacuo Spatio* (Amsterdam, 1672) have been more often reproduced than the text has been read. This book must have been rare in England, but Oldenburg gave a two-page account of it in *Phil. Trans.*, No. 88, 18 November 1672.
7. Robert Boyle, *New Experiments Physico-Mechanical on the Spring of the Air and its Effects*, Oxford, 1660.
8. *Histoire de l'Academie Royale des Sciences, II*, 1686–99, Paris, 1733, 202–3. First published in the *Journal des Scavans*, whence it was reproduced (in English) in *Phil. Trans.*, No. 136, 25 June 1677.

9. Probably the damp atmosphere of seventeenth-century houses and the organic composition of the materials used within them prevented the ordinary appearance of the flashes, discharges, and accumulations of charge on the person so familiar domestically to us.

10. The colours in mica were observed with the microscope. Hooke has to make *ad hoc* changes to his original theory about colour and the pulses in order to account for the relationship between colour and the thickness of the transparent layer (of mica and air).

11. The quotations are from Oldenburg's account of the book in *Phil. Trans.*, No. 79 (22 January 1672), 3068–70. Possibly he was the only man in England who actually examined it at this time.

12. After a prehistory of suggestions, the Gregorian form of reflecting telescope was described by James Gregory in *Optica Promota*, London, 1663; this design Newton rejected in favour of his own. The Newtonian reflector requires only one curved surface and no loss of light at the objective mirror. Gregory had tried in vain to have his design realized by the London instrument-makers, who also failed to produce a good, large version of the Newtonian.

13. The quotations in the last paragraphs have been from this letter (*Correspondence of Newton*, I, 1959, 92–102). Neither Newton nor any of his critics had encountered Marcus Marci's *Thaumantias Liber* (Prague, 1648; reprint, ed. Jiri Marek, Prague, 1968) which contains many new experiments on colours, including those of soap-bubbles and diffraction, as well as the discovery of dispersion and the assertion (Theorem XX, p. 100): 'Refraction affecting a coloured ray does not change the species of its colour'. Marci's theoretical ideas about his observations were confused.

14. Ibid., 378.

15. Ibid., 385

16. I. A. Sabra, *Theories of Light from Descartes to Newton*, Oldbourne: London, 1967.

17. Henry Guerlac, *Essays and Papers in the History of Modern Science*, Johns Hopkins University Press: Baltimore and London, 1977, 479–88; *Correspondence of Newton*, VII, *passim*.

18. F. Hauksbee, *Physico–Mechanical Experiments on Various Subjects* (2nd ed), London, 1719, Preface.

19. R. Boyle, *Usefulness of Natural Philosophy*, Pt. II, Essay 5, Ch. 6; *Works*, 1772, II, 134–5; quoted in Marie Boas, *Robert Boyle and Seventeenth Century Chemistry*, Cambridge U.P., 1958, 214.

20. Marie Boas, ibid., 106–7.

21. Boyle, *Works*, 1772, I, 564, 494. Among transformations, Boyle was naturally very interested in that which might produce gold from base materials. Towards the end of his life he thought he possessed a clue to rendering gold other than (almost) chemically inert. Newton seems to have shared Boyle's basic philosophy of stability/mutation, but ended in strong scepticism of any practical possibility of goldmaking. Cf. Marie Boas, op. cit., 102–7.

22. Boyle *Works*, 1772, I, 474–5, 506–7.

23. *Certain Physiological Essays* (1661); *Works*, 1772, I, 356.

24. *Origin of Forms and Qualities* (1666); *Works*, 1772, III, 95–6.

25. Sendivogius in turn attributes his *Novum Lumen Chymicum*, Prague 1604, to a Scottish confrère, Alexander Seton. See Henry Guerlac, *Essays and Papers in the History of Modern Science*, Johns Hopkins University Press: Baltimore & London 1977, 245–59.

THE REVOLUTION IN SCIENCE 1500–1750

26. See Robert G. Frank, *Harvey and the Oxford Physiologists*, California University Press: Berkeley and Los Angeles 1980.
27. *General History of the Air*, (1692): *Works*, 1772, V, 627.
28. Huygens to Leibniz, 4 February 1692. *Oeuvres Complètes de Christiaan Huygens*, X, 239; A. R. and M. B. Hall in *Mélanges Alexandre Koyré*, Hermann: Paris, 1964, II, 241–56.
29. Marie Boas (op. cit., Note 19), 230, 231.
30. The words are from Power's title-page; see Henry Guerlac (op. cit., Note 17), 208–215.
31. Newton, *Correspondence*, I, 209; 6 July 1672. The words strictly apply to optics only, but Newton would surely have extended them to the *Principia* also, at a later date.

CHAPTER ELEVEN

Nature and number

Today it is commonplace to present information in quantitative form, using perhaps tables or graphs, and to express theories so far as possible by mathematical functions, by the manipulations of which the potentiality of the theory can be fully brought out. Even in the social sciences mathematical models are perfectly acceptable, outmoding the purely descriptive approach to economics or anthropology. In the seventeenth century the idea that mathematical methods were appropriate to the physical sciences made at first slow progress, even though before the close of the century John Graunt, William Petty and Gregory King had introduced the idea of social statistics. No one disputed the rightful place which the Greeks had assigned to geometry – in making astronomical computations, in treating certain questions of optics, and in such applied sciences as architecture, cartography and mechanics. Conflict occurred when the attempt was made to extend mathematics into natural philosophy, for this implied that geometry (in particular) was not merely a tool to be employed along with set-square and level, or a basis for aesthetics, or useful in constructing a model which like a flat map of the Earth's surface, had no claim to be real, but could represent the true physical nature of things, or be used as a valid logic to determine the nature of things.

The question whether or not our knowledge of the universe can be 'mathematized' (to use Alexandre Koyré's word) is metaphysical; a cognate question, nearer our own time, might be: is there anything in living processes not explicable by the laws of physics and chemistry? But it is also a programmatic question, for if the natural philosopher asks whether colour is substantial or accidental in light he enters upon one kind of technical argument, whereas if he asks for a mathematical analysis of the rainbow he enters on a quite different realm of thought detestable alike to Peripatetics and Romantics. The mathematical picture of the universe does not answer the questions that non-mathematical philosophers asked, and vice versa. This is quite clear with Galileo, who was the founder of the mathematical philosophy of nature. When Galileo created a mathematical theory of the strength of beams, this had nothing to do with the Vitruvian tradition of architecture, though that too was in its way mathematical: for Galileo considered the properties of things, the architects the human way of looking at things. More importantly, as we have seen, Galileo's treatment of motion in terms of quantitative velocities, accelerations and momenta has nothing to do with the prevailing Aristotelian and post-Aristotelian account of motions in terms of cause. To ask the philosopher therefore to believe the universe capable of mathematization was asking him to pose new questions, accept new answers, and abandon the old issues as no longer interesting, perhaps utterly meaningless.

Thus we can face the historical problems involved in the creation of a mathematical physics during the seventeenth century – for that is what mathematization of the universe entailed – in two ways: we can consider shifts in metaphysical positions, or the operational evolution of new segments of knowledge, which only the mathematical approach could bring into existence. The first way has been recommended and adopted by E. A. Burtt:

We must grasp the essential contrast between the whole modern world-view and that of previous thought, and use that clearly conceived contrast as a guiding clue to pick out for criticism and evaluation, in the light of their historical developments, every one of our significant modern presuppositions.[1]

More recently Koyré has in many of his writings, notably *From the Closed World to the Infinite Universe* (1957), addressed himself to similar problems. This chapter will, however, concentrate on the development of new knowledge, as indeed Koyré did in other writings. But, first, we may note with the historians of metaphysical ideas that a mathematical rather than a qualititive physics implies acceptance both of the fundamentally mathematical character of nature itself, and of the unreality of qualities. Both these points Galileo clearly emphasized many times. Galileo would not have said that philosophers can interpret the data *as though* the universe were mathematical or, alternatively, qualitative; quite on the contrary, he assures us, as does Kepler, that the mathematical relations and quantities are really part of nature itself. We may call this the Pythagorean position. Then, the inadequacy of verbal logic as an instrument of true science becomes evident: the mathematical logic of demonstration is superior because it corresponds to the actual structure of the universe. The philosopher rightly believes that events in nature follow a logical pattern: but it is the logic of number.

Beyond this, to account for the universe's being of this sort, Kepler and many others taught that God himself is a geometer, not of necessity but of choice (it would be geometrically feasible, for example, to arrange the geometric solids defining the planetary orbits in a different pattern). This is the Platonic position. The answer to the question: how did the universe acquire this mathematical character? is, accordingly: From the Supreme Intellect. It is because the mind of God thinks mathematically, conceives of physical relations mathematically, that the actual parts and properties of physical nature are mathematical.

We might pursue this line, touching on Galileo's assurance that the human mind understands the truth of a geometrical proposition as completely as the divine mind can do, or examining the role of the mathematical deity in his universe after its creation, or discussing the very difficult interrelations of space, matter and number. Can either space or matter be infinitely divided: indeed, can the concept of infinity, essential to mathematics, be comprehended by the human mind at all? All these questions were significant for seventeenth-century science, and with regard to all of them the seventeenth-century philosophers differed from their predecessors.

In what follows, this important substratum of intellectual change will be taken for granted. Scientists were not themselves always very self-analytical about it: when Boyle wrote: 'A competent knowledge in mathematics is so necessary to a philosopher that I scruple not to assert, greater things are still to be expected from physics, because those who pass for naturalists have been generally ignorant in that study', he was (probably) not so much advocating a particular metaphysical or epistemological position as making a common-sense point about the interpretation of experimental and other data. The discovery of Boyle's Law proves the point. But it was not only necessary that, as he said, the naturalist should master mathematics; there had to be accessible to him a useful kind of mathematics. The geometry of the Greeks had sufficed for Kepler's ellipse and Galileo's parabola, but by the end of the century new, more powerful methods would be required. Although a great deal of Newton's *Principia* was within the classical mould he deliberately adopted for it, some of the most important reasoning was not, and with that book advanced physics passed forever beyond the reach of the innumerate.

Before the nineteenth century only a few areas of science could make any interesting use of mathematics: chiefly, the various branches of mechanics, optics and astronomy. Simple uses of mathematics occurred more frequently, of course, for example the use of ratios in musical theory which was, in this century, extending in its experimental part to become the science of acoustics. More interesting are the studies of tessellation patterns made by Kepler as an offshoot from his celestial physics, and also Kepler's hypothetical construction of the snow-crystal from close-packed spheres, an idea taken up by Hooke (1665). No main lines of work resulted. But with regard to mechanics and astronomy one may say that the great achievements characterizing the scientific revolution would have been impossible in the absence of the enormous elaboration of pure mathematics which took place, and was to some extent inspired by realization of the fact that it was essential. Nearly all the great mathematicians of the sixteenth and seventeenth centuries, from Tartaglia and Stevin to Cavalieri, Descartes, Newton and Leibniz, were at least partly interested in the physical sciences. One of the unexpected discoveries of the time was that a number of regular mathematical curves (some long familiar), such as the ellipse, the parabola and the cycloid, or the algebraic functions which Descartes associated with such curves, appeared in the investigations of the astronomer and the physicist, so that their study proved to have a double interest. The calculations performed by the physical scientist frequently required the calculation of an area bounded by a curve of some type, and so in turn stimulated investigation of the operation of integration in which perhaps the success of seventeenth-century mathematicians was most striking. A number of their advances in method were first denoted by the solution of some problem in mechanics, which offered from about 1650 onwards a most rewarding opportunity for the display of mathematical inventiveness, formerly more commonly devoted to the improvement of the mathematical procedures in astronomy.[1]

The progress made in mathematics in the seventeenth century can be very easily illustrated from the fact that, about 1600, it had hardly as yet reached a form intelligible to modern eyes.[2] The writing of Arabic numerals was indeed nearly stabilized in the modern style, but the Roman were still commonly employed, especially in accounting. The use of the modern symbols for the common operations of multiplication, division, addition and so forth was standardized only in the second half of the seventeenth century. Previously mathematical arguments were set out in a diffuse rhetorical form. Algebraic notation was settled at about the same time, the practice of employing letters to denote unknown or indeterminate quantities having been introduced by the French mathematician Viète shortly before 1600. Arithmetical operations, particularly those involving long division or the handling of fractions, were still performed by cumbersome methods, and 'reckoning with the pen' (rather than with the abacus or other aid) was still regarded as a somewhat advanced art. One of the earliest calculating-devices, the so-called 'Napier's bones', was designed to obviate the memorization of multiplication tables and the labour of handling long rows of figures. Again, at a higher level, tables of functions were very deficient. In trigonometry, the Greeks had known tables of chords alone; during the late Middle Ages tables of sines and tangents became available, and during the sixteenth century other trigonometrical functions were tabulated. But the methods of computing and of using the tables were both very tedious. From an attempt to facilitate calculations involving these functions developed the invention of logarithms, perhaps the most universally useful mathematical discovery of the seventeenth century, as it was certainly the least expected. Napier's tables, published in 1614 (*Mirifici logarithmorum canonis descriptio*), give logarithms of sines which are effectively powers of a base e^{-1}, the reciprocal of the base of modern Napierian logarithms. A table of logarithms to the base 10 for the first thousand numbers was published by Henry Briggs in 1617. Logarithms offered a compelling instance of the utility of the decimal system of fractions, of which Stevin had been a most forceful advocate some thirty years earlier.

It is curious that the prevailing mechanism of seventeenth-century thought governed Napier's mathematical discovery, for he defined the logarithm as a line-length determined by the different continuous motions of two points; it 'involved concepts of time, motion, and instantaneous speed'.[3] The Cambridge mathematician Isaac Barrow (1630–77), Newton's early patron, returned to somewhat the same procedure; indeed, that Barrow 'might put me upon considering the generation of figures by motion, tho I not now remember it' was the only debt to Barrow that Newton ever acknowledged. In October 1666 Newton was to prepare an (unpublished) tract headed 'To resolve Problems by Motion these following Proportions are sufficient', a tract marking an important stage in the evolution of his method of *fluxions*, or flowing quantities, formed by the motion of a point or line. Conversely, the early applications of fluxions (or differentials) were in large part to problems in mechanics.

Since the Greeks had excelled in geometry and trigonometry, little more than the assimilation, with some slight extension, of their methods in these branches of mathematics had been accomplished by 1600. Renaissance scholarship had devoted itself to the recovery of the pure classical tradition in this as in other departments of learning, with the result that the texts, particularly those describing the more advanced Greek studies of geometrical analysis and the conic sections, were far more completely available by the middle of the sixteenth century than before. Here, at least, pure scholarship caused an immediate rise in the level of competence. Even in the mid-seventeenth century the practice of 'restoring' a lost or fragmentary work by means of the methods presumably used by the ancient author did not seem absurd, and when Newton wrote the *Principia* the synthetic geometry of the Greeks was still held to be a more reliable form of mathematical demonstration than the recently developed analytical method.

Algebra, on the other hand, represents a native European development from Hindu and Islamic sources made known to the Latins by medieval translators. Considerable progress in the sixteenth century, for example in the solution of equations of higher powers than the quadratic, was unaffected by humanistic influences; indeed, Greek geometric procedures for solving equations were supplanted by algebraic methods. Operations with proportions and series, also known to the Greeks solely in the geometric expression, were similarly transformed into a more convenient arithmetic or algebraic form.

This is no place for even an outline account of the development of pure mathematics in the seventeenth century, but attention must be at least drawn to the existence of two main lines of activity. The first, which everyone knows to be linked with Descartes's *Geometrie* (1637), was the introduction of what came to be called 'analytical geometry', that is, the identification of quantities in a geometrical figure representing the problem to be solved with algebraic quantities from which an equation can be formed. Or in Descartes's own words:

wishing to resolve some problem, it is first considered as solved, labelling all the lines which seem necessary for its construction, both those which are known and those which are unknown. Then, without making any distinction between the known and the unknown lines, one must set out the problem following that order which of all others most naturally shows how the lines are mutually related one to another, until a means has been found of expressing one quantity in two different ways, which is called an equation because the terms of one of these two expressions are equal to those of the other.[4]

Although analytical geometry was long to be regarded by the more conservative mathematicians (Huygens, Barrow and Newton among them) as simply a useful tool, a means of discovery but not a means of demonstration, its importance in that former capacity was enormous, totally transforming the rate of mathematical discovery. In particular it vastly increased the usefulness of mathematics in problems of mechanics.

The second line of activity was the development of infinitesimals. Here the turning-point was the publication by Bonaventura Cavalieri (1598–1647) of his *Geometria* (1635), a work stemming from the drive to re-create the method of discovery employed by Archimedes and, for the first time, systematizing the method of indivisibles.[5] Torricelli called it 'the royal road through the mathematical briar-patch, one that Cavalieri first opened up for the public'. His best known successor was John Wallis (1616–1703), long professor at Oxford, whose *Arithmetica infinitorum* (1656) was carefully annotated by Newton; in these annotations, D. T. Whiteside has remarked, 'there is no true dividing line between the summarized impact of the original and the following wave of new ideas which became a piece of original research'.[6] In Newton, who made a thorough study of the *Geometrie* of Descartes and other mathematicians of his school as published by Frans van Schooten, the two lines of activity were to marry and create the concepts of his method of fluxions, or calculus. Gottfried Willhelm Leibniz (1646–1716), whose differential calculus was to see the light of day (1684) before Newton's fluxions, though subsequent to fluxions in epoch of discovery, came into existence by a different route, making use for example of the arithmetical work of Pascal which, in the mid-1660s, was unknown to Newton.

So brief a sketch as this is very unjust in making no note of the accomplishments of other mathematicians of great fertility, both of the generation just before that of Leibniz and Newton, like Pierre de Fermat (1601–65), correspondent (through Mersenne) and rival of Descartes, and contemporaries like James Gregory (1638–75) whose innovations in method so often went parallel to those of Newton.

The transformation of mathematics – though not complete until about 1720, by which time the whole of mechanics had been re-stated in the language of calculus by the joint efforts of Pierre Varignon (1654–1722) of the Paris Academy of Sciences and the brothers Jakob and Johann Bernoulli – gave to mathematical physics a hitherto unprecedented subtlety and richness. The first new steps, however, in Kepler's *Snowflake* (1611) or Descartes's *Dioptrique* and *Meteores* (1637) were straightforward enough. The modern study of the geometry of lenses had begun in Kepler's *Dioptrice* (1611) which not only explained how the existing Dutch telescope yielded an enlarged image but proposed a new, astronomical telescope using two convex lenses. Descartes took the basic treatment of refraction much further on the basis of Snel's Law, which enabled him to compute, for example, the width of the rainbows as well as their diameter on the basis of two refractions and a single or double reflection at the raindrop. (The coloration was left to Newton to account for by dispersion.) The argument by which Descartes shows how the light falling uniformly in parallel rays upon the drop, is after refraction and reflection concentrated into bands, is most ingenious. Geometrical optics was taken much further in subtlety by Barrow (1669) and by Newton in his *Optical Lectures*, which were to remain unpublished until 1728.

Although Newton's experiments on light had yielded the discovery that colour has a mathematical connotation, along with many other quantitative results obtained with consummate precision, he was unable to formulate a general mathematical theory of light and its transmission. Perhaps his most successful approach towards one starts from the ideas later expressed in Query 29 of *Opticks*:

Are not the Rays of Light very small Bodies emitted from shining Substances? Pellucid Substances act upon the Rays of Light at a Distance in refracting, reflecting, and inflecting them, and the Rays mutually agitate the Parts of those Substances at a distance for heating them, and this Action and Reaction at a distance very much resembles an attractive Force between Bodies.

In the *Principia* a group of propositions explores the hypothesis as an aspect of the general theory of attractive forces, supposing the light-particles to be accelerated positively or negatively after passing through an interface; they yield the ordinary optical conditions, including Snel's Law, and Newton accommodated in the same way what he took to be the phenomena of diffraction. However, in the *Queries* Newton also wrote:

Nothing more is requisite for producing all the variety of Colours, and degrees of Refrangibility, than that the Rays of Light be Bodies of different sizes, the least of which may make violet . . .

which will not work, at least on the normal gravitational supposition that the force between two bodies is proportional to the product of their masses, since the large and the small light-corpuscles will be equally accelerated and no dispersion will occur. Newton never found his way out of this *impasse*, and so only left the unsatisfactory sketch in the *Principia* of a mathematical force-theory of light.[7]

Christiaan Huygens succeeded better, to the extent that his work (again, only a part of a large endeavour) has been admired and reproduced down to the present day. It appears in his *Treatise of Light* (1690), sketched as early as 1673 (the period of his controversy with Newton). Like Hooke, Huygens started from the supposition of an analogy between light and sound, hence arguing that light is a movement of the aether-particles radiating outwards from its origin. Although Huygens's analysis of the pulse – or longitudinal wave-motion – was in some ways less satisfactory than Newton's mathematical theory of sound-waves in the *Principia*, it enabled him to explain, by 'Huygens's principle' of the formation of the travelling wave-front, how the pulses might travel through an aperture so as to produce a rectilinear beam, because outside the beam the individual waves 'do not at the same instant concur to compose a wave terminating the motion, as they do precisely at the circumference which is their common tangent'. He also succeeded in the far more difficult task, which in fact always defeated Newton even when he had Huygens's example before him, of explaining the twin rays of double refraction in terms of his own theory. A limitation should be noted, however, that emphasizes the purely mathematical character of Huygens's wave-theory: it considers only the movement of a single expanding wave or pulse, and cannot be extended to the physically appropriate case of a train or succession of periodic waves.[8]

In view of the deep differences, alike philosophical and technical, between the two great mathematical physicists of the seventeenth century, it is hardly surprising that the theory of light remained in debate until the final triumph of the Young – Fresnel transverse wave-theory. True, the ascendancy of Newtonianism from about 1720 entailed a widespread acceptance of his particle or emission theory, which was more philosophically plausible besides carrying Newton's seal of approval; but some continental mathematicians of great influence, notably Leonhard Euler (1707–83), continued to defend the wave-theory, which was always stronger than Newton's in its mathematical formulation. The first real check to Newton's authoritarian rectitude in this matter was curiously enough to come from the English Newtonian experimenters, when they discovered the error of his apparent confidence that dispersion (for any one colour) is always proportional to refraction. Their discovery (1759) made achromatic lenses possible.

The greatest weakness of the philosophy of nature put forward by Descartes had been in its treatment of light, which could not stand up against Huygens. From 1712, indeed, the philosopher Malebranche adopted the Newtonian theory in preference even to Huygens in his *Recherche de la Verité*. The antithesis between the dynamic basis of Newton's 'optical' propositions in the *Principia* and the kinematic basis of the Cartesian theory, maintained by Huygens, was the fundamental issue in mathematical science generally through the period of Newton's later lifetime. Should the philosopher hold, with Descartes, that endless motion was inherent in nature so that he might with freedom postulate any initial condition of motion that he pleased, his only duty being to study its transmission and modification; or should he, as Newton insisted, believe that forces are at work in nature, conferring, modifying or halting the motions of bodies? Could the latter philosophy, in its failure to explain the origin or mode of action of forces, be properly called a mechanical philosophy at all? Of course, no one doubted that 'force' is a properly mechanical expression, as when it is said that air pressure exerts a force upon a piston, or when a body moving at speed exerts a force by impact upon others; in its driest sense the difference of view turned on the question whether *all* forces must be reducible to the impact of particle upon particle, or whether it is proper also to speak of forces as dynamic causes that produce effects of motion, without making any assumption about impact. Newton himself was categorically always cautious in maintaining an agnostic position, that is, he formally in mathematical contexts declared that he believed in the existence of forces, while remaining ignorant of whether or not the postulated forces (gravity, magnetism and so forth) could in turn be reduced to impact processes, for example, by imagining some sort of impelling aether. Thus, in the *Principia*, Newton excuses his constant repetition of the word 'attraction':

For attractions are generally made towards bodies . . . For which reason I now go on to explain the motion of bodies mutually attracting each other, by considering the centripetal forces as attractions although perhaps if we use the language of physics we may more truly call them impulses. But we are now dealing with mathematics, and on that account we employ the ordinary speech, setting aside physical arguments, in order to be more easily understood by mathematical readers.[9]

While it may be debated whether or not readers of 1687 would have ordinarily spoken of the Sun attracting the Earth, or the Moon the sea, it is certain no critic of Newton was ever dissuaded from castigating him as the father of attractive forces by this piece of legerdemain and others of the same sort. In the Queries to *Opticks*, though purportedly in a conjectural spirit, Newton seems to reveal more openly his true understanding of the nature of things when he asked

Have not the small Particles of Bodies certain Powers, Virtues, or Forces, by which they act a distance, not only upon the Rays of Light for reflecting, refracting, and inflecting them, but also upon one another for producing a great Part of the Phenomena of Nature?[10]

This passage may be coupled with that published long before in the Preface to the *Principia*, where Newton after speaking of the forces from which he had deduced the motions of the planets, comets, the Moon and the sea, had continued

I wish we could derive the rest of the phenomena of Nature by the same [mathematical] kind of reasoning from mechanical principles, for I am induced by many reasons to suspect that they may all depend upon certain forces by which the particles of bodies, by some causes hitherto unknown, are either mutually impelled towards one another, and cohere in regular figures, or are repelled and recede from one another.

If we generalize from the macroscopic to the microscopic, as the Fifth Rule of Reasoning in the *Principia* justifies us in doing, then Newton invites us to perceive a simple basic pattern in nature formed by the motions of particles (and gross bodies) caused ultimately by interparticulate forces, both attractive and repulsive.

Now it is not hard to believe that each particle affects others in multifarious ways, so that if one were annihilated all the rest of the universe would, in principle, feel the loss. It is much harder to believe that the universe is so constructed that it, from outside, makes each particle of matter the centre of multifarious forces. Newtonianism based on the attractive and repulsive force was intelligible to a Huygens or Leibniz, though they refused to believe it; a Newtonian kinematic universe is simply incomprehensible. It is not surprising that his contemporaries, pro and con, thought him to take as physically real the centres of attractive force of which he so often spoke.

This discussion of the emergence of the Newtonian idea of force as something ontologically real, and perhaps even an absolute like matter itself, has been necessary because of the novelty in its day of an idea that seems so familiar to us. In the early seventeenth century the word 'force' (in its technical uses) had no more than a mechanical significance: a screw-press exerts force on a bale. In his admirable book on *The Metaphysical Foundations of Modern Physical Science* E. A. Burtt wrote that Galileo was primarily concerned with accelerated motions 'and these always presuppose . . . some force or forces as cause'.

Hence the cause of every motion which is not simple and uniform must be expressed in terms of *force*.[11]

This is a natural view, but one unjustified by history. Galileo had not only no mathematical conception of 'force' as the name given to the product formed by multiplying the mass and acceleration of a body, but he had no ontological conception of 'force' as the name of an active, conservative agent in the universe either. He knows only one single ontological force, gravity, which he does not call a 'force', though he does speak naturally of the force of projectiles. He is very far, therefore, from being able to see constant acceleration as an effect, constant force as its unique cause; in that passage of the *Discourses* where he disclaims interest in determining the cause of uniform natural acceleration he does not suggest that the cause must be a force, and the name of this force gravity. In fact, since gravity is natural, it could only improperly have been classified as a force by Galileo. [12]

If a generalized idea of force is sought in vain in Galileo, still less would one expect to find it in Descartes, though (like Galileo) he uses the word in analysing the action of machines and (qualified) as a synonym for momentum. For Descartes the problem of force in mechanics became a problem of mechanical cause, since every kind of motion was specifically accounted for in his system by assigning an impelling flight of particles to produce it. Hence Descartes could never agree with Galileo though he opens his comments on Galileo's *Discourses* (1638) with the bland praise:

I find in general that he philosophizes much better than the ordinary person, in that he abandons as far as he can the errors of the Schools, and tries to examine physical questions by mathematical reasonings. In that I am wholly in accord with him, and think there is no other means to find out the truth.

This aspiration Descartes would never fulfil in his own philosophy of nature, to be published six years later. But to be more specific:

All that [Galileo] says about the speed of bodies falling through the void is built without foundation, for he ought in the first place to have determined what weight is, and if he had known the truth of it, he would have known that it is zero in the void. [13]

Obviously there is a quibble about the meaning of 'void' here; Galileo meant a space free from an atmosphere resisting motion, while Descartes takes it as a space from which the impelling particles causing bodies to fall are excluded, so that there can be no 'weight'. Thus Descartes, pursuing causation which Galileo had renounced, isolated himself from the Galilean tradition of analysing in mathematical terms the concepts of acceleration and velocity. On the other hand, his system emphasized the importance of the laws of impact governing the exchange of motion. The combination of the two first of Descartes's Rules of Motion as stated in his *Principles of Philosophy* (1644) was to form the first of Newton's Laws of Motion. Before Descartes, Galileo too had attempted without attaining concrete results to formulate a general theory of collision; the French philosopher's Rules were quantitatively expressed but, after the first three, all false. He admitted himself that they did not conform to experience, partly because Descartes became thoroughly confused in his ideas about the effect of size on the collision of bodies.

If the workings of the world depended on such phenomena, the situation was absurd. In 1668 the Royal Society asked three of its Fellows who were known to have examined the matter to report their findings. John Wallis dealt with inelastic collision only: here he correctly established that – regard being had to direction – the sums of the momenta (weight times velocity) are the same before and after collision, and stated the case aright. Huygens and Wren, on the other hand, considered perfectly elastic collision again stating the cases correctly, Wren arguing from a rather strange postulate of a dynamical balance, Huygens (looking into the whole business more explicitly) expressing exactly the general dynamical principles: (1) the sum of the kinematic energies before and after collision is the same (2) the velocity of the centre of gravity of the two bodies is also unchanged.[14] Thus were the 'laws of motion' (then so dominated) found out, though perfectly useless in any kind of physical theory. It is interesting that at this late date, and without impairing his ultimate conclusions, Wallis could choose as his second postulate:

if a force V moves a weight P, a force nV will move nP, all things being equal, that is, through the same distance in the same time, or with the same speed:

which is a perfectly Aristotelian principle!·

When inviting Huygens to communicate his ideas on collision Oldenburg had premised the belief in London that Huygens 'had already discovered a theory which explained all kinds of phenomena concerning motion', and in reply Huygens asked, what sort of motion did the Royal Society wish discussed? 'For there are several sorts, most of which I think I have considered: that is, the ratio of the fall of heavy bodies, both with and without the resistance of air; the motion of pendulums; centres of oscillation; circular and conical motion and centrifugal force; the communication of motion by impact.'[15] Though only a part of all this work in mechanics was to be printed in his lifetime (in *Horologium Oscillatorium*, 1673) Huygens was the foremost authority in applied mathematics before Newton. His determination of the magnitude of centrifugal force went back to 1659; his fundamental theoretical study of the simple, compound and conical pendulum to 1657. Equally stimulated in his early studies by Galileo and Descartes, Huygens in later life justified the brilliant promise of his youth (the elucidation of Saturn's rings), perhaps with age tending more towards a Galilean methodology, for as he relates:

M. Descartes had found the way to get his conjectures and fictions accepted as truths. And to readers of his *Principles of Philosophy* much the same happened as to those who read romances that please and create the impression of being true narratives. It seemed to me when I first read this book of the *Principles* [being then 15 or 16] that everything in it was splendid, and I felt on encountering some difficulty, that it was my fault for not understanding Descartes's thought properly. But since then, having from time to time discovered some things that are obviously false in that book, and others highly improbable. I have recovered a good deal from the infatuation I had for it.[16]

Pascal too spoke of the *Principles* as a romance of physics. But if Descartes's demonstrable mistakes and absurdities were renounced by Huygens, the Netherlander was far from losing faith in the principle of the plenistic, kinematic universe which was at the root of Descartes's philosophy of nature, preferring it strongly to the principle of attractive and repulsive forces which he later found in Newton's *Principia*, much as he admired Newton's mathematization of physics. We may feel sympathy for Huygens's conservatism in this regard, in that it is beyond doubt that Newton's physics created problems of a profound character (What is the origin of forces? What is the cause of gravity?) which he could not resolve, and which were never to be resolved because they define the boundaries of that physics, but equally – and with worse consequences since it obstructed further development – Huygens was trapped as all the neo-Cartesians were trapped in a disparity between the microcosm and the macrocosm. At the macrocosmic level Huygens effected important advances and set the theory of motion on a sounder footing, and he knew that *if* the laws and methods of mechanics were general, as well applicable to fundamental particles as to billiard balls, then a unity of explanation would be attained:

if nature as a whole consists of certain corpuscles, from the motions of which every diversity of things aries . . . as many philosophers believe to be probable, then it will prove no small help in reflecting upon this if the true laws of motion were to be discovered, and if it were known how motion is transferred between bodies.[17]

This was written in 1656; but in all the rest of his life Huygens could not find his way from theoretical mechanics to experimental physics. Newton was to succeed in this. True, Newton's successful penetrations to the microscopic level in order to show the congruity with the macroscopic are few, but they are decisive, and his fundamental concept – that the ultimate particles of matter exert forces on each other – has remained from his day to ours the starting principle of scientific explanation, even though the forces are no longer Newtonian.

Thus in the end Huygens like Leibniz after him failed to detach himself from the metaphysical shackles of the Cartesian preoccupation with mechanistic causation, and his achievements in the mathematization of nature were to remain disconnected and incomplete: when the issues became really deep, Huygens retreated once more into the aetherial conjectures of Descartes's *Principles*. In this formal analysis of mechanics, according to Westfall, Huygens similarly diminished through the years the dynamical content of his investigations in favour of the purity of kinematics:

Huygens held the very concept of force under suspicion for the occult tendencies he felt to be implicit in it. More even than Galileo, he tried to base the kinematics of heavy bodies on the fact, to be accepted as empirically given, that heavy bodies descend with a uniformly accelerated motion.[18]

At one here with both Galileo and Descartes, gravity was not to be reckoned a force, but simply as its linguistic synonym, weight. Huygens's liberation was further impeded by the limitation in his mathematical imagination noted before; the geometrical way of thinking that brought him rich rewards in mechanics and even allowed him to develop his own informal methods of integration of considerable power, as in his investigation of resisted motion, prevented his finding any merit in others' elaboration of the infinitesimal calculus.[19] This is very evident in Huygens's exchanges with Leibniz, Newton and Fatio de Duillier. Always he was to be what his father had called him, the Archimedes of this new age.

This is distinction enough. In the mid-seventeenth century distinguished by so many excellent studies in the field of mechanics – by Borelli, Hooke, Marci, Wren, Wallis, Fabri – Huygens is invariably singled out as the one essential link between Galileo and Newton, and he was one of the few men whom Newton publicly praised. Their personal relations were cordial though the two men were in different worlds of physics. Hard upon the intensive study by several mathematicians of the cycloid – a 'mechanical' curve and the first new curve to be mastered since antiquity – Huygens had proved (1659) that the simple pendulum is only isochronous in its swings if it describes a cycloidal arc; further, that the evolute of a cycloid is the same cycloid. Thus, by confining the flexible suspension of the pendulum between cycloidal 'cheeks', the arc becomes an identical curve and the construction of the pendulum clock invented by Huygens two years before was mathematically justified; but it is perhaps more important that Huygens had devised the mathematical concept of the evolute.[20] He also solved the problem of determining the centre of oscillation (thereby permitting comparison of experimental pendulums with the ideal single pendulum): 'As for the vibrations or centres of oscillation', he wrote, 'Roberval found out a very little, that is to say the centre of oscillation of the sector of a circle. M. Descartes did nothing. I have acomplished everything related to this matter, and gave the demonstrations in my treatise on the clock [*Horologium Oscillatorium*].'[21] The relation of the length to the period of the pendulum and the gravitational force was easy for Huygens to unravel, by which he ascertained the value of g at Paris to be 981 cm/s^2 (in equivalent measure).

Several currents, not least his reading, bore Huygens towards the appellation and discovery for which he is best known, centrifugal force. On this too he wrote a treatise in 1659, to be published only posthumously, in 1703, when no longer significant. Its chief propositions had been stated without proofs in *Horologium Oscillatorium*, so that Newton was aware from 1673 of certain analogies between Huygens's course and his own. Galileo had not been able to demonstrate why objects are not thrown off – as from a sling – by the swiftly rotating Earth; he had simply replied, in effect, that a rotation of one revolution per day is not swift. Descartes too had failed to deal with his issue quantitatively, though he had explained that 'centrifugal force' (to use Huygens's name out-of-place) is a manifestation of a body's inertia. Although he also held that a body suspended in a fluid, as he imagined the Earth to be, is not moving because it does not leave its immediate environment, Descartes drew attention to the planet's tendency to recede from the centre of the vortex in which it is borne and arranged an opposite, centripetal tendency in the matter of the vortex to retain the planet in its orbit.

Huygens started from the position that centrifugal force is comparable to gravity, or rather (and the point is of some significance) that the endeavour (*conatus*) of a body to recede from a centre about which it revolves is of the same kind as that with which the body tries to approach the centre of the Earth.

Geometrical considerations show that if the body could escape along the radius-vector by which it is tied to the centre, it would, in successive equal times. traverse distances increasing in the series of odd numbers, just as Galileo had proved for falling bodies. By examining the effect in circles of different radius, or of the same radius revolved with different velocities, Huygens proved that the *conatus* is as v^2/r, or specifically, that the endeavour to recede from the centre is equal to the body's weight, when the peripheral velocity in the circle is that which the body would acquire in descending half the radius ($v = \sqrt{(gr)}$). Thus the *conatus* even at the Equator is hundreds of times less than gravity.

There is a curious, if well-known, aspect of Huygens's analysis. He began by postulating (as indeed had Galileo, and slings depend upon it) that if suddenly released the revolving body 'flies off at a tangent', the tangent to the radius-vector at the point of detachment. Its motion along the tangent is, as correctly expressed by Huygens himself, inertial and uniform. Its acceleration in relation to the former centre of revolution is an illusion, just as a train approaching along a straight track appears to accelerate if we are standing a little to one side, there is no force within, or acting upon the body, to accelerate it from the centre, as Huygens supposed and always maintained in speaking of 'centrifugal' force. On the other hand (as Newton appreciated) there does have to be a constant force – the resistance of a string, say – a *centripetal* force, to retain the body in its circle. One has to imagine the body being constantly accelerated *inwards* from the tangent (where it would otherwise be) to its position on the circle. Although Huygens spoke of the revolving body 'having an endeavour to recede in the direction of its string with an accelerated motion' its only 'endeavour' is, in fact, tangential. The distinction of point of view is essential for the understanding of planetary motion.

As a neo-Cartesian, his celestial bodies swimming in vortices, Huygens never broached the question of planetary mechanics. Yet after the publication of Descartes's *Principles* in 1644 the crude elements of the problem were completely assembled. The essential step – ignoring for the present the question of non-circularity in the orbits and non-uniformity in the planets' motions – was to substitute for Descartes's centripetal pressure in the vortex some other 'endeavour' of force in the planet directed towards the sun. About twenty years after the *Principles* appeared, three men addressed themselves to this issue.

But before turning to them, the background of the concept of celestial attractive force must be sketched in. Descartes had forcibly excluded it; all supposed attractions and repulsions were in his system effected by the impact of subtle matter (or aether) upon solid bodies. In the celestial vortex the positions of the planets were not assumed to be wholly arbitrary, but Descartes had made no attempt to accommodate to his philosophy the laws derived by Kepler from observation which precisely stated the planetary pattern. Equally he had abandoned the somewhat vague idea of Copernicus that gravity might be seen as a universal, though specific, cohesive principle in nature. A different tradition, however, had preserved it. Gilbert had appealed to it as the cause of bodies keeping their integrity. 'Cohesion of parts, and aggregation of matter', he had written, 'exist in the Sun, in the Moon, in the planets, in the fixed stars', so that in all these bodies the parts tend to unite with the whole 'with which they connect themselves with the same appetence as terrestrial things, which we call heavy, with the Earth'.[22] This means that gravitation is a universal property of matter, but peculiar to each body; the same gravity is not common to all, in Gilbert's view, because a piece of lunar matter would always tend towards the moon, and never adhere to the earth.

It might seem that after Galileo's contention that the matter of Earth, Moon and Planets – the non-luminous heavenly bodies – was of the same kind, it would have been a straightforward step to argue that all this earthy matter shared a common attraction, like drawing like. But against such an argument the teleology of the theory of attraction – which was in no way required to explain the known behaviour of lunar or solar matter, apart from in cohesion – was doubly effective. In the first place, if the matter of the Moon, for example, were attracted towards the earth, the theory would cease to explain the cohesion of the parts of the Moon. Secondly, a common gravitational attraction would suggest that all the earthy matter in the universe would collect in one mass – this was Aristotle's view, which Galileo opposed. Thirdly, Galileo and his followers were reluctant to introduce into astronomy the esoteric principle of attraction, which would disturb the perfect inertial revolution of the heavenly bodies. The theory of specific attractions remained far more plausible.

This theory had been used by Gilbert, and by Copernicus before him, as an alternative to the Aristotelean causation of the motions of heavy terrestrial bodies. It was less a new cosmological principle, than a new physical principle applied to cosmology. As such it is also used by Kepler:

A mathematical point, whether it be the centre of the universe or not, cannot move heavy bodies either effectively or objectively so that they approach itself . . . It is impossible, that the form of a stone, moving its mass [corpus], should seek a mathematical point or the centre of the world, except with respect to the body in which that point resides . . . Gravity is a mutual corporeal affection between cognate bodies towards their union or conjunction (of which kind the magnetic faculty is also), so that the Earth draws a stone much more than the stone seeks the Earth. Supposing the Earth to be in the centre of the Universe, heavy bodies would not be borne to the centre of the Universe as such, but to the centre of a cognate spherical body, to wit the Earth. And thus wherever the Earth is assumed to be carried by its animal faculty, heavy bodies will always tend towards it.[23]

So far Kepler has said nothing very new. He has repeated that the concept of attraction of like to like can replace the Aristotelian concept of matter being attracted to specific places, and he has limited his use of this concept to heavy bodies cognate with the Earth. But he has stated, for the first time, that the attraction is mutual (the analogy between gravity and magnetism, so fruitfully begun by Gilbert, is now being extended), and this point he amplified further:

If two stones were placed close together in any place in the Universe outside the sphere of the virtue of a third cognate body, they would like two magnetic bodies come together at an intermediate point, each moving such a distance towards the other, as the mass of the other is in proportion to its own.

Here an original conception of the magnitude of the motion due to gravitational attraction was introduced ($d_1/d_2 = m_2/m_1$), in which it was related to the ratio of the masses of the two bodies. Kepler, therefore, began the investiture of the theory of attraction with a definite dynamical form. Further, he postulated that the Earth and the Moon were cognate matter, like the two stones:

If the Moon and the Earth were not retained, each in its orbit, by their animal or other equivalent forces, the Earth would ascend towards the Moon one fifty-fourth part of the distance between them, and the Moon descend towards the Earth about fifty-three parts; and they would there join together; assuming, however, that the substance of each is of one and the same density.[24]

Kepler then went on to demonstrate, from the ebbing and flowing of the tides, that this attractive force in the Moon does actually extend to the Earth, pulling the waters of the seas towards itself; much more likely was it that the far greater attractive force of the Earth would reach to the Moon, and greatly beyond it, so that no kind of earthy matter could escape from it.[25]

Clearly no one invented the theory of gravitational attraction; it grew through many diverse stages. And clearly also the genesis of the theory of universal gravitation is found in Kepler. Newton's hasty calculation of 1666, his later theory of the Moon, and his theory of the tides, are all embryonically sketched in the *Astronomia Nova*. But the attraction was still specific, applicable only to heavy, earthy matter; Kepler himself did not go so far as to suppose that the Sun and planets were also mutually attracting masses, or that the dynamical balance he indicated as retaining the Earth and Moon in their orbits with respect to each other also preserved the stability of the planetary orbits with respect to the Sun. He failed as Copernicus, Gilbert and Galileo failed, to see the full power of gravitational attraction as a cosmological concept.

Nevertheless, Kepler's idea that the satellite revolving round a central body is maintained in its path by two forces, one of which is an attraction towards the central body, although applied only to the Earth–Moon system, holds the key to all that followed and to the *Principia* itself. Galileo, like Copernicus, had believed the planetary revolutions to be 'natural', i.e. inertial; the celestial bodies were subject to no forces. Kepler, however, believed that the motive force of the universe resided in the Sun which, rotating upon its own axis, 'emits from itself through the extent of the Universe an immaterial image [species] of its body, analogus to the immaterial image [species] of its light, which image is itself rotated also a most swift whirlpool and carries round with itself the bodies of the planets.[26] Each planet, moreover, was endowed with its own 'soul' which influenced its motions.'[27] Such notions confused the dynamical elements of the situation for Kepler – since the Sun's force operated tangentially upon the planet, he did not imagine that a centripetal force was neccessary to retain it in the orbit. In the singular case of the Earth and Moon, it was neccessary for him to suppose that the 'animal or other, equivalent force' of the Moon was sufficient to overcome the attraction towards the Earth which would have distorted path. This physical, attractive property of heavy matter could not as yet be made the basis the stability of the celestial system; rather it was a disturbing feature which the cosmological properties of the heavenly bodies had to overcome.

However imaginative, however prescient Kepler's dynamic ideas might be, they were certainly confused, not least by starting from the Aristotelian assumption that a constant force was required as cause of a constant speed. Nevertheless, readers of his works could find in them a possible answer to Descartes' problem of the planetary orbits: might not the philosopher postulate as the centripetal force required to hold the universe together just such a 'corporeal affextion between cognate bodies towards their union' as Kepler had described?

The first of the three to take the issue of the dynamical balance in planetary motion before the public, Giovanni Alfonso Borelli (1608–79, often mentioned before), marched even closer in Kepler's footsteps by regarding the rays of light radiating from a rotating Sun, and so revolving with it, as levers pressing upon the planets and urging them in their circles. Light, in this sense, had to be regarded as a material emanation. Borelli explained that no matter how small the impulse applied, it would impart some motion to the greatest mass (though Descartes had said exactly the opposite) and so, in the absence of any resistance, the planets would move with a speed equal to that of the light impelling them (there is no question of constant force here: the planets are swept along like boats in a current of water):

These very effective rays can surely seize upon the planetary bodies and drive them round in a solar vortex; for if light is a corporeal substance diffused by the body of the sun like some perpetual wind, this radiating substance must also like the body of the sun, turn in a circle and then it is certainly possible, indeed necessary, that the planetary bodies balanced and floating in the celestial aether should be impelled into locomotion by these corporeal rays.

Why then do not all the planets revolve at the same speed? Borelli again reminds us that the rays are like levers – the further the point of application is from the fulcrum (the Sun) the weaker the impulse of the lever – and so, the further the planet from the Sun, the weaker the driving force and the less its speed, for Borelli *now* insists, with remarkable inconsistency, that the planet's reluctance to move increases with its distance from the centre. However, instructed by Descartes, Borelli knew that to retain the planets in the solar vortex a centripetal impulse was necessary: he found it – again echoing Kepler – in a 'natural instinct' in the planet to approach the Sun in a straight line

as we see all heavy bodies have a 'natural instinct' to approach our Earth, that is, driven by the force of gravity natural to them, or the iron which moves straight towards the magnet. For this reason, it would not be impossible for the body of the planet to possess a certain faculty, like the magnetic faculty, by means of which it moves towards the solar globe . . .

Note that Borelli carefully avoids the word *attraction*, applying the term *force* also only indirectly, preferring an almost animistic phraseology; nor does he precisely identify the instinct with either gravity or magnetism. The instinct is not mutual, for it does not affect the central body, and evidently it is constant at all distances, as no doubt Borelli also supposed gravity to be.[28]

He had yet a further difficulty to surmount. Borelli was the first writer on the system of the world to take Kepler's two first laws of planetary motion seriously. Therefore he had to explain how, in this curious vortex, the orbits are not circular but elliptical. His explanation is ingenious: Borelli imagined that each planet was created outside its hypothetical orbit circle. Then, he supposes, the centripetal force he has postulated will be in excess of the centrifugal force: the planet, as it circles the Sun, will tend to approach it and its momentum will cause it to overshoot, so that after half a revolution the planet will be inside its orbit. There the situation is inverse, the centripetal force being the lesser, and so the planet now receding from the Sun returns to its original station, and the cycle is repeated. As the planet gathers and loses speed in successive half-revolutions, its speed at perihelion must be greater than that at aphelion, in accordance with observation. Thus the ellipse – of course, Borelli did not prove that the curve would be an ellipse rather than an eccentric circle – is the consequence of the planet's oscillation about a mean concentric orbit, an oscillation compared to that of a floating body depressed into the fluid, then released, or to that of a pendulum passing through the stable position of rest at the centre. Later, Hooke, was to illustrate this second analogy with the conical pendulum, which can also display rotation of the line of apsides.

At the time of developing this only loosely mathematical theory, Borelli was in Florence, where he had a small observatory and made careful studies of Jupiter's satellites, having obtained a copy of Galileo's tabulation of their motions some twenty years before. Though best known as a mechanistic physiologist he was, as a pupil of Benedetto Castelli at Rome, in the Galileo tradition. He taught for some years at Messina whither he returned for a while after the collapse of the Accademia del Cimento. Political intrigues compelled him to spend his last years in Rome, in part patronized by the abdicated Queen Christina of Sweden. To avoid trouble with the clerical censorship by providing himself with a minimum of 'cover', Borelli wrote as though he were discussing only the movements of Jupiter's satellites, entitling his book *The Theory of the Medician Planets Deduced from Physical Causes* (Florence, 1666) though, as in the quotations above, he was not at all hesitant about referring to the Sun – perhaps silently to be conceived by those who so wished as circling about a stationary Earth – as the centre of a similar, larger system. Indeed, the nonsense involved in thinking of the Earth or Jupiter as centres of vorticles of radiating light is conspicuous. As a writer on mechanics Borelli was discursive and long-winded, as well as muddled. While adopting the propositional format for his books, clearly apprehended axioms and continuous mathematical argument are both lacking. Borelli himself was inclined to think of mechanics as merely a staircase by which to mount to the admirable science of the motion of animals. It has been said, fairly, that he 'played an important part in establishing and extending the new experimental-mathematical philosophy' but he gave it neither clear principles nor logical methods. To attempt to reduce all dynamic action to impact, and to analyse it by Borelli's one constant resource, the law of the lever, was to embroil himself in impossible difficulties. Yet Borelli was certainly read; Newton who mentioned 'Borel's hypothesis' in the *Principia*, owned three of his books at the time of his death, including that on the Medician satellites.[29]

Other philosophers of mechanics, such as Marcus Marci and Robert Hooke, were just as deeply embroiled in imprecise notions and perilous analogies as was Borelli. Hooke's conceptual precision was by no means equal to his fertility, nor did his mathematical capacities match his experimental skill. Nor did he ever perceive his own deficiencies, or appreciate the distance to which mechanics during the late seventeenth century would lead the geometer, far beyond the bounds of Euclid and Apollonios. This was to be the cause of Hooke's tragedy.

There is ample evidence that by 1685 Robert Hooke had a very complete picture of a mechanical system of the universe founded on universal gravitation. In the early days of the Royal Society he performed unsuccessful experiments to discover whether gravity varies above and below the Earth's surface. In *Micrographia* (1665) he conjectured that the Moon might have a 'gravitating principle' like the Earth. In a discourse read to the Royal Society in 1666 Hooke improved on Borelli with the supposition that a 'direct motion' might be inflected into a curve by 'an attractive property of the body placed at the centre'. Like earlier writers he compared this centripetal attraction to the tension in the string of a conical pendulum, which retains the bob in its circular path. In 1678 he wrote: 'I suppose the gravitating power of the Sun in the center of this part of the Heaven in which we are, hath an attractive power upon all the planets, . . . and that those again have a respect answerable.'[31] This is the first enunciation of the true theory of universal gravitation – of gravity as a universal principle that binds all the bodies of the solar system together. The same force whereby the heavenly bodies 'attract their own parts, and keep them from flying from them', also attracts 'all the other celestial bodies within the sphere of this activity'. It is this force which, in the Sun, bends the rectilinear motions of the planets into closed curves. And this force is 'the more powerful in operating, by how much nearer the body wrought upon is' to the attracting body.[32]

These ideas, Hooke claimed, he had expounded as early as 1670. But it was not until 1679 that he hit upon a hypothesis to describe the rate at which the gravitational attraction should decrease with distance. In that year he renewed his correspondence with Newton, discussing an experiment to detect the Earth's rotation through the deviation of falling bodies. This in turn led to a debate on the nature of the curve which a heavy body would describe if it were supposed to be able to fall freely towards the centre of the Earth, during which (in a letter to Newton dated 6 January 1680) Hooke stated the proposition that the force of gravity is inversely proportional to the square of the distance measured from the centre of the gravitating mass. He was convinced that this 'inverse square law' of attraction, combined with the ideas he had already sketched out, would be sufficient to explain all the planetary motions.

We shall return to these exchanges in the next chapter, devoted wholly to the third man who was tempted by Descartes's problem of the dynamics of the planetary orbit: Isaac Newton. Hooke's scientific intuition was certainly marvellously exact, on this as on other matters. Of all the early Fellows of the Royal Society his was the mind most sparkling imaginative. Schemes for new experiments and observations occurred to him so freely that each day was divided between a multiplicity of investigations, each in rapid succession subjected to his ingenuity and insight. He had a view – often, it must be said, a self-regarding view – on every topic raised at the Royal Society's meetings. The obverse of this endless and creative curiosity was that Hooke completed nothing to perfection; his first large work, *Micrographia*, was also his last. His longitude clock, his meticulously exact astronomical instruments, his forty ways of flying, were to remain as projects lost to posterity. More fortunate in mechanics than Borelli – for at least we recall Hooke's Law, *Ut tensio sic vis*,[33] his outline of celestial mechanics, so impressive when summarized and rationalized by an historian *a posteriori*, was to remain forever fragmentary, disconnected; unproved. As Isaac Newton bitterly acknowledged later, much more was needed than mathematical expertise in order that a true mechanics could have been derived from Hooke's hints. The conceptual structure available to Hooke (as to Borelli) was wholly inadequate, and he could neither define nor enrich it. Only an intellect of supreme clarity and percipience could erect a sharply defined, classical edifice from the jumbled materials available to mathematical physics in the 1660s.

NOTES

1. E. A. Burtt, *The Metaphysical Foundations of Modern Physical Science*, Routledge: London, 1949 [1924], 16.
2. For seventeenth-century mathematics in general see D. T. Whiteside, 'Patterns of mathematical thought in the later seventeenth century'. *Archive for History of Exact Sciences*, 1, 1961, 179–388.
3. Margaret E. Baron in *D.S.B.* IX, 611 (2).
4. *Geometrie*, 1637, 300.
5. Cavalieri was like his teacher Benedetto Castelli, a religious; Castelli had been a pupil and friend of Galileo's, whose disciple in turn Cavalieri considered himself. He was the first to publish the parabolic trajectory.
6. D. T. Whiteside, *Mathematical Papers of Isaac Newton*, I, Cambridge U.P., 1967, 11.
7. *Principia*, Book I, Props. 94–98. *Opticks*, 1934 reprint, Query 29, 370, 372. A. R. Hall in R. Taton (ed.), *Roemer et la Vitesse de la Lumière*, Vrin: Paris, 1978, 188–9.
8. A. E. Shapiro in H. J. M. Bos *et al.* (eds), *Studies on Christiaan Huygens*, Swets and Zeitlinger Lisse, 1980, 200–20.
9. *Principia*, Book I, Introduction to Section XI.
10. *Opticks*, Query 31.

11. E. A. Burtt, *The Metaphysical Foundations of Modern Physical Science*, Routledge: London 1949, [1924], 89.

12. Galileo Galilei, *Two New Sciences*, trans. Stillman Drake, Wisconsin University Press: Madison & London, 1974, 159; Compare R. S. Westfall, *Force in Newton's Physics*, Cambridge U.P., London & New York, 1971, 7–8, 40–41.

13. Descartes to Mersenne, 11 October 1638; Ch. Adam & Paul Tannery, *Oeuvres de Descartes*, re-issue Paris 1975, II, 380, 385.

14. Huygens did not use the words kinetic energy nor even *vis viva* (introduced later by Leibniz) but the sense is plain. See R. Dugas, *La Mécanique au XVIIᵉ Siécle*, Dunod. Paris, 1954, 287–93. All the documents are printed in Hall & Hall, *Correspondence of Oldenburg*, V, University of Wisconsin Press: Madison and London, 1968.

15. *Oldenburg*, 104, 127.

16. *Oeuvres Complètes*, X, 403. Quoted in Dugas, op. cit., 284–5.

17. Alan Gabbey in Bos *et al.* (Note 8), 166–99; quotation from *Oeuvres Complètes*, XVI, 150 on p. 189, and in Westfall (op. cit. Note 12), 147.

18. Westfall loc. cit., 161 ff.

19. Bos (Note 8), 143.

20. Within a short space the anchor escapement, oscillating the clock pendulum through only a few degrees, would render the cycloid mechanically redundant in even the most perfect timekeeper.

21. *Oeuvres Complètes*, X, 402, quoted Dugas (Note 14), 319.

22. *On the Magnet*, trans. S. P. Thompson (London, 1900) Basic Books: New York 1958, 219, 229.

23. *Astronomia nova; Gesammelte Werke*, III, 24–5.

24. The implied ratio of the diameters of the two bodies is not quite right.

25. *Astronomia nova*, 25–7.

26. Ibid., 34.

27. *Harmonices Mundi* (1619); *Gesammelte Werke*, VI, 264ff.

28. Besides the article of A. Koyrè in *Revue d'Hist. des Sciences*, 5, 1952, see the section on Borelli in his *La Revolution Astronomique*, Hermann: Paris, 1961, 488, 501.

29. Thomas B. Settle in *D.S.B.* II, 306. Westfall (op. cit., Note 12), 213 ff – the best general study of Borelli's science. Since only one copy of the *Theory of the Medician Satellites* existed in London in 1668 (in the possession of Lord Brouncker) Newton probably only knew of it much later.

30. R. T. Gunther, *Early Science in Oxford*, VI, Oxford 1930, 266. Printed for the author.

31. Ibid., VIII, 228.

32. Ibid., VIII, 27–8, 229–30, etc.

33. 'As the tension, so the [applied] force', or in modern terms, stress (such as the extension of a spring) is proportional to strain. Boyle's Law is a specialized version.

CHAPTER TWELVE

Newton

Newton's work was not perfect, nor was it complete; neither the *Principia* nor the *Opticks* were ever to be, in any edition, absolutely finished treatises. In the ground he had surveyed he left many blank areas for his successors to fill up, and indeed a number of important mistakes for them to correct. Nevertheless, with his work the scientific revolution reached its climax, and a model for future natural philosophers had been created. Galileo's and Kepler's confidence in the mathematical structure of nature was by it fully justified and 'mechanical principles' were proved to be a sufficient basis for explanation universally throughout physical science. Thus the unity of nature was made manifest in a grand synthesis revealing the applicability of the same laws, the same principles of explanation, in the heavens and on the Earth. The planetary revolutions of Copernicus, Kepler's laws, the discoveries made by Galileo and Huygens relating to the phenomena of gravity and motion, were all shown to follow from these laws and principles, and to be embraced within the same synthesis. In a new form, reshaped by Newton's concept of force, the mechanical philosophy was vindicated; shown now to be capable of mathematical development, its range was extended to include the theory of wave-motion and even light itself. Newton's *Mathematical Principles of Natural Philosophy* (1687) was the culmination of the scientific endeavour of the seventeenth century, of its efforts to experiment and mathematize, of its reaction against tradition and its search for new and firmer conceptual foundations. Newton proved that the world was much as the 'new philosophers' had suspected it of being: the giants on whose shoulders he stood had been looking in the right direction, though he had seen further than they.

In Newton, conceptual and mathematical strengths united in a combination of extraordinary power, a combination for which neither heredity nor environment offers any satisfactory explanation. Born (on Christmas day, 1642) an only child into a widespread family of Lincolnshire farmers, barely gentry, some of them illiterate, the only obvious inference from his childhood is that he possessed capacities for reflection and for making mechanical devices. He was, apparently, sent to Cambridge because his mother (a widow, remarried, some suppose to the deep distress of the infant Isaac) could find no practically useful

abilities in him. At Cambridge his undergraduate years seem equally unre-
markable, yet in 1669 he became the second Lucasian professor of mathematics
in the University. Something in this step must have been owing to the interest
of his predecessor, Isaac Barrow (who went off to become a royal chaplain,
returning as Master of Trinity, Newton's College, four years later); Barrow was
never Newton's tutor, nor perhaps his mentor in any way, but he knew Newton's genius and aided it. For almost thirty years Newton remained as an
industrious, though virtually non-teaching, academic fulfilling his professional
duties conscientiously enough by the standards of the day.

Whether Barrow really had a clear inkling of how much Newton had actually
accomplished by 1669 is very uncertain. One of Newton's own summaries of
his youthful creativity, written long afterwards, reads:

July 4th 1699. By consulting an accompt of my expenses at Cambridge in the years
1663 & 1664 I find in ye year 1664 a little before Christmas I being then senior
Sophister, I bought Schooten's Miscellanies & Cartes's Geometry (having read this
Geometry & Oughtreds Clavis above half a year before) & borrowed Wallis's works and
by consequence made these Annotations out of Schooten & Wallis in winter between
the years 1664 & 1665. At which time I found the method of Infinite series. And in
summer 1665 being forced from Cambridge by the Plague I computed ye area of ye
Hyperbola at Boothby in Lincolnshire to two & fifty figures by the same method. Is.
Newton.[1]

The essence of this Barrow knew; he it was who sent the paper *On Analysis* by
Newton to Collins in London, in July 1669; it was followed by a *Treatise on
the Methods of Series and Fluxions*, written in 1671. He may not have been so
well aware of other studies, also recollected by Newton many years later:

In the beginning of the year 1665 I found the Method of approximating series & the
Rule for reducing any dignity of any Binomial into such a series. The same year in
May I found the method of Tangents of Gregory & Slusius, & in November had the
direct method of fluxions & the next year in January had the Theory of colours & in
May following I had entrance into ye inverse method of fluxions. And the same year
I began to think of gravity extending to the orb of the Moon, & having found out how
to estimate the force with wch a globe revolving within a sphere presses the surface
of the sphere: from Kepler's Rule of the periodical times of the Planets being in a
sesquialterate proportion of their distances from the centres of their Orbs, I deduced
that the forces wch keep the Planets in their Orbs must be reciprocally as the squares
of their distances from the centres about wch they revolve: & thereby compared the
force requisite to keep the Moon in her Orb with the force of gravity at the surface of
the earth, and found them answer pretty nearly. All this was in the plague years of
1665 and 1666 For in those days I was in the prime of my age for invention & minded
Mathematicks & Philosophy more than at any time since.[2]

Some events in this draft written from memory, then struck through, seem to
be dated a year too late; what is more significant is that all have been broadly
speaking confirmed by examination of Newton's notebooks, letters and papers.
The outlines of a great part of Newton's future work were sketched in the years
1665–66, though it is certainly true that many particular results of importance
were first obtained in later years, and that his thoughts in the area of mechanics

and gravitation, particularly, matured slowly. In 1666 Newton was much more favourable to the Cartesian philosophy than he became later. But perhaps the most important point of all is that Newton was formed as a mathematician. It would always be natural for him, even when handling the business of the Royal Mint late in life, to think in terms of quantity and number. Newton did not give utterance to such statements as Kepler's about the geometry of the creation, yet, no less convinced of the reality of the image of the Divine Architect, he certainly viewed the universe as profoundly ordered, in space and in time, and accordingly believed that the mathematical relationships inherent in its physical structure had been willed by God:

For while Comets move in very excentrick Orbs in all manner of Positions, blind Fate could never make all the Planets move one and the same way in Orbs concentrick, some inconsiderable Irregularties excepted, which may have arisen from the mutual Actions of Comets and Planets upon one another, and which will be apt to increase, till this System wants a Reformation. Such a wonderful Uniformity in the Planetary System must be allowed the Effect of Choice.[3]

Barrow knew something, then, of how far Newton had pushed mathematics in the methods of infinitesimals and infinite series, so did John Collins who entered into correspondence with Newton and copied some of his papers on fluxions (that is, calculus) and so finally through Collins and Oldenburg did some continental mathematicians, including Leibniz, although these understood far less of what Newton had done than he himself supposed. English and Scottish mathematicians too, especially the latter (David Gregory, James's nephew, and John Craig) were permitted to study Newton's papers privately. But John Wallis in the early 1690s was still ignorant of Newton's work now a quarter-century old, and rebuked him severely for not publishing material that would have brought credit to his country. Finally, Wallis in 1695 and 1699, Newton himself in 1704 (by attaching two short mathematical treatises to *Opticks*) and William Jones in 1711 broke the long silence. By this time almost everything that Newton had pioneered in 1660s and 1670s had been duplicated by others. His old papers were only of historical interest.

Late in 1675 Leibniz, then residing in Paris and rapidly making up for defects in his mathematical education under the guidance of Huygens, had hit on the idea of using differentials (infinitestimals) as algebraic quantities, his approach being arithmetical, rather than geometrical like Newton's. He worked out and developed the implications of his idea with extraordinary rapidity. By June 1677 he was able to address to Oldenburg[4] (for Newton) a letter praising briefly some of the 'really very elegant theorems' and comments on Wallis's method of interpolation previously sent him by Newton, and going on formidably, after the opinion 'I agree with Newton that Sluse's method of tangents has not yet been brought to perfection', with a full account of elementary differentiation and its application to the problem of drawing tangents. 'In my opinion', he added, 'what Newton chose to conceal about the drawing of tangents is not far off these'. Leibniz rightly guessed that Newton was ahead of him in methods of root-extraction and infinite series, all involved in the 'inverse method' of tangents, or integration. He appealed in vain for Newton's willing cooperation in perfecting these promising new techniques.[5] Newton did not, perhaps could not, reply to this letter. All then remained quiet – Leibniz was making a new career as an official historian in Hanover – until Leibniz printed a complex account of his method of differentials in the *Acta Eruditorum* (1684). Newton rejoined with a note on his own prior system in the *Principia* (1687).

How did the discoveries of Newton the pure mathematician ease the task of Newton the physicist? The question is far from simple. True, the method of fluxions (which is a kind of algebra) is not employed at all in the *Principia* (which is wholly geometric). True also that the claim later put forward by Newton himself that the propositions of the *Principia* had been discovered by analysis (fluxions) and then rewritten in the conventional geometrical form then familiar to mathematicians generally is entirely without substance: the *Principia* as published was the *Principia* as composed, there was no antecedent algebraic version. On the other hand it is not (Whiteside has argued) a book dependent for its results on a peculiarly profound knowledge of Greek geometry.[6] Rather, the chief characteristic of Newton's mathematical style in the *Principia*, so different from the purely traditional style of Huygens in *Horologium Oscillatorium*, has been defined as

his developing expertise with (and to be sure, firm preference for) arguments involving one or more orders of the infinitesimally small.

Recognition of the *Principia* as a great work of the Leibnizian calculus – in content, that is, not in form – was common in the late seventeenth and eighteenth centuries. As Whiteside points out, the elements of this infinitesimal method were neither fluxions nor differentials but geometrical limit-increments of variable line-segments. We might crudely say that this was calculus in geometrical dress, rhetorically rather than symbolically argued, and without a precise formal structure.

At a rough count [writes Whiteside] some half of the problems posed in the *Principia's* three books are reduced to determining an appropriate equation involving two fluent variables and their first-, second-, and occasionally third-order infinitesimals and then computing the relationship which connects the fluent variables alone.[6]

Thus, though the *Principia* has little or no bearing on the question of Newton's evolution and use of a formal calculus or algorithm, it provides ample evidence that Newton's success as a theoretical physicist was conditioned by his originality as a mathematician, for it can hardly be doubted that in the main period of composition of the book (1685–86) Newton was beyond all rivalry in his mastery of infinitesimal methods.

Into the texture of his personal life mathematics brought Newton great trouble and distress. A young Swiss mathematician, Nicholas Fatio de Duillier, after first meeting Newton in London ten years before and becoming the most intimate friend Newton is known to have had, in 1699 accused Leibniz of having plagiarized the idea of the differential calculus from Newton, and published it as his own. Such an accusation against a scholar who was recognized as one of the greatest intellects in Europe and whose mathematical innovations had been adopted and improved by distinguished younger men, could not but be scandalous; yet Leibniz's reply was calm and modest. He had no quarrel with Newton, he wrote, and went on to praise him while surrending nothing of his own position:

No geometer that I know of [he wrote] before Mr Newton and myself, had that method; just as no one before that geometer of great fame had proved by any public example that he possesed it [in the *Principia*, that is]; and before Mr [Johann] Bernoulli and myself no one communicated it.[7]

So the dispute simmered, until in 1705 Leibniz made use in a review of the mathematical treatises published with *Opticks* of certain expressions that, when brought to Newton's attention by officious friends, enraged him by seeming to impugn his own priority. Newton now mobilised that power of concentration and mastery of detail, so remarkable in a man of nearly seventy years, to prepare a collection of correspondence, the *Commercium Epistolicum* (1712), going back to Barrow's knowledge of his early communication (at least by sufficient hints) to Leibniz. The battle that ensued consumed the aged philosopher's energies – in part, for he was still active in other ways too – almost to his eightieth year. Leibniz died part-way, in 1716.

We can now be certain that Newton was both right and wrong, and that perhaps in the last ethical analysis Leibniz was more injured than he was. For if Newton was beyond doubt the prior inventor of calculus methods, Leibniz was equally the first to make them public; his independence of discovery is also beyond doubt, as is the falsity of the devious larcenies Newton and his friends attributed to Leibniz. It may be said that Leibniz and his followers provoked the Newtonians, belittled them, and refused to allow Newton the priority which the *Principia* at least attested; on the other no man of genius has ever mounted so unscrupulous a campaign against an opponent as Newton organized against Leibniz.

A curious feature of this extraordinary affair, which the literate of Europe followed with amazed amusement, is its relation to Newton's previous experience. As already noted in Chapter 10, the printing of Newton's first optical letter swept him into a seemingly endless controversy, to the point where Newton threatened to give up philosophy altogether, as too litigious a lady to deserve his devotion. He proposed to resign from the Royal Society, to which his reflecting telescope had not long before won him election, though this was prevented. However much one may sympathize with the bewilderment and incredulity of the critics of Newton's prismatic experiments and the 'doctrine' he founded upon them, their persistence, blindness, and loyal adhesion to preconceived ideas (which, if strengthened by familiarity, were certainly not better supported by experiment and reason than his own) was tedious in the extreme. Newton wrote many thousands of words of reply, some of it indeed necessary reformulation but little of it creative. He never forgot this experience, never got over the feeling that most 'philosophers' were pointless, opinionated fumblers, never forgave Robert Hooke for leading the chorus of uncomprehending criticism from the premise that his own theory of light as described in *Micrographia* was perfectly satisfactory so that no more need be said about it.[8] Long years after, when the *Principia* was before the world and Newton (as was his way) had spent a few years privately reworking the text, he took out his old optical papers and notes and rewrote them more or less into the shape *Opticks* has now. But he put that book in a drawer for ten more years until death ended Robert Hooke's powers of criticism.

He had, by then, endured a priority row with Hooke (1686) in which everyone allowed victory to Newton. His earlier discomposure had not prevented him from serious efforts to get some of his optical and mathematical work printed at Cambridge in the early 1670s, or sending a second very long communication on light to the Royal Society at the end of 1675 – which, however, he did not permit to be printed.

Meanwhile, almost from the moment of his election to the Lucasian chair, Newton had plunged into chemical experiments, of which no word was said in any of Newton's autobiographical recollections; public indication of his interest and expertise in this branch of science is mostly to be found in Query 31 at the end of *Opticks*, apart from a little paper 'On the nature of acids' probably published without his knowledge. Chemical experimentation was quite normal: Charles II had a laboratory at Whitehall, his nephew Prince Rupert was accomplished in practical chemical arts, there were many other amateurs and there was the lofty example of Robert Boyle. Everyone had to begin, as Newton did, by buying some retorts and other apparatus, building a furnace, and buying chemicals. There is nothing very mysterious in this, nor in Newton's acquiring as not uncommonly happened a sort of valetudinarian skill in preparations and dosages. In recent years a great deal has been made of Newton's chemical investigations and their supposed bearing upon his mature natural philosophy, because they were (seemingly) accompanied by the purchase and careful study of alchemical authors, and by the development of acquaintance with alchemists, as well as with less extravagant chemists such as Boyle and John Vigani (also at Cambridge). Newton certainly devoted his uniquely powerful brain to a huge mass of material which those who have an eye to the progress of natural science find superannuated, pointless and repellent. He was not himself above using the conventional vocabulary (the planetary names for the metals, of course; the oak, Diana's doves and so forth).

What was the meaning of this activity, wherein (as in his theological writings) Newton may seem to be looking backwards, rather than forwards? One might reply that the 'backwardness' is only from our point of view: Newton was certainly no more of an alchemist than Boyle (if the term can sensibly be applied to either) and each knew of the other's interest; likewise Newton and the philosopher Locke shared recondite scriptural interpretations. Newton's *Chronology of Ancient Kingdoms* was in its day regarded as a literary property worth stealing. Be that as it may – and the unreliability of both classical myth and the Bible as exact, chronological guides to history was only to be established a century or more after Newton's death – the desire of the great Lord

Keynes to demonstrate that Newton was a man as well as a mathematician by displaying him as magus, alchemist and heretic has certainly encouraged misunderstanding. Some cause for doubt might be found in the fact that Newton left half a volume of mathematical annotations and seven and a half volumes of his own work; by contrast, he left a million words of transcripts from alchemical authors, among which two or three short pieces are supposed to be of his own composition.[9] It is an odd fact that although Newton kept careful note of his chemical experiments,[10] contrary to his universal practice otherwise he composed little of his own. Nevertheless, some recent writers have argued that the assignment of 'powers, virtues or forces' to the particles of matter reflects the influence of the Hermetick tradition on Newton's thought.[11]

Certainly Newton built a furnace in the little garden by the Great Gate of Trinity College, from which an outside stair ran up to his room above, and watched his fires for long hours; certainly he pored over the crystalline 'star' of antimony, and pursued the art of rendering metals volatile. Nothing in the philosophy of his day forbade the possibility of chemical changes far more dramatic than any we now know to be possible, including altering the species of metals. No one then believed metals to be elements; it seemed that just as brass and bronze (being alloys) are known to be composed of at least two kinds of particles, so 'simple' metals like copper might consist of more than one kind, and so have an (in principle) alterable composition. The question was, supposing this to be hypothetically true, could human agency so operate on the metal as to *de facto* change its composition? Newton may well have believed or hoped that the disguised wisdom of the alchemical authors could be decoded to reveal the answer, as he also tried to decode historical and biblical sources. If so, he was certainly disappointed. However, in a letter to John Locke after the death of Robert Boyle, Newton wrote (August, 1692):

I have forborn to say anything against multiplication in general because you seem persuaded of it: tho there is one argument against it wch I could never find an answer to.

Unfortunately we do not have the subsequent letter in which Newton promised to set out this argument; 'multiplication' being a step towards transmutation, an artificial increase of the metallic bulk. In this instance Newton shows himself more sceptical than Boyle or Locke, and evidently he had been so for some time; he was reluctant to try a method which the deceased Boyle had hoped Newton would pursue.[12]

Chemical experiment clearly filled a space of some four years in Newton's life (1675–79) of which little otherwise is known. His experimental and mathematical study of light was already complete (the latter represented by the posthumously published *Optical Lectures*), he was reluctant 'to devote more than a minimal amount of his creative effort to mathematical research', and indeed as he wrote to Robert Hooke at the close of this phase 'had been endeavouring to bend myself from Philosophy to other studies in so much that I have long grutched the time spent in that study unless it be at idle hours sometimes for a diversion'. As far as possible Newton at this time cut himself off from the outside world and stayed fast at Cambridge.[13]

From this seclusion he was drawn by Robert Boyle,[14] to whose friendship Newton thought he owed 'my thoughts about the physical qualities we spoke of' which he expressed in the form of an elaborate neo-Cartesian aetherial hypothesis, even though 'my notions about things of this kind are so indigested that I am not well satisfied myself in them', and later in the same year 1679, ironically enough, by Robert Hooke, who had been appointed Secretary of the Royal Society in succession to the late Henry Oldenburg a couple of years before. Newton's reply to Hooke's invitation to a philosophical correspondence was discouraging; he had 'shaken hands with philosophy'. However, though (to quote words used to another correspondent somewhat later) 'I am of all men grown the most shy of setting pen to paper about anything that may lead into disputes', Newton could not resist rewarding Hooke's importuning with a thought of his own:

I am glad to hear that so considerable a discovery as you made of ye earth's annual parallax is seconded by Mr Flamstead's Observations. In requital of his advertisement I shall communicate to you a fansy of my own about discovering the earth's diurnal motion.[15]

He reasoned that an object falling from a high tower ought to deviate slightly eastwards of the perpendicular line of descent, and in doing so sketched a spiral curve running from a point above the Earth's surface to terminate at its centre. Clearly Newton had drawn no mental analogy between a projectile on Earth and a satellite in the heavens, though a few years later he would make this comparison very explicit; Hooke, however, had made it already and in forceful terms pointed out Newton's error. The falling body would, in the absence of air-resistance (and if the Earth were cut in two so as to leave a space between the two halves) describe an *ellipse* and return to the starting-point. Clearly, Hooke had learned something from Kepler.[16]

Hence to understand this situation, something must be said of Kepler's laws in the seventeenth century, before Newton embodied them in celestial mechanics. They were not ignored: for example, they are summarized quite well in a multi-volume mathematical textbook, Pierre Herigone's *Cursus Mathematicus* (1634–42).[17] The mathematicians Ismael Boulliaud (in France) and Seth Ward (in England) and numerous others after them adopted Kepler's elliptical orbit but without the second law; finding, as Kepler had, that the area-law was not amenable to mathematical handling they abandoned it in favour of various arbitrary theories by which the position of the planet on the ellipse was related to the radius-vector between the planet and the *empty* focus. If this radius-vector is specified as revolving in fairly simple ways, then the motion according to the area-law can be reproduced quite exactly. This was how Newton at first understood Kepler's hypotheses − of which he learnt from the *Astronomia Carolina* (1661) of Thomas Streete − experimenting with various devices of this sort himself, since Streete did not state the area-law, though Newton could have found it in such well-used books as G. B. Riccioli's *Amagestum novum* (1651) and in a little tract by Wren published by Wallis (1659). Indeed, as late as 1679 Newton was still investigating the arbitrary empty-focus treatment of Kepler's second law and thus − as his first reply to Hooke, just quoted, confirms – was as yet quite innocent of attaching any dynamical significance to the first and second laws. How crude, how un-Newtonian his ideas were at this stage is evident from the letters he exchanged with the Astronomer Royal, John Flamsteed, in 1681 about cometary motion. [18]

It was very different with the third law: $T^2/r^3 = k$, which Newton also learned from Streete, probably in 1664. [19] For, presumably at no very distant time, Newton had already taken up the Cartesian problem of centrifugal force (in ignorance of what Huygens had already done privately but would only publish in 1673), and discovered the V^2/r proportionality. [20] To anyone coming across Kepler's third law with this proportionality in mind it is almost self-evident that the centrifugal forces of the planets with respect to the Sun must be inversely as the square of the distance. Further than this, in his first statement of the inverse-square relationship, Newton did not go and the evidence suggests that for many years he still retained the notion of the aetherial vortex – a concept he mentions without hesitation in letters of 1681. [21] The reality of the vortex was further suggested by the discrepancy (recorded autobiographically) in his calculation of the effect of gravity reaching up to the Moon (? 1669, 1670): supposing the Moon to be distant 59 or 60 Earth-radii, an inverse-square law would make terrestrial gravity at that distance no more than 1/3,600 of gravity on Earth, but Newton calculated it from the Moon's speed in her orbit as at most 1/4,000. [22] Even if the accidental discrepancy had not been present in this version of the 'Moon-test', Newton would still have been far from gravitation as a universal force, and the mathematical demonstration that the elliptical shape, the area-law, and the inverse-square law of force were all consistent parts of a single dynamic unity.

When, after the first part of the *Principia* had been rapturously welcomed by the Royal Society in London, Robert Hooke complained that Newton had received the notion of the inverse-square law of gravity from himself, 'though [Hooke] owns the Demonstration of the Curves generated thereby to be wholly your own', Newton was able to produce assurance and evidence that he had known it before; what, after all, he went on angrily had Hooke done but publish 'Borel's hypothesis' in his own name:

Borel did something in it & wrote modestly, he has done nothing & yet written in such a way as if he knew & had sufficiently hinted all but what remained to be determined by ye drudgery of calculations and observations . . . tis plain by his words he knew not how to go about it. Now is not this very fine? Mathematicians that find out, settle & do all the business must content themselves with being nothing but dry calculators & drudges & another that does nothing but pretend & grasp at all things must carry away all the invention as well as those that were to follow him as of those that went before . . .[23]

Newton's rage had urged him to this third outburst, in the furious invective that was to lash Leibniz in future years. One sees his point: Hooke had been *almost* as vague as Borelli, and certainly could never have produced dynamical demonstrations applicable to planetary motion: yet we may allow that the idea of a terrestrial projectile becoming a satellite in elliptical orbit was Hooke's own, though a 'guess' indeed as Newton rightly called it, moreover Hooke had

said (in a muddled way, it is true) that 'the Velocity [of the hyp
body under discussion] will be in a subduplicate proportion
[$V \propto 1/f^2$] and Consequently as Kepler Supposes Reciprocal to
which is another way, inferior but Keplerian, of formulating th
for the ellipse.

Hooke twice asked Newton to work all these ideas out for him n
ically. Newton maintained a dignified, uncooperative silence; nevertheless,
solved the problem. Quite how, we shall never know, because less than five years
later when the young astronomer Edmond Halley (who had worked with Flamsteed at Greenwich) took horse to Cambridge to visit Newton (August 1684)
that demonstration was already lost. But Newton was able to assure Halley
that the curve produced by an attractive force varying as the inverse square of
the distance would be an ellipse, and shortly after supply a demonstration of
this fact and a good deal more besides. The turning-point was the proposition
that comes first in Book I of the *Principia*: when a body revolves round a centre
of force the areas described by the radius-vectors are proportional to the times
taken, no matter what the law of force the curve described. This is a wonder-
fully general dynamic form of Kepler's second law, and it occurs already in the
Propositions on Motion which Newton wrote in the autumn of 1684 and sent to
the Royal Society; this is an outline sketch of the future *Mathematical Principles
of Natural Philosophy*. The proof of this fundamental proposition depends on
reasoning about infinitesimal straight-line segments and areas bounded by
them, and a central force acting in infinitesimal, instantaneous impulses (whose

Fig. 12.1   Newton's demonstration of the generalized Kepler's second law. The triangles ASB,
BSC, CSd are shown by geometry to be equal. The points B, C, D are reached after
equal successive times; the lines Bc, Cd, De are the inertial components of motion,
equal respectively to AB, BC, CD. The impulses (not necessarily uniform) towards
the centre S are directed along the lines BS, CS, DS and are represented vectorially
by Cc, Dd, Ee . . . The resultants AB, BC, CD, . . . form a continuous curve and
the action of the central force becomes continuous also, when the time elements
become infinitely small. (*Principia*, Book I, Proposition 1).

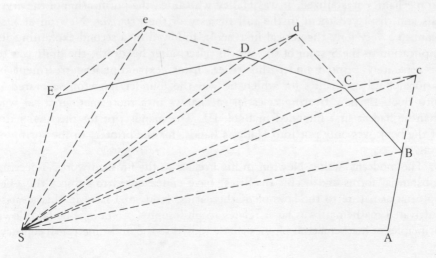

gnitude does not have to be considered), interpreted with the aid of the
arallelogram of forces. It is almost childishly elegant.

In the succeeding eighteen months Newton wrote a great part of the *Principia*, though not all in the form in which it was to be printed. This was an amazing achievement, which we can measure the more exactly by comparing the *Propositions* – dynamically still somewhat naive, showing some sophistication in the mathematics – with the mature *Principia* : using too an incomplete manuscript version pretty close to the final text. But if this was an almost incredibly rapid period of maturation, even more enigmatic is the evolution of Newton's thought between 1679, when he ceased to reply to Hooke, and August 1684 when he revealed his opinion with so much confidence to Halley. In one of Newton's angry ripostes about Hooke, he wrote to Halley:

I never extended the [inverse] duplicate proportion [the inverse-square law of gravity] lower than to ye superficies of the earth & before a certain demonstration I found the last year [1685] have suspected it did not reach accurately enough down so low: & therefore in the doctrine of projectiles never used it nor considered the motions of the heavens . . . [24]

Historians have for long agreed that Newton had in mind Proposition 71 of Book I of the *Principia* (as it was ultimately numbered in print) wherein he demonstrates the certainly counter-commonsensical result that a massive sphere attracts at points immediately adjacent to its surface as well as its points distant from the surface as though the whole mass of the sphere were concentrated at its centre; this, even though the lines of forces from the particles of the sphere to a point almost touching its surface are far from being mutually parallel. This is the only proposition singled out by Newton as particularly essential to the general theory of gravitation, after the discovery of the dynamics of Kepler's second law, and the correlation of the inverse-square law with conic-section trajectories. And this Proposition 71 is indeed not to be found in the early *Propositions on Motion*.[25]

If Hooke provided the irritant nucleus about which Newton's nascent ideas on mechanics crystallized, it was Halley who aided the purification of the crystals and displayed them in the full majesty of the *Principia*. Newton at first planned a very long theoretical first book, followed by a second explaining its application to the System of the World (later, after his death, the draft was to be separately printed under this title). Later, expanding the treatment of rational fluid mechanics (of which he was the founder) Newton separated it into Book II, now treating celestial mechanics in a more mathematical way than he had at first intended in Book III. The manuscript for the final parts of the book was only put into Halley's hands, for the printer, in the spring of 1687.

'The moderns' writes Newton in his Preface to the finished work, 'rejecting substantial forms and occult qualities, have endeavoured to subject the phenomena of nature to the laws of mathematics, [and so] I have in this treatise cultivated mathematics as far it relates to philosophy'. So doing, he laid down principles of mathematical physics that endured to the mid-nineteenth century.

He might also have as well written that he had cultivated philosophy so far as it served as the essential foundation for mathematical physics. Book I opens with Definitions of the fundamental concepts of mechanics: mass, quantity of motion, inertia, impressed force and centripetal force. We nowadays know how unsatisfactory Newton had found, already at some fairly early stage of his development, the basic concepts of nature and motion that Descartes had provided, not least the Cartesian identification of matter and extension.[26] In the *Principia* Newton's rejection of Cartesian relativism is evident in the celebrated Scholium to the Definitions, where Newton argues that absolute time, space and motion are to be distinguished from their relative counterparts that we ordinarily measure; for he held that reason and the stability of scientific theory alike required the existence of dimensions that are universal and unchanging (and which, indeed, correspond with the universal and unchanging character of the Creator of things): in Newton's view space and time have a being independent of the material universe which exists relatively within them. The distinction between absolute and relative, almost perversely confused by Descartes as Newton saw it, permitted him to affirm the absolute rotation of the Earth and planets and the relative fixity of the Sun as the centre of their motions, that is, to offer a proof of the Copernican hypothesis. For Newtonian dynamics demonstrates that the centre of gravity of the whole solar system is located within the body of the Sun, and because the planets exhibit a centripetal acceleration towards the Sun, they must be in absolute motion around it.

After the Definitions follow the Laws of Motion and their corollaries, the contingent principles of nature upon which the consequent mathematical theory is based. In both Book I and Book III (in the 'Rules of Reasoning') Newton stated explicit principles of scientific method, but not less influential was his implicit exemplification of a way of proceeding in science that was at once theoretical and experimental, mathematical and mechanical. Newtonian theoretical science was weakened neither by the loose articulation of Cartesian natural philosophy (since it was cemented step by step by geometrical demonstrations) nor by the latter's arbitrariness (since its conclusions were verified by experiment or observation) For example, in Book II the speed of sound as worked out from the theory of wave-motion Newton had established and the known density of air, 298 m/s (979 ft/s), is compared with experimental estimates of the speed of sound made by Newton (using echoes) and later by Sauveur (using organ pipes). Here, in fact, there was a serious discrepancy of about 46 m/s (150 ft/s) for which Newton attempted to account by *ad hoc* speculations, the true reason being found by Laplace at the end of the eighteenth century (Proposition 50). Or in Book III one finds at the very beginning of Newton's careful comparison of the periodic times of Jupiter's satellites as ascertained by several observers with the Third Law of Kepler and gravitational theory.

After these preliminaries, the bulk of Book I is taken up with the general theory of dynamics and the pure mathematics needed for its development. Here Newton studies the limit-case of a mass-point moving under the action of a force, especially a central attractive force, without commitment to a physical theory of force. Here, among other riches, one finds (Book I, Prop. 13) that where the central force obeys the inverse-square law, the orbit described by the mass-point will be elliptical, parabolic or hyperbolic; in Book III the second case will be applied to the motion of comets (Prop. 40). This had certainly not been known to Newton in 1684 when he had proved the Keplerian elliptical case only. Many propositions in Book I prepare the mathematical groundwork for the celestial mechanics demonstrated in Book III, but Newton is by no means wholly concerned with the gravitational case of the inverse-square law. He shows how Galileo's parabolic trajectory for projectiles is a special case of the operation of a constant force, and in Section 14 extends this idea to the 'optical' propositions concerning the motion of a light-particle (as previously mentioned).

Book III demonstrates the conformity of this dynamical theory of motion with the phenomena of the heavens, the tides, and the shape of the Earth. Newton once wrote that Kepler 'guessed' that the planetary orbits were ellipses, meaning that Kepler had generalized for all the planets the laws which he had actually confirmed by observations only in the case of Mars. He set himself, particularly, to demonstrate Kepler's second and third laws emphatically from measurements. In this he succeeded. He could now also confirm by a very exact calculation that the Moon is held in its orbit by a force corresponding to ter-restrial gravity. With much else in his programme, however, he encountered insurmountable difficulties. His theoretical calculation of the ratio between the Earth's polar and equatorial axes was excellent, but (for lack of adequate geo-detic information) he could not convince all contemporaries that the polar axis is geographically the shorter. This issue was only to be decisively settled in the mid-eighteenth century, thanks to the expeditions led by Maupertuis (in Lap-land) and Bouguer (in Peru). Similarly the whole problem of tidal ebb and flow was one not to be settled in a few months, even by a Newton, and (as he recognized himself) local topographical features commonly disguise the overall dynamic pattern. The principles, but not the details, of Newton's gravitational interaction between Sun, Moon and oceanic water were to be proved correct. The three-body problem latent here (Sun, Moon, Earth) and admitting no facile solution, was far more grave in relation to the motion of the Moon itself. This was the only part of the *Principia*, Newton confessed afterwards, which had made his head ache. The problem of the Moon was to trouble him over some thirty years, so long as the *Principia* was actively working in his mind; it was to bring about a furious and fatal quarrel with the Astronomer Royal, Flam-steed, whom Newton bullied unmercifully to produce observations, and it was finally to defeat Newton remaining as the one imperfection of the *Principia* to tarnish its glory, until Clairaut removed it.

The Moon's motion is, in detail, very complex so that the problem of pre-dicting with exactitude its position at some future time, or even the precise path of an eclipse on the surface of the Earth, is some orders more difficult than the problems of planetary motion. Two periodic irregularities in its motion had been known to Ptolemy; Tycho Brahe found two more. In the brief time avail-able to him, and with scarcely any suitable observational material, Newton could give hardly more than a promise of a dynamical theory of the Moon in the *Principia*'s first version (1687). Between then and 1713, when the second edition was published, he strove relentlessly to attain an objective which he felt must, in principle, be within his grasp, the establishment of a group of interlocking equations which, with the parameters measured, would define the Moon's motion accurately. Again, he did not succeed, though he defined three further irregularities making seven in all (these three Newtonian inequalities required telescopic instruments for their detection). As the French astronomer Lalande put it half a century later, 'it was reserved for Newton to take the greatest step forward in the theory of the Moon as in all the rest', yet the state of that theory at Newton's death was very unsatisfactory, incomplete and arbitrary-seeming as he had left it. When the mathematician Alexis-Claude Clairaut (1713–65) took it up in the 1740s, he at first supposed that only a modification to the inverse-square law of gravitation could reconcile Newton's theory to the observed movement of the lunar apogee but later after finding a new method of analysis he was able fully to vindicate the inverse-square law once more (*Théorie de la Lune*, 1752).

Clairaut was equally involved in the most spectacular of all the vindications of Newtonian astronomy – the prediction of the return of Halley's Comet. Its perihelion passage actually took place on 13 March 1759, having been predicted by Clairaut for 15 April, put back by slight revisions of the computations *post facto* to 31 March. Before Newton comets, popularly regarded as the most evil of portents, had been the mavericks of philosophical astronomy. Kepler had guessed that they travelled in straight lines through the heavens. Descartes regarded them as slipping round the edges of stellar vortices, Hevelius and Dörffel suggested conic-section orbits, Auzout proposed for one comet a circular orbit centred on Sirius. Amid this wild speculation no one had proposed any reliable means for determining the path of a comet from the observed places; this was first accomplished by Newton, although so late as 1681 he thought that the comet before and after its closest approach to the Sun was two distinct bodies, until Flamsteed convinced him otherwise. Newton's dynamical theory made it clear that a comet drawn to the Sun from an immense distance would pursue a visible path that was imperceptibly different from a parabola, whether or not it was an elongated ellipse in fact. Halley had been the first to guess that comets recorded at different dates in the past, if their elements proved to be roughly the same, might be the same recurrent body; he undertook the great and doubtful labour of computing from the meagre historical evidence their characteristic motions. In 1705, in his *Synopsis of the Astronomy of Comets*, he argued that the comets seen in 1531, 1607 and 1682 were the same object with a period of some 75 years (more than twice that of Saturn) and predicted its return in 1758, though well aware that the masses of Jupiter and Saturn would so influence the comet's motion as to imperil any preciser estimate. This was the problem that Clairaut had taken up and so closely solved, though (as Halley hoped) 'candid posterity will not refuse to acknowledge that this was first discovered by an Englishman'.[27]

To have brought comets within the scope of the laws of mechanics was a great triumph for Newton. They have nevertheless not ceased to amaze mankind, and Newton himself continued to regard them as mysterious bodies, involved in the destinies of our world. That none (as he thought) strike our globe was a sign of the divine governance. Still more interesting are the physical speculations about comets that he added to his ever-increasing monograph on their observed motions, beginning with the estimation that comets must be heated about 30,000 times hotter than our summer heat by their proximity to the Sun (say to 900,000° C). Therefore much matter will be volatized from them and the solid heads must retain their heat for a very long time – an earth-sized globe of red hot iron, Newton states, would hardly cool (to what temperature?) in 50,000 years (an estimate of interest to speculative cosmogonists later). The tail, therefore, is 'nothing else but a very fine vapour, which the head or nucleus of the comet emits by its heat', and which ascends from the Sun by a kind of repulsion, as all smokes and vapours must do (or so Newton alleges, without explanation). This very rare vapour must become diffused about the whole heavens, and be attracted to the planets by their gravitation and mixed with their atmospheres, since

for the conservation of the seas, and fluids of the planets, comets seem to be required that, from their exhalations and vapours after condensation, the diminution of the planetary fluids devoted to vegetation and putrefaction and so converted into dry earth, may be continually supplied and made up . . . and hence it is that the bulk of the solid earth is continually increased, and the fluids, if they are not supplied from without, must be in continual decrease and quite fail at last. I suspect, moreover, that it is chiefly from the comets that spirit comes, which is indeed the smallest but the most subtle and useful part of our air, and so much required to sustain the life of all things among us.[28]

Who would imagine that the writer who was only a few pages later to write the immortal sentence 'I do not feign hypotheses' would here, in this first sketch of chemical astronomy ever to be penned, link the willow-tree experiment of Van Helmont and Boyle, together with the aerial nitre hypothesis of Sendivogius, to the question of the constitution of the tails of comets?

Undoubtedly, however, the implication in the *Principia* for the physical theory of the universe that most struck contemporaries was Newton's attack on the prevailing aetherial theory of vortices. Here the antithesis between the attraction of Newton and the kinematic hypotheses of the neo-Cartesians became most stark, though Newton did not seek to press the fact, merely remarking: 'The hypothesis of vortices is pressed with many difficulties.' His own dynamical system of the world did not require rhetoric for its defence, for in the latter part of Book II of the *Principia* Newton had shown that a continuous solar vortex was totally incompatible with Kepler's laws of planetary motion.

Book II contains more difficult mathematics than Book I, including the only proposition in the whole *Principia* (on the shape of the solid of least resistance) for which Newton could find no synthetic demonstration. It is all concerned with fluids, but the various main problems are unrelated (resistance, flow, wave-motion, Boyle's Law, sound, vortices) and as Truesdell has pointed out, Newton's view of a fluid – for mathematical purposes – is not consistent; 'Almost all of the results are original' he remarks 'and but few are correct'. Perhaps, as there was no rational fluid mechanics before Newton apart from hydrostatics, this is hardly surprising; even a century's further work by mathematicians of genius building on Newton's foundations did not solve satisfactorily all the problems he tackled.[29] Vortical fluid motion is briefly tackled in Section IX. Newton makes the assumptions that the resistance due to viscosity in a fluid increases with the velocity, and that the extent of the fluid is infinitely great: then, he proves, the periodic times of portions of fluids in the vortex – or of bodies carried round in the fluid of the vortex, obviously – will be as the squares of the radii to the centre. But in the universe they are always as the $3/2$ power of the distance. Therefore the planets could not be borne in such a fluid vortex. Newton had done what all his predecessors had failed to do: he had made a mathematical model of a fluid vortex which, he said, could be confirmed by trials in deep water. If anyone could have devised an alternative model, conforming to Kepler's Laws, it would have been possible to argue that the celestial aetherial vortex was of *this* kind, not like the Newtonian model. No one took this step. Instead, two years after the publication of the *Principia* (but before reading more than a full review of Newton's book) Leibniz proposed to avoid Newton's criticism by dividing the vortex into separate layers, slipping without friction or viscosity one over the other, and each containing a planet.[30] These were fluid rather than solid, Ptolemaic spheres. It seems, in hindsight, an oddly elaborate and implausible mechanism to choose in order to salvage the mechanism of the universe from the destructive menace of attraction.

Efforts, ingenious if cumbersome, to save the vortices continued long after Newton was dead. None of them, surely, could meet the other direct and obvious point he had made against them, based on his dynamics and supported by observation:

The motions of the comets are exceedingly regular, are governed by the same laws with the motions of the planets, and can by no means be accounted for by the hypothesis of vortices; for comets are carried with very eccentric motions through all parts of the heavens indifferently, with a freedom that is incompatible with the notion of a vortex.[31]

We may perhaps link with the arguments against vortices Newton's dynamical proof that the Copernican system is physically true: the centre of gravity of the whole solar system is well within the body of the Sun, and therefore the planets revolve around the Sun. At the end of the Scholium on space and time Newton had insisted on the importance for philosophy of distinguishing real from apparent motions which (in the case of solar system) his analysis enabled him to do. His insistence is directed against Descartes who, by a piece of ingenious sophistry, had formally relieved his system of a possible pro-Copernican condemnation by authority. This casual treatment of a serious question had long irritated Newton, who was no relativist. In his youthful, unpublished tract 'On the Gravitation and Equilibrium of Fluids' – which, if it had ever been completed, might have considered the vortex theory – Newton wrote:

The Philosopher is hardly consistent who uses as the basis of Philosophy the motion of the vulgar which he had rejected a little before, and now rejects that motion as fit for nothing which alone was formerly said to be true and philosophical, according to the nature of things.[32]

This is a fundamental criticism. If Descartes, Newton says in the passage, chooses to treat motion in only relative terms, as though it is of no significance whether the Earth is, or is not, at rest at the centre of the universe, can one judge him a serious philosopher of motion? The *Principia* was to prove in mathematical detail that one could not.

In the fourteenth of his *Letters on the English Nation* (1734) Voltaire listed among the opposite beliefs held in Paris and London besides the shape of the Earth and the matter of vortices the question of the plenum and the void: the former espoused by Descartes and the neo-Cartesians Huygens, Malebranche and Leibniz, the latter by the Newtonians. The last-named, as we have just seen, confirmed his adhesion to the fluid universe in 1689, Huygens was to do so in his *Discourse on Gravity* and *Treatise on Light* of the following year. There is no doubt of their position and so long as neo-Cartesianism survived, so did its confidence in the aether-filled universe – which was, of course, to be revived with the victory of the wave-theory of light in the nineteenth century. The position of Newton and his followers is more obscure. An aetherist himself before embarking on the dynamics of the *Principia*, his success with a mathematical force-philosophy of nature led him to abandon aetherial mechanisms as empty, useless speculations. Whether or not space was really empty or really contained some extremely rarefied form of matter was a question the mathematical physicist could afford to ignore; he could be confident that space was certainly not filled with any kind of dense fluid capable of resisting the motions of the celestial bodies. This point was clearly made by Newton in Book III, Proposition 10: at a height of 320 km (200 miles) above the Earth's surface, Newton calculates (using Book II, Proposition 22) the density of the atmosphere is so reduced that the planet Jupiter passing through it would loose only a millionth part of its motion in a million years. But, 'the celestial regions being perfectly void of air and exhalations', the celestial bodies meet effectively zero resistance and continue their motions for an immense tract of time.

Could there be, nevertheless, an effective aether able to impel physical bodies in this space void of air and exhalations? What would it be like, and could it both impel bodies, and not resist them? Many worthy souls were uselessly to crack their brains over such problems, Newton did not. In 1692, however, pressed by the philosopher Richard Bentley, later to be Master of Newton's own College, Newton was brought to face directly the consequences of his denial of the aether. Bentley at first took it to be Newton's view that gravitation was essential to and inherent in matter. Not so, Newton assured him, only its own inertia was essential to matter; as 'for the cause of gravity [it] is what I do not pretend to know, and therefore would take time to consider it'. Furthermore, the notion of inherent gravity seemed to entail, as Newton put it, 'that one body should act upon another at some distance through a vacuum, without the mediation of anything else by and through which their action and force may be conveyed from one to another', and such material action at a distance was (he declared to Bentley) 'so great an absurdity, that I believe no man who has in philosophical matters a competent faculty of thinking, can ever fall into it'.[33]

Is not this an impasse? On the other hand Newton says that no aetherial means, or presumably any kind of material mechanism occupying the celestial spaces, can exist; on the other he says that the existence of gravitational force within a void without 'mediation' between the masses is absurd. Some of his friends thought that Newton meant that because God is omnipresent He everywhere causes the gravitational force to operate between bodies, Fatio de Duillier, the only Newtonian to frame an aetherial hypothesis for gravity in Newton's lifetime, which he believed Newton approved, nevertheless added

tho he would often seem to incline to think that Gravity had its Foundation only in the arbitrary Will of God.

At least one other Newtonian, David Gregory, also recorded this as being Newton's view. It squares with the idea certainly entertained by him that 'matter' is simply 'space' endowed by God with the properties of impenetrability, inertia and so forth. As the final passages in the ultimate versions of both *Opticks* and the *Principia* make crystal clear, Newton could not conceive of the Creator as a merely historical person. For him the Creation was not an event in time, over and done with, after which the universe was to run like a wound-up clock; he believed that constantly through time God wills the existence of the universe, and as Providence rules it. When this belief made its way to Leibniz's ears he mocked Newton as one who would make nature a perpetual miracle, and God an imperfect workman forever tinkering with his handiwork.[34] The Newtonians replied that to make the universe perpetually God's creature was necessary in religion, and that a miracle was a departure from the normal course ordered by God.

The pilotage in these high-flying metaphysics Newton (after a little) handed over to his friend Samuel Clarke, a divine.[35] They illustrate the danger as well as the necessity (in that age) of Newton's belief that to discourse of God belongs to natural philosophy. In the end they could not provide a way out of Newton's impasse, for to avow publicly that God's will was the only explanation of gravity was (for all his protests) to admit the other defect of favouring 'occult causes', that is, to admit desperately that the cause of gravity lay beyond the limits of natural philosophy. Other Newtonians were less inclined to metaphysics than Newton himself, among them Roger Cotes (1682–1716), who took charge of the second edition of the *Principia*,[36] where, in the explanatory preface he was persuaded to place before it, he declared in downright fashion

either gravity must have a place among the primary qualities of all bodies, or extension, mobility and impenetrability must not. And if the nature of things is not rightly explained by the gravity of bodies, it will not be rightly explained by their extension, mobility and impenetrability.

What Newton thought of this one we do not know, but friends had certainly advised Cotes to moderate his sentiments on this point before the preface was printed. In fact, time was to be on his side: the mathematical physicists of the late eighteenth century were perfectly content to think of gravitation thus pragmatically, as a universal phenomenon of nature, indeed a universal constant whose magnitude can be evaluated, without searching for any cause, physical or metaphysical, behind gravitation.

We should read the title of Newton's masterpiece, *The Mathematical Principles of Natural Philosophy*, in the simplest and most literal sense, not forgetting those aspirations which its author expressed in his Preface (and still more fully in rejected drafts)[37] for the general extension of the mathematical theory of forces and motions to other branches of philosophy than those to which he had addressed himself in that book. Newton's topic was not simply rational nor celestial mechanics, and gravitation was far from being the only force he had in mind. The seemingly disparate problems of which he was to furnish the synthetic solution were derived not from Kepler and Galileo alone, but from Descartes also. If the significance of the last-named for his early intellectual development was in his mature years diminished by Newton himself, and passed over by his successors, it has been rediscovered by modern scholars who have pointed out that even the title of the *Principia* is a reminiscence of Descartes's *Principia Philosophiae*. It is surely beyond question that Newton did not mean to replace the kinematic view of nature by a dynamic view merely with respect to the celestial spaces, rather he clearly intended this transformation to be of universal validity. In the *Principia* the burden of extending the dynamic view beyond gravitation falls on Book II, where moreover Newton takes a sophisticated use of quantitative experiment, paralleling for the same purposes of illustration and verification his use of astronomical and geodetic data in Book III. By moving into the theory of fluids, by showing how precisely the theory of motion in fluid mediums could be confirmed by experiments on the oscillation of pendulums or the fall of heavy bodies in air and water, he shifted his discourse from the mathematical world of abstractions to the real world of physics. In successive editions of the book Newton took trouble to improve the factual data by quoting the experiments of others. With increasing and perhaps over-anxious refinement Newton sought to show that when based on mathematical principles and when using correctly chosen and accurately determined parameters, the scientific model of nature could be fitted as accurately as one wished to the measured phenomena.[38] In Book II, Proposition 50 of the second edition, Newton took excessive pains to adjust his calculated value for the speed of sound in air to the latest experimental determination by Joseph Sauveur (1653–1716), the adjustment involving arbitrary physical assumptions that could not have been quantified even if they had been correct. In fact, as Laplace was to prove, the dynamic derivation of the speed of sound in this proposition was perfectly correct (at 298 m/s (979 ft/s)) and when appropriate allowance was made for thermodynamic effects unsuspected by Newton, this can be raised to match the experimental values.

With Galileo, the agreement between the mathematical expression and the world of experience had been, as it were, in principle only while the physical factors obstructing and complicating the elegance of a simply geometrical universe had resisted evaluation and calculation. Newton proved that by successive approximations they could all be brought within the terms of a comprehensive theory. Ours cannot be an ideal Platonic universe as Galileo and Kepler supposed:

Each time a planet revolves it traces a fresh orbit, as happens also with the motion of the Moon, and each orbit is dependent upon the combined motions of all the planets, not to mention their actions upon each other. Unless I am much mistaken, it would exceed the force of human wit to consider so many causes of motion at the same time, and to define the motions by exact laws which would allow of an easy calculation.[39]

The rich and complex universe we inhabit is, nevertheless, capable of mathematical analysis: Newton meant this to be true of the whole range of phenomena not only extensively but intensively, from the microcosm to the macrocosm.

This, surely, is implied in the Rules of Reasoning as well as in many mathematical propositions of the *Principia* (where the passage from particles to gross bodies corresponds to that from the infinitestimal to the integral), and in numerous discursive passages not least in the Queries to *Opticks*. Celestial mechanics logically required a foundation in rational mechanics: only so could it properly become a branch of natural philosophy. Here again Newton and Descartes were more alike than the crude antithesis of their philosophies would allow. Descartes had proceeded, in his *Principles of Philosophy*, from his clear ideas of what must be in the world through the laws of motion and the properties of moving bodies to his celestial machine. Newton did likewise: developing his mathematical method from the Definitions and the Laws, through the long series of analyses of the motions of bodies in many different conditions, until he could at last discern in the heavenly motions special cases of those principles of motion that he had already elucidated. Thus, on the one hand the theory of universal gravitation was rendered intellectually respectable by its deductive relation to a universal dynamical philosophy of nature, while on the other hand this philosophy was given experiential substance and quantitative confirmation by its inductive relation to astronomy. But for this latter relation the dynamical philosophy would have been merely speculative; but for the former relation the theory of the planets would have been a phenomenalistic as Hooke's 'supervening attractive principle'.

What is to be said of *Opticks* in this connection? First, the inherent contrast between the aspect of Newton's scientific mind revealed in that book, and what is discerned in the *Principia*, can be overstated even though later Newtonians were conscious of inheriting a dual tradition. *Opticks* like the *Principia* begins with axioms and continues through propositions in the Euclidean manner though, Newton promises, these are to be proved 'by Reason and Experiments'; in his university lectures of 1670–72, however, Newton had covered the same ground in a far more traditionally geometrical manner in satisfaction of Newton's 'wish to create a sophisticated mathematical theory of optical phenomena (rather than merely to describe observed effects)'.[40] The change of style between the *Optical Lectures* and *Opticks*, like that between Book III of the *Principia* and the *System of the World*, is a result of policy rather than of difference in content or method. Secondly, as already noted, Newton surely hoped to create an optical mechanics which would have been the bridge between geometrical and physical optics, had it been in his power to build it. Had it matured, it might have stood as a 'Book IV' in the *Principia*. Fourthly, we must not overlook the Queries in *Opticks*, Newton's last and most enigmatic scientific testament, occasioned by the incomplete state of that book

since I have not finished this part of my Design [concerned with diffraction] I shall conclude with proposing only some Queries, in order to a farther search to be made by others.

The Queries link *Opticks* firmly with the *Principia*, especially Query 29 where Newton asks:

Are not the Rays of Light very small Bodies emitted from shining Substances? . . . Pellucid Substances act upon the Rays of Light at a distance in refracting, reflecting and inflecting them and the Rays mutually agitate the Parts of those Substances at a distance for heating them; and this Action and Re-action at a distance very much resembles an attractive Force between Bodies. If Refraction be performed by Attraction of the Rays, the Sines of Incidence must be to the Sines of Refraction in a given Proportion, as we shewed in our Principles of Philosophy: And this Rule is true by Experience.

In this last sentence Newton of course refers to Section XIV of Book II of the *Principia*, whose not wholly apposite propositions were to stand for ever as the only published hint of what such on optical mechanics might have been. Later in the same Query he put new touches to the notion connecting colour with the size of the light-particle (as we saw before), and suggesting that the particles 'by their attractive Powers, or some other Force' create vibrations in what they act upon, so creating the 'Fits' responsible for Newton's Rings.

Now indeed Newton ran into qualitative speculations. In Query 31, where he dealt at some length with the last of the interparticulate forces considered in any detail, 'attraction' becomes almost as general an idea as 'shape' had been for Descartes. Three general ideas emerge: firstly,

there are Agents in Nature able to make the Particles of Bodie stick together by very strong Attractions. And it is the Business of experimental Philosophy to find them out.

The point of this is that we must suppose all physical bodies to be compounded of different kinds of particles held together by these powerful short-range attractions: chemical change is the process by which these attractions (and therefore the combinations) are modified. Secondly, Newton supposes that there may be an ordered structure in matter:

the smallest Particles of Matter may cohere by the strongest Attractions, and compose bigger Particles of weaker virtue; and many of these may cohere and compose bigger Particles whose Virtue is still weaker, and so on for divers Successions, until the Progression ends in the biggest Particles on which the Operations in Chymistry, and the Colours of natural Bodies depend, and which by cohering compose Bodies of sensible Magnitude.

326

In a draft Newton explained this notion further and related it to crystal structure: the particles do not coalesce at random 'into heaps' but like 'snow and salts coalesce into regular figures. From the very smallest particles bigger ones are formed, and from these the largest ones, all in a lattice structure'. If the attractive forces become weaker as the particle assemblies become larger, they also exhibit qualitative variation, and this principle of variable affinity is the third of Newton's ideas about the structure of matter, heavily illustrated by chemical examples in Query 31:

When Salt of Tartar *per deliquim*, being poured into the Solution of any Metal, precipitates the Metal and makes it fall down to the bottom of the Liquor in the form of Mud: Does not this argue that the acid Particles are attracted more strongly by the Salt of Tartar than by the Metal, and by the stronger Attraction go from the Metal to the Salt of Tartar?

Indeed the qualitative variation may go all the way from positive to negative, Newton hints, so that there may be short-range repulsive, as well as attractive forces; in optical phenomena he suggests further, some bi-polar force like magnetism may be at work.

Here is a splendid and many-faceted vision. Newton in his *Opticks* had to leave it as such, as he had in the rejected long Preface to the *Principia* in 1687. He there 'proposed the inquiry whether or not there be many forces of this kind, never yet perceived, by which the particles of bodies agitate one another and coalesce into various structures'. If more could be learned of such forces, then the dynamic view of nature could be firmly extended far beyond the theory of gravitation, essentially limited to large masses:

For if Nature be simple and pretty comfortable to herself, causes will operate in the same kind of way in all phenomena, so that the motion of smaller bodies may depend upon certain smaller forces just as the motions of larger bodies are ruled by the greater force of gravity. For if all natural motions can be explained through such forces, nothing more will remain than to enquire the cause of gravity, magnetic attraction and the other forces.[41]

This was the great philosophical and experimental programme of enquiry that Newton bequeathed to posterity, to be considered again in the last chapter of this book.

He must have clearly perceived that the problem of treating the transformations effected in chemical experiments in terms of particle dynamics must be very different from those which he had solved in relation to gravitation. Long before his death two attempts had been made by faithful adherents of the Newtonian philosophy to push it further into chemistry. The first was John Keill (1671–1721), a competent mathematician who was to be Newton's advocate in the quarrel with Leibniz over the invention of the calculus, and who published a quasi-mathematical paper on chemical attractions in the *Philosophical Transactions* for 1708, that is, two years after Newton had first introduced them into the Latin *Optice* of 1706.[42] Keill's 'theorems' despite a few cross-references to the *Principia* are nothing more than a combination of the Newtonian concept of varying affinity with the Cartesian idea of varying particle size and shape; so his Theorem 18:

The size of a body more dense than water may be so diminished that in the end it will remain suspended in water and not descend under the force of its own gravity. From this the reason appears, why salt or metallic particles and others of the same kind, reduced to the smallest size, remain suspended in their solvents.

This seems to be an empty and pointless hypothetical exercise, of which no one ever made any effective use. Not much more can be alleged on behalf of the *Chymical Lectures* (1709) of the physician John Friend (1672–1728), 'in which' the title continues, 'almost all the Operations of Chymistry are reduced to their true Principles, and the Laws of Nature'. It is true that Friend did account for distillation, fermentation, precipitation and all the other technically-named chemical processes by combinations and permutations of the ideas of Query 31, but apart from enriching the exemplification it cannot be said to have made the reader any wiser, or to have got any closer to disclosing the nature of the non-gravitational forces of which Newton had written. Not surprisingly, such a dubious but Newtonian production received a devastating review by Leibniz.

In fact, as we know, nature is less conformable to herself than Newton supposed for the homology between large-scale and small-scale forces that he imagined does not exist. And though his injunction to investigate the nature of forces more thoroughly in the future may have had some immediate effect in the electrical studies which so much interested Newton in his last years, they were to prove irrelevant to the progress of chemistry. Just as, in the eighteenth century, 'experimental natural philosophy' was increasingly to be marked off by its separate character from 'mathematical philosophy', so too it was to be divided at least as rigorously from the 'theory of matter', increasingly (among the last post-Newtonians like Boscovich and Priestley) a topic of philosophical speculation, the Newtonian equivalent of neo-Cartesianism. Not for the last time, Newton in 1726 seemed to have placed all physical science within the mathematicians' grasp; not for the last time – think of Faraday or Rutherford! – physical theory would escape from the embrace.

NOTES

1. University Library, Cambridge MS. Add. 4000, 14v. Quoted in D. T. Whiteside, *Mathematical Papers of Isaac Newton*, Cambridge U.P., 1967–81, I, 7–8.
2. ULC, MS Add. 3968, f. 85, from I. Bernard Cohen, *Introduction to Newton's Principia*, Cambridge U.P., 1971, 291. Both this passage and the last quoted had been printed many times previously. This passage probably belongs to 1718: see A. Rupert Hall and Laura Tilling, *Correspondence of Isaac Newton*, VI, Cambridge U.P., 1976, 454–62.
3. *Opticks*, London, 1931 reprint, 402.
4. In fact, Oldenburg had died in September 1677.
5. Newton, *Correspondence*, II, Cambridge U.P., 1960, 212–31.
6. D. T. Whiteside, 'The Mathematical Principles underlying Newton's *Principia Mathematica*', *Jour. Hist. Astronomy*, 1, 1970, 116–38; (quotations, 119, 120 (slightly abbreviated)).

7. A. Rupert Hall, *Philosophers at War*, Cambridge U.P., 1980, 125.

8. Newton, *Correspondence*, III, Cambridge U.P., 1961.

9. The mathematical comparison is from Whiteside's edition: the million word guess (often repeated) is from J. M. Keynes in Royal Society, *Newton Tercentenary Celebrations*, Cambridge U.P., 1947.

10. A. R. and M. B. Hall in *Archives Inst. d'Hist. des Sciences*, 11, 1958, 113–52.

11. B. J. T. Dobbs, *The Foundations of Newton's Alchemy*, Cambridge U. P. 1975; R. S. Westfall, *Never at Rest*, Cambridge U.P., 1980 – by far the best life of Newton.

12. Newton, *Correspondence*, III, 217–9. It is not easy to discern what was in Newton's mind in writing this letter, except lack of enthusiasm for Boyle's 'recipes' – 'one of them a considerable Expt. & may prove of good use in medicine for analysing bodies, the other is only a knack'.

13. D. T. Whiteside, *Mathematical Papers of Isaac Newton*, IV, Cambridge U.P., 1971, General Introduction. A major mathematical effort of Newton's in these years was preparing his two large letters of 1676 for Leibniz, but the basic materials for these were all at hand.

14. Newton to Boyle, 28 February 1679 (*Correspondence*, II, 288 ff.).

15. Newton to Hooke, 28 November 1679, ibid., 300–3. Hooke's supposed observation of annual parallactic shift in α Draconis proved to be worthless.

16. Ibid., Vol. II, pp. 305 ff, and III, 438 ff.

17. J. L. Russell, 'Kepler's laws of planetary motion', *Brit. Jour. Hist. Sci.*, 2, 1964, 1–24.

18. D. T. Whiteside, 'Newton's early thoughts on planetary motion', *Brit. Jour. Hist. Sci.*, 2, 1964, 117–37: and *Jour. Hist. Astronomy*, 1, 1970, 5–15.

19. *Astronomia Carolina*, London, 1661, 39.

20. J. W. Herivel, *The Background to Newton's Principia*, Oxford U.P., 1965.

21. *Correspondence*, II, 331, 341.

22. Ibid., I, 297–303. Newton's error arose from his taking (from Galileo's *Dialogo*) too small a value for the Earth's radius. No doubt Newton read this book in the English (1661) or Latin (1635) version; he never read the *Discourses*, which were almost inaccessible in English.

23. Ibid., II, 438. Newton to Halley, 20 June 1686.

24. Ibid., II, 435. Newton's interest in projectiles, mentioned here, went back to 1674; see Whiteside, *Math. Papers*, VI, 1974, 6–8 and A. R. Hall, *Ballistics in the Seventeenth Century*, Cambridge U.P., 1952, 120–21.

25. Newton's emphasis on this demonstration is partly directed against Hooke; he could have chosen others for the same purpose, however.

26. See *De Gravitatione* in A. R. and M. B. Hall, *Unpublished Scientific Papers of Isaac Newton*, Cambridge U.P., 1962, 1978.

27. A. Armitage, *Edmond Halley*, Nelson: London, 1966, 161–7. Halley first proposed his identification of this recurrent comet to the Royal Society in 1696. He also proposed a period of 575 years for Julius Caesar's comet (44 BC:)–AD 531, 1106, 1680, 2255 (*Principia*, 3rd edn, 1726, 501)

28. *Principia*, 1726, 515–6. Newton seems to have written this expanded version of the physical theory of comets after finishing the *System of the World*. It is found in the printer's MS. of Book III of the *Principia*.

29. Clifford Truesdell, 'Rational fluid mechanics, 1687–1765', Editor's introduction to *L. Euleri Opera Omnia*, Ser. II, XII, Orell Füssli: Zürich 1954, xii.

30. G. W. Leibniz, 'Tentamen de motuum coelestium causis'. *Acta Eruditorum*, Feb. 1689,

an essay hotly criticized by Newton. E. J. Aiton, *The Vortex Theory of Planetary Motion*, Macdonald: London and New York, 1972; Westfall, *Force in Newton's Physics*, 308–10.

31. Opening of General Scholium concluding the *Principia* (added to 2nd edn, 1713).
32. Hall and Hall (op. cit. Note 26), 124.
33. I. Bernard Cohen, *Isaac Newton's Papers & Letters on Natural Philosophy*, Harvard University Press: Cambridge, Mass., 1958, 1978, 298, 302.
34. Hall (op. cit., Note 7), Ch. 10. A Koyré, *From the Closed world to the Infinite Universe*, Johns Hopkins University Press: Baltimore, 1957.
35. H. G. Alexander, *Leibniz-Clarke Correspondence*, Manchester University Press: Manchester, 1956.
36. A. Rupert Hall in *Proc. R. Soc. London A*, **338**, 1974, 397–417.
37. Hall and Hall (op. cit., Note 26), 305–8.
38. R. S. Westfall, *Never at Rest*, Cambridge U.P., 1980, 733–9.
39. Hall and Hall (op. cit., Note 26), 281.
40. Cambridge University Library, *The Unpublished First Version of Isaac Newton's Lectures on Optics*, 1973, Introduction.
41. Hall and Hall (op. cit., Note 26), 306, 307.
42. *Phil. Trans..* **26**, 1708, 97–110.

CHAPTER THIRTEEN

The range of life

Biological study, as it is practised today in laboratories and field stations, is essentially a creation of the nineteenth century. The work of Darwin on evolution, of Mendel on genetics, of Schleiden and others on the cell theory, so transformed the texture of the biologist's thought that it would be appropriate to attribute to the period 1830–70, rather than to any earlier age, the 'biological revolution' which completed the modern scientific outlook. The belief in the fixity of species was no less respectable than the belief in the fixity of the Earth; the belief that the Creator must have personally attended to the fabrication of every kind of diatom and bramble was no less primitively animistic than the belief that His angels governed the revolutions of the planetary orbs. Exactly as the mechanistic philosophy of the seventeenth century was accused of encouraging scepticism and irreligion, on a greater scale (because the issue was more clear and more decisive) the mechanistic biologists of the nineteenth century met the full force of ecclesiastical wrath. The liberty of the scientist to direct his theories in accordance with the scientific evidence alone was equally at stake. But there is this difference. Biology was certainly 'modern' – in some respects if not all – before the nineteenth century. A great Renaissance had already occurred, which itself far surpassed all that had gone before. Materials had been heaped up from which a great generalization such as evolution could be drawn. Above all, the scientific method of biology was already in existence – that was not the creation of the nineteenth century. The researches of Leeuwenhoek and Malpighi, the systematics of Ray and Linnaeus, were preliminaries as essential to the syntheses which introduced the truly modern outlook as the work of Copernicus and Galileo was to that of Newton.

None of the ancient founders of biology was primarily interested in collection, description and classification as ends in themselves. Aristotle the zoologist and Theophrastus the botanist were always philosophers – their purpose was to investigate the functioning of living organisms; Dioscorides studied botany as the servant of medicine. Partly, perhaps, because the range of species examined was comparatively small – neither Aristotle nor Theophrastus knew more than about five hundred distinct kinds of animals or plants – the problem of cataloguing them did not become of overriding importance, though much thought was given to order and arrangement. Since the Greek empire extended into India, exotic species were available, but they did not attract great attention. To the Greek mind, the attempt to answer the questions that living nature posed was more important than the compilation of information, and for this the materials close at hand were sufficient. Over-leaping a great space of time, in the last century and taxonomy have again become no more than specialized branches of biology. The study of function, of the processes of growth and differentiation, has assumed a more fundamental importance. The experimental has replaced the encyclopaedic method, so that a modern zoologist may find a greater interest in the works of Aristotle than in those of any natural historian of the pre-Darwinian age.

The intervening period has, indeed, very special characteristics. For long there were no adequate successors to the Greek botanists of the fourth century BC. The Romans were competent writers on agriculture, but such an author as Pliny added nothing beyond the cult of marvels to the existing texts which he pillaged. The philosophic spirit of the Greeks almost perished, and was only revived in the botanical work of Albert the Great (*De Vegetabilibus et Plantis*, *c.* 1250). Albert was an Aristotelean botanist – at least, his main authority was a translation of two books on plants then attributed to Aristotle.[1] He was interested in the philosophy of plant growth, in the variety of their structures and (as he believed) in their constant mutations. Care in the morphological analysis of plants for purposes of description and identification was combined with renewed attention to the problem of classification, but Albert was not greatly impressed by the importance of cataloguing. Such an emphasis was then unusual, for in his time herbalism – medical botany – had already become a principal interest.

Herbalism looked to Dioscorides, rather than to Aristotle and Theophrastus. Before the fall of Rome the tradition he founded had already suffered debasement and the decline, both in matter and in illustration, continued throughout the early Middle Ages. In the thirteenth century, however, there were already skilful herbalists with a good knowledge of Dioscorides and his commentators, some familiarity with exotic drugs, and an interest in description and identification. The herbal of one of them, Rufinus, serves to show that he, at least, did not scruple to add remarks of his own to the literary tradition, and that he was aware of distinctions in kind unknown to the more famous compilers of the sixteenth century. Rufinus was clearly well acquainted with drug plants and druggists, but he made no attempt to classify, merely arranging his notes in alphabetical order. The greater part of his text was made up of quotations from earlier pharmacological authorities (Dioscorides, the *Circa instans* of about 1150, the *Tables* of Salerno, and others).

The herbal flourished, to become enormously popular soon after the invention of printing. But the herbalist's interest in the plant was always in knowledge of means to an end. Some of his medicaments were minerals, or derived from animal sources, and it was only because such a large proportion of medieval physic was derived from vegetables, that the pharmacopoeia assumed a preponderantly botanical form. Thus descriptive zoology was a poor relation of herbalism, though animals were also described as the immediate companions and servants of man, because they offered useful moral lessons, and because some of them had an exotic or symbolic fascination. Conceiving that the world was created for the use and instruction of man in working out his own salvation, the medieval mind naturally adopted a somewhat functional approach to the living state. The task of the naturalist was simply to describe living things, with their particular uses (or wonders, or edifying properties) so that other men might use them (or wonder at them, or be edified). Despite the occasional philosophic questioning of an Albert, there was no powerful motive to elevate him above a lexicographical mentality. And the naturalist was less interested in collecting facts about creatures that might form the material of a science, than in human reactions to this and that, in the diseases against which a given plant was supposed to be beneficial, in the moral to be drawn from the habits of the ant-lion.

Thus the origins of natural history were essentially anthropocentric, in the Roman Pliny, in the early Christian compilers like Isidore of Seville, in the thirteenth-century encyclopaedia of Bartholomew the Englishman, in the late medieval herbalists. Human interest in nature was limited to the production of a *catalogue raisonné*.

The early stages of the Renaissance brought no important reorientation. Occasionally the representational art of a 'Gothic' stone mason or wood carver had enriched a cathedral with a recognizable likeness of a living species. About the beginning of the fifteenth century the graphic artist began to realize the aesthetic possibilities of exact imitation of nature in the illumination of man-uscripts – here were the roots of both the naturalistic art of a Dürer, and biological illustration. By 1550 the technique of life-like illustration had been mastered, with greatest distinction in the herbals of Brunfels (1530) and Fuchs (1542). This technique was ultimately as necessary to botany and zoology as to human anatomy, but it did not occasion any immediate enhancement of the level of botanical knowledge. Brunfels, indeed, tried to find some more natural arrangement than that of an alphabetical list, but the latter was by no means abandoned as yet. The botanists of the sixteenth century, with the exception of Cesalpino and Gesner, were still herbalists, and the herbal was still an adjunct to the pharmacopoeia, enabling the apothecary to identify such medi-cinal plants as Swallow-wort and Fennel, Sage and Fumitory, whose names are perpetuated on the majolica drug-pots of the time.

Humanism had its effect upon biology, as upon all branches of science, without challenging the main emphasis on collection and classification. The authority of Dioscorides and Theophrastus was reinforced rather than weakened; their texts were better understood, but did not encourage originality in ideas. Mediterranean botanists particularly took up the task of identifying more exactly the species described by Dioscorides; some, like Mattiolo, Cordus and Conrad Gesner, were content to put forward their own work as expansions of his, with considerable display of philological learning. Gradually it was learnt that Greek names had been abused by application to species quite different from those formerly known to the Greeks themselves; and that, moreover, the names often covered a whole group of similar plants, not a specific type. North-ern botanists now acquired knowledge of plants not included in the traditional Mediterranean flora; Charles de l'Écluse alone is reputed to have found two hundred new species in Spain and Portugal (1576), and later he was equally successful in Austria and Hungary. Cataloguing and description were extended far beyond the range of the merely useful. Decorative plants, like daffodil and horse-chestnut – this last one of many importations into Western Europe at this period – were noticed as well as the medicinal, along with many new species reported by the explorers to the Far East and the Americas. The common and uncommon plants of hedgerow, pasture and upland were no longer neglected. A garden was now judged by the multitude, rarity and beauty of the species represented in it, while the *Hortus Siccus* became a repository of trophies exchanged among collectors. For the men of the Renaissance collected plants, plumages and skins as they amassed coins, antique statuary and manuscripts.

Though the character of the product of this vastly increased activity in botany, or herbalism, was not greatly changed in the sixteenth century, the character of the new herbalist was certainly modified. As he attached less importance to medicinal value, he became more keenly interested in fine dis-tinctions; whereas the ancient and medieval herbalist had hardly been concerned with a unit smaller that the genus, their successors began to discriminate between different species within the genera, and even between varieties of the same species. Again, the new naturalists were often scholars and gentlemen, they had therefore greater opportunities for botanizing over wide areas, even despatching emmissaries for this purpose; they could acquire a more extensive literary knowledge and employ the best draughtsmen. Such men felt the aesthetic appeal of nature keenly. As Fuchs wrote:

There is no reason why I should expatiate on the pleasure and delight of acquiring knowledge of plants, since there is no one who does not know that there is nothing in this life more pleasant and delightful than to wander over mountains, woods and fields garlanded and adorned with most exquisite little flowers and plants of various sorts. . . . But it increase that pleasure and delight not a little, if there be added an acquaintance with the virtues and powers of these plants.[2]

Fuchs's observation ends with a touch of that pedantry which very often divides the scientist from the artist; the scientific tendency is, after all, to dissect and destroy the thing of beauty, but there is no reason to doubt that the intellectual inquisitiveness which leads *via* microscope and herbarium to the unreadability of a *Flora*, may have its aesthetic foundation. This also links naturally with the urge to collect and preserve, the emphasis upon the rare and the expensive, which are so typical of biology from the sixteenth to the nine-teenth century. The botanist's character was complex. He could claim that his activities were useful to man, and contributed to the worship of God. In nature he saw abundant evidence of Design, and so created the tradition which led through Ray's *Wisdom of God* to Paley's *Natural Theology, or Evidence of the Existence and Attributes of the Diety, collected from the Appearances of Nature*. There was thus a variety of arguments for commending biology to the attention of a serious and devout mind, of which medical utility was not the least important. Few naturalists in this period would have given whole-hearted support to the views of the Bohemian, Adam Zaluzian (1592):

It is customary to connect Medicine with Botany, yet scientific treatment demands that we should consider each separately. For the fact is that in every art, theory must be disconnected and separated from practice, and the two must be dealt with singly and individually in their proper order before they are united. And for that reason, in order that Botany, which is (as it were) a special branch of Natural Philosophy, may form a unit by itself before it can be brought into connection with other sciences, it must be divided and unyoked from Medicine.[3]

The task of the descriptive biologist was also far more complex than that of the cataloguer of human artefacts, indeed, it was this complexity which enforced the development of systematics. Problems of nomenclature, identification and classification rather suddenly became acute between 1550 and 1650, and constituted one of the main theoretical topics in biology for nearly three hundred years. Naturalists tried to follow a 'natural' order of groupings – which meant that they were long deceived by superficial characteristics. Aristotle had distinguished, in zoology, between viviparous and oviparous creatures, between the cephalopodia and other molluscs; Dioscorides had distributed plants among the four rough groups of trees, shrubs, bushes and herbs. Lesser distinctions, between eggs-with-shells and eggs-without-shells, between deciduous and non-deciduous, flowering and non-flowering, were also very ancient. In the main such distinctions were preserved as the basis of arrangement until late in the seventeenth century. Nomenclature was equally in need of reform, if standardization were to be obtained, and the name to have a logical connection with the system. Description was the very basis of a communion of understanding in biology, for on it depended the hope of arriving at a single comprehensive *Flora* which would enable all men to agree upon the identity of any given specimen. Here the classical tradition was very frail, partly owing to the defects of its language in referring to the parts of animals and flowers.

No consistent answers to the problems of taxonomy were produced before the eighteenth century; even today the concept 'species' cannot be exactly defined, and many systems of classification have succeeded that of Linnaeus. Nevertheless, the great compilers of the sixteenth century, in their attempts to make an encyclopaedic survey of all living things, more than mastered their Greek inheritance and demonstrated the fruits of exact observation. Their view of their undertaking was of course far from strictly biological. Thus Conrad Gesner, in his enormous *Historiae Animalium* (published 1551–1621), besides naming and describing the animal, discussed its natural functions, the quality of its soul, its use to man in general and as food or medicine in particular, and gave a concordance of literary references to it. The Italian naturalist Ulissi Aldrovandi strove for even deeper omniscience when (for example) writing of the Lion he noted at length its significance in dreams, its appearance in symbolism and mythology, and its use in hunting and tortures. But Aldrovandi was also one of the first zoologists to give a skeletal representation of his subjects where possible. Along with the spirit of sheer compilation there developed a growing tendency to specialize, exemplified in Rondelet's book on Fishes

(1554), in Aldrovandi's treatise on the different breeds of dog, in the Englishman Thomas Moufet's *Theatre of Insects* (1634). All these works, and some portions of the vast encyclopaedias, were written with conspicuous attention to the kind of detail that could only be obtained through systematic personal observation. Most of the old fables debasing natural history – the birth of bees from the flesh of a dead calf, and of geese from barnacles, the inability of the elephant to bend its legs, and the tearfulness of crocodiles – were at least doubted, though they lingered long in popular books.

The classification of animals in accordance with Aristotle's scheme presented no great difficulties. The Latin names gave sufficient identification, superficial distinctions were marked. In the group of oviparous quadrupeds for instance, Gesner had only a few divisions – frogs, lizards, tortoises – and he knew only three or four different kinds in each. Plants were more recalcitrant. Alphabetical lists had their uses, and so had others in which the groups consisted of plants having a similar habitat or function. When the attempt was made to render identification easier by adopting arrangements based on form and structure, more profound difficulties were encountered. In general, it seemed desirable to make the arrangement as natural as possible, by taking into consideration the maximum number of characteristics, but it was difficult to decide what the most important of these were. Reliance on superficial features, like the possession of prickles, or habits like climbing, was apt to prove very deceptive. The early systematists consequently tended to make increasing use of a single characteristic of the plant as a determinant – de l'Obel chose the leaf, and Cesalpino the fruit. One advantage of this method was that it led to the more intensive study of particular parts of the plant, especially the flower, and to the improvement of descriptive terminology. Such systems, of which Linnaeus's was the logical and highly successful climax, were artificial, convenient indices to the prodigality of nature; but they did promote conscious study of the problems of taxonomy. Before 1550 there were hardly any firm principles by which species were distinguished, while the arrangement of the species was a matter for the discretion of each author. By 1650 there was a great measure of agreement on specific identities, and it was gradually becoming clear that there was a difference between a search for a *method*, which would make identification easy, and an endeavour to trace the natural affinities between species and larger groupings.

Attention to systematics was partly enforced by the sheer multiplicity of species. Some six thousand distinct plants had already been described by 1600, and the number trebled during the following century. Since it was the pride of the good botanist to be able to identify every plant presented to him, or if it were a new species to indicate its relationship to known ones, there were strong reasons for correlating identification and arrangement with one or more morphological characteristics. Caspar Bauhin, in 1623, outlined the natural groupings of botanical species more clearly than any of his predecessors, and made more extensive use of the binomial nomenclature in which one element of the name was shared by the *genus*, or group of closely related species. A little later Jung, at Hamburg, greatly improved the technical description of the disposition and shape of leaves, and of the various parts of the flower. A younger contemporary, the Englishman John Ray (1627–1705), laid the foundations of modern descriptive and systematic biology, in botany at least owing something to Jung's methods. Ray had some experience of dissection, but he was not an experimenter, nor a microscopist. Though his interests extended to the ecology, life-history and physiology of his subjects – thus he was much more than a plain cataloguer – he did not himself do much to advance the newer branches of biology growing up in his time. On the other hand, his philosophic and general scientific outlook was wider than that of most succeeding naturalists; like many other Fellows of the Royal Society, he was fascinated by technological progress, accepted the broad picture of a mechanistic universe under divine surveillance, and joined in the expulsion from biology of myth and mystery.

Ray was perhaps the first biologist to write separate treatises on the principles of taxonomy.[4] These were exemplified in his great series of descriptive volumes, the *Historia generalis plantarum* (1686–1704) and *Historia insectorum* (1710), with the *Ornithologia* (1676) and *Historia Piscium* (1686) in which he collaborated with his patron, Francis Willughby. Taken together – for all these books were actually finished and published by Ray – they represented by far the most complete and best arranged survey of living nature that had ever been attempted. Ray had exercised his keen faculty for observation intensively over the whole of England, and extensively over much of Western Europe; he was deeply learned in the writings of ancient and modern naturalists; above all, he welcomed new ideas. From Grew he accepted as probable the sexual reproduction of plants; from Redi and Malpighi the experimental disproof of spontaneous generation; and he himself taught that fossils were the true remains of extinct species, not mere 'sports' of nature nor God-implanted tests of man's faith in the truth of the Genesis story. If the enumeration of species was his principal task – which still left him room for his *Collection of English Proverbs*, *Topographical Observations*, and *Wisdom of God* – Ray was very far from supposing that classification was the end of biology.

In botanical systematics Ray favoured a 'method' which was more natural than those of his contemporary Tournefort and his successor Linnaeus. He admitted that the familiar triple distinction between trees, shrubs and herbs was popular rather than scientific, though he continued to use it while also recognizing the far more fundamental distinction between mono- and dicotyledonous plants. For finer discrimination he relied upon no single characteristic but appealed to the forms of root, leaf, flower and fruit. The necessity for a formal method of classification was fully apparent to him – it was particularly required by beginners in botany – but he did not expect that all living forms could be perfectly accommodated within it. Taxonomists would always have difficulty with 'species of doubtful classification linking one type with another and having something in common with both'.[5] In zoological classification Ray was perhaps even more successful, through basing his groups upon decisive anatomical features. He was the first taxonomist to make full use of the findings of comparative anatomy, particularly among mammals[6] and with regard to such

Fig. 13.1 Ray's Classification of Animals

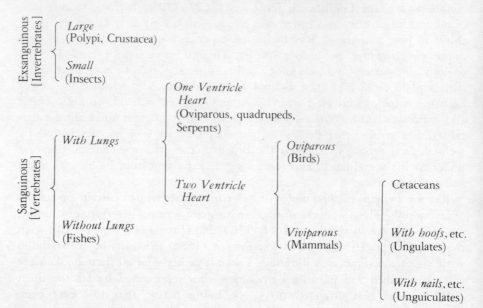

characteristic features as feet and teeth, thereby discerning such groups as the Ungulates, Rodents, Ruminants, etc. (Fig. 13.1).

Meanwhile, the naturalist's range of observation was being vastly extended by the microscope (Ch. 9). In the use of this instrument the primary emphasis was still on description; at this stage, attempts to construct elaborate theories upon the new evidence were infrequent and misleading. There was opportunity for the ramification of activity, and it was not neglected. The study of plant anatomy, originally enforced by the need for classificatory systems, could now proceed to the structure of tissues and reproductive mechanisms; zoological anatomy, likewise, stimulated by the fertility of the comparative method as shown by Harvey and many before him, was extended to strange creatures like the 'orang-outang' (dissected by Dr Edward Tyson),[7] and, with the aid of the microscope, to levels of detail inaccessible to the naked eye.

Most of this new work prolonged existing tendencies. Marcello Malpighi (1628–94), for example, completed Harvey's discovery of the circulation of the blood by following its passage from the arterial to the venous system through the capillary vessels, at the same time observing its red corpuscles. He was also able to go further than Harvey and Fabricius in examining the microscopic foetus of the chick within the first hours of incubation, from which he was led to believe that growth was a process of enlargement or unfolding only: the foetus was 'pre-formed' in the unfertilized egg.[8] As a pioneer of histology Malpighi entered on less familiar ground, in his microscopic examinations of the liver, the kidney, the cortex of the brain, and the tongue, whose 'taste buds' he discovered. In the study of insects – where Aristotle had shown wonderful insight – the serious scientific curiosity in which Malpighi was joined by Jan Swammerdam (1637–80) had already been anticipated by Hooke in *Micrographia*, and by even earlier virtuosi with their 'flea-glasses'. These two naturalists, however, were the first to explore fully the internal anatomy of minute creatures, demonstrating that their organs are as highly differentiated as those of large animals. Malpighi's treatise on the silkworm has been described as the earliest monograph on an invertebrate; in it he indicated the function of the *tracheae* first observed by him, which distribute air about the insect's body, and of other tubes by which the products of metabolism are excreted. He did much work on the anatomy of the larval stages of insects, and observed their evolution to maturity, but here he was excelled by Swammerdam, who also denied that there was any true transformation, even in the emergence of the butterfly from the caterpillar, or of the frog from the tadpole – processes which he studied with enormous care. In sheer technical skill – exemplified in the quality of his drawings as well as in the fineness of his dissection under the lens and his unique methods of injection – Swammerdam foreshadowed the greater manipulative resources of the mid-nineteenth century. Leeuwenhoek is chiefly remarkable for his work at much higher magnifications and the discovery of a new world inhabited by Infusoria and Bacteria (p. 253), but the ubiquitous curiosity which led him to examine hairs, nerves, the bile, parts of plants, crystals – indeed almost everything that could be brought before his lenses – induced him to make some observations comparable to those of Malpighi and Swammerdam, among which those on the compound insect eye and on ants were particularly novel. From observations on aphids he discovered parthenogenesis in animals – reproduction by the female parent alone.

In the plant kingdom, the microscope could not reveal a new order of magnitude within the living state, as it did in the animal; on the other hand, a much clearer idea of the structure of plant tissues emerged – including the description of their minute components, the cells – than was yet obtained in zoology. The presumed anatonomical and physiological analogies between animals and plants were indeed powerful incentives to enquiry at this time. Sometimes analogy was wholly misleading, as with the theory (popular until disproved by repeated experiments) that the sap in plants circulates like the blood in animals, but in other aspects, as when the 'breathing' of plants was compared with that of animals by Malpighi and later by Stephen Hales (1679–1761), it led towards a more correct understanding. Malpighi, despite the excellence of his descriptions of the differing structures found in wood, pith, leaf and flower under the microscope, and of the germination of seedlings, thought too exclusively in terms of the animal form. Thus he wrongly identified the function of the spiral vessels that he observed in plant tissue with that of the tracheae in insects, and erected upon this identification a broad theory of the increasing specialization of the respiratory organs, reaching its climax in mammals. He also tried to find in plants the reproductive organs familiar from vertebrate anatomy. The Englishman, Nehemiah Grew (1641–1712), whose independent work is closely parallel to that of Malpighi, and of equal quality, was a more restrained observer, though he believed (as he quaintly wrote) 'that a *Plant* is, as it were, an *Animal* in Quires, as an

Animal is a *Plant*, or rather several *Plants*, bound up into one volume' – a remark which, however strange the metaphor, expresses profound intuition.

Grew was well aware, not only that the attainments of ordinary naturalists still fell far short of their aims, but that these aims by no means amounted to a true *'Knowledge of Nature'*. His *Philosophical History of Plants* (1672)[9] sketched a new and more ambitious programme. Many of the problems he proposed remain unsolved:

First, by what means it is that a *Plant*, or any *Part* of it, comes to *Grow*, a *Seed* to put forth a *Root* and *Trunk*. . . How the Aliment by which a *Plant* is fed, is duly prepared in its several *Parts*. . . How not only their *Sizes*, but also their *Shapes* are so exceeding various . . .Then to inquire, What should be the reason of their various *Motions*; that the *Root* should *descend*; that its descent should sometimes be *perpendicular*, sometimes more *level*: That the *Trunk* cloth *ascend*, and that the ascent thereof, as to the space of *Time* wherein it is made, is of different *measures* . . . Further, what, may be the Causes as of the *Seasons* of their *Growth*; so of the *Periods* of their *Lives*; some being *Annual*, others *Biennial*, others *Perennial* . . . and lastly in what manner the *Seed* is prepared, formed and fitted for *Propagation*.

Some of these questions Grew himself tried to elucidate, most brilliantly deducing that plants reproduce sexually, the flowers being hermaphrodite like snails, with the stamens acting as the male organs.[10] Nor did he neglect the possibility of examining the plant substance by combustion, calcination, distillation and other experimental methods of chemistry, though these were as yet too primitive to be of real service. In this way he showed that the matter of the pithy or starchy part of the plant was quite distinct from that of the woody or fibrous part. Like Ray and other naturalists Grew saw no reason to reject mechanism as a working hypothesis which he developed (for example) in his account of plant nutrition; as he put it, with a familiar simile:

[We need not think] that there is any Contradiction, when *Philosophy* teaches that to be done by *Nature*; which *Religion*, and the Sacred *Scriptures*, teach us to be done by *God*: no more, than to say, That the Ballance of a *Watch* is moved by the next *Wheel*, is to deny that *Wheel*, and the rest, to be moved by the *Spring*; and that both the *Spring*, and all the other *Parts*, are caused to move together by the *Maker* of them. So *God* may be truly the *Cause* of *This Effect*, although a Thousand other *Causes* should be supposed to intervene: For all Nature is as one Great *Engine*, made by, and held in His Hand.[11]

A general sketch of the horizon in biology about the year 1680 would show virile activity, a steady expansion of the sphere of interest, and the fruitful exploitation of new techniques. Admittedly, man was still the prime focus of attention, whether in the Royal Society's endeavour to introduce a scientific spirit into agriculture, or in the relics of the belief (still held by a plant-anatomist like Grew) that all vegetables have 'virtues', or in the frequent backward glances of the zoologist at the human body. Nevertheless, as the peripheries rapidly became more remote they assumed, as it were, a territorial autonomy. The survival of anthropocentricity in the feverish concentration of Swammerdam was small. It is significant that naturalists no longer defended their preoccupations as useful, but rather as contributions to knowledge of the universe, of the organic part of the divinely created machine. And, though description and cataloguing of macroscopic flora and fauna remained their principal tasks, natural history showed clear signs of entering into partnerships in which the skills of the human anatomist and physiologist, the chemist, and the physicist, should be placed at its service. Gradually, through the seventeenth century, biology had returned to the philosophic attitude of an Aristotle; now it seemed likely that the borrowing of modern knowledge and techniques would permit the ancients to be as greatly excelled in these sciences as in physics and mechanics.

Briefly, there was promise — a promise of growth in depth and extent that was hardly fulfilled during the next century and a half. That it was not fulfilled may be attributed partly to the fallaciousness of the early hopes, for neither microscopic technique, nor chemical experiment, was capable of changing the pattern of activity so permanently as the work done during the two decades 1660–80 would suggest. These crude tools were soon blunted. The close connection between biology and medicine, which had encouraged study of the former science in the seventeenth century, tended to hamper its later development, for as medical studies were permeated by the influence of Galen's ideas until the nineteenth century, it was impossible that animal and plant studies should escape the limitations of those ideas. Unable, as yet, to build freely upwards upon the half-finished foundations of their predecessors, eighteenth-century naturalists might well be discouraged by the splendour of their inheritance. Discouragement was all the more harsh because this inheritance included such a feeble element of hypothesis to serve as a scaffolding for their own researches. Thereafter it is not surprising that they felt strongly a positive attraction that was both old and new. Like the sixteenth-century encyclopaedists, they were subjected to a vast incursus of new species, fruit of a renewed urge towards exploration that drove Linnaeus into the sub-arctic tundra, and Joseph Banks to the Pacific and Australasia. Moreover, this invasion synchronized, not with a sense of confusion before the profligacy of nature, but with an increasingly dogmatic confidence in a system, the system of Linnaeus. Quite suddenly, about the middle of the century, classification became one of the easiest, instead of one of the most difficult, biological exercises. Not for the first or the last time in science there was a rush to gather the harvest, while the unbroken fields were neglected.

The great debate between Ovists and Animalculists was more widespread, and even less fruitful. Harvey had believed in epigenesis, that is, that the growth of the embryo proceeded both by the gradual differentiation of its parts, and by their increase in size: 'there is no part of the foetus actually in [the egg], yet all the parts of it are in [the egg] potentially.' The effect of microscopy, soon after Harvey's death, was to give immediate advantage to the alternative theory of preformation, according to which the embryo merely swelled from being an invisible speck which was from the first completely differentiated; as Henry Power said: 'So admirable is every organ of this machine of ours formed, that every part within us is intirely made, when the whole organ seems too little to have any parts at all.' Preformation was developed especially by Mal-

341

pighi and Swammerdam. Since the embryo, among oviparous creatures, develops in the maternal egg, and microscopists believed that the first signs of its future form could be detected as soon as the egg appeared, it was naturally assumed by them that the embryo, or potential embryo, was solely derived from the female. This view conveniently opposed the unfashionable Aristotelean conception that the male, supplying the active 'form', was the prime agent in generation, and the female responsible merely for the passive 'substance' of the offspring. Aristotle seemed to be further confounded by the discovery of the mammalian ovum attributed to De Graaf (1672). This supposed discovery was premature – De Graaf saw the follicles since known by his name, and the true ovum was first described by von Baer a century and a half later. However, it brought about an essentially correct change of thought. to the view that both viviparous and oviparous reproduction begin with the fertilization of an egg formed in the female. According to the Ovists, the ovum contained the embryo not potentially but actually, and in the version of their theory known as *emboitement* they supposed that this held within its own organs the ova of the next generation, and so on *ad infinitum* like a series of Chinese boxes: in the ovaries of Eve were confined the future forms of all the human race.

The discovery of spermatozoa opened up a contrasting but parallel theory. Leeuwenhoek, in one of his rare flights of hypothesis, suggested that these 'little animals' were the living embryos, which were enabled to grow by transplantation into the egg: 'If your Harvey and our De Graaf had seen the hundredth part they would have stated, as I did, that it is exclusively the male semen that forms the foetus, and that all that the woman may contribute only serves to receive the semen and feed it.'[12] He supported this doctrine by reference to well-known cases where the offspring was strongly marked with the characteristics of the male parent. Hartsoeker (1694) and Plantades (1699) – the last perhaps as a deliberate fraud – published illustrations of a 'homunculus' enclosed in the head of a spermatozoon. *Emboitement* was also taken up by the Animalculists in the eighteenth century. Rival interpretations of observations that were commonly very imperfect and carelessly recorded continued for over a hundred years. Some regarded the spermatozoa as products of corruption, like the eel-worms in vinegar, for it was only in 1824 that they were proved essential to fertilization by Dumas and Prévost; at about the same time the experiments of Geoffroy Saint-Hilaire on the production of monsters proved that the morphology of the embryo is neither preformed nor predestined. By this time preformation as an embryological theory was moribund, having declined ever since Caspar Wolff had strongly revived epigenesis (1768), pointing out that unbiased examination with the microscope showed the formation of structures taking place out of previously undifferentiated tissues.

Long before this time the lead in biological experimentation had decisively passed to the continent from England and the successors of William Harvey. It would be difficult to find adequate English counterparts to the work of Spallanzani on digestion, of Lavoisier and his collaborators on respiration, and of Ingenhousz on photosynthesis, the English talent at this time running rather to speculative cosmogenies. But in Newton's last years one Englishman, Stephen Hales (1677–1761), established himself as the founder of a new brand of science, plant physiology, and exercised also a potent influence on the development of chemistry. His intellectual links with Newton were close, as we shall see further in the next chapter, though their personal contacts were slight, for Hales was a student at Cambridge in the time of William Whiston, Roger Cotes, John Francis Vigani and especially William Stukeley (1687–1765), later Newton's friend and notable as an antiquary. It was Stukeley who introduced Hales to botany and animal dissection. They joined in some wild pranks, according to Stukeley:

We took up old Hoyes that hangd himself & was buried in the highway, & dissected him, & afterwards made a sceleton of his bones, & put them in a fine glass case with an inscription in Latin.[13]

At Cambridge, also, Hales began the experiments on the pressure and flow of blood in animals, later described in *Haemostaticks* (1731) and always regarded by him (a most humane philosopher) as disagreeable, which inspired his cognate enquiries into the flow of sap in plants. His technique goes back in direct lineage to Torricelli and Pascal only, instead of balancing the weight of a column of mercury against the pressure of the atmosphere, Hales linked his manometer (as we may now call it) to the blood vessels of animals or the stems of the plants. Beginning these experiments in 1719, Hales first measured the great height to which, in spring, the sap would ascend in a tube cemented to a branch of a grapevine and noted its variation according to time and weather. Later he investigated the volume of fluid passing through an actively growing plant, and transpired through its leaves into the atmosphere, relating this to the total leaf-area which he ascertained by a careful counting and sampling process. He also measured the growth of the leaves themselves. Hales found that the sap was vigorously pushed up the stem of the plant by an active pressure in the root, then urged forward by the 'vastly attracting power' in the fine, capillary vessels until finally transpired at the leaf-surface. Starting from an experiment of Francis Hauksbee's described by Newton in Query 31 of *Opticks*, Hales applied his technique to the actual measure by his mercurial manometer of the 'imbibing force' of a column tightly filled with wood-ash: it raised the mercury column 18 cm (7 in.), equivalent to 2.5 m (8 ft) of water. Another line of enquiry, starting from his noticing bubbles of air within sap-filled tubes, made him think it

very probable, that the air freely enters plants, not only with the principal fund of nourishment by the roots, but also thro' the surface of their trunks and leaves, especially at night, when they are changed from a [transpiring] to a strongly imbibing state.

Some of this air, he thought, was mixed with the soil, some fixed in an inelastic state in the ground:

Being desirous to make some further researches into this matter, and to find what proportion of this Air I could obtain out of the different substances in which it was lodged and incorporated[14]

Hales set about a process of analysis of very many substances, some like oyster-shells and oak quite hard and dense, which he subjected to distillation, for the first time collecting the 'air' emitted in the process by the method of the pneumatic trough, which he invented.

Despite the fluid and pneumatic aspects of analogy between the properties of plants which Hales investigated, and the better-known ones of animals, he finally renounced any idea of there being a regular circulation of the sap in the plant, like that of the blood, though fifty years before many had been inclined to believe the analogy was complete in this way.

In his Conclusion to *Vegetable Staticks* (1727), in which Hales's experiments were set out in a manner that surely owed as much to the example of Boyle as to that of Newton, he principally discussed the useful lessons which gardeners and fruit-growers might derive from his discoveries. As with his predecessors, Hales combined the mechanical philosophy with veneration for the supreme Creator; 'the specific difference of vegetables', he asserted 'is doubtless owing to the very different formation of their minute vessels, whereby an almost infinite variety of combinations of the common principles of vegetables is made'. Moreover, he went on,

could our eyes attain to a sight of the admirable texture of the parts on which the specifick differences in plants depend, what an amazing and beautiful scene of inimitable embroidery should we behold? What a variety of masterly strokes of machinery? What evident marks of consummate wisdom should we be entertained with?[15]

The intricate, minute perfection of biological mechanism, the superb adaption of particular plants to particular conditions of soil and moisture on which Hales insists, and the wonderful adaptability of the organisms' responses to changing environmental conditions, all this stood as no substitute for divine providence, but rather as the most sublime and refined proof of providence and design.

Probably few historians would wish to argue that the anatomists and naturalists from Harvey to Hales wrought in their studies a 'scientific revolution' in the sense of Thomas S. Kuhn.[16] There was no set of paradigms about the constitution and distribution of living things overthrown, nor an alternative put in its place. If anything, there was more deep disagreement about all possible issues of that sort in 1750 than there had been in 1600. On the other hand, it is nearly as indisputable that the study of living things did participate in the scientific revolution, whose typical core was certainly in the mathematical sciences. One familiar quotation serves almost uniquely to prove the point, the words with which Newton concluded the second edition of his *Principia*:

Now some remarks might be added about a certain very subtle spirit pervading dense bodies, and lying within them; by the force and actions of which the particles of bodies attract each other mutually at the least distances and cohere when they touch; and electric bodies operate at greater distances . . . and light is emitted, reflected . . . and all sensation is stimulated; and the limbs of animals are moved at will, namely, by the vibrations of this spirit spread through the solid filaments of the nerves from the external sensory organs to the brain, and from the brain back to the muscles. But these matters cannot be dealt with in a few words, nor do we have a sufficiency of experiments available by means of which the laws of action of this spirit ought to be accurately determined and demonstrated.

Precisely what Newton meant by these strange sentences is, admittedly, far from clear. A longer, unpublished passage indicates Newton's thought that the 'visual spirit' must be continuous from transparent medium transmitting light into the eye and the nervous system, and that because electrically charged bodies might shine, this 'visual spirit' and the 'electric spirit' were identical.[17] But what is more important in the present context is that he so plainly homologizes physics and animal physiology. He makes as bold an assertion of the fundamental unity of causal explanation in the organic and inorganic realms as can be found in Descartes, and indeed the unacknowledged debt to Descartes's philosophy in this passage is very evident. Here we see the deep and metaphysical sense in which the idea of life and living action was by no means absent from the intellectual processes of the scientific revolution. To say that Newton, like Descartes, treated the animal as a machine would be to run far beyond the evidence; what is certain is that, while avoiding any such rhetorical and (in fact) empty affirmation, Newton accepted without hesitation the continuity and homogeneity of the living organism with its non-living environment, at least so far as all their interactions are concerned. (This leaves open the question of *will* – denied by Descartes to animals – among others.) That is, in so far as the organism is composed of physico–chemical structures and exhibits physico–chemical properties, it is at one with and in no way distinct from the rest of the universe, save in (to go back to Hales's words) the 'almost infinite variety of combinations of the common principle'.

Here we have a potentially powerful metaphysic, shared by Ray, accepted by Hales, Christian and providential yet firmly maintaining the explanatory powers of the mechanical philosophy. And in factual science it was strongly buttressed by Baconian observation and experimental research, the transforming features of the biological sciences during the sixteenth and seventeenth centuries, which have (not inappropriately) been seized upon by apologists as worthy to stand comparison with the achievements of astronomers and mathematicians. Thus Charles Raven justly complained of the Whiggishness of historians of science, in assessing the events of the past in terms only of their anticipations of and contributions to 'the current orthodoxy of their own day'.[18] At the simplest, antiquarian level it is a due tribute to the naturalists of the past to record and understand their accomplishments, particularly towards their exemplification of their rational belief that the phenomena of living things were to be enumeratively, experimentally and analytically investigated like the properties of the organic world; at a deeper historical level it is even more important to understand that if (as Raven allows) the sixteenth and seventeenth centuries contributed little enough in a direct, factual way to the laboratory and evolutionary biology of the nineteenth century, nevertheless the shifts in perspective about life and its phenomena then occurring did contribute in an important way to the eighteenth century world-view. To read a vitalist–mechanist dichotomy back into the last years of Newton is a major historical mistake, which would render the harmony of endeavour between men of varied interests and religious beliefs incomprehensible.

345

NOTES

1. Now assigned to Nicholas of Damascus, first century BC

2. L. Fuchs, *De historia stirpium*, Basel 1542, Preface. Quoted by A. Arber, *Herbals*, Cambridge U.P., 1953, 67.

3. A. Zaluzian, *Methodi herbariae libri tres*, quoted Arber, op. cit., 144.

4. *Methodus plantarum nova* (1682): *Synopsis methodica animalium quadrupedum et serpentini generis* (1693): *Methodus insectorum* (1704).

5. See the Preface to *Methodus plantarum* and C. E. Raven, *John Ray, Naturalist*, Cambridge U.P., 1950, Ch. 8.

6. The Class was recognized by Ray, though not so named.

7. Cf. M. F. A. Montagu, *Edward Tyson, M.D., F.R.S. 1650–1708* (Memoir XX, Amer. Phil. Soc., Philadelphia, 1943). The creature was in fact a chimpanzee. Tyson also published monographs on the 'porpess', rattlesnake, opossum, etc.

8. Joseph Needham: *History of Embryology* (Cambridge U.P., 1934), pp. 144. *et seq.* F. J. Cole, *History of Comparative Anatomy*, Macmillan: London, 1949. H. B. Adelmann, *Marcello Malpighi and the Evolution of Embryology*, Cornell University Press: Ithaca, 1966.

9. Reprinted in *The Anatomy of Plants* (London, 1682).

10. Op. cit., pp. 171–3. Hermaphroditism is not, of course, universal among plants, as Grew thought.

11. Ibid., 80.

12. Letter to Nehemiah Grew, 18 March 1678. Leeuwenhoek, *Collected Letters*, vol. II, Swets and Zeitlinger: Amsterdam, 1941, 335. See on all this Jacques Roger, *Les Sciences de la vie dans la pensée française au 18ᵉ siécle*, Armand Colin: Paris, 1963.

13. Michael Hoskin, Foreward to Stephen Hales, *Vegetable Staticks* [1727], reprint 1961, xi.

14. Ibid., 87–9.

15. Ibid., 205.

16. T. S. Kuhn, *The Structure of Scientific Revolutions*, Chicago University Press: Chicago, 1962.

17. Newton, *Correspondence*, V, Cambridge U.P., 1975, 366–7. Cf. Henry Guerlac, *Essays and Papers in the History of Modern Science*, Johns Hopkins University Press: Baltimore & London, 1977, 120–30.

18. C. E. Raven, *Natural Religion and Christian Theology*, Cambridge U.P., 1953, 7.

CHAPTER FOURTEEN

The legacy of Newton

In the first year of the eighteenth century, fourteen years after the publication of the *Principia*, two years after the reorganization of the French Royal Academy of Sciences had brought Newton in as a Foreign Member, anyone looking back to review the scientific inheritance from the seventeenth century would have found it rich and varied. Neo-Cartesianism was the prevalent natural philosophy, with Leibniz and Malebranche active and influential figures, and the lessons of Huygens still cogent. Largely as yet confined to Germany was an evolving tradition of chemical mysticism rooted back in Van Helmont and Paracelsus, represented by Johann Joachim Becher (1625–82), Johann Kuñckel (1630–1703) and Georg Ernst Stahl (1660–1734); in Germany too interest in medicine was particularly strong, while comparative anatomy had flourished under the aegis of the Academy in Paris, and in Holland, where Frederick Ruysch (1638–1731) was the active master. Astronomy was cultivated not only by Flamsteed (an enemy of Newton's, now) at Greenwich, but at Paris where the Cassini family acquired the Observatory almost as an hereditary fief, and by many 'amateur' astronomers. In the mathematical sciences Leibniz, his associates and their pupils dominated the academic world from Padua to Groñingen, and especially in the person of Pierre Varignon (1654–1722) were firmly established in the French Academy. It would have been a fair judgement on the previous fifty years to conclude that a great deal had been learned, not least in the descriptive sciences, and that pure and applied mathematics had made very swift advances indeed. But only to a relatively small number of Englishmen would it have appeared that the character of scientific work and thought had undergone any very radical change in that time; any European in 1701 discerning such a change would have attributed it to Huygens and Liebniz.

Half a century later still the retrospective view would have seemed wholly different; much that seemed exciting in 1701 would have receded into insignificance, while the English empirical and mathematical traditions, known earlier to continental philosophers but generally regarded as idiosyncratic or even bizarre, were seen as conveying the message of truth. Bacon, Harvey and Boyle had acquired new importance as precursors of the Newtonian method.

By 1750 English philosophy and English science, even English social customs and political institutions, were being praised and practised by those who had begun to think of themselves as enlightened. Contrary to all historical precedent, the almost barbaric off-shore islanders were proving themselves intelligent, cultured and prosperous, and their light seemed to irradiate Europe.

A convenient and conventional date for this change in perspective is 1734, when Voltaire published his *Letters on the English Nation*, wherein the French read, for example,

Very few people in England read Descartes, whose works indeed are now useless. On the other side, but a small number pursue those of Sir Isaac Newton, because to do this the student must be deeply skilled in the mathematics, otherwise those works will be unintelligible to him. But not withstanding this, these great men are the subject of every one's discourse. Sir Isaac Newton is allowed every advantage, while Descartes is not indulged a single one . . . In a word, Sir Isaac Newton is here as the Hercules of fabulous story, to whom the ignorant ascribed all the feats of ancient heroes.[1]

Two years before, Pierre Louis Moreau de Maupertuis (1698–1759) had published *A Discourse on the different Shapes of the Stars*, the first Newtonian treatise by a Frenchman, while Voltaire returned with his *Elements of Newton's Philosophy* in 1738. Both men had visited England, indeed Voltaire lived there 'for the good of his health' from 1726 to 1729. But these were far from being the first Frenchmen to inspect, and yield their allegiance to, the prevailing English philosophy. It is easy to forget that war, almost as much as ideas, separated French and English intellectual life during almost twenty-five years from 1698 to 1714. Soon after the restoration of a settled and peaceful order in Europe, a group of Frenchmen (Rémond de Monmort, C-J. Geoffroy, and the Chevalier de Louville) came to London to observe an eclipse of the sun visible there but not at Paris, and to learn more of English science. They were able to confirm by experiment that Newton's accounts of his colour-separations and measurements in *Opticks* were exact, and Louville became a convinced Newtonian. Not long after his return home he expressed himself fulsomely to Newton:

thanks to you, we are now permitted to be initiated into the mysteries of nature, and are allowed knowledge of its most recondite secrets. But with your discoveries it is not as with those famous systems which are founded only upon guesses, and which may be as easily overthrown by other guesses. You have erected the magnificent edifice of your philosophy upon unshakeable foundations.[2]

However, until Maupertuis came to England in 1728 *Opticks* had attracted more interest than the *Principia*. It reached Paris in 1706, after twenty-five years of silence there concerning Newton's optical theories, ever since Edmé Mariotte in *On the Nature of Colours* (1681) had claimed the experimental falsity of Newton's assertion that a pure spectral colour could not be further split up by refraction.[3] E-F. Geoffroy prepared a French summary of the book which was read at the Academy of Sciences, and rapidly secured a notable convert in Father Malebranche, after the experiments had been confirmed on his behalf by Dortous de Mairan. Ten years later any reasonable suspicion that Newton had been mistaken in his reports was laid to rest by J-T. Desaguliers' careful repetition (elaborately reported in the *Philosophical Transactions*) of these now classical experiments, provoked, it seems certain, by Leibniz's again reviving Mariotte's scepticism in a review of 1713. Yet at the instigation of various great personages they were then formally re-enacted twice more in Paris, the continued success and vindication of Newton's theory preparing the way for his first great public success in France, the publication of a handsome French translation of *Opticks* in 1722.[4] No less a man than the Chancellor of France urged it on, and the actual editor was Varignon, associate both of Malebranche and Leibniz.

Thus, at roughly his eightieth year, pressing endeavours were made to bring Newton actively within the orbit of French science: he was urged to communicate the results of his researches and generally treated *en prince*. The leading role of the Oratorians, who some twenty years earlier had been learning the differential and integral calculus from Leibniz and Johann Bernoulli, in commencing the naturalization of Newton in France in opposition to the unrelenting orthodox Cartesians, can hardly be doubted; to quote Henry Guerlac: 'Malebranche and his followers broke down the initial barriers of the Cartesian fortress, and made the way easier for radical Newtonians like Maupertuis, Clairaut, and Voltaire.'[5] The Oratorians' veneration for mathematics as 'the foremost and fundamental discipline of all the human sciences', which had made them pupils of Leibniz, afterwards made them admire and find truth in Newton's achievement in the *Principia*, the only universal and compelling essay in the mathematization of philosophy. They were soon eager to transform Newton's geometrical formulations into their own mathematical language of the calculus, a task again undertaken by Varignon and published in the *Mémoires* of the Paris Academy between 1700 and 1710. Another Oratorian mathematician, Charles René Reyneau (1656–1728) evidently thought highly of the technical aspects of the *Principia*, though like others of this group he could not bring himself fully to share Newton's philosophy of nature.[6] The Malebranchistes adopted an essentially positivist stance; accepting the idea of the inverse-square centripetal force and the mathematical theory of its action, they were prepared to let all discussion of the reality or ontology of force pass them by. They were willing radically to modify their aetherial speculations so that they should cause no conflict with Newton's mathematical theorems, whose precise agreement with phenomena they admired, but not to admit the dreadful idea of 'attraction'. For this reason they may be classed as transitional Newtonians.[7]

The trend towards Newtonianism in the rest of Europe (outside Germany) was similar, but less protracted. The Italian mathematician Guido Grandi (1671–1742) may have been teaching the mathematical aspects of the *Principia* at Florence before the end of the seventeenth century. At Padua in 1716 Jakob Hermann, in a book on mechanics dedicated to Leibniz and the members of the Berlin Academy, permitted a friend to address him in a poem noting that 'Newton, a dweller in that rich isle which yet contains nothing more golden than himself, had been the first to follow that path'. And more significantly an Italian, Francesco Algarotti, composed in *Newtonianism for the Ladies* (1737) one of the Enlightenment's most successful popularizations. Cartesianism had never been very strongly rooted in Italy: with the weakening of sterile clericalism from about 1720, Italy moved rapidly into the Newtonian phase. Again, the transition was aided by the strong predilection of the Italian natural philosophers for mathematical arguments and their steadily increasing pride in Galileo, whom they began to understand as the great forerunner of Newton.

In Holland, in whose universities Cartesianism first became academically respectable but with a considerable leaning towards experimental demonstration and justification rather than rational argument, the influence of Newton is closely linked with William Jacob 'sGravesande (1688–1742), professor of mathematics and astronomy at Leiden from 1717. He had begun to express the originality of his outlook by founding, with others, the *Journal Litteraire de la Haye* (1713) which soon opened its pages to the English Newtonians: he spent a year in England (1715–16) where he became acquainted with them personally. He was an extremely successful teacher developing the demonstrative class-instruction methods already devoted to Newtonian mechanics in England by John Keill and J-T. Desaguliers. These methods received very wide publicity through 'sGravesande's *Mathematical Elements of Natural Philosophy confirm'd by Experiments; or An Introduction to Sir Isaac Newton's Philosophy* (1720), immediately translated into English. An even greater teacher, Hermann Boerhaave (1668–1738), who extended further the high repute of the medical school at Leiden, also adopted certain Newtonian ideas; not those of Newton's exact physics, but the ideas about the corpuscular structure of matter which Boerhaave found in the Queries of *Opticks*, for which he was already prepared by familiarity with the corpuscular chemistry of Robert Boyle. The third of the trio of Newtonian Dutch professors was Petrus van Musschenbroek (1692–1761), a friend of 'sGravesande, who also paid a visit to England in 1715; he taught at Utrecht and Leiden, perfecting the empiricist tradition established by his friend. He was a great designer of experimental apparatus, immortally associated in electrical science with the discovery or invention of the 'Leyden Jar'.

The Dutch seem to have been almost unique, at first, in supporting the English Newtonians' case against Leibniz concerning the discovery of the calculus. If the first great boost to Newton's fame on the continent was given by the Latin *Optice* (1706) – and not least the generous speculative range of its Queries – the increasing heat and publicity of the public quarrel between the two great philosophers and their partisans certainly brought Newton's name to the attention of many who would have been but dimly conscious of the existence of the *Principia* (not reprinted after 1687 until 1713, then quickly pirated at Amsterdam). After the death of Huygens in 1695, all Europe except the English recognized Leibniz as its leading intellectual light: mathematician, philosopher, inventor, historian, friend and counsellor of monarchs, unlike Descartes always eminently respectable. That an English mathematician should set up his pretensions against such a figure was remarkable; that these pretensions should be upheld, widened and justified by an ample printed justification with, it seemed, the unaminous confidence of the Royal Society behind them was almost incredible.[8] We know that Newton was right to claim priority of discovery, Leibniz right to claim independent discovery and priority in publication. It is also obvious that despite some flashes of magnanimity between the two rivals, each behaved extremely badly. Before his death in 1716, which did not determine the quarrel, Leibniz had failed to convince the world that he had learned nothing from the mass of early mathematical material, including the letters addressed to Leibniz in 1676, which Newton now set out (by and large, not inaccurately as regards the texts though Newton's glosses on them contain gross distortions). Given the facts of admitted access by Leibniz to Newton's unpublished materials, the technical features of the discovery which were difficult for any but considerable mathematicians to assess, the apparent candour of Newton and his personal authority which won over almost all visitors to London to his side, and the complete failure of Leibniz to lay before the public a narrative of how and when he did come independently to the concepts of the calculus, it is hardly surprising that many who were not ardent partisans for Leibniz came to believe that Newton's mathematical discovery had been equally as epoch-making as that of Leibniz, though not so extensively developed, and that Newton's discovery had produced the *Principia*. So, for example, Voltaire in his *Letters on the English Nation:*

For many years the invention of this famous calculation [calculus] was denied Sir Isaac Newton. In Germany Mr Leibniz was considered as the inventor of the differences or moments, called Fluxions [by Newton], and Mr Bernoulli claimed the integral calculation. However, Sir Isaac is now thought to have first made the discovery, and the other two have the glory of having once made the world doubt whether it was to be ascribed to him or them.[9]

Newton's now outmoded mathematical writings began to come before continental eyes from 1708 onwards. The translator of Newton's *Method of Fluxions and Infinite Series* (written in 1671, first printed in 1738) wrote in 1740:

in the manner with which topics are treated the hand of the great Master will be recognized, and the genius of the discoveries; and the conviction will persist that Newton alone is the author of these marvellous modes of calculus, as he is also of many other achievements which are quite as wonderful.

The Comte de Buffon (1707–88) was, it must be explained, a very fervent Anglophile, and also the translator of Stephen Hales's *Vegetable Staticks*. But it was, after all, the evident power of Isaac Newton's mind that created intellectual Anglophilia, rather than the other way about.

Another striking confirmation of that mind's power did much to seal the Newtonian victory, and it was wholly effected by the French. In the *Principia* (Book III, Proposition 19) Newton had calculated from the Earth's rotational force at the Equator that its equatorial diameter should exceed its polar diameter by about 0.44 per cent, or 27 km (17 miles); similarly in Jupiter, rotating more than twice as fast, the disparity of the diameters was shown to be even greater (in the third edition the ratio was put at about 13 to 12 and confirmed by astronomers' measurements). In France, however, the Cassinis from geodetic measurements stretching along the meridian of Paris from the Channel to the Pyrennees came to exactly the opposite conclusion – that the polar diameter of the Earth was the greater. After Maupertuis had examined this incompatibility in 1733, the Academy of Sciences decided that it should be settled by measures of a degree of latitude taken in two widely separated parts of the globe. Maupertuis, with Clairaut, took a party to the Gulf of Bothnia. La Condamine, with Bouguer, took another to Peru. Maupertuis departed in May 1736 and was absent for a year; only in December 1739 was he able to announce the result that, in accordance with Newton's dynamical theory, the degree in the far north was longer than that in Paris. More years elapsed before the degree in Peru was found to be shorter. As Voltaire put it in a wrily witty (but un-Baconian) couplet addressed to Maupertuis:

> Vous avez confirmé dans des lieux pleins d'ennui
> Ce que Newton connut sans sortir de chez lui. [10]

These twin expeditions, glorious manifestations of the wealth and technical expertise of French science, removed the last serious factual obstruction to the universal acceptance of Newtonian mechanics.

Acceptance, that is, as a basis for further investigations. Newton himself was well aware that what he had accomplished in the *Principia* still fell far short of perfection. At the very basis of his mechanical theory there was, for example, an awkward, unsolved problem – the measurement of force. The root of it went far back to 1669, when it had become apparent that in inelastic collision the total product of mass times velocity was conserved, whereas in elastic collision a greater quantity, mass times velocity squared, was conserved: the missing 'force' had vanished in the deformation of the inelastic bodies. Similarly, if the force of a moving body is thought to be proportioned to its velocity, it is consistent with the first of the former measures; if (as Leibniz preferred) force is considered proportional to the height of the ascent or descent, it is consistent with the second measure. Leibniz named the former (momentum) 'dead force', the second 'living force' (*vis viva*). Half the *vis viva* ($\frac{1}{2} mv^2$) is our kinetic energy. From 1686, when Leibniz condemned the Cartesian (and later, Newtonian) measure of force, declaring that *vis viva* contained the only true and mathematical conception of force, until 1743 a vast and inchoate debate ranged over this question of definition. In that year it was ended by Dalembert's argument that both definitions 'worked' mathematically, and that neither mv nor mv^2 was a uniquely true definition of force. The two expressions simply reflected different ways of looking at the same thing, so that the dispute was about names only, not realities. To avoid confusion it was best to avoid the use of 'force' in the old sense of 'force' of a body's 'motion'.

There are of course other examples of conceptual problems that needed much clarification after Newton, notably again by the introduction of the idea of 'work' near the end of the eighteenth century. Then the principles of mechanics had to be extended and rendered precise in relation to such topics as hydrodynamics, friction and the behaviour of systems of bodies. As already noted in connection with the theory of the Moon, much remained to be done for the perfection of celestial mechanics; finally, the science of mechanics received its ultimate classical form at the end of the century in the works of Joseph Louis Lagrange (1736–1813) and Pierre Simon Laplace (1749–1827). Among their predecessors and contemporaries, in all this magnificent post-*Principia* achievement, the names of French, Swiss and German analysts stand out: the Bernoulli family, Pierre Bouguer, Lazare Carnot, Clairaut, Dalembert, Leonhard Euler, and numerous others associated with the Paris, Berlin and St Petersburg academies. No British mathematician stands comparison with these. John Keill is remembered only as Newton's champion. Roger Cotes's youthful promise was in a kindly moment praised by Newton but he died at the age of 34 without striking achievement. Brook Taylor and James Stirling, both remembered as pure mathematicians, certainly merit no more than third-rank places in the history of mechanics. Benjamin Robins (1707–51), a late Newtonian partisan, an energetic enemy of *vis viva*, was rather an engineer than a mathematician. Only of the Scot, Colin Maclaurin (1698–1746), the last British mathematician to have a tenuous personal link with Newton, can something more positive be said. His *Treatise of Fluxions* (1742) has been praised for its rigour, and confirmed the singular use of this Newtonian system in Britain; Ernst Mach wrote that this work marked 'a very important advance' in analytical mechanics beyond the *Mechanica* (1736) of Euler and 'invests the computations of this subject with a high degree of symmetry and perspicuity'.[11]

The historical reasons for this collapse of British mathematics during and after Newton's lifetime have not been made clear; certainly it was not caused simply by total lack of interest – for trivial kinds of mathematical activity attracted much support – and though the English did not pursue the differential and integral calculus of their continental colleagues, they need not have completely isolated themselves (as in fact they did). What is certainly discernible in Britain is a strong preference for interpreting Newton in Baconian terms. As Newton's fame had increased enormously in the years since the publication of *Optice* (1706), it had absorbed and subsumed all that had gone before that was not in conflict with Newtonianism. The mechanical philosophy was Newtonian; mathematical philosophy took its origin from Newton; experimental philosophy was Newtonian also. Not that the pronouncements of Galileo, Kepler, Boyle and Huygens were forgotten or the complexity of the pre-Newtonian development of science wholly ignored, rather, these men were seen as precursors of the true founder of modern science who had each seen partial glimpses of the truth. Above all, Newton had defined a definitive and infallible *method* of science, where the others had merely groped uncertainly after particular truths.

The eighteenth century understood that Newton's method while avoiding misleading claims to omniscience offered a pathway to certain, undebatable truths. Eschewing hypotheses, or rather setting hypotheses and conjecture in their proper places as stimulants to inductive investigation, distinguishing rigorously between hypotheses and firm, supported theory (which Newton called 'doctrine'), it set the latter on a basis of axioms confirmed by experience or experiments:

For if anyone may make a guess at the truth of things from the bare possibility of hypotheses, I do not see how anything certain can be determined in any science, since it is always possible to think up more and more hypotheses, which will seem to answer new difficulties.[12]

A doctrine, however, invokes no hypotheses and is confirmed by experiments. These apparently simple rules were, for many, clear and sufficient definitions of the true method of science, discovered once for all. The English mathematician William Emerson argued that if it was a 'mere joke' to talk of Newton's philosophy ever being supplanted; it might

indeed be improved, and further advanced; but it can never be overthrown, notwithstanding all the efforts of all the Bernoulli's, the Leibnitz's . . .[13]

In fact, Newton's was the first *positive* philosophy in the meaning of Auguste Comte. The fact that Newton had refrained from assigning a cause to gravitation was a matter·of congratulation rather than criticism. 'Doomed as we are to be ignorant of the essence and inner contexture of bodies' wrote Dalembert in anticipation of Comte, 'the only resource remaining for our sagacity is to try at least to grasp the analogy of phenomena, and to reduce them all to a small number of primitive and fundamental facts'.[14]

Modern scholars have not unjustly praised Newton's wealth of physical insight, his wide-ranging speculations about atoms and stars that they find in his manuscripts. These were not the features that his immediate successors found most admirable in the printed works which they read, either in his deliberate pronouncements on method or in his examples of research. Some even asserted that the thoughts Newton had expressed in *Opticks* as Queries he really knew to be true. They believed that Newton had set before his readers the most confidently certain interpretation of nature that could ever be formulated, not a structure dependent on metaphysical presuppositions, and welcomed it on this understanding.

The Newtonian view of nature was indeed doubly rigorous, for not only was it soundly based upon induction from experience but it possessed in its development the rigour of mathematical argument. To quote the first Dutch Newtonian, William 'sGravesande, writing in 1720:

In Physics we are to discover the Laws of Nature by the Phenomena, then by Induction prove them to be general Laws; all the rest is to be handled Mathematically. Whoever will seriously examine, what Foundation this Method of Physics is built upon, will easily discover this to be the only true one, and that all Hypotheses are to be laid aside.[15]

Henry Pemberton (1694–1771), editor of the third edition of the *Principia* (1726) and another early popularizer of Newton in his *View of Sir Isaac Newton's Philosophy* (1728) similarly explains that 'the nature of those discoveries made it impossible to prove them upon any other than geometrical principles' hence the necessity of such a book as his own to enlighten the non-mathematical reader. Madame du Châtelet in her *Institutions de Physique* (1740) more than once explains that the principle of attraction – gravitation – was mathematically derived by Newton from Kepler's Laws, a statement which if not strictly correct in history at least takes us to the roots of things in mechanics as a mathematical science. Once discovered and defended the principle of attraction could stand as a concept, and so Stephen Hales for example accepted and used it, but however useful a concept attraction might be (as liberally shown by Newton himself in Query 31) it was perfectly obvious that attraction could only be *proved* in the mathematical theory of gravitational mechanics.

Modern commentators have refined, without radically modifying, the opinion that Newton's great methodological accomplishment was to unite the inductive and deductive processes, that is, experiment and the axiomatic method of geometry, though they are more conscious than Newton could be (as he had never read the *Discourses*) of the extent to which the necessity for such a union had been anticipated by Galileo. E. A. Burtt defined the essence of Newton's innovation as follows:

By his intimate union of the mathematical and experimental methods, Newton believed himself to have indissolubly allied the ideal exactitude of the one with the constant empirical reference of the other. *Science is the exact mathematical formulation of the processes of the natural world.* (Italics in original)[16]

What Newton intended is better gathered from a study of his actual practice than from his *obiter dicta*, for he certainly never meant to compile an essay on the philosophy of science: Burtt, indeed, complains that 'his words are disappointingly inadequate'. One of the sharpest direct indications appears near the beginning of the posthumously-published *System of the World*, where Newton explains his purpose to 'trace out the quantity and properties of this [gravitational] force from the phenomena, and to apply what we discover in some simple cases as principles, by which, in a mathematical way, we may estimate the effects thereof in more involved cases'. He then elucidates his own expression with a gloss:

We said, *in a mathematical way*, to avoid all questions about the nature or quality of this force, which we would not be understood to determine by any hypothesis, and therefore call it by the general name of a centripetal force . . .[17]

One might express this more shortly by saying that mathematics, the science of quantity, is not concerned with ontology. Let us postulate a centripetal force, Newton is saying, and then explore in a systematic group of propositions the motions that may arise from it.

If that is really what Newton meant, his statement is rational and Galilean, but somewhat in conflict with his earlier-quoted pronouncements about hypotheses. For is not the centripetal force a mathematical hypothesis, comparable to Archimedes' definition of a fluid or Galileo's of a naturally-accelerated motion, since it is not declared to be justified by induction from experience? True, as with Galileo, the mathematical propositions will *a posteriori* be shown to correspond to experience, so that in the end we agree that a centripetal gravitational force exists, but this is not the same thing as starting from axioms experimentally proved, the method Newton did in fact adopt in *Opticks*. The Newtonian methodological legacy seems less clear and confident — at least for non-mathematical natural philosophers — than Burtt would have us believe.

Then again, by breaking off the unfinished *Opticks* and launching himself in to what became a series of thirty-one Queries, Newton seemed to countenance the method of conjecture he had disallowed in others, providing the distinction from 'doctrine' was still maintained. These start, indeed, with simple questions:

Query 1. Do not Bodies act upon Light at a distance, and by their action bend its rays . . .?

but before long became little experimental essays:

Query 10. Is not Flame a Vapour, Fume or Exhalation heated red hot, that is, so hot as to shine? . . . In distilling hot Spirits . . . the Vapour which ascends out of the Still will take Fire at the Flame of a Candle, and turn into Flame . . .

and so on, with many chemical examples for two pages. The later Queries get longer and longer, the suggestion that a conjecture may be confirmed by the recitation of innumerable apparently positive instances more and more compelling. To many of the English, who knew their Bacon and their Boyle and their *Philosophical Transactions* but could make nothing of the *Principia* except its concluding General Scholium, this was inspiring prose. A majority, probably, of those who eagerly professed the title of 'Newtonian' made no pretence of practising Newton's experimental–mathematical method. Some, like the chemical philosophers Keill and Friend (p. 328), engaged in speculations about the play of attractive forces; others, like the rather absurd Bryan Robinson (1680–1754), constructed a towering house of cards on the hints of aetherial mechanisms that Newton left behind. If the alchemists had known of Newton's interest in their fantasies no doubt they too would have claimed to be Newtonians. As Bernard Cohen pointed out long ago,[18] it was fatally easy to divide where Newton had joined, mathematical science going one way and experimental science another. For such a division *Opticks* seemed to provide authority; had not Newton himself developed his discoveries about light and colours by a purely experimental investigation? So Hales – by no means unique in this – takes his philosophical stand on a wholly non-mathematical version of attraction:

there is diffused thro' all natural, mutually attracting bodies, a large proportion of particles which, as the first great Author of this important discovery, Sir Isaac Newton, observes are capable of being thrown off from dense bodies by heat or fermentation into a vigorously elastick and permanently repelling state: And also of returning . . . into dense bodies . . .It is by these properties of the particles of matter that he solves the principal Phenomena of Nature.[19]

We would be inclined, perhaps, to say that Hales himself had made 'this important discovery', the origin of pneumatic chemistry; but what a curious peep this gives into Hales's image of Newton; certainly not that of any mathematician ever, nor of any modern philosophical analyst. Yet, as Cohen has shown, something of this strange image was held by the physician and chemist Herman Boerhaave (1668–1738) of Leiden, a keen admirer of Newton, by

J.T. Desaguliers, an experimental assistant to Newton in his last years, by the translator (and chemist) Peter Shaw and no doubt by Benjamin Franklin. All of these tended, in some degree, to make the discovery

That these properties of bodies, such as gravity, attractions, and repulsions by which we shall hereafter explain several phaenomena, are not occult qualities or supposed virtues, but do really exist

the central core of Newtonian philosophy, proved by experiments. They took the meringue for the whole pudding.[20]

To see Newton in this light was certainly in keeping with the English empirical tradition, for it made him a philosophical brother of Robert Boyle, a Boyle whose mechanical philosophy had been enriched by the concepts of attraction and repulsion. As a mathematical philosopher Newton was not intelligently received in England. To some it seemed (as we have just seen with 'sGravesande) that the *Principia* itself could very well be 'demonstrated by experiment': one could then have a very good grasp of all the Newtonian philosophy enforced by cogent experimental demonstrations without any troublesome theorems and lemmas at all. Such a popularization is the negation of the Newtonian method, but it did not seem so, in an age when the competent readers of the *Principia* never numbered more than a few dozen. And it was certainly true that only in a non-mathematical presentation could Newtonian science reach a large audience.

It is inconceivable that such a result was foreseen and intended by Newton, or that even if he saw the 31st Query as the corner-stone of his philosophy in some sense, as it was his final (1718) scientific utterance of any importance, he intended it to be read as a guide to methodology. Far from *Opticks* being Newton's own testimony to the excellence of the qualititative experimental method, there is much evidence of his effort to make the structure of the book not only axiomatic, but as quantitative and mathematical as the subject would allow. This seems to be the necessary interpretation of a number of remarks in Newton's books and correspondence, such as the following passage at the end of Proposition III in Book I, Part 2 of *Opticks*, where Newton has discussed the mathematical proportionality of the coloured refracted rays:

And these Theorems being admitted into *Opticks*, there would be scope enough of handling that Science voluminously after a new manner, not only by teaching those things which tend to the perfection of Vision, but also by determining mathematically all kinds of Phaenomena of Colours which could be produced by Refractions. For to do this, there is nothing else requisite than to find out the Separations of heterogeneous Rays, and their various Mixtures and Proportions in every Mixture. By this way of arguing I invented almost all the Phaenomena described in these Books . . .
As is done in our Author's Lect. Optic. *Part I Sect III and IV and Part II Sect II.*

By a strange irony of fate, the mathematization of the theory of light and optics when it came in the nineteenth century was to be founded on that physical concept of light as wave-motion that Newton had – in a different form, it is true – rejected as impossible; while this left much of Newton's own descriptive exploration to stand as a classically valid example of experimental research, it further confirmed the artificial division of Newton's natural philosophy into 'experimental' and 'mathematical' branches, as though physics had been and must be a dichotomy. That was never Newton's own view.

However, if, more legitimately, we classify Newton's immediate heirs as either 'experimenters' or 'mathematicians' – though some, like Bouguer, were successfully both – it is clear that the latter were not only working more authentically in the tradition of the *Principia*, but that their work has better stood the test of time. The Newtonian experimental tradition as pursued by Hales and by the very many eighteenth-century electricians from Stephen Gray onwards was of course perfectly sound, and produced innumerable notable discoveries, but it did not produce either in *Vegetable Staticks* or Benjamin Franklin's *Experiments and Observations upon Electricity* (1751) anything that could really be qualified as Newtonian science. Good science certainly, but only Newtonian if all good science is to be classed as Newtonian; for the objective of the mathematization of nature, set by Galileo and realized by Newton, had been completely abandoned. The English electricians especially were to all intents neo-Cartesians, with their hypotheses of fluids, and once again it was left to the French to introduce a Newtonian mathematical order into electrical science.

The multitude of other speculations generated more or less directly by the Queries in terms of particles and their powers, virtues and forces, including the various attractive and repulsive aetherial hypotheses, which play large roles in both the philosophical and popular scientific writing of the eighteenth century, need not detain us long. Attempts to reach the deeper substrata of physical understanding through such speculations failed, and it is hard to believe that Newton himself would have hoped for their success, especially as few of these writers heeded his plea for further *experimental* elucidation of these knotty problems. It is worth noting, however, that one trend amid these speculations – making endless permutations of the same conceptual devices – particularly linked with the names of Roger Boscovich and Joseph Priestley, powerfully reacted against materialism, favouring the ontology of forces as the basis of phenomena. Exploiting a hint from Newton himself, they cured the heresy of thinking that the activity of nature might be dependent on the lumpishness of matter by visualizing matter as a kind of artefact created by the spatial distribution of forces. Thus the problem of action at a distance between atoms disappeared. This was an idea with a future.

As Arnold Thackray has demonstrated,[21] the application of a qualitative theory of attraction to chemistry was at least as sustained and highly developed as its application to electricity: the theoretical chemists adhered to the notion of forces, while the electricians took up the idea of the subtle, elastic fluid or aether. Although the writings of Keill and Friend furnished no adequate specific model, the general principle that chemical reactions could be interpreted as particle-rearrangements (from Boyle) and such rearrangements caused by short-range Newtonian forces, was widely diffused at home and abroad by Query 31 and other subsequent vehicles. Buffon, the Newtonian translator and subsequently voluminous naturalist, also fostered this idea and in turn his 'vision profoundly affected Guyton de Morveau, Lavoisier, Fourcroy and the whole school of French chemists',[22] that is, the revolutionaries who replaced phlogiston by hydrogen and antiphlogiston by oxygen, altered the whole nomenclature of science, and brought about a chemical revolution. These Newtonian principles had nothing to do with chemical research in the laboratory and the identification of the elements, but they continued to form the natural-philosophical basis of experimental chemistry until the weighty chemical atom of John Dalton replaced, early in the nineteenth century, the Newtonian fundamental particle. Dalton was not interested in attractive and repulsive forces between atoms, though he clothed them in atmospheres of heat; albeit (it seems) himself rather a poor hand with a balance, he brought in chemical statics and pushed chemical dynamics into the background for three generations. This was the end of what Thackray has called the Newtonian dream of a quantified chemical mechanics:

Dalton's work was to shift the whole area of philosophic debate among chemists . . . The replacement of the fruitless endeavour to qualify the forces of chemical *mechanism* by his astonishingly successful weight-quantification of chemical *units*, undercut the whole Newtonian programme.[23]

Thus, a glance round the scientific world of the first years of the nineteenth century would have found the Newtonian world of macroscopic forces elegantly described in mathematical language, precisely and repeatedly justified by experience. The astronomers particularly possessed a virtually complete mastery of planetary dynamics. Far otherwise with that microscopic world which Newton had entered by the door of experiment and analogy and had viewed through conjecture: the sciences of chemistry, of light and of electricity were already moving happily on neo-Newtonian paths. To relate the conceptual and mathematical evolution of these various branches of science, still essentially descriptive in 1800, and their attainment of a view of the microcosmos different from anything envisaged by Newton, would be to write a large part of the history of physical science during the nineteenth and twentieth centuries.

It has become a truism to assert that the development of natural science has been the most significant and enduring feature of Western civilization. Western scientific ideas have penetrated, at least partially, into the culture of all peoples, and almost all have contributed something to their evolution; Western scientific technology has influenced the lives of all peoples. Much else that has seemed essential to the life of the West – Christianity, capitalist industry, personal freedom and political democracy – has been rejected by non-European nations. Even in the West, the society that gave birth to science and encouraged its growth has quite vanished, yet science has survived and thriven. At one time it seemed that it must continue to survive, having established an inviolable position for itself whatever the vicissitudes of social structure and ideology. That now seems far less certain. The enemies of the rational scientific exploration of nature are more numerous and stronger than they were thirty years ago, and many intelligent people today would deny that the words 'scientific truth' have any definable or absolute meaning. At the extreme, some philosophers appear to regard the scientific idea of nature as an artefact of the society entertaining it.

The very opposite was the guiding principle of the scientific revolution. The men considered in this book believed in a real, ordered natural creation, independent of man but rationally knowable by man so that its properties and laws could be discovered. They would have rejected as both irreligious and unphilosophical the notion that nature might be in a fundamental sense unknowable and indeterminate. Their belief was universally prevalent until some half century ago and although it is no longer justified by the mathematical principles of natural philosophy, it still in practice provides the metaphysical substrate for much scientific work. This being so, it is unfortunate that we understand the genesis of modern science as little as we do, even now. We see that earlier civilizations, preceding that of modern Europe, each in its own way responded to the challenge of the natural environment, both practically (in order to live) and intellectually. None succeeded in freeing its idea of nature from the complexities and uncertainties of philosophical debate nor from the preconceptions of religion. None made more than a slight beginning in the mathematical understanding of nature, or discovered any procedure for satisfactorily discriminating between less, and more well-founded propositions about the natural order. Nor did the range of factual knowledge in these early civilizations extend far beyond the ordinary experience of men. From such an intermediate state of knowledge, a state between primitivism and science, only the modern European society and those other societies subjected to its influence during the last two centuries, have made an escape. It is this singular passage from philosophic rationality to scientific rationality that historians do not fully comprehend, any more than philosophers are agreed on the solution to the problem (which is of course related) of the breakdown of allegiance to one complex of principles, explanations and methods which leads to the transfer of credence to an alternative complex.

All historical explanations are problematic. Historians of science are not at much of a disadvantage as compared with other historians trying to explain (say) the occurrence of the French or Russian revolutions. And just as political historians might, after explaining the evolution of a certain social and economic condition and the pressure of certain political necessities at a particular moment find it necessary to superpose an account of ideas and principles that suddenly seemed to demand implementation, if only because they operated in the mind of a Robespierre or a Lenin, so the historian of science has to consider within a certain form of society (which, in various material or intellectual ways permits or forbids this or that kind of investigation) the role of ideas, ideas that move linearly through time changing their character and force as they evolve and become modified. This book has been about ideas, rather than about society and about particular individuals rather than anonymous masses. I believe that we can only properly understand the course of scientific — and for that matter, political — change in this way. Many admired Newton, many more cheered Lenin; without those who read and those who cheer revolutions would not happen. But without ideas there would be no Newtons or Lenins in history.

NOTES

1. *Lettres sur les Anglais* (1734), Letter 14.
2. Newton, *Correspondence*, VI, 1976, 398.
3. Henry Guerlac, *Newton on the Continent*, Cornell University Press: Ithaca, 1981, 78–163.
4. It was based on the French version of Amsterdam, 1720.
5. Op. cit., Note 3, 73.
6. Newton, *Correspondence*, VI, 1976, 188–9.
7. Guerlac (op. cit., Note 3), 61–2.
8. A. Rupert Hall, *Philosophers at War,* Cambridge U.P., 1980, especially Ch. 11.
9. Letter XVII.
10. 'In tedious deserts you were forced to roam To find the truth that Newton knew at home.'
11. Ernst Mach, *The Science of Mechanics* [1893], Open Court Publishing Co. La Salle Ill., 1942, 562.
12. Newton to Pardies, 10 June 1672, *Correspondence*, I, 164. See H. Guerlac, *Essays and Papers in the History of Modern Science*, Johns Hopkins University Press: Baltimore & London, 1977, 131–45.
13. Quoted by L. L. Laudan in R. E. Butts and J. W. Davis (eds), *The Methodological Heritage of Newton*, Blackwells: Oxford, 1970, 104, note.
14. Guerlac (loc. cit., Note 2), 141, quoting the *Discours Preliminaire* to the *Encyclopédie*.
15. W. J. 'sGravesande, *Mathematical Elements of Natural Philosophy* (trans. J. T. Desaguliers), 4th edn, London, 1731, xvi–xvii.
16. E. A. Burtt, *Metaphysical Foundations of Modern Physical Science* [1924], Routledge and Kegan Paul: London, 1949, 223. Cf. E. W. Strong in *Jour. Hist. Ideas*, 12, 1951, 90–110.
17. F. Cajori (ed.) Newton's *Principia*, University of California Press: Berkeley, 1946, 550. This celebrated passage does not figure in the Latin edition of the *Systema* in Newton's *Opuscula*, Tom II, Lausanne & Geneva 1744, and may be an addition. It is curious that it should have been in the *System* at all, since this was (supposedly) composed *methodo populari*. The printed Book III of the *Principia*, which replaced it, was written *more mathematico*.
18. I. Bernard Cohen, *Franklin and Newton*, American Philosophical Society: Philadelphia, 1956.
19. M. A. Hoskin (ed.), *Vegetable Staticks*, Oldbourne: London, 1961, xxvii.
20. Cohen, op. cit., 254 quoting Desaguliers, *Course of Experimental Philosophy*, I, 1734, 21.
21. Arnold Thackray, *Atoms and Powers*, Harvard University Press: Cambridge, Mass., 1970.
22. *Idem*, in D. S. L. Cardwell (ed.), *John Dalton and the Progress of Science*, Manchester University Press: Manchester, 1968, 101.
23. *Idem, Atoms and Powers*, 276.

Index